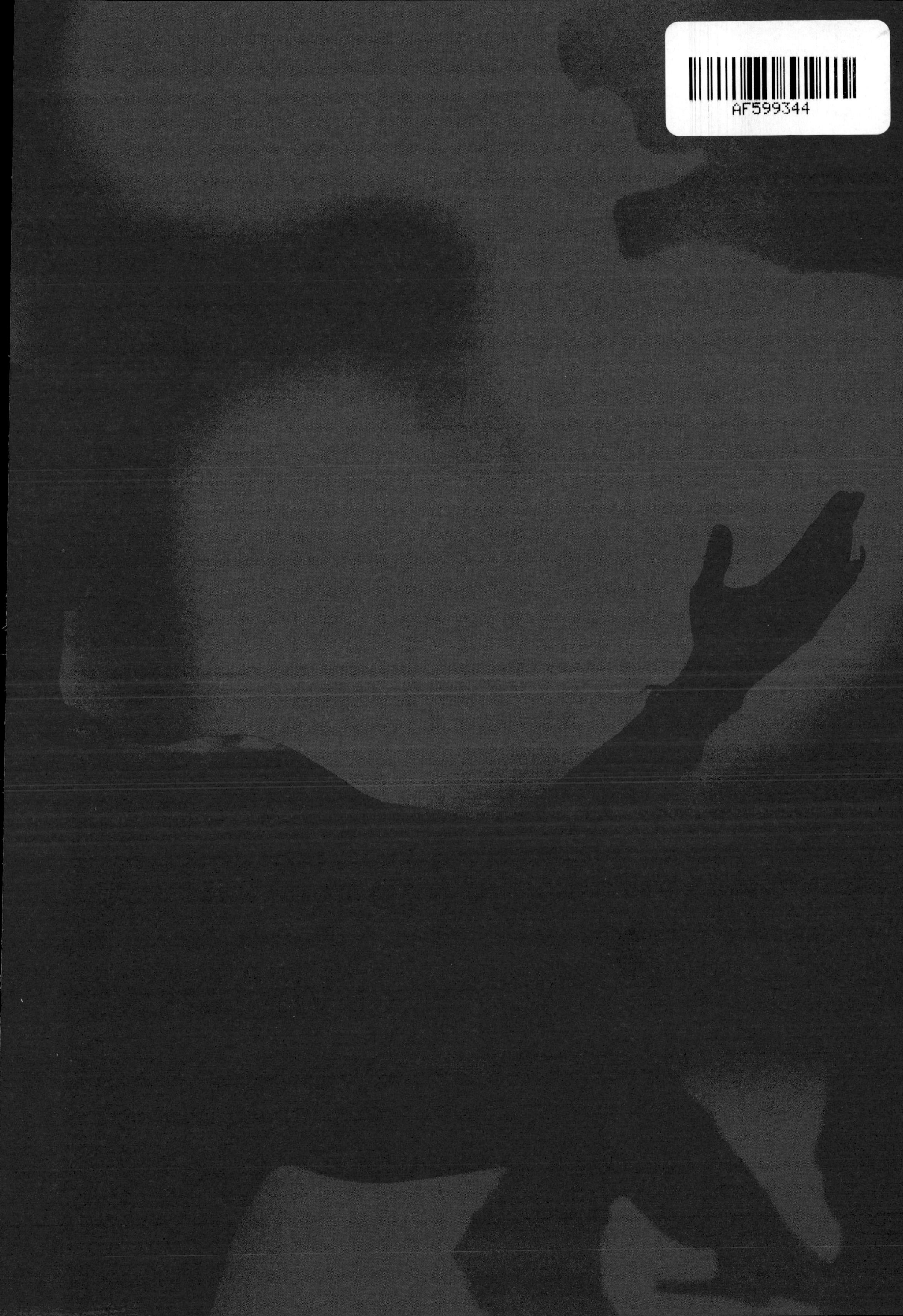

What to Let Go?

Para Site 藝術空間

Sternberg Press

What to Let Go?

EDITED BY
COSMIN COSTINAŞ &
INTI GUERRERO

Introduction: What to Let Go?

6

COSMIN COSTINAŞ
&
INTI GUERRERO

This book gathers voices that intervene in current discussions on what gets counted within the category of heritage, who gets to do the counting, and more broadly on issues of cultural sovereignty. The authors and artists populating these pages unpack historical narratives and political memory linked to objects, sites, and ceremonies that have either been lost, looted, restituted, repatriated, revived, or even reinvented. Each contribution is an entry point to rethinking forms of memorialization and patrimony in our current era of dangerous revisionism, when history has seemingly become a major battlefield both for the left and for the right, in different ways and with different stakes. In this landscape of politics and memory, we are asking ourselves how can art reconfigure collective foundational myths? And what should we let go of along this journey?

The making of this publication comes from a wish to weave together in a broader thematic spectrum several subjects that are not always considered simultaneously. It is also motivated by a desire to help bring into the same conversation different geographies where distinct and often disconnected discourses are taking place in cultural and academic institutions. All these, against the backdrop of an increasingly public debate and of a far more modest array of actions regarding the repatriation and restitution of looted cultural belongings held in museum collections in former colonial metropolises (or in the established institutions of settler colonies). This moment has overlapped with processes of renaming or removing symbols of past eras, including the toppling of statues. Less obviously connected are recent social upheavals and political processes which this book tries nevertheless to associate. It does so by straddling discourse, poetry, and original artistic contributions as interlaced vantage points from which to perceive and unpack societal contradictions of the past and present.

Departing from a political reflection on the act of cataloguing Filipino material in ethnographic collections outside of the country, cultural theorist and curator Marian Pastor Roces takes an X-ray of the Filipino psyche's internalised islamophobia, describing the ghosts of colonial violence and its resurrection in the "archaic leadership" of former president Rodrigo Duterte. Curator and writer Bonaventure Soh Bejeng Ndikung's carefully considered selection of poems from different contexts offers transversal sensitivities as antidotes to institutionalized processes of history writing. Curator and art historian Maia Nuku proposes possibilities for institutions to manage translation of Indigenous technologies and systems of knowledge from cultures of the Great Ocean (Pacific) region by activating kinship. Connectedly, Pablo José Ramirez reflects on ideas of custodianship of Maya belief systems when collecting works by contemporary artists of Indigenous descent who in their practice are using temporality and value systems outside of the market logic. Alutiiq anthropologist and curator Sven Haakanson shares the revival story of boatmaking in his community linked to an experience of repatriation, while outlining principles and recommendations for communities seeking reinvigoration living heritage. Curator Vivian Ziherl delves into contemporary politics of restitution by presenting concepts of possession and ownership for First Nations Australians, and how these discussions manifest in the production, circulation, and monetization of Aboriginal art.

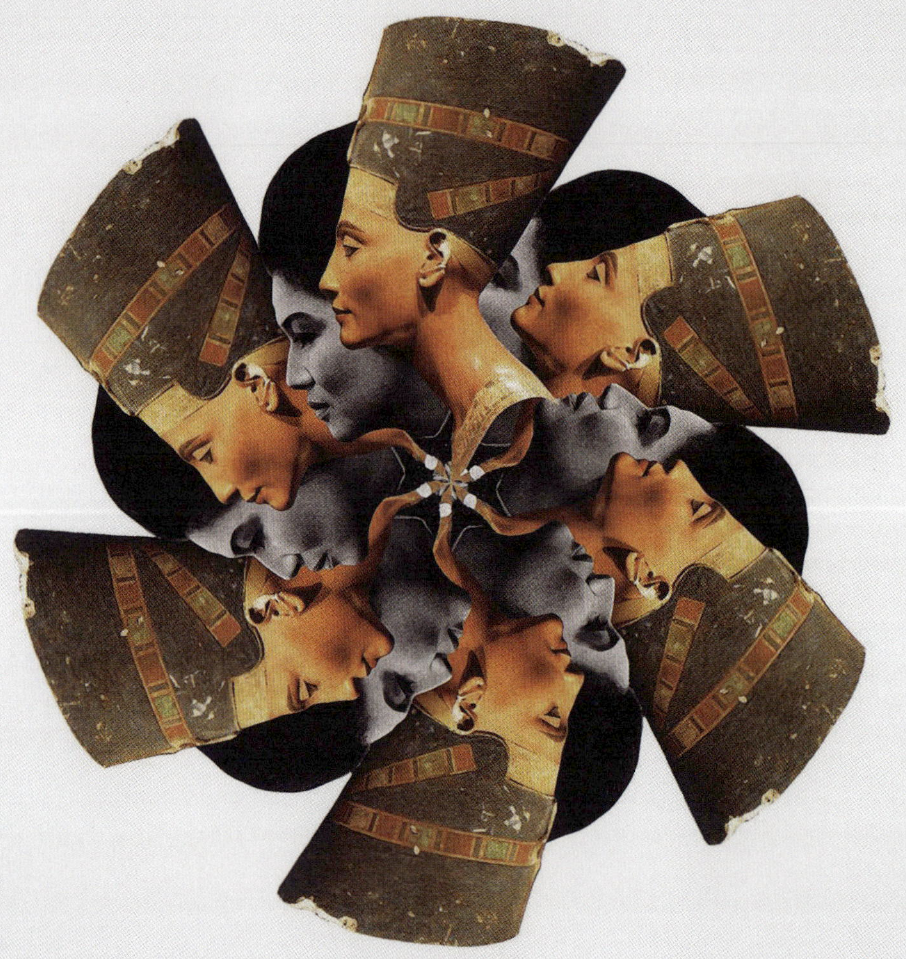

FIG 1 Pio Abad, Design for ceramic plate depicting Imelda Marcos as Semiramis, mistakenly depicted as Nefertiti, 2012.

Social upheavals and street protests often embody contradictions and historical traumas of societies when they appear as outbursts of a past that is refusing to remain silent anymore, manifesting at times violently, but also euphorically and celebratory. Heritage and political memory is embodied here in the flesh of the protesters, in particular in contexts where mass movements and rallying have historically marked the consciousness of a group or place. In her text, curator and writer Natasha Ginwala maps the sonic memory linked to protests by Black and Brown communities in the US and the UK, as well as the ethnic divides and history of rioting in India and Sri Lanka. In the same vein, artist and poet Cecilia Vicuña takes us to the palpable euphoria on the streets of Chile's *estallido social* (social outburst) of 2019—a multivoiced eruption that fought for letting go of centuries of repression against Indigenous Mapuche matriarchal heritage, alongside other systems of power. The conversation with historian Thongchai Winichakul walks us through how generations of protest since the 1930s in Bangkok and historical revisionisms by Royalists and military governments ever since have defined cycles of political remembrance and amnesia in Thai society. He carefully discusses the at times humorous history of placement and removal of commemorative signs and monuments in public space, both by official forces and clandestinely by protesters.

Historian Hong Lysa shares the experience of memorialization of colonial heritage in Singapore through the bicentennial celebrations and counter-celebrations of Stamford Raffles's arrival to the Southeast Asian territory. Hong argues that the bicentennial was a seemingly paradoxical nation-building ritual that favored colonial melancholy while turning its back on the postcolonial Malaya history—a strategy of nationalist remembrance, glorifying British imperialism and a Eurocentric Columbus complex that the late Lee Kuan Yew had already carried out on the 150th anniversary of Raffles's arrival. Art historian and curator Carol Yinghua Lu traces the complexities around meanings of tradition and heritage in post-1949 China, looking at how art mediums such as ink painting became part of, and were transformed by, the ideological battlefields of communist nation-building. Academics and filmmakers Xiaoxuan Lu and Bo Wang's associative text unpacks the interconnectivity of present-day politics and the vestiges of Cold War ideology in the Korean peninsula, departing from the ancestral significance of the spiritual waters of Heaven Lake that is considered to be the natural heritage of both Koreas. Cold War ideology in the Asia Pacific region is further analyzed by artist Pio Abad as he looks at how the archeology of luxury artifacts amassed by the Marcos dictatorial family in the Philippines ended up representing the nation's treasure, and at a never-ending search for justice and reparations.

Rich in transhistorical research, art historian and curator Naman P. Ahuja's essay presents modes in which curating archeological artifacts together with art and vernacular visual culture can critique dominant processes of writing Indian religious and cultural histories. It talks about how constructs of what constitutes "national treasures" have been heavily coopted by reductionist, nationalist, and misogynist interpretations. Curator and researcher Lia Colombino's text introduces the pioneering work of Museo del Barro in Asunción, Paraguay, as an early museum model of decolonization in which Indigenous material culture and works by contemporary artists of Indigenous descent are at the core of the insti-tution's presentation of art and living heritage. Curator Vali Mahlouji's nostalgic revisiting of the Festival of Arts, Shiraz-Persepolis, staged in Iran from 1967 until 1977, in the context of other internationalist art festivals taking place outside the West, reveals an era of culture, solidarity, and new artistic forms bridging various forms of artistic heritage on a diverse and often conflicting political spectrum.

Closing the book is an interview with philosopher Yuk Hui, in which he debates different moments when cultural traditions caused friction with modernity, and how a future of techno-diversities would embrace a plurality of cultural lineages and defy colonially-generated universalisms.

Losing the Discourse of Loss

10

MARIAN PASTOR ROCES

> Animism has thus proven to be tenacious, as the relationships cultivated in animist rituals and discourses are often constitutive of sociality as such. This is true for modern contexts as well.
>
> — Guido Sprenger, *Dimensions of Animism in Southeast Asia* (2016)

It is the undetected flow of malignancy from acts of impunity—which includes those perfectly legitimate scientific expeditions of consecutive colonial administrations—through random channels to surprising termini and further. The multi-directional and non-linear dynamic precludes predictability.

I worry about surprise trajectories, which are legion; each trajectory a compacted history which nevertheless sends tendrils into different domains. Such as, for example, the arc this essay tracks. In this particularly snaky case, old notions such as causal links show up as inadequate. But the arc is perceptible, given some writerly doggedness. Given some attentiveness to the bizarrely mutable.

A Howl, A Hum

Things lost live elsewhere, sub-atomically in due course. But this inscrutable eternity is consolation to no one. Consolation is in any case a too-thin salve. A Spanish-Tagalog coinage describes a pointless solace, *consuelo de bobo*. Cold comfort of fools, in this pidgin rendering. Because loss is inevitable and aspiration invariably thwarted, surrender is likely the wise posture, with either a wan smile or operatic rage, to the jokes of gods.

Concerning purloined cultural material, choice is quite the cosmic prank. There is nowhere to seriously ask *What to let go?* Other than in huddles of artists and intellectuals, and UNESCO delegates, hypothesizing is unreal fuss. Indeed only shamans, astronomers, physicists, philosophers, and perhaps very old people in their states of grace have purchase on calmness while meaningful things and ideas disappear.

This foreclosure is originary violence: that aggrieved communities are by sheer weight of history consigned to spaces outside any choice about future prospects. But the violence can only be palpated; the detected pulse, arhythmic and faint. It is an often indiscernible murmur, despite the passionate hue and cry over stuff acquired by empire builders and capital hoarders with exquisite aesthetics. Sometimes the cries for restitution intensify, but these are quickly inaudible. The near impossibility of sustaining processes of restitution over many decades may itself be a violence as great as the loss.

The intergenerational relay to pass forward the mental archives of negotiations for repatriation—including accounting for reasons why the initiatives neither flourished nor happened at all in the majority of cases—is caught in a tautology of forgetting. Pried out from the life of source cultures, the cultural material in museum storages and collectors' salons and bedsides, snarls and ghosts numerous streams of cultural possibility for the progeny of the makers. The many streams convey the force of that originary violence.

But this is known violence: the toxicities produced by absent symbolic materials where these have been vacuumed up. Rather, my object in this essay is less obvious.

Counts, Arcs

In 1998 I undertook a global inventory of Philippine cultural materials deposited in museums outside the country.[1] My volatile republic was celebrating the centennial of its declaration of independence from Spain in 1898, and the government was unusually open to cultural projects of substantial scale. The Department of Foreign Affairs facilitated this inventory project, guided by a Secretary who instructed ambassadors in specific posts to request copies of the relevant accession records from specific museums, and photographs if available. I provided the Secretary with the list of museums of interest. All addressees responded, and the project was accomplished by 2000.[2]

This project exists today in hard copy (twenty years ago, digital databasing was yet to be the norm globally). Happily, two decades after the records were first gathered, the School of Oriental and African Studies (SOAS) at University of London built the website "Mapping Philippine Material Culture Overseas," bringing forward the experience of the inventory project into the digital open access world. The SOAS site continues to seek permission for online publication of Philippine cultural material from owner museums that the old project contacted, and then some, one museum at a time.[3]

---

1 The global inventory did not include articles in private collections, nor natural history collections.

2 Secretary of Foreign Affairs Domingo Siason gave the *Global Inventory of Filipiniana Artifacts, Artworks, and Selected Documents in Foreign Museums* an office and a small staff at the Foreign Affairs building. Initiated by Marian Pastor Roces, the project was endorsed by Senator Leticia Ramos Shahani, formerly Assistant Secretary General for Social Development and Humanitarian Affairs of the United Nations (1980–86).

3 https://philippinestudies.uk/mapping/. Cristina M. Juan, PhD, head of the SOAS Philippine Studies Program, University of London, has taken up the task of contacting, negotiating, and communicating with the museums with Philippine holdings. Dr. Juan initiated, organized, and heads the *Mapping Philippine Material Culture Overseas* website at SOAS. I assist Dr. Juan, create virtual exhibitions, and co-edit the site.

A meta-museological project, the 1998–2000 inventory was of interest to people gravitating to museums and only a few others. The ongoing SOAS-run mapping project communicates much more widely, and is already registering a generational shift from disinterest to enthusiasm for a literally unknown Philippines in things secreted in obscure storages. Also, open-access digitization is a worlding project that changes the complexion of tropes of loss. Accessed intimately as pixels in digital images on home computers, loss now emanates strangely from the materials. The things are within grasping distance of the Filipino imagination but well outside the possibility of touch. They are as entombed as ever, although additionally today in a two-dimensional digital universe, apropos the times. Three-dimensionality exists in an apparently permanent and forever elsewhere.

A curious postmodernity obtains in the inherent, extended modernity of the SOAS website's encouragement and facilitation of a comparative imagination, today through global access. Encompassing both private and public collections, it offers users a comparative field of considerable breadth. Jose Rizal's and Benedict Anderson's *el demonio de las comparaciones*, the spectre of comparisons—to these authors the very sensibility that defines the modern—haunts the field of pixels.[4]

Comparison allows users a haunting grasp of immensity. Comparison also makes a hum audible: the "sound" from long-ago instances of extraction. The immense numbers are heard, so to speak. More than 8,000 Philippine articles belong to the holdings of the Peabody Museum of Archaeology and Ethnology at Harvard; over 10,000 at Chicago's Field Museum of Natural History. Another over 10,000 items are stored by the Smithsonian Institution. The Spanish collections remain difficult to count. And even the relatively small collections, such as those at the Leiden Museum, Berlin's Museum für Völkerkunde, Vienna's Weltmuseum, and so forth, comprise materials, some quite humble but critical to Filipino self-regard.

Audible, however faintly, in the resonances produced inside emptied cultural spaces, the sound of emptiness is extraordinarily important in all talk of dislocated things and meanings. The numerical and meta-physical hugeness of the emptying is comprehensible only in its epic scale. Also, in its epic form as a long, complex, persistent chanting, encompassing voids. It is for instance important to persist mentioning the 350+ ikat-dyed textiles with the American Museum of Natural History, New York City. These were collected in the first years of the twentieth century from a single language group—the Bagobo—and represents an absence so vast in the Bagobo homelands that only a handful of their weavers in the second half of the twentieth century have had physical references of the virtuoso dyeing achieved by their antecedents.[5]

The exquisite levels of Bagobo ikat-dyeing is not only extinct today; little about its peak achievement is remembered. This one arc, totally unintended, inclined towards extinction. Only the sound of an emptied cultural landscape hints of unexpected turns and matters unaccounted for.

Liver and Vinegar, Oil and Bones

Another arc impales Philippine current events. I refer to a spear-like tracery that runs from losing weapons long ago to the shock of having a sociopath democratically elected as president. Rodrigo Roa Duterte was elected after what in the Philippines is a typically brutal winner-take-all tournament. His case, however, was an even more savage arrival in national politics than experienced earlier. Duterte was mayor for decades of the country's third city, Davao. He ruled in the manner of a nineteenth century Latin *caudillo* materialized in a twenty-first century banana and *abaka* plantation city between the Philippines and Indonesia.

He promised to murder narc dealers and users equally, as well as miscellaneous underlife, rebels, and political enemies—including activists—by his own hand if he pleased. And indeed he did. Control was exercised thus, and the elite ranks of businessmen and the Davao middle class enjoyed his version of peace. He then foisted this tyranny on the entire nation. The underground economy flourished unrestrained.

4 Anderson, Benedict, *The Spectre of Comparisons: Nationalism, Southeast Asia, and the World*, (Quezon City: Ateneo de Manila University Press, 2004) [Reprint].

5 American researcher Laura Watson Benedict lived among the Bagobo-speaking people of Davao Gulf in the first decade of the twentieth century. As the author of *Bagobo Ceremonial Myth and Magic*, she gathered an immense number of Bagobo textile specimens and subsequently negotiated with the American Museum of Natural History for the permanent home of these ikat-dyed textiles.

Duterte's sewer mouth drew enough laughs for him to slither past serious scrutiny. When with a warped braggadocio, he let loose about eating an enemy's liver—just pass him salt and vinegar—he is the Joker, *sans maquillage*, playing for a pass. Although infantile, Filipinos think it harmless enough. But he is letting on about something true and horrific. Duterte may not himself be a cannibal, but he most certainly knows one *ilagâ* or another—killers who gained ghastly notoriety in the late 1960s and early 1970s, for de facto ethnocide and attempted genocide against Muslim communities. These agents of ethnic cleansing self-identified as Christian. They killed entire villages, mutilated the bodies of victims, and indeed ate some human liver and other parts of Muslim bodies.[6]

There is enough verifiable recollection that these were state-sponsored murderers. About these horrors, it can be said that the President Ferdinand Marcos period Constabulary forces supported the terror strategy for political gain. We can further argue that this Constabulary initiated the formation of these bands and accompanied them on their rampages. Duterte's reign of grisly murders can be recognized as culturally rooted in these precedent terror campaigns.

During the long days of the ilagâ, ethnic cleansing attempted to wipe a clear space for the ascendant political power of Christian settlers who were becoming demographic majorities in Mindanao towns and provinces, and who then helped buttress the Marcos dictatorship. Still, something far more horrific was unleashed than petty rulers with bloodstained hands. The *ilagâ* and their Constabulary enablers tapped into mangled animisms. They activated quasi-mystical systems that drove ritualized murderousness. Ilagâ personalities were—and are—by definition amulet-bearing men with tattooed bodies, armed with specific knife forms and whatever guns their military allies made available to them. With their talismanic bottles of sacralized oil containing herbs, written arcana, and bits of human bones, worn as pendants or in multiples as bandoliers, they believed themselves impermeable to knives or bullets.

The fifty-year war of secession waged by two Muslim liberation fronts in succession began in the same period as the ilagâ assaults.[7] Mid-twentieth century, the

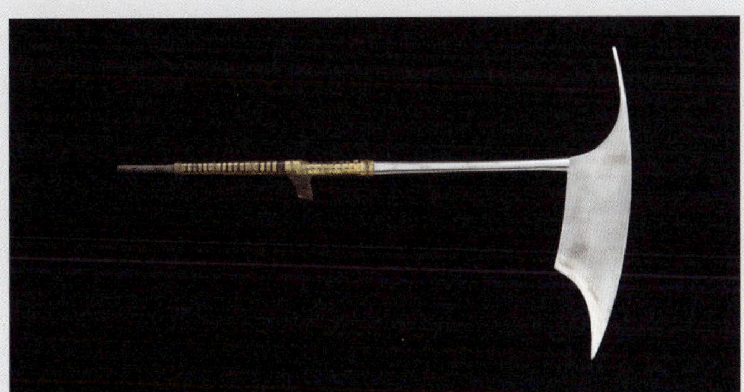

FIG 1 Battle-axe; Philippine, Kalinga; Axe, head axe, curved steel blade, steel tang, wood handle with brass sheeting; 59.3 × 35.5 × 4.3 cm, Gift of Edward Bowditch, Jr., 1916. © President and Fellows of Harvard College, Peabody Museum of Archaeology and Ethnology, 16-55-70/D449.

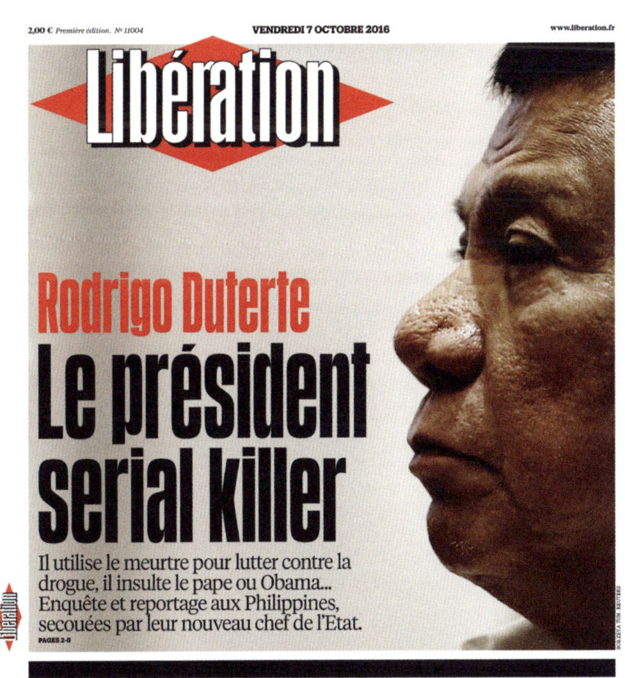

2,00 € Première édition. Nº 11004 VENDREDI 7 OCTOBRE 2016 www.liberation.fr

Libération

Rodrigo Duterte
Le président serial killer

Il utilise le meurtre pour lutter contre la drogue, il insulte le pape ou Obama... Enquête et reportage aux Philippines, secouées par leur nouveau chef de l'Etat. PAGES 2-8

2017 : Najat Vallaud-Belkacem se prépare au cas où...

La ministre de l'Education nationale restera loyale à François Hollande jusqu'au bout. Mais s'il devait renoncer, elle entend bien jouer les premiers rôles pendant la campagne présidentielle. Jusqu'à se présenter elle-même à la primaire ? ENQUÊTE, PAGES 14-15

Foot : les faux-semblants des Bleus

L'équipe de France se frotte à la Bulgarie, ce vendredi, en éliminatoires de la Coupe du monde 2018. Un retour au Stade de France, trois mois après la défaite en finale de l'Euro face au Portugal. PAGES 18-19

Casques blancs : un Nobel pour la Syrie ?

Les volontaires secourant sous les bombes les habitants d'Alep pourraient être primés à Oslo. PAGE 8

FIG 2 *Libération* cover from 7 October 2016: "Rodrigo Duterte Le président serial killer," © *Libération*.

6 I am preparing a book-length description of ilagâ atrocities for publication titled *WaO Whispers*, available in limited edition in 2023.

7 The war commenced with the establishment of the Moro National Liberation Front (MNLF) in 1969. The Moro Islamic Liberation Front (MILF) was founded in 1977 with a theologically-inclined state-building project. Both fought to secede from the Philippine Republic. The MNLF negotiated a *détente* with the Philippine Government in 1996 but factions have since returned to belligerent status. It was the MILF that successfully brought the protracted peace negotiations into a viable settlement, with the enactment by 17th Congress of the Philippines of the Bangsamoro Basic Law in 2018, and the subsequent creation of the Bangsamoro Autonomous Region in Muslim Mindanao (BARMM), ratified by plebiscite. BARMM was established in 2019.

barbarity of the Christians and the ferocity of Muslim responses explosively accelerated four centuries of conflict between the parts of the Philippines colonized by Spain and the United States, and the smaller Islamicized regions. Because religious difference rang strongest about this war in the Filipino imagination, it is habitually characterized as Muslim-Christian conflict. This characterization is inadequate, of course, because forces of marginalization, penury, and dispossession in Muslim communities, and the impoverished cultures brought by settlers, are arguably stronger drivers of extreme aggression in Mindanao.[8] Historical injustice was perpetrated by more than religious differences.

Uncontained, unapologetic Islamophobia figured significantly in this history. Inherited from the strain of Spanish culture that flowed into *las islas filipinas* in the sixteenth century, together with a Medieval Christianity that survived well past the Spanish Reconquista, anti-Muslim prejudice nearly foreclosed peaceful coexistence in the Philippine south.[9] This bigotry is a much more insidious social toxin than religious ideology. Bigotry drove ilagâ impunity, dehumanizing Muslims, consigning them to an ancient fearsome stereotype, and conjuring reason for their elimination. It was classic fascist impunity sustained by tropes of a godless, savage other. The Marcos dictatorship worked these tropes well—paradoxically as it celebrated "colorful" diversity in its institutions for cultural production.

8 For work inquiring after Mindanao's underground economies that have complicated conflict, see, among others: Francsico Lara and Steven Schoofs, ed., *Out of the Shadows: Violent Conflict and the Real Economy of Mindanao*, (London: International Alert, 2013).

9 Prosecuted by the Roman Catholic monarchs of northern Spain, the Reconquista that replaced Islam in the Iberian Peninsula during the tenth to sixteenth centuries impacted *Las Islas Filipinas*, which received a triumphalist Christianity with little infusion of a modern sensibility. What arrived in the Philippines was the Christianity of the Holy Inquisition. The "reconquest" of Iberia after 800 years of Muslim Spanish culture was a protracted process that at some points was brutal in the extreme, notably the expulsion of first the Sephardic Jews and then the Muslim Spanish into diaspora in North Africa and beyond.

Sleeping Blades

The dispersal of Philippine cultural material to global capitals, draining cultural landscapes of physical references to local cosmologies (orders of being that continued to mutate), has had a somnambulant trajectory. The blades were put to sleep, bloodless, with a few words attached about their removal from conflict sites (sometimes from the hands of the dead). During their sleep, the weapons appeared to their museum or aesthete owners to have transitioned completely from tribalisms to *haute* culture. For more than two centuries, therefore, the work of the Southeast Asian *panday* ("smith" in many Philippine languages) was understood only in the occulted precincts of connoisseurs, and only for its aesthetic and historical character—along with its aura of contained violence. In their interment, tens of thousands of swords, daggers, head axes, spears, and other lethal projectiles and blades, were themselves severed, as though amputated limbs from the body of the Philippines' tribalisms and martial arcana.

However, in the last two decades, intensive collecting projects concentrated on Philippine weapons have brought substantial numbers to private hands in North America, Europe, and the Philippines. Splendid pieces dating from the 19th century and earlier, matching those in museum holdings, turned up in dealerships and auction houses. Collecting aficionados are typically martial arts practitioners, deep-diving into related martial forms *arnis*, *kali*, *eskrima*, and *kuntao*—by all indications indigenously developed and possessed of as yet incomprehensible complexity. (These martial forms include weaponless hand-to-hand combat as lethal as that with blades.) The new collectors are, as it were, waking up the blades. Contrasting with connoisseur and museological acquisitiveness, this new collecting is impelled by resurrected belief in the weapons' anima, mobilizable within Philippine male combat traditions. Many weapons are back in the hands of individuals as capable in combat as learned jousting.

Thus far paying scant attention to this martial dimension of local culture, Philippine museums and cultural centers are late to the upswell of popular interest. Other than the stray *kris* or *kampilan* in general exhibits, the occlusion of the arts of killing and their instruments has been nearly total. But this would have been expected of cultural institutions invested in a nationalist civilizational agenda. It is hence only as of late that the links between and among the following have become obvious to the culturati: tattooing practices; ritual utterances; the "charging" of talismanic oils on mystical nights; the sharply defined persona of the individual who kills; and the exquisite weapons made by virtuoso smiths.

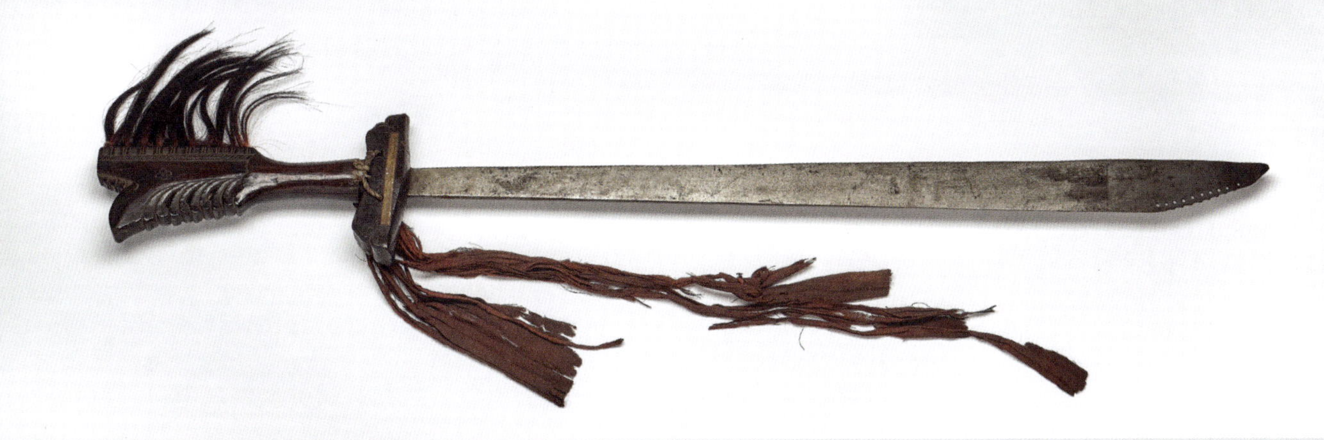

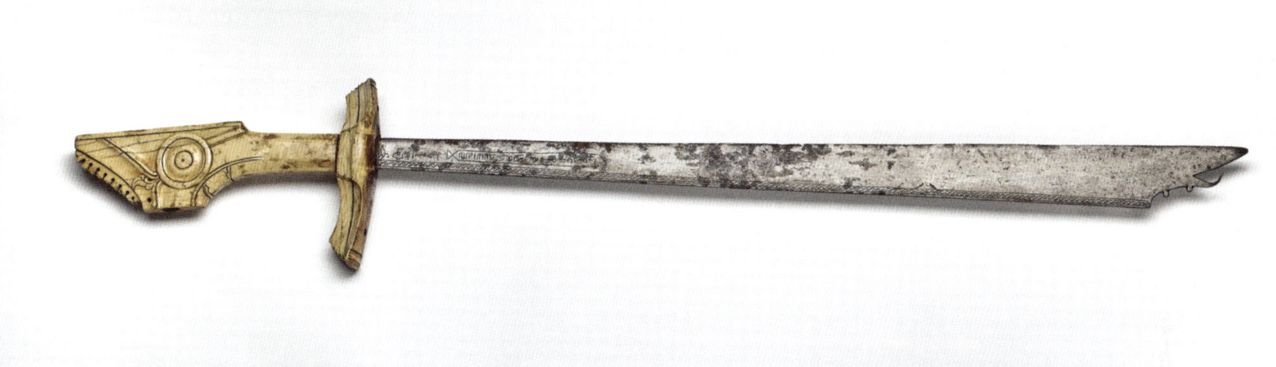

FIG 3 Sword, the hilt carved and ornamented with tufts of human hair. Likely found in Borneo, it is probably Iranun and called a kampilan. It is a Sulu / southern Philippines sword. Eighteenth to nineteenth century. 100.5 × 13.2 × 4 cm © The Trustees of the British Museum.

FIG 4 Sword ("kampilan") made of gold-inlaid steel with ivory hilt; blade engraved on one side with the name of the maker, Isma'il, and the "shahada" (Muslim profession of faith) and on the other side with the Arabic names of the four archangels: Jibril (Gabriel, angel of revelation), Mika'il (Michael, angel of fertility and rain), Israfil (Raphael, announcer of the end of time), and Azra'il (Azrael, angel of death); ivory hilt features a stylized figure (Jawa demam), possibly the legendary Garuda, a part-human, part-eagle figure from Southeast Asia's ancient past. Approx. 1800s–1920s, Made in: Philippines (south), Found / Acquired: Indonesia (East) 101 × 16 × 4.5 cm © The Trustees of the British Museum.

Emerging awareness is quick to recognize that the blades previously interred in cabinets of curiosities represent, in fact, a materiality that immediately limns the powerful immateriality of lethal force. Austronesian animism appears to exceed or bleed out of the bisection of body and spirit. The blades slash through simple dualisms.[10]

So long as—or wherever—that transition from tribalisms to haute culture appears to have solidified and become permanent, ilagâ ritualized killings are inexplicable. Yet these killings—however twisted and eccentrically linked to what is known of Philippine martial traditions and Austronesian concepts of battle, leadership, and death—cohere within the Southeast Asian animism still shaping reality for Christians and Muslims of the Philippines. At present, Duterte's fixation on the macabre (as actualized rather than only metaphorically figured) will only be grasped ineptly, feebly, and as mere aberrant behavior, thought of as sociopathy in a modern world, and as accessible to psychoanalysis in time.

10 Guido Sprengler discusses the inadequacy of the material / immaterial, body / spirit dichotomy in Southeast Asian animism in "Dimensions of Animism in Southeast Asia," Århem, Kaj and Guido Sprengler, eds., *Animism in Southeast Asia* (New York: Routledge, 2016), 32.

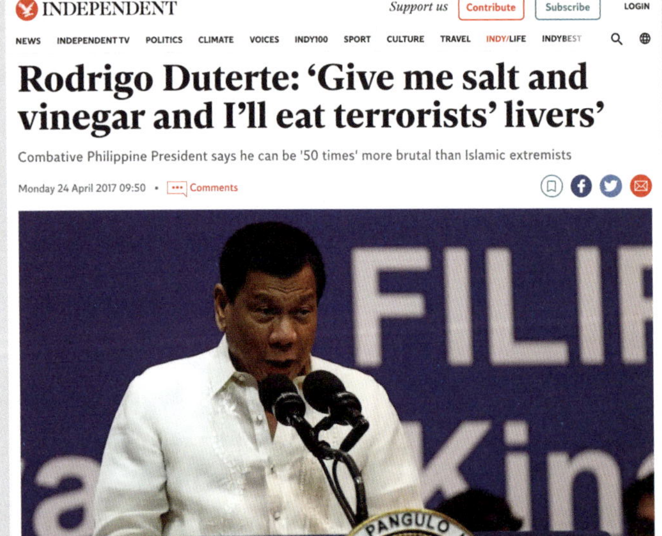
INDEPENDENT
Support us Contribute Subscribe LOGIN
NEWS INDEPENDENT TV POLITICS CLIMATE VOICES INDY100 SPORT CULTURE TRAVEL INDY/LIFE INDYBEST

Rodrigo Duterte: 'Give me salt and vinegar and I'll eat terrorists' livers'

Combative Philippine President says he can be '50 times' more brutal than Islamic extremists

Monday 24 April 2017 09:50 • Comments

FIG 5 ***The Independent*** **website, "Rodrigo Duterte: 'Give me salt and vinegar and I'll eat terrorists' livers'" April 24, 2017. © The Independent.**

Hypothetically, however, had the antique weapons remained in full view of Filipinos through the last centuries, their collective, breathtaking beauty would have preserved in mainstream Philippine discourse an understanding of ecosystemic interconnections among: the power to kill as possible only with ritualized personal and social states; the male force in Austronesian-speaking societies typically expressed as a spiritualized warriorhood; and the tattooing of signifiers as passages through states of ritual maturity.

This is not to say that Duterte is entirely explicable as an archaic warrior-leader (although there is value in accounting for this possibility). I am however suggesting that Duterte took something very old, and alchemized it for contemporary fascistic ends. Because he lived among Mindanao's legend-ary killers when he was young, Duterte viscerally grasps ritualized killing as signifying the power over the life and death of a magnetic violent *datu*, the precolonial male leader metamorphosed in Mindanao into the Malay *orang besar* (strong man), typically leading through a barely controlled or theatrical ferocity.[11] Duterte presided over murders with a fear-producing call, *tokhâng*: executions, not hidden from view, unlike during the Marcos period, when "salvaging" anonymized political murders.[12]

Duterte's instructions to slaughter were brazen and vulgar. Following the fascist template, his targets were vilified ahead of their murder, but then furthermore set up for display in his Grand Guignol spectacles, matter-of-factly contrived with the victim's head covered as though in mummy bandaging, in packing tape. Torsos are usually decorated with a placard showing words of warning: "Do not imitate me."

The datu reincarnation in Duterte's mayor-as-president theater is a garbled version of a precolonial cosmology that was bilaterally organized with a male-female aspects its archaic formulation (that is, the warrior and priestess interplay), and empowered by ritual procedures substantiating the emergence of compelling personae—not the contrivance of spectacle. But in the symbolic power of killing, the mangled and ancient versions overlap. This is, in any case, the insight to be drawn from simultaneously seeing the horrific Duterte administration and the reappeared arrays of stunning old weapons. The lacuna produced by the absence of the weapons in the Philippines is precisely the chasm in which Philippine politics is impossible to comprehend.[13]

The operations of symbols on the national imagination escape detection and analysis. Killings as symbols of correct cause and the righting of disequilibrium are as deep a taproot as can be pulled from the past in island Southeast Asia. It is unlikely to have been comprehended even by Duterte, even as he watered that ground with blood.

---

11 Among the intersections between President Rodrigo Duterte's biographical information and accounts of Mindanao's killer-leaders is the young Rodrigo's mentorship by Octavio Parojinog Sr., 1986 founder of anti-Communist vigilante group *Kuratong Baleleng Gang* (KB). 1980s KB and 1970s ilagâ impunity were at the very least related in similar and historically consecutive terror tactics that included grisly murders. In 2017 President Duterte, through operatives of the Philippine National Police, massacred nearly the entire family of Reynaldo Parojinog Sr., for accusations of drug trafficking. See, among others, Bea Cupin, "The Parojinogs and the tangled webs they wove," Rappler, August 1, 2017, 9:31 AM PHT, https://www.rappler.com/newsbreak/iq/177294-parojinog-kuratong-baleleng-links/.

12 The website drugarchive.ph, run by a consortium of the Ateneo de Manila University, the University of the Philippines, De La Salle University, and the Stabile Center for Investigative Journalism at Columbia University's Graduate School of Journalism, writes: "The police say they have killed more than 4,000 drug suspects. In addition, more than 22,000 deaths were under investigation as of May 2018, unsolved killings that may be related to the anti-drug campaign." Current estimates from various sources are as high as 30,000 killings. Drugarchive.ph continues: "The complete impact of the [Duterte initiated and operated anti drug campaign remains unclear." In September 2021, the International Criminal Court at The Hague authorized an investigation of President Duterte for crimes against humanity.

13 The Museo ng Kaálamáng Katutubò was recipient of a remarkable bequest of more than a thousand swords from the banker Edwin Bautista. Two other collectors sold their collections of bladed weapons to this museum, which has published a seminal volume: Corazon S. Alvina, ed., *A Warrior's Armament and Adornment* (Manila: Museo, 2019). These acquisitions finally repatriated a substantial number of this part of Philippine material culture. The MKP now holds a 2,000-piece reference collection.

Lethal Beauty

The beautiful bladed weapons in collections of major North American and European museums are the work of masterful smiths. The wavy, double-edged kris form, shared with the Islamicized cultures of Indonesia, was typically executed with bird-like pommels in precious woods and bone, hilts wholly filigreed or inlaid or carved; incised mythic symbols on the blade, and codified cuts along the guard. Philippine weapons scholar Mark V. Wiley writes: "Kris blades are forged from finely tempered steel of different grades, giving it the appearance of the revered Damascus blades. This forging method produces a blade with dark and light wavy lines called pamor (pattern)."[14] The scabbards were often elaborately articulated, including overlays of fine silver *repoussé*.

At more than a meter, the second-longest bladed weapon made in the Philippines, the kampilan, is distinctive for its tapered blade that is wider at the thrusting tip, where it splits into two points. The kampilan's pommel carving reveals ethnolinguistic origins, the most dramatic of which is a Muslim Philippine abstracted crocodile head profile with mouth agape. This pommel type immediately begs the questions about the overt reptilian reference held in the hand of a Muslim man and how much animism shaped Islam—or any other belief system—in the Philippines. And in fact, swords from Christian Philippines bring up the same questions.

Nearly unknown to most Filipinos are the distinctive sword traditions of the island of Panay in the Visayas, Central Philippines, and of the Bicol Region. The Panay *tenegre*, sometimes chisel-ground (flat on one side and beveled on the other), was always provided with a carved pommel in the form of a monstrous mythic figure about the size of the user's balled fist. The Bicol *minasbád* also shows up with riveting small sculptures for pommels, and is distinguished by a blade with a curved belly. Both minasbád and tenegre are admired for ease of thrust.

Tagalog swords are similarly aerodynamically perfect, most notably the slim *dahong palay*. In another now-rare form, the steel is worked for full-blade incised floriate patterning matched with cut-openwork carved scabbards. And the longest of the Philippine blades, the *panabás*, has a blade some four feet long, clearly used for ceremonial executions rather than battle. It is quite the opposite form of the Kalinga head axe, a slim instrument with a long handle and stunning curvature, ending in a sharp, long, thin point: a weapon for lethal effect on the run.

These weapons' dispersal is an art historian's treasury of research possibility. Indeed this work is called for by the simple fact of substantial collections held by important museums. Wiley writes of the University of Pennsylvania Museum of Archaeology and Anthropology collection: "Although none of these materials are currently on display, the museum has in its storerooms nearly 1,000 martial artifacts from the Philippines, including swords, knives, spears, shields, helmets, and armor." Scholarship will eventually have to square this with what Filipino martial arts practitioners understand as the relevant belief structure. The weapons were, and continue to be, invested with the warrior mythos, symmetrical with the priestess mythos, that constituted the physical and metaphysical universe of island Southeast Asia, in turns re-shaping Buddhism, Hinduism, Islam, Christianity and, in fact, modernity in this part of the world.

What the exhumed weapons are collectively saying from out of the void, in example after example through thousands of examples, is that they belong to a complex metaphysics. And while the lethal beauty re-encountered today exhibits features of globalized ideas, materials, and processes, island Southeast Asian animism emanates from how they were made. These are bespoke weapons custom-made for individual bodies by pandays with highly individualized skills. These were not made by proto-factories for armies. Each owner and each maker indicated belief in the talismanic properties of the shapes and ciphers. Each weapon, distinct from agricultural blades and small women's knives, killed with clear ergonomic logic.

---

14 Wiley, Mark, https://philippinestudies.uk/mapping/about.

This 19th c. shield from Muslim Mindanao, with inscriptions on the handle / interior side, gives powerful clues to the spiritual qualities of warfare. This animist relationship of the mystical and martial traditions is shared by all peoples of the Philippine archipelago. It continues to exist within Islam, Christianity, and modernity. Update: In February 2023, just prior to publication of this essay, Dr. Zeus Salazar suggested to the author to turn the shield in the photograph upside down for a better reading. (Private correspondence)

FIG 6 Shield from the British Museum with annotations by Information Technology specialist Abdulhamid "Gaddi" Alawi Jr., who works as an archivist with the Bangsamoro Autonomous Region in Muslim Mindanao. (Original Image: Wooden Shield with Arabic inscription; Object reference: As1894,–.389; © The Trustees of the British Museum).

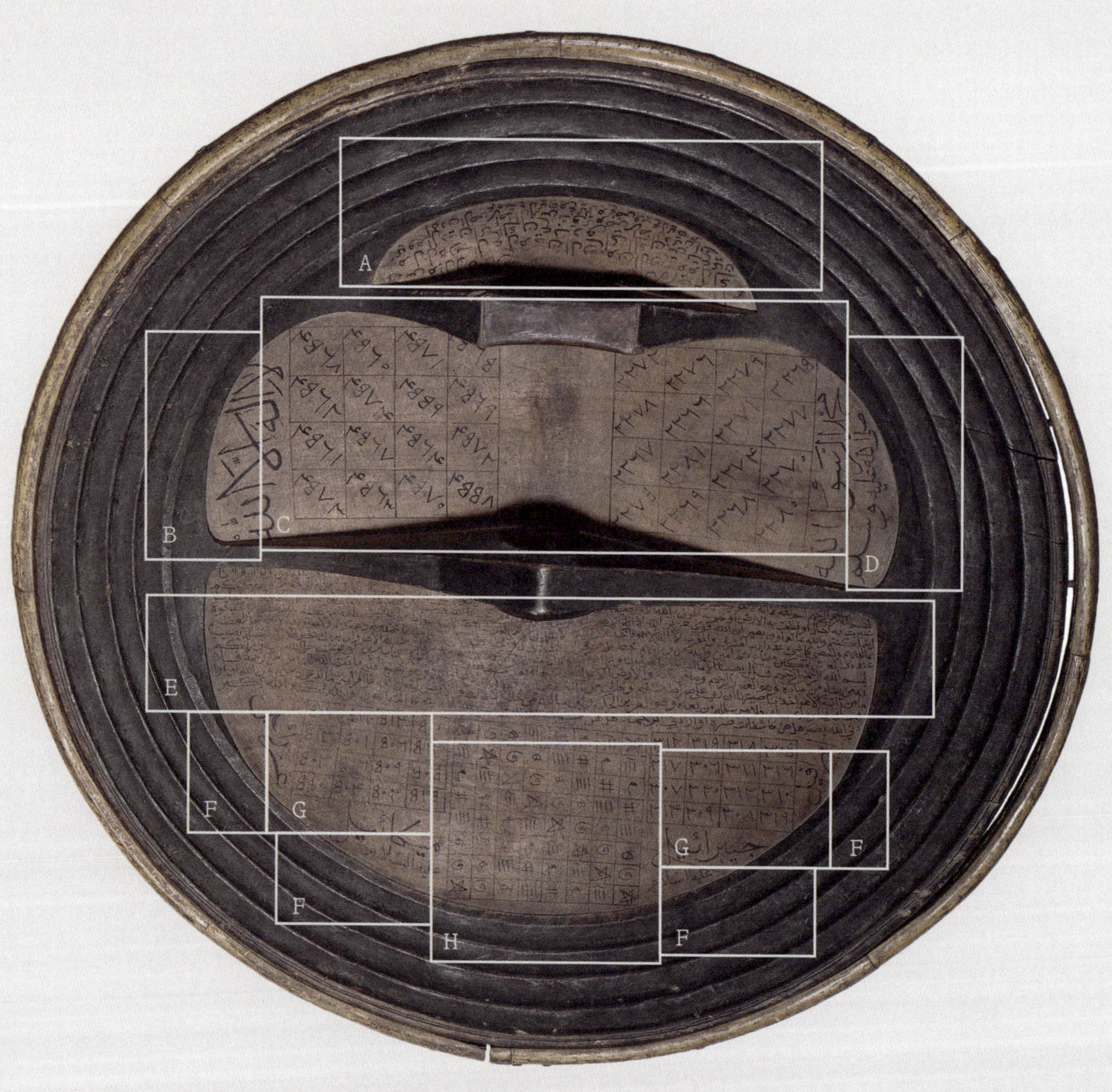

A. Al-Fatiha or The Opening—the first verse of the Quran. While usually written in joined or cursive script, this is in isolated or disconnected form. Such is done to invoke fully the intrinsic power of each letter to improve the potency of the charm or amulet.

B. "There is no God but Allah"—the first phrase of Shahada, the islamic profession of faith.

C. A Pair of four-by-four tables with three-digit number combinations in each cell. Square table builds are considered to be magically potent patterns. If the numbers are ascriptions to certain characters/ words from Islamic text, it is done for talismanic purposes.

D. "Muhammad is the Messenger of Allah, Peace and Blessings be upon Him"—the second phrase of Shahada, the Islamic profession of faith.

E. Various verses or phrases from the Quran for protection or power. About 20% of the text is unreadable but is in Arabic script.

F. The names of angels Israfil (Raphael), Aza'il (Azrael), Jibril (Gabriel), and Mika'il (Michael). The latter two have the salutation "Upon Him be Peace" that follows.

G. Another pair of four-by-four tables with three-digit nuber combinations in each cell.

H. An eight-by-eight table with one symbol in each cell. These symbols come from a version of the Seven Seals characters found in the works of the thirteenth-century mathematician and philosopher Ahmad Al-Buni.

FIG 7 Development specialist Momo Miguel suggested that the numbers on the shield were most probably from the Gurmukhi system of writing, "particularly, ੯ is no. 9." After a series of exchanges, further annotations were made on the posted image. (Original Image: Wooden Shield with Arabic inscription; Object reference: As1894,-.389; © The Trustees of the British Museum).

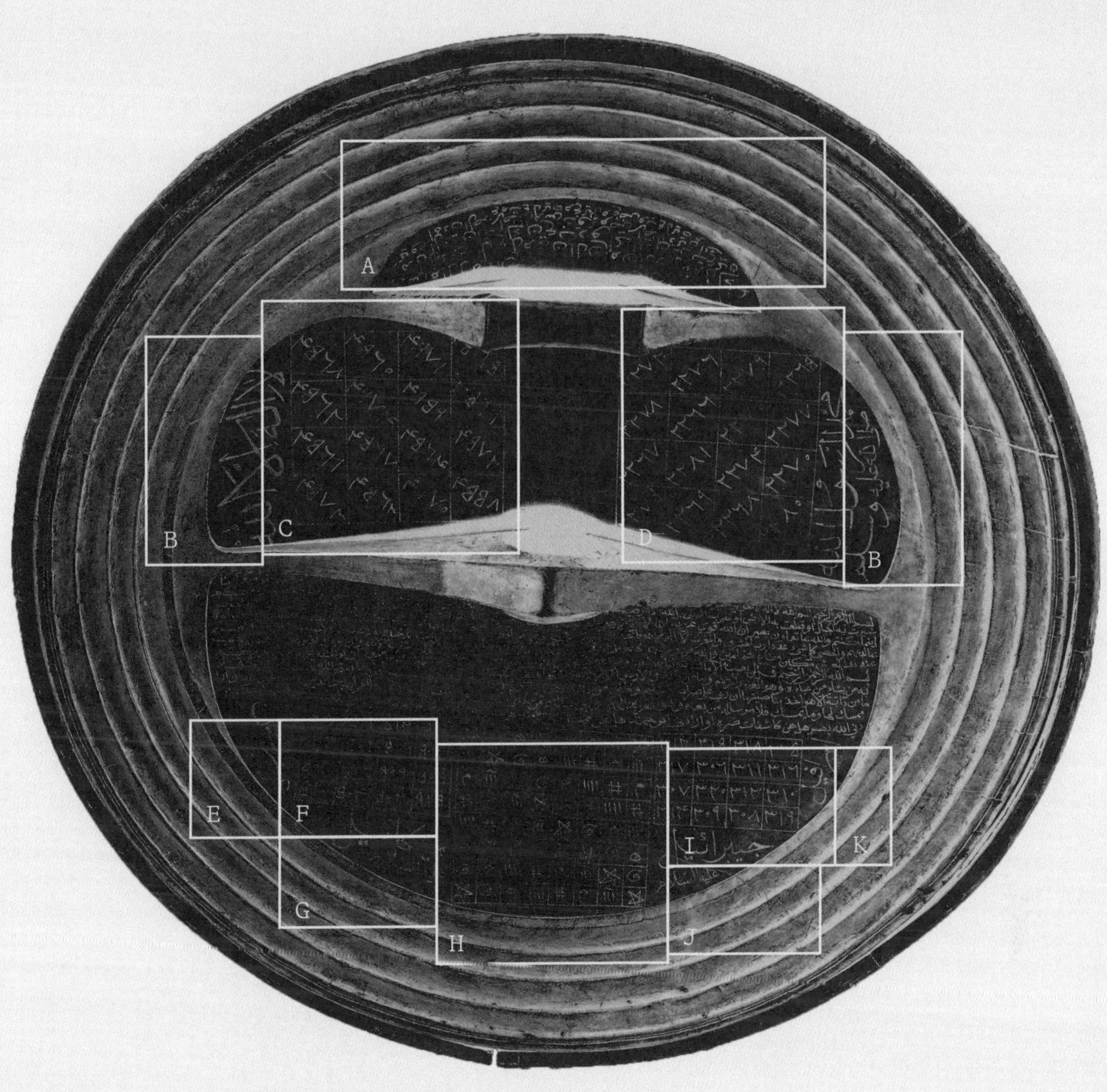

A. The Quran's Fatiha (Opening) Prayer with letters disconnected but lacking the last three words.

B. (Left) "No God but Allah." (Right) "Muhammad is the Messenger of Allah."

C. Four-digit (early Sanskrit?) numbers all starting with "45" on a four-by-four table.

D. Four-digit Arabic numbers all starting with "22" on a four-by-four table:
2279 2267 2278 2272
2269 2281 2266 2276
2268 2272 2271 2279
2270 2270 2277 2269

E. Azrail—Archangel of Death.

F. Three-digit (early Sanskrit?) numbers all starting with "5" on a four-by-four table

G. Mikhail/Michael–Archangel of Mercy.

H. Eight-by-eight table of symbols and characters on a Vigenère cipher-like pattern.

I. Three-digit Arabic numbers all starting with "3" on a four-by-four table

J. Jibril/Gabriel—Archangel of Reveiation.

K. Israfil (Raphael)—Archangel who will blow the trumpet to signal the Day of Resurrection.

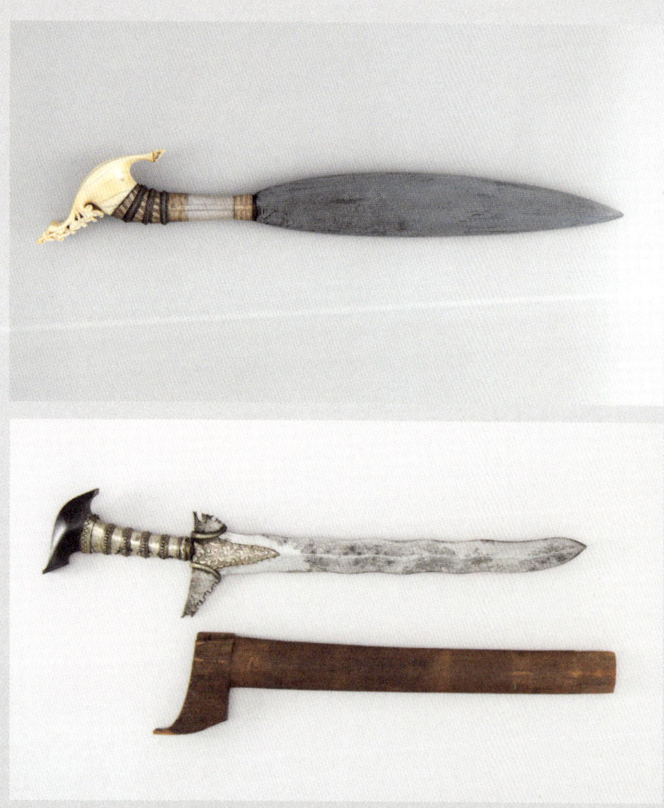

FIG 8 Knife (Barong) with Sheath; 19th century; Sulu; Philippine, Jolo Island or Zamboanga Peninsula; Steel, wood, ivory, silver, copper, gold; L. with sheath 28 in. (71.1 cm); L. without sheath 24 in. (61 cm); L. of blade 15 in. (38.1 cm); W. 3⅝ in. (9.2 cm); © The Metropolitan Museum of Art. Image source: Art Resource, NY.

Dhū al-fiqār, or the Sword of ʻAlī, is the key element of the decoration and symbolism of this barong, a single-edged short sword from Jolo Island in the Sulu Archipelago of the southern Philippines. A stylized depiction of Dhū al-fiqār, inalid in silver, is shown in the center of the barong blade. It is recognizable by its characteristic forked tip, here rendered as two curved prongs.

Also known as the Sword of the Prophet, Dhū al-fiqār was originally the name of one of the personal weapons of the Prophet Muhammad, which later belonged to his son-in-law, ʻAlī. Following Muhammad's death Dhū al-fiqār attained legendary status, its ownership conferring legitimate temporal and spiritual power. Representations of the sword came to symbolize the victory of Islām and to serve as powerful talismans. The forked tip with which Dhū al-fiqār is invariably depicted seems to have resulted from interpretations of a dream the Prophet was said to have had prior to the battle of Uhud in 625 CE. In the dream he reportedly described the tip of his sword as having a notch or dent. Later, artists represented this as a sword with two points, making it the standard iconographical form found throughout the Islamic world in works of art and on flags, armor, and weapons such as this barong.

The barong is a type of sword unique to the Islamized peoples of the southern Philippines, the Moros. It is distinguished by a heavy single-edged blade of elliptical shape and a gracefully curved pommel that resembles the stylized head of a cockatoo or parrot. The finely carved ivory pommel, silver grip, and plentiful silver inlay decorating the blade of this barong suggest that it was not intended for use in battle but rather as a sign of social status.

Inlaid in Arabic in the center of the Dhū al-fiqār motif is the word "Allāh." Surrounding it are numerous groupings of letters and numbers. These are not intended to be read per se, but were probably chosen in accordance with formulas derived from an Arabic book of talismans. Belonging to the gray area between magic, folk beliefs, and religion, talismans were published in Arabic books as early as the fourteenth century and are still used in some parts of the Islamic world today. Each letter and number in such a system has a mystical significance. Arranged in specific combinations, sometimes in conjunction with Qurʻanic passages and other pious phrases, talismans are believed to ward off various dangers. The most common form of talisman is written on a paper, which is folded up, placed in a small container, and worn as an amulet. Talismanic formulas and motifs were used on various types of objects, and were often incorporated into the decoration of Islamic sword blades. This baron, however, appears to be unique in terms of Philippine weapons because its decoration combines talismanic inscriptions and the Dhū al-fiqār motif.

FIG 9 Kris with Sheath; 18th-19th century; Philippine, Maguindanao; Steel, wood, horn, silver; H. with sheath 14 9/16 in. (37 cm); H. without sheath 13⅞ in. (35.2 cm); H. of blade 10⅛ in. (25.7 cm); W. 11/16 in. (1.7 cm) © The Metropolitan Museum of Art. Image source: Art Resource, NY.

The body of knowledge thus embodied by these bladed weapons is no less than the complex of mysticisms enshrouding life and death. The weapons were deployed to manifest visible and invisible realities as interpenetrated. Life and death are overlapped but yielded to the volition of warriors and priestesses who take up positions in the overlapped zones.

Loss does not show up in these reflections at all. Certainly the weapons themselves presided over harsh loss: life, possibility, visibility. But to an island Southeast Asian animist, the anima of things escapes form yet persists—and the notion of loss may have been inconceivable. Speculating further, what would have been imaginable to the makers and wielders of these instruments was instead metamorphosis. There is enough explicit suggestion in Philippine epics and rituals to follow the transformations of humans to animals, things to animated entities, reality into dreams, absence to presence. And vice versa.

Observers of this form of animism are inevitably persuaded to therefore think of loss as the utterly incommensurable. Matters disappear but don't. Life is taken, but not exactly. What appears to matter most is the symbolic power of the transitions, whether these are violent or gentle or something else from a vast range of possibility. And, depending on the character of each dynamic of transition, the arcs that are set in motion can be fugitive indeed.

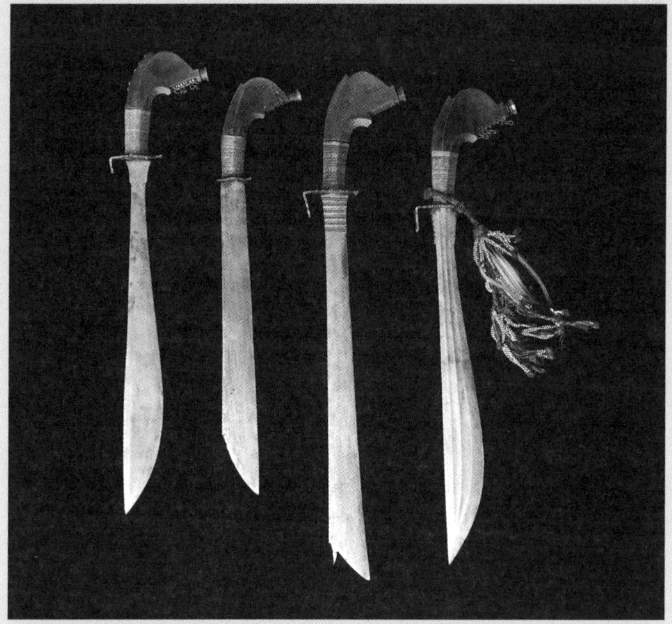

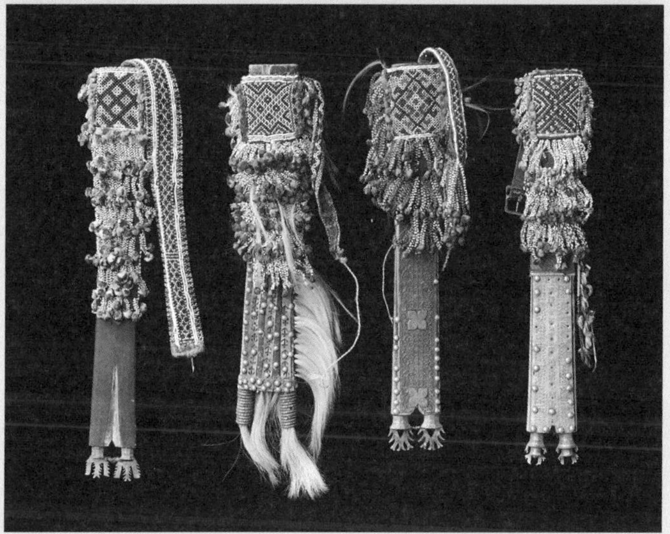

FIG 10-11 Philippine Islands, Davao Gulf, Mindanao; Bagobo; Sinan kabau: Man's fighting knife with fine grooved blade. Fret work near ferrule. Incised brass ferrule. Wooden handle. Heavy bead tassel attached to ferrule. Wooden sheath has lower part carved with fine; Source / Collector: Fifth R.F. Cummings Ethnological Expedition to Philippines Islands 1909–1911 © The Field Museum, Image No. CSA36942, Cat. Nos. 129137, 129135, 129138, 129140.

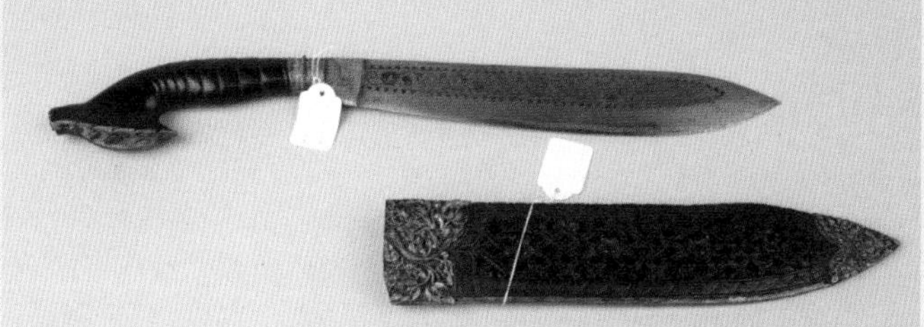

FIG 12 Dagger, knife; Philippines, Luzon; Kris with the blade straight at the bottom, 6 mm thick back and slightly curved edge, widened towards the tip, next to the mount 30 mm. On one side stamped decoration in the form of a leaf vine, on the other a flower vine, partly inlaid with brass. The blade covered with brass at the hilt. Mount of black horn with incised, transverse rings, at the tip widened backwards and covered with a leaf-shaped silver shell, at the blade silver band; 42 cm long; Accession Number 1889.04.4249. Image Courtesy: Etnografiske Museet, Stockholm.

The Mystical and the Raw

The lost weapons of the Philippines was such a case: untrackable until the pieces themselves reappeared to at least some publics. By the time they resurfaced, their arc into history had already moved through realms of unknowing that produced incomprehensible violence. The loss of the materials to Filipinos obscured archaic mysticisms whose features were transmogrifying—while arguably the animist structure was sustaining itself—creating non-mystical forms in which only the rawness of killing remains.

To the question, *What to let go?*, the answer is: to let go of the discourse of loss. Entropy will take the form of loss, at least to human eyes. From the perspective of living through Philippine contemporary history, the small, humanly useful question to mull is: How do we live out the violence of entropy to get to some point of negentropy?

The discourse of loss loses sight of this question in its focus on the hope in reversibility and restitution. But these possibilities—very real in many cases and needing to happen in one or other form—will not recreate a previous order. Best, to my mind, to take the local animist's view: keep materiality and immateriality indistinct and hence recognize reorderings of elements of chaos and anarchy. The reorderings currently abroad in the Philippines have given power to modern-esque bloodthirstiness, a warped mirroring of archaic leadership.

But if archaic leadership can be recognized in the haze, or through the viscosity of blood, and not automatically yielded to discourses of recuperation or loss, an order might be obtained that recasts virtuoso object-making in its relation to community-making. To return to this essay's example artifact group, weapons may no longer be weapons in any new scheme of things, and certainly not icons of past notions of the hero. But the alternative fantasy—or future prospect—might see them transmogrify into signs towards a philosophy of death and the exquisite in postmodernity.

DUSADEE HUNTRAKUL

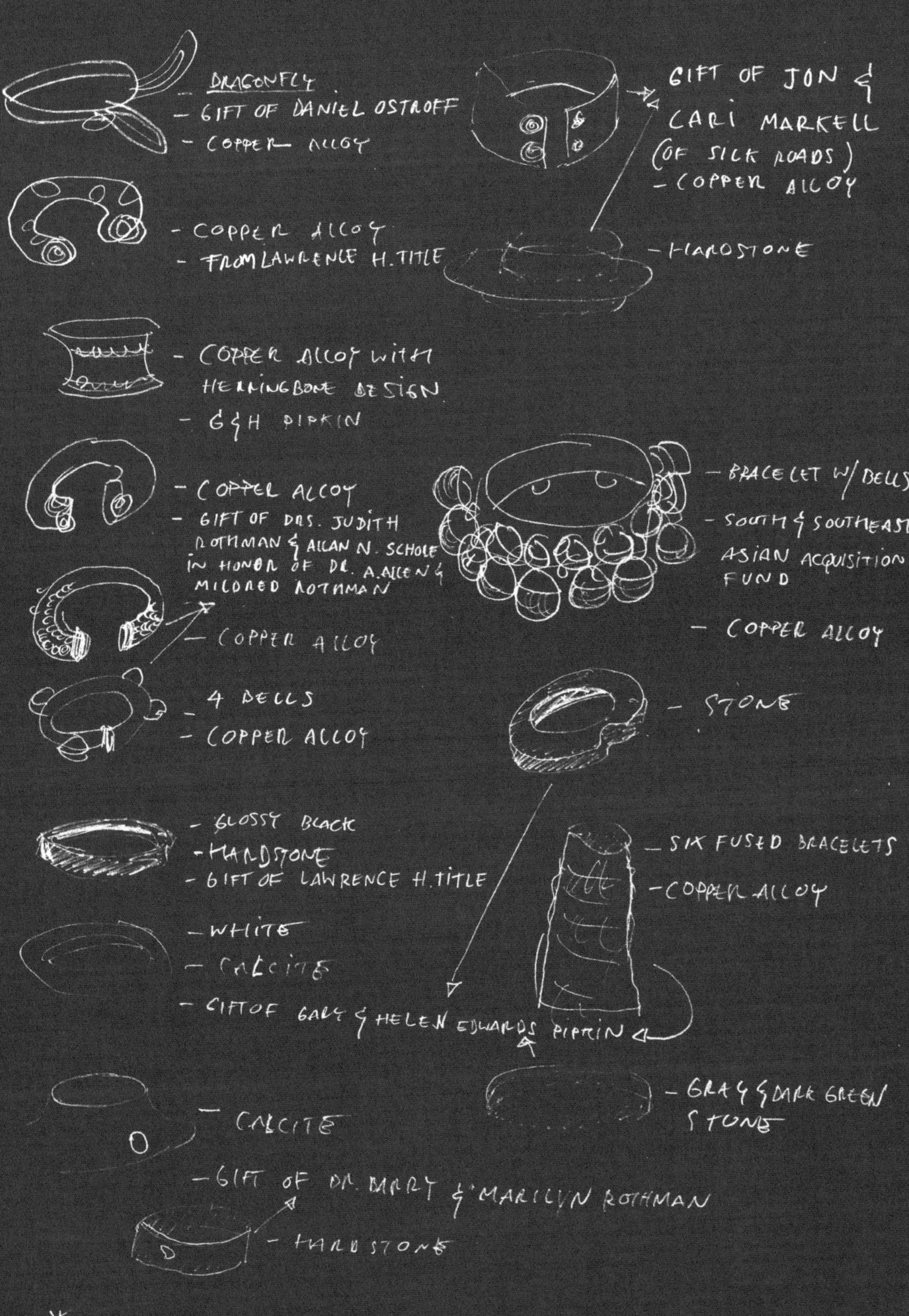

There are More Monsoon Songs Elsewhere (16 Ban Chiang bracelets from LACMA Collections found at www.lacma.org), 2018. 30 × 21 cm each. Charcoal powder, soft pastel, dry pigment, white chalk, and color pencil on paper. Collection of Singapore Art Museum.

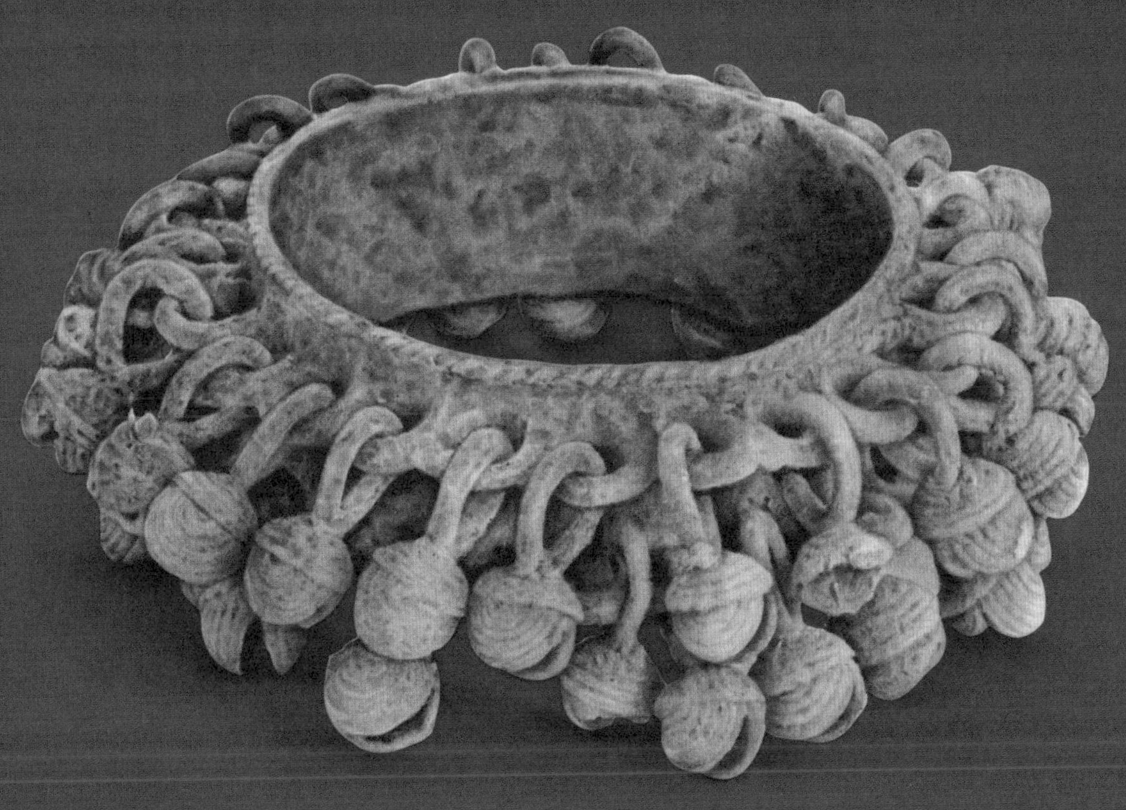

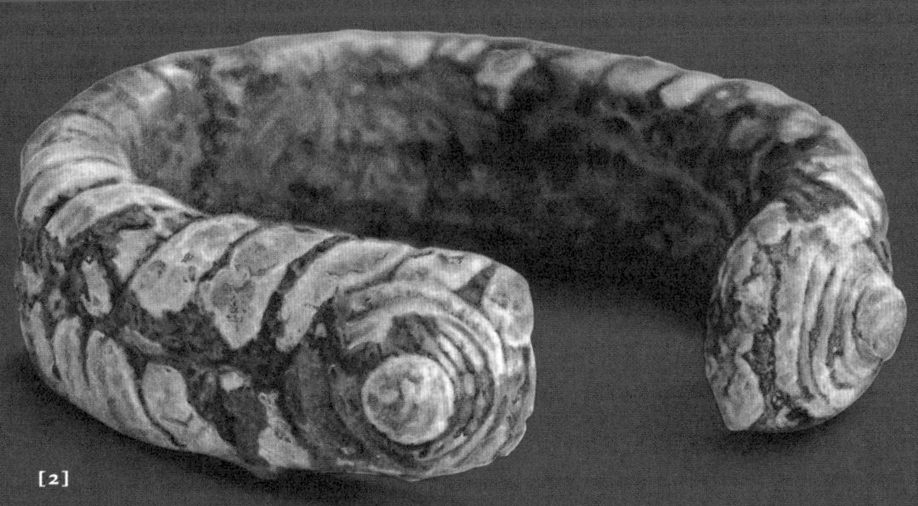

[2]

[1] Copper alloy (bracelet with bells). South and Southeast Asian Acquisition Fund.

[2] Copper alloy. Gift of Lawrence H. Title.

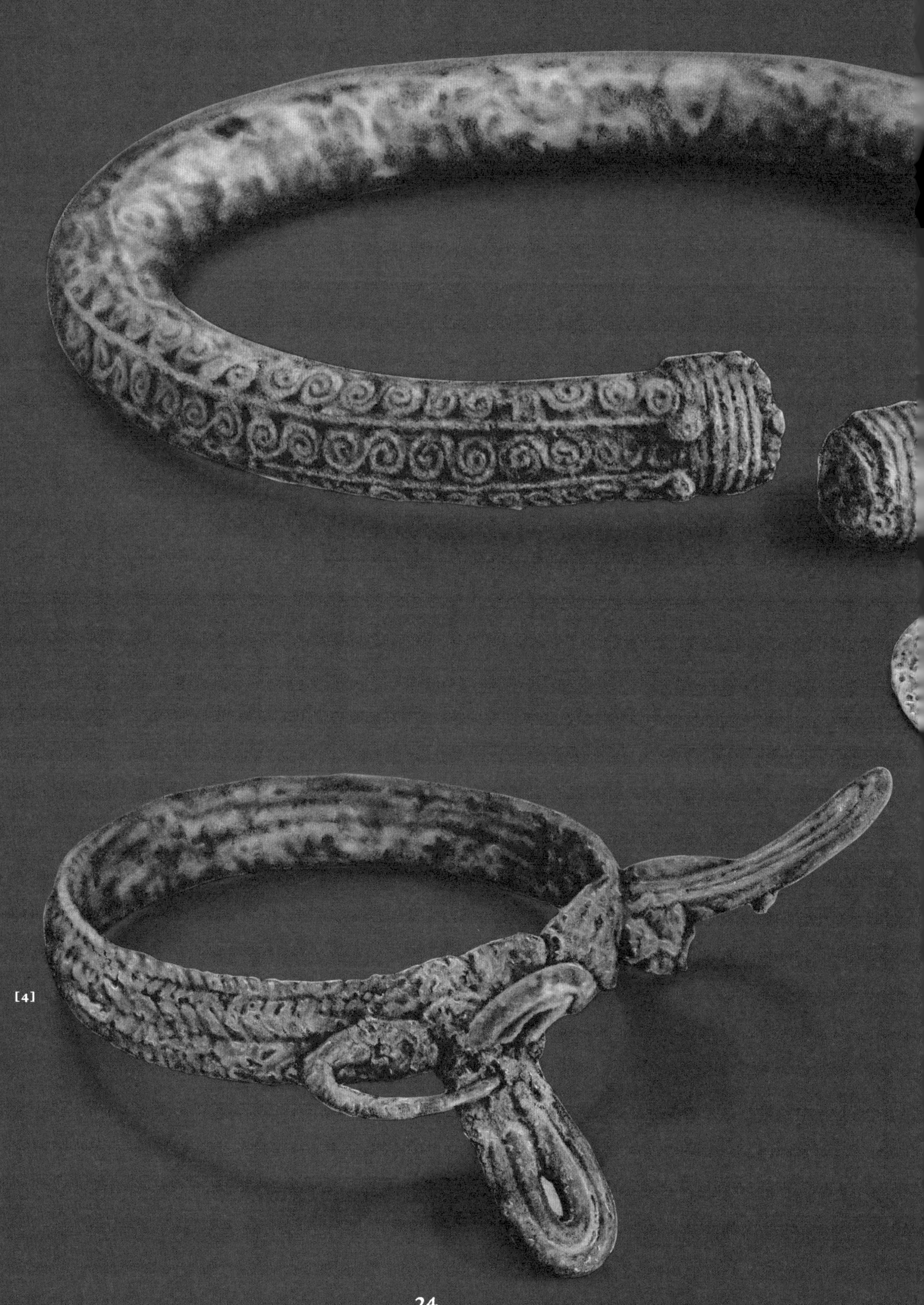

[4]

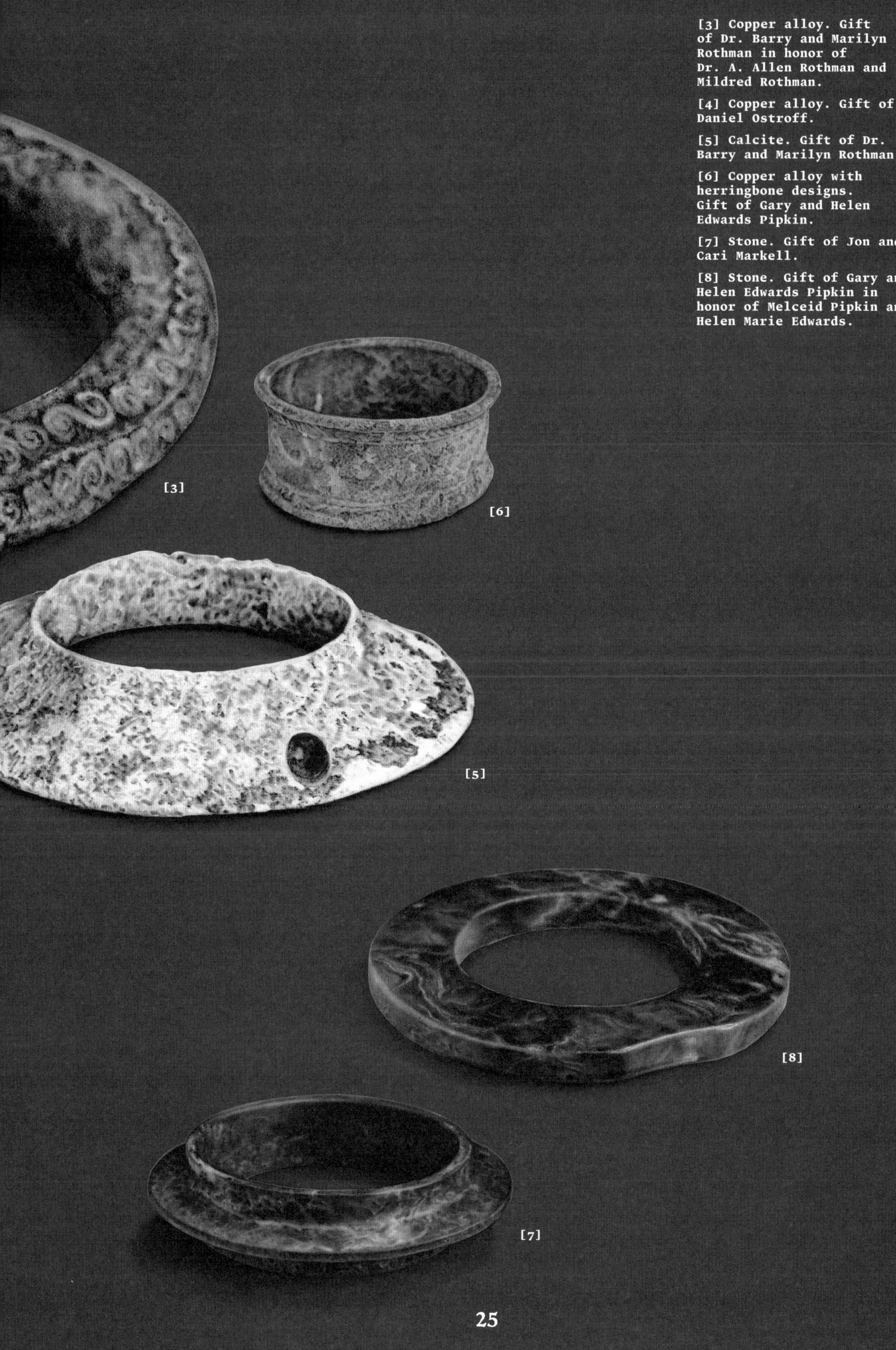

[3] Copper alloy. Gift of Dr. Barry and Marilyn Rothman in honor of Dr. A. Allen Rothman and Mildred Rothman.

[4] Copper alloy. Gift of Daniel Ostroff.

[5] Calcite. Gift of Dr. Barry and Marilyn Rothman.

[6] Copper alloy with herringbone designs. Gift of Gary and Helen Edwards Pipkin.

[7] Stone. Gift of Jon and Cari Markell.

[8] Stone. Gift of Gary and Helen Edwards Pipkin in honor of Melceid Pipkin and Helen Marie Edwards.

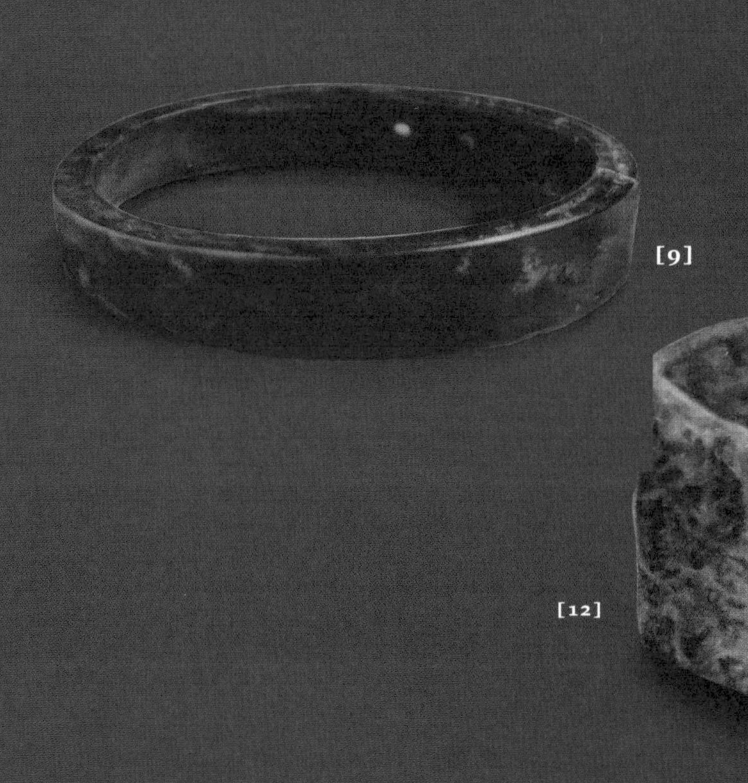

[9] Stone. Gift of Lawrence H. Title.

[10] Calcite. Gift of Gary and Helen Edwards Pipkin.

[11] Copper alloy (bracelet with four bells). Gift of Drs. Judith Rothman Schore and Allan Schore in honor of Dr. A. Allen Rothman and Mildred Rothman.

[12] Copper alloy. Gift of Jon and Cari Markell (of Silk Roads).

[13] Hardstone. Gift of Dr. Barry and Marilyn Rothman.

[14] Copper alloy (six fused bracelets). Gift of Gary and Helen Edwards Pipkin.

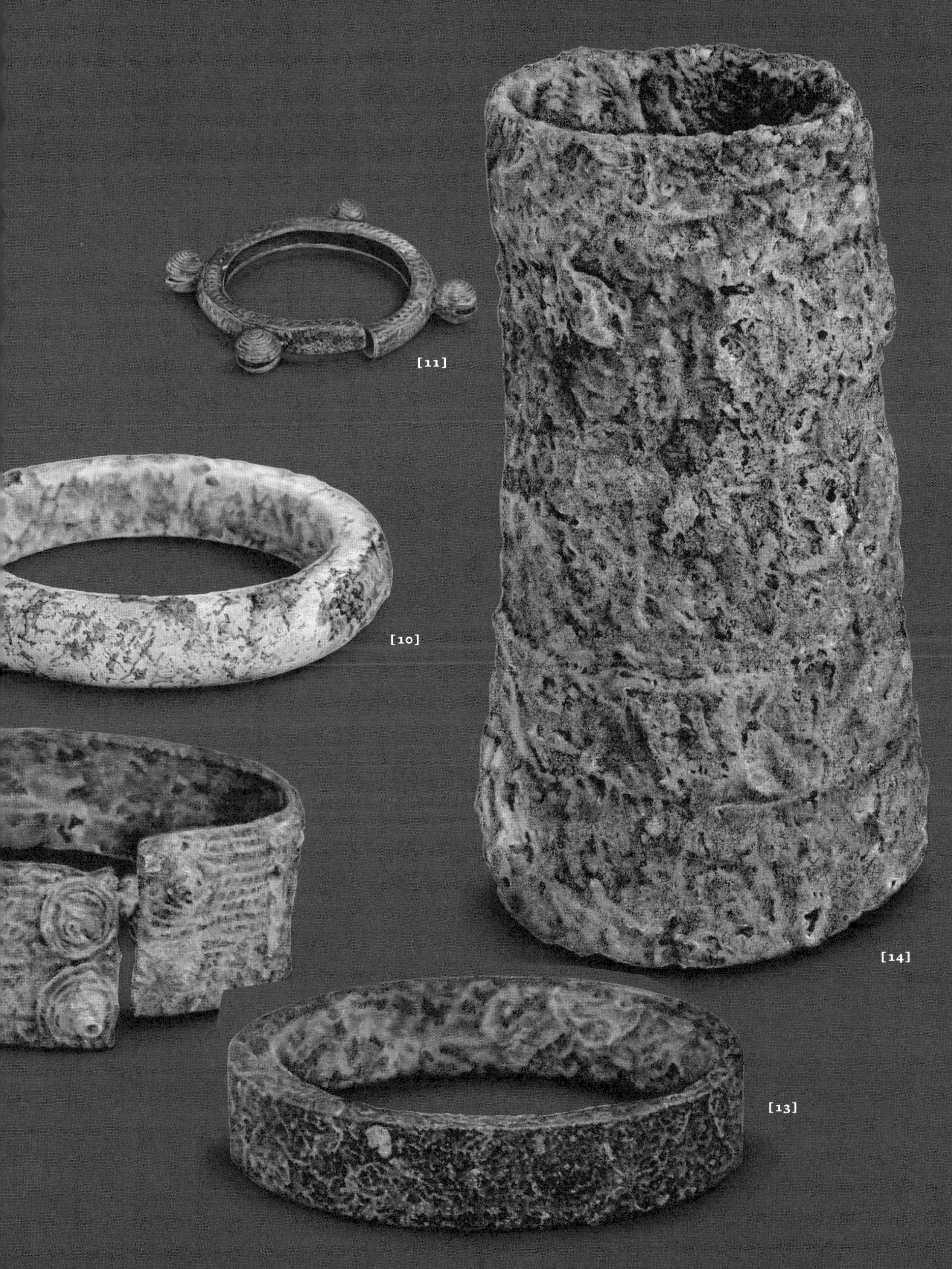
[11]
[10]
[14]
[13]

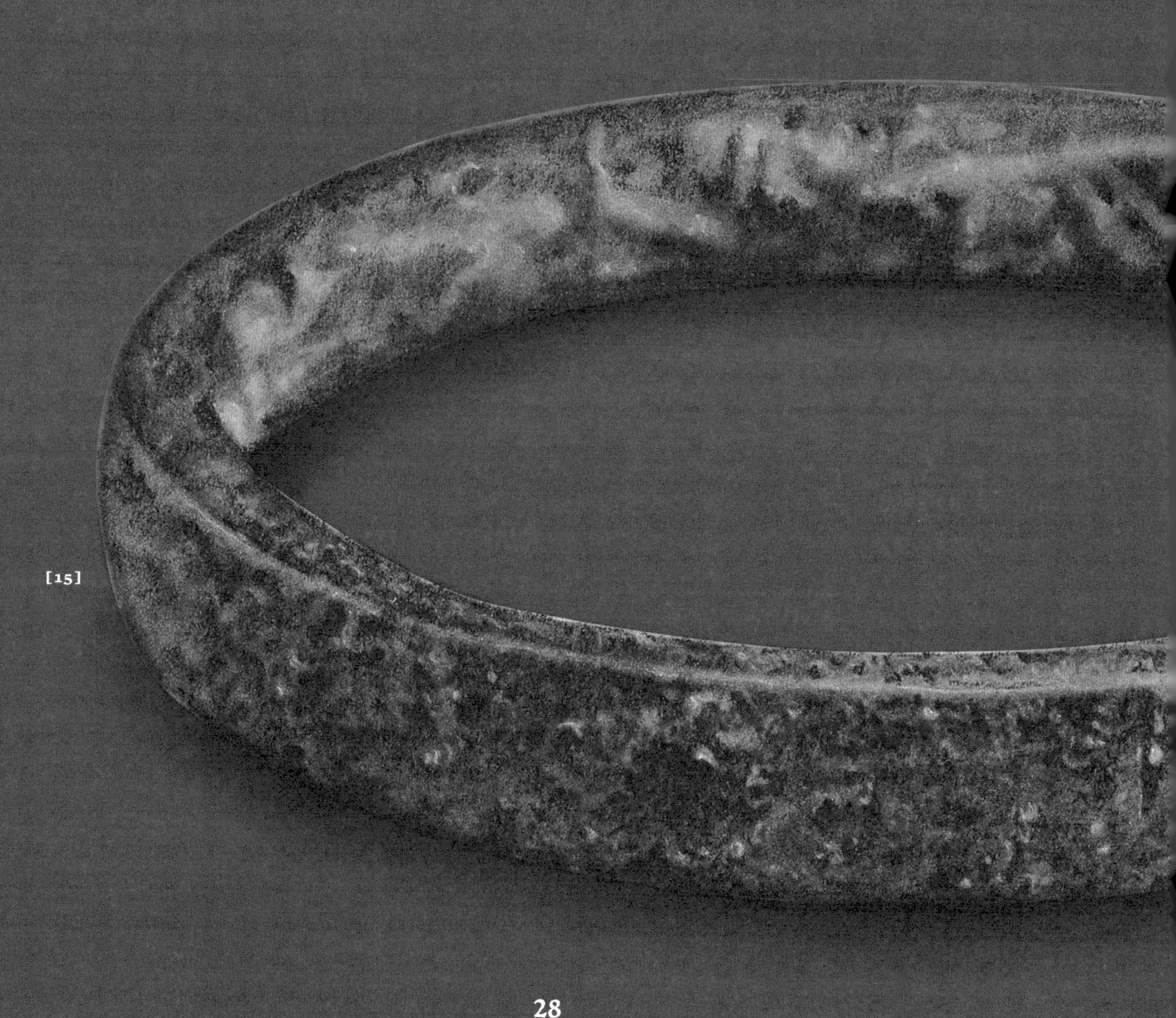

[15]

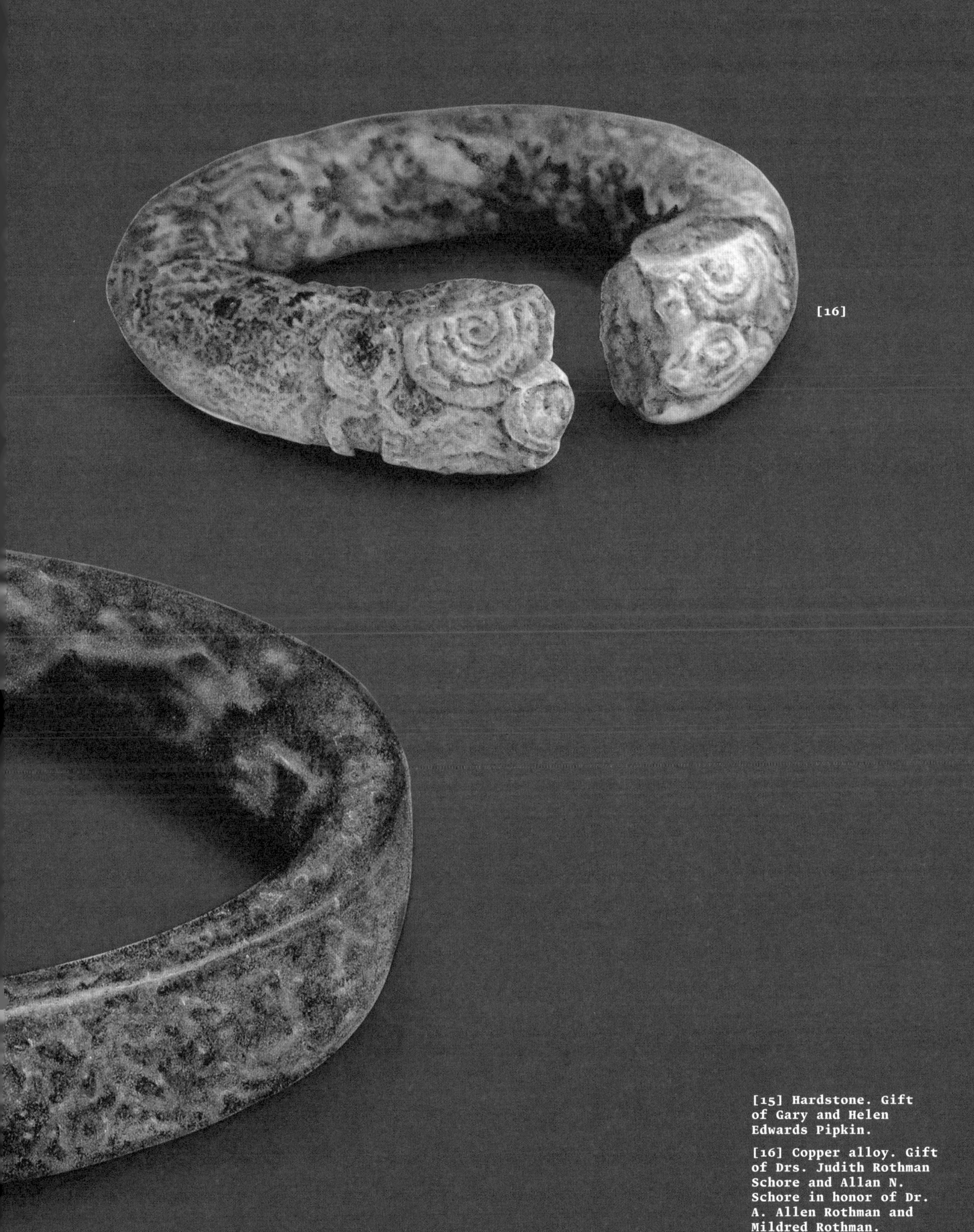

[16]

[15] Hardstone. Gift of Gary and Helen Edwards Pipkin.

[16] Copper alloy. Gift of Drs. Judith Rothman Schore and Allan N. Schore in honor of Dr. A. Allen Rothman and Mildred Rothman.

That Fresh Kernel of Things, That Quintessential Spirit: A selection of Poetry on Patrimony and Heritage

30

BONAVENTURE
SOH BEJENG NDIKUNG

Introduction

The title is borrowed from a poem by Wang An-Shih. So … what to let go? While I am not really sure about what to let go, when to let go or whom, I would like to think that Wang An-Shih answers, or at least attempts to answer the question in the poem "Reading History"!

It is said that the most essential issue of sculpting is the decision of what to take out. The sculpture is thus the residue of the whole after that which to the sculptor is superfluous is taken out. This is how I would like to understand Wang An-Shih's statement. But the fundamental question is the procedure, the methodology, the practice of recognizing what is superfluous in the writing of history and distilling from those dregs "that fresh kernel of things, that quintessential spirit" which is at the core of subjective and collective memory rather than institutionalized historicization. All the poets chosen in this composition—Wang An-Shih, Lee Maracle, Tishani Doshi, Sandra Cisneros, Taban Lo Liyong, and Jenny Xie—have found in very lyrical, personal, familial, communal and even colloquial ways, possibilities of telling the "non-dits" of history. They do, in a plethora of ways, capture those fresh kernels of things and those quintessential spirits that make up human relations irrespective of times, geographies, and politics (BSBN).

Reading History
WANG AN-SHIH

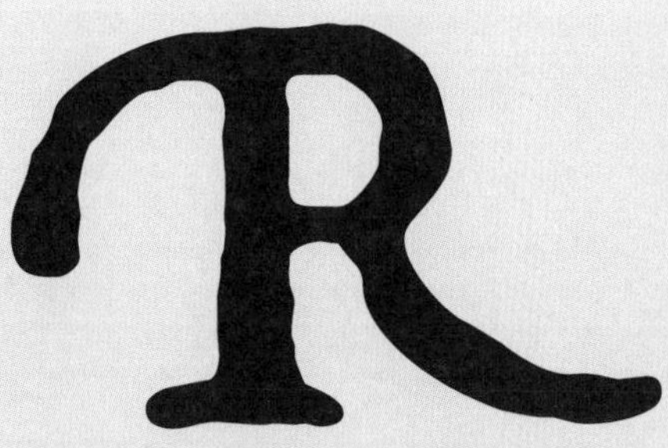

enowned achievement's been
bitter business from the beginning.
Who can you trust to tell the story
of all you've done and not done?

Whatever happens is already
murky enough, and full of distortion,
then small minds muddle the
truth further, and it's utter confusion.

They only hand down dregs. Their green-azure and
        cinnabar inks can't capture that fresh kernel of things,
        that quintessential spirit, quintessential
and how could they fathom a lofty sage's ch'i-mind,
those witless sentinels guarding thousand-autumn dust
        on their pages of paper?

Abuelito Who
SANDRA CISNEROS

Abuelito who throws coins like rain
    and asks who loves him
    who is dough and feathers
    who is a watch and glass of water
    whose hair is made of fur
is too sad to come downstairs today
who tells me in Spanish you are my diamond
who tells me in English you are my sky
whose little eyes are suing
    can't come out to play
sleeps in his little room all night and day
    who used to laugh like the letter k
    is sick
    is a doorknob tied to a sour stick
    is tired shut the door
doesn't live here anymore
    is hiding undemeath the bed
who talks to me inside my head
    is blankets and spoons and big brown shoes
who snores up and down up and down up and down again
    is the rain on the roof that falls like coins
    asking who loves him
    who loves him who?

Solitude Study
JENNY XIE

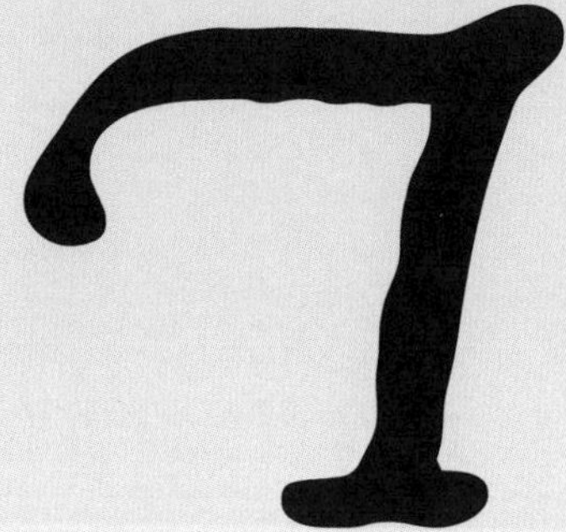

imes when I think a mind uncluttered with others
is the only condition for gentleness

or that memory sticks like cartilage
to the meat of those with the most words.

Yet I know we can hold more in us than we do
because the body is without core

and when I can no longer keep dividing
the odds are in my favor to strike it out alone.

Seeing the collars of this city open
I wish for higher meaning and its histrionics to cease.

If only the journey between two people
didn't take a lifetime.

Naturalization
JENNY XIE

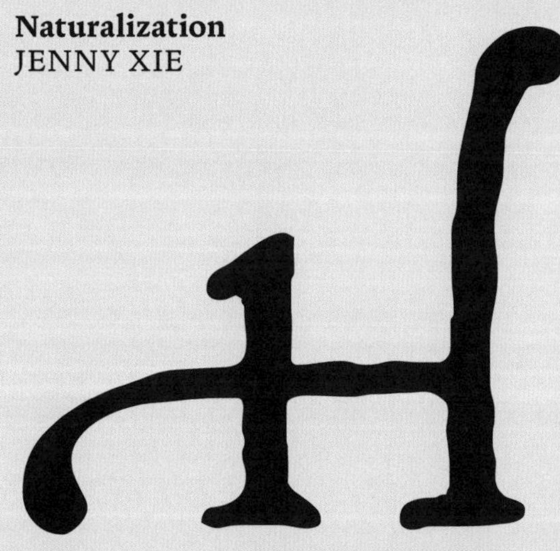

is tongue shorn, father confuses
snacks for *snakes*, *kitchen* for *chicken*.
It is 1992. Weekends, we paw at cheap
silverware at yard sales. I am told by mother
to keep our telephone number close,
my beaded coin purse closer. I do this.
The years are slow to pass, heavy footed.
Because the visits are frequent, we memorize
shame's numbing stench. I nurse nosebleeds,
run up and down stairways, chew the wind.
Such were the times. All of us nearsighted.
Grandmother prays for fortune
to keep us around and on a short leash.
The new country is ill fitting, lined
with cheap polyester, soiled at the sleeves.

Portrait of the Poet as a Reclining God

TISHANI DOSHI

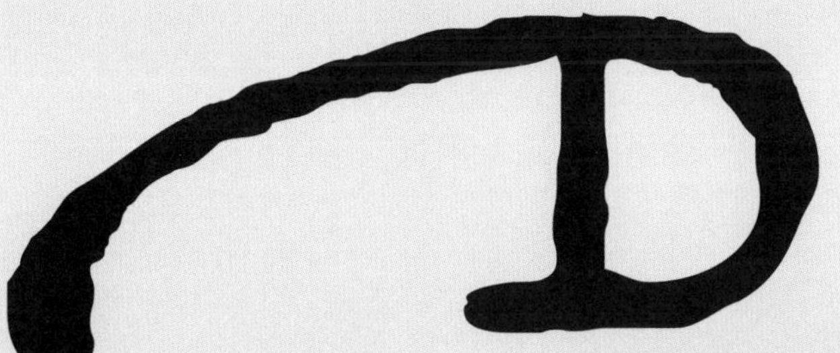

on't make much of the fact that recline
rhymes with decline. Do it anyway.
Stretch out sideways. Think Titian's
Venus, but with clothes. Better still,
think Hindu gods. Press mound
of palm up to lake of ear. Imagine
legs of blue, legs of Vishnu,
serpent skin susurrating against
your back. Belly? But of course,
Ganesha's. Breasts or no breasts,
that is the question. Ardhanarishvara.
Grow serious as we sweep towards
the eyes. Focus inwards, Avalokiteshvara.
Cradle that palm against your ear as if
it were a telephone. Whisper into the velvet
air: *Hello heart! You still there?*

The Day Night Died
TISHANI DOSHI

Bats, voles and vampires threatened
to strike. Insomnia leaned over a balcony,
shrieking, *What the...?* before vanishing
into a wormhole created by Jan Van Eyck.
Stars exposed themselves like pervs.
Forests under duress released
nyctohylophobia from their nerves.
Bonfires staged a minor revolt.
Sea said, *I'm done*, and rolled herself
back to a valley of plums. Discos
and motels schemed to Take Back
the Night, but got knifed by Brutus
in broad you-know light. Houses
reared up and slammed their blinds shut.
Dreams free-associated in corridors
of smut. Dadaists shrank against mighty
Surrealists. Jung went for Freud in the sands
of a kabaddi pit. And it was only until
the Subconscious stepped in, with
what looked like the world's tiniest violin,
whose strings he plucked like Lolita
grown up, that everyone fled from the room
in their heads, to a field where an almost extinct
species called poets, previously known
for worshipping the moon,
sat in a churlish circle of gloom.
Dead is dead, is what they said.

Your Body Language Is Not Indian! or Where I Am Snubbed at a Cocktail Party by a Bharatnatyam Dancer

TISHANI DOSHI

Lady, do you know how long I've roamed
this world like a saw-toothed shrew, sans hubby
and kids? Do you understand the kind of resistance
involved in arriving at 37—alone, two white hairs,
the onset of wrinkles. To have withstood barricades
of scolding aunties and so many diabolical winters
of social conditioning? To have said N-O
to the effervescent sortie of evolution,
which twitches in me even as I cling to a puppy,
or sing lullabies to birds. I've thought about it,
sure—of a warm body that might save me,
of these teeth of mine, which could go on and on.
But I bowed out of the race, said thanks, but no,
to History and Biology. I decline the invitation
to breed. And when the situation got aggressive,
I gave a giant finger to Genes, to centuries
of women before me who patiently flexed
their shoulders and hoiked up their knees.
To all of them I've written letters of apology.
And before all this, Lady, I was a teenager!
No picnic, as you know—a decade of crawling
through slums in the gloaming; all those neuroses
and goddamn deficiencies. How many nights
of fevered fantasies? And before that—
childhood—transparent days
of burrow and play. Being carted around
like a lady's lapdog, peeing and being petted,
paying no heed to the hours in the woods,
to subterranean skills of survival and moulting.
And this is saying nothing of the tremendous
caravan of Time, which mutters velvet aphorisms
as you sleep, like, In extreme solitude men perceive
again the touch of immortal wings. Or, Civilization seems
to be the invention of a species now extinct.
So, having arrived this far, spare me, please,
if I choose to be mysterious. If I delight
in dilutions and the vagaries of neither here
nor there, and display no seals of authenticity.

What right have I, after all? Part sea creature,
part peach tree, to take this cocktail chatter
seriously? But Lady, truly, you offend,
when you say: Your body language is not Indian!
You demolish me by quartering my paltry
ancestry into territories of wetland, desert,
marsh, city. My legs and arms, banished,
poor things, for incorrect mudras and aramandis.
And why? Because I refuse to wear the sins
of my progenitors in the topography of my chin?
Because the wobble of my head is too perfunctory?
Must I be more like you, who has so clearly
embezzled the coronary stance of your turgid
mama and faint-hearted papa; who carries
all those failed proteins in your body
like an identity card? And just how far
will you go to ensure generations of Bharatnatyam
domination? Eliminate me if you must,
for I will always prefer the pale underside
of the past to a future of grass. And when
I die, which is a fate no mammal can escape,
it will be far from home in a nest underground.
There will be tremors and some confusion
as I hang these muddy bracelets of existence
around the wrists of an easterly wind. We will dance,
the wind and I—our bodies like rosebushes alight
in the sky, clanging against the geometry of stars.

Below is a Song
LEE MARACLE

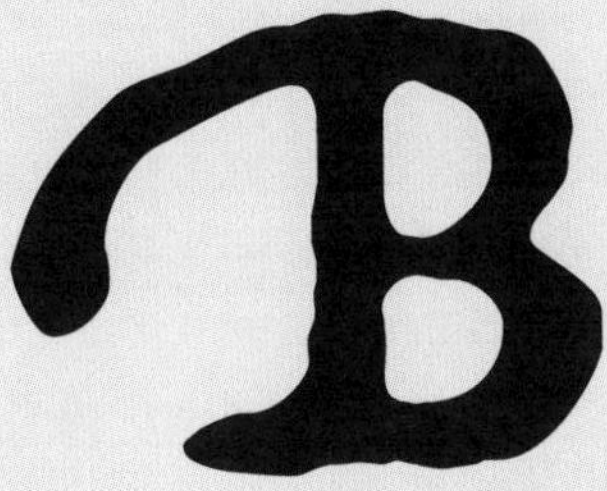

elow is a song
 It is yours
I glued it to your future
bound familial memories
 in its melody
Below is a moment
 time
moving breath time
 lost time
 dead time
 present time
 future time
 any time you want
 Below is a clock
keep time
count time
embrace time
make time
make time sweet
Below the clock is a key
 Grab the key
 find a lock
 open it
 open your throat
 unlock your song

"Below is a Song" and "Remembering Mahmoud 1976" by Lee Maracle, from *Talking to the Diaspora*.

Remembering Mahmoud 1976

LEE MARACLE

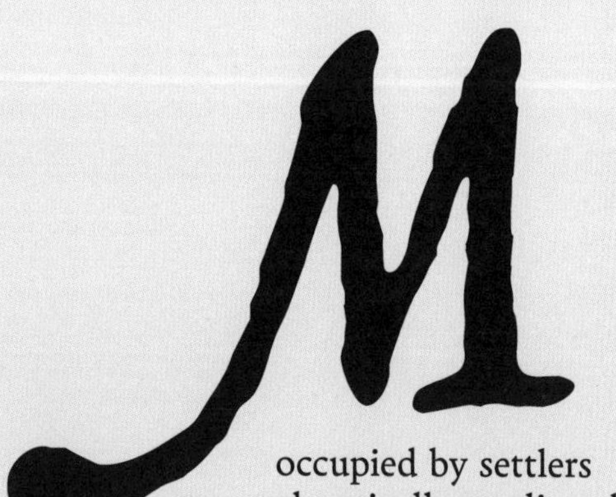

ahmoud's poems are beads of sweat
dripping from stressed and weathered foreheads
to fall near silent amid incessant Israeli bombs
to rise—blood—from between the bits of rubble
clutched by Palestinians chasing a livelihood
from a shrinking land base
They become desperate word flowers
blooming nonetheless from a land
occupied by settlers
chronically stealing the lives of children

It's December
            Toronto
Gaza is on fire
            again
another Wounded Knee
another massacre
no muskets this time
tanks, monster machines
bombs and missiles pummel the children
How brave is that?

-40 Celsius in Winnipeg
Palestinians and Indigenous children wave placards
Stop killing children in Palestine
Free Gaza
My tears freeze on my face
my daughter is there
just as she was there 35 years ago
chanting Free Palestindians
my frozen tears cut pain lines on my face
In between the rubble
Darwish's last words look at the world
say good-bye to Edward Said

peer past the camps, the bombs, the hypocrisy
stubborn
resistant
eternal

There is no tomorrow in yesterday,
so let us advance

I stare at a photo
a small boy cradles a pair of stones
gleaned from the rubble
I imagine him hearing
Darwish's ghostly words
these stones testify
this is his home
he clutches them
he looks set to advance
the stones are no longer simply rubble
they cradle a story
they cradle his memory
they cradle his hope
they cradle Darwish's last testament:

There is no tomorrow in yesterday,
so let us advance

In this boy's hands the stones transform
they are the story markers of his future
they are his beginning
beloved stones, last bits of a place called home
they become stones of conscience
they are his stones of pride
they will become his stones of belonging
they are the rocks of justice for all of us
His face is set
his eyes see past this rubble
they see forward to his return
forward to the restoration of his homeland
forward to the right of return
In his eyes I see Indigenous global tenacity
I touch the stones in the photo
caress his face
commit to building a bridge
an arc of light
under this wind of war
of dispossession
I want to build a pathway
and blow us all toward freedom and justice
I want the wind of freedom to echo
the resonance of Mahmoud's breath tracks

Let us pick up this stone of justice
build this bridge
that will lead us to the laughter of belonging
of being where we belong
of being who we are and always will be
This light shines back at me from his eyes
the light illuminates his stones
bound as these stones are to his resolve
to traverse across the abyss
between his refuge and the tanks
My commitment to Palestine floats
the light emanating from his eyes captures my heart
I whisper Palestine, Palestine—Free Palestine
Wounded Knee, no more Wounded Knees
I imagine him listening, hearing me
nearly smiling
just before he throws his stones

Carrying Knowledge up a Palm Tree
TABAN LO LIYONG

31

Which is more dangerous:

to profane the host of God and risk losing heaven
to dare intimate tabooed names in public and out of season
to call a State house spade a Statehouse spade of all trade
to go to bed with an adder and hope you'd smother it to death?

Reader
the first two dangers are universal
you'd need to be particularly daft, to incur the wrath of the third
and would need a zoologist to permit you date an adder.

Contrary to syllogists
dangers do not sprout in every backyard.

32

Snakes, unable to dig their holes
Appropriate the hedgehog's underground garage
And hibernate there when times are bad.

Addis Ababa looks like a pod
Without the seeds. I don't like
The poor aesthetics of makers of coups
Who know (or think they do) how
To return seeds to pods.

52

The colonizer had his ways learned from the Greek states;
The colonizer trained his sons in the Tripos learning Roman history;
The colonizer used the popes to bless genocides before they were done;
The colonizer had no personal qualms, history had already absolved him;
The conscience of the colonizer was already tailor-made by the time
Shakespeare was born.

Blame the Greeks and their mini-states for forging links;
Blame the practicality of Romans for expanding far beyond Italian foot;
Blame the universal dream of Saul for creating Paulinity and Popes;
Blame the Arabs for closing land-routes to the East for Europeans;
In the process of finding routes to Eastern markets we were found
and taken in stride.

If Marco Polo's camel route to Sinna was still in use, America
would still have lain virgin;
If the world map still revealed a flat world, nobody dared
sail far to tumble eternal;
If the Crusades were won by Europe the gold, nutmeg, myrrh
of India would have sufficed;
If Atalantis had not lived in myths nagging, quests westwards
would not have arisen;

If—if what?
Stop iffing. The hunchback is already created.

RADCLIFFE BAILEY

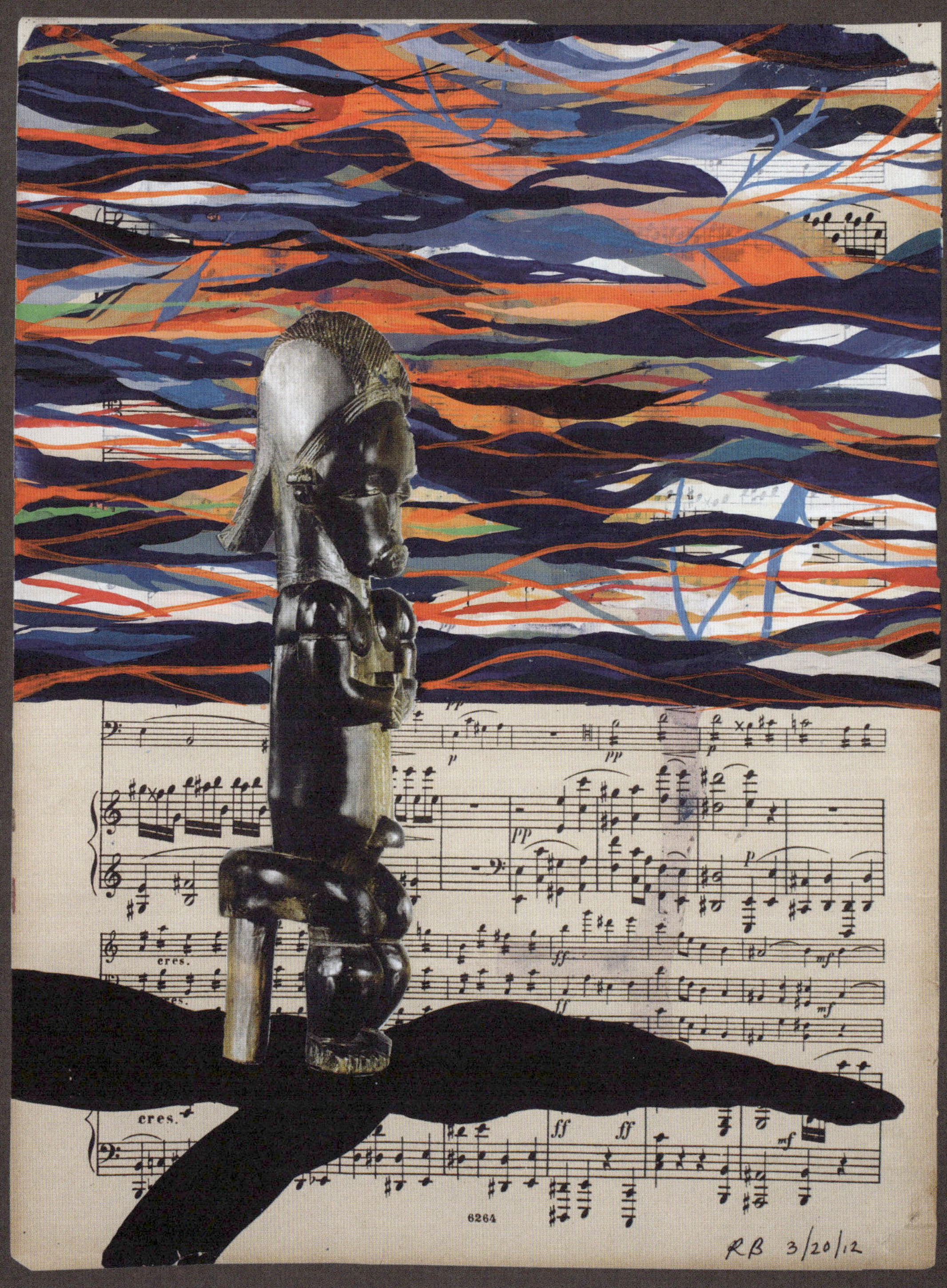

LEFT
Notes from Tervuren, 2011. Gouache, collage, and ink on sheet music.

RIGHT
Notes from Tervuren, 2013. Gouache, collage, and ink on sheet music.

NEXT PAGE
Notes from Tervuren, 2013. Gouache, collage, and ink on sheet music.

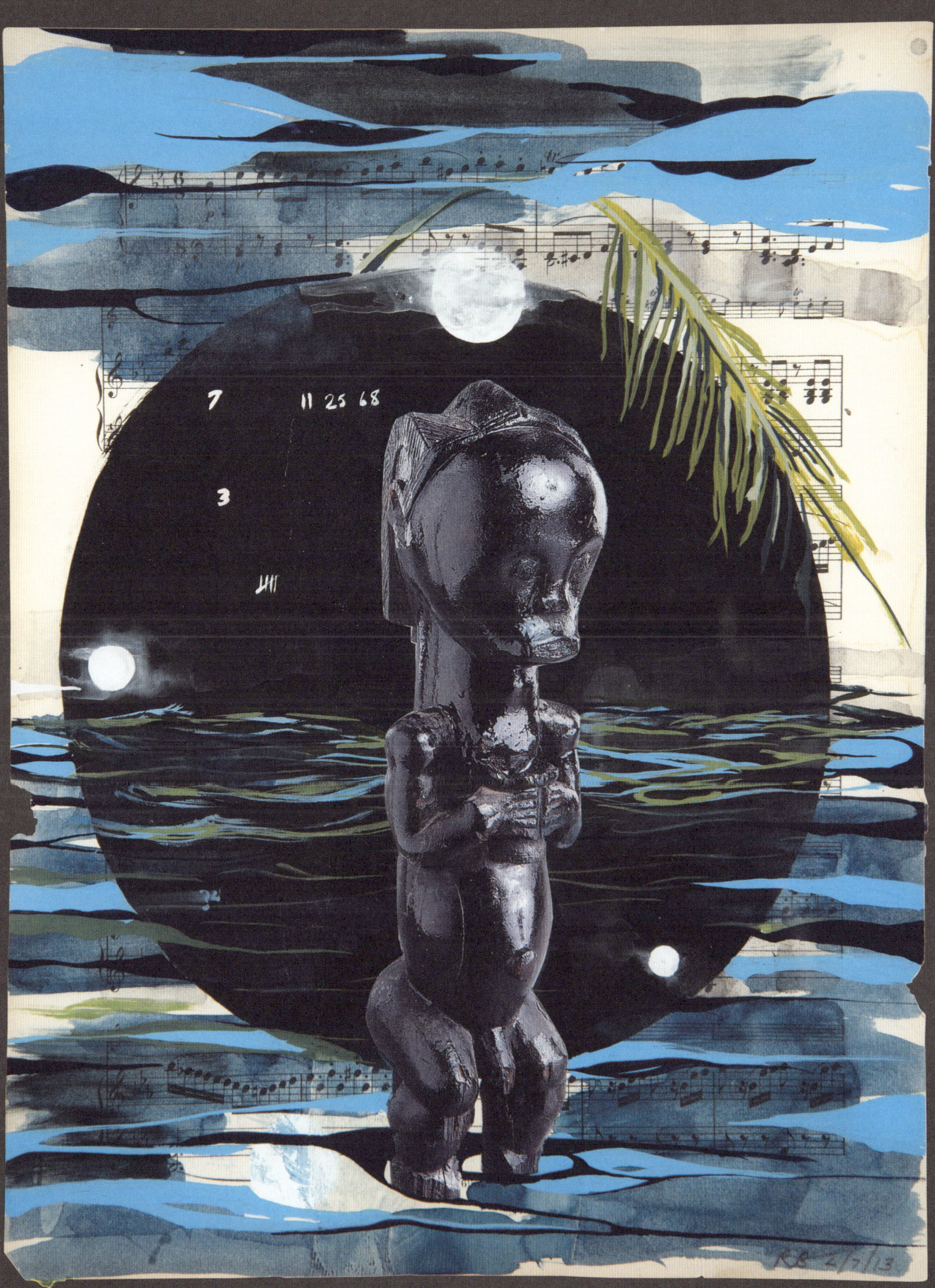
7
11 25 68
3
RB 2/7/13

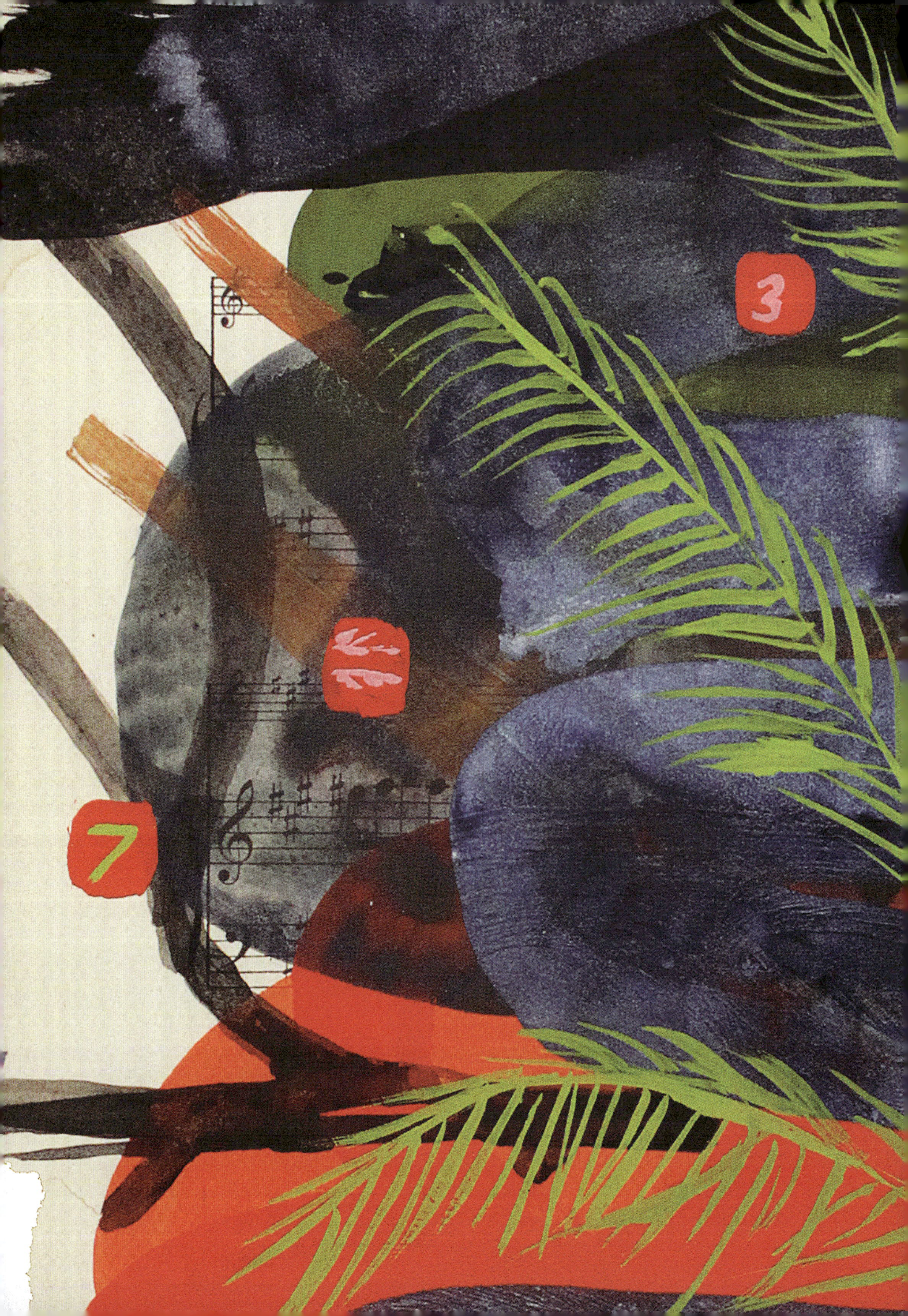
3
7

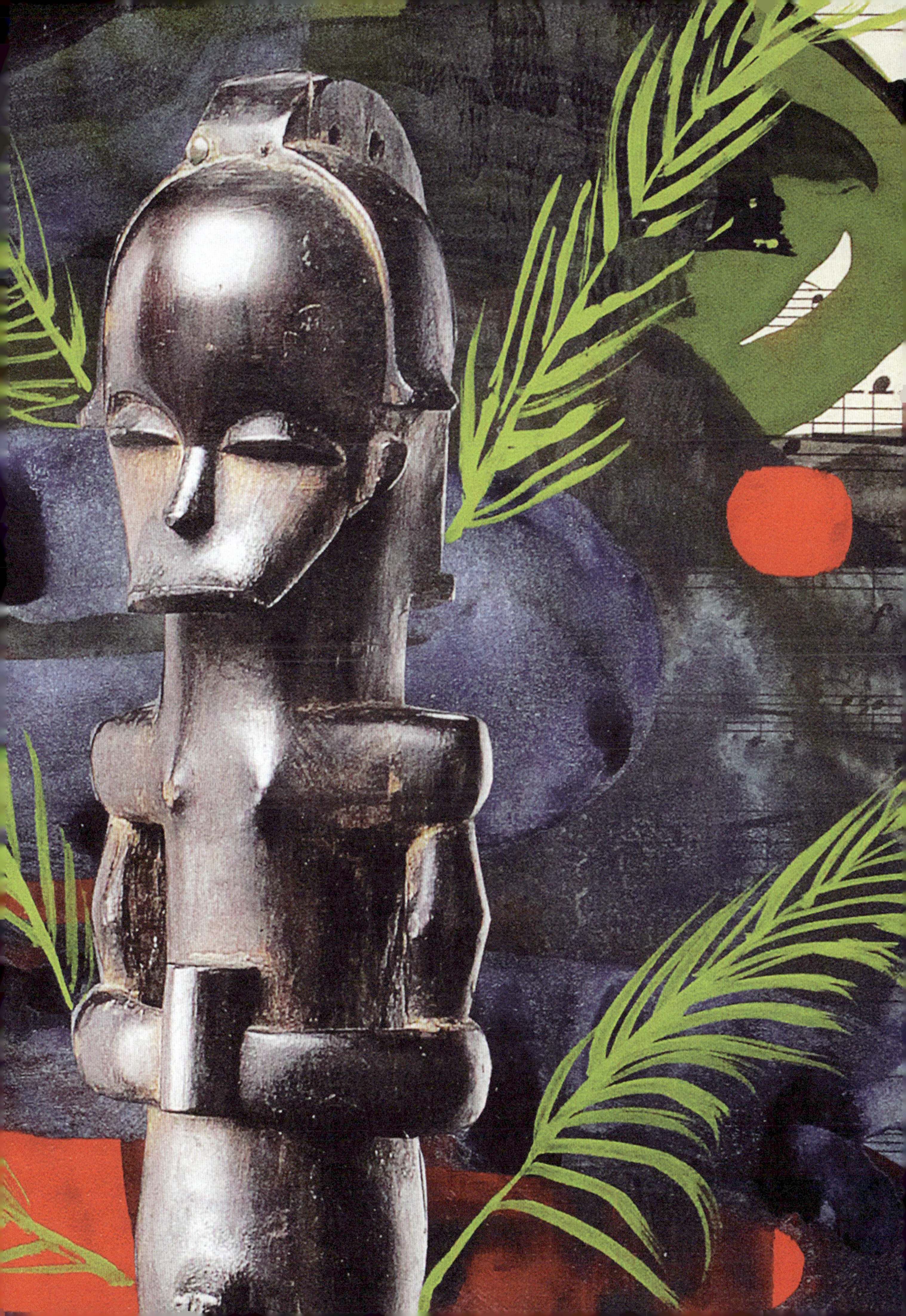

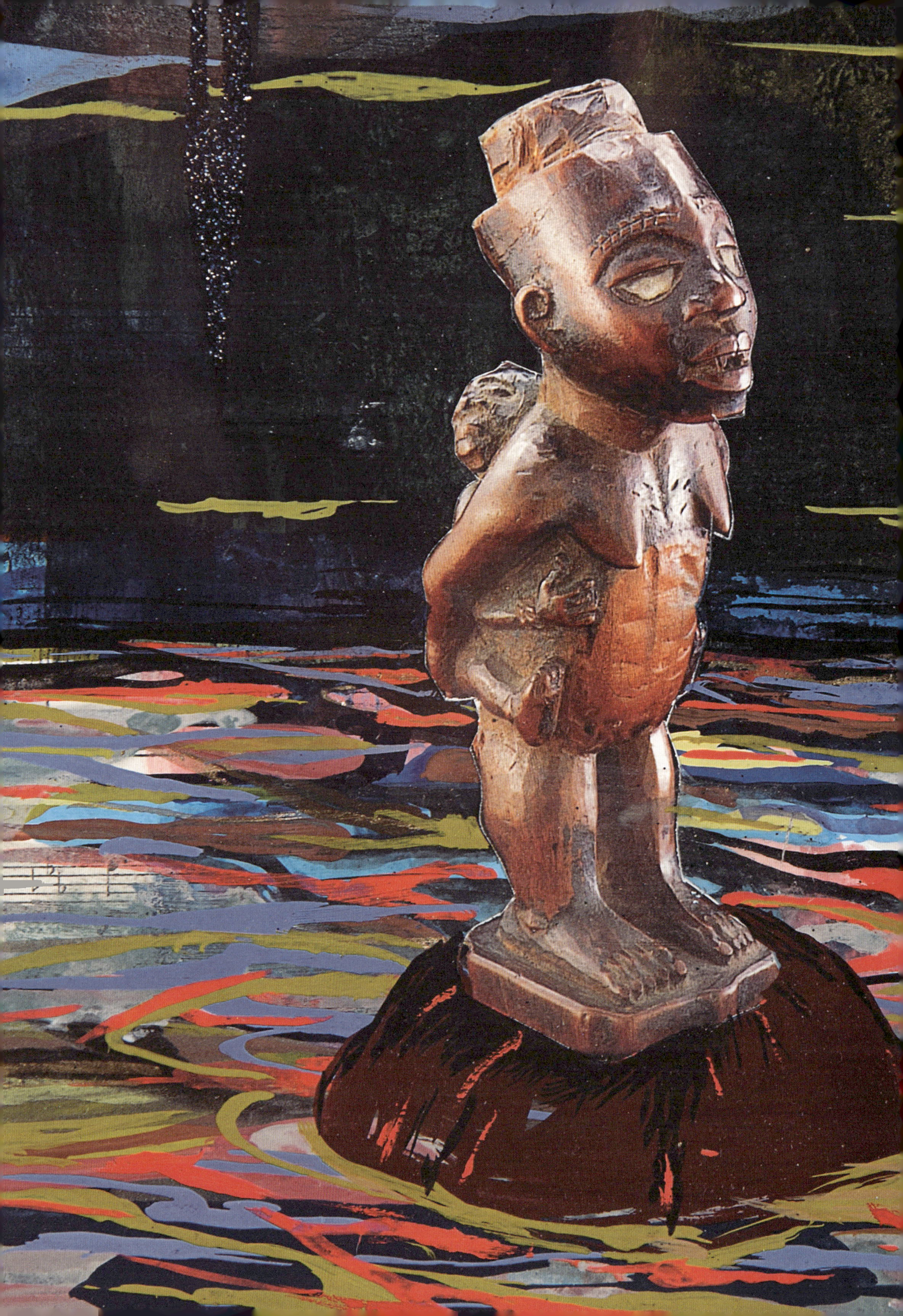

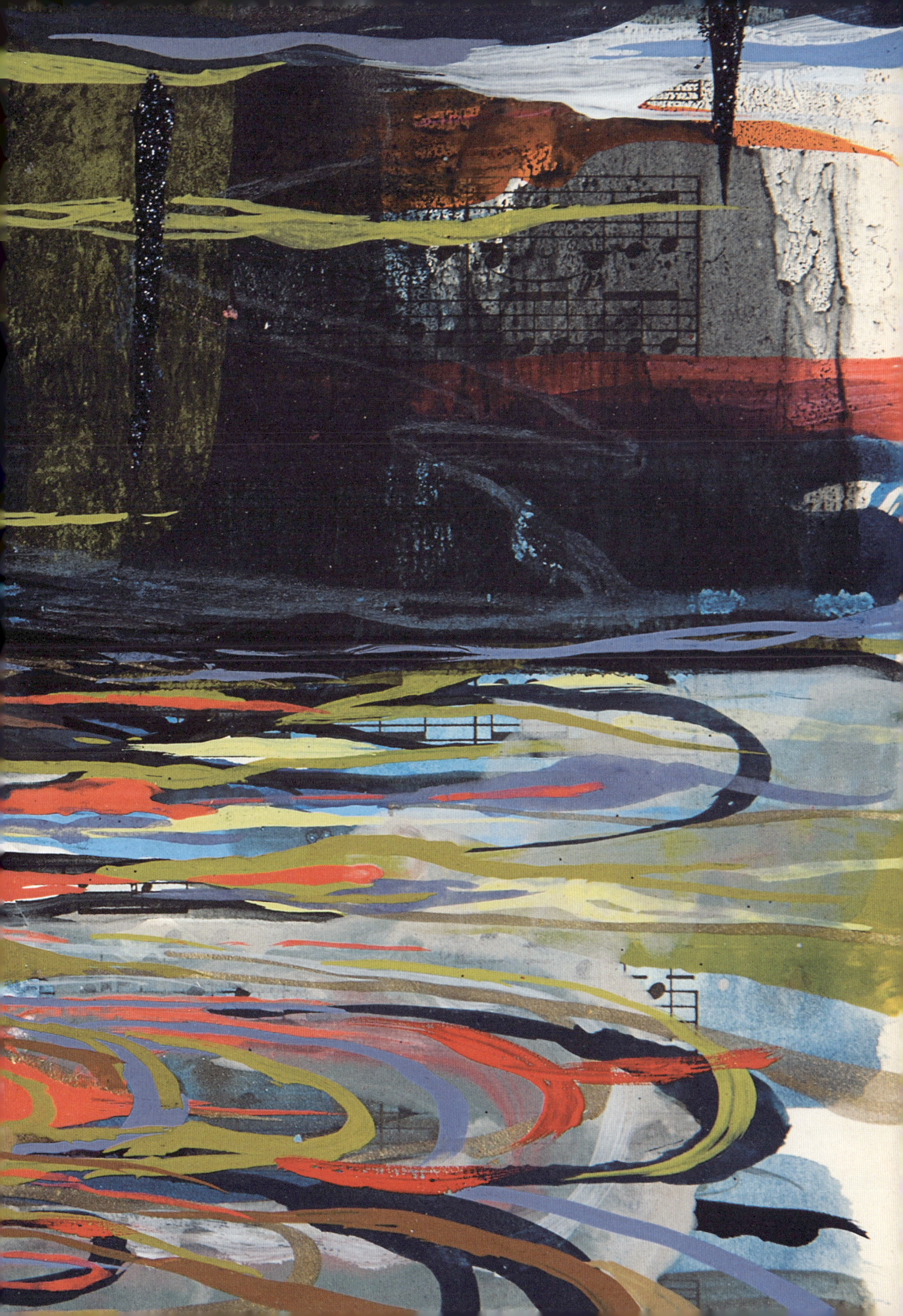

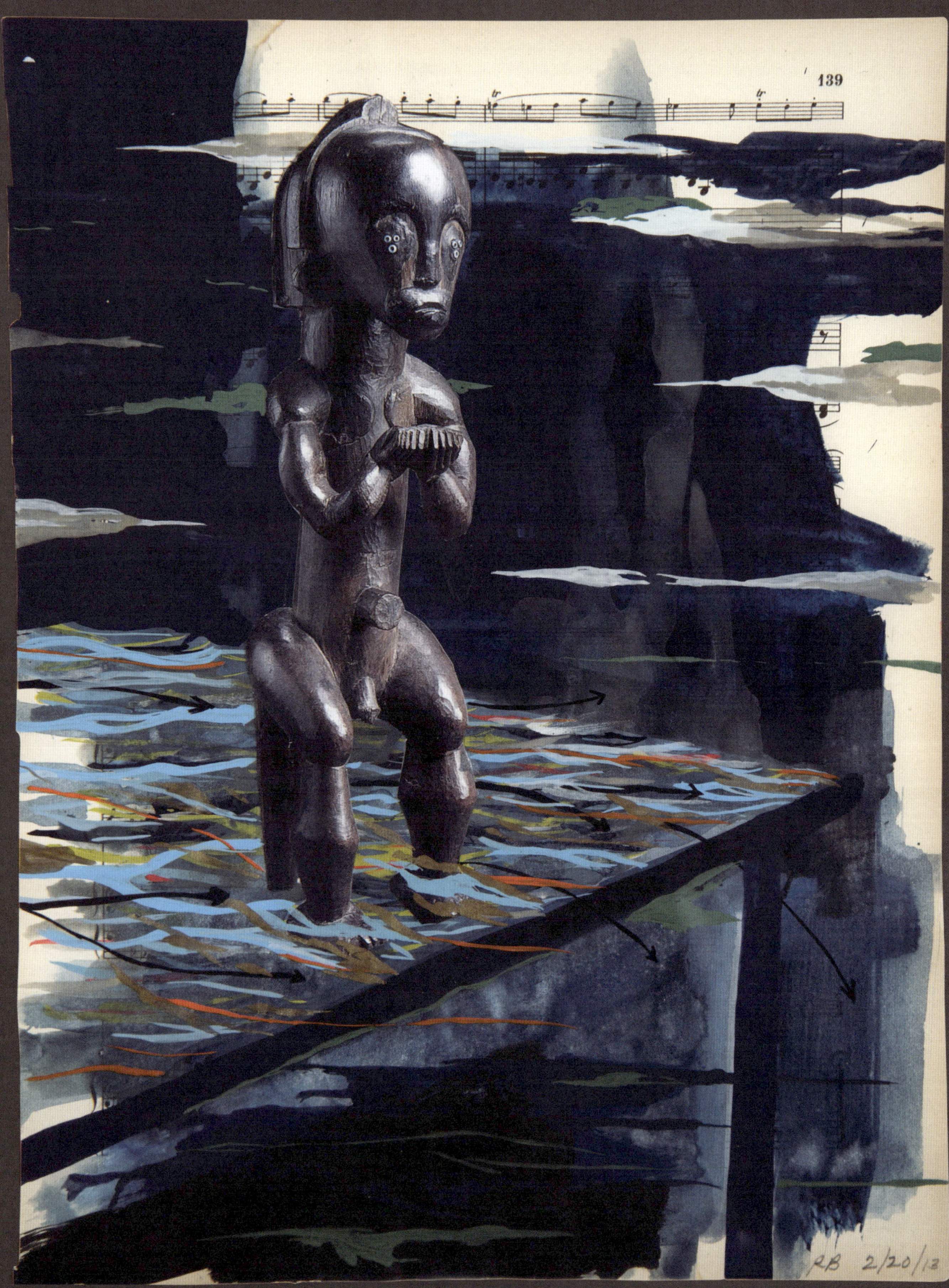
139
RB 2/20/13

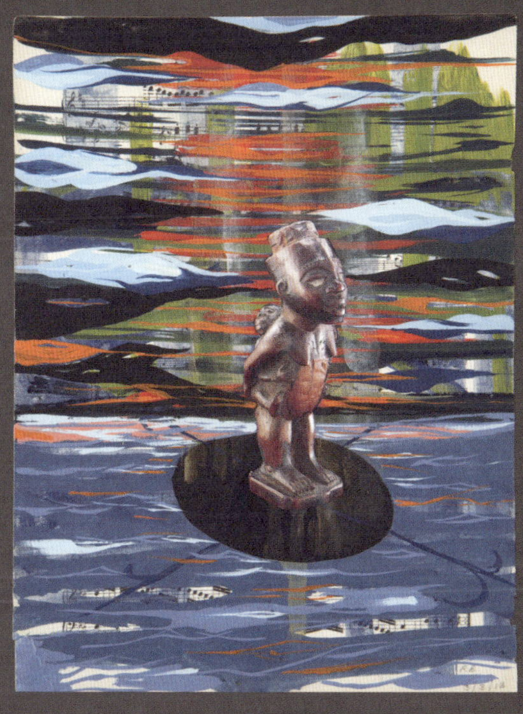

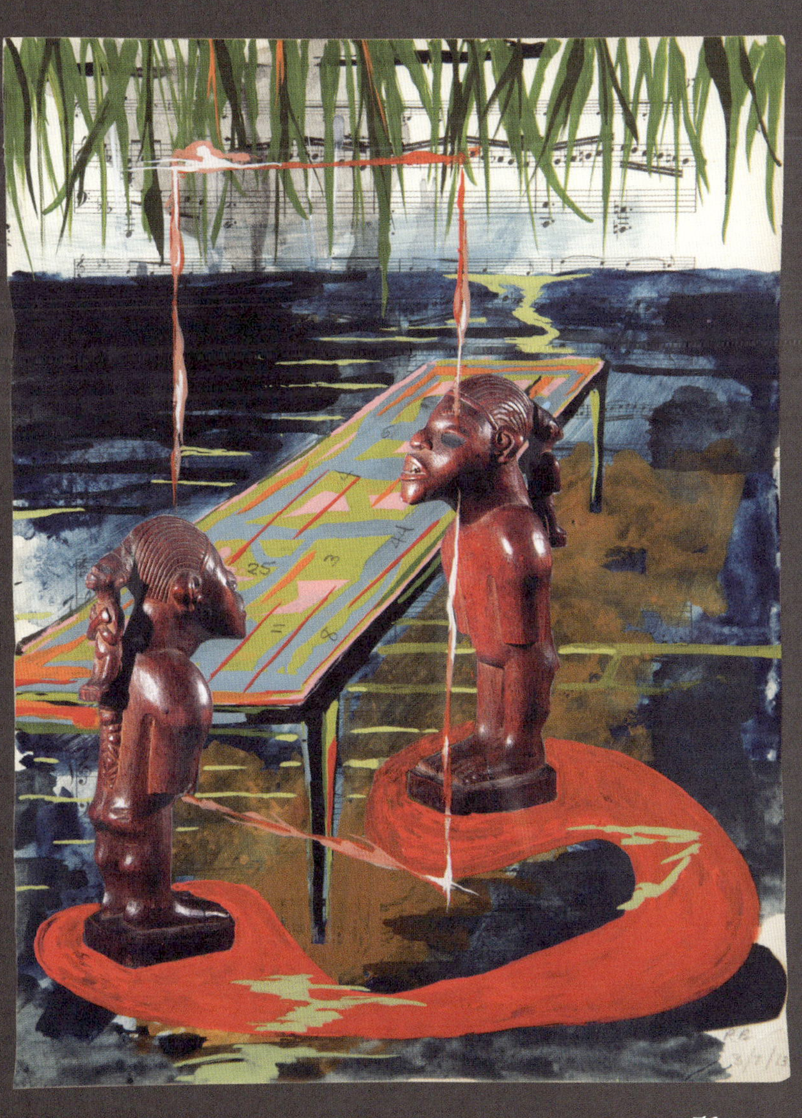

PREVIOUS PAGE
Notes from Tervuren, 2013. Gouache, collage, and ink on sheet music.

LEFT AND RIGHT
Notes from Tervuren, 2012. Gouache, collage, and ink on sheet music.

Indigenous Pacific: Co-Creation and Collaborative Stewardship in Today's Museum

52

MAIA NUKU

We cross with only these possessions
And look for something familiar
Yet so much belongs to a separation
Unlike definitions I lose what objects mean
In time I could almost say:
We belong to what we lose.

— Craig Santos Perez, Guåhan (Guam) [1]

I begin with these powerful words by CHamoru poet Craig Santos Perez as a way of grounding us in the immediate challenges one faces as a museum curator caring for a collection of Pacific art in an overseas institution. The words are pertinent, prompting ideas of loss and separation. They encapsulate many of the acute issues that we necessarily confront in our daily work at the interface of museums, collections, and their communities. Considerations come thick and fast: Can we continue to make museum collections relevant and pertinent to our times? How can we create more expansive access to artworks in the collection and the narratives associated with them? How might we reconcile the histories of ethnography and collecting with the contemporary issues and challenges facing Pacific peoples today? Far removed from the region, collections of Pacific art located in museums in the United States and Europe present a material record of the historical and geographical fracture, violence, and creativity enacted by encounter—the rupture and dissonance of colonial histories, the divisive nature of missionary enterprise, and the unforeseen imaginative outcomes of cultures conjoined. Collections present a unique and valuable window onto that past. Exploring artworks in collections gets us close to confronting those histories; each individual artwork—so charged with the cosmological underpinnings of its Indigenous conception and manufacture—brings the coordinates of the culture clearly into focus for those of us seeking them out today. From painful and uncomfortable to joyous, emotions run the gamut. There remains much to do in connecting dispersed collections with their descendants so we can continue piecing together full and complex histories (nuanced, not partial or selective) and make sense

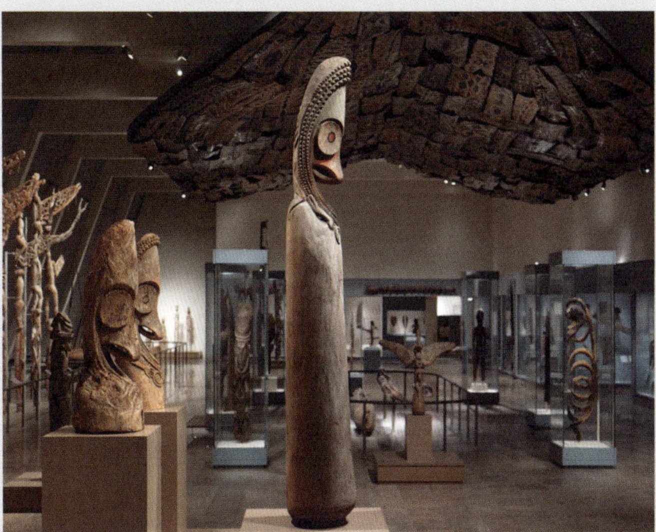

FIG 1 Oceania galleries in the Michael C. Rockefeller Wing, The Metropolitan Museum of Art (now closed for renovation and reopening in 2025). Photo: The Metropolitan Museum of Art, New York.

1 Excerpt from a poem by CHamoru poet Craig Santos Perez, who represented Guåhan (Guam) at the Poetry Parnassus, a spoken word event held at London's Southbank Centre as part of a series of cultural events linked to the London Olympics in 2012.

of these in our present. Knowledge and history, objects and memory—these relationships may be fraught with tension but there is value, and I hope optimism, in their reunion. Implicit within the question "What to let go?" lies the equally fraught issue of "What to keep?," which we might rephrase for this set of reflections on museums as "How best to keep?."

In New York I look after a collection of just over 2,800 works of Pacific art—ancestral treasures (or *taonga*, to use Māori terminology) that have passed down through the generations FIG 1. These cultural heirlooms come from a range of islands and archipelagos that spread across a vast expanse of ocean taking up over a third of the globe. The outstanding mobility of Oceanic peoples over the course of several thousand years was the catalyst for the flourishing of a kaleidoscopic range of cultures and art traditions—some 20,000 islands and close to 1,800 different cultures and language groups, all of which share common ancestry. The interconnectedness of the Pacific and its people, wrought from many centuries of dynamic engagement, is a strand that unites all the art. Voyaging (both in its literal sense as "travelling across the open seas" and its more conceptual aspect of "spiritual voyaging") is evoked in much of the art of Oceania. The production and display of art continues in the region as a vital means to stage necessary journeys into other realms—from life to death, for example, from the landscape of uninitiated youth to that of knowledgeable elder. Sculptures, masks, textiles, the dynamic accoutrements with which individuals adorn themselves—all are the focal point of ritual protocols that assist a transition across spiritual borders. Once carved, sculptures such as this remarkable female figure from the Inyai-Ewa people of the upper Korewori River in Papua New Guinea FIG 2 would have been animated with the words and gestures of her descendants. Created as early as the sixteenth century, the sculpture represents the founding female ancestor of the clan group. Figures such as this owe their survival to the fact that they were generally displayed away from the village proper, and kept tucked away in rockshelters. Exposed to the elements, they were protected from the rain by overhanging rock, and the drying force of the wind prevented them from rotting. The majority of these flat carved sculptures portray primordial beings whose actions collectively shaped the features of the landscape and established the rules and institutions of human society. An integral part of both past and present, these beings inhabit a supernatural realm that exists parallel to the human world. Art in Oceania is a channel for these fundamental aspects of the culture: customary knowledge, oral tradition, and the constantly proliferating landscape of genealogical relationships amongst the people inhabiting an area. All this, and more, embeds itself into an artwork. The sculpture itself can be understood, in that sense, as a concrete, tangible, more "visible" component of knowledge, events, and experience—a solid armature on which to hang the active elements of encounter. This, then, is the "stuff" of collections, the material residue of the myriad interactions that take place within community, between individuals and their gods, ancestors, and clan spirits.

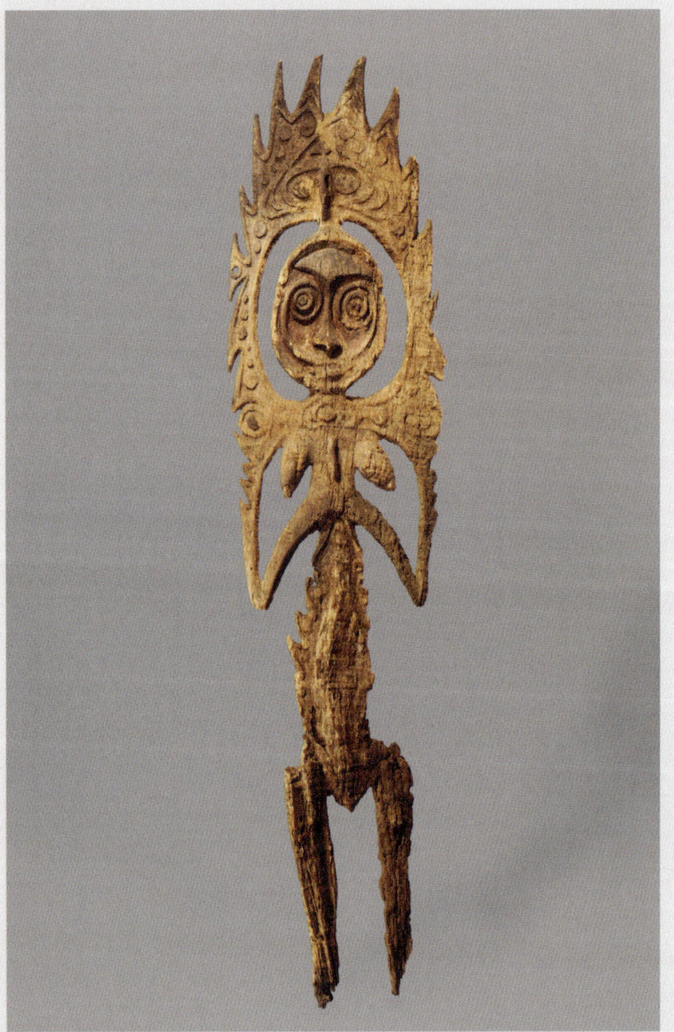

FIG 2 Female figure, Inyai-Ewa, Korewori River, Middle Sepik region, Papua New Guinea. H. 168 cm. Acquired in 1964 from Father Heinemans of the Catholic Mission, Wewak, Papua New Guinea. Photo: The Metropolitan Museum of Art, New York (1978.412.857).

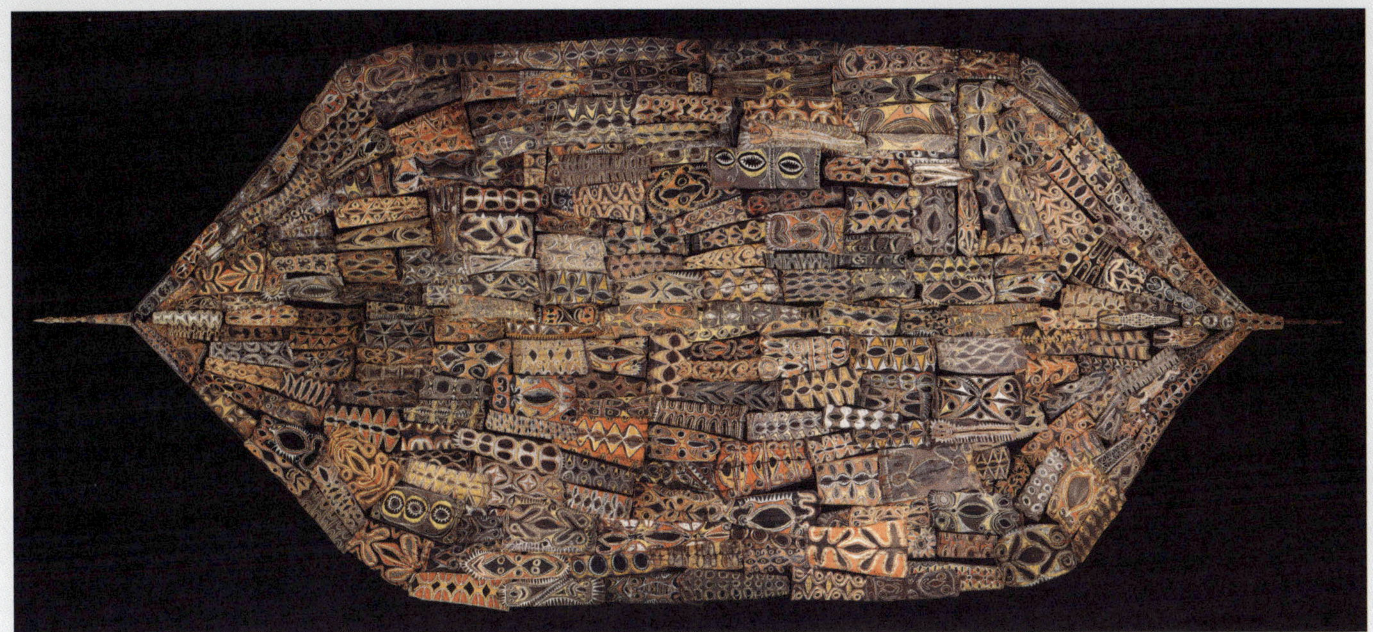

FIG 3 Paintings for a ceremonial ceiling commissioned from Kwoma artists (1971–3), Mariwai village, Washkuk Hills, Upper Sepik region, Papua New Guinea. Dims. 2469 × 930 cm. Photo: The Metropolitan Museum of Art, New York (1974.Kwoma.Ceiling).

Alongside ancestry and mobility, storytelling is the other great connector that unites the collection I look after. Broadly speaking, all Oceanic art is a vital means to access story. Acting as a mnemonic to memory, the artworks act as a crucial conduit by which current generations can pass important knowledge from the past into the present and future. One of the most dramatic examples of this in the museum in New York is the large-scale installation of more than 270 individually painted sago palm petioles (*pangal*) that evoke the dynamic polychrome interior of a Kwoma men's ceremonial house in the Sepik River region of Papua New Guinea. Each painting represents a specific animal, plant, or ancestral being to which stories attach. Iconography may relate to a specific phenomenon associated with one of the village clans, such as a shooting star. Whilst some of the paintings employ explicitly figurative imagery, such as a crocodile, many others employ more abstract, geometric designs derived from specific features of the animal or plant subject they portray, such as the extended wings of a flying fox. All are part of the genealogical fabric of the clan community. There is no one correct way to "read" these motifs. Identical geometric patterns can depict different subjects and the precise interpretation of a design can vary according to the intention and clan affiliation of the artist. Individual artists have rights to certain designs and the knowledge and associated authority that relates to it. Commissioned by former curator Douglas Newton during two trips he made to Mariwai village in the Washkuk Hills between 1971–73, the Kwoma Ceiling FIG 3 is the largest contemporary art installation in the Metropolitan Museum and speaks boldly to this idea of art as a powerful and active agent through which knowledge, ideas, and stories can continue to be generated.

New Precedents for Indigenous Art: *Te Maori*

One of the challenges of looking after a collection of art in a museum is the static nature of display. How do we convey to visitors the interior landscape of an artwork when so much of the sensual repertoire of words and gestures originally conceived to accompany it is now absent? When I arrived in New York to take up the position of curator of Oceanic art at the Metropolitan, I was keen to work with Pacific artists as a way to animate the galleries, to populate the space with Pacific voices. I had wondered about the Met's institutional memory of *Te Maori: Maori Art from New Zealand Collections* (Metropolitan Museum of Art, September 1984 – January 1985), the landmark exhibition FIG 4 that established important new precedents for consultation and shared decision-making between Indigenous communities and museums almost forty years ago.[2]

It turned out many recalled that auspicious morning of September 10, 1984. With the traffic stopped on Fifth Avenue, a small crowd had congregated before dawn, watching as a delegation of Māori leaders gathered themselves on the front steps of the museum and prepared to enter. The *karanga* (call) of the women went out and a group of *kaumātua* (elders) climbed the front steps, flanked by two younger men wielding their *taiaha* (long weapons or staffs) FIG 5. The highly esteemed group of *tohunga* (ritual experts) proceeded steadily through the museum towards the exhibition galleries, ensuring the appropriate ceremonial rites (*whakaheke tapu*) were enacted in order to lift the *tapu* (potent sacred quality) of the ancestral works, rendering them spiritually safe for the public to encounter FIG 6–7. Once inside the galleries, rousing speeches (*whaikōrero*) of welcome and tributes honoring long-departed ancestors followed, with the delegation formally entrusting the *taonga* to the care of the Met as host institution. In his reciprocal speech, curator Douglas Newton acknowledged the Met's ongoing commitment to the custodial care of these precious works of art and assured the Māori delegation, on behalf of the Met's staff and Trustees, that the Museum would honor their obligations. East Coast *kaumātua* (elder) Monita Delamere confirmed how deeply moving it had been to walk into the Met's galleries FIG 6–7 and experience their *taonga* on display for the first time that morning: "[I] felt that all [my] *tūpuna* were alive there."[3] With the strict conventions of Māori protocol established within the museum that morning, a subtle yet unprecedented shift had come into effect: the gallery space became a *marae* for the duration of the exhibition FIG 8–9.

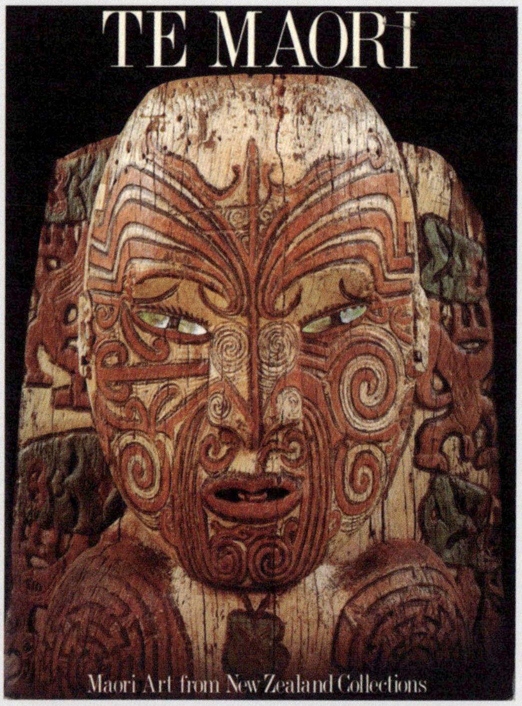

FIG 4 **"Te Maori: Maori Art from New Zealand Collections" exhibition catalogue.**

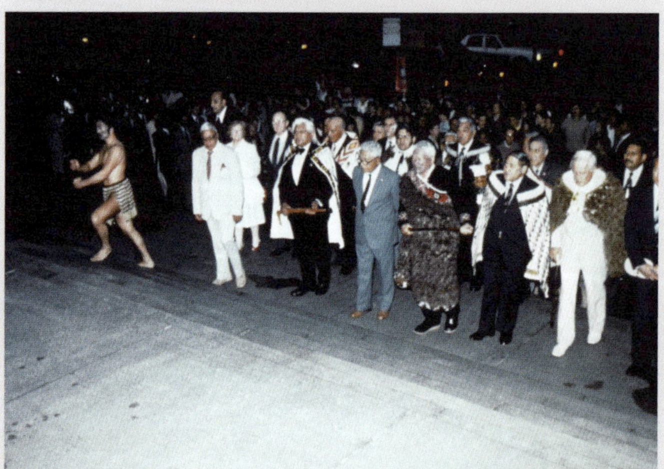

FIG 5 **Opening protocols for "Te Maori: Maori Art from New Zealand Collections" at dawn on September 10, 1984. Henare Tuwhangai (fourth from right wearing feather cloak) completes the first cycle of chants and prepares to hand over to tohunga Sonny Waru (to his right, also in cloak) for the second phase of chants to accompany the delegation as they proceed up the front steps to the main entrance of the Met. Photo: The Metropolitan Museum of Art, New York.**

2 Nuku, Maia "Te Maori: New Precedents for Indigenous Art at The Met," *Metropolitan Museum Journal*, vol. 56 (2021), 32, 50.

3 Recounted by Con Te Rata Jones to Conal McCarthy August 19, 2002; cited in Conal McCarthy, *Exhibiting Maori: A History of Colonial Cultures of Display* (Wellington: Te Papa Press / Oxford: Berg, 2007), 141.

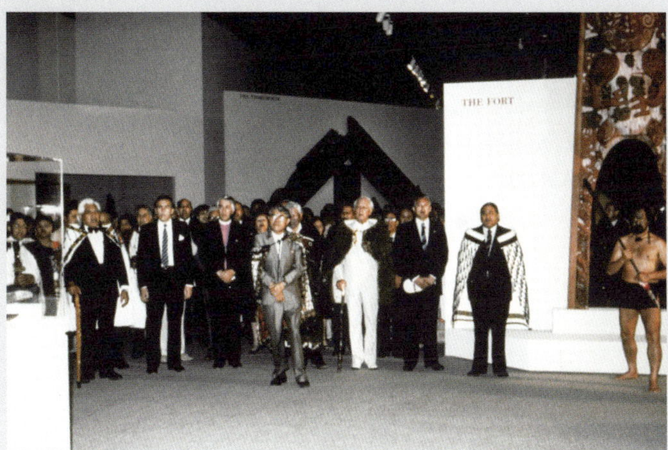

FIG 6 Kara Puketapu (center, in front) stands with the delegation of kaumātua (senior Māori leaders) in the exhibition galleries, 1984. Photo: The Metropolitan Museum of Art, New York.

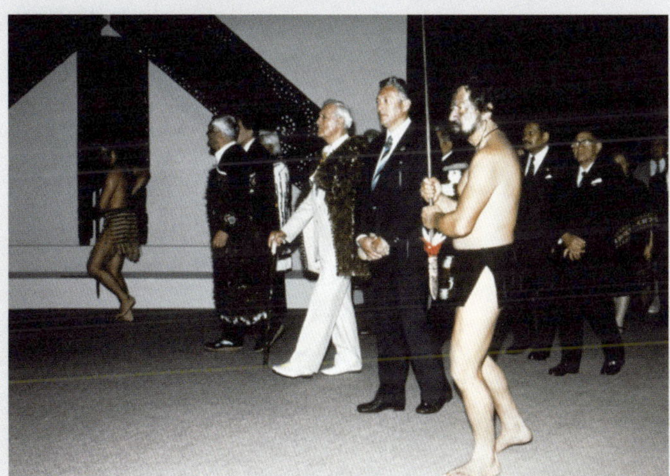

FIG 7 The Māori delegation, led here by Henare Tuwhangai and Sir James Henare (in cloaks, from left), guide the party of Government officials and Met Museum officials through the exhibition galleries. Senior statesmen are flanked by Jerry Rautangata and Pita Sharples (in foreground), two manutaki (armed sentries) who accompanied the group throughout the formal proceedings, 1984. Photo: The Metropolitan Museum of Art, New York.

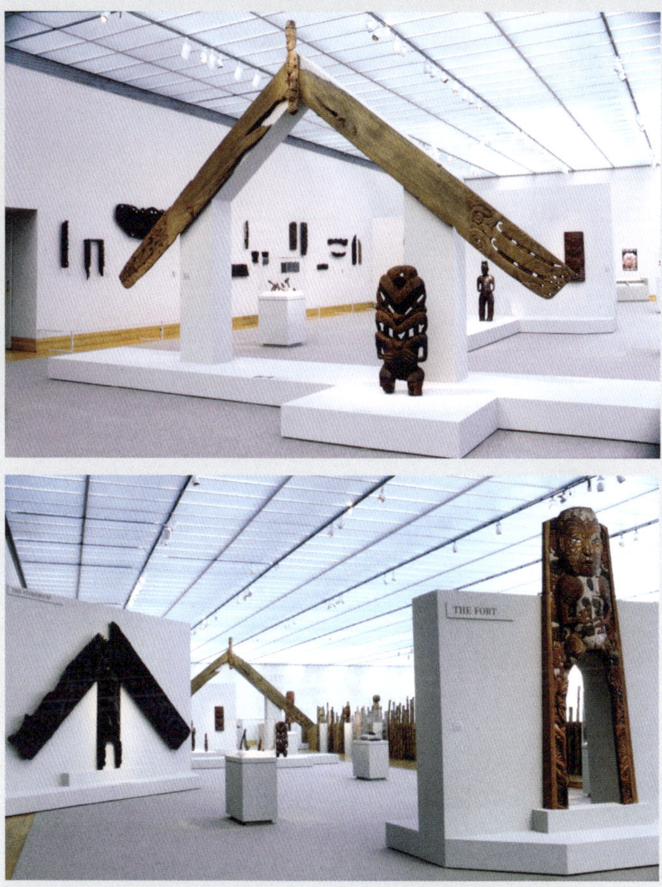

FIG 8–9 Installation views of Te Maori at the Met, 1984. Photo: The Metropolitan Museum of Art, New York.

So how had this come about? From the outset, an extensive dialog with *iwi* Māori (tribal authorities) was established. This was at the insistence of the management committee created to oversee the project. This close engagement with Māori was sustained throughout the planning and installation of the exhibition, and directly impacted the selection of works and their availability for loan. Whilst curators in New Zealand shared images and ideas for major works of art that they believed should be included, these were all, they explained, subject to final approval by the tribal authorities for whom they were held in trust. This process of consultation with Māori was a crucial new initiative and one in which regional museums throughout New Zealand outlined their distinct role as custodians of *taonga* (ancestral treasures) on behalf of the Māori communities within their districts. Each institution acknowledged that, alongside any nominal claim to legal ownership of Māori artifacts (what we might determine the "physical" component), full spiritual and cultural custodianship (the "metaphysical" aspect) was vested in a variety of local Māori tribal groups. This stance established a precedent that has had a phenomenal impact on the way museums in the Pacific engage with their local communities as partners.

Having opened to great acclaim in New York, the exhibition traveled for the next two years to three further venues in the US (San Francisco, St. Louis, and Chicago). Māori continued to organize formal protocols at each venue and led impromptu cultural performances in the galleries alongside the *taonga* on display. The constant presence of Māori and their insistence on overseeing appropriate *tikanga* (protocols) ensured that museum staff and audiences alike were introduced to the unique relationship of Māori with their art—that sculptures are not simply relics of a forgotten past but living spiritual ancestors who remain in close relation with their living descendants. What the exhibition did so deftly was vividly highlight this distinctive interaction to audiences in real time, driving home the ancestral connections that bind the peoples of the Pacific to their art.

Animating Collections—Activating Relationships

In the decades since *Te Maori*, our work as museum curators has seen many exciting developments. The disciplinary boundaries within which we operate work productively on the thresholds of art history, anthropology, and museum ethnography, so the attendant theoretical framework of each flourishes towards becoming ever more expansive. Artifacts and objects have taken center stage in this "material turn," opening up pathways to different kinds of knowledge and understandings so that written documents are no longer perceived as the only valid primary sources through which to interpret art. The new methodological tools that center materiality and an analysis of "things" (in and of themselves) now direct a discourse acknowledging the active agency of objects. Indigenous epistemologies have been encouraged to take root so that one can attend to the cosmological and cultural coordinates of an artwork alongside its formal attributes. Several decades of collaborative research projects led by museums in the United Kingdom have enhanced research and curatorial practice so that Pacific artists, scholars, and cultural practitioners work alongside museum curators and conservators to access major collections of Pacific art together.[4] Pooling their diverse knowledge bases, these projects have brought dynamic new perspectives to the study of collections that lessen the gap—and deaden the accepted hierarchy—between knowledge and practice so that scholars in the Academy now take seriously the perspectives and viewpoints of these collaborators.

---

4 The following examples are a selection of research projects spearheaded by curators working with collections of Oceanic art in UK museums to give a sense of their scope and range. These projects all took place within the last twenty years and specifically engaged Pacific interlocutors as collaborators for collections research in museums across the UK and Europe, as well as specific outcomes in publications, digital and multimedia stories, art exhibitions, and the reinstallation of new permanent displays. They include: *Pacific Pathways: Multiplying contexts for the Forster ("Cook-Voyage")* Collection at the Pitt Rivers Museum (2002–3) led by Jeremy Coote; extensive and ongoing collaboration with Torres Strait Islanders to commemorate the centenary of the *1898 Cambridge Expedition to the Torres Strait* (1998), Museum of Archaeology and Anthropology (MAA), University of Cambridge, led by Anita Herle; *Pasifika Styles: Artists Inside the Museum* (2006–8), curated by Amiria Salmond and Rosanna Raymond at the Museum of Archaeology and Anthropology (MAA), University of Cambridge; *Pacific Encounters* 1760–1840 (2003-6) and *The Fijian Art Research Project* (2011–14), led by Steven Hooper at the Sainsbury Research Unit, University of East Anglia; *Melanesian Art: Objects, Narratives and Indigenous Owners*, British Museum and the Museum of Archaeology and Anthropology (MAA), University of Cambridge (AHRC, 2005–10) led by Lissant Bolton and Nicholas Thomas; *Artefacts of Encounter* 1760-1840 (2010–13), led by Amiria Salmond, and *Pacific Presences: Oceanic Art in European Museums* at the Museum of Archaeology and Anthropology (MAA), Cambridge University (2013–18) led by Nicholas Thomas. *Engaging Objects: Indigenous communities, museum collections and the representation of Indigenous histories* was a joint research project with a focus on Indigenous Australian art undertaken by the British Museum with the National Museum of Australia and the Australian National University in Australia (2011-14), led by Lissant Bolton, Howard Morphy, John Carty, Maria Nugent, Ian Coates, and Michael Pickering. Frances Lennard at the Centre for Textile Conservation and Technical Art History at the Hunterian Museum, University of Glasgow, Scotland, led a joint research project *Situating Pacific Barkcloth in Time and Place* (2016–19) in collaboration with the Royal Botanic Gardens at Kew and National Museum of Natural History (NMNH) at the Smithsonian Institution, Washington, DC. These projects all have publications and/or websites associated with them for further reference.

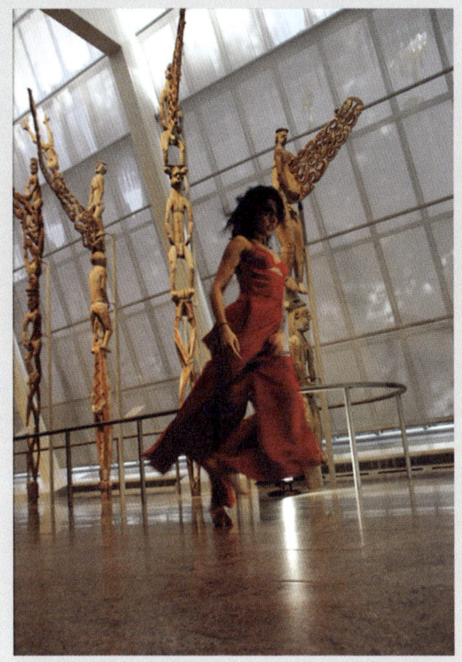
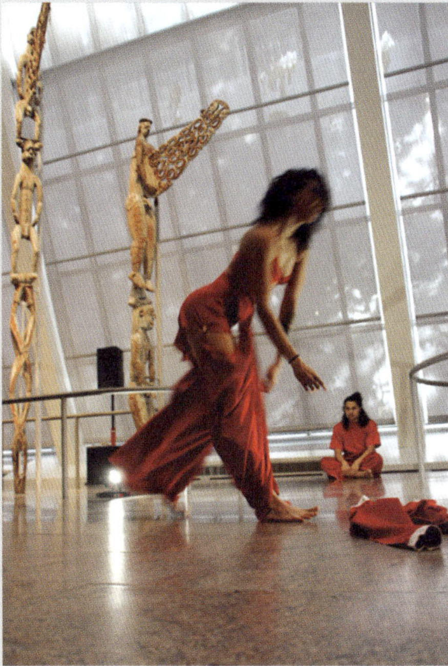
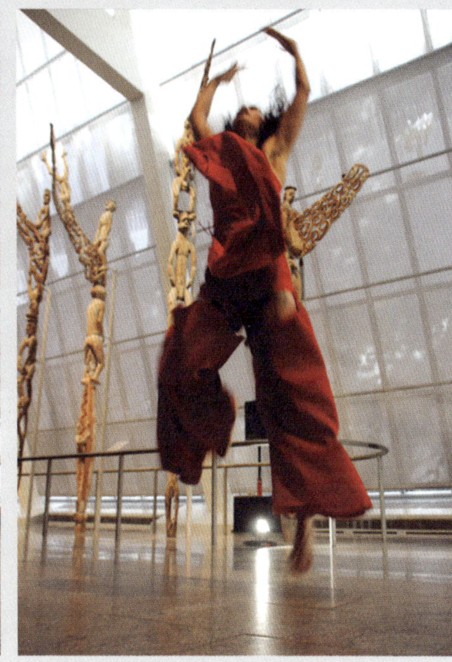

FIG 10–12 Jahra Wasasala performing "Bure Kalou: God House" in The Metropolitan Museum of Art Oceania galleries as part of the World Cultures Festival (October 26–27, 2019). Photo: Dan Taulapapa McMullin.

Broadly speaking, my own curatorial practice seeks to amplify Pacific voices and perspectives so that visitors can begin to understand the art with the visual aesthetic and conceptual underpinnings of its origin. One major impact of my own curatorial work has been a shift in my perception of the gallery as simply a place where we present art from a particular region or time in history, towards understanding it as a place of encounter. I do see the gallery as a place where we can come together in dialog: a place to confront complex, painful, and conflicting histories. A place to acknowledge and work through colonial legacies and their ongoing violence. A place to explore and celebrate Indigenous epistemologies. A place where we might encourage the latter to "land" and take root, nurturing them so they flourish within the ecosystem of the museum and its interface with the public. A place to *host* artists, and I use that term "host" advisedly, that is, in its rich Pacific sense, and three key Māori concepts now strongly align with the way I relate to an engaged curatorial practice in the museum today. These are the concepts of *manaakitanga*—that is, hosting people as a way to nurture relationships; *whanaungatanga*—the idea of kinship, coming together in acknowledgement of our relationship with each other; and *kaitiakitanga*—the duty of care inherent in stewardship (of people, land, the environment). This framework is attended by a range of specific obligations and duties of care. Indeed, the ongoing stewardship of collections requires that institutions actively accommodate the reciprocal relations necessary for Indigenous interlocutors to advocate for the ways in which they would like their art and culture—and own selves—to be represented.

Relationships are part and parcel of Oceania. In the early twentieth century, anthropologists such as Bronisław Malinowski and Marcel Mauss wrote famous analyzes of the power of the gift in Pacific communities, revealing the profound implications of gift culture, i.e., that Pacific Islanders present each other with things in order to create and extend *relationships*. Their work outlines a central objective in gifting, the intention of which was not merely to exchange and secure goods but rather to create a formal means by which individuals could gain prestige and create partnerships and connections. These exchanges were inextricably bound up with identities, which people were then able to negotiate throughout their lives; "Gifts forged connections ... the gift was never just a transaction: it was also a spectacle, and frequently a highly aestheticized one."[5] I have found one of the most productive strategies for highlighting this kind of engagement with the Met's collections has been to oversee collaborative projects with Pacific performance artists, poets, writers, and visual artists. Two such projects by Pacific women will suffice as recent examples.

In 2019 we commissioned a newly choreographed work with the Met Live Arts team as part of our programming for the *ATEA: Nature & Divinity in Polynesia* exhibition. The commission was an imaginative new dance work from a fiercely talented young Fijian performer Jahra Wasasala, and was inspired by the eighteenth- and nineteenth-century Polynesian *atua* (or deities) featured in the exhibition. Jahra felt a particularly strong connection to one of the Fijian fiber god houses (*bure kalou*) which formed the foundation for her development of the work. "Bure Kalou: God House," the powerful twenty-minute piece she produced, was an intensely personal response to what she described as the "extraordi-nary ancestors" on display FIG 10-12. Using her own body as a point of connection and expression, she explored her genealogical links to the artworks in the exhibition.

Jahra executed a series of startling performances in the Oceania galleries during the closing weekend of the *ATEA* exhibition, which coincided with the Met's "World Cultures Festival" (October 26–27, 2019) and used the performances to open up a dynamic and critical space for her own voice in the galleries where she could respond in a profound way to the works gathered there. Visitors who attended described the performances as "visceral" and "revelatory," and expressed their delight at having witnessed such an honest and intimate response to the art. Jahra performed three times in the Oceania galleries and again at the closing of the exhibition during the *poroporoaki* (farewell) that Leali'ifano Dr. Albert Refiti and I arranged with the Polynesian community in New York on the final day of the exhibition FIG 13-14. Over the course of the afternoon the gallery became an active space of creative renewal. Real and conflicting emotions were aired in a powerful and moving performance that spoke directly to Jahra's feelings about the works on display and her singular relationship with them. Those present were able to confront and reflect upon the full range of complex emotions conjured from the entangled histories on display. The audience joined Jahra in a rollercoaster ride as grief and anguish washed over us all, with pride segueing into anger followed by a melancholic and spent exhaustion. This kind of intervention—in which Indigenous perspective is centered—has huge transformative potential in helping audiences reflect more deeply on the role of collections and what they can mean for different constituencies. This exposure to Jahra's distinctive practice is precisely the kind of extension of boundaries that I am dedicated to promoting at the Met.

5 "Spirit of the Gift," in Nicholas Thomas and Peter Brunt, eds., *Oceania* (London: Royal Academy of Arts, 2018), 182.

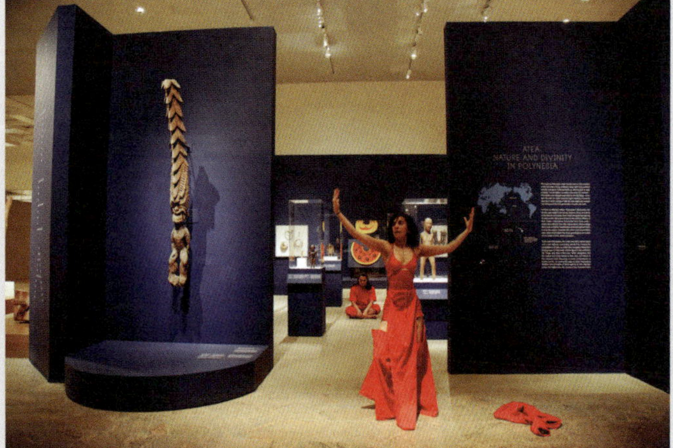

FIG 13 Jahra Wasasala performing for the Polynesian community at the closing ceremony (poroporoaki) for ATEA: Nature and Divinity in Polynesia (October 27, 2019) at the Metropolitan Museum of Art, New York. Photo: Sophie Chalk.

Two years earlier, in 2017, the artist, poet, and fashion activist Rosanna Raymond arrived in New York to take up a six-month residency at the Met as the Chester Dale Fellow in Education and Public Practice. From the outset she established her interest in responding to the institution of the museum itself and the opportunity arose for her to resurrect her haughty and mischievous "Back Hand Maiden" from her sassy "One-a-Day Maiden Rave On" series, which she had conceived in London almost a decade earlier.[6] **FIG 15–16**

---

6 Raymond and the author were interviewed by esteemed colleague Dame Professor Anne Salmond for an episode of a new series, *Artefact* (Greenstone Productions), for Māori Television in New Zealand. See https://www.maoritelevision.com/shows/artefact/S01E001/artefact-series-1-episode-1. The series presents case studies exploring specific stories pertaining to Pacific history, art, and culture as they inhere in and around "artifact"—objects, art, and people. Aspects of the complex histories and relationships brokered by artists, researchers, and curators working in museums fell naturally within the scope of the program.

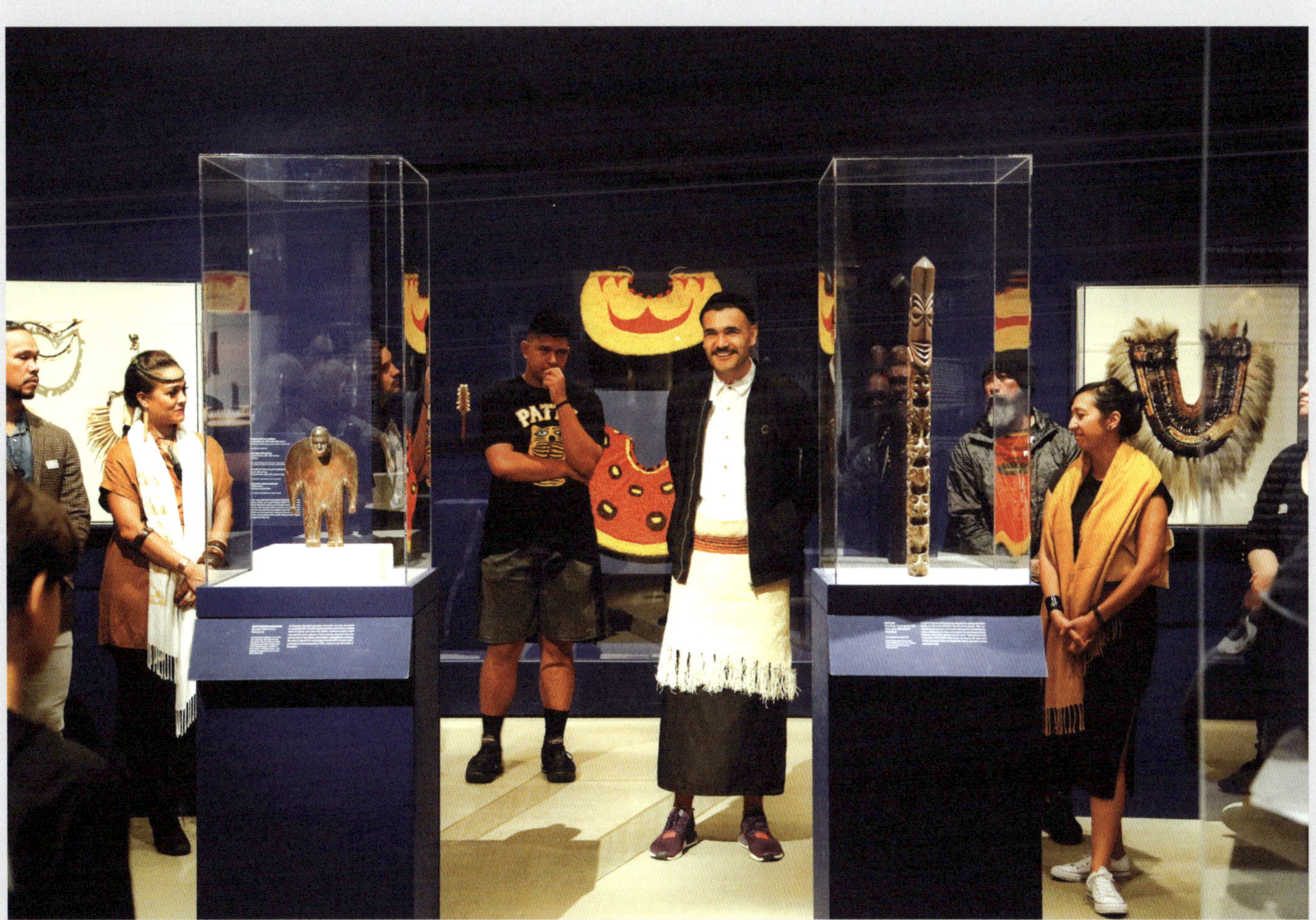

FIG 14 Artist Benjamin Work addressing the Polynesian community in New York at the closing ceremony (poroporoaki) for ATEA: Nature and Divinity in Polynesia (October 27, 2019) at the Metropolitan Museum of Art, New York. Photo: Sophie Chalk.

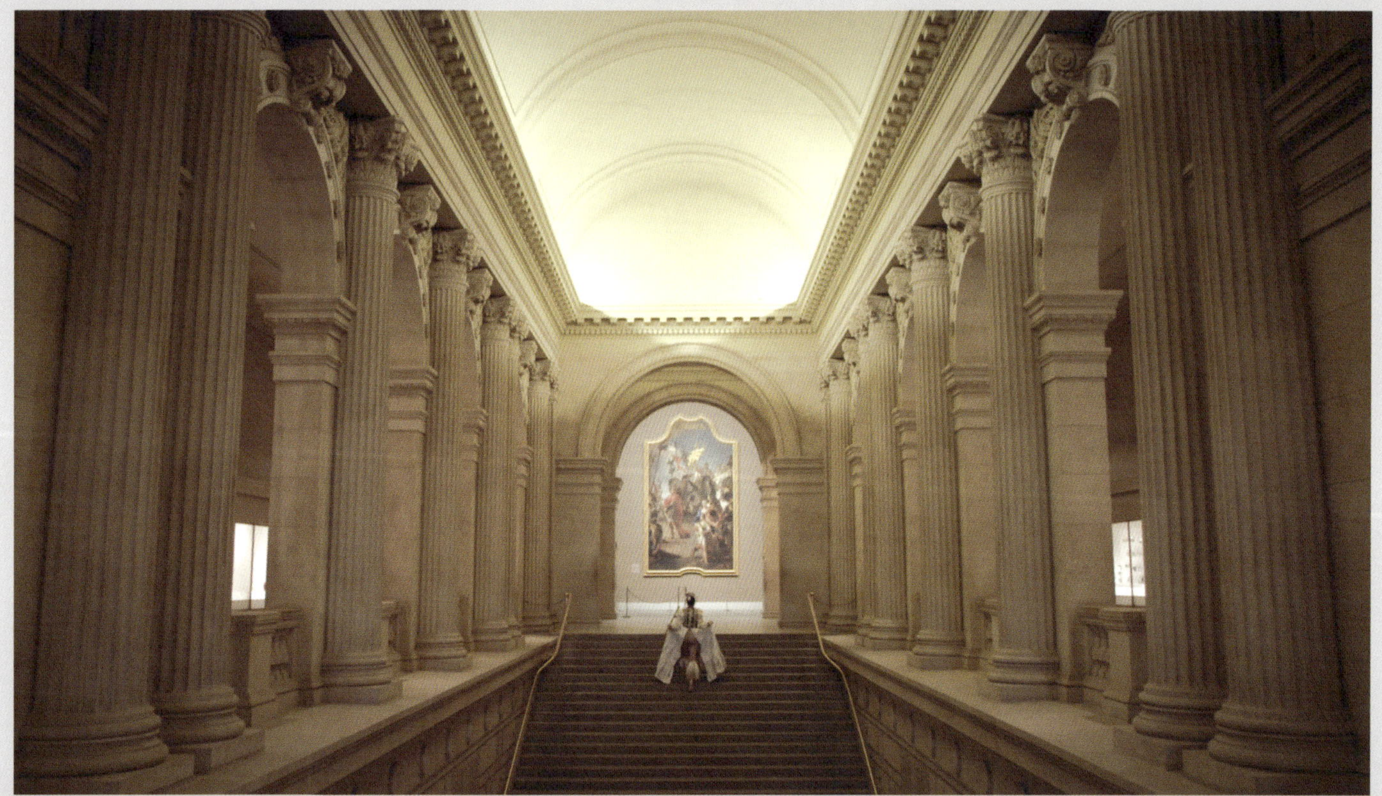

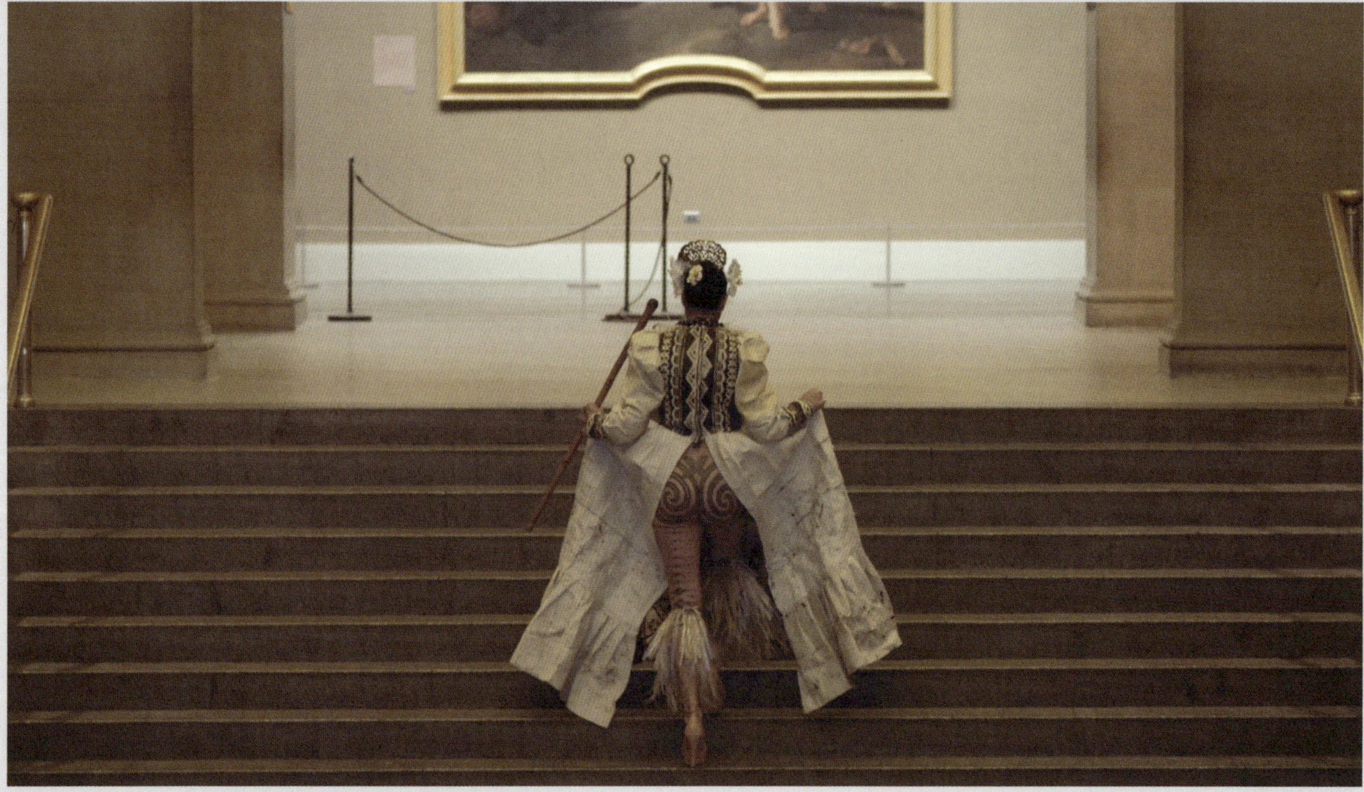

FIG 15–16 Rosanna Raymond as Back Hand Maiden ascending the steps towards the galleries for European Paintings (May 29, 2017) The Metropolitan Museum of Art, New York. © Artefact, Greenstone TV Ltd.

Fascinated with the architecture of the museum interior, we had talked about the difference between the wood, plants, and fiber of Pacific art in the Oceania galleries, and the cool, smooth stone statuary of the classical world on display in the Greek and Roman galleries immediately adjacent. The sense of permanence in the idealized portraits that once braced the architecture of political power during the Roman Empire seemed completely at odds with the transience and ephemerality of much Pacific art. In many instances, art in the Pacific is conceived to exist only for a short period of time—designed as a conduit, materials are assembled into a dynamic visual display that will bring the community together before being disassembled and returned to the environment. Fiber and barkcloth; stone and bone; male beauty and dusky female power—something was taking root in Rosanna.

The moment when "Back Hand Maiden" appeared in her full barkcloth bustle was a powerful one. Rosanna had described her as haughty and austere, a mistress of the manor. A towering turtleshell comb sat atop her scooped up hair. Wielding her *tokotoko* defiantly, she walked through the galleries as if she owned the place FIG 17–18. Stopping to curtsy gently, she paused to pay her respects to the youthful beauty of a series of male nudes, their taut buttocks laid bare in an avenue of smooth plinths and stone. The back of her dress split open to reveal her own behind clothed in the dark green ink of the *tatau* that marks her Pacific skin, neither naked nor nude but marked with the stories and genealogies of the Pacific. The statement was subtle and an effective way to infuse the beautiful austerity of the stone galleries with the warmth and vigor of a Pacific body—a female body moreover, that highly contested site so central to the earliest European encounters with the Pacific. Wrapped in natural fibers, this strong Pacific body, clothed in the skin of trees, disrupted time to unfold its own storied past into the present, introducing its ancestors to those of ancient Rome FIG 19–21. It was a memorable occasion.

The sketched fragments of maidens in her series built a profile of strong and vulnerable women—each in some sense an aspect of her own self.

> She got big bones and big hair,
> when she breathes her breasts rise and
> fall like the swell of the shallow sea,
>
> Loves wearing mother of pearl and
> pounamu all at the same time,
> so she chimes when she walks,
>
> Always busy so can seem a bit distracted,
> never the less, a no fuss, no bother,
> can-do, sort of a girl.
>
> Pretty in a strange sort of a way,
> you can't help stare at her eyes,
>
> They are vast and can light up the night sky,
>
> You see she has no pupils, they are vessels
> containing old gods ...
>
> Just don't trip over and fall in them ...
> you won't come back alive.[7]

7 Excerpt from "Fully Laiden Maiden," a poem by Rosanna Raymond from *One-a-Day Maiden Rave On ... or The Dusky ain't Dead she just Diversified*, a compilation that inspired a series of photographic portraits exhibited as "EthKnowcentrix: Museums inside the Artist," October Gallery, London (September 10–October 10, 2009), with Lisa Reihana, Shigeyuki Kihara, and George Nuku that explored each artist's ongoing relationships with museums as a site of research and reflection.

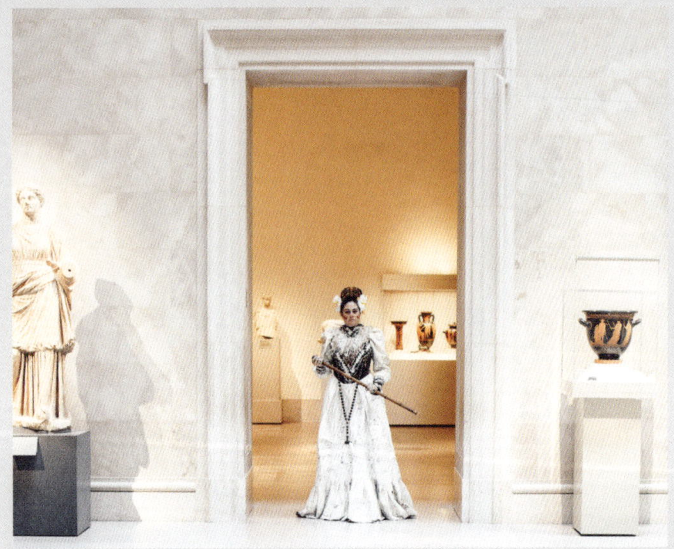

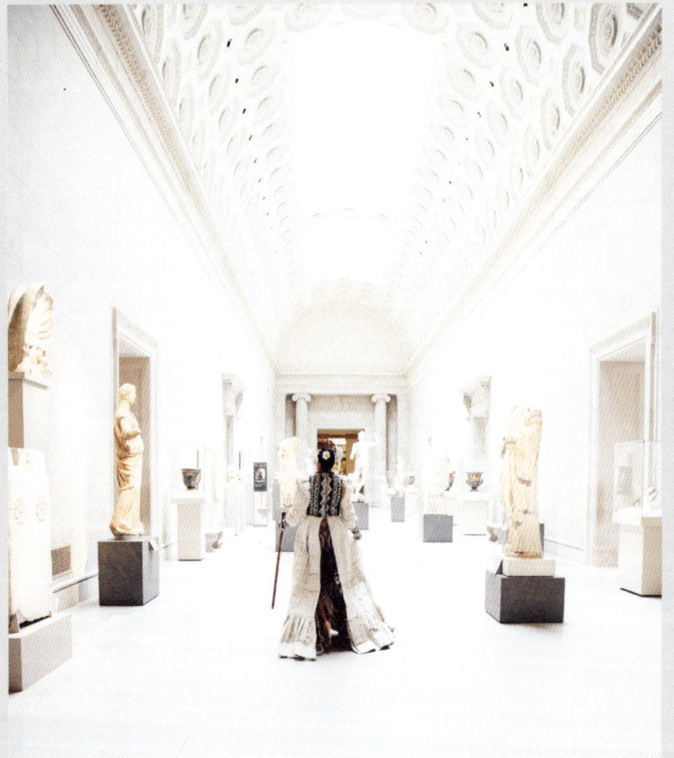

FIG 17–18 Rosanna Raymond as Back Hand Maiden in the Greek and Roman galleries (May 29, 2017) The Metropolitan Museum of Art, New York. Photo: Richard Wade.

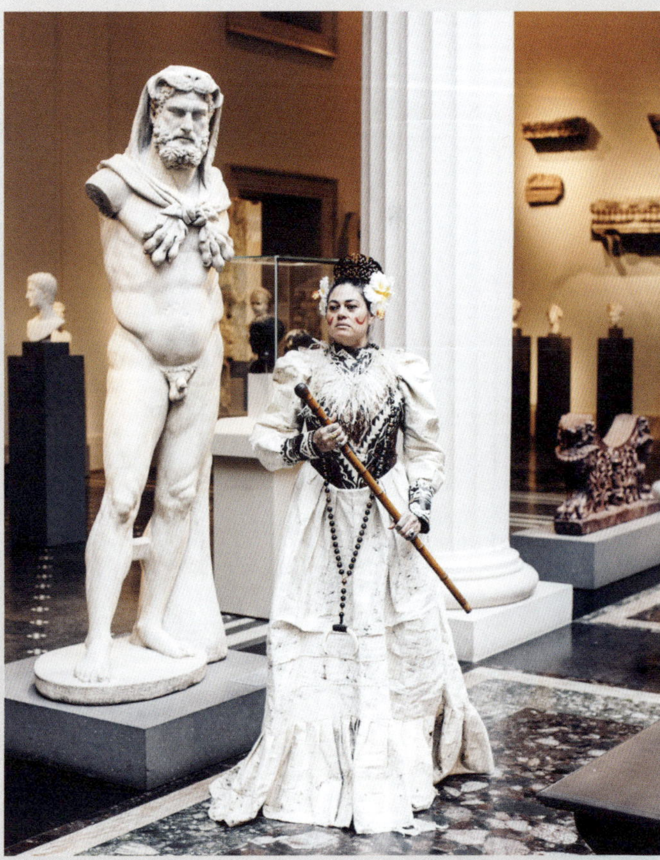

FIG 19 Rosanna Raymond as Back Hand Maiden in the Greek and Roman galleries (May 29, 2017) The Metropolitan Museum of Art, New York. Photo: Richard Wade.

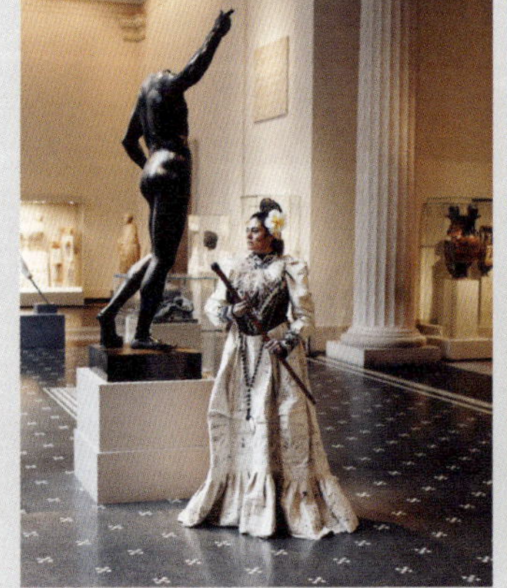

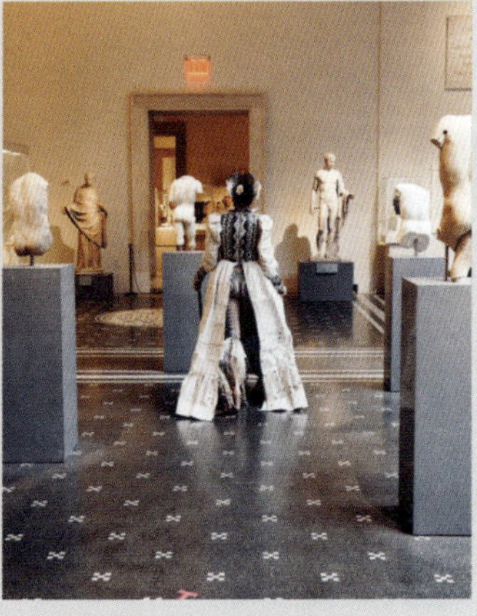

FIG 20-21 Rosanna Raymond as Back Hand Maiden in the Greek and Roman galleries (May 29, 2017) The Metropolitan Museum of Art, New York. Photo: Richard Wade.

Conclusion

If *Te Maori* showed that museums and their galleries have the potential to become active and dynamic spaces, Pacific peoples understand that in many respects, art—these ancestral heirlooms, our *taonga*—were in fact *designed* to leverage these kinds of relationships. This is their role and agency. A new appreciation of this has played a vital role in initiating an expansive cultural dialog in relation to museums with collections of Māori and Pacific art that now extends far beyond the region. For those of us born overseas, the Pacific art encountered in the galleries and stores of variously located museums can act as anchor points that connect us to home. They are a vital link creating a connection to the *whenua* (land) that brings us back into relationship with one another. Our Pacific ancestors had the imagination to visualize these deep networks of ancestral relations, expressing the lineages that meshed a current generation into the intricate folds of time and space. The power of Pacific art is unleashed when we help join up that history with its people. Bringing people—physically or digitally—into the space of the museum helps to activate and enliven these relationships. The projects that invite this participation signal the need for dialog to better accommodate the next wave of change that must come.

As well as a repository of the past, collections are living resources for creative interventions that have the power to effect change. These projects—and the people they center—push at the boundaries of an institution, forcing it to re-assess itself and become self-reflexive. The work is cross-cultural and interdisciplinary, and we are all rightfully committed to engaging with it. At its heart is an acknowledgement of the value in leveraging relationships, in connecting the living dynamic of people with the art in our collections. It is these ongoing, exciting, and rewarding relationships that drive participation in a critical dialog forward. Rather than trying to confine collections, a more productive strategy must be to continue to engage them in active and dynamic ways.

NIKAU HINDIN

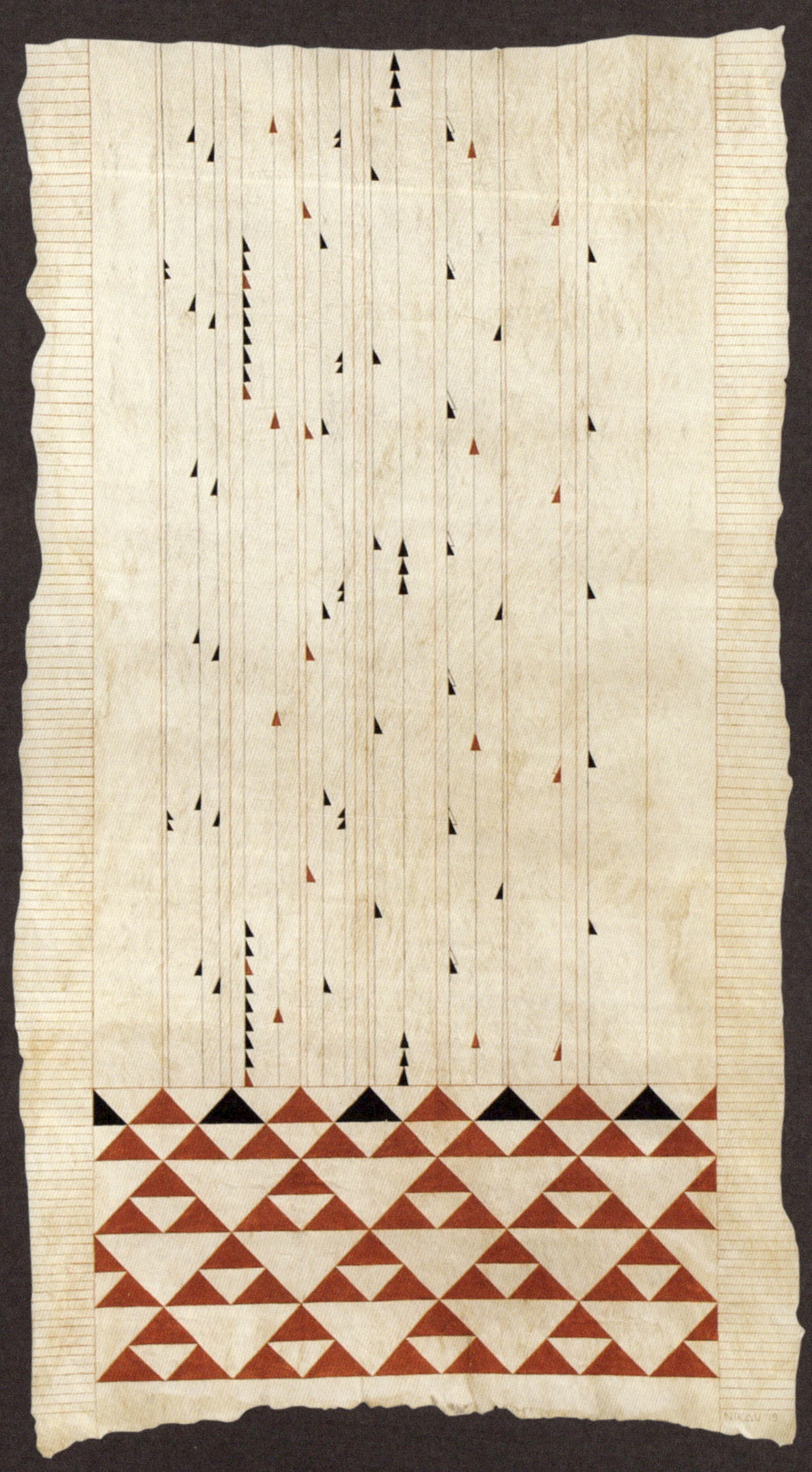

LEFT
Arorangi, 2019.
Kōkōwai and ngārahu
on aute.

RIGHT
Pō Ngārahu, 2019.
Soot Black Night.

NEXT PAGE
Pō Ngārahu, 2019.
Soot Black Night.

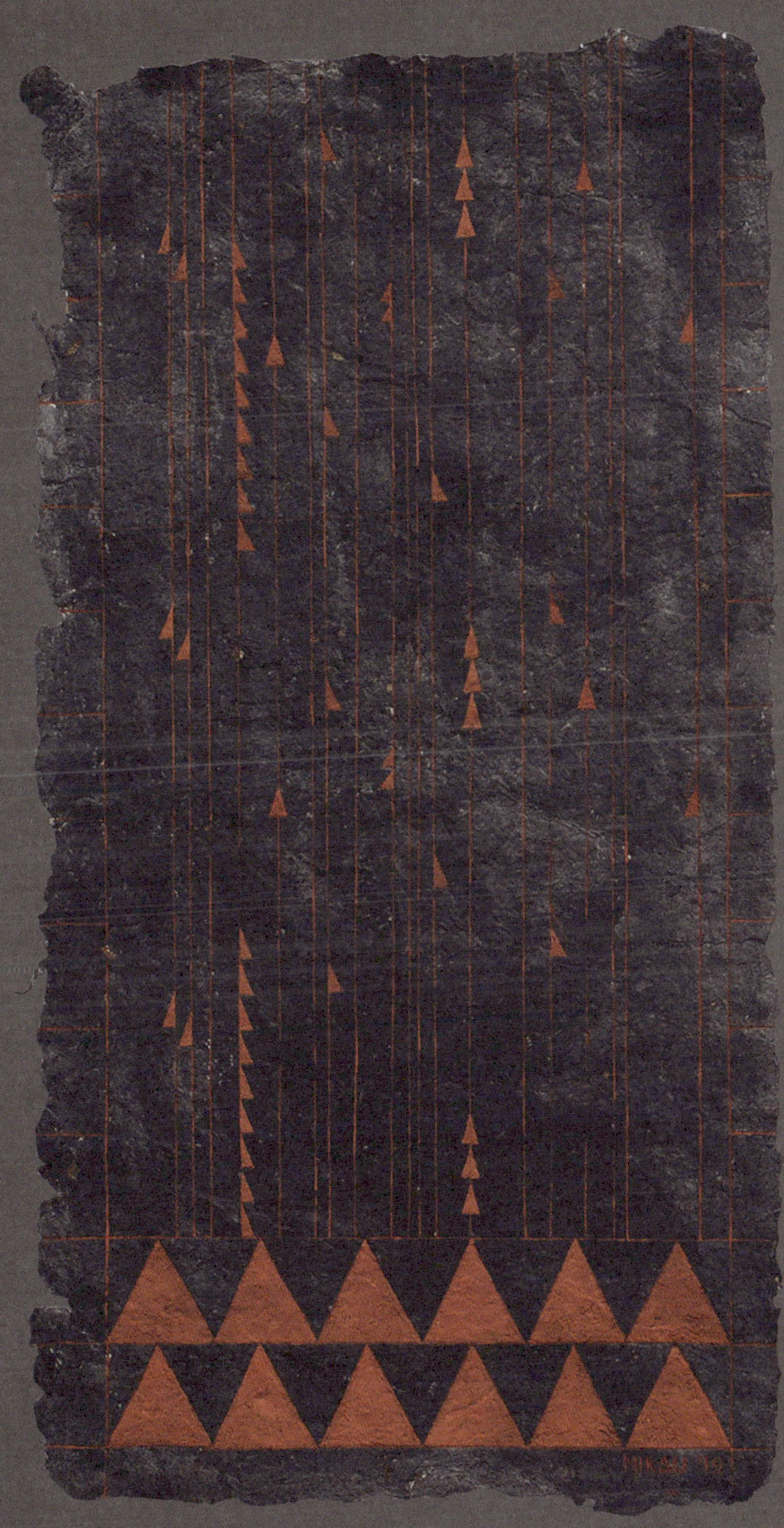

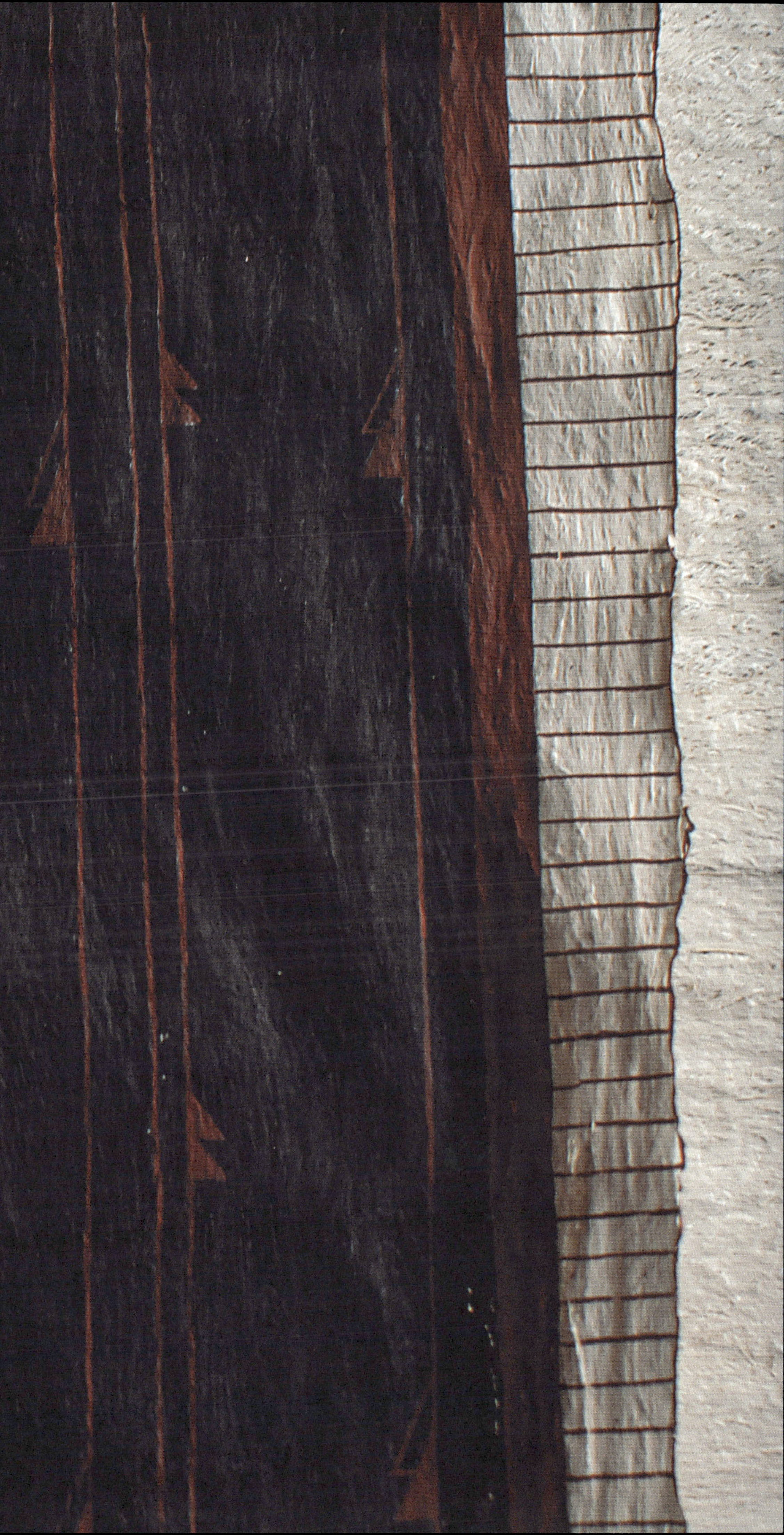

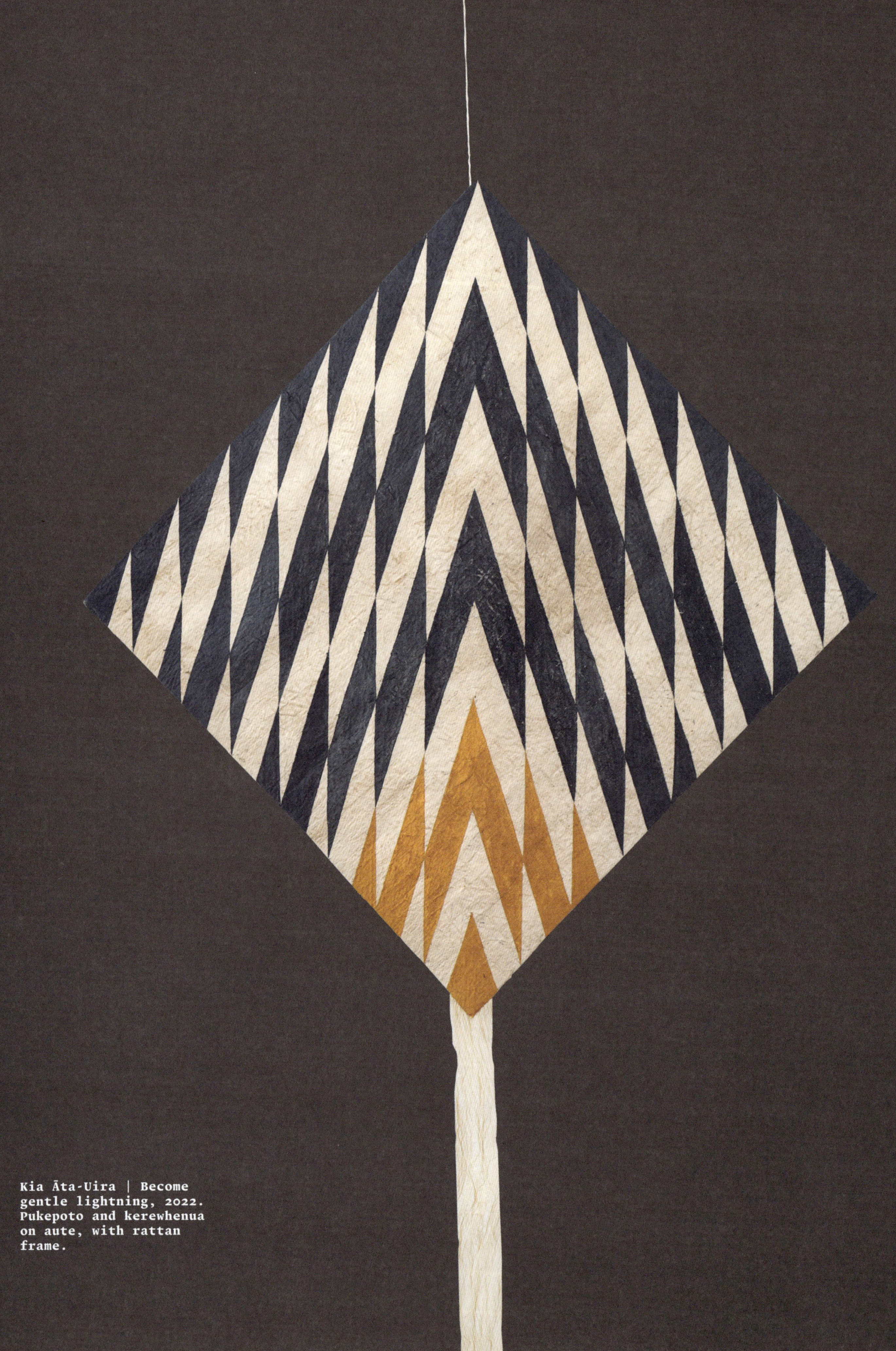

Kia Āta-Uira | Become gentle lightning, 2022. Pukepoto and kerewhenua on aute, with rattan frame.

LEFT
Te Tīpare o Hine Takurua (The Winter Solstice), 2020. Kōkōwai (red ochre) and ngārahu (soot pigments) on bark cloth.

MIDDLE
Te Ia o te Ao II (The divine flow of energy in the universe II), 2020. Kōkōwai (red ochre) and ngārahu (soot pigments) on bark cloth.

RIGHT
Ira (Life Principle), 2020. Kōkōwai (red ochre) and ngārahu (soot pigments) on bark cloth.

NEXT PAGE
Nikau Hindin laying out finished pieces for her solo exhibition "Kōkōrangi ki Kōkōwai," 2020.

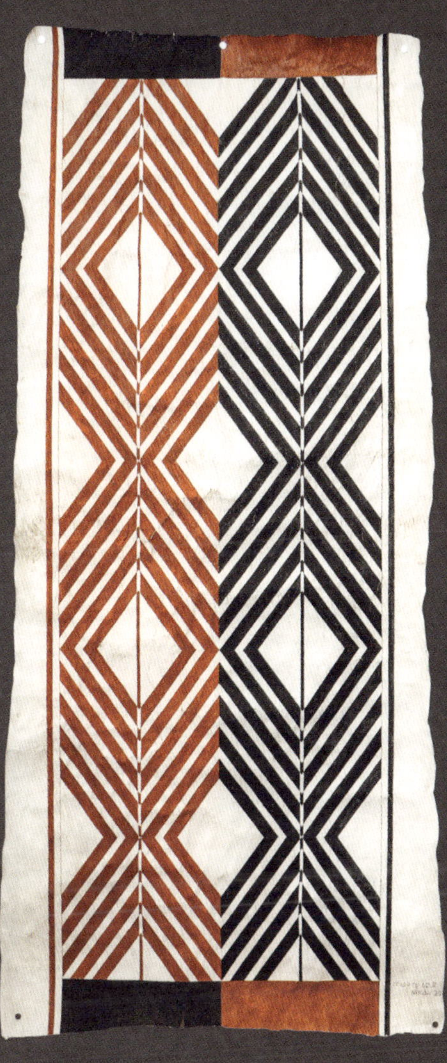

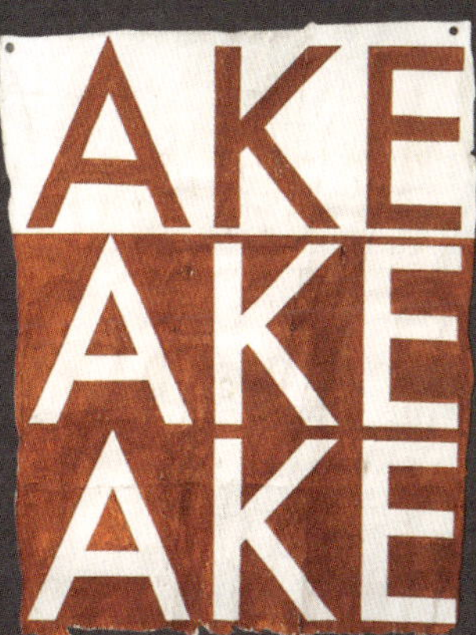

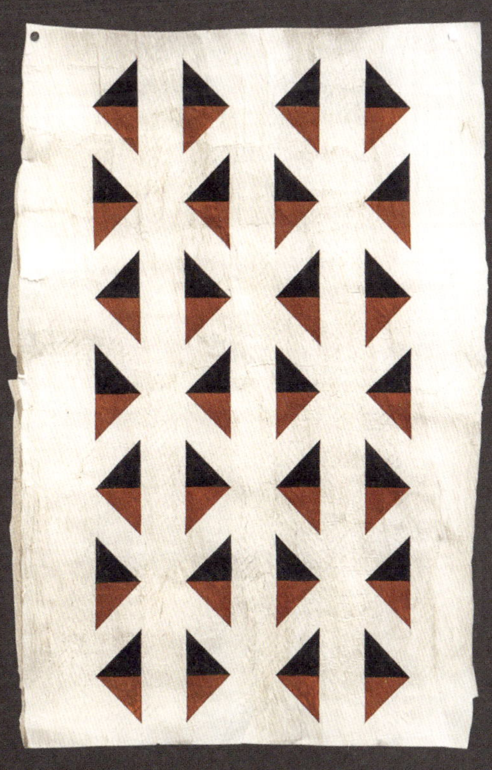

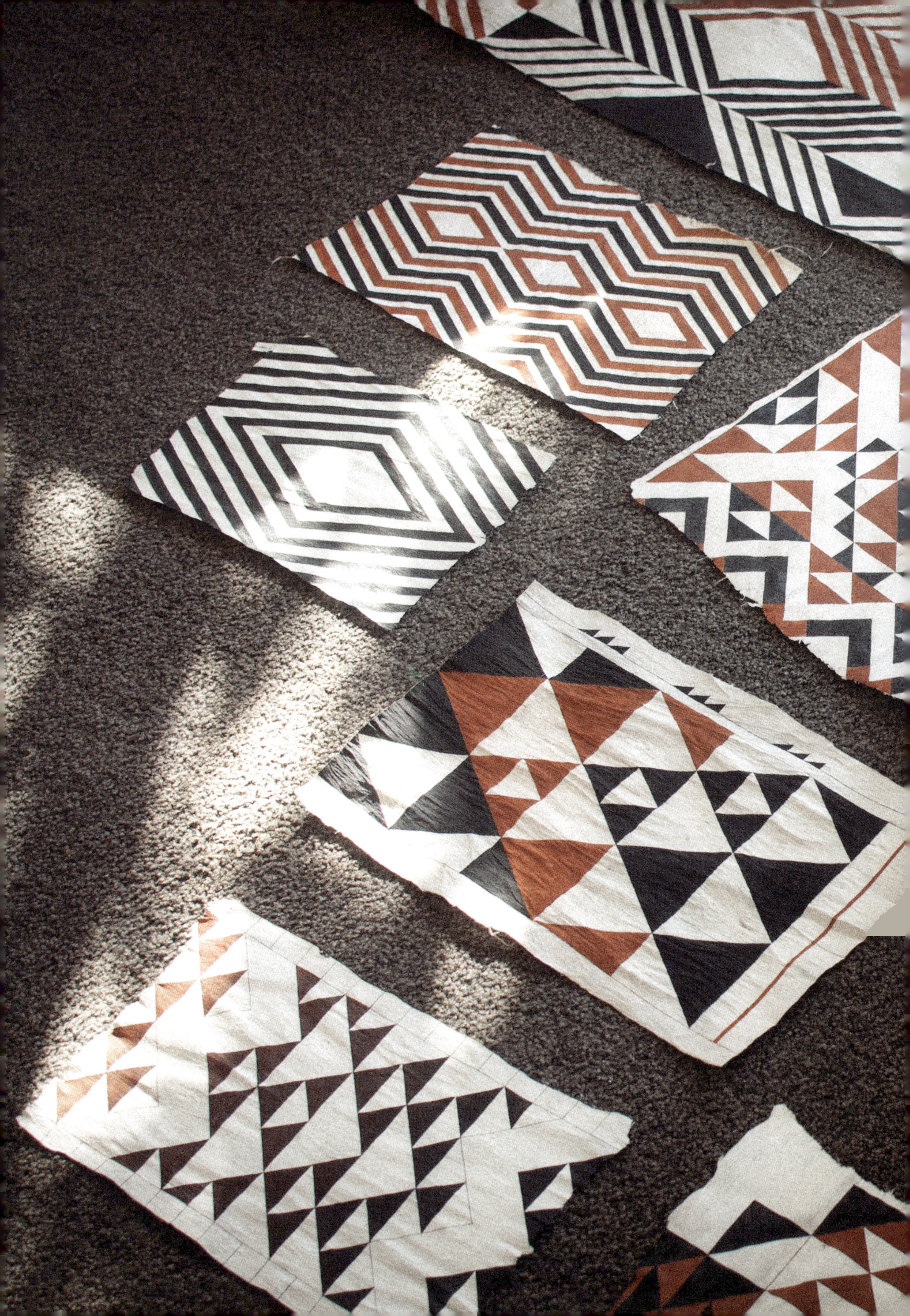

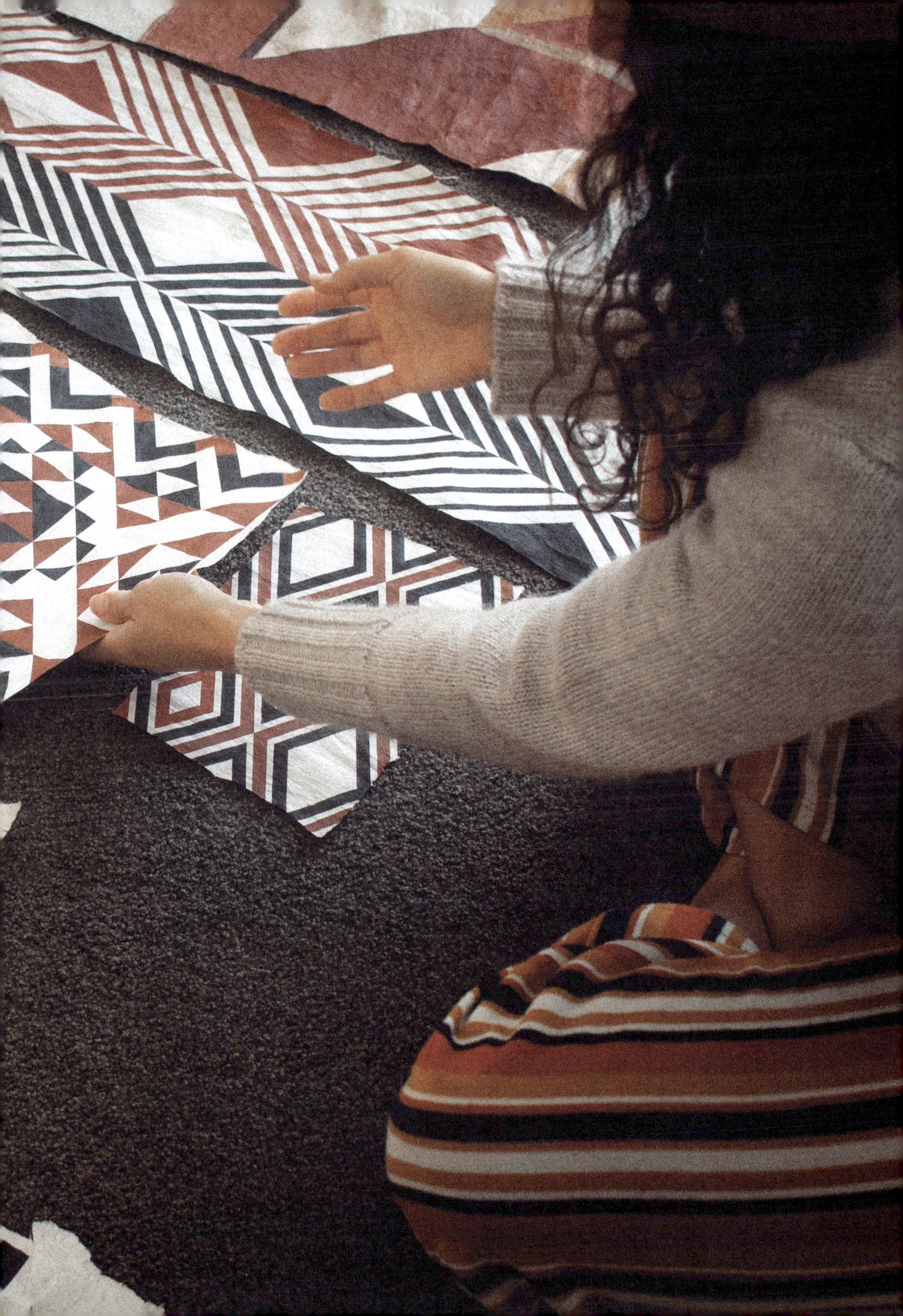

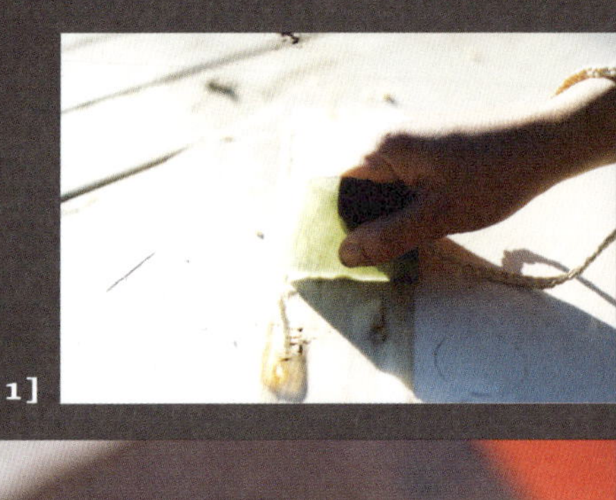

[1]

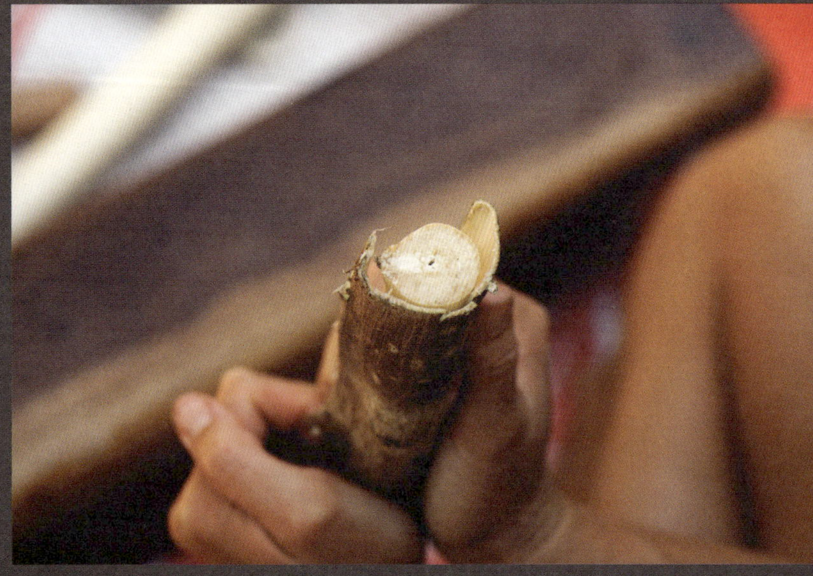

[2]

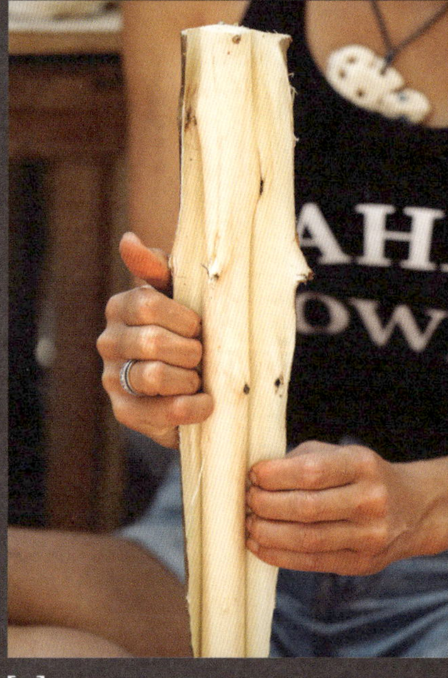

[3]

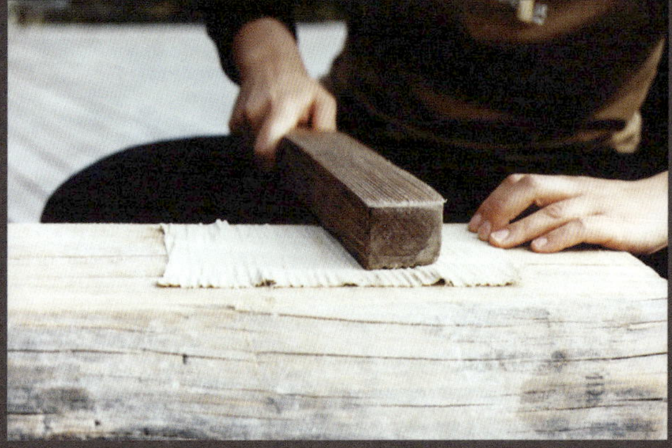

[4]

[5]

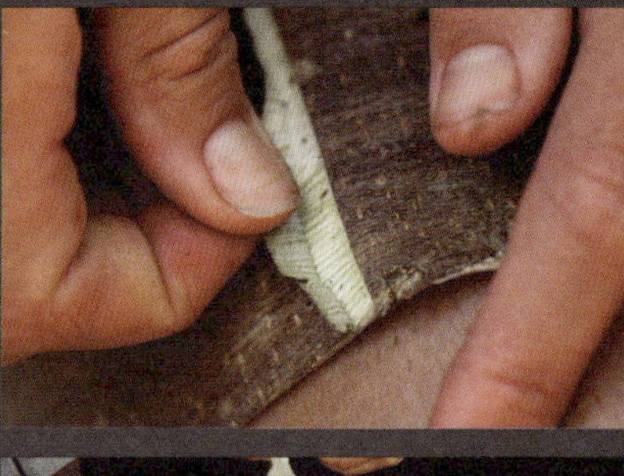

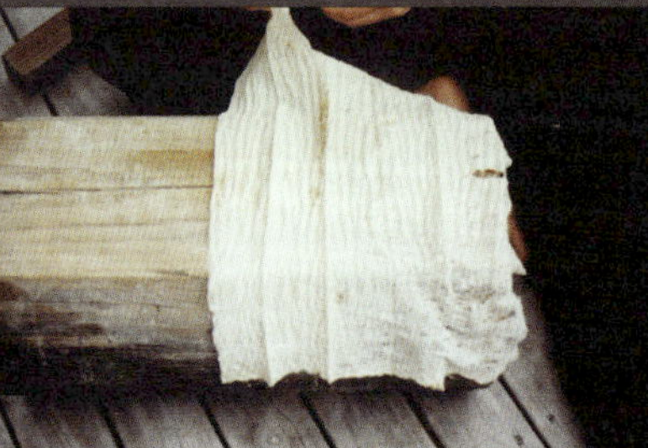

[6]

[9]

[1] Haylee Koroi uses a *pounamu* (greenstone) scraper to soften and remove water from the bast of the aute (Step 1).

[2] After making the lengthway cut along the stalk Hindin is peeling back the bark (Step 1.0).

[3] Here Hindin is removing the bast off the inner stalk of the paper mulberry (Step 1.1).

[4] Here Haylee is beating the cloth with a beater made from *pohutukawa* (Step 2).

[5] The process is called *whakapaa*, and after making a light cut in the bark Hindin has flicked up the edges of the brown bark (Step 2.0).

[6] This is Haylee unfolding her piece of cloth after the folding and beating process. This is the final reveal (Step 2.1).

[7] Here Hindin is peeling the outer bark off the inner bast of the mulberry paper (Step 2.2).

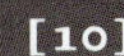
[10]

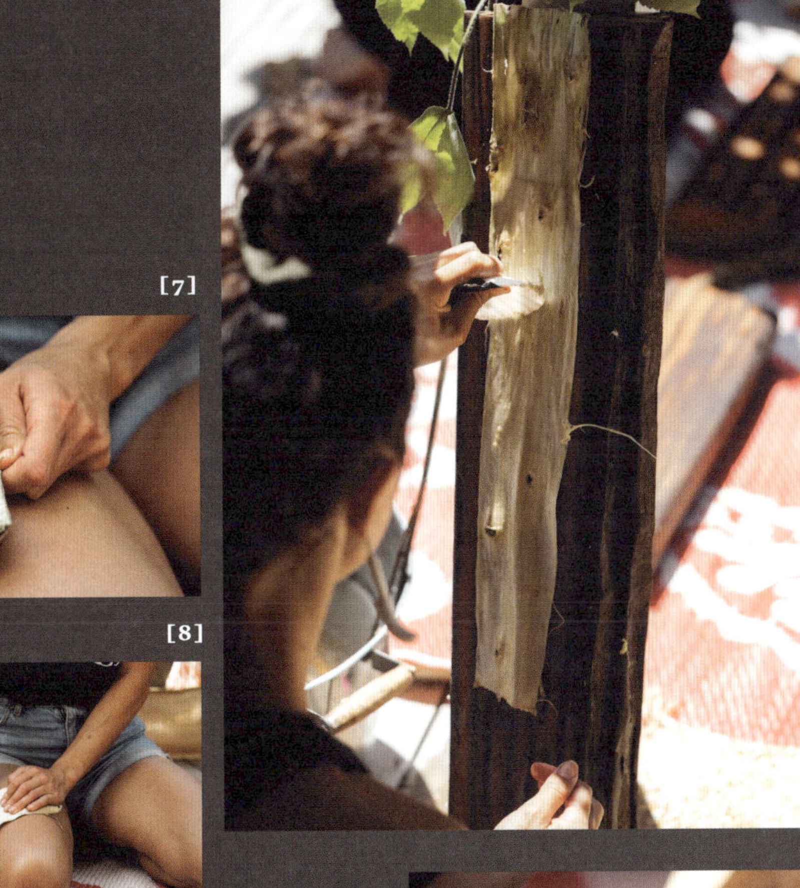

[7]

[8]

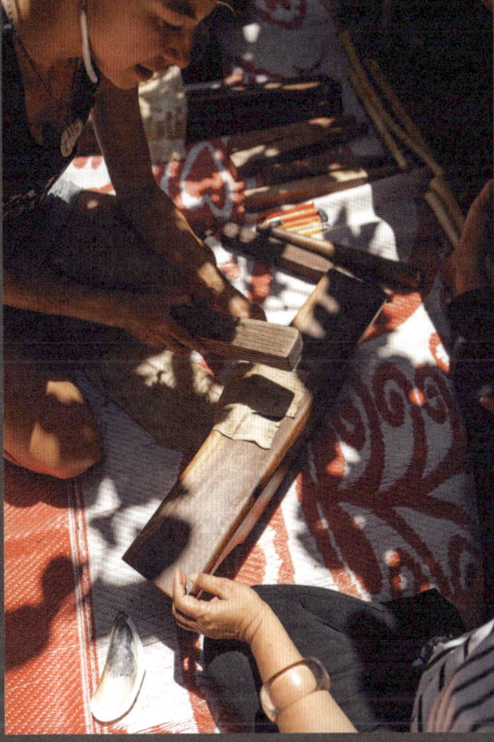

[11]

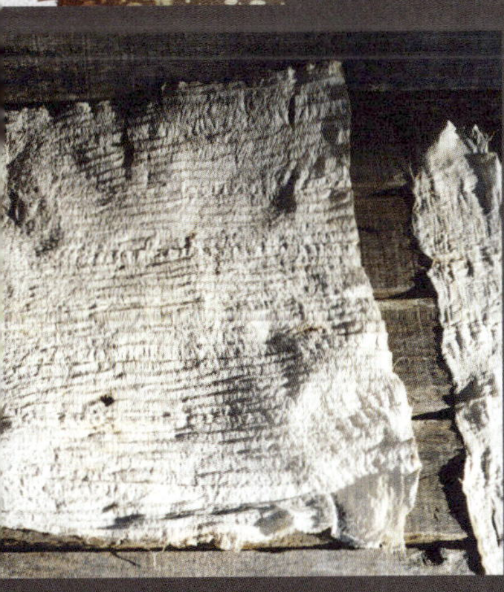

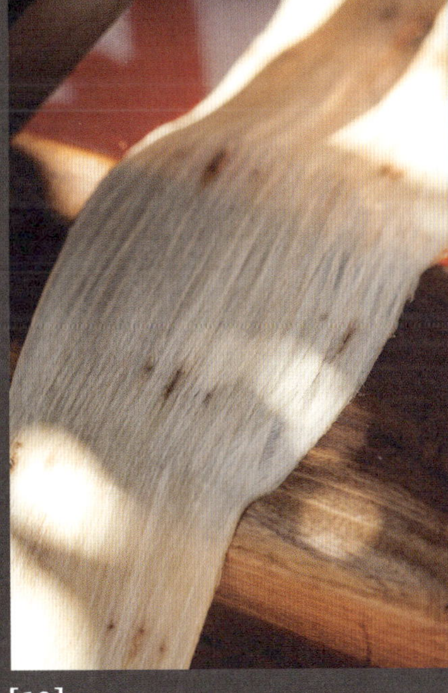

[12]

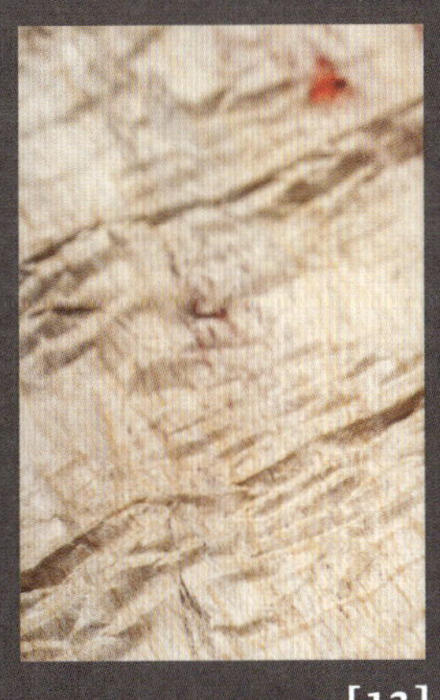

[13]

[8] Here Hindin has managed to grip the edge of the bark and is pulling it in a downward motion against her thigh (Step 2.3).

[9] This is Haylee's piece. The creases come from the folding and beating process (Step 3).

[10] Scraping the bast and removing all the excess water. This is the step right before beating (Step 3.1).

[11] Demonstrating the beating process for Aitutaki Pa'oa revivalist Lulu (Step 4.0).

[12] Close-up of the bast that has been thoroughly cleaned and scraped being beaten on the anvil. You can see the grooves of the beater making imprints on the bast as the fibers spread out (Step 4.1).

[13] Close-up of the beaten cloth drying in the sun (Step 5.0).

Stones. Transduction. Fermentation: Edgar Calel and the Case of Ownership in Art Ccollections

76

PABLO JOSÉ RAMÍREZ

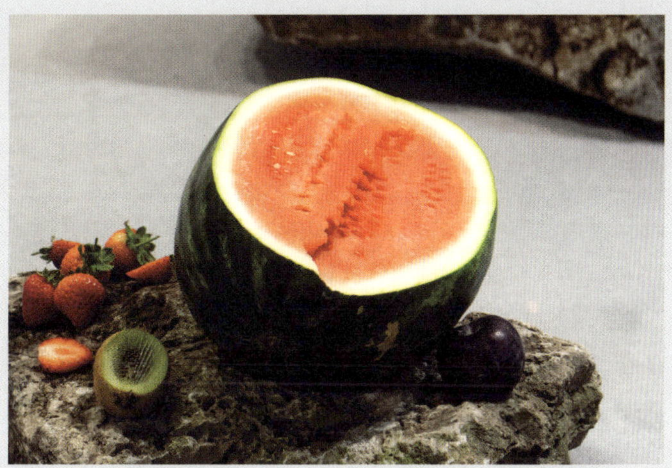

FIG 1 Edgar Calel, *Ru k' ox k'ob'el jun ojer etemab'el (The Echo of an Ancient Form of Knowledge)*. Frieze London, 2021. Image courtesy of the artist and Proyectos Ultravioleta. Photo: James Retief.

Throughout the agitated halls of Frieze London 2021, Proyectos Ultravioleta presented the work *Ru k' ox k'ob'el jun ojer etemab'el (The Echo of an Ancient Form of Knowledge)* (2021), by Maya Kaqchikel artist Edgar Calel. The work consisted of a constellation of stones of different sizes distributed across the booth's floor. Atop the stones sat sliced fruit collected from Brixton Market. By cutting the flesh, a fermentation process was initiated; the piece breathed.

Looking at Indigenous Art from the safe distance of ethnographic colonial methodologies and the prescriptive explanatory logics of curatorial practice perpetuates the recitation of colonial translation endemic largely to Western museums. Institutional infrastructures are moving toward the acknowledgment of their foundation myths, understanding that their axioms have in part obliterated the aesthetic manifestations of large groups of populations on the planet.

The formal features of the piece are insinuated through a condensed silence whose utterance is possible in the agency of the work itself, in the time it possesses, in the histories it articulates. Crucially, it was not on sale at this international, well-established art fair; it was not to be owned by a collector or a museum.

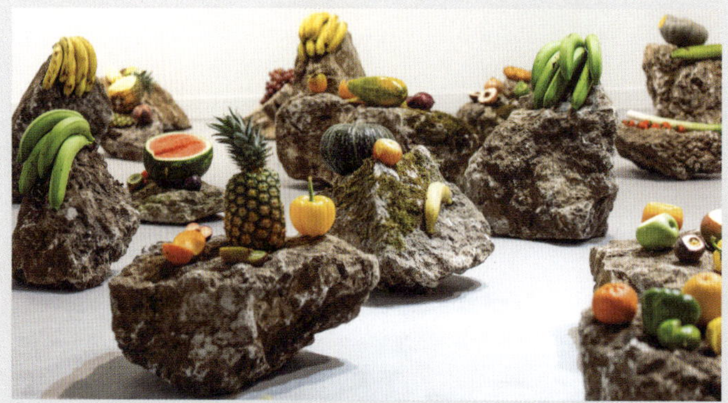

FIG 2 Edgar Calel, *Ru k' ox k'ob'el jun ojer etemab'el (The Echo of an Ancient Form of Knowledge).* Frieze London Image courtesy of the artist and Proyectos Ultravioleta. Photo: James Retief.

Edgar Calel is an artist from San Juan Comalapa, in the central highlands of Guatemala. The history of the town goes back to anti-colonial resistance and the history of the Maya Kaqchikel population. The town has been a true artistic breeding ground since the early twentieth century. Artists such as Andrés Curuchich and Paula Nicho Cumez stand out as iconic figures who transformed the way we see and understand so-called naif painting. Comalapa has also been pivotal to an intellectual Mayan movement of thinkers whose work has combated the forces of neoliberalism within the country. Calel's practice doesn't stand alone. It is part of an unprecedented movement in Latin America, which, alongside artists such as Manuel Antonio Pichillá, Marilyn Boror, Angélica Serech, Angel Poyón, Fernando Poyon, and many others, has established a vibrant epicenter for contemporary art production in the continent.

Modern Guatemalan history is tainted by the blood of thirty-six years of internal civil war, one of the cruelest in Latin America. Under decades of military dictatorships, the Indigenous population endured the stigma brought by the modernization processes, facing the idiocy and cruelty of the military mind. In countless cases, counterinsurgent attacks obliterated entire villages under the so-called *politicas de tierra arrasada*, murdering hundreds of thousands and displacing millions of rural workers, precarizing the living conditions of large portions of a population that by now have endured more than five centuries of colonial violence.[1]

It's important to point out that the racial axioms of Guatemalan contemporary society are dialectical sides of the violence mentioned above. Colonial violence requires of the conceptual articulation of Mestizo and Creole, as antagonistic to the Indigenous one, configurations from which the machinery of the nation-state is conceived. They extend from its operational racist protocols. In the Guatemalan theoretical production of the twentieth century, the Indigenous and the Mayan have been widely discussed notions, whose critical genealogy can be traced in the contributions of Marxist historian Severo Martinez Peláez and in the articulation of the Mayan subject, developed with sharpness in the work of Guatemalan anthropologist Carlos Guzman-Böckler:

1 The "politicas de tierra arrasada" were military plans led by dictator Efrain Rios Montt, who justified genocidal actions under the argument that Indigenous populations were supporting and providing resources to the guerrilla leftist movement. Under this pretext he ordered the genocide of entire communities (as with the Ixil people) and a permanent persecution against Indigenous communities, which continue today under different strategies.

> As a consequence of colonization, there was therefore a change in the economic assumptions accompanied by a breakdown of the valuation patterns, which since then have not found a substitute in the axiological system of the peninsula, and whose effects became increasingly acute in the Creole and the Mestizo. From there, the exploiter (whether peninsular, creole or mestizo) throws on the indigenous a veil of contempt that, in reality, only conceals the unspeakable contempt that very deep down he feels for himself.[2]
>
> — Guzman-Böckler and Herbert

Regarding the Indigenous-Mestizo relationship, the following statement is illuminating:

> In short, the colonial system, by striving to create, with a life independent of its human managers, a world based on the exploitation of the land for the benefit of a minority, which in turn rests on the exploitation of a human group found defeated and stripped away, has given life to a fetish, in the Marxist sense of the term. In support of this fetish, it has created the concepts of ladino and indigenous: mental constructions to which it has also given a life independent of those who conceived it and that have taken on the character of ideological abstractions with real appearance [...] fetishes are also the terms ladino and Indigenous. Consequently, within the colonial system, the relationship between fetishes and man manifests itself to the latter as his alienation from himself, as the loss of himself. It is a clear process of alienation.[3]

---

2 Carlos Guzman-Böckler and Jean Loup Herbert, *Guatemala: una interpretación histórico-social* (Guatemala: Cholsamaj, 2002), 58.

3 Guzman-Böckler and Herbert, *Guatemala*, 62.

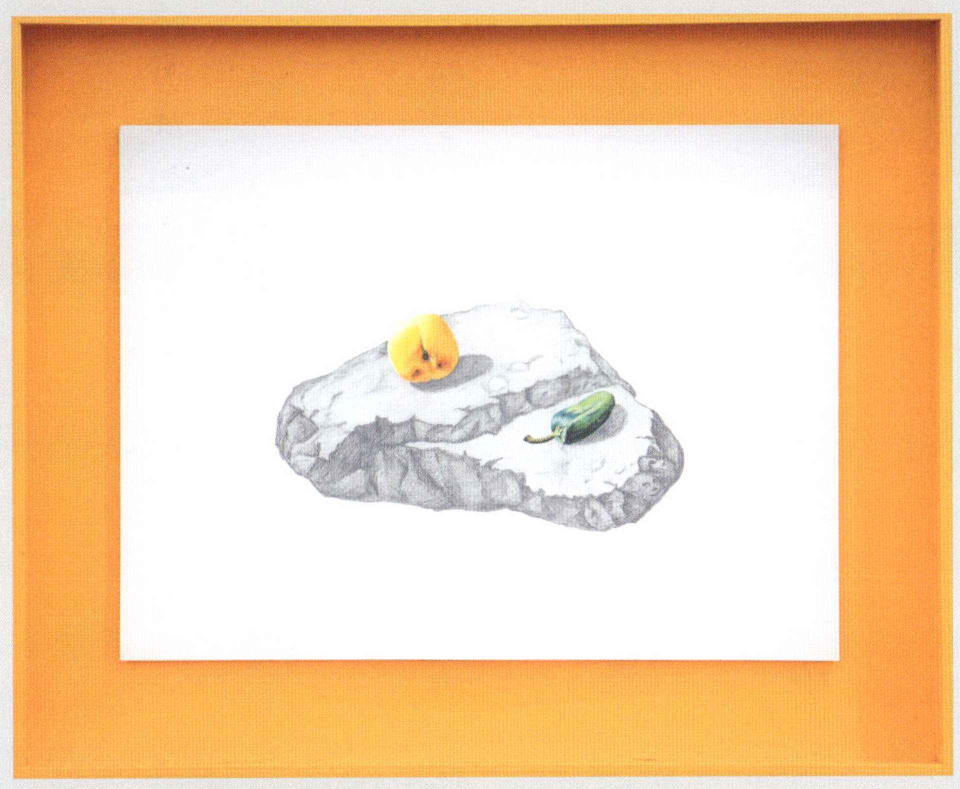

FIG 4 Edgar Calel, *Ru k' ox k'ob'el jun ojer etemab'el (The Echo of an Ancient Form of Knowledge)*, 2021. Frieze London. Image courtesy of the artist and Proyectos Ultravioleta. Photo: James Retief.

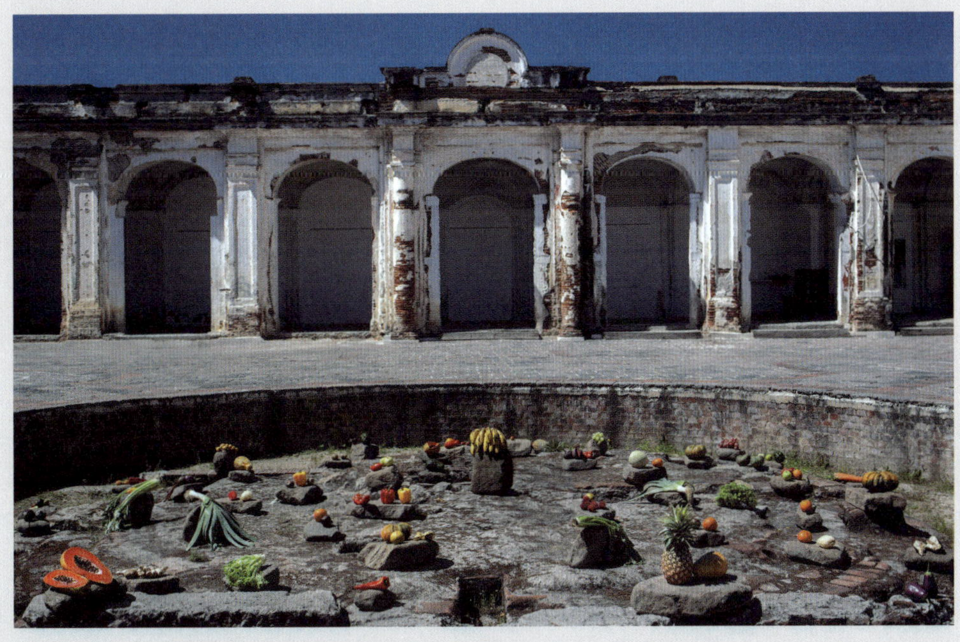

FIG 5 Edgar Calel, *Jun Kio Oxi qi Munib'al ri qatit qa Mama' (Some Two or Three Offerings for Our Ancestors)*, 2018. Digital photography on cotton paper. Image courtesy of the artist and Proyectos Ultravioleta, Guatemala City. Photo: Jose Wolff.

Calel is an artist who troubles this colonial categorization, sabotaging common assumptions associated with a Western construction of the Indigenous subject. He seems to be comfortable working within different formal approaches, ranging from performance, sculpture, painting, drawing, time-based media, and everything in between. His practice grasps the intricacies of the art world and its Western axioms with boldness, clarity, and humor.

I have been close to Calel's practice for over a decade. Witnessing the way he considers art has made me realize that if one thing is certain, it's that Indigenous Art holds the potentiality to debunk some of the myths that the automatism of curatorial practice has forgotten to question when it comes to race politics. Within Calel's practice, some may see an intersection of art and life; a resemblance to the ritualistic dimension of performance tradition, perhaps embodied in modernist icons such as Joseph Beuys or Ana Mendieta. However, there's something that this approach cannot grasp. Calel's work brings forward a dimension of rituality embedded in the fabric of the communal, in the semantic DNA of Kachikel culture, debunking the categorical binarisms of the colonial mind mentioned above.

One of the first iterations of the piece was presented at the 19th Paiz Biennale curated by Cecilia Fajardo-Hill, Anabella Acevedo, Rosina Cazali, and myself. Since then, the work has had different manifestations and iterations. The stones were moved from one place to another and distributed differently. The fruit was sourced from local markets. The rituals activating the piece varied with each specific temporalization. During Frieze London 2021, the activation of the work was performed by Ulrik Lopez, a Puerto Rican/Mexican artist. With alcohol and incense, López "opened" the piece, setting the work in motion to be presented at the art fair. The work was accompanied by a group of drawings inspired by the installation.

The decision to show the work but not put it on sale is not insignificant. It responds to a bold gesture recurrent in Calel's practice, converting Indigenous Art into much more than a commodity. The artist creates agency within the matter of the object, downplaying the role of an art fair as a vitrine for commodified objects. The piece shows such subtle irony that it could even be mistaken for naivety. The work speaks for itself, and while it is so exposed, it cannot be owned, resembling the familiar paradox of the exotifying eye; the implosive impossibility of desiring something that cannot be possessed.

We've witnessed over the last several years at Frieze, and particularly Frieze Masters, an increasing presence of non-Western art and objects such as textiles and a wide range of crafts. This could be read as a symptom—an unconfessed desire that art world infrastructures seem to have with objects belonging to other cultures. The cognitive stimuli of non-Western aesthetics, when displayed in cosmopolitan centers, powers the revitalization of the art experience, which on its flipside can be read as an old vampiristic habit.

This not only borders ethnographic practices of decontextualization and commodification, it furthermore abstracts cultural complexity to the taxonomic ruling of identity and diversity. This is not a new paradox, although it has mutated as a phenomenon traced back to neoliberal reforms and the fall of the Berlin Wall in 1989. The semiotic global experience of "diversity," namely *multiculturalism*, has mutated, and the simulation of cultural diversity in a controlled space of display seems to be a feast difficult to resist, especially when it comes to global art events such as an art fair.

When it comes to *Ru k' ox k'ob'el jun ojer etemab'el*, this is a conundrum which could be easily addressed by arguing this is a move that artists have made in the past. The more resistance to the market or the institution, the more desirable an object becomes, foreseeing its destiny as a work that surrenders its antagonistic force to the stream of art snobbism. There are two things we must consider before rushing to make an assessment in that direction. One is that this work responds to a collective force, namely the Kaqchikel community in Comalapa. It is not a collectively authored piece, but its aesthetics are informed by the episteme of an Indigenous culture. Calel is accountable to that community. The second factor to consider is that the work itself represents a rather uncomfortable place for ownership and conservation, bringing forward seminal questions yet to be solved. How to preserve a fermenting work? How to display a piece that requires activation to be displayed? What are we actually collecting with such a piece?

In Mayan Kaqchikel communities, non-animated objects such as stones are matter with agency. The silence held by stones teaches and transmits knowledge. Take, for instance, the case of the *Cerro Quemado* in the southwestern highlands of Guatemala. The relationship of the K'iche community with that *cerro* dates from ancestral (precolonial) times, as do their very relationship with the stones in the hills. People honor the stones through rituals that speak of the complex and rich relationship between people, the mountain, and the stones. They pray with the stones, chat with them, hug them, and cry. From the 1980s onwards, US interventionism brought about the expansion of evangelical neo-Pentecostal churches. Many evangelical churches have used the space to attract more followers. Their improvised structures had to convene with the rugged and uneven terrain of the mountain.

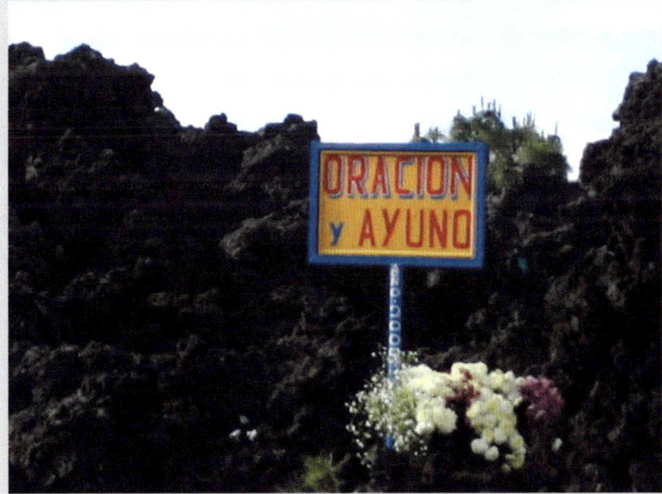

FIG 6 *Cerro Quemado*, Guatemala, 2020.
Photo: Andrés Rodríguez.

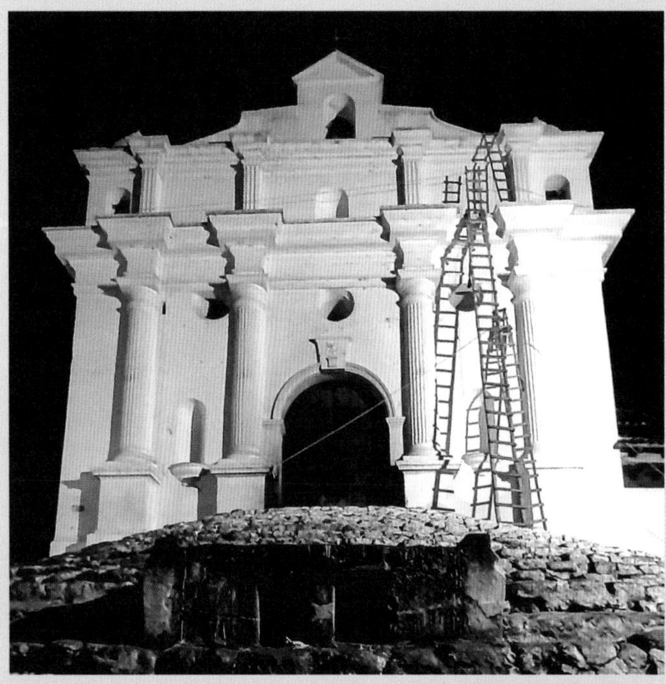

FIG 7 Iglesia de Santo Tomás, in Chichicastenango, Guatemala. Image courtesy of Edd Tol, Chichicasteco.

The relationship that Mayan communities hold to stones is complex and in many cases is associated with places of cultural resistance. Another example is the Iglesia de Santo Tomás in Chichicastenango, Guatemala — a Catholic church founded in 1540 and installed in a ceremonial pre-Hispanic sacred site of the K'iche people. Inside the church, a sober hall is surrounded by wooden carved saints above altar structures. The saints are completely covered by the soot of the smoke emanating from a group of stone bonfires allocated along the halls of the church. These are the stones where Ajq'ij' [4] lead ceremonial encounters, right in the middle of

4 According to professor Pedro Juan Toc Barreno, Ajq'ij is a contracted word composed of two concepts: Aj, a prefix that indicates action, and Q'ij Sun, from day or light. Etymologically, the word Ajq'ij derives from the ancient Mayan language K'iche', indicating who works with the Sun or with the day. In other words, who works with clarity; clarity is the truth; the truth is science. Therefore the person Ajq'ij is a scientist and a person of Light. The Ajq'ij person in Mayan culture is known as a Spiritual Guide.

the Catholic imagery. More than a syncretic practice, this can be understood as a historical strategy of survival. The community fought for the right of continuation, the right to keep practicing the ancestral ceremonies they have known for centuries. The stones where they perform the ceremonies serve as a passage, breaking apart the architectural weight of the colonial church. The stones operate as a transductive object.

In this context transduction is a concept borrowed from sound theory, one that can easily be applied to certain views on aesthetics. Stefan Helmreich, preoccupied with sound and energy, sees transduction

> as a form of energy transmitted through a medium. Often, that energy moves across or between media—from an antenna to a receiver, from an amplifier to an ear, from the lightness of air to the thickness of water. With such crossings, sound is transduced. The word comes from Latin transducere, "to lead across, to transfer," out of trans, "across, to or on the farther side of, beyond, over" + ducere, "to lead."[5]

5 Stefan Helmreich, "Transduction," *Keywords in Sound*, ed., David Novak and Matt Sakakeeny (Durham, NC: Duke University Press, 2015), 222–31.

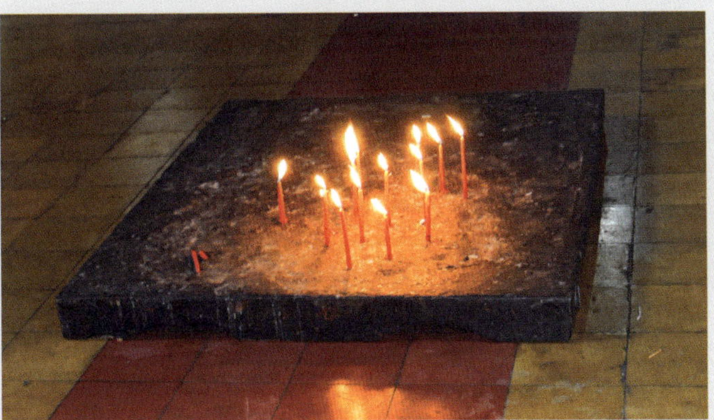

FIG 8 Syncretic K'iche' Maya offering inside Iglesia de Santo Tomás (St. Thomas Church) Chichicastenango, Guatemala.

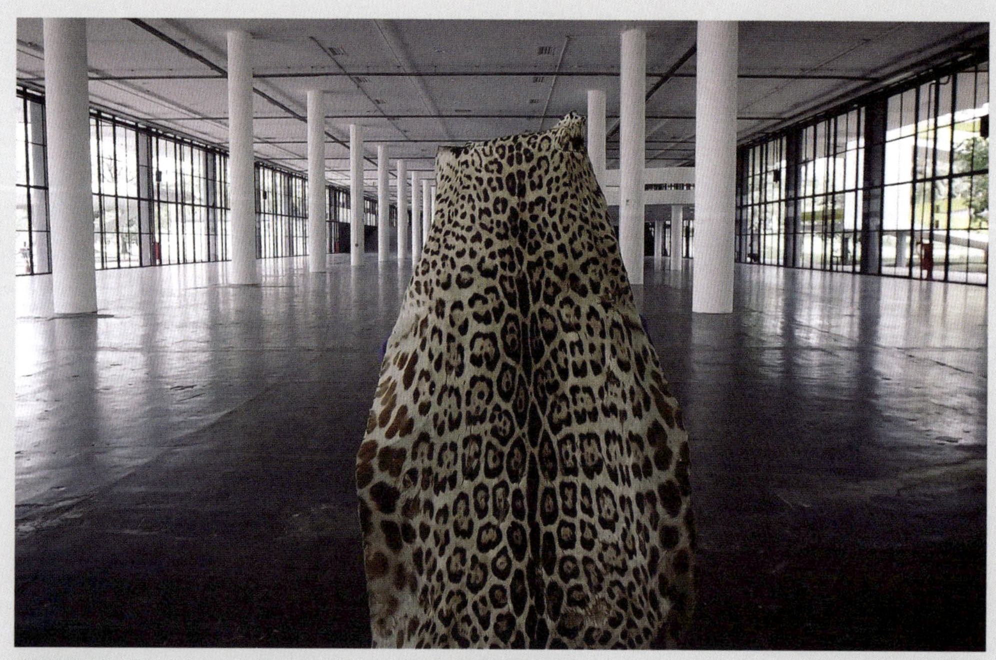

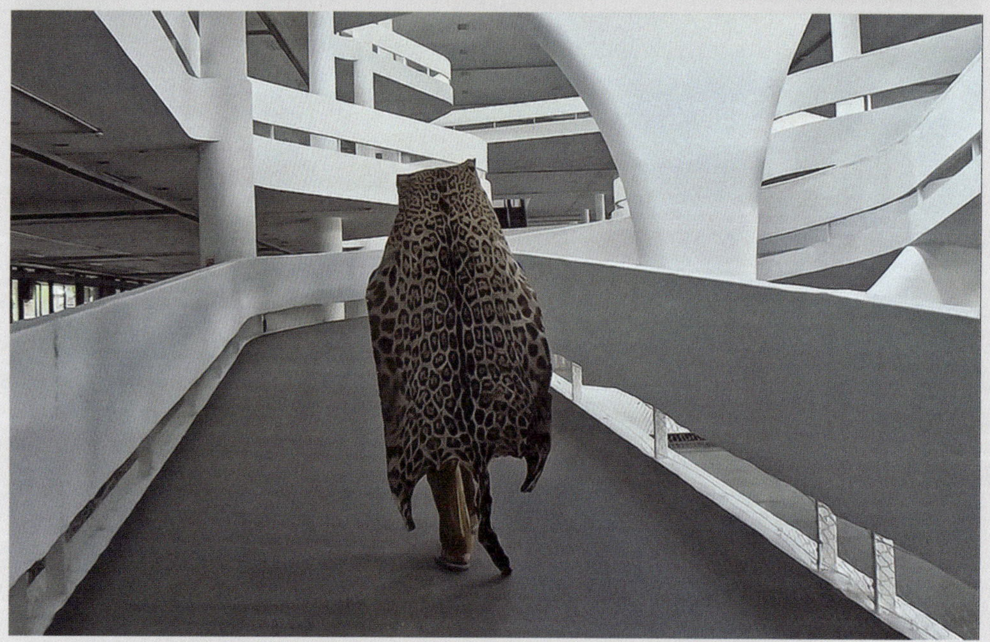

FIG 9-10 Edgar Calel & Fernando Pereira Dos Santos, *Xar Obsidian Dream*, 2020–21. Single Channel HD Video Loop. Courtesy of the artists and Proyectos Ultravioleta, Guatemala City.

At the core of *Ru k' ox k'ob'el jun ojer etemab'el*, the stones hold transductive energy. They belong to a place and are the keepers of that energy. While being transported, they—as the artist does—work as a nomadic piece whose immanence is contingent to the place of display. They might return to the same place or they might be permanently moved to another location. As they belong to a place they are also placed, hosting cut fruit whose process of fermentation is observed and allowed by those very stones. New fruit will come and the stones will continue playing their role as keepers and transmitters of that energy.[6]

To understand Indigenous Art as a Cosmopolitan Utterance means to sabotage the ethnographic colonial gaze, obstructing the violent operation of translation that abstracts cultural complexity to the axioms of Western civilization. At the foundation of the colonial mind is the explanatory logic around cultural difference that performs the gesture of cultural inclusivity while holding the power to name the world, to name things. This is a piece that names itself. The emergence of Indigenous Art in international circuits has exposed the cracks and limits of Western universalism. We are witnessing a unique moment in history where those very meanings are being disputed.

---

6 It's difficult also not to think of the reference that fruit has held as a signifier in Central America. Being a commodified production, subjected to the imperial and colonial social relations of production in Guatemala, as in the well-known case of the US interventionist company UFCO (United Fruit Company), which controlled the monoculture of bananas and other fruits in the country, supporting dictatorial regimes and landowners.

After conversations between the artist, the artist's gallery, and the Tate, *Ru k' ox k'ob'el jun ojer etemab'el* was acquired via custodianship for thirteen years through the Frieze Tate Fund. This approach is unprece-dented when it comes to the institution and its relationship to Indigenous Art. The work will not be owned but will exist in custo-dianship at the museum, and after thirteen years, custodianship of the piece will either be extended through a new agreement for another thirteen years, passed on to another institution, or returned to the earth. The Mayan calendar holds thirteen energies, which also represents the conjectures in the human body. Calel insinuated this number as it is significant for the Kaqchikel culture.

Although this is just one step forward, it opens the window to consider something that has been troubling me for some time. How can we move beyond questions of representation when it comes to Indigenous Art and museum collection, towards a view that understands Indigeneity as a force capable of transforming and questioning the very structures that have given shape to the way we understand art history and its curatorial repertoires? In this case, yes, acquiring the work of Indigenous artists is essential, but the ethos of such practice should go beyond questions of how many Indigenous artists an art collection has.

To Indigenize a collection might then mean to have a different understanding of museum practice not rooted in ownership, but in sharing certain values. The idea of custodianship might require a new set of theoretical tools and curatorial practices that treats the art object as matter with agency, with a history, and a social vibrancy. To hold these stones in the collection, to collect the fruit from a market and take care of their process of decay brings forward the need for a different type of awareness of the art object and also of how time acts within a piece. The fact that the piece depends on a temporality of fermentation, decay, and transformation, means it is alive, therefore it has agency.

The answers to these questions are not to be found in an alternative reading of art history, but rather in an altered understanding of our relationship with objects; that is to say, a different understanding of the way we live the subjectivation of art. The foregrounding of a term such as Indigeneity in a museum context brings forward a set of questions that institutions might not be ready to respond to. Even if not through a radical gesture of vulnerability, there is a need for opening up the very foundations that ascribe museums' legitimacy as gatekeepers of history in the first place.

A new approach should propose alternatives to the teleology of Western time when it comes to how we read art history. To Indigenize a collection is to trouble the fixed Western categories and its temporalizations, thinking of *the contemporary* as the paradoxical conjuncture of ancestral, colonial, and Western globalized time. Such potentialities are contained in Calel's work, and collecting this piece makes evident the wounds of this diachronism. The stakes are high.

* With thanks to the community of artists in Comalapa, Fernando Poyon, Angel Poyon, and Edgar Calel for the countless conversations, and to my admired colleagues Catherine Wood, Tamsin Hong, and Stefan Benchoam.

Starting with an Honest Conversation

92

SVEN HAAKANSON

How does a museum change its practices so it can truly engage with Indigenous communities and their cultural heritage?[1] The process is messy when institutional practices are centuries old and based on antiquated ways of seeing, treating, interpreting, and sharing Indigenous worldviews.[2] Many museums were established as institutions to show how exotic and "primitive" other cultures were compared to colonialists' own. I ask the reader to consider the practice of "othering" others simply by exhibiting their cultures and histories from an outsider's view. Anthropological and ethnographic museums' emphasis on Indigenous collections has led to a public impression of Indigenous cultures being in the past, and museums are now grappling with how to change this. As this fundamental shift is happening, we are all learning new paths towards engaging with each other. I want to share my path in this process and stress how important it is to continue to support this change within our institutions.

As an Indigenous person in a position to raise awareness of the "othering" practices that I have personally experienced, I had to teach myself how to change my own practices and overcome the distrust that communities held towards museums as unfeeling collectors of "objects." I realized that to change these practices, museums must systematically engage and collaborate directly with communities *by listening to and integrating what communities want*, not just doing what the museum wants. What happens when a museum engages in these changes? In my experience it opens and creates new ways forward for all of us to change our practices, roles, and ways of caring for Indigenous Heritage. It also gives museums a route for changing their past exhibiting practices openly and systematically. It allows museums to acknowledge all the issues and opens the door to dialog. Below are some suggestions for ways one can start to better engage with communities.

---

1 To me, "Cultural Heritage" means the intangible and tangible knowledges that are embodied within the cultural works created by Indigenous peoples.

2 Antiquated or as the terms are used today "colonial" practices that control what and how we learn; colonial practices that control what and how we learn.

1. **Hold listening sessions** to hear what communities are saying, and learn what they need and want from your museum.
2. **Engage** with cultural leaders and listen to how they want their culture to be shared with the world.
3. **Research and share** the history of collecting, both good and bad. Don't hide any of the issues; allow difficult histories to be a conversation starter.
4. **Give communities access** to the collections so they can learn from them on their terms, not yours.
5. **Find funding opportunities** for communities to re-engage with collections. Within these, look for ways to complete a collaborative project together.
6. **Give them space** to learn from the collections and to explore the knowledges embodied within each cultural piece. Don't rush the process.
7. **Step back and listen**. Don't extract knowledge for a paper. This falls into the practice of extraction done over the past several centuries. Don't do this.
8. **Let things come together naturally**. They will play out within the community on their terms.
   Also, be ready to support communities when they ask. Don't force things.
9. **Know our roles are changing**. It is now important to help facilitate communities in taking back their knowledge for them to use within their community. They own this knowledge and should have access to collections whenever they want.
10. **Understand that building trusting relationships takes time** and is based on personal human interactions.

I have shared these points because over the past thirty years of working with and within museums I have seen change start when the employees within institutions have collectively agreed to change their practices with communities.[3] It's not easy to change, especially when you have policies and generations of work done in certain ways. It takes time to completely shift to another way of thinking and working with communities. To make this become part of new institutional memory and practice we must do this work collaboratively.[4] We need to create projects that can be shared and built on over time: our institutions and communities are not going anywhere. Think beyond your time so that the institutional work carries these memories forward, with the staff and community remembering these changes. Your engagements will continue over time, as long as you build this work in trust and openness with communities.

My Path

I'd never considered a career in Anthropology until I was given an opportunity to attend the Sixth Inuit Studies Conference in Copenhagen, Denmark, in 1988.[5] There I was able to attend a lecture by Dr. Lydia Black, one of the foremost scholars in Russian-American History at that time. Dr. Black was presenting what she had found in storage in museums across the world from the "Aleut" people. As I sat listening to her talk, I asked myself why I was on the other side of the world learning about my own cultural heritage when I should have already known about it? This trip and her lecture changed the direction of my career. I now wanted to learn more about what happened to my ancestors and their knowledge. Why did we lose so much after our contact with Europeans? Was it too late to get this knowledge back? These questions inspired me to get involved in archaeology and eventually with museums, where I have been able to make a difference in how this knowledge is shared within my community.

3 This work starts with individuals within institutions. We all want to do right by what we do, and this starts with being aware of others and how important it is for people to interact with each other over time.

4 This is where accountability and funding comes into play in how an institution moves forward.

5 Dr. Gordon Pullar and Dr. Rick Knecht called me up in the fall of 1988 to ask if I would be interested in attending this conference and I agreed.

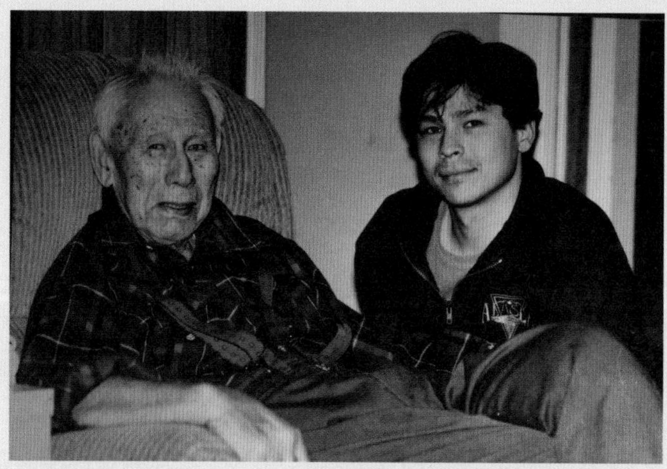

FIG 1 Larry Matfay and Sven Haakanson Jr. at Old Harbor, Alaska, 1997.

The mission of allowing the community to speak for their objects starts with making sure that native naming conventions are recognized, honored, and investigated. From the 1740s until the mid-1980s, the people of the Kodiak region were labeled "Aleuts," a name used to describe us by the Russians. This was an imposed name used only by colonizers; people were never asked what they originally called themselves. Sadly, this was in line with the European mode of interacting with Indigenous peoples globally. When I was seventeen, I was told by an elder from my village of Old Harbor, Larry Matfay, that this name was wrong, yet no one had previously listened to him or other elders on the subject. I did not understand what he was saying at the time because at that point we called ourselves Aleuts as we had learned from schools, the government, and history books. This naming convention would not change until the communities created their own museums that shared their histories and true ethnonyms. In the Aleutian Islands, the people's real name is *Unangan* in the Eastern region, and *Unangas* in the Western region, while from the Alaska Peninsula and Kodiak to the Prince William Sound the name is *Sugpiat*. For over two centuries, colonial terms and suppression controlled how the people would see and identify themselves. This open erasure of our ethnonym unconsciously influenced how we saw and treated ourselves for several generations. In the museum world, properly naming people and their pieces would be a solid place to begin improvements.

In Kodiak we are now starting to use “Sugpiat” over other names to identify ourselves, especially among the younger generation as they have become aware of its power, meaning “true human being.” The simple but powerful act of knowing who they are and where they come from grounds people in their communities and gives them strength in themselves. The global reclamation of Indigenous names and cultural heritage has become a powerful beacon for starting to reverse colonial practices of suppressing and erasing traditional ways of knowing, languages, and the cultural heritages of people over several centuries.

Our Unspoken Histories

It was during my graduate studies that I started to learn about our rich material cultural heritage, which primarily existed in museum collections scattered across the world. Having the privilege and opportunity to research museum collections has allowed me to explore, learn, and piece together history while bringing back this knowledge to our communities.

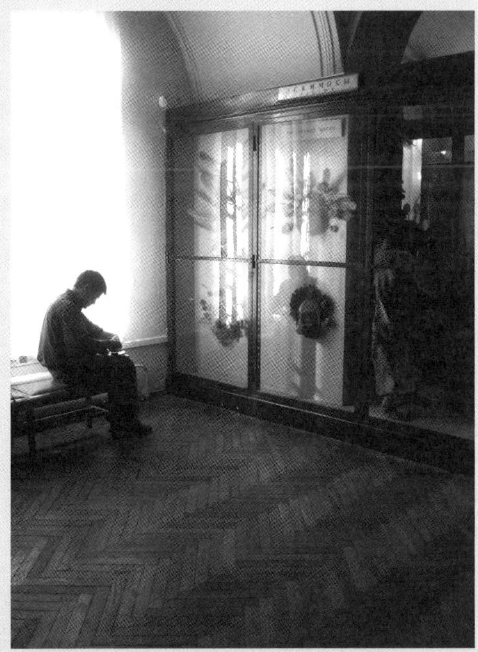

FIG 2 Sven Haakanson studying Sugpiat masks at the Museum of Anthropology and Ethnography (MAE), St. Petersburg, Russia, 2009. Photo: Nadia Jackinsky.

After finishing my PhD in 2000, I started working as the Director of the Alutiiq Museum, and the first project I was involved in was to create a traveling exhibition that went out to five villages on Kodiak Island to share the cultural knowledge that we cared for in our museum. It was a simple and straightforward project in which we designed a small traveling exhibition to share with the community, and a small project on the topic for students to engage with.

In the end this became more about sharing and giving back knowledge to communities, and it changed the way I viewed the role of our museum within our community. As museum professionals we are responsible for stopping the extraction of knowledge and for starting to rebuild and heal community memory, which are essential for language and heritage reclamation.

Starting in the early 1990s, village tribal councils across Kodiak got together and demanded that rural schools teach their youth about our Alutiiq culture for at least one week during the school year. This led to the creation of what is called "Alutiiq Week," held annually in all village schools. Because I was from the village of Old Harbor, I learned about this from my sister who has been a teacher's aid there for over thirty years. When I started as Director of the Alutiiq Museum, I saw an opportunity for how we could share the cultural knowledge in our museum with communities across the island.

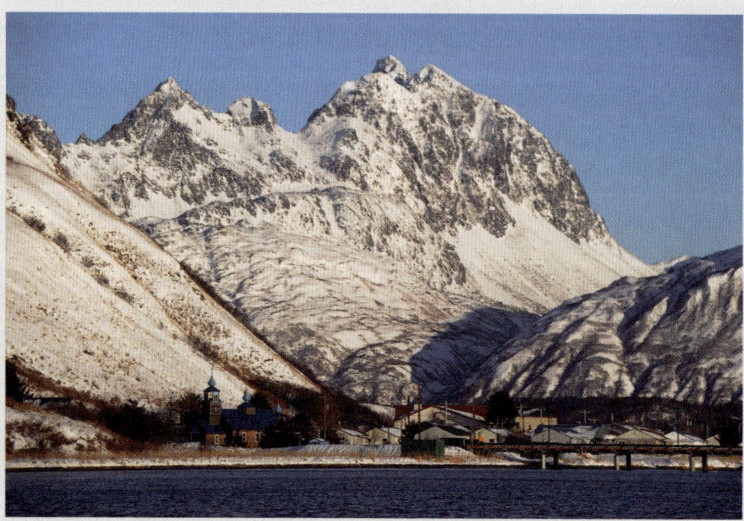

FIG 3 Old Harbor, Alaska, 2016.

My goal was for us to go out to communities rather than wait for them to come to us, thus reversing our role as a museum by bringing the knowledge back out to where it originated. During our first year I learned that we needed to coordinate our projects and travel time to match the dates that each school decided to hold their Alutiiq Week. We started working with the tribal councils and teachers in the fall to learn what the community wanted to do during their Alutiiq Week and what we could contribute. For over thirteen years I collaborated with the villages by sharing what we had learned that year about our cultural heritage. As I conducted research within museum collections from around the world, I would figure out how to create a new project from this knowledge that we could then share during the Alutiiq Weeks. We shared how to weave baskets, carve masks, make games, create hunting tools, model kayaks, paddles, bent wood boxes, and drums, and sew fish and reindeer skin bags and clothing. We shared what we had in our collections with the communities, and worked to ensure that they knew it was their knowledge and belonged to them. Every year we collaborated with the villages and it showed them that the museum was here for them, not the reverse. In the end, Alutiiq Weeks became about more than simply creating a cultural piece with our youths; it became about bringing our elders, parents, and children together around an object and theme, which resulted in storytelling, community connections, and ultimately, growing the museum's knowledge base. This in turn led to a stronger connection with and support for the museum and its mission to share and celebrate our cultural heritage in a living context.

The first project was to try to teach traditional basket weaving, which in hindsight was not the easiest project to start with, because we only had one week. Aleut-style basket weaving is not something that can be completed within a week, even for more seasoned weavers. By any standards, I would say that this project wasn't successful because only two students completed their baskets, and we worked with six schools that first year. What we learned from this first experience were some very valuable lessons that we used for the next thirteen years about creating projects that students can complete within one week, building on the previous year's project, and establishing an atmosphere in which kids enjoy themselves in the learning process. The projects should never be forced. I also developed four simple rules: 1. We are here to have fun; 2. Please don't play with the knives; 3. If you are playing with the knives, please sit out for five minutes; and 4. If you are caught playing with the knives again I will ask you to leave the class, no questions asked. Across thirteen years of teaching carving in communities, I have only had to ask one student to leave, and they did. Sadly, the student later regretted their behavior.

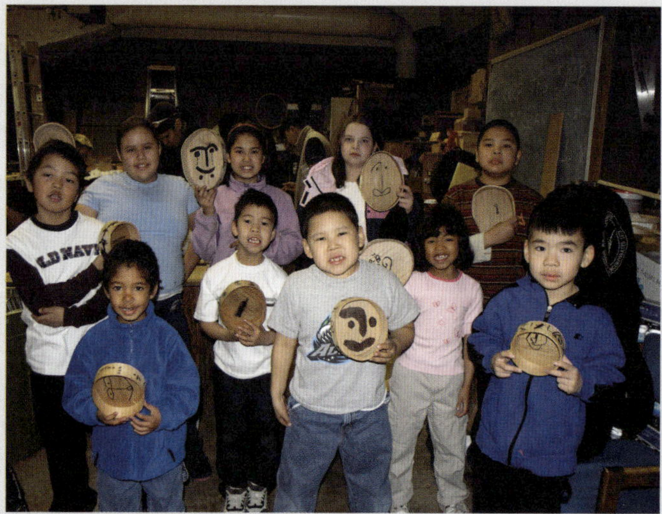

FIG 4 Youths in Akhiok holding up bent wood boxes they made inspired by the Karluk collections at the Alutiiq Museum.

What I did not realize at the time was how powerful this way of sharing, teaching, and collaborating would become for our museum and myself. What we were doing was reversing the colonial practice of taking things out by bringing this knowledge back and empowering the communities to not only celebrate but own and use this knowledge for themselves. By collaborating with tribes through schools and the museum we were collectively taking back the knowledge of our histories and putting it into the hearts and minds of our Sugpiat communities.

Future Directions

Our museums are not going anywhere and neither are our communities. Keeping this in mind I changed how we were using individual projects, making them tools for generational learning that built on our collaborations with and within our communities. How do we lift up and carry forward our cultural knowledge in ways that celebrate and allow for our communities to grow with this knowledge over time and learn who we are and how our ancestor's knowledge has allowed us to thrive within our region for thousands of years?

Our knowledge was set aside during colonization, however when I was doing this work, I did not use this term because it wasn't openly expressed in such a blunt way. We were still under the control of colonial expressions—and we are even now. Our material cultural heritage was destroyed, our language forbidden, and our ways of being were systematically suppressed in order to assimilate us into white society. The knowledge of our cultural heritage, language, and material culture was not openly shared beyond stories or in museums. We have created a path for our communities to take back their knowledge and celebrate it in their own ways.

In 2013 I changed jobs and moved with my family to Seattle, Washington, where I took a position as Professor of Anthropology at the University of Washington and Curator of North American Anthropology at the Burke Museum. Over the past nine years I have seen, tried, and experienced many approaches for how larger institutions handle and engage with Indigenous/Native peoples from across the world. I understood when I took my job that I had to show my work and to build trust with the local Coast Salish community. Being Native does not give me a pass to come into another Native community to do the same work I was doing within my community. I had to start anew and show the local community that my work was focused on changing the way our museum engaged and collaborated with Indigenous communities. I had to show this, not talk about it. It has taken me over a decade to build this trust locally and the work never stops.

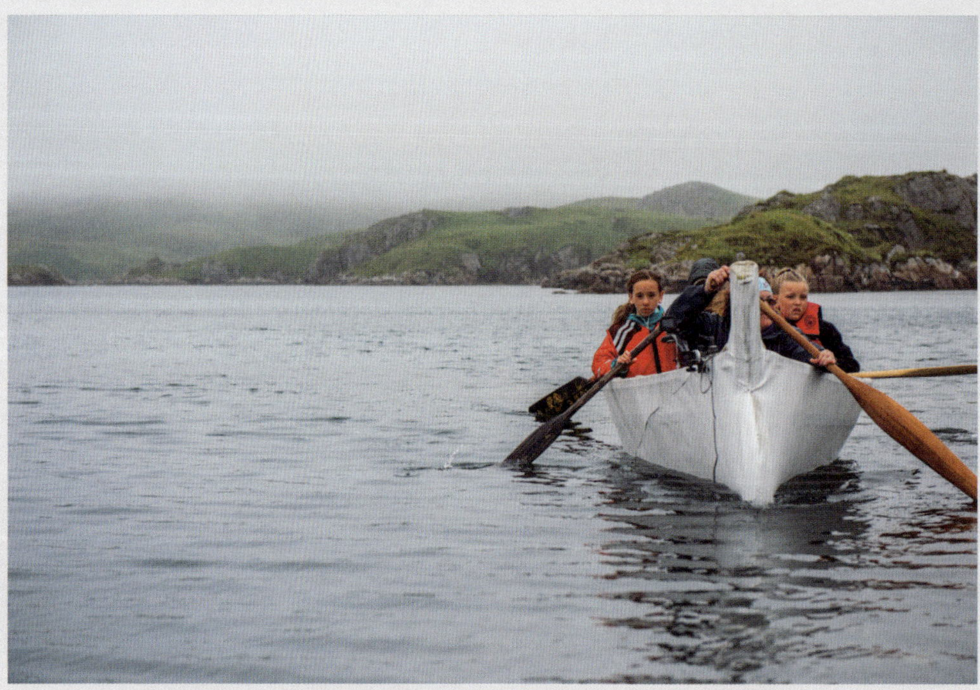

FIG 5 Youth paddling the *angyaaq* we made at the Akhiok Kids camp 2015–16.

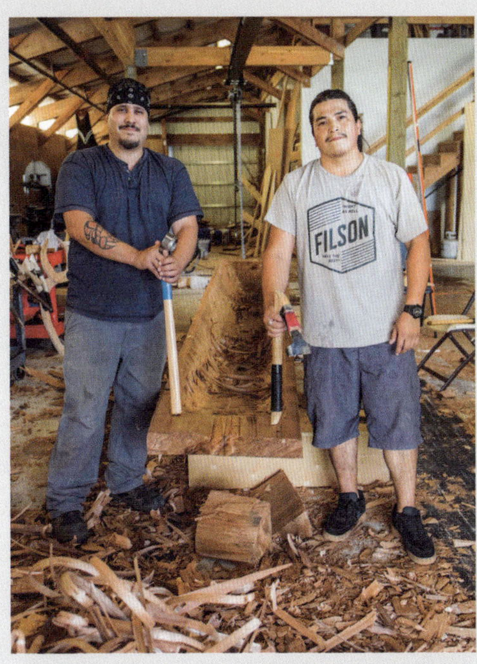

FIG 6 Keith Stevenson and Tyson Simmons making an *Äalay* (a shovel-nose canoe) for the New Burke Museum's "Culture is Living" gallery, 2018.

My strategy for this work is to dedicate time to creating a space for collaboration that is based on listening, patience, trust, being consistent, building a relationship, and supporting the community on what they need, not what I need. When we were designing the new gallery for the New Burke Museum, we started by going out to the communities to listen to and learn what they wanted us to share with our visitors. We shared what we had in our collections and let them decide what they wanted us to exhibit. We also changed our text. We put the original name of the piece first, then a translation and a quote from a community member telling the visitor what the piece means for them now, not what it meant for them in the past. We titled our gallery "Culture is Living," and we are holding ourselves accountable to the communities we are engaged with because it is the right way to collaborate with communities that have been marginalized for decades.

Our work is never done within museums, but if we create a culture of change that is based on trust and long-term relationships we can change the way we share, exhibit, and celebrate the diversity of our world through all museums. Each exchange is unique and should be respected. What I shared above is my own personal experience and some living examples of what can be done through trust and collaboration. I know it can work because I have personally experienced it through the Alutiiq Museum and now the Burke Museum in the work I have the privilege to do with communities.

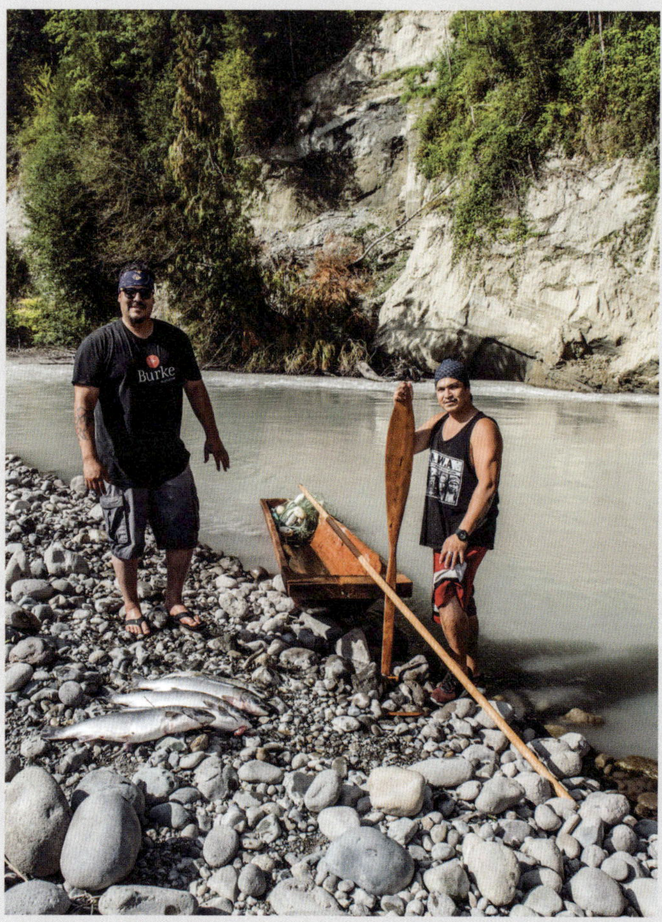

FIG 7 Tyson Simmons and Keith Stevenson fishing in the White River with the *Äalay* after finishing it, 2018.

References

Haakanson, Sven "Caretakers of Our Histories." In *Change Is Required: Preparing for the Post-Pandemic Museum*, edited by Marsha Semmel, Avi Decter, and Ken Yellis. 111–16. Lanham, MD: Rowman & Littlefield and AASLH, 2022.

Haakanson, Sven, Holly Barker, and Sara Gonzalez. 2021. "Changing museum narratives: a conversation with culture curators at the Burke Museum of Natural History and Culture." In *Routledge Handbook of Indigenous-Colonial Interaction in the Americas*, edited by Lee M. Panich and Sara L. Gonzalez. 524–41. New York, NY: Routledge, 2021.

Haakanson, Sven, *Living Knowledge in Cultural Collections in Conserving Active Matter: Essays*, edited by Peter Miller and Soon Kai Poh. 234–45. New York, NY: Bard Graduate Center, 2022.

Haakanson, Sven. "Kanaglluk: The Original Gut Skin Rain Jacket for Kayakers." In *Ghhúunayúkata / To Keep Them Warm: The Alaska Native Parka*, edited by Susie Jones and Melissa Shaginoff (Forthcoming).

Haakanson, Sven, "Translating Knowledge: uniting Alutiiq people with heritage information," in *Museum as Process: Translating Local and Global Knowledges*, edited by Raymond A. Silverman. 123–29. London: Routledge, 2015.

Haakanson, Sven, "Can there be such a thing as an Alutiiq anthropologist?" In *Looking Both Ways: Heritage and Identity of the Alutiiq People*, edited by A.L. Crowell, A.F. Steffian, and G.L. Pullar. Fairbanks, AK: University of Alaska Press, 2001.

Haakanson, Sven, and Amy Steffian. *Giinaquq: Like A Face. Sugpiaq. Masks of the Kodiak Archipelago*. Fairbanks, AK: University of Alaska Press, 2009.

Haakanson, Sven, Amy Steffian, Marnie Leist, and Patrick Saltonstall. *Kal'unek—From Karluk. Kodiak Alutiiq History and the Archaeology of Karluk One*. Fairbanks, AK: University of Alaska Press, 2015

MYRLANDE CONSTANT

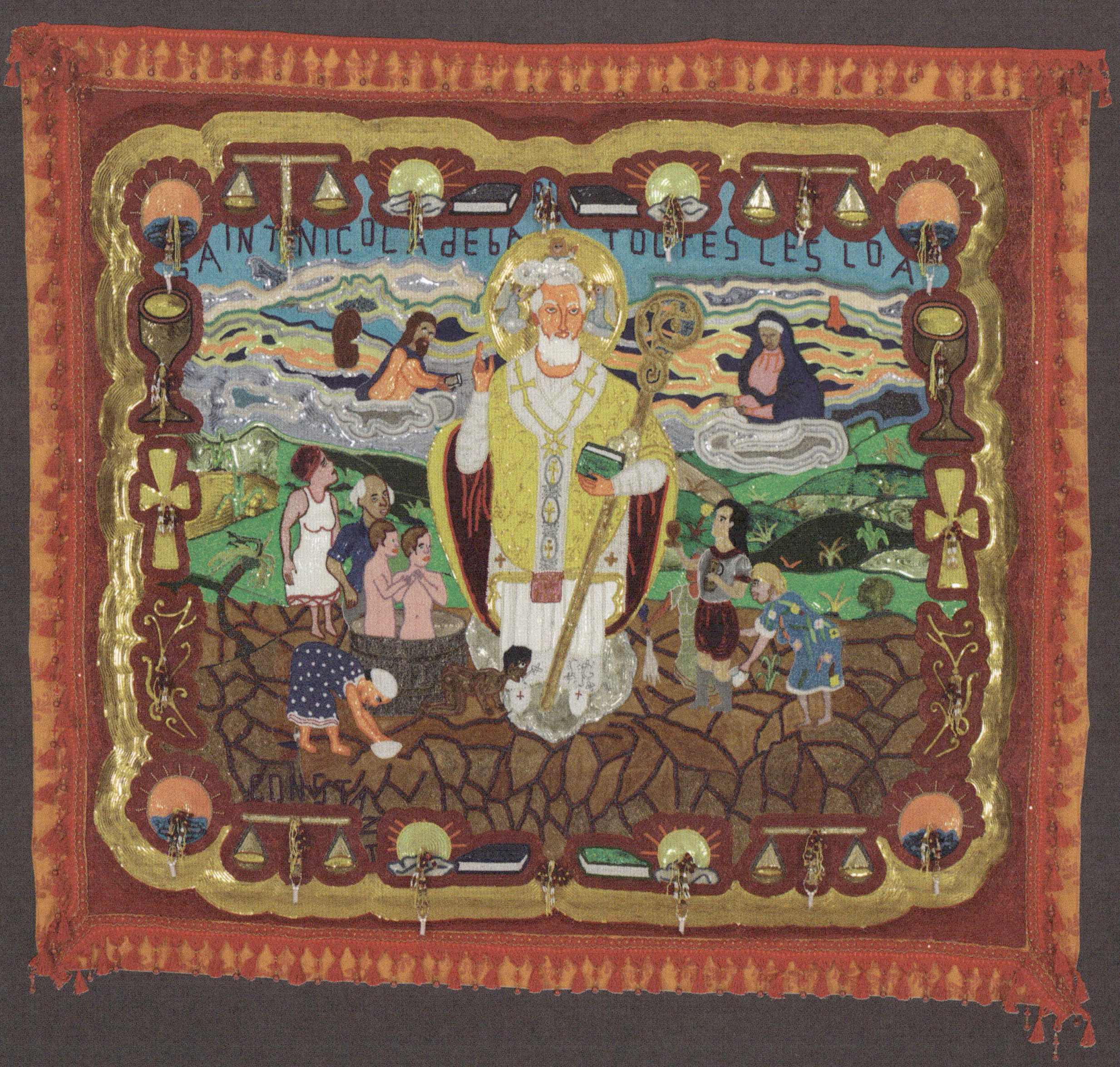

Saint Nicola, 2020.
Sequins and beaded flag.

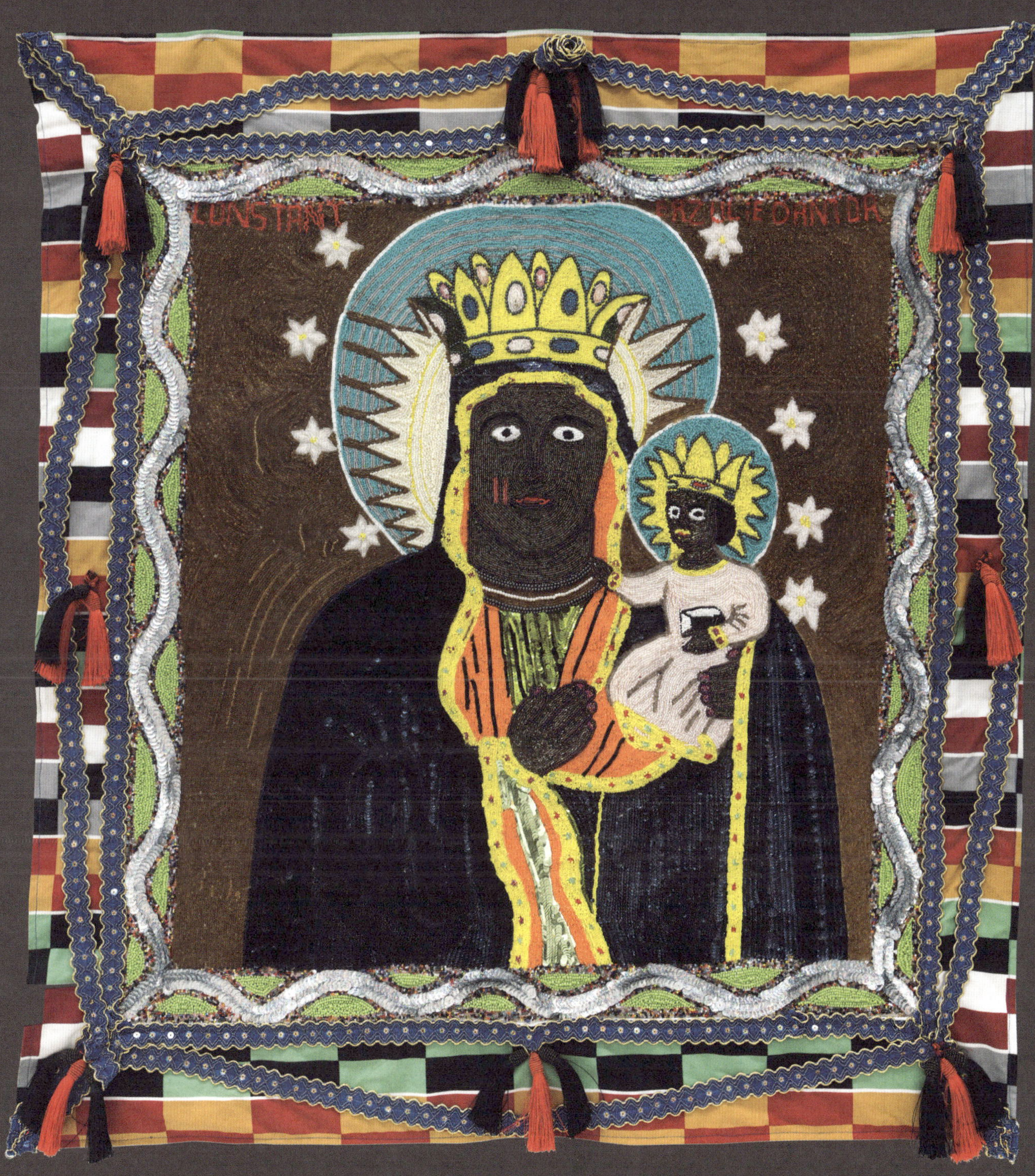

Erzulie Dantor, 1995–2020. Sequins, glass beads, and silk tassels on cotton.

NEXT PAGE
Saint Nicola (detail), 2020. Sequins and beaded flag.

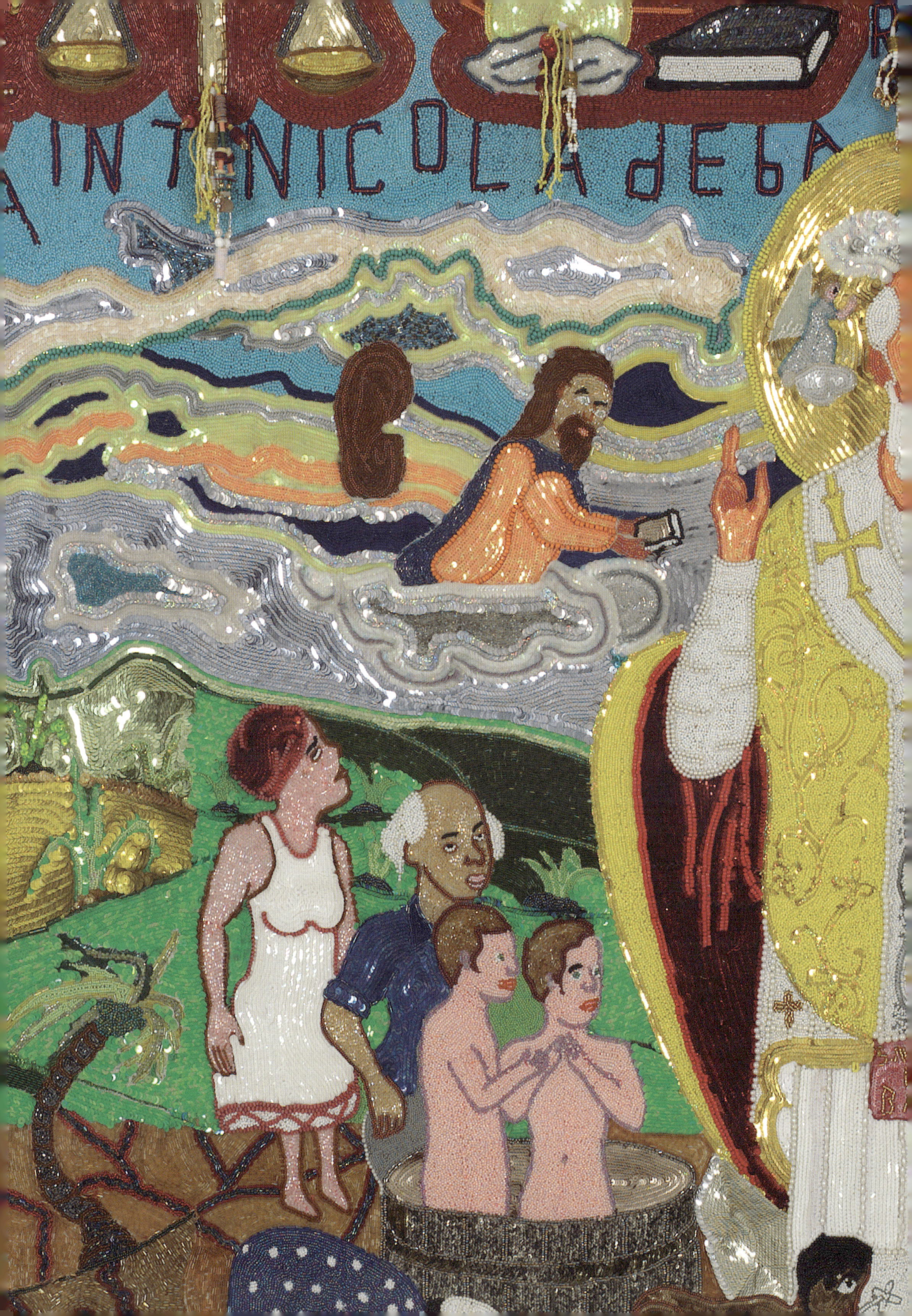
AINT NICOLA dEbA

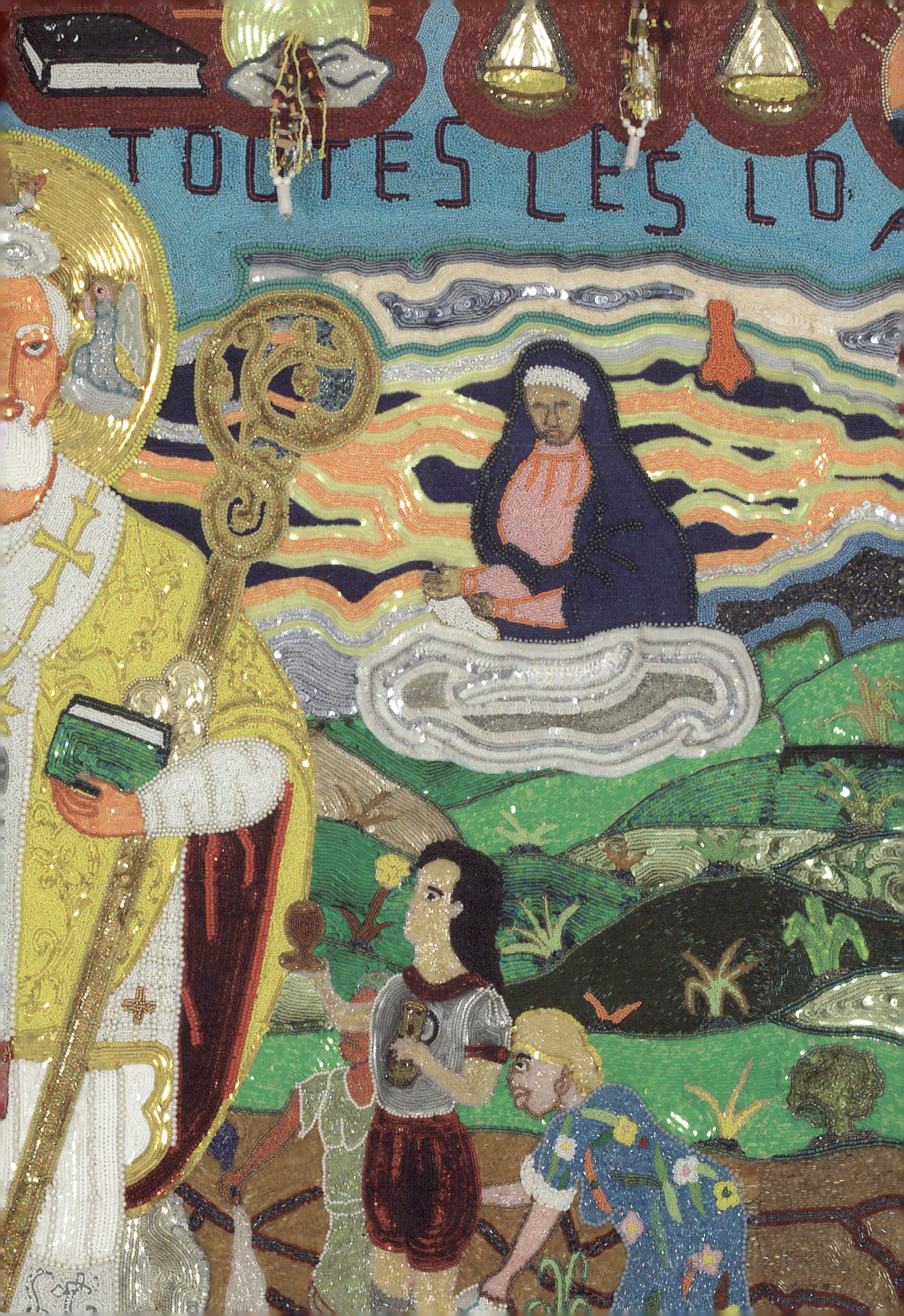
TOUTES LES LOA

LEFT
Guede, 2020.
Beads, sequins, and silk on cotton.

TOP RIGHT
Scene with Brigitte and Baron, 2010–17. Sequins, beads, and silk on cotton.

BOTTOM RIGHT
Invocation of Saint Anthony, 2015–19. Beads, sequins, and silk on cotton.

NEXT PAGE
Scene with Brigitte and Baron (details), 2010–17.Sequins, beads, and silk on cotton.

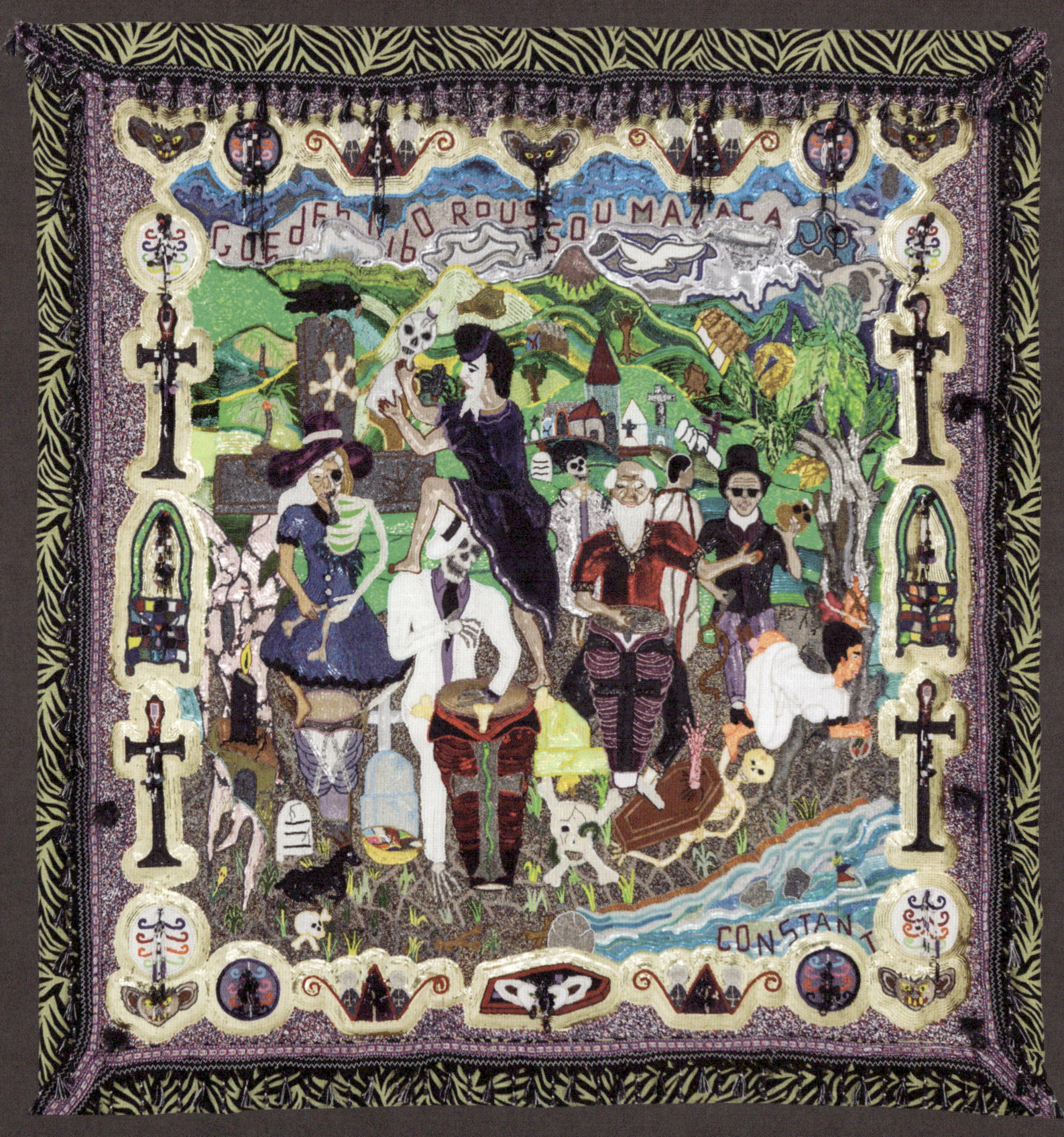

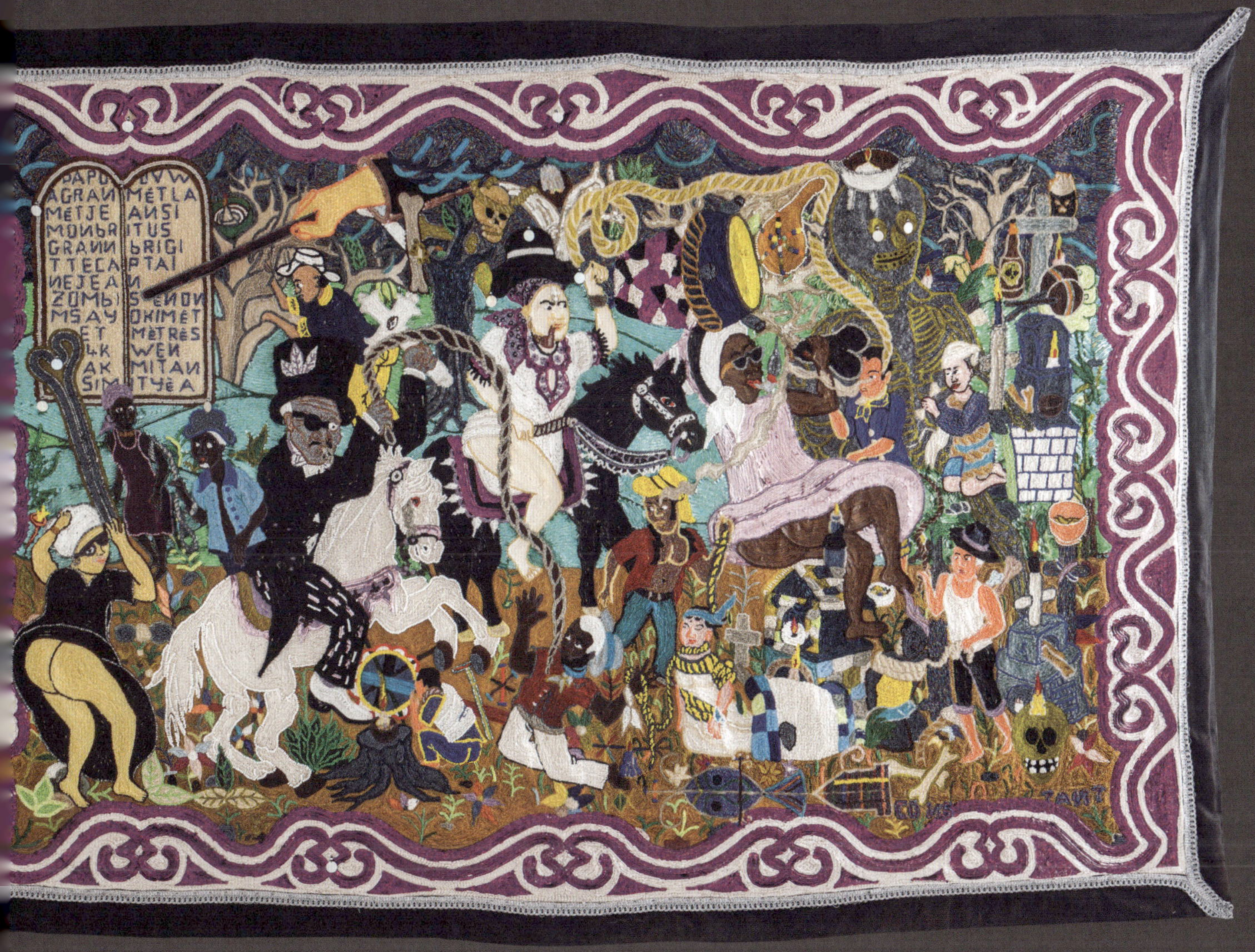

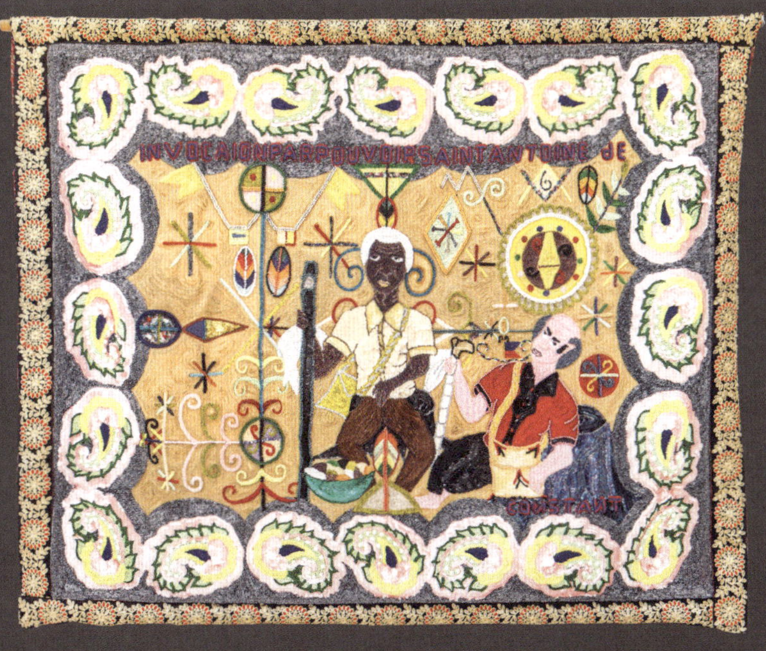

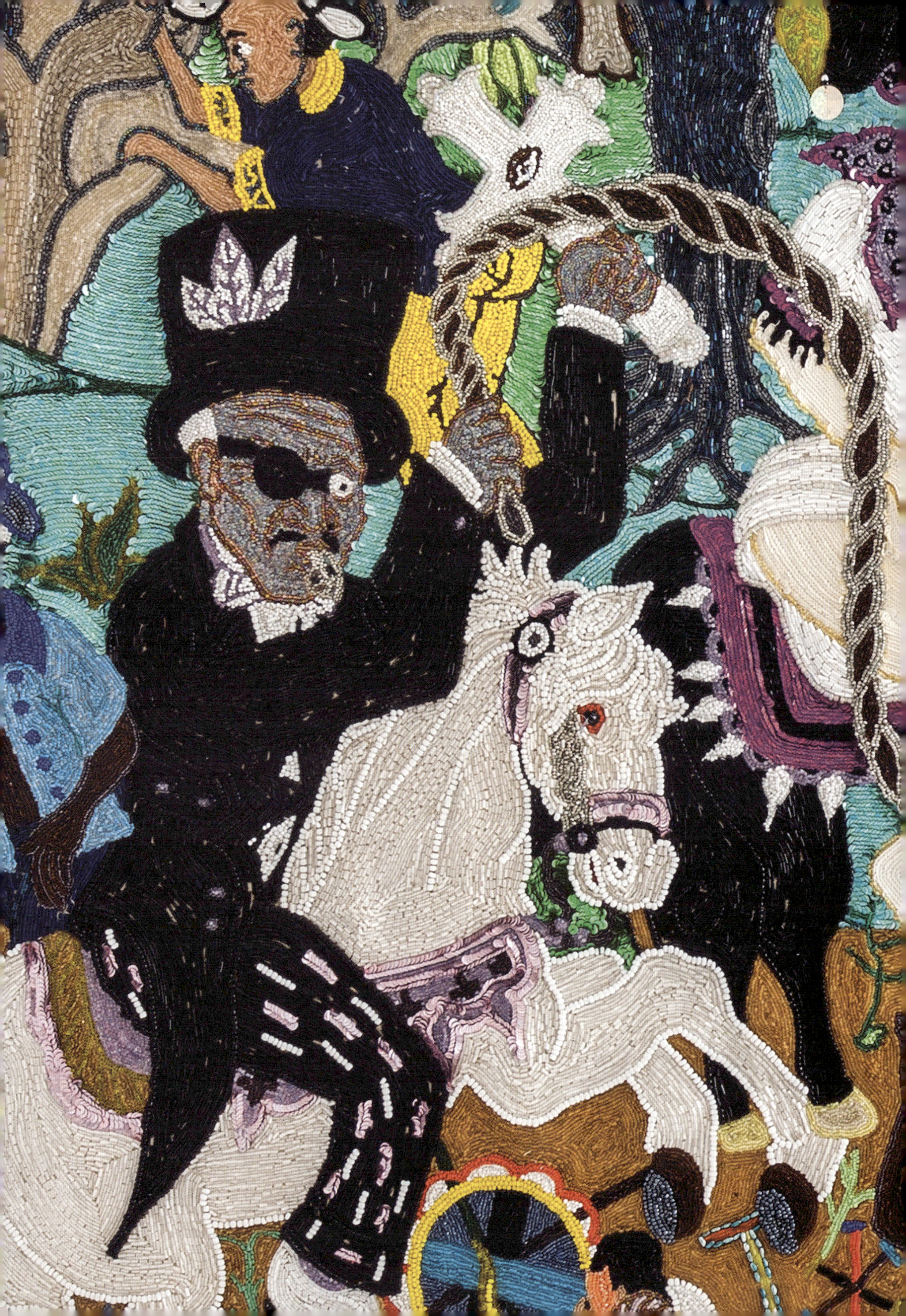

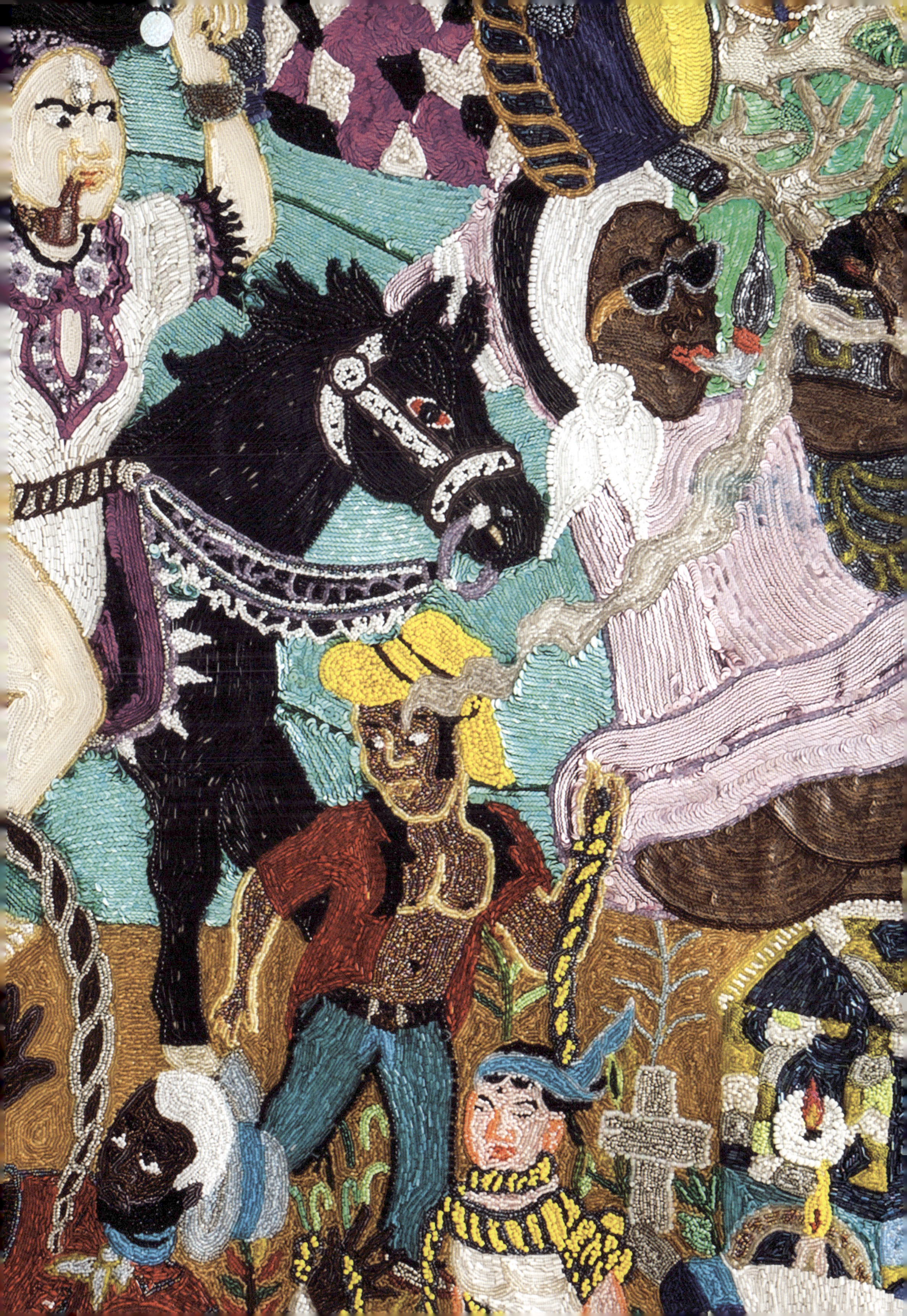

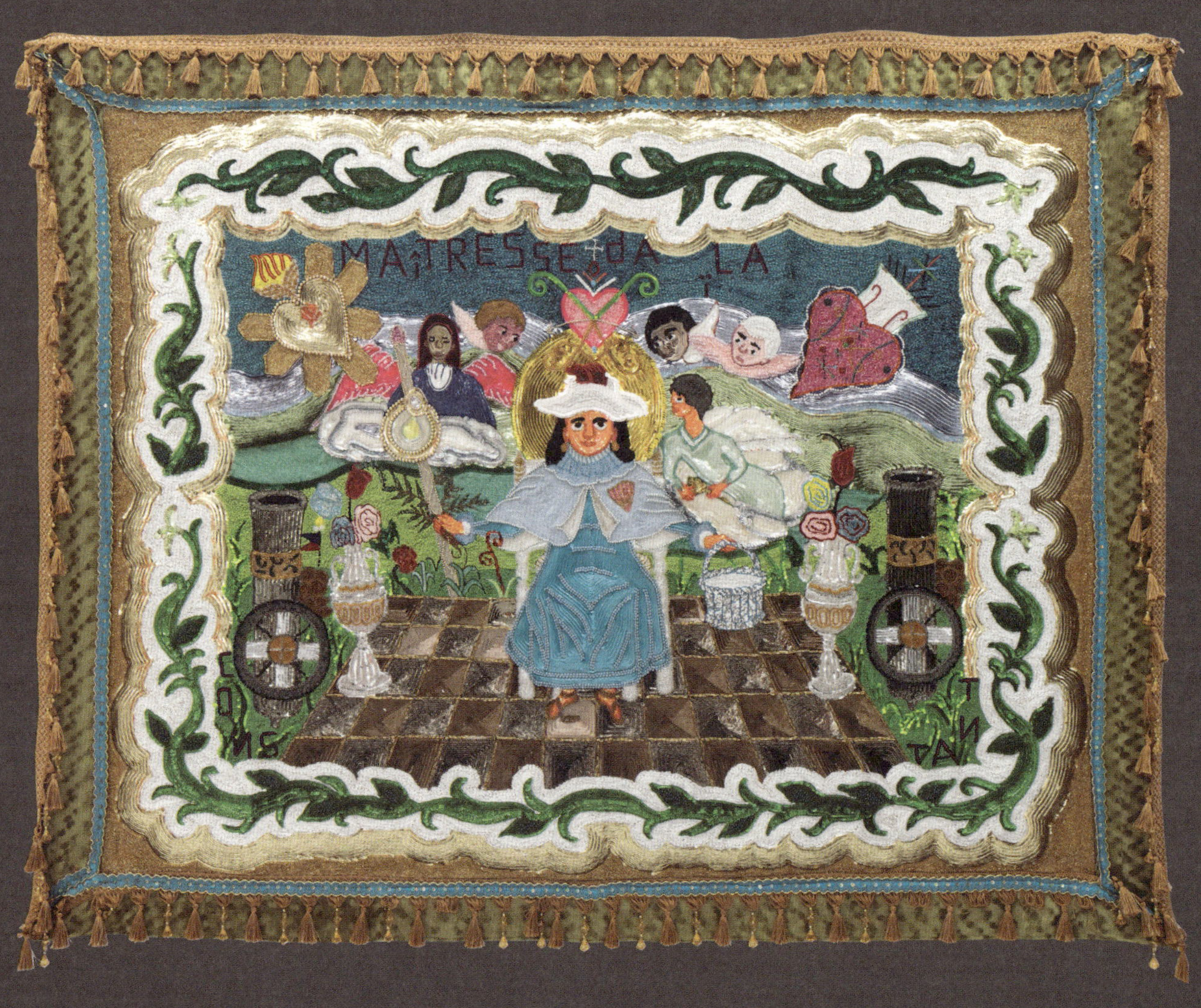

LEFT
Maitresse Dalia, 2021.
Sequins, beads, and cotton.

RIGHT
Maitresse Dalia (details).

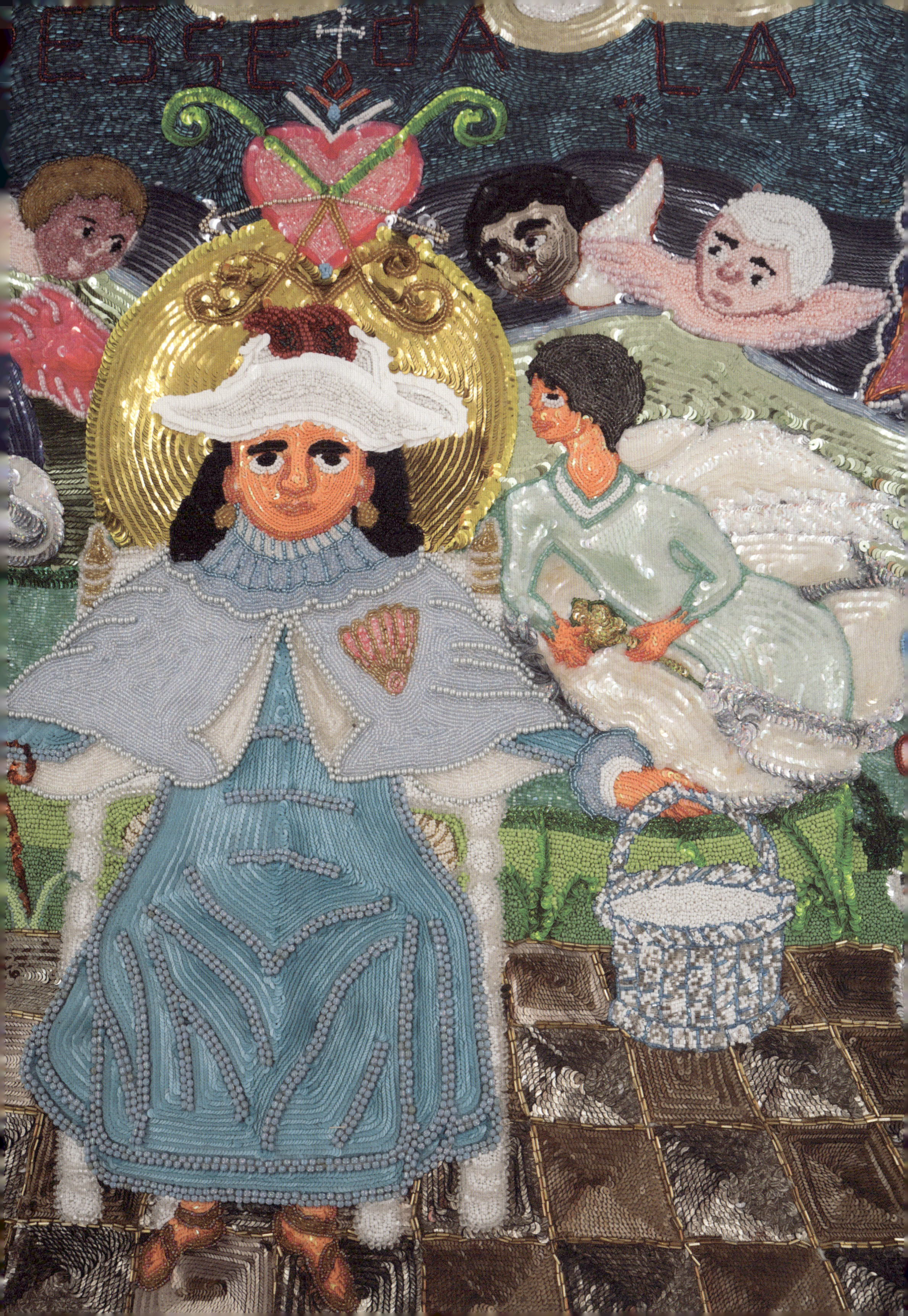

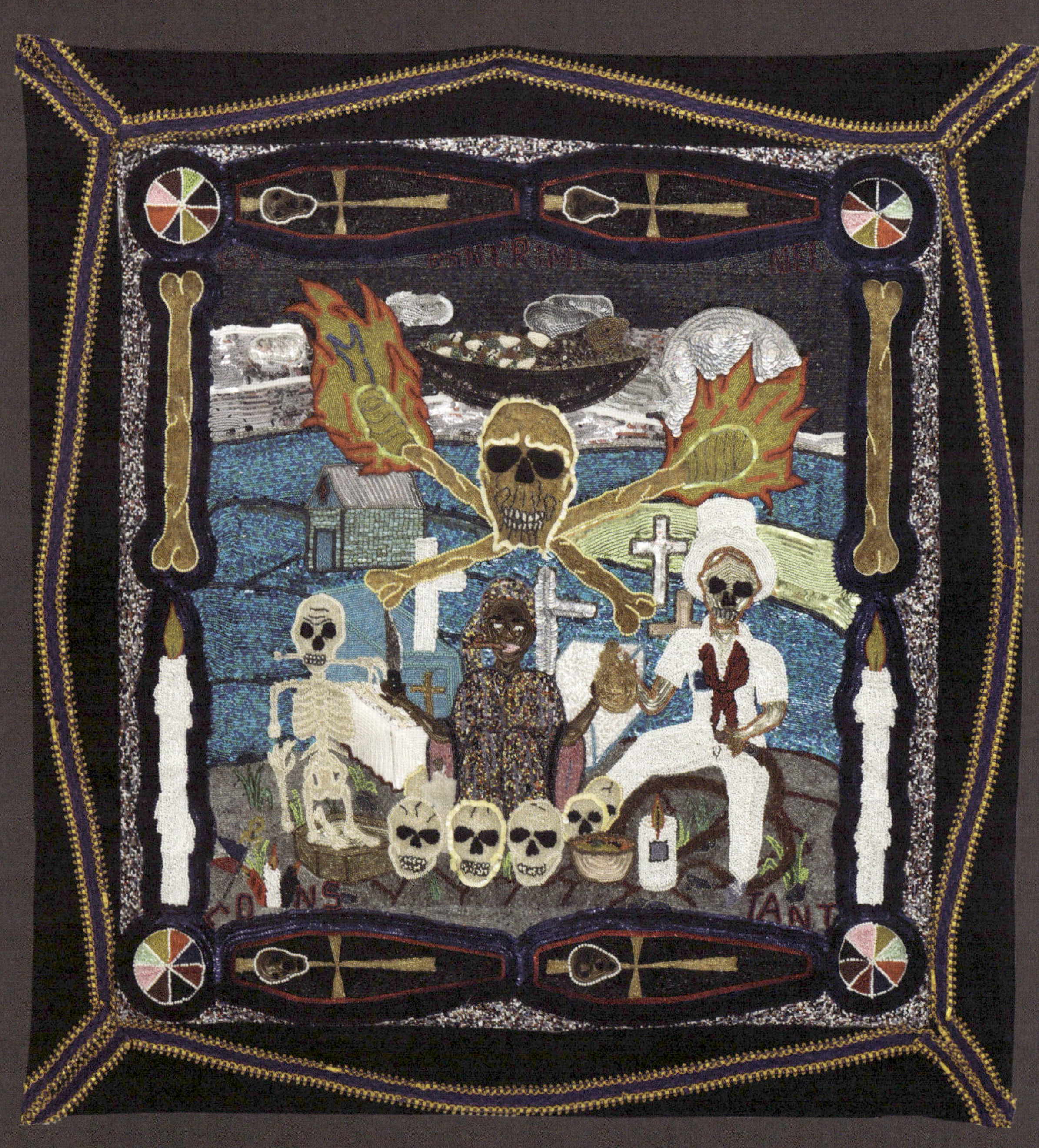

Baron Crimenel, 2021.
Sequins, beads, cotton.

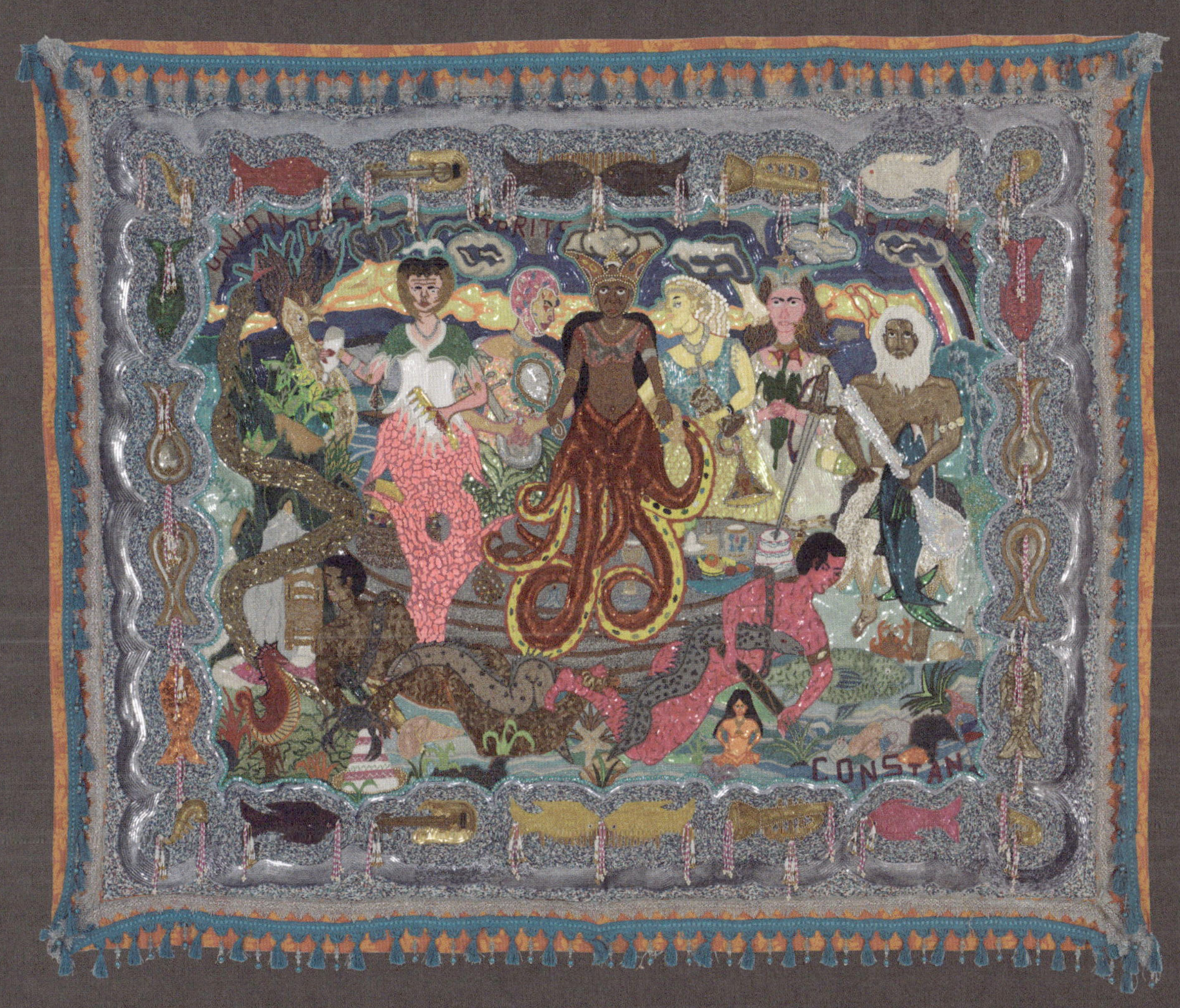

***Sirenes*, 2020.**
Sequins and beaded flag.

NEXT PAGE
***Sirenes* (details), 2020.**
Sequins and beaded flag.

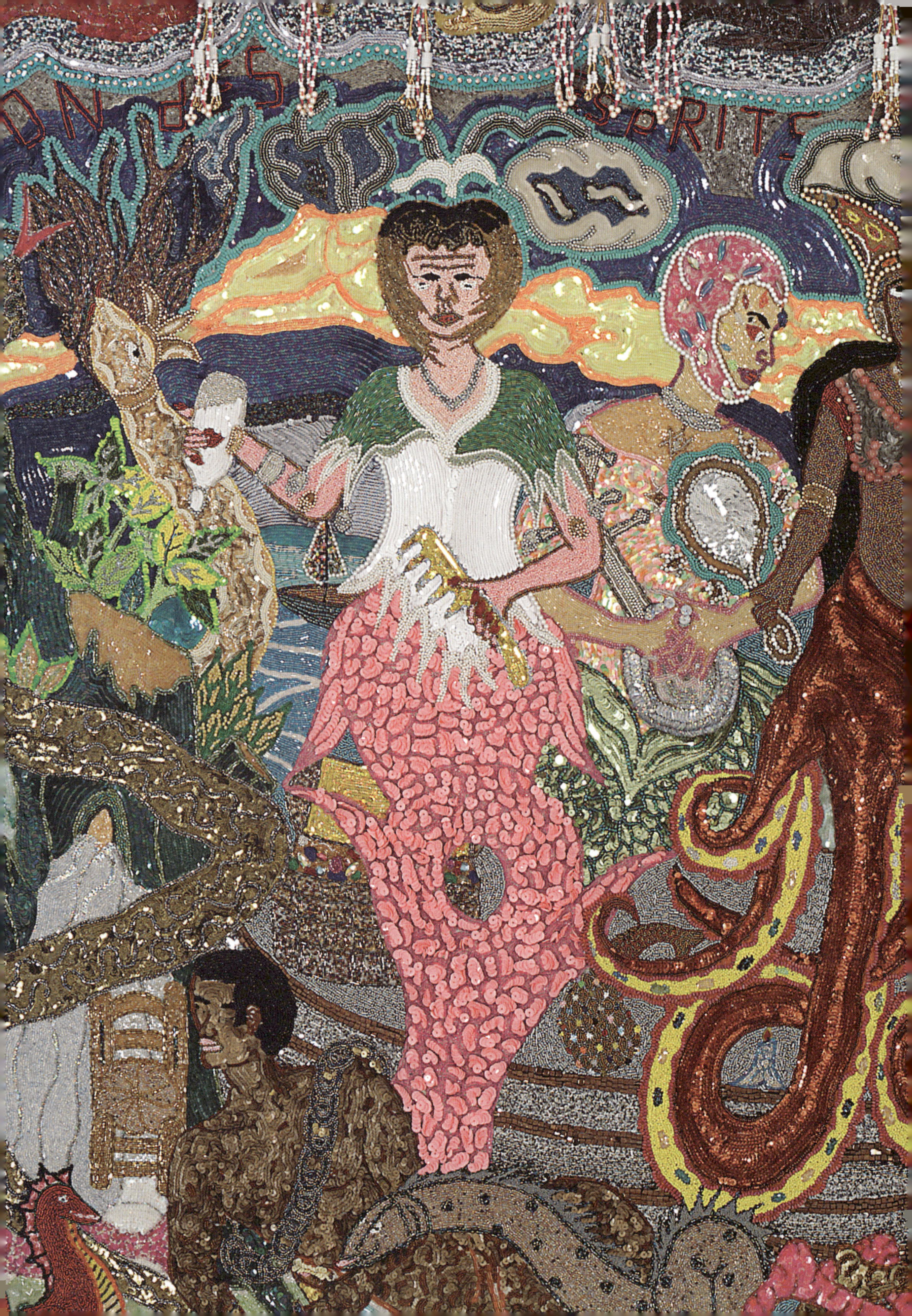

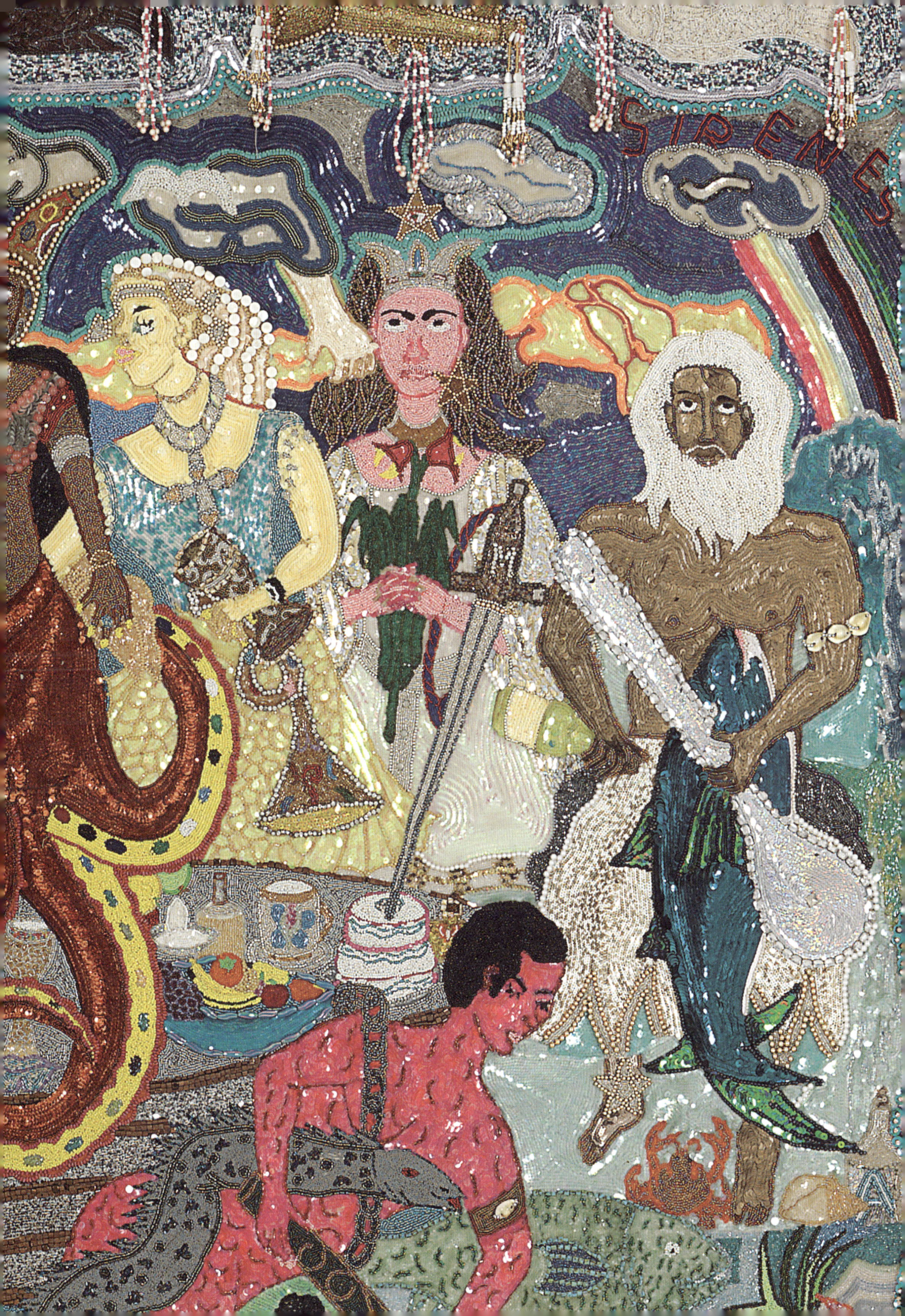
SIRENES

Frontier Imaginaries: Property, Art, and Alibi

120

VIVIAN ZIHERL

In the work *Poly-Si* (2018) by the Otolith Group, a small infrared video feed sits positioned amid a wallpaper printed with a field of nano-scaled computer chips. The video feed—sourced from the website asml.peregrines.nl—displays live footage of a nesting box placed on top of a corporate tower in Veldhoven, in the Netherlands' south-east. On display over the spring of 2018, a peregrine falcon could be seen nesting, hatching, nurturing, and eventually abandoning the box before migrating, most likely north to Scandinavia.[1] The computer chips magnified on the wall-paper were of the kind produced by semiconductor giant ASML, and in the same tower on which the eagle nurtured its hatchlings, "Building 8," that has local fame in hovering over an otherwise low-lying landscape. Tiled across a wall, the differentiation of any particular chip merges in a patternation of markings. Its indiscernibility was inspired by an encounter with a spectral lithography engineer who had formerly worked at the tower. When asked by the group's members Kodwo Eshun and Anjalika Sagar, "How can we see what one of these microscopic chips looks like?," the engineer had gestured all around himself. He swung his hand past our mobile phones, towards the lighting grid of the cafetaria and past its cash machines, and said, "It's everywhere, everything you see."

Peering at the video feed amid the vertiginous wallpaper, spying on the falcon and its hatchlings, the viewer is brought to focus on overlays of relationality. Through a traffic of consumption, transit, transfer, and reproduction, the world of the falcon inscribes its terrain, at the same time as the world of the nano-scaled chip draws towers, roads, and networks of digitized exchange. Their inhabitation of a particular parcel of land is summoned together and tied up with places farther afield. The place of the tower and the falcon is bound-up and undone through circulations. With what Elizabeth Povinelli stresses, following her Emmiyengal colleagues, as country comprised by "routes" rather than "roots."[2]

1 The artwork *Poly-Si* was commissioned as part of the exhibition "Trade Markings," held at the Van Abbemuseum, April 7–July 1, 2018, co-curated by Charles Esche and Annie Fletcher. It was the final chapter in "Frontier Imaginaries," an internationally roaming set of commissions, exhibitions, and collaborative research projects, with stations in Meanjin/Brisbane, Al Quds /Jerusalem, Lenapehoking/New York, and Eindhoven /Valkenswaard. See: www.frontierimaginaries.org.

2 Elizabeth A. Povinelli, "Routes/Worlds," 2011, *e-flux journal*, no. 27, https://www.e-flux.com /journal/27/67991/routes-worlds/.

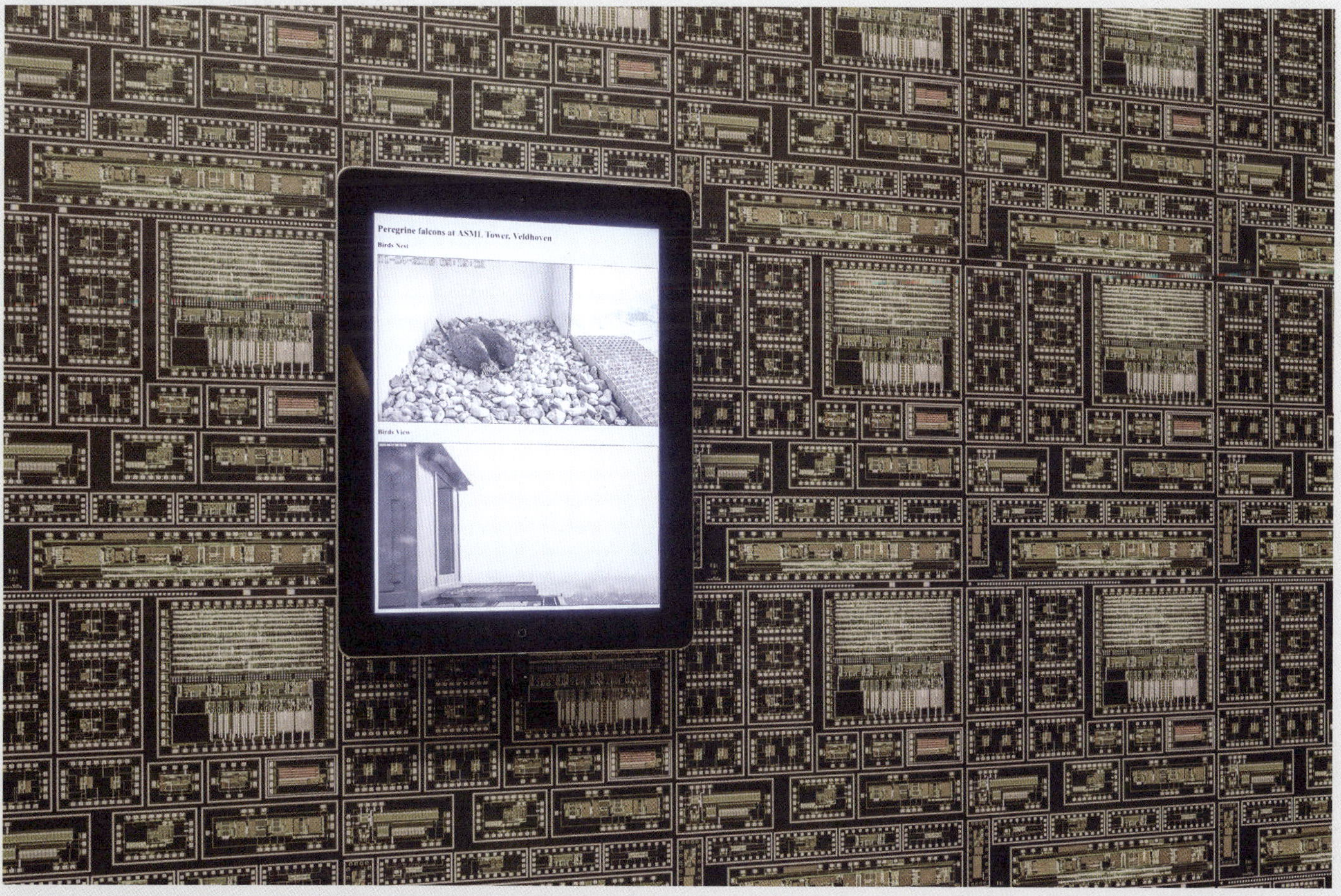

FIG 1 The Otolith Group, *Poly-Si*, 2018. Archives Van Abbemuseum, Eindhoven, The Netherlands. Photo: Marcel de Buck, The Netherlands.

This is an instrumental reading of the work, which could just as easily be discussed in terms of Warholian screenprint reproduction and popular defamiliarization, as the artists themselves do. But it is one that serves a discussion of the contemporary politics of restitution—namely the repatriation of cultural belongings, often cultural treasures, by European and settler collections and institutions. It frames a consideration of the transfer of items across fields of relationality. This rests upon a loop of world-making and of creation through the signification of exchange. When an item crosses from its place amid social congress into a colonial collection—often by theft—what world of relation is produced?

Political theorist Kōjin Karitani has made a case for "mode of exchange" as the determining aspect for a macro-analysis of social systems, pivoting and expanding on Marx's "mode of production."[3] For Karitani, exchange is what drives the regulative force of social value, and it is exactly systems of non-credit-based relationality that are dispossessed in the system of capital and its political support structures. Yellowknives Dene scholar Glenn Sean Coulthard arrives at a similar formulation when he argues towards an Indigenous "resurgent sovereignty" based not on "modes of production" but "modes of life."[4] In *Red Skins, White Masks*, Coulthard arrives at this formulation through an analysis of the diminution of radical Indigenous claims to sovereignty into narrowed "cultural rights." His analysis places a focus on the cunning of the Canadian state to splice powerful Indigenous demands between the worlds of culture and politics proper. In so doing, Coulthard pinpoints a certain fissure around aesthetics and politics as conceived in the epistemologies of liberal governance.

3 Kōjin Karitani, *The Structure of World History: From Modes of Production to Modes of Exchange* (Durham, NC: Duke University Press, 2014).

4 Glen Sean Coulthard, *Red Skin, White Masks: Rejecting the Colonial Politics of Recognition* (Minneapolis, MN: Minnesota Press, 2014).

This structure of mind also appears in Marcel Mauss's *The Gift*, a foundational comparative anthropological study. In describing "the gift," Mauss repeatedly defines his research as trained upon the "total social fact," which he defines as encompassing four domains: "economic, legal, political, and religious spheres."[5] Only elsewhere and in the margins does Mauss mention aesthetics, and does so in order to bracket it from discussion. Strange, given the undeniably aesthetic dimension the items and ceremonies that are the primary subject of his work have. Many of these subjects, at the time and until now, were residing in collections such as Musee de l'Homme in Paris, and Mauss's work coincides with the creation of that institution. And so again the question arises, what worlds of relation might transpire if the items are returned?

5 Marcel Mauss, *The Gift: The Form and Reason for Exchange in Archaic Societies* (Abingdon: Routledge Classics, 2005).

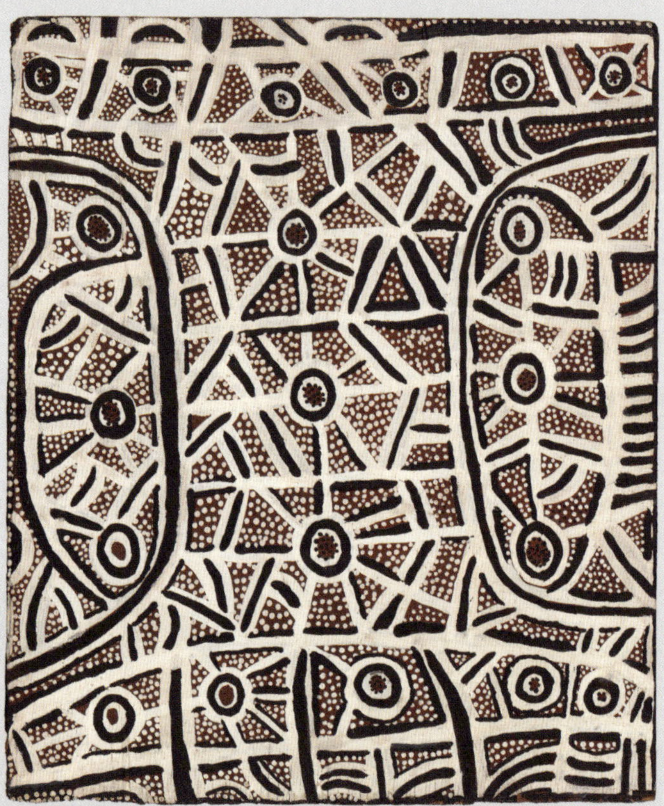

FIG 2 Charlie Tarawa (Wartuma) Tjungurrayi, *The importance of fire*, 1973. Synthetic polymer on plywood, 42.0 × 50.0 cm. Confirmed for acquisition in the QAGOMA Collection in August 2020. © Charlie Tarawa (Wartuma)Tjungurrayi / Licensed by Aboriginal Artists Agency Ltd Sydney.

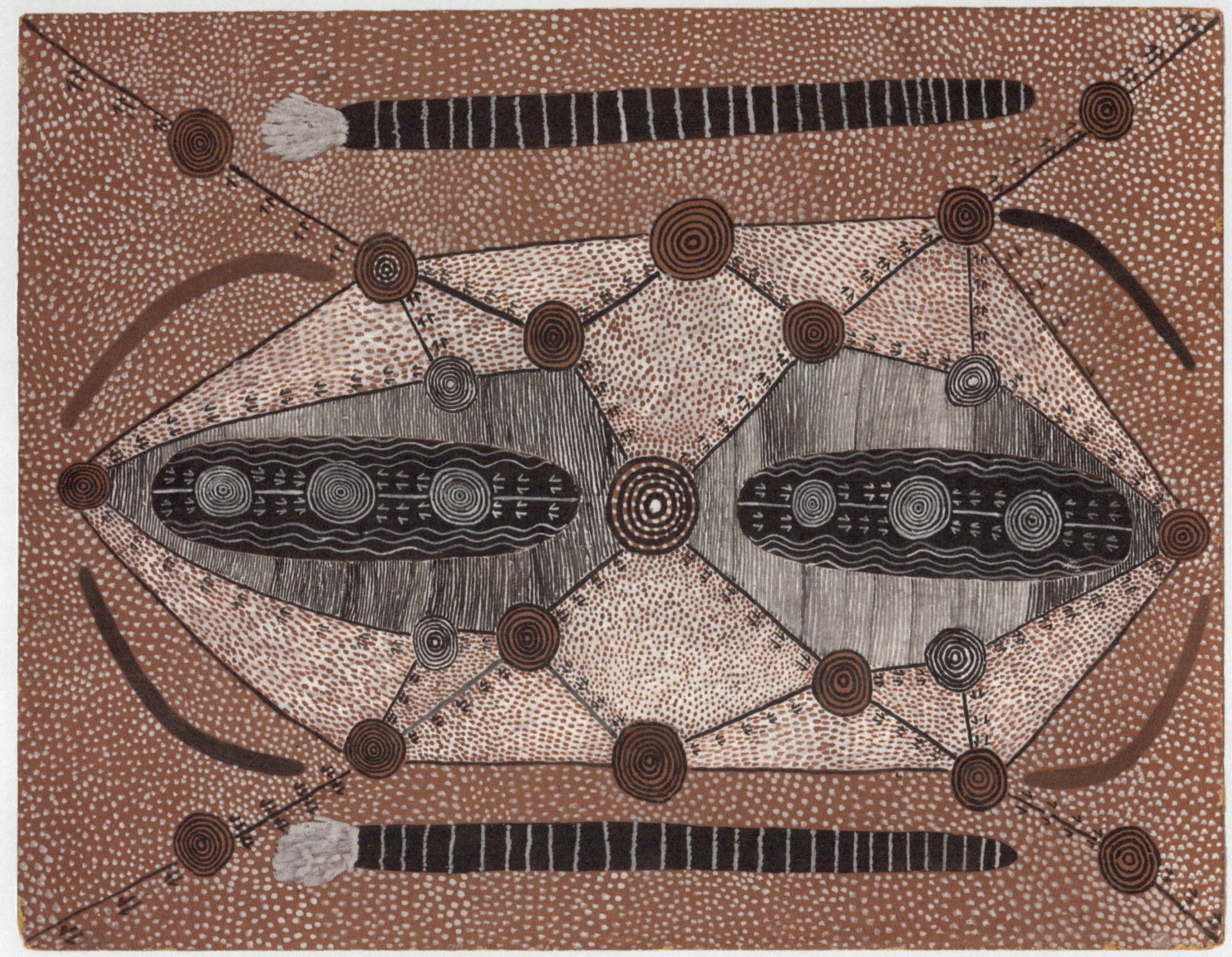

FIG 3 Tim Leura Tjapaltjarri, *Untitled (Euro Dreaming Ceremony)*, 1972. Synthetic polymer paint on compressed fiberboard, 61.0 × 48.0 cm. Confirmed for acquisition into the QAGOMA Collection in August 2020. © Estate of Tim Leura Tjapaltjarri / Licensed by Aboriginal Artists Agency Ltd Sydney.

~

An art institutional reckoning with this two-sided problem has been underway in Australia since the 1980s. The problem is a double-knot, for the matter of restitution conjoins two problems. First, the dubious legitimacy of items acquired through dispossessive processes; and second, the historical evaluation of these holdings as "ethnographic" rather than as "art."

It was in the 1980s in Australia—in the wake of 1970s land rights movements and Whitlam government policies—that a market for Aboriginal art emerged both within the country and overseas. In 1982, Sotheby's auction house opened branches in Sydney and Melbourne, led by Robert Bleakly, an enthusiast for "tribal art," and by the mid-1990s it began holding lots under the title "Important Aboriginal Art."[6] These auctions became celebrity events in which works consistently and meteorically broke records. Paintings increasingly sold for prices "that look like telephone numbers," artist Richard Bell wryly noted.[7] This rocketing market culminated in 2007 with the sale of Clifford Possum Tjapaltjarri's *Warlugulong* (1977) for $2.4 million.

6 Shireen Huda, *Pedigree and Panache: A History of the Art Auction in Australia* (Canberra: ANU Press, 2008), 105.

7 Richard Bell, *Aboriginal Art: It's a White Thing!* (2002), http://www.kooriweb.org/foley/great/art/bell.html.

Such auctions, in this context, raised the specter of a "primitive accumulation" of aesthetics—to lean on Marx once again.[8] In this early phase, many of the most sought-after paintings had been produced through the education initiatives of colonial missions and were picked up at prices from $60–220.[9] Two or three decades later, the same paintings were auctioned at prices in the hundreds of thousands. Meanwhile, none of the benefits of this market adjustment returned to the artists who'd produced the work from and remained in impoverished conditions, enduring ongoing cycles of dispossession. The painters of the famous Papunya Tula movement, for example, had been forced off their lands in the 1950s by a combination of policies of assimilation and the interruption of traditional water springs by pastoralists boring new wells during a time of drought.[10] It should not be possible to look at the appearance of Aboriginal art as paint and canvas without bearing in mind the assimilationist period that it arose through and that acts of survival that it inscribes.

The paradox is that these paintings' value was to a considerable degree attributed to perceived innate or "uninterrupted" Indigenous knowledge held within its aesthetics. Yet, as the market for Aboriginal art accelerated, the fields of art history and criticism were left scrambling for discourses to match. The cultural critic, ethnographer, and AIDS diarist Eric Michaels put a fine point on the problem in his 1988 essay, "Bad Aboriginal Art." After glossing over the surging "dot painting" market and its newsreel hype, he wrote, "I want to consider the curious fact that almost nothing of this work is ever designated 'bad'."[11]

8 Within chapter twenty-six of Marx's *Das Kapital*, the concept of "primitive accumulation" denotes an originary phase of dispossession by which the preconditions of capitalism are produced—in this instance the preconditions of a commodity market for Australian Indigenous art.

9 For example, among the Pintupi, Luritja, Walpiri, Arrernte, and Anmatyerre artists of Papunya Tula movement. There, a body of panels were created in 1971–72 in a process that was inseparable from a real movement of Indigenous peoples from their lands, and to a government-managed settlement. A detailed history of this art movement and its political circumstances can be found in Vivian Johnson's *Once Upon a Time in Papunya*, 2010, (Sydney : NewSouth Books, 2010).

10 Johnson, *Once Upon a Time in Papunya*,2010.

11 Eric Michaels, "Bad Aboriginal Art," in *Bad Aboriginal Art: Tradition, Media and Technological Horizons* (Minneapolis, MN: University of Minnesota Press, 1994), 144–5.

The diagnosis that Michaels reaches is economic and rooted in a mistaken European understanding of a purchasable painting for a relational world. Michaels distinguishes that in meeting the sudden market *revaluation* of Aboriginal art, its critics had failed to sufficiently also *reevaluate* their own aesthetic terms.[12] His point—informed by the knowledge of Warlpiri artists and elders—is that the phenomena ascribed to Aboriginal art reveals more about the epistemologies of Western art theory and art economies than the other way around. He writes, "Considering Aboriginal art practice as problems in contemporary discourse —problems of production, circulation and exchange—may indicate that something about world economics and ideology is also centrally involved here."[13]

Aboriginal artists themselves have led the charge in describing and challenging this *mise-en-discourse*. In 1996, the Campfire Group, a collective of Indigenous and non-Indigenous artists from Meanjiin/Brisbane, staged the performative installation *All Stock Must Go!*. The collaborative installation featured a carnivalesque marketplace of art and tourist items that flouted the neatness and decorum of fine art display. Presented at the Queensland Art Gallery as part of the Asia Pacific Triennial, the work lampooned the frameworks encountered by Aboriginal artists and their communities at the time.[14]

Ultimately, the Australian dramaturgy of Aboriginal art in this phase from the 1970s to the 2000s rests on a transfer of cultural material into the property form and the exchange relation of commodity. The interval is one that has historically frustrated European thinkers, or turned them to various forms of mystic aversion. Eventually the matter yields as one of European desire at the limits of its own partitions of knowability from the senses. What James Clifford delineated as "the predicament of culture," here captured as a problem of eros.[15] As Aboriginal artist Richard Bell warned in his classic text of the era, "Bell's Theorem," the challenge for Aboriginal art is its emplacement

12 The terms "revaluation" and "re-evaluation" are emphasized by Michaels in a typically deft use of language. See: Michaels, "Bad Aboriginal Art."

13 Michaels, "Bad Aboriginal Art", 143.

14 Michael Eather, ed., *SHOOSH!: The History of the Campfire Group* (Brisbane: Institute of Modern Art, 2005).

15 James Clifford, *The Predicament of Culture: Twentieth Century Ethnography, Literature and Art* (Cambridge, MA: Harvard University Press, 1988).

amid European and settler worlds of enterprise—that is to say, attributed valuation by markets and inscribed in European aesthetic styles. Contemporaneous with the Campfire Group, Bell's early art-making experience had been painting boomerangs for the tourist market, and he well understood the occult operations of market forces. With sardonic wit, Bell grasped latent drives behind the well-meaning desire to purchase and possess art as operative at the scale of relational worlds. It is especially unwise to offer up spirituality as the alibi for Aboriginal art, "Bell's Theorem" cautions, for this suggests "that the purchaser can *buy* some" (original emphasis).[16]

~

To return to the artwork *Poly-Si*—and its place within this mesh of possession and propriety in art presentation—occasions a longer lens. The piece was commissioned as part of the exhibition "Trade Markings" held at the Van Abbemuseum in the spring and summer of 2018. It was the final chapter in a cycle of exhibitions called "Frontier Imaginaries" that had travelled from Meanjin Brisbane via Al Quds/Jerusalem.[17] The project had mobilized the term "frontier" as an intervention into the curatorial and museological field so as to pull into focus its unspoken limits and thresholds, along with those of historical and ongoing colonial projects. As a concept-image, "the frontier" foregrounds real colonial projects of the settler colonies, while at the same time asking how a frontier frame of mind —an imagined vision of futurity, progress, and supremacy— continues to shape globalizing processes.

16 Richard Bell, "Aboriginal Art: It's a White Thing!" (2002), http://www.kooriweb.org/foley/great/art/bell.html.

17 Edition No.1 of "Frontier Imaginaries" had been commissioned by the Institute of Modern Art in Brisbane, with the support of an Australia Council for the Arts Fellowship. Its presentation took place in partnership with the QUT Art Museum, and the Australian Cinematheque. Edition No.2 was staged as the eighth edition of the Jerusalem Show, upon the invitation of Al Ma'mal Foundation for Contemporary Art, and as part of the 3rd Qalandiya Biennial. Two further editions—staged as symposia—took place in New York with e-flux projects and Columbia University, and in Amsterdam with Masters of Curatorial Practice of Bergen University, the Veem Theater, and Amsterdam Art Weekend respectively.

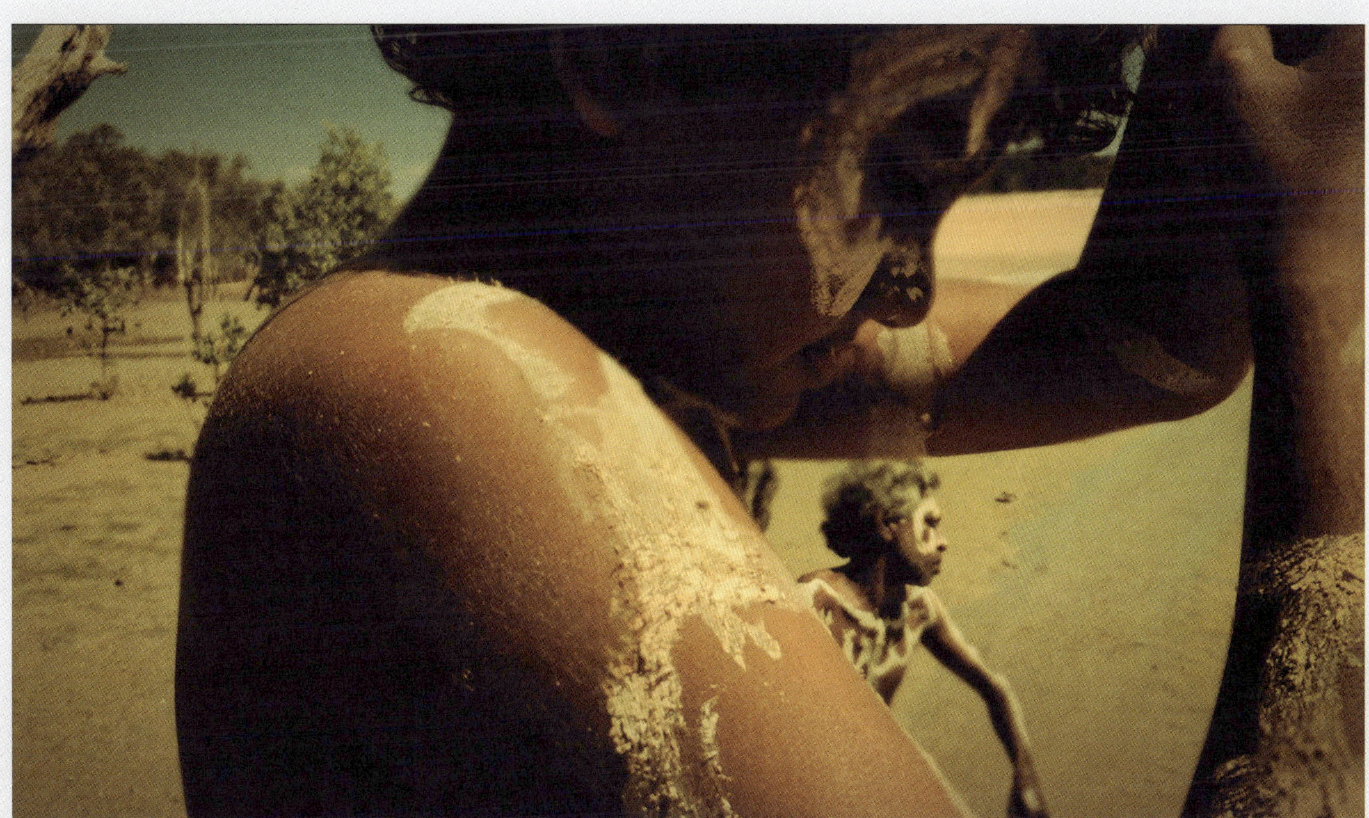

FIG 4 Film Still. Karrabing Film Collective. *The Mermaids, Mirror Worlds*, 2018. Two-channel installation, 34'50". Courtesy of the Karrabing Film Collective.

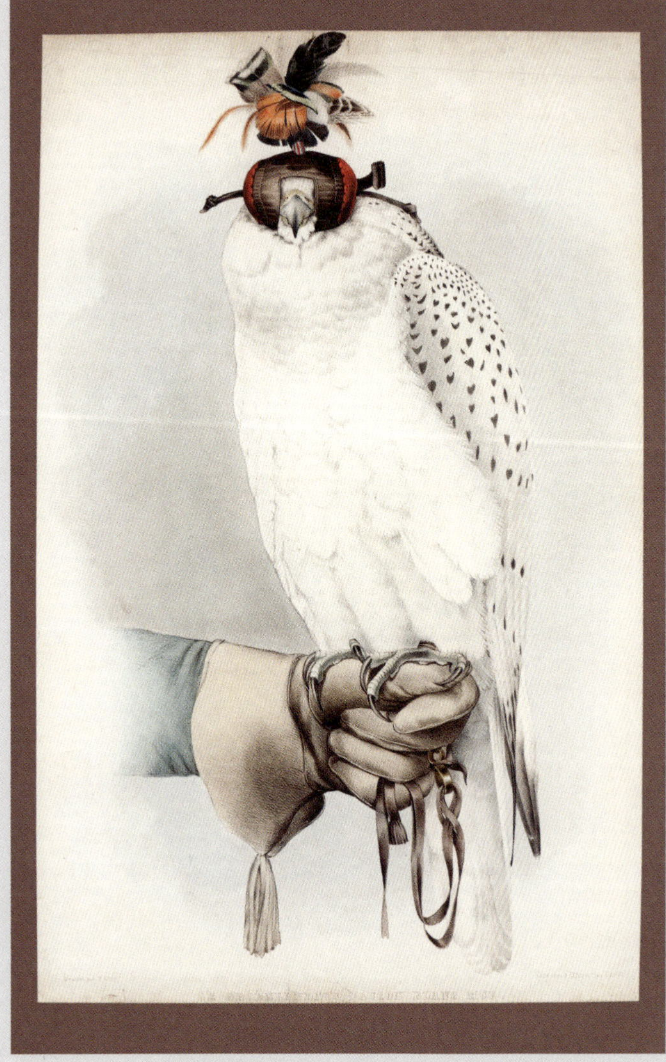

FIG 5 Falconry apparel from *Traité de Fauconnerie*, 1844. Courtesy of the Falconry and Cigar-maker's Museum of Valkenswaard.

In Australia an image of territory, bodies, intimacy, and extraction had emerged through artist commissions and archival materials of "Frontier Imaginaries" there—in Meanjin/Brisbane. The notion of frontiers conjured recognized realities of colonial histories as well as present day encroachments. Materializations of frontier dispossession were near at hand, for example as traced by oyster shells in the establishment of settler architecture not so much *on* as *through* Indigneous lands. In Palestine the appearance of frontiers took a turn towards narrative structures, configured through the project of nationhood. There, images of archeology, mythos of sites, and of the numerous forms of story-telling occasioned by checkpoints charachterized the exhibitions of "Frontier Imaginaries" held in al Quds /Jerusalem. Notions of frontiers were connected to the l egal, political, and economic anchoring of settler expropriation in narratives of origin.

In the Netherlands, however, "the frontier" was an altogether more elusive figure to apprehend. Having innovated speculative capital at the outset of the seventeenth century, its assumptions appear engineered deeply into the Dutch landscape and culture. As such, frontiers seem inexorably "far off" and "over there" .... With "Frontier Imaginaries" in Eindhoven, the frontier emerged in a recursive formulation of propriety, possession, and dispossession. These spanned three clearly delineated eras: feudal, industrial, and digital; and three commodities: falcons, cigars, and computer chips.

While *Poly-Si*'s falcon in the nesting box was beamed into the museum foyer, another falcon stood, taxidermied, resting on a sheet of corrugated iron in a far corner room as part of a video installation by the Karrabing Film Collective, from Australia's Top End region. The tin formed the roof of a makeshift shed, its outer walls covered in graffiti. Sprawling about the shed was a long-necked sea-monster crafted in chicken wire and zip ties. Meanwhile, a giant sea turtle scaled the shed's anterior side. Within the shed *The Mermaids, Mirror Worlds* (2018) played—a two-channel film also commissioned for the exhibition. The film alternates between promotional videos for chemical conglomerates such as Monsanto, and the story of a young Indigenous man, Aiden, taken as a baby for scientific experimentation to save the white race, who is then released back into the world of his family. The falcon hovers above as an avatar, once again threading through an overlay of three relational worlds that surround Eindhoven and nearby village Valkenswaard.

First had been the feudal phase, when cunning locals had devised traps that took advantage of the tree-less, low-lying landscape to catch peregrine falcons on their migratory paths. Valkenswaard had been named after its preeminent position in the early modern trade in hunting falcons as courtly effects, with a few families holding a lucrative trade network spanning Vienna, Versaille, Coimbra, Stockholm, and Istanbul, depending upon the prevailing politics. As tides turned in the European system, falconry was replaced by cigar manufacturing, with small brick factories spread across the region.

Second was an industrial phase, when the comparative poverty and generous labor force of the Catholic region lent itself towards becoming the Dutch home for manufacturing. Hollandish merchants, such as Henri van Abbe, whose collection founded the Van Abbemuseum in the 1950s, established factories where workers rolled cigars at small wooden desks. Their inner tobacco was sourced from Virginia, and outer leaves sourced through continuing colonial networks in occupied Sumatra.

As second international socialist and poet Henriette Roland Holst held in her 1902 classic *Kapital en Aarbeid in Nederland*, industrialization in the Netherlands was late-coming and partial. Unlike the United Kingdom, for example, the Netherlands had entered into modernity foremost not through industrialization, but through an earlier modernity of mercantile trade.[18] For Holst, this compromised the basis of workerism as a revolutionary project. Instead she turned towards a questioning of European spiritual consciousness and alliances with independence movements in Indonesia and India.

These layers can be found one above the other in the double-barreled museum, The Falconry and Cigar-maker's Museum of Valkenswaard. Visiting the museum as research for the show, Karrabing Film Collective members Rex Edmunds, Gavin Bianamu, and Elizabeth Povinelli, found their Emmiyengal worlds recognizable and woven among these layers. Pausing among the dioramas and taxidermied falcons, they discussed the falcon story of Ridem Koi who had swooped down and wrested back fire from the jealous sea monster Therrawin who had attempted to steal it away. Upstairs, among the yellowed cigar tins and desks, a retired cigar factory worker, Jacques Delis, sat at a desk telling stories as he rolled each member a cigar, playfully pretending not to offer one to Beth as the woman of the group. Receiving their gifts, the members had reflected on the appearance of tobacco in their communities during the mission days when Aboriginal workers had been unwaged and paid in rations of sugar, flour, and twists of tobacco.

18 Henriette Roland Holst van der Schalk, *Kapital en Aarbeid in Netherland* (Nijmegen: Socialistische Uitgeverij Nijmegen, 1971 [1902]).

Through Karrabing, an exchange was brokered between the Van Abbe and the Falconry and Cigar-maker's Museum. A diorama of a wealthy falconning couple, as well as a set of eighteenth-century C etchings, was presented in the Van Abbe, along with cigar factory portraits and a desk. In return, the Falconry and Cigar-maker's Museum featured Karrabing's film *The Jealous One*, which tells the story of Ridem-Koi and Therrawin while a Karrabing member, Rex, struggles with the corporate and bureaucratic red tape that bars his way to a funeral. Various other items were available in the exchange. And this is how it was that Karrabing incorporated a taxidermied falcon into their installation at the same time as the falcon brooded on ASML's Building 8, as viewed in the Otolith Group's *Poly-Si*.

And here the corporation ASML gives the third twist to the region, adding to the falcons and the cigars the high-tech economy of the computer chip. Located nearby to Valkensward, ASML is a company that develops the machines and ever-shrinking lithography technology that is used by brand names such as Intel and Samsung to manufacture chips. With a sixty-two percent monopoly of the market share since 2005, the global footprint of the company is hard to overestimate.[19] A recent article in *The Economist* put it this way: "If chips make the world go round, ASML may be the closest the multi-trillion-dollar global tech industry has to a linchpin."[20]

19 "How ASML became chipmaking's biggest monopoly", *The Economist*, February 29, 2020, https://www.economist.com/business/2020/02/29/how-asml-became-chipmakings-biggest-monopoly.

20 "How ASML became chipmaking's biggest monopoly."

~

The company had started out as a research lab of the Phillips corporation, which itself had been established in Eindhoven in the 1890s as a light bulb manufacturer. In the late 1990s, with Operation Centurion, Phillips restructured and moved much of its manufacturing offshore. Various research departments were placed on the market at this time, such as the semiconductor unit that became ASML. Today, the workforce of the corporation is overwhelmingly international, highly educated, and mobile through research networks including the CERN particle research project in Switzerland. The main product of the company, the engineer explained to the Otolith Group, is patents. In order to maintain the ever-accelerating rate of change that underpins digital economies, the main object is to chart out new directions in technology and secure potential technoscientific leaps as proprietary knowledge. The obdurately physical—if ever-shrinking—computer chip is downstream of the maximally dematerialized object of "intellectual property."

In a stack, or set of layers, the falcon, the cigar, and the computer chip trace three worlds of modernity that issue from and through the city of Eindhoven, the village of Valkenswaard, and the new techno epicenter of Veldhoven as anchored in the fields, habitats, and lowlands of its surrounds. Each traces an international—indeed globalizing—circulation, as much as the falcon was traded in a notably pre-national context. A consistent although mutable feature among these is that of trade—of these items as commodities and subjects of proprietary worlds of relation.

In his exceptional comparative work, "Theft is Property! The Recursive Logic of Dispossession," political theorist Robert Nichols undertakes a careful reconstruction of the deployment of the term "dispossession" within the arguments of Indigenous scholars and activists across the Anglosphere and within earlier European attempts to critique inherited wealth inequality. What Nichols yields is an insight into the radical Indigenous use of dispossession as revealing a "recursive" logic of colonial modernity. Here what is dispossessed is not merely land but the possibility of relating to land as anything other than property per se. The works of Quandamooka political theorist Aileen Moreton-Robinson, for example, find an ipso facto argument in Australian conservative discourses, "that, because Australian Aborigines had no word in their languages for 'property' as prevailing Western legal and political systems understand it—or indeed, in some cases lacked any conception of land as a discrete entity in which one could claim property—there could be no meaningful subsequent claim to theft of that land".[21] Whereas eighteenth-century thinkers such as Rousseau, Proudhon, and Marx critiqued the aristocracy as beneficiaries of ancient acts of theft, Nichols holds that the figure of dispossession in Indigenous scholarship recursively points to European forms of ownership as themselves a dispossession of life-worlds; "Not only the forcible *transfer of* property but *transformation into* property."[22]

21 Robert Nichols, "Theft Is Property! The Recursive Logic of Dispossession," *Political Theory* (April 2017): 1–12.

22 "How ASML became chipmaking's biggest monopoly."

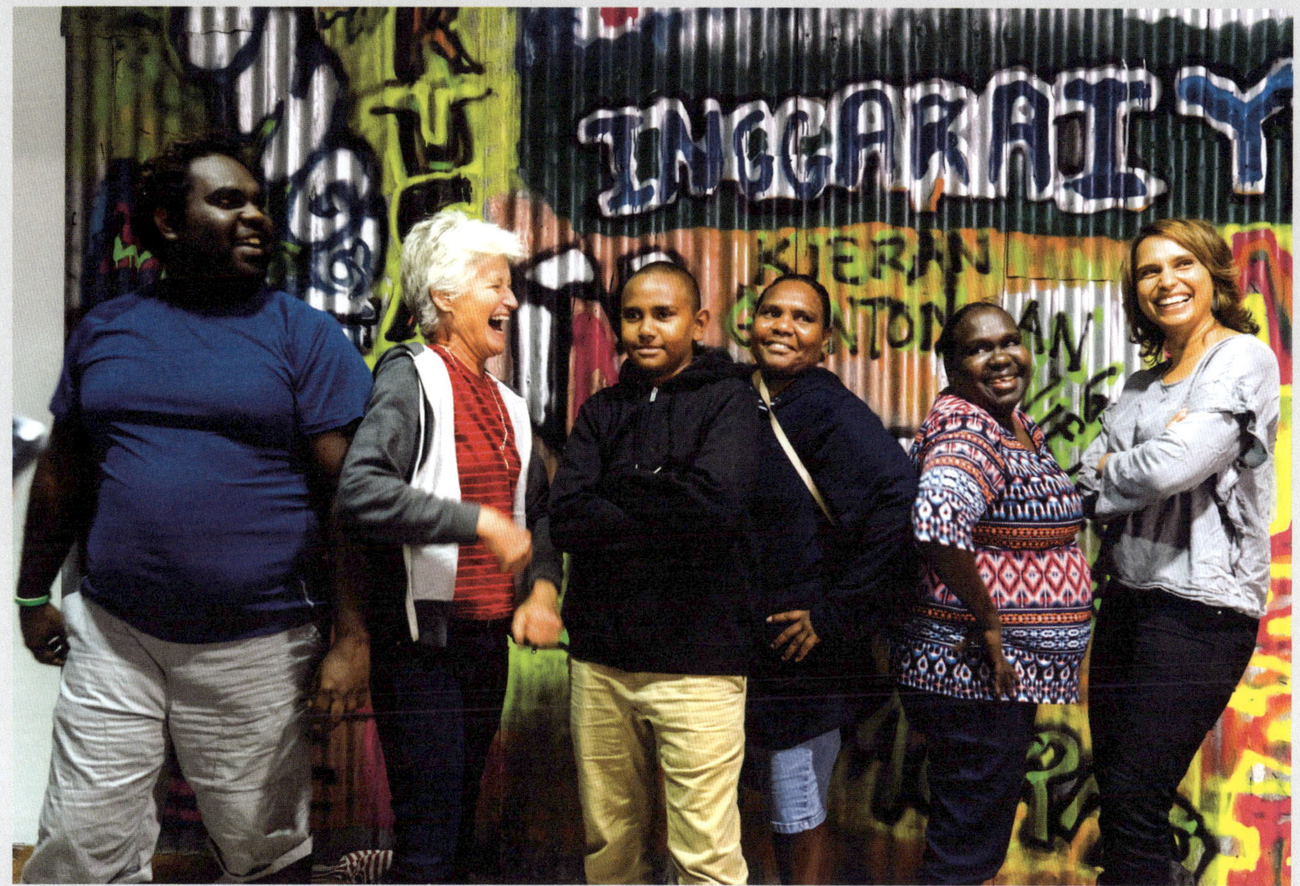

FIG 6 Karrabing Film Collective members and Delvene Cockatoo-Collins. Installation view, Karrabing Film Collective, *The Mermaids: Mirror Worlds*, Institute of Modern Art, Brisbane, 2018. In view: *Graffiti Dreaming*, 2018, corrugated iron, spray paint. Photograph: Louis Lim.

In framing a conference on the subject of restitution with the title "What to let go?," the organizers at Para Site beautifully and deftly constructed the problem of restitution as one of relationality. What does it mean for items to have been seized from their location among the congress of cultural, geo-social spaces, and to have entered the holdings of European and settler collections? And what does the event of their return mean also for the social and political spaces that they leave behind? In response to the question, "What to let go?," a meaningful response hinges on specific objects but goes far beyond these terms. It concerns a relationality, a "mode of exchange," marked historically and down to the present in dispossession as a subjective structure. To clarify what exactly this means, we might refer to the frontispiece of Aileen Moreton Robinson's crucial publication *The White Possessive: Property, Power and Indigenous Sovereignty*. There she offers an epigraph: "The problem with white people is they think and believe that they own everything."[23]

---

23 The source of the remark is cited as "Dennis Benjamin Moreton, personal communications, April 10, 2015," in Moreton-Robinson, *The White Possessive: Property, Power, and Indigenous Sovereignty* (Minneapolis, MN: University of Minnesota Press, 2015), xi.

Dissonant Chords of Riots

130

NATASHA GINWALA

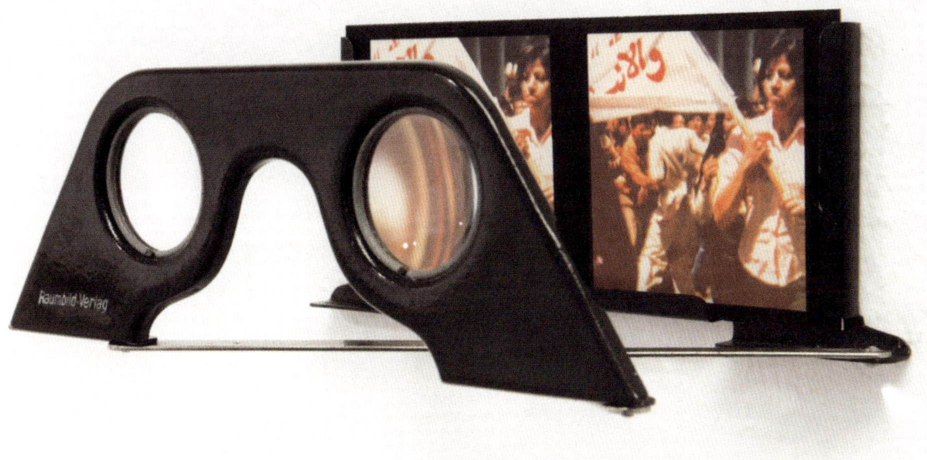

FIG 1 **Ala Younis, *Pat-riot–against the slow cancellation of the future*, 2018. Photo: Wataru Murakami. Courtesy: ifa Gallery Berlin.**

The learning process is something you can incite, literally incite, like a riot.

— Audre Lorde

The riot is an open wound located across legacies of coloniality as well as nation building.[1] It is an extraordinary setting, yet one that is recursive. As a transformative and polarizing ground, riots often perform as decisive sequences within prolonged conflict—in the shape of mass rebellions, anti-colonial struggles, civil war, and genocide. Exploding beyond definition, the riot has tended to remain that unresolved chapter, strategically buried in the subconscious of divided cities and civil society. Dilip Gaonkar asks, "How might one account for the persistence of rioting and the rioting crowds of people within the evolving trajectory of capitalist time and terrain? In my judgment, our time and terrain is caught in an inextricable paradox: coveting crowds and fearing riots."[2] It is in reflecting on this double bind that I initiated the exhibition "Riots: Slow Cancellation of the Future" at ifa Gallery (Berlin and Stuttgart) in 2018, which led to discursive collaboration and the anthology *Riots Unbound: Nights of the Dispossessed*, coedited with political theorist and researcher Gal Kirn, and architect, researcher, and writer Niloufar Tajeri. We chose to study the power dynamics and "politics of disorder" that surrounds, and in turn comes to determine, the social ferment, dispossession, and traumatic fallout unleashed through riots and uprisings.

---

1 Keller Easterling, "Shake the Ground: A Foreword" in *Riots Unbound: Nights of the Dispossessed*, ed. Natasha Ginwala, Gal Kirn, and Niloufar Tajeri (New York, NY: Columbia University Press, 2021). My utmost gratitude to Krisztina Hunya who has accompanied this endeavor from the outset and strengthened artistic as well as editorial pursuits.

2 Dilip Gaonkar, "After the Fictions: Notes Towards a Phenomenology of the Multitude," *e-flux journal*, no. 58 (2014).

The first part of this essay draws on the sonic corporeality of riots—returning to their quality of overflow as noise, rallying calls, and echoes in the public sphere, but also in poetry, dub, and performance cultures that have endeavored to express from the mouths of turmoil, addressing gaps in state records and cracks in governability within the dominant fold of violence.

> Madness, madness
> Madness tight on the heads of the rebels
> The bitterness erup's like a heart blas'
> Broke glass, ritual of blood an' a-burnin'
> Served by a cruelin' fighting
> Five nights of horror and of bleeding
> Broke glass, cold blades as sharp
> as the eyes of hate
> And the stabbin', it's
> War amongs' the rebels
> Madness, madness, war
>
> Night number one was in Brixton
> Sofrano B sound system
> I'm was a-beatin' up the riddim with a fire
> I'm comin' down his reggae reggae wire
> It was a sound checkin' down
> your spinal column
> A bad music tearin' up your flesh
>
> — Linton Kwesi Johnson

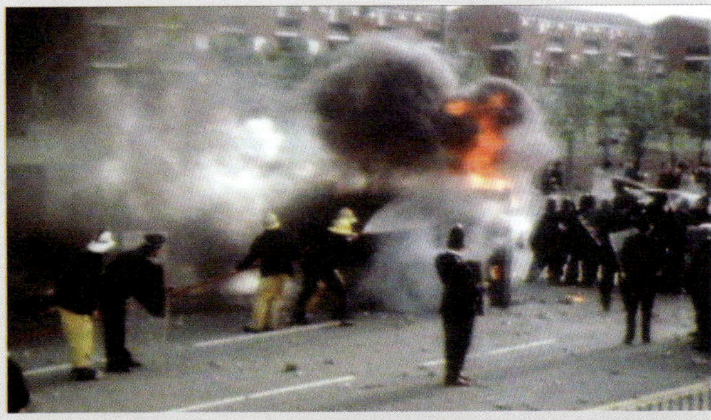

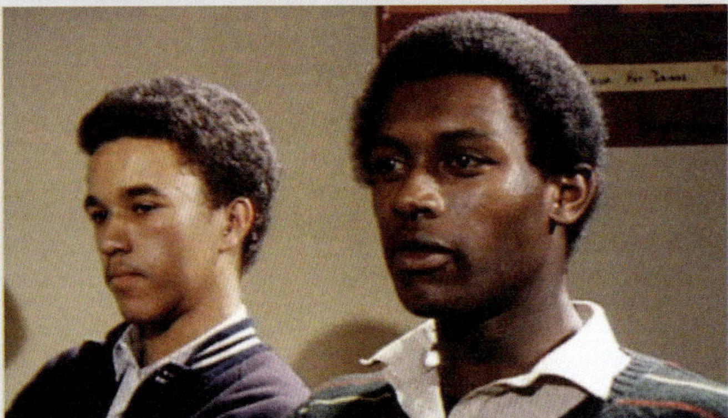

FIG 2-3 John Akomfrah, *Riot*, 2000, © Smoking Dogs Films, All Rights Reserved, DACS / Artimage 2022.

Linton Kwesi Johnson's track *Five Nights of Bleeding* (1985) evokes how dub-and-reggae-infused poetry have fearlessly described the truth on street corners, chronicling the escalation of bloodshed and animosity in ghettoized neighborhoods while also addressing how Black and Brown lives have been subjugated to tactics of "divide and rule" for centuries. While the sound system acts as a resonance chamber and protection shield through rhythms mixed and spun, it also livens a poetics of refusal.[3] Even Bob Marley thought Kwesi Johnson ("LKJ") was "too" militant and didn't root himself enough in Rastafarian philosophy. Rather, he most believed in the revolutionary potential of poetry and struggle music, mixing reggae grooves, testimonial narration, and dub that is in between languages: Jamaican Patua and English. In *Five Nights of Bleeding*, LKJ calls out to the "madness" and knife fights, persistent rituals of bloodshed and burning that rang in communal memory, and shared scars (in truth there is madness and in madness there is truth). This violence traversed from systemic oppression and was rife, especially through the 1970s and 1980s, between promoters of rival sound systems, and youth shielding from the lingering threat of police brutality. LKJ noted: "Fanon wrote about violence in the anti-colonial struggle. I transferred that to what was happening around me, the violence at the hands of the police and among Black youth. Thirty years on it hasn't changed; now they're killing each other with guns."[4] We need to actively recall how uneven operations of the law proliferate and go far back in computing furies of the dispossessed—centuries even, as long as the colonial enterprise has existed. How is it that in the United States especially, but also beyond, the white aggressor, often labeled a "lone wolf," is never seen as part of a wider systemic terror, while police shootings and gun violence continue to threaten the racialized subject as a moving target?

---

3 Audre Lorde, "Poetry is Not a Luxury," 1985.

4 https://www.theguardian.com/books/2002/may/04/poetry.books.

John Akomfrah, founding member of the Black Audio Film Collective, made his debut as a director with *Handsworth Songs*, which examined the fallout from the 1985 Handsworth riots. Akomfrah's seminal film *Riot* (1999) is lesser known and made for British Television. It traces the riots in Liverpool during July 1981 in a climate of economic recession under Thatcher's regime. Akomfrah captures this turning point in Britain's struggle towards multicultural democracy through interviews revealing the ghettoization and racial abuse in Toxteth that escalated with stop-and-search policing tactics following the "sus" laws. Chronicling Thatcher's response to the riot and the continued oppression of Black residents, Akomfrah's film charts the drawn-out impact of this riot, which becomes even more urgent to dissect today—a rupture that still bleeds as the post-Brexit landscape begins to take shape.

Arriving years later, Louis Henderson's *Evidence of Things Unseen but Heard* (2018) is an audiovisual collage conducted as a sonic archeology into the music scene of the city of Bristol, specifically plotting "The Bristol Sound" and braiding it with the mnemonic weight of uprising. The predominantly Caribbean community of St. Paul's protested in April 1980 against the brutality of the police forces in particular, and against the racist institutions and conditions of economic oppression of Margaret Thatcher's government more broadly. The centuries of colonial violence echo back, entangled with the nights of unrest resulting from a complex security apparatus activated through networked police surveillance and newly implemented Stop and Search laws across Bristol and other parts of England.

This filmic collage, which includes music video clippings, digs into the Bristol city archive and visits sites that have witnessed rebellion and brutality, arguing that measures of social control used against the St. Paul's community were first developed on Caribbean slave plantations. Rippling and reverberating through time are the sonic acts that unleashed rhythms of defiance, against the police/plantation state. The reggae sound system is imagined as an alternative public sphere with dub as its technological invention, creating, as Fred Moten has described, the "Sound [that] gives us back the visuality that ocularcentrism had repressed." [5] On a Sunday afternoon, June 7, 2020, the five-and-a-half-meter-high statue of slave trader and merchant Edward Colston, that had stood on Colston Avenue in Bristol since 1985, was pulled off its pedestal by a group of Black Lives Matter protestors. Colston was a member of the

5 Louis Henderson, "Evidence of Things Unseen but Heard" in *Riots Unbound: Nights of the Dispossessed*, eds. Natasha Ginwala, Gal Kirn, and Niloufar Tajeri, (New York, NY: Columbia University Press, 2021), 348–54.

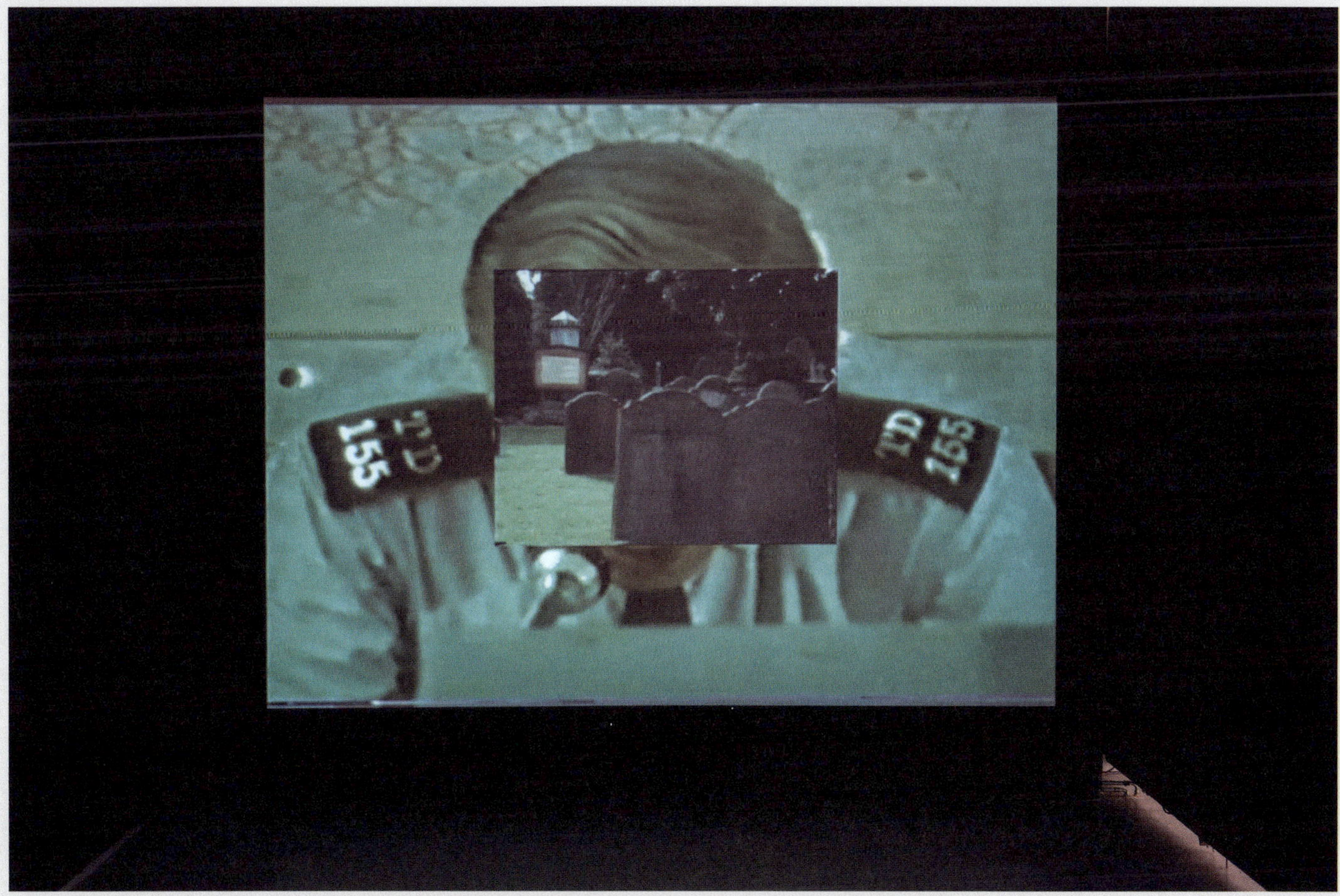

FIG 4 Louis Henderson, *Evidence of Things Unseen but Heard*, 2017, installation view, ifa Galerie Stuttgart. Photo: Henrike Hoffmann, © ifa–Institut für Auslandsbeziehungen.

Royal African Company, which had a monopoly on the West African trade in the late seventeenth century.[6] As Henderson states: "With a strong sense of poetic justice, the statue of a slave owner sunk to the bottom of the water in which slave ships were once docked."[7] Among the latest tunes to emerge from Bristol is Grove's queer dancehall track "Black," which they wrote as a response to the Colston statue being dragged down and thrown into the river.[8]

Guy Debord's "The Decline and Fall of the Spectacle-Commodity Economy" was published in *Internationale Situationniste* as an analysis of the Watts rebellion in Los Angeles during the summer of 1965, when the city's Black population rose against law enforcement agencies, the police, and National Guard. He notes, "Even those prepared to acknowledge apparent justifications for the black anger in Los Angeles (though not, of course any real ones)—all the theorists and spokesmen of the international Left (or, rather, its nothingness)—deplored the irresponsibility and disorder; the looting—especially the fact that liquor and weapons were the first targets of plunder; and above all; the estimated 2,000 fires started by the Watts petrol-throwers to light up their battle and their celebration. Who has defended the rioters of Los Angeles in the terms they deserve? Well, we shall. Let us leave the economists to grieve over the 27 million dollars lost and the town-planners over one of their beautiful supermarkets gone up in smoke, and McIntyre over his slain deputy sheriff; let the sociologists weep over the absurdity and euphoria of this rebellion. The task of a revolutionary journal is not only to endorse the Los Angeles insurgents, but also to help supply them with their reasons: to offer a theoretical account of the truth sought implicitly by their practical action."[9]

6 https://www.theguardian.com/uk-news/2020/jun/08/who-was-edward-colston-and-why-was-his-bristol-statue-toppled-slave-trader-black-lives-matter-protests.

7 Ibid.

8 https://www.loudandquiet.com/interview/grove-bristols-radical-new-voice-in-queer-dancehall/.

9 Guy Debord, *A Sick Planet* (Kolkata: Seagull Books, 2008), 1.

Much-loved rebel diva Vaginal Davis witnessed the Watts rebellion and Los Angeles Riots. In conversation, she spoke of earlier episodes of race riots and how they impacted cultural icons: "When the East St. Louis race riots happened, I think Josephine (Baker) was just about ten or eleven years old. It was horrific. Those riots also affected Miles Davis, who was from St. Louis as well. The ability of those people to attack and scream at the Blacks—men, women, and children—in St. Louis affected her very much. I think that's one of the things that led to Josephine Baker wanting to leave America altogether."[10] Davis considers longer trajectories of queering in reading the languages of uprising, rioting, and police violence in Los Angeles, and in her strategies of "terrorist drag" (as José Esteban Muñoz termed) that included making parties, queercore punk zines, and iconic works such as *The White to be Angry*.

10 "Vaginal Davis in Conversation with Natasha Ginwala," in *Riots Unbound: Nights of the Dispossessed*, (New York, NY: Columbia University Press, 2021), 74–76.

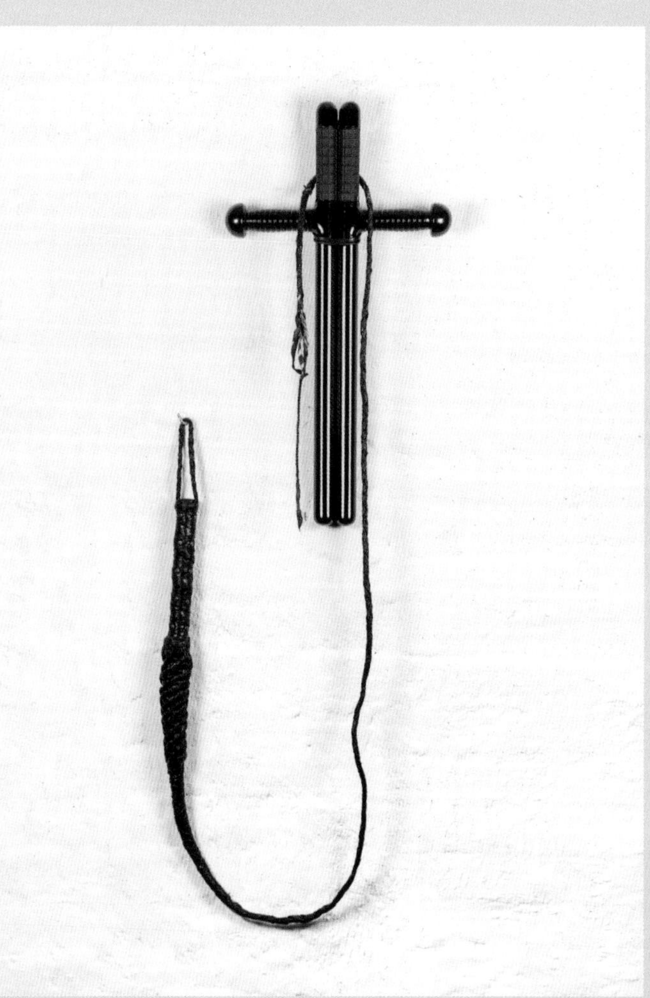

FIG 5 Satch Hoyt, *Bula Matari*, 2013. Police batons, bull whip, rubber. 140 × 40 × 5 cm.

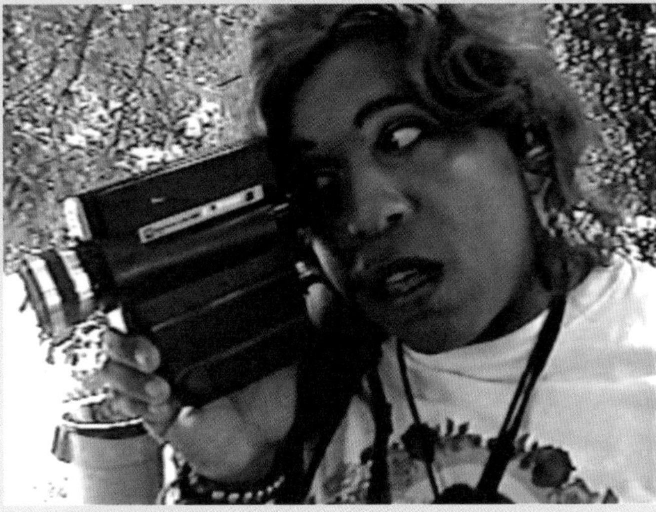

FIG 6 **Still from Vaginal Davis as G.B. Jones in the "Beggars of Life" segment of *The White to be Angry*, 1999. Courtesy the artist and Galerie Isabella Bortolozzi, Berlin.**

The manifesto, dog eared, unwritten
The charter sadly still unread.
Yeah we been drowned in cold derision
Yeah we been classified as dead.
Too many centuries of revolutions
have been fought in dis ere head
Memory capacity done imploded
into confusion undefined.
Let's huddle close this morning breakfast,
count our limbs, pick scabs off sores,
Pay respect to the ancestors,
place offerings at secret shrines.
Know, little sister, little brother,
libations can open closed doors ...

— Satch Hoyt

When alluding to the "cold derision" and death worlds that oppressed subjects must pass through, Satch Hoyt recalls the brutality that has proliferated across generations. He calls for attunement with the suffering ancestors, of offerings made, and restitution of memory that might sustain thresholds into recovery. Through musicality as a space of mimesis and rupture, the sculptures, sonic mappings, and poems of Hoyt appropriate and "puncture" the flow of circulating emblems of corporal punishment: the whip, police batons, and water hose. Hoyt positions the viewer in a way that is both conceptually grounded and atmospherically visceral—in facing up to the accounts of bare life against the oppressive tools exercising power and restraint. [11] Into the face of an off-white retro water hose, the artist spells the word "RIOT" using Swarovski crystals—this gesture doubles as a reminder of armed ferocity but also, as he lightly puts it, that "every riot has some bling." The sculpture *Bula Matari* (2013) is composed of police batons forming a cross and a bullwhip that threatens to crack down, recasting the wild forces of animality. However, in the title loosely translating as "breaker of rocks," we are also reminded of the administrative terror and forced labor brought about by colonial agent-administrator Henry Morton Stanley in the Belgian Congo under the reign of Leopold II throughout the nineteenth-century.

11 Giorgio Agamben, *Homo Sacer: Sovereign Power and Bare Life* (Stanford, CA: Stanford University Press, 1998).

I'm reminded of a passage in Ta-Nehisi Coates's, *Between the World and Me*: "There is nothing uniquely evil in these destroyers or even in this moment. The destroyers are merely men enforcing the whims of our country, correctly interpreting its heritage and legacy. It is hard to face this. But all our phrasing—race relations, racial chasm, racial justice, racial profiling, white privilege, even white supremacy—serves to obscure that racism is a visceral experience, that it dislodges brains, blocks airways, rips muscle, extracts organs, cracks bones, breaks teeth. You must always remember that the sociology, the history, the economics, the graphs, the charts, the regressions all land, with great violence, upon the body." [12]

12 Ta-Nehisi Coates, *Between the World and Me* (New York, NY: Random House, 2015).

~

The second part of this essay revisits a set of cultural practices and secular activism in the context of India and Sri Lanka. In particular, it considers the production of communal rioting and pogroms as a live sphere of ethnic divides, civic alienation, political complicities, and the weaponized mob. Official accounts of these events have neglected the veracity of public memory, and often, reigning political factions have manipulated sentiments and data and exploited policing measures. Further, military leadership and authoritarianism have galvanized riots with a zealous fervor as part of "vote bank politics," particularly in South Asia. Comparative timelines that analyze historical and recent riots as well as pogroms as part of a common historiography of violence are often lacking. The previous riot, therefore, brims to the surface as blistering recall when the next one is already causing wreckage. The search for truth amid such pogroms can remain a blood-soaked, torturous, and highly dangerous inquiry. To those who are active witnesses, "the right to remembrance" and access to justice frequently remains a lonely battle. Testimonial production occurs beyond the juridical apparatus, especially as the temporality of communal trauma composes a circuit that is out-of-joint with the news cycle, reparations, and legal remedy.

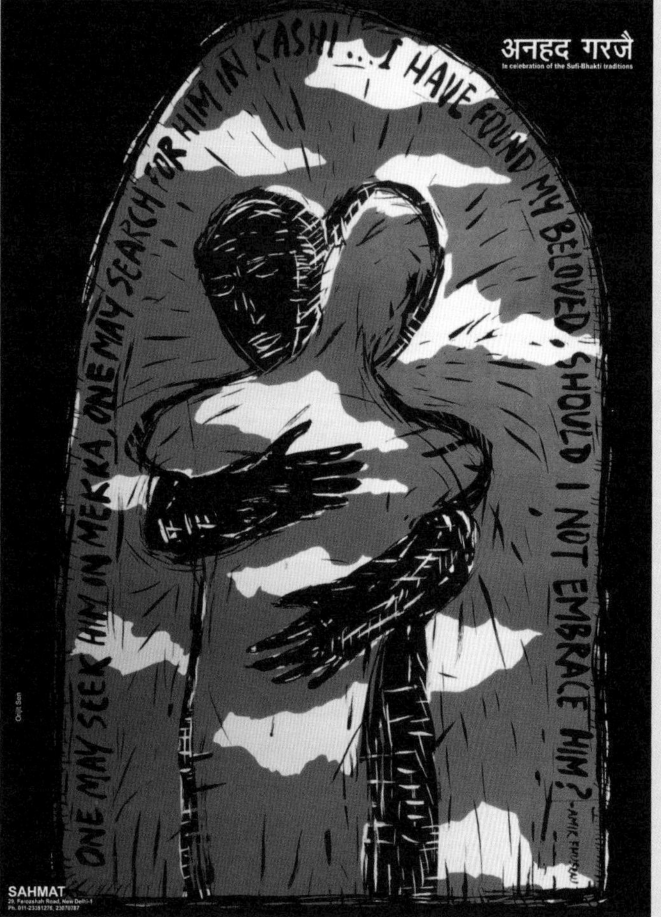

FIG 7 Sahmat poster in Angad Garje series, 1993. Design: Orijit Sen.

As was the case with the Gujarat Pogrom of 2002: several victims who lost family and neighbors, and had severe damages to property, continued to face stigma and alienation in the aftermath of mass carnage. Twenty years later, during the pandemic, rioting broke out in the Indian capital at the hands of armed Hindu mobs, while former US president Donald Trump dined with Prime Minister Narendra Modi. Incited by political players, the police force was filmed breaking CCTV cameras, while Muslims were openly targeted.[13] Citizen and activist networks' footage has increasingly produced modes of public evidence against the law and order establishment. As an exhibition project and growing archive led by artistic vocabularies, *Riots: Slow Cancellation of the Future* interrogates the veracity of the dominant image, especially given the failures of majoritarian democracies and deeply-sown ethnic divisions within societies chronicled in realtime by algorithmic intelligence, media censorship, and mobile phone cameras. How may we evolve possible narrations around riots and uprising through collaborative witnessing in choosing to stir acoustic memories, in filmic evidence, through reading images against the grain to unearth the systemic burden of contemporary mass violence? And moreover, sustain complex dialogs so that oral histories are not consumed entirely in those lost bodies, incarcerations, and fires.

Feminist historian Uma Chakravarti insists that the heated debates around India's history, including several instances of revisions to textbooks, fabrication of curricula, altering the names of roads, and civilizational orientation of heritage sites, face a shortfall of source material and comprehensive argumentation. These are indications of the desperation of authoritarian forces to dismantle syncretic languages of faith, coexistence, and acculturation. Chakravarti notes, "They can write mythology, but not history, they have no sources to show us [...] how many libraries and research institutions will they target and get rid of? They cannot do that. History is being pressed from various places and directions. Women and Dalits have been rewriting their histories since a long time."[14] These forms of anti-systemic historiography seek to counter master chronicles, distortions generated through nationalism and inequity caused through terms of citizenship laws such as India's implementation of National Citizens Registry and Citizen Amendment Act.

---

13 https://www.theatlantic.com/ideas/archive/2020/02/what-happened-delhi-was-pogrom/607198/.

14 Uma Chakravarti, "They can write mythology, not history," Indian Cultural Forum, https://www.youtube.com/watch?v=2FmgCMWo4Qs.

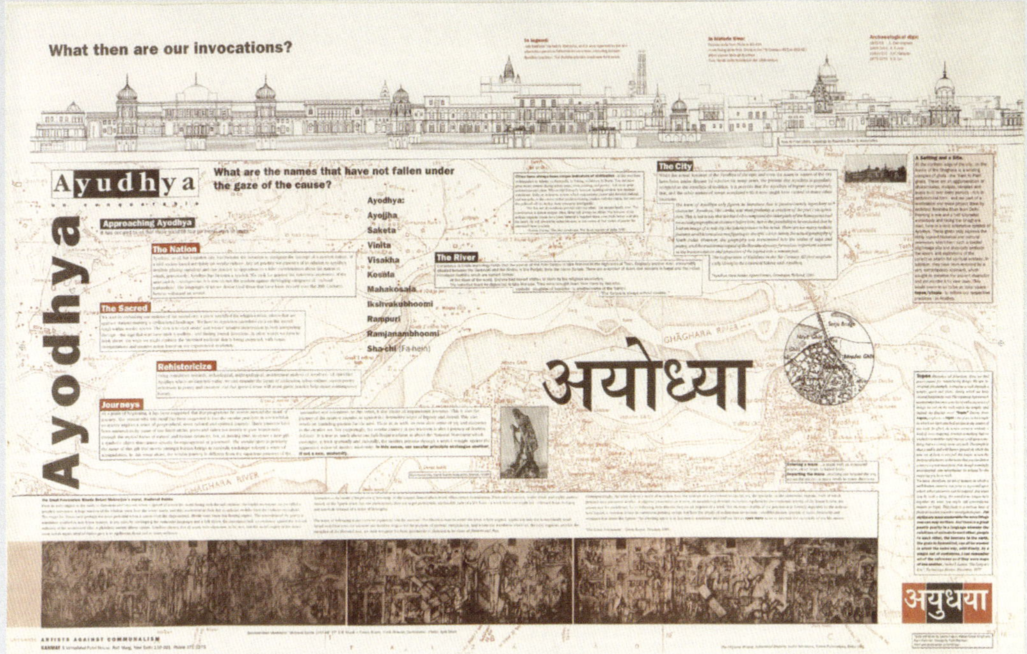

FIG 8 ***Ayodhya: What then are our invocations?*, poster, 24 × 38 in. Design: Ram Rahman. Texts: Charles Correa, Geeta Kapur, Madan Gopal Singh, and Ram Rahman, with contributions from Rajendra Prasad, May 1993. Courtesy: Sahmat.**

In the posters, publications, music concerts, and exhibitions organized by the Delhi-based Sahmat collective (since 1989), we find aesthetic strategies and forums striving against the rise of communal forces, defending artistic freedom, secular traditions, and plurality in history-telling. The exhibition display at ifa Gallery highlighted some of the key interventions realized by Sahmat after the demolition of the sixteenth-century mosque Babri Masjid by "Kar Sevaks" and inflammatory speeches by members of the BJP and Vishwa Hindu Parishad (VHP) on December 6, 1992. While the archeological status and sacred origin of this site was disputed already during the colonial period, causing combative claims, it was the ascent of Hindutva groups in the political arena that led to the desecration of this monument as well as the Bombay Riots of 1992–93.[15] Vivan Sundaram's multi-part installation *Memorial* (1993–2014) is a seminal work that attests to this period of strife and the social aesthetics which echoed as part of Sahmat's activities. The key image in Sundaram's project is a newsprint photograph, taken by photojournalist Hoshi Lal, of a man lying on the street side next to a garbage dump after the cycle of riots in Mumbai during 1993. It is interpreted materially in various ways to form commemoration gestures and acts of mourning toward known and unknown victims of this carnage. A detail of it also features on the cover of *Justice Now Bombay Riots 1992–93*, The Srikrishna Commission Report copublished by Combat and Sahmat.

Sahmat planned a programme of Sufi-Bhakti performances for January 1993, titled *Anhad Garje* (a phrase used by the medieval saint-poet Kabir that roughly translates to "the silence reverberates"). In the immediate aftermath of the demolition, Anhad Garje became Sahmat's synergetic response to, and protest against, the demolition of the mosque. The seventeen-hour stretch of performances took on an additional resonance by promoting communal harmony and serving as a reminder of the voice as an organ of resistance. Musician and vocalist Shubha Mudgal expresses how the concert stage for the programme *Anhad Garje* was under the shade of a large tree. The musical repertoire and banners spread around the venue invoked lines from Kabir, Bulleh Shah, and Baba Farid, professing humanity, love and secular spirit.[16]

15 https://cjp.org.in/bombay-riots-timeline/.

16 Hum Sab Sahmat in collaboration with Indian Cultural Forum, uploaded to YouTube, December 6 2020. https://www.youtube.com/watch?v=BF9nmc5wgc4.

After a High Court ruling in 2010 said that the disputed land in Ayodhya, where the Babri Masjid was, shall be divided into three parts, historian Romila Thapar noted, “The verdict has created a precedent in the court of law that land can be claimed by declaring it to be the birthplace of a divine or semi-divine being, worshiped by a group that defines itself as a community. There will now be many such *janmasthans* wherever appropriate property can be found or a required dispute manufactured. Since the deliberate destruction of historical monuments has not been condemned, what is to stop people from continuing to destroy others? The legislation of 1993 against changing the status of places of worship has been, as we have seen in recent years, quite ineffective.”[17] Further judgments confirmed Thapar’s concerns, as under the present regime the Supreme Court pronounced its verdict in the Ayodhya title dispute case on November 9, 2019, saying that Hindu parties will be given the disputed land where the Babri Masjid once stood; and that the Sunni Waqf Board, the biggest Muslim litigant in the case, will be given five acres at a separate “prominent” location in Ayodhya. As the pandemic raged on in August 2020, an unveiling on an opulent scale and a prayer ceremony were held at the Ram Temple, conducted at the Babri Masjid demolition site, headed by the Prime Minister and telecast to several news channels and widely circulated via social media.

17 https://www.thehindu.com/opinion/op-ed/The-verdict-on-Ayodhya-a-historians-perspective/article15523346.ece.

Thapar explains that when dealing with ancient India, “The past is not another country, the past is still with us.” Her analytical course at Jawaharlal Nehru University, titled “historical method,” examined how past genealogies connect to the present and what we do with these records as precedents in times we are living through.[18] Students were invited to explore evidence-led methods that assume causal links rather than stories that string events together. In recent years, this university campus, along with other educational establishments in India, has become a target for fascist administrators planted in leadership roles, as well as Hindu nationalist student organizations such as the ABVP (Akhil Bharatiya Vidhyarthi Parishad). As protests against the Citizenship Amendment Act gained momentum across cities and campuses, these sites of intellectual life and dissent became even more prone to repressive measures. On January 5, 2020, over fifty masked persons carried out an armed attack on the JNU campus, injuring more than

18 https://www.youtube.com/watch?v=zJqjb4NzFRU.

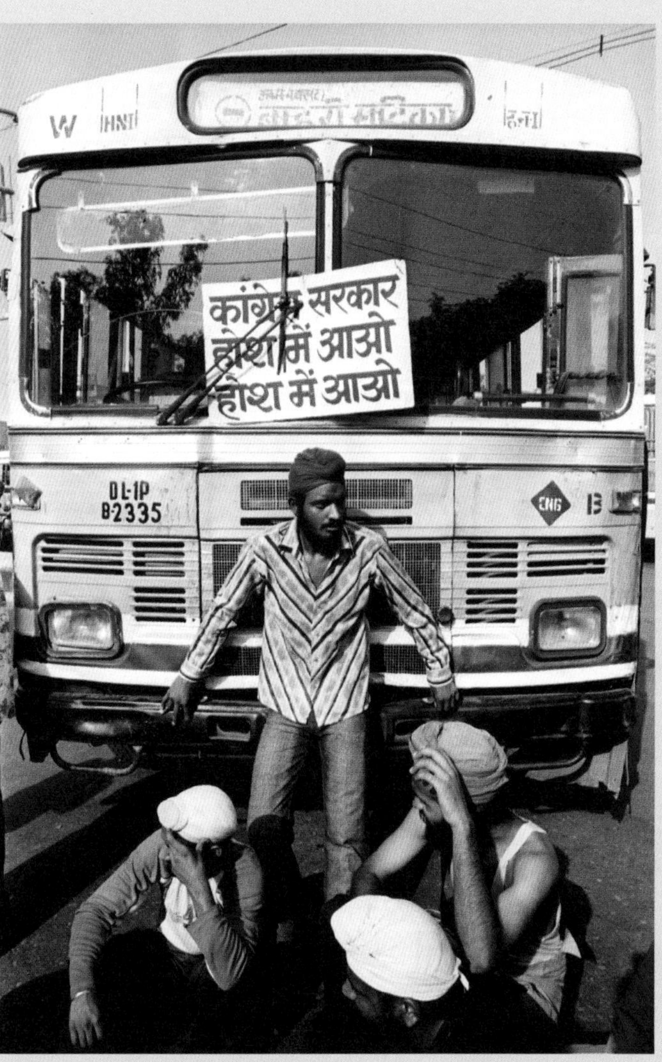

FIG 9 Sikhs protesting against the Nanavati commission report in New Delhi, 2005, from the 1984 notebooks by Gauri Gill. Copyright Gauri Gill.

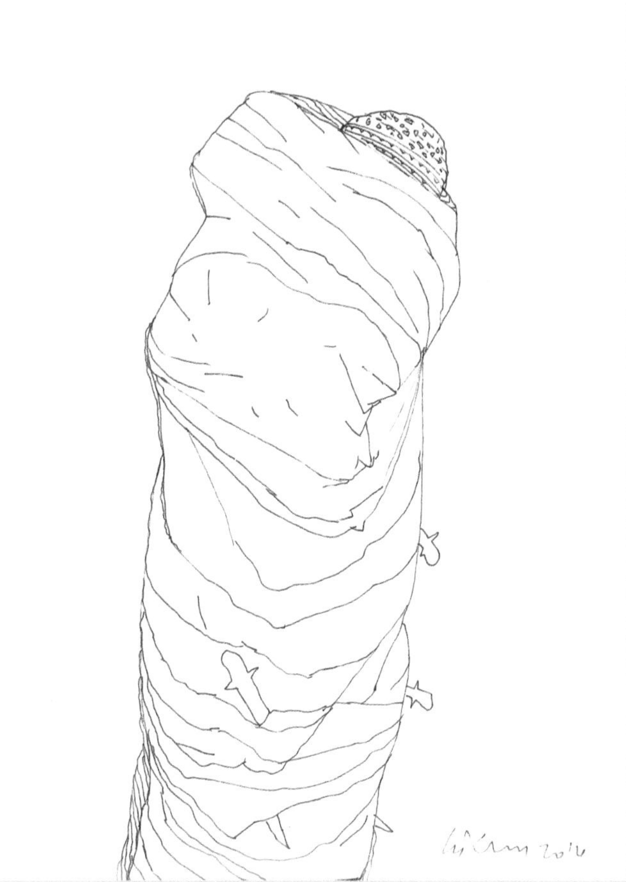

FIG 10 Chandraguptha Thenuwara, *Untitled I (Assassination)*, 2014. Ink on paper, 29.7 × 21 cm. Courtesy of the artist and Saskia Fernando Gallery.

thirty-nine students and teachers, chanting against them as "anti-nationals." Such is the state of affairs where an emboldened mob can stride into a campus that has for decades sustained room for disagreement and visionary political agency, and leave it as a shattered ground. [19]

Among the recent exhibitions by Sahmat is *India is Not Lost* (2021), exhibiting the collective's initiatives over the decades observing iconic moments of India's long struggle for independence. The question that emerges in such presentations, given the system failures of the nation-state, is how our political imagination may move beyond the classic and well-rehearsed representation of "national heroes" that leaves out a multitude of class positions and caste stratifications. As a case in point, one may pore over the resources generated by P. Sainath's initiative "Foot-Soldiers of Freedom" on the People's Archive of Rural India (PARI) site. [20] While this is beyond the scope of the present reflection, it is crucial to attend to how the virtual sphere and people's movements on the ground have been conceiving aesthetic strategies of resistance and remembrance in recent years. These act as counter-currents to the routine indoctrination and fabrication of fascist media portals. Some examples include the graphic visual analysis of Orijit Sen, who has been part of Sahmat initiatives, and younger voices that include gender-diverse and dalit practitioners who act within and beyond the artistic realm, such as Bakery Prasad (Siddhesh Gautam), Posters Unite!, and Smish Designs, as well as grassroots media organizations and literary archives such as Dalit Camera, Dalit Poetry and Literature, and Buffalo Intellectual.

19 https://time.com/5760597/what-happened-during-jnu-attack-india/.

20 https://ruralindiaonline.org/en/stories/categories/foot-soldiers-of-freedom/.

Gauri Gill's long-term project 1984 (2014– ongoing) assembles a range of voices, including artists, writers, poets, and filmmakers, with survivors' testimonies recalling the anti-Sikh genocide that led to the murder and torture of over eight thousand Sikhs in Delhi and other cities in India. During the course of three days in November 1984, following the assassination of Prime Minister Indira Gandhi and just months after operation Blue Star marking the Indian Army's attack in June 1984 at the Darbar Sahib, the "Golden Temple" in Amritsar. This genocide sent shockwaves across the Sikh and non-Sikh community, while sowing seeds of communal discord that continue to fuel antagonisms and bloodshed today. Lawyer and writer Mallika Kaur notes, "In contravention of their usual practice of not revealing information that might incite communal violence, All India Radio quickly noted that the prime minister had been gunned down by her Sikh bodyguards. Images of her corpse were rerun on state-run television, cementing Sikhs as violent 'others' in the Indian imagination, even as armed gangs marched to deliver death on Sikhs." [21]

21 https://www.aljazeera.com/gallery/2014/2/4/in-pictures-delhis-widow-colony.

Here, the boundary of terminology between the communal riot and genocide are vitally recodified from the community perspective, witnessed in contrast to the mainstream media and state narrative. Gill invites a dialog between her photographs, first published in print media, and resilient modes of response from cultural actors in her midst, that together form a notebook and an expansive bibliography countering the void left by necropower. In 1960, Elias Canetti wrote, “One of the most striking traits of the inner life of a crowd is the feeling of being persecuted.”[22] However, what happens when state forces instigate persecution from within the crowd? Orchestration by statist forces in inciting mob violence leading to the Sikh massacre remains covered up, with perpetrators belonging to major political parties still moving freely. Balbir Singh relates to Gill’s work in terms of “Mourning as Antagonism.” [23] One might also ask: “how does a community wrestle with state accountability and mainstream amnesia while carrying a common traumatic wound?” This too is a question of heritage and loss.

Over several years, Sri Lankan artist and activist Chandraguptha Thenuwara has marked the changing significance of the 1983 Black July pogrom that preceded three decades of civil war in Sri Lanka. His endeavor has included creating installations and exhibitions annually as ways to demarcate room in the civic sphere to memorialize ethnic violence and alert people to the engulfing threats of entrenched militarism and postwar developments that have exacerbated religious intolerance and class-based fragmentation. Asynchronous and often competing historical legacies of different religious and language groups in Sri Lanka, especially of the Tamil and Sinhalese peoples, and centuries of coloniality, led to divergent ideals of sovereignty, economic imbalances between the north, south, and east of this island geography, ingrained mistrust, and oppressive strategies of domination by the Sinhala Buddhist majority in political power. Thenuwara observes the 1983 carnage as part of a palimpsest of event cycles and warfare. Adopting camouflage and pixelation as a satirical tool, his works map these discrepancies in Sri Lanka’s social milieu and checkered lineage.

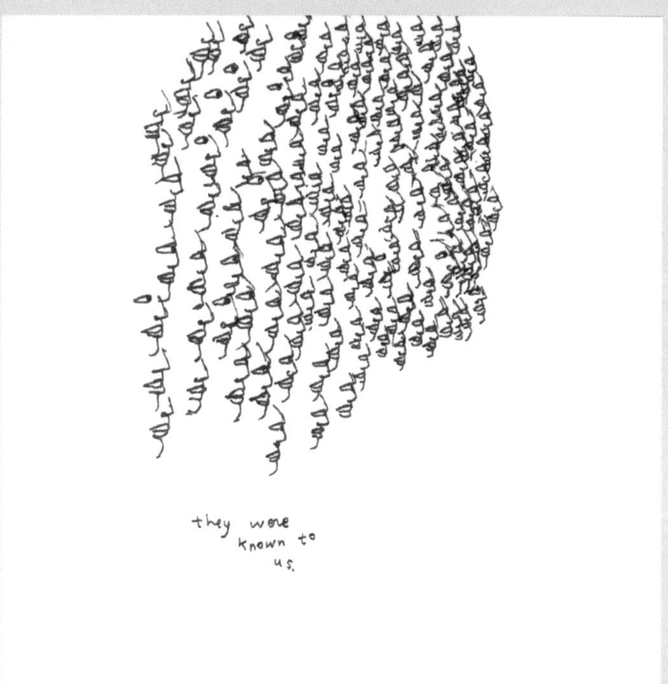

FIG 11 Drawing about 1984 contributed by Gagan Singh to the 1984 notebooks by Gauri Gill. Copyright Gagan Singh.

Thenuwara’s artistic conceptualism, in a series coined as “Barrelism,” includes paintings and installations made through the 1990s, that were realized against the backdrop of the spatial topography of civil war years, with checkpoints and army-green barrels at blockades as part of battleground ideology, perpetuating a militarized landscape, and disconnecting parts of the island in the north and east where genocidal violence was executed by state forces in conflict with the LTTE, as well as for several years with the presence of the IPKF (Indian Peacekeeping Forces) in Sri Lanka.

The artist comments, “A new form of barricades appeared across the country—painted camouflaged Barrels, and based on this form, and I coined the term ‘Neo-Barrelism.’ My Neo-Barrelism exhibitions started after 2006, and continued until 2008 July. I also exhibited most of my camouflage paintings and the *Dhammapada* (sayings of the Buddha) painting during this phase. As the war escalated and Buddhist monks stridently supported it, I criticized this phenomenon through three selected verses from the Dhammapada preached by Buddha. Dhammapada verses were written on the canvas but also camouflaged; the viewer with difficulty had to identify the verses. That kind of visual suggestion was to show how difficult it was to both see and follow the Buddha’s words and preaching which forms the basis of Buddhism on the island which has a history of

22 Elias Canetti, *Crowds and Power* (London:Phoenix, 2000), 20–21.

23 Balbir K. Singh, “Unjust Attachments: Mourning as Antagonism in Gauri Gill’s 1984,” *Critical Ethnic Studies*, vol. 2, no. 2 (Fall 2016): 104–28.

more than 2,500 years."[24] The leitmotifs in Thenuwara's recent drawings are often ironic: a bunch of microphones without an orator, an ensnarement of thorns and lotuses that recollect mechanisms of subjugation and minorities' displacement, as well as the dragon and lion more recently, conveying Sinhalese Buddhist leadership in cahoots with China's grip on the Sri Lankan economy and infrastructure.

The event horizon widens as he observes modes in which the military apparatus continues to flex its muscle. Through drawings made after the antimuslim riots in Aluthgama in 2014, and the installation work *VIP Convoy*, he uses traffic police gloves and a coffin beneath to plot how the monstrosity of ethnic violence returns to life, indicating that kidnapped and disappeared bodies still haunt as policing of urban spaces continues to pave ways for political incumbency. Even as this installation was on view in Berlin, communal violence broke out in Kandy district in Sri Lanka against Muslims in the area, with identified suspects involved in the ultra-nationalist Buddhist organization BBS (Bodu Bala Sena).[25]

As I write this, mass protests and a citizen struggle have gripped the island in recent days, owing to the corruption, war crimes, and nepotism of the Rajapaksa and Wickremesinghe regimes advancing the country's worst economic crisis. The yellow barricades blocking protestors from nearing the parliament and on main thoroughfares now face the pressure of mass disenchantment even by the erstwhile partisan Sinhalese voter base.[26] A critical notion floated by Franco "Bifo" Berardi and Mark Fisher: "The slow cancellation of the future" brings forth the hauntings of predatory social relations that damage multi-ethnic terrains of life-making. Through its paradoxical lens we find ourselves wrestling with lost futures and the languages of uprising that refuse the "loophole of retreat."[27]

Frederick Douglass argues, "Those who profess to favor freedom yet deprecate agitation, are men who want crops without plowing up the ground; they want rain without thunder and lightning. They want the ocean without the awful roar of its many waters."[28] The question for our present is how to comprehend a thermodynamics that simultaneously governs burning cars and flaming forests. What kind of future comes after such violent scenarios?[29]

A vital lesson from climate history is that ruling classes don't always survive climate transitions, or at least are slowed on their path into barbarity. Feudalism's class-enforced monocultures crumbled in the face of the Little Ice Age: famine and disease quickly followed. As a result, with the onset of the Black Death, webs of commerce and exchange didn't just transmit disease—they became vectors of mass insurrection.[30] Almost overnight, peasant revolts stopped being local affairs and became large-scale threats to the feudal order. "Unlike the strike, it is hard to tell when and where the riot starts and ends," writes Joshua Clover. "This is part of what allows the riot to function both as a particular event and as a kind of holographic miniature of an entire situation, a world-picture."[31] Today, the declaration of a state of emergency is no longer exceptional and becomes part of adjacent implosive trajectories in the planetary gridlock of systemic violence and authoritarian governance. This certainly does not mean we are all affected in an identical manner; rather, the struggles between defensible and defenseless bodies intensify existing asymmetries and with that can radicalize into an age of riots.[32]

April 2022

24 Chandraguptha Thenuwara, "Re-looking at Riots in Contemporary Sri Lanka," in *Riots Unbound: Nights of the Dispossessed*, ed. Natasha Ginwala, Gal Kirn, and Niloufar Tajeri (New York, NY: Columbia University Press, 2021), 369–85.

25 https://www.bbc.com/news/world-asia-43305453.

26 https://www.aljazeera.com/opinions/2022/4/5/sri-lanka-gota-needs-to-go-but-so-does-the-ethnocratic-state.

27 Loosely borrowing from: https://www.e-flux.com/journal/105/302556/the-loophole-of-retreat-an-invitation/.

28 From his "West India Emancipation" speech, delivered in Canandaigua, New York, on August 4, 1857. Frederick Douglass, *Two Speeches by Frederick Douglass* (Rochester, NY: C. P. Dewey, 1857), 22.

29 Editorial *Riots Unbound: Nights of the Dispossessed*, ed. Natasha Ginwala, Gal Kirn, and Niloufar Tajeri, (New York, NY: Columbia University Press, 2021).

30 Jason W. Moore and Raj Patel, "Unearthing the Capitalocene: Towards a Reparations Ecology," *ROAR Magazine* 7 (Autumn 2017), https://roarmag.org/magazine/moore-patel-seven-cheap-things-capitalocene.

31 Joshua Clover, *Riot. Strike. Riot: The New Era of Uprisings* (New York, NY: Verso, 2016), 123.

32 https://booksandideas.net/A-Call-to-Arms.html.

Monu-Mental

142

CECILIA VICUÑA
Translated by Christopher Winks

The forgotten history of the word “monument” contains a code, a potential future.

A long time ago, I wrote: “An object is not an object, but a witness to a relationship.”

“A place is not a place, but a relationship to a place.”

Etymology is a journey to the *etymon*, the “true meaning” of a word, a word imagined as an origin, a hypothetical reconstruction, or an observatory of language.

The word “monument” is the witness to a relationship; it comes from the Latin *monumentum*, from *monēre*: to counsel, warn, admonish. The question is: of what does it wish to warn us?

The meaning of “monument” oscillates and transforms itself through the energy of the mother morpheme **mēn* which gave it its origin, from which were born its derivatives, the variability of a living current.

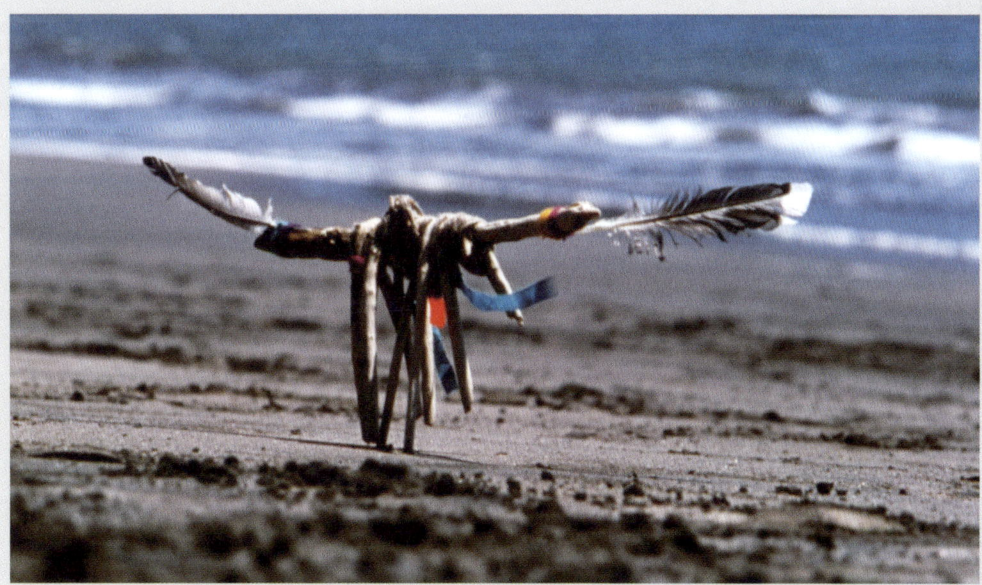

FIG 1 Cecilia Vicuña, *Guardián*, 1967. Precarious site-specific performance installation, *Con Con*, Chile, 1967. Photo: Ricardo Vicuña.

Etymological dictionaries sing in chorus as they survey the most ancient roots:

Monument: "A structure erected as a memorial...
venerated for
a certain reason."

"An admirable achievement ..."

From the Latin *monēre* and *mŏnĕo*, to warn, make known, advise, recall to memory,
and even earlier, from the Proto-Indo-European **mēn*, to think, the linguistic zero of the Greek menos: spirit and *mentor*, *mnasthai*, to recall and *Mnemosyne*, Goddess of Memory, mother of the nine Muses, and of its contrary: amnesia, and other variants:

monitor
monster
and premonition.

To predict, augur, prophesy, says Virgil's "Horrenda monere."

If the human soul's capacity for prediction reactivates itself, the monument's imponderable, ungraspable meaning, the greatness of the human dream could reemerge.

Does the monument advise the mind what to think? And does the mind resist because it detests admonitions?

Every revolution or evolution begins by pulling down monuments.

Recent events in Chile—the social explosion of October 2019—demonstrate the precarious life of the monument during historical transition.

The rebellion of the forgotten: the Indigenous and Mestizos attacked and transformed military and colonial monuments, from south to north, from Arica to Magallanes, transforming them into a question and a multivalent expression of joy and rage.

The collective body of the revolt turned them into launch pads for poems and performances in which predominated the hitherto-unseen flourishing of Mapuche flags flying in the squares of Chile, a belated recognition of the suppressed and despised part of our country: the Indigenous peoples.

> " ... from the beginning of the social movement, monuments were understood anew in their political dimension and the protest used them as an amplifier of its demands."
>
> "In particular, the monument to Baquedano, which could be understood as the principal stage-setting of the revolt and territory in permanent contestation."
>
> "... a monument changed into a sign submitted to successive interventions, to changes, in transit."
>
> — Luis Montes Rojas, sculptor and professor at Universidad de Chile

Seeing the monuments attacked, clothed, painted, and punished as if they were living beings reminded me of the testimony of John Osborne, an archaeologist dedicated to the study of three-thousand-year-old statues in Turkey, destroyed by their contemporaries, who cut off their noses, eyes, ears, and hands, so that they could not "see," "hear," or "touch."

Violence against a symbol of power lasts longer than the desire to glorify it, because the symbol, in ancestral vision, "sees and hears," interacting with reality.

Losing their prior meaning and acquiring new ones, monuments entered into life.

The cyclical movement of a "monument's" life, from its conception to its destruction, is a language that demands attention to the questions contained in the mutations of its history.

~

The monument is not an object, it is the inexhaustible texture of a fertile root, the *men* of the "thinking" that resists being reduced to fixity.

The idea of an ephemeral or immaterial monument may be found under various names in multiple cultures. In the Andean world, the *ceqe* system of imaginary lines uniting the *wakas*, the sacred spaces across long distances. Or the *Alcheringa* (Arunta) in Aboriginal Australia, translated as *The Eternal Dream Time*, an ancient oral narrative of what happened in a primordial era, which the Aboriginal wise ones "read" as invisible writing in the landscape. Even in European classical antiquity, certain impermanent forms of knowledge, like the hanging gardens of Babylon, were considered one of the seven wonders of the world.

The real monument is memory, the wonder of the relationship between the two parts of the noun: *monu* & *mentum*.

The monument is the idea of the monument: speaking to the mind, contemplating the power of naming as action.

Contemplating the mind: the true monu-mental space.

The consciousness of a relationship.

The fractal of an act: seeing seeing.

~

The ephemeral monument is the moment, or the memory of the moment, which mobilizes the very nature of remembering,
to touch the heartstrings again.

The *etymon* of the "moment" is born from the contraction of *movimentum*, from *movere*, "mover," whose root is **meue*: to push outside.

The moment dissolves in order to be.

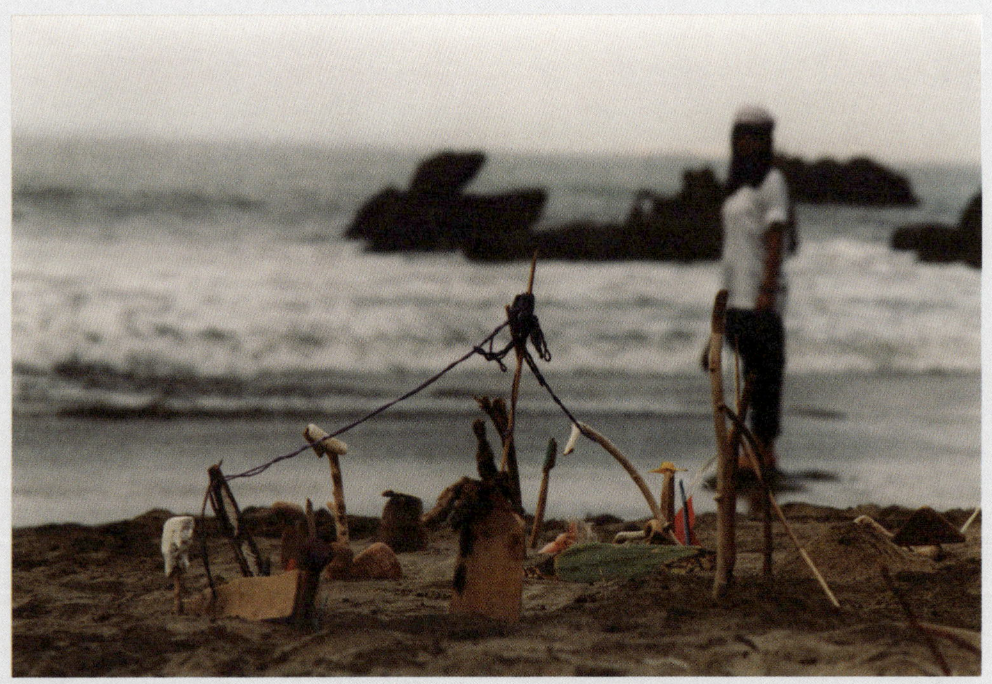

FIG 2 Cecilia Vicuña, *Basuritas en la playa (Debris on the beach)*, 1987. Precarious site-specific performance installation, *Con Con*, Chile, 1987. Photo: Ricardo Vicuña.

The memory of the moment is movement in reverse: to bind together leaving and holding back.

A reflection of going and coming that returns us to a possible future.

The value of remembering is monumental.

Going against history, against the memory of a people: a monumental error.

~

If the monument is not only for others, but counsels one's own mind as to what to think, its dual potential demands that we be careful of imposition, the violence of an authority that imposes a definition.

Transforming a monument by seeing the idea that animates it from another place is precisely what the formless movement of the human crowd rising in revolt does, going to the crux of the matter, dismantling the idea that it or the established powers wished to exalt.

~

To think of the word “monument” reveals a tension expressing itself in us. For whom or what does the monument exist?

I don’t know if I accepted this invitation because of its absurdity, or because of what happened to Baquedano and the Plaza Italia of Santiago’s changing into Plaza Dignidad.

> Hours away from the first anniversary of the social explosion of October 18, 2019, in Santiago de Chile, a symbolic dispute occurred at the monument to General Manuel Baquedano, in the epicenter of the capital’s protests, the Plaza Italia zone. On Friday evening, the day of the week when the mobilization started up again, a group of masked demonstrators dyed red the 19th-century sculpture created to honor the soldier. Hours later, the Chilean army, through a communique, denounced the “vandalization” of the statue, which awoke newly repaired this Saturday: both the sculpture and its pedestal had been painted by the municipality.
>
> — Rocío Montes
>
> https://elpais.com/internacional/2020-10-18/la-disputa-simbolica-en-chile-porel-monumento-del-epicentro-de-las-protestas.html

Perhaps I am stirred by the secret idea that my “precarious little messes” had been considered “monumental,” although they are slight nothings, or tiny nothings towering in their fragility. I have heard that they manage to suggest a lost civilization, or the beginning of a future.

That which falls and disappears, the precarious swallowed by the sea is perhaps that which is monumental, which makes us see, advising the mind as to where we are. Not in the illusion of perpetuity, of the continuity of human culture, but in its dissolution, extinction sought after at full speed.

~

What is the monumental now?

Drought? Extreme heat? No snow on the cordillera? Dried-up rivers?

Species extinction?

The fight against Chile's progressive conversion into a sacrifice zone?

The collective will to write a new constitution?

The search for a new way of "being with" earth, water, and all beings?

In a performance I made in Santiago in 2019, dedicated to the mutilated youths who lost their eyes seeking justice, I said:

> "They murdered a phrase ...
> That I don't know if you heard ...
> The phrase said: 'Now we are we.'
> That 'we' has been reborn,
> Here and now among us ..."

Young people desired the lost memory of a time when collectively seeking justice was not a cause for persecution. They said, "we are no longer afraid," and in their songs, the "we" was reborn,
the desire to be with.

When I think of the erased and reborn "we," in the monumental "being with," I think of my father, who died a few days ago. He said: "Chile is two waves: snow on the cordillera and the breakers on the sea."

His vision nurtured me. The lesson was not to see towards but *from* the landscape, from an imaginary flight that rises and sees the totality from the starry immensity, the gaze that belongs to this land of two parallel abysses.

From childhood, I saw from this very place. I remember that the North American writer Barry López once asked me in a letter: "Why are there so many poets in Chile?" I responded: "Maybe because Chile is two abysses: the highest mountain range in the Western Hemisphere and the deepest pit of the sea." And we, inhabitants of this extreme fragility and creativity, always subject to the sway of the clashing tectonic plates, are beings on the edge.

From this fissure and conjunction are born the fear and delight of our being.

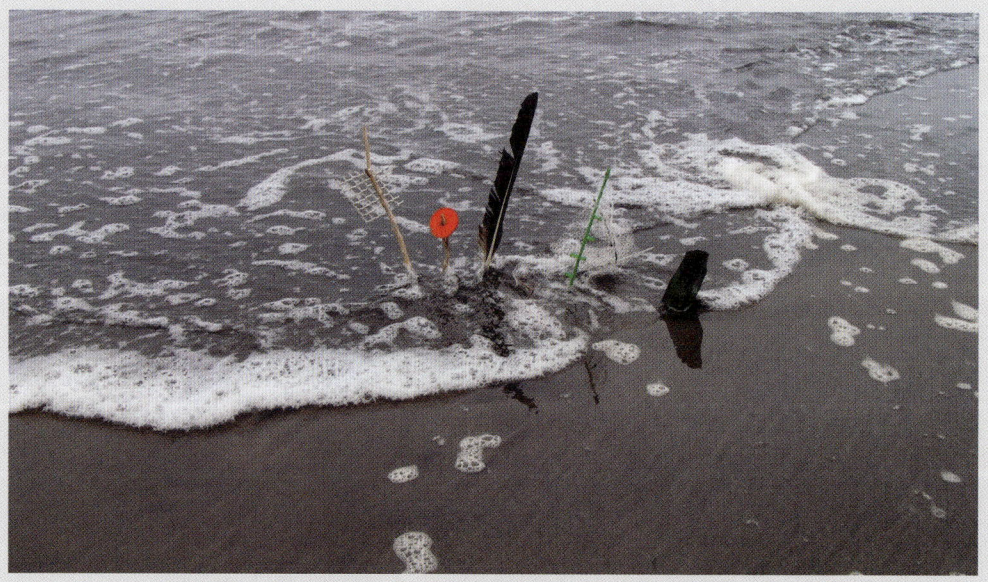

FIG 3 Cecilia Vicuña, *Dissolution*, Precarious site-specific performance installation, Con Con, Chile, 2010. Photo: James O'Hern.

I remember that as children we played on the edge of the sea, feeling the pit where the earthquakes and tidal waves came from. We always left behind a boy or girl guardian who had to look towards the horizon to see whether rough seas heralded a tidal wave. The scale of our childhood dream was already tuned to this magnitude.

I recognize the monumental scale of this dream in the images of our poetry, and in the science that conceived *autopoiesis* in Chile—the foundation of a new biology—as well as in the political power that imagined a participatory democratic revolution, without violence or persecution, in Salvador Allende's Unidad Popular. This magnitude is reborn today in the Constituent Assembly, democratically elected to write a new constitution.

Imagining without limits changes us into "dangerous dreamers" in the eyes of the dominant powers. The colonialism that still pursues the dreaming emanating from the monumental scale somehow transmitted to us mestizos, cyclically expressive itself from colonial times till today in the liberatory movements and visionary works of often-murdered authors and leaders.

I think of our Independence, of the fervor that inflamed the hearts of the impoverished Chilean *patipelados*, capable of crossing the *cordillera* without shoes or shelter, with the aim of "freeing the nation," or the young men and women who lost their eyes dreaming of seeing another reality in the social explosion of 2019.

I remember—or I imagine I remember—an image communicated by Alexander von Humboldt—which my memory is surely distorting—who observed the scope of the Amerindian gaze capable of visualizing the totality of the landscape, beyond the visible. It's unlikely that these were his words, but something in his text made me recognize this gaze, without which it would not have been possible to conceive the Nazca lines, the geoglyphs of the Atacama Desert, the geometrical cities connected by straight lines of Amazonia, the *Qhapaq Ñan*, the Inka road network or the *ceqe* system of Perú, an invisible *quipu* that organized the duties and responsibilities of communities by connecting Cusco with the sacred sites and water sources in the glaciers at thousands of kilometers' distance.

Simón Rodríguez, the sage who educated Simón Bolívar, saw this greatness in the Inkas:

> "After Bolívar's death, Simón Rodríguez continued his submergence in the Inca dimension ... he knew that the deepening of this dimension would result in the clarification of the American space ... [that] continues to win the most decisive battles for the image, the secret pulsations of the invisible toward the image, as anxious for knowledge as it is for being known."
>
> — José Lezama Lima, "Imagen de América Latina," in Moreno, *América latina en su literatura* (Mexico: Siglo XXI Editores/UNESCO, 1972), 468.

~

Our lives are besieged by the small-mindedness of hatred, which only the grandeur of the soul, the magnanimous art of a collective invention that erupts with the force of a volcano, can counter.*

I think of the *pillán*, a Mapuche concept that is so vast and searing that no definition can contain it. To look for it in a book is to look for the sun in a spark; however, some books are also a *pillán*-echo.

> "This is a Mapuche term that has had various meanings through time, but which almost always refers to a powerful spirit that dwells in the mountains or volcanoes. Like all numinous beings, the *pillán* possesses positive and negative connotations. It has been defined as the spirit of the great ancestors who continue to watch over their descendants."
>
> — Sonia Montecinos, *Mitos de Chile, Diccionario de seres, magias y encantos* (Santiago: Editorial Sudamericana, Biblioteca del Bicentenario, 2003), 366.

May my Mapuche friends forgive me for this appropriation, but years ago I heard a Mapuche elder say that the *pillán* was in all of Chile, in the cordillera, and that it existed for all Chileans. His generous gift impressed me.

*As I write these lines, an announcement arrives of a new agreement of collaboration between the Constituent Convention and the Pontificia Universidad Católica of Valparaíso, through which there will be further discussion of digital contents on the process of eradicating hate speech.

I heard him again when I listened to Elisa Loncón Antileo on the day she was elected President of the Constituent Convention. Her words, in mapudungun and Spanish, offered a possible future that stirred in her emotional voice, because all the forces of the earth were present in this trembling, and those who listened to her, whether in Chile or New York, knew it, like the volcano knew it. The *pillán* made itself present in the tone of her voice and in what she said; the intention that moved her included multiple dimensions that wished to be heard, recognized in a speech directed at all of Chile, at the earth as a whole, and at all beings who wanted to hear.

In her words, there was neither vengefulness nor reproach, only the invitation to share, to converse on terms of equality and gender parity—that is, to do what has never been done before. Her breaking voice was the monu-mental act created by Chile's awakening, by herself, and the history of all those who suffered for centuries so that this moment could be possible.

She said:

> "We are here *pu lamngen*, to thank the support of the different coalitions that placed their confidence in us, who placed their dreams in the call ...
>
> We are very happy about this power you have given us, but this power is for all the people of Chile ... for all women and men ... we are putting in place here a way of being plural, a way of being democratic, a way of being participatory ...
>
> This Convention that I am called upon today to preside over will transform Chile into a plurinational Chile ... a Chile that cares for Mother Earth, a Chile that cleans its waters, in a Chile free from all domination ... this is a dream of our ancestors, this dream has been made a reality today ... All of us together, *pu lamngen*, we will remake this Chile."
>
> — Elisa Loncón Antileo, President,
> Constitutional Convention

The future depends on hearing these words, the collective *pillán* that comes to our aid, calling upon us to leave behind death, violence, and extinction and return to life, the music of the waters in the saliva that attends to the sound of the waterfalls.

~

The memory that we still do not recognize as "memory" contains the information and language we will need for what is to come.

A few days after her speech, I said the following in London:

> Elisa Loncón is also an oral poet ... and this comes from the tremor, from suffering, the terrible suffering that women have borne—especially the Indigenous women of Chile—for so long. From this emerges a *Pillán* ... the erupting strength of volcanoes regardless of conditions: positive, negative, or bad, no matter—the volcano emerges and changes everything. It is the unstoppable creative energy that characterizes the cosmos, earth, and the inner human being. So when a person like Elisa completely aligns herself with this force, an unstoppable beauty emerges .... Her speech was broadcast by CNN, but they did not translate it for the entire planet. Though this is precisely the speech this earth, this entire earth, needs, because it includes everything .... It is simply about how to build a future with real justice for all. And this concept is what this earth needs. Justice for earth, justice for water, justice for the protectors and defenders of water. Very few people know that the defenders of water are not only being murdered with impunity throughout the world, but that many countries are making laws to turn the defense of water into a crime. How will this earth that is being subjected to total destruction be ready for someone like Elisa Loncón?
>
> — "Art & Text as a Political Device: The Work of Cecilia Vicuña," Amalgama, Art London, July 13, 2021. Conversation between Camila Marambio and Cecilia Vicuña, forum TRAMA: Art & Language in Latin America.
>
> https://www.youtube.com/watch?v=nLwA-2Nxbck

The monu-mental task is to con-template the difference between what is and what could be. To re-imagine the humidity of the soil and our human humility guiding us towards the re-discovery of the senses of being.

New York, August 22, 2021

CECILIA VICUÑA

Poetry Inter-Actions

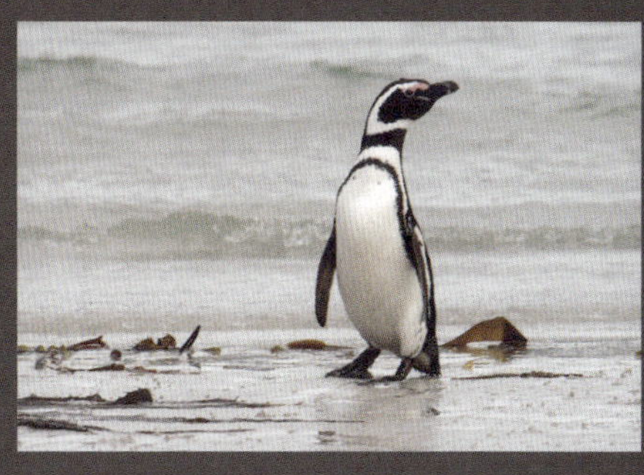

Magellanic penguin from ebird Macaulay Library ML 51753271.

Poetry inter-acts with history and time in non-linear ways. A poem is composed and lies in a corner, censored or forgotten, yet it acts just by existing.

The Sleeping Gypsy (A Lion Guards Her Dream Journal)

The Gypsy has been writing for many years
a secret text no one will ever
read, but which has begun
to materialize in real life.
While she continues dreaming
her dreams create the world.
The lion, however,
cannot sleep.
If he ceases to watch her,
she could awaken
and we vanish
instantly.

— Cecilia Vicuña (Translated by Rosa Alcalá)
Santiago, 1970

In 2006, high school students in Chile revolted against the inequality of an education system that favors the rich and abandons the poor. People dubbed their movement "La Revolución Pingüina" (The Penguin Revolution) because they had to navigate the schools' flooded hallways in their blue-black uniforms.

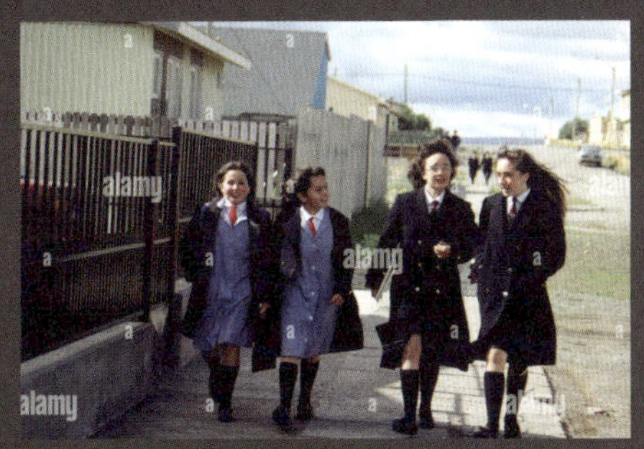

Schoolchildren in uniform, Punta Arenas, Chile.

En la mañana del 25 de abril, los estudiantes del liceo A-45 Carlos Cousiño, de la ciudad de Lota, toman su plantel en protesta por las malas condiciones de la edificación. El "liceo acuático," como lo llamaron, se haría famoso gracias a algunos videos que mostraban el agua corriendo por sus pasillos (Ramírez, 2016). Era el inicio del estallido social derivado de la precaria situación existente en los liceos municipales, con infraestructura y presupuestos insuficientes.

https://cubaxdentro.wordpress.com/2017/11/14/la-revolucion-chilena-de-los-pinguinos-y-la-tecnologia/
Por MS. Waldo Barrera Martínez

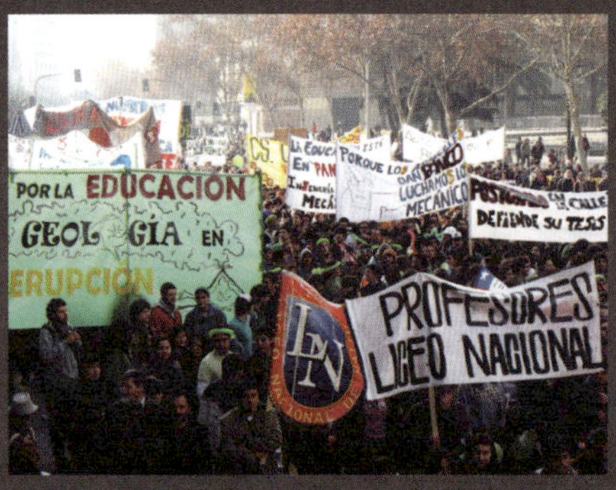

Chilean student protesters marched down La Alameda, the main avenue in Santiago in July 2011.

Thousands of students joined the movement demanding educational reform. They paralized cities for a few moments, and got a "reform" on paper, but no real change.

In 2011, college students rose all over Chile, demanding the end of education for profit: free education for all.

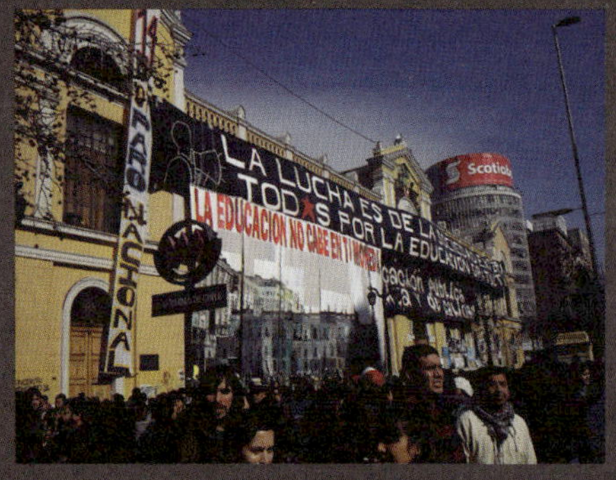

The sign reads: *La lucha es de la sociedad entera / Todos por la educación gratuita* (The fight is of the whole society / Everybody for free education).

The massive protests led to no structural change, but the students transformed the protests into collective performance art. On June 5, 2015, the students called a "besatón," a universal kissing event against violence.

Seeing this collective kissing of strangers reminded me of a censored poem I wrote in the 1970s, published in 2013, although the students most likely never read it.

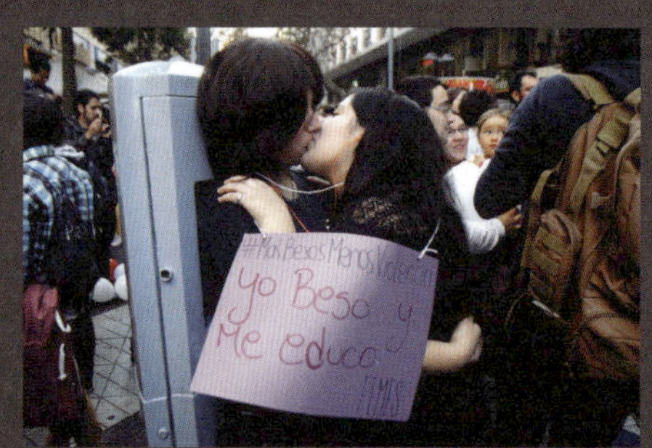

A group of Chilean students participates in the "Kiss-a-thon for education," convened on Friday, June 5, 2015, by the Federation of Secondary Students of the Metropolitan Region (Femes) in the center of Santiago de Chile.

Research Project

I propose we take a trip around the world,
to be officially designated:
"Socialist government
research project."
You and I will be
the "kissers."
We kiss better than anyone,
having developed
a meticulous
and carefully researched
method for perfecting the kiss.
There is no woman who kisses like me
nor man who kisses like you.
As THE KISSERS we'll kiss
every person
we meet
to determine
who does it better
and learn accordingly
from their technique,
we'll practice it
and without delay bring it back
to our socialist country,
which will be land of The Kissers.

April 1971

— Cecilia Vicuña
(Translated by Rosa Alcalá)

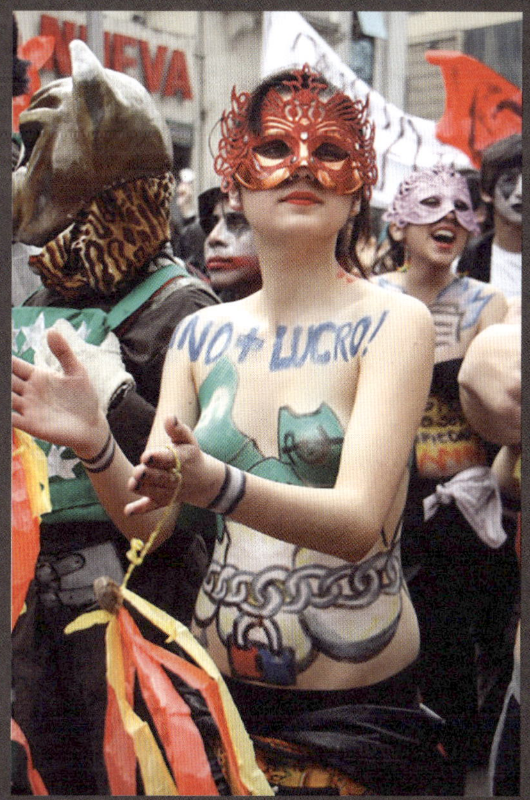

Naked and semi-naked rallies: "No + Lucro" (No More Profit), Santiago de Chile, 2011.

Naked and semi-naked rallies began soon after: "No + Lucro" (No More Profit).

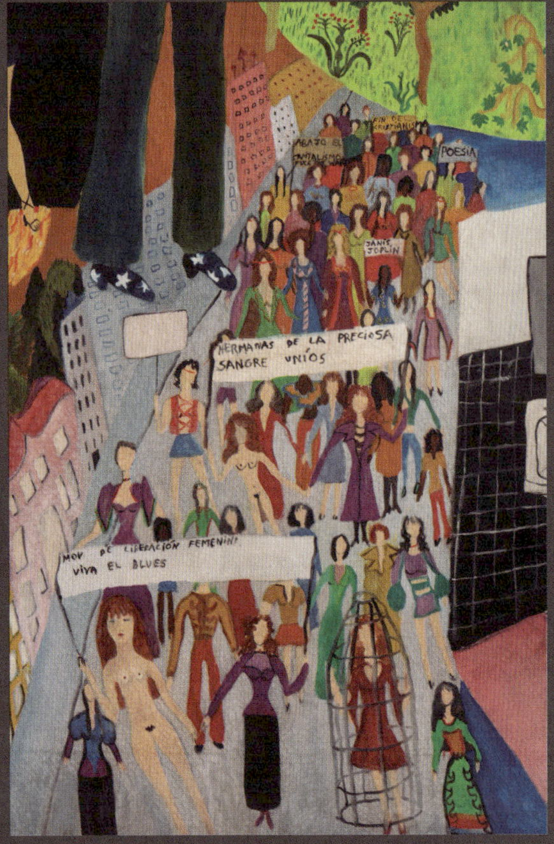

Cecilia Vicuña, detail of *Janis-Joe*, 1971.

The body language of young girls in the streets reminded me of a work I painted in 1971, depicting naked women rallying with banners saying: "Down with Capitalism," "End Christianism," "Poetry," "Women's Liberation," "Janis Joplin," "Long Live the Blues," "Sisters of the Precious Blood."

The dream images created before the military coup of September 11, 1973, and the new struggles, met in the streets.

Celebrating the students' protests, I joined them with my red threads.

In May 2018, el "Mayo Feminista" (The Feminist May) began in the south of Chile, and spread like a tsunami, with young girls demanding an end to sexual harassment in universities.
A different kind of feminism emerged, riding the strength of the #MeToo and #NiUnaMas movements, to stop gender violence.

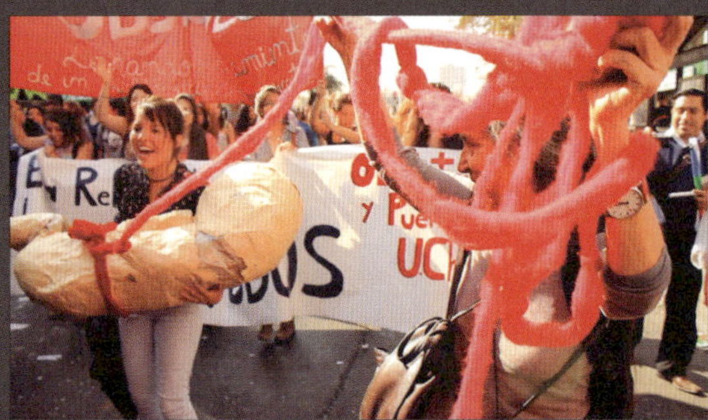

Student rally, Santiago 2015. Standing for reproductive rights, a girl with a fetus, and my red threads.

Until then, my poetry had been censored and ignored in Chile, yet an anonymous photo posted on Instagram showed my work being handed over by feminist students in the southern city of Temuco.

In October 2019, high school students, led by young girls, suddenly jumped a turnstile in a subway station in Santiago to protest a fare hike, and this act spread in no time through the whole of Chile, initiating the "Estallido Social" (Social Explosion), the greatest movement Chile had seen since the 1970s.

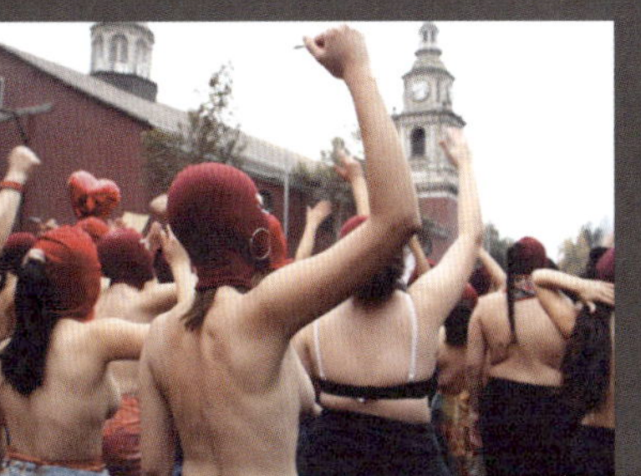

Gender and Equity Watchdog, Santiago de Chile, 2018.

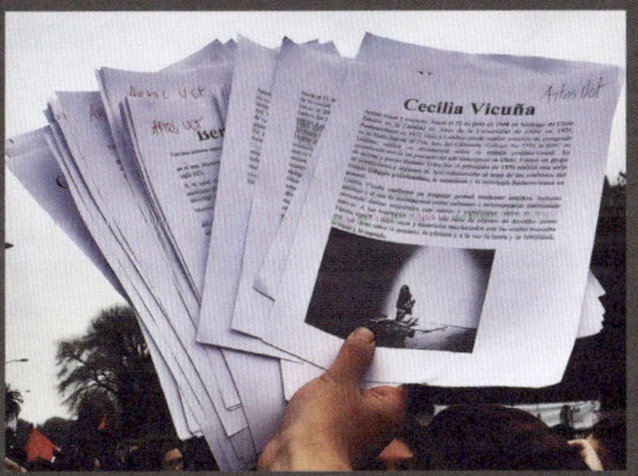

May 16, 2018, action carried out during the "March for a non-sexist education."

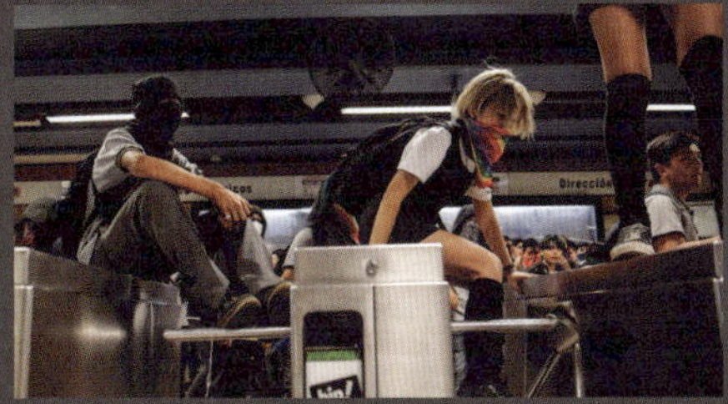

In early October 2019, high school students in Santiago started jumping turnstiles to ska music all over the city, ostensibly in protest against a public transit fare increase.

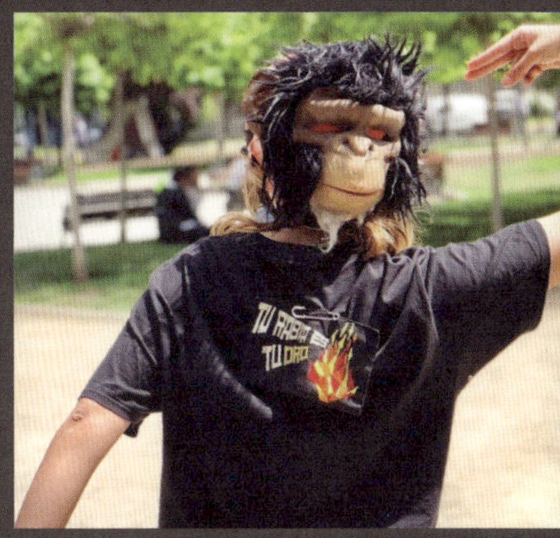

"Tu rabia es tu oro" (Your rage is your gold) palabrarma by Cecilia Vicuña.

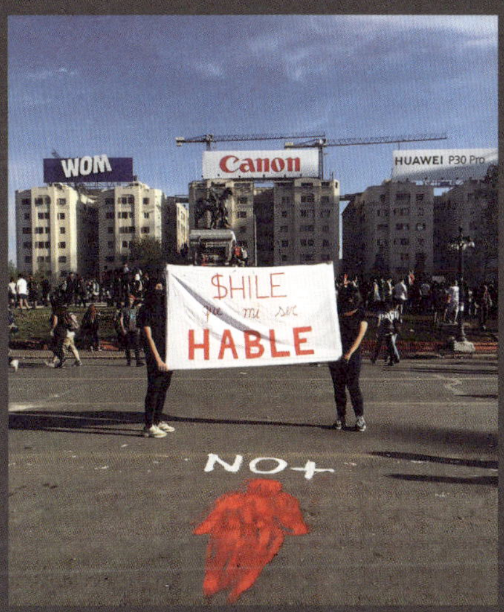

"Miserable, que mi ser hable."(Miserable, let my being speak.) palabrarma by Cecilia Vicuña; October 21, 2019; "Demonstrations during the social revolt," action carried out by the Artistic Collective "Corporeal Intimacy;" Mar Valderrama, Paula Tramolao, Eduardo Filún, and Matías Fuentes.

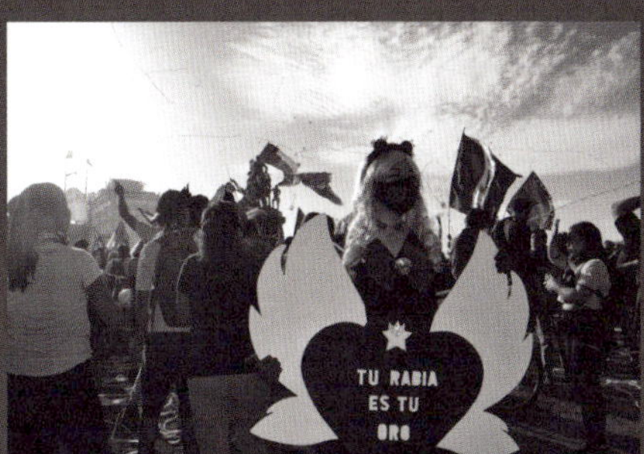

"50 dias en Plaza Dignidad" (50 days in Plaza Dignidad), performance by Leslie Núñez in Plaza Dignidad, Santiago de Chile. "Amuletos en resistencia: ¡Transformación!" (Amulets in resistance: Transformation!), Balmaceda Arte Joven, 2020.

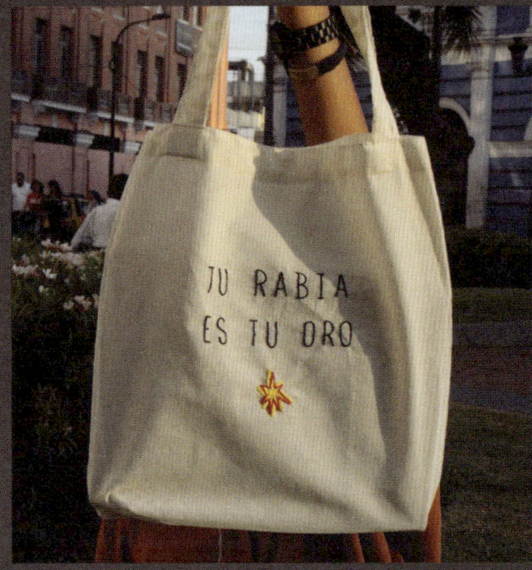

"Tu rabia es tu oro" (Your rage is your gold) palabrarma by Cecilia Vicuña.

Things culminated with 1.2 million people defying violent police repression "No son thirty pesos, son thirty años" (It's not thirty pesos, it's thirty years) was a leitmotif; the thirty-peso fare hike broke the promise that democracy had made over thirty years earlier.

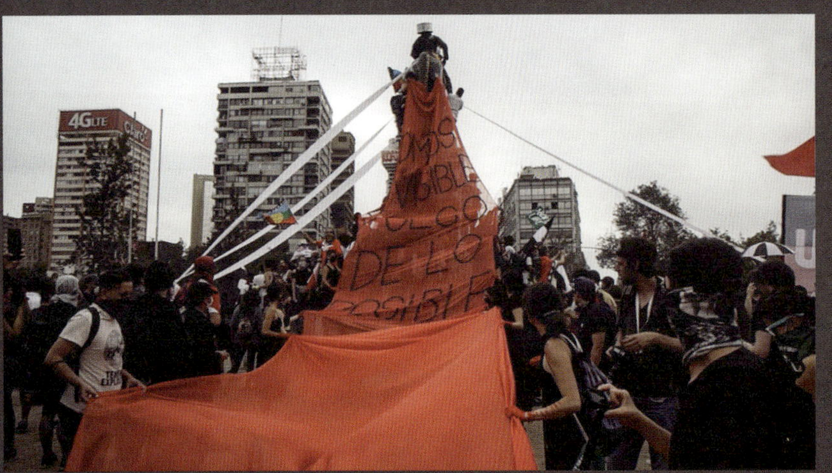

"Somos el Visible Pulso de lo Imposible"(We are the visible pulse of the impossible) palabrarma by Cecilia Vicuña, displayed by the Colectivo La Casa de las Recogidas, en Plaza Dignidad, Santiago, November 22, 2020.

The massive protests included not just the young, as older generations joined too. The city walls became a site for poetry and art made by all, and the rallies evolved into multiple performances.

In this context my "Palabrarmas," the word-weapon-poems I'd created in 1974 to oppose the dictatorship—opening words to reveal their inner metaphors—began to appear on the walls and people's bodies as well as in massive performances.

More complex poems of mine were also transformed into large collective performances.

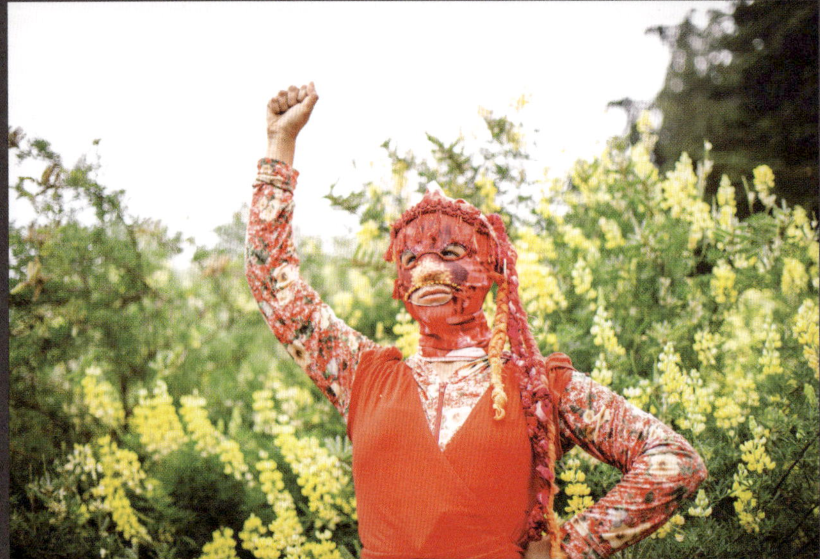

"Somos el Visible Pulso de lo Imposible" (We are the visible pulse of the impossible) palabrarma by Cecilia Vicuña, Performance de Capuchas Rojas (Performance of Red Hoods) in resistance in the petrel wetland, Pichilemu. Performer: Cata Conejo.

Despite the violent response of the police, the uprising against injustice and inequality went on in the streets of Chile with people chanting "Despertó, despertó" (the people awoke) until COVID-19 hit. But even after lockdown, people persisted and won the right, in a national plebiscite, to create a new Constitution for Chile, drafted by a constituent assembly elected by popular vote. A right achieved through the sacrifice of hundreds of people jailed, murdered, or blinded by the police aiming at young people's eyes, as if seeing the truth of the unfair system had become a crime.

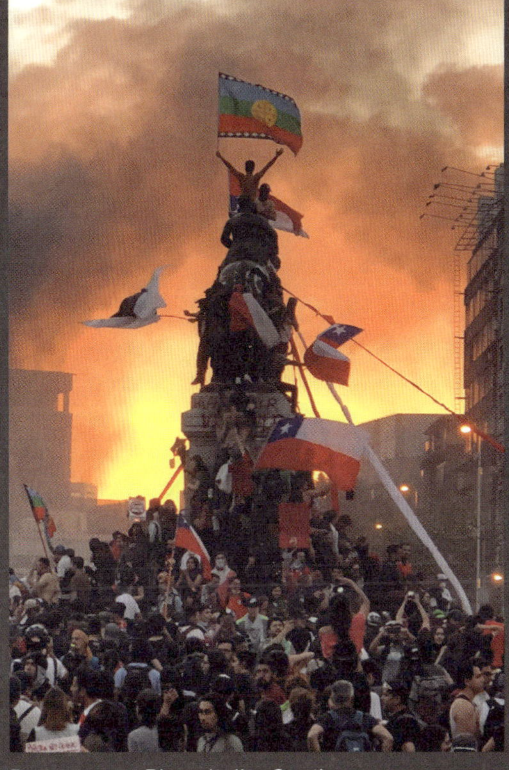

Protesters at Plaza Italia, Santiago on October 25, 2019 during Chile's Estallido Social (Social Outburst) with a protester flying the Mapuche flag on top of the Baquedano monument.

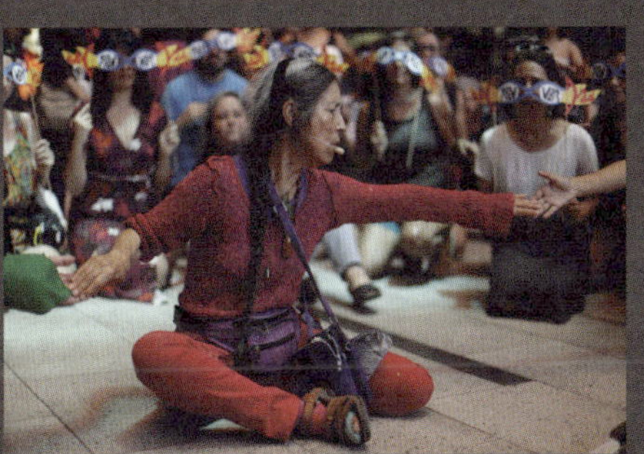

"El Veroir Comenzó" (Seehearing began), reactivating the Palabrarmas Ver dad (Truth), GAM Gabriela Mistral Cultural Center in Santiago, 2019.

In December 2019 I joined the Estallido Outburst in Santiago to perform a collective ritual homage to the hundreds of people who lost their eyes to police brutality: "El Veroir Comenzó" (Seehearing began), reactivating the palabrarma "Ver dad" (Truth): to give sight—"glasses to see the truth"—that I had created in exile in 1974. Together and crying, we experienced the verb "veroir" (seehear) now embodied by the awakened people of Chile.

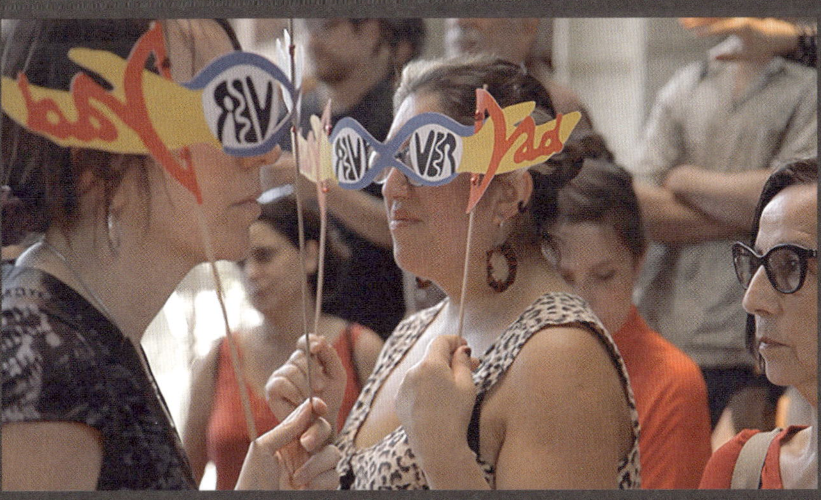

Performing a collective ritual homage to the hundreds of people who lost their eyes to police brutality, Santiago, December 2019.

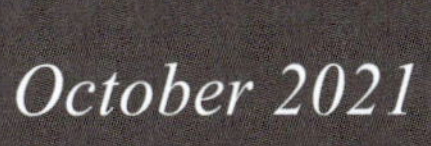

October 2021

Big Brother Knows No Joke: the Battle to Control the Past in Bangkok's Streets

168

THONGCHAI WINICHAKUL
Interview by Cosmin Costinaş and Inti Guerrero

COSMIN COSTINAŞ & INTI GUERRERO

The events of Sunday, September 20, 2020—when student activists cemented the commemorative People's Plaque close to the royal field, which read, "The people have expressed the intention that this country belongs to the people and not the King"—were an important gesture in relation to the contemporary conversation around monuments and how they affect historical memory and ideas of heritage, as well as in the context of this time when monuments are being torn down around the world and simultaneously other objects of heritage are being reclaimed.

In this transfer of objects—this up and down, from pedestal to ground, from colonial museums to post-colonial states and Indigenous communities—we are fascinated by this example of a transitory monument, nevertheless employing the most official language of monumentality, albeit humorously, being used in the context of a protest, and moreover in a protest set along the lines of dismantling a certain dominant idea of the nation. Humor has been another important part of strategies of protests across Asia in this new wave of Pan-Asian discontent, from Thailand and Hong Kong to Myanmar, which has nevertheless turned very dark in most instances. While acknowledging the role of humor, you've also expressed that humor might not be an appropriate key for dealing with current political issues in light of the repression that's now occurring.

THONGCHAI WINICHAKUL

Leading up to September 20, 2020, the protest movement called for an overnight gathering (to which somewhere between 30,000 and 50,000 people would show up) at the place we call in Thai *Sanam Luang* (Royal Ground). It is a place of traditional significance, a huge field in front of the Grand Palace, used in the past for public events and the cremation of high royalty. That's why it is also sometimes called *Tung Pra Me'ru* (Crematory Ground). It's probably the largest public space in Bangkok, about four or five soccer fields big, so in the last forty to fifty years it became the place for key political gatherings. It was also a site for general public gathering, for purposes like the weekend market that was held for about twenty years when I was young. During weekdays, it was a place where kids went cycling, playing soccer, flying kites. Then they closed the market down because it had become unsanitary. They first tried to gentrify it, but ended up moving the whole market. In the last decade or so they've been closing off this space from public use in daily life, reserving it only for state events.

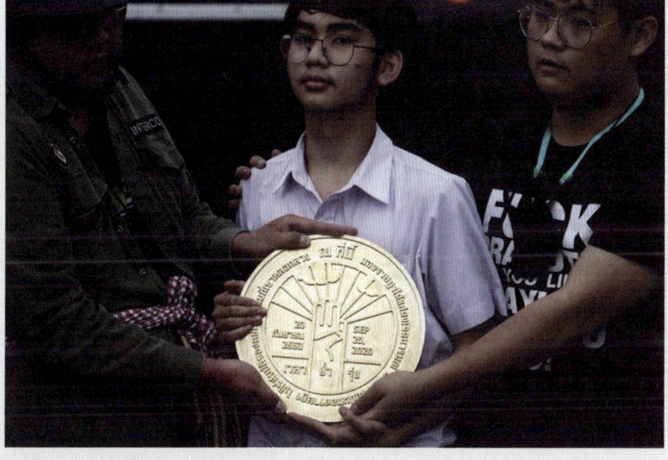

FIG 1 Student leaders install a plaque declaring "This country belongs to the people" during a mass rally to call for the ousting of Prime Minister Prayuth Chan-ocha and reforms in the monarchy, near the Grand Palace in Bangkok, Thailand, September 20, 2020. Photo: Reuters/Athit Perawongmetha.

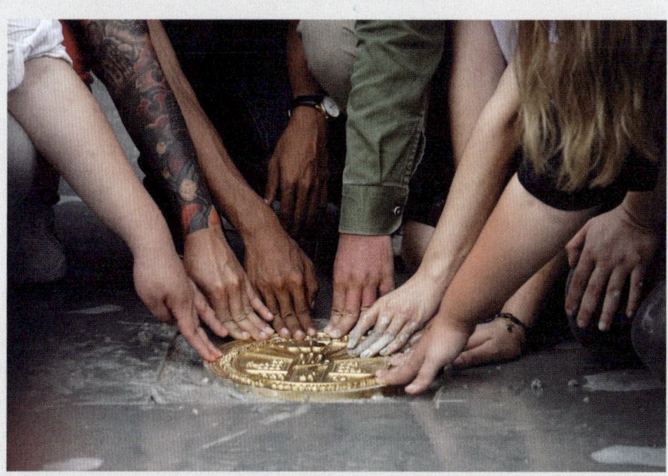

FIG 2 Protest leaders place a commemorative plaque at the Royal Grounds in Bangkok, September 20, 2020. Courtesy Nontarat Phaicharoen / BenarNews.

Last year, after people had protested in a few other places, they wanted a bigger gathering place for a large protest, so they came to the Royal Ground. They renamed the place (which none of the officials cared about) to "People's Ground." After protesting all night, with speakers and music etc., in the early morning, around 6 a.m., they held an unannounced symbolic gesture in the form of a ritual, installing a plaque onto the Royal Ground to declare it the People's Ground.

Now, in relation to this plaque I need to give a bit of context. In recent years, Pierre Nora's *Realms of Memory* (1981–98), the three-volume treatise on sites of public memory, has somehow become alive in Bangkok. There were attempts to remove what we can consider as the "sites of memory" of the People's Party, which launched a successful revolution in 1932, ending the absolute monarchy. Thailand has been officially calling itself a democracy since then. Of course, unofficially it's another story: so many coups represented the push and pull between royalists/conservatives and various democratic movements over the past ninety years. The former has tried to establish some form of regime that gives the monarch increasing political power, although it stops short of the official, direct, overt political authority over elected officials or formal government. In 1947 the People's Party was ousted. Thailand did not return to an absolute monarchy, but to extended periods of military rule with the royalists as partners to the ruling regime. Officially, the King was separate from politics, but in fact he was part of it. From 1947–73, Thailand was under military rule most of the time. In 1973, a People's uprising brought democracy, but at the same time this was a turning point from which the royalists have had the upper hand over the military until today, gaining influence over it and within its ranks. Since 1992, under the leadership of King Rama IX (who passed away in 2016), this dominance accelerated, with the royalists becoming the leading force in Thailand. While they allowed elections, in effect the government has been subservient to the authority of the monarch. Since the 1980s, in terms of social and cultural conditions, a phenomenon which I call "hyper-royalism" developed, a stronger and intensified royalism based on hyperbole about royal members, exalted glorification, "the king is the best at so many things," "Thailand, an ode to the monarchy," etc. And a great number of monuments were erected for the royals. Royalism controls the time, becoming the seasonal and annual staple, including public holidays. They even changed the National Day to the King's birthday, Father's Day and Mother's Day to the King's and Queen's birthdays. Almost every year, invariably, there is a huge celebration of something to do with Kings and Queens. Anyone who said that modernity is more secular is, I think, mistaken. In Thailand, the monarchy is still sacred.

The elected government of prime minister Thaksin Shinawatra (2001–6) tried to reform the government and the bureaucratic system in ways that undermined the royalists' ability to interfere with policy, personnel, and big projects, as they had regularly done. Thaksin wasn't anti-royalist, far from it, yet somehow his projects in effect undermined the royal dominance. Hence the royalist military coup in 2006. In the elections the year after, Thaksin's party came back to power again, but without Thaksin. In 2008, the PAD (People's Alliance for Democracy), the misnomer right-wing royalist movement, clashed with the police. One of the protesters died. The Queen visited her funeral praising her as a national hero. The growing disillusion with the monarchy since the coup was then confirmed. That day was called the Eye-opening Day or Day of Awakening. Since then, all histories that were critical to the monarchy have been revived, especially the 1932 revolution. Somehow the democratic popular movements before 2006 didn't pay much attention to the 1932 revolution, probably because those people grew up during the time when the royalist domination had erased the memory and damaged the meaning of the revolution. But since 2006, the memory of the 1932 revolution has had a new life.

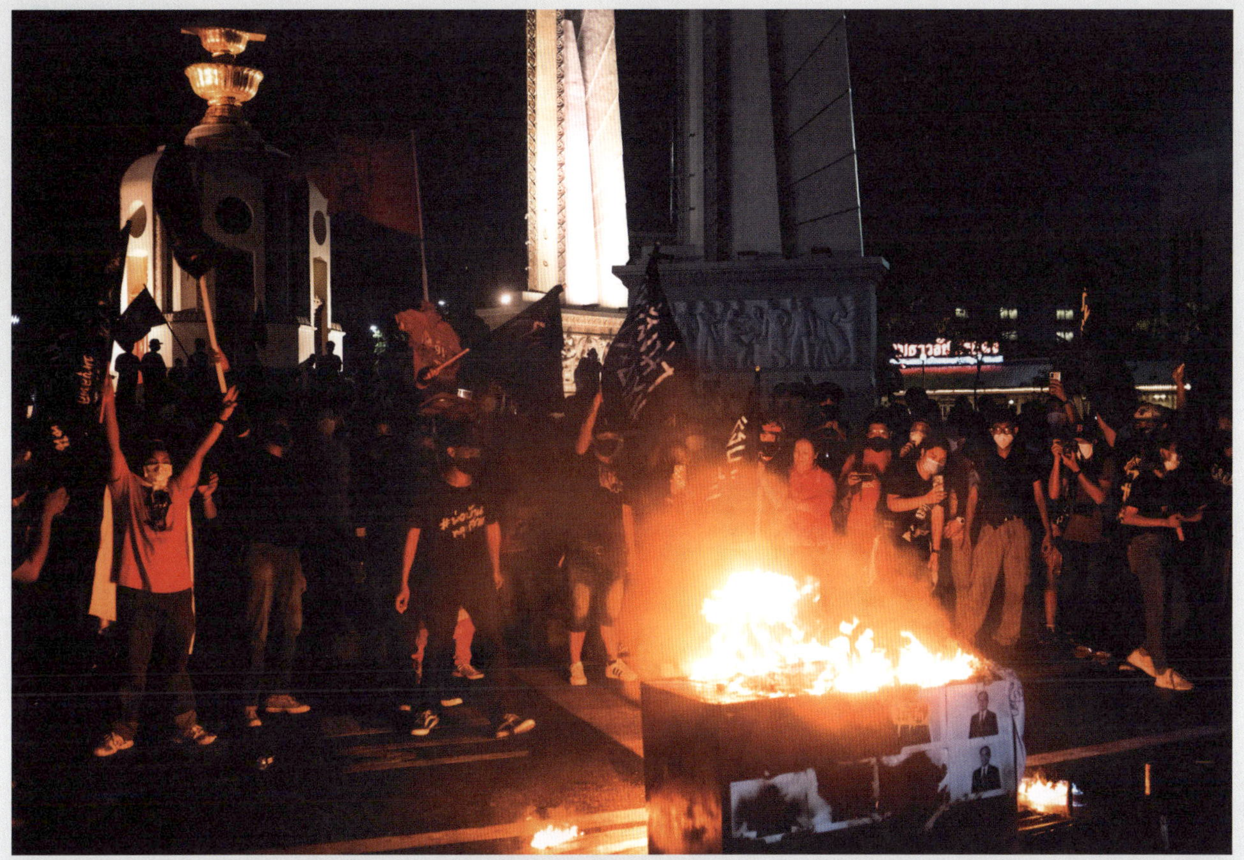

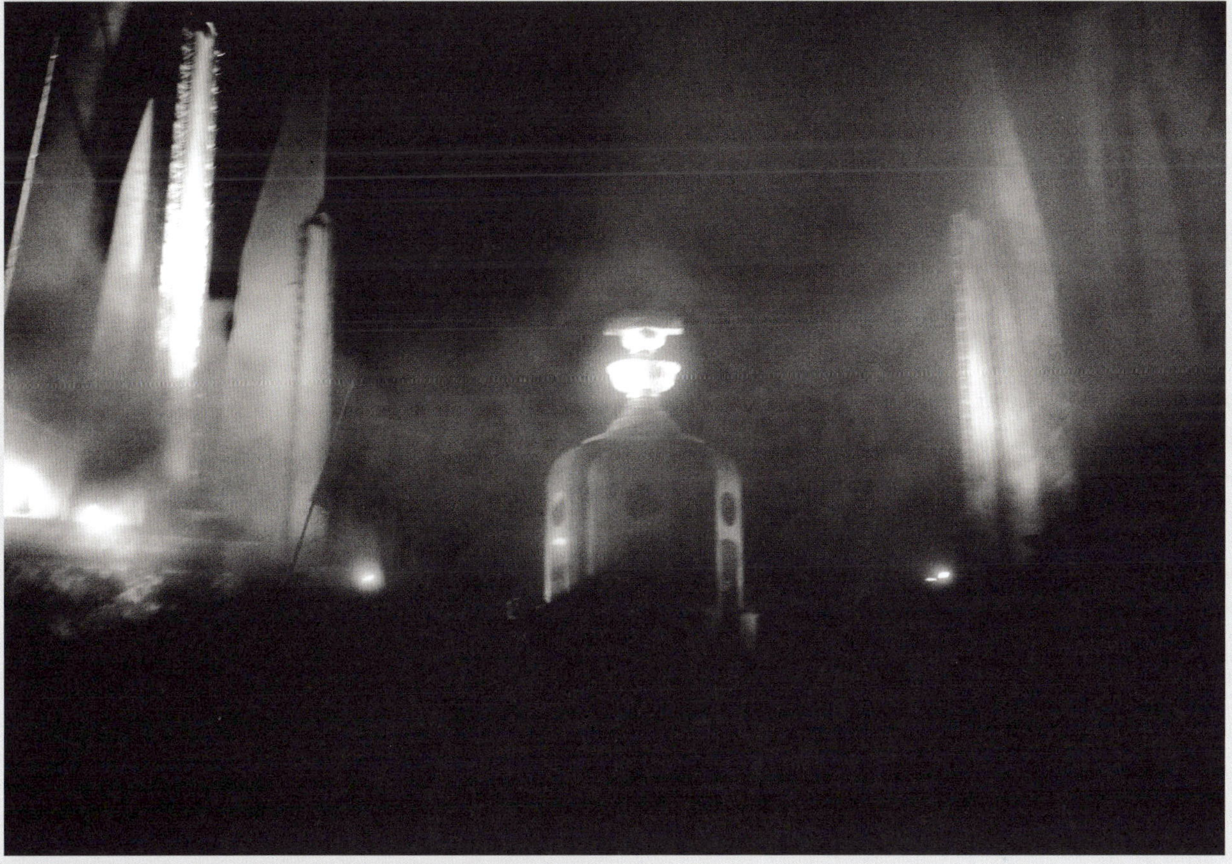

FIG 3-4 April 10, 2022: Youth pro-democracy anti-government protesters joining with the Red-shirt protesters, or Thailand's United Front for Democracy against Dictatorship (UDD), reacted as they burned a mock coffin decorated with portraits of Prayut Chan-o-cha, the Prime minister of Thailand, during the rally at the Democracy Monument in Bangkok, in memory of those who died in the 2010 military crackdown. Image courtesy Vinai Dithajohn.

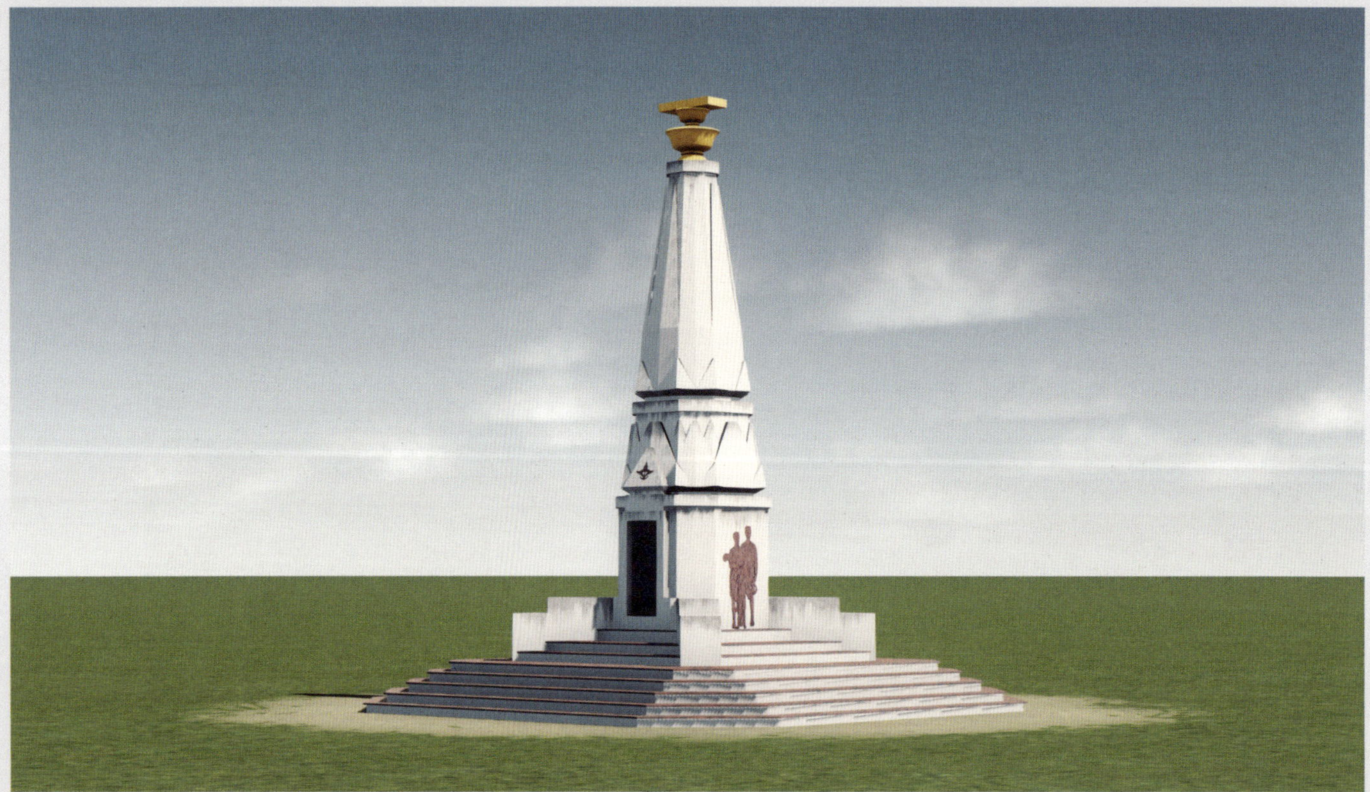

FIG 5 Lak Si Monument. Image courtesy Marconok19 (Nensat C.), amateur asset creator for Cities: Skylines.

Despite the royalist coup in 2006, the royal-military regime failed to subdue the huge popular democratic movement. Hence, another royalist coup occurred in 2014, backed by the palace, which was one of the most oppressive, comparable to the 1957 coup, putting hundreds of people in jail—dozens of them for *lèse-majesté*. Many measures were implemented trying to restrict freedom of speech and public gatherings. The severe suppression by the royalist regime was the immediate context of the removal of the 1932 sites of memory. However, these removals backfired, sharply raising the public awareness of the revolution and its relevance in the present.

Thanks to the revival of public interest in recent years, publications of historical studies have become popular. Some of them sold like hot cakes, particularly since the 2014 coup. An interesting phenomenon I have observed is that, for some reason, quite active works critical to the monarchy have come from the fields of art and architectural history. As the royalists have begun to demolish People's Party buildings and removed many 1932 sites of memory, we see the increase of publications, lectures, theses, and walking tours, about the People's Party sites and their philosophy, implying of course why the demolitions happened.

CC

I was reading that they're planning to add Thai decorations to the modernist buildings lining the boulevard around the Democracy Monument ...

TW

That's right, because the idea is to make it a royal boulevard again, the "Royal Avenue," as it is officially called. This avenue links the old Grand Palace with the modern palace. The Grand Palace was the Monarch's residence until Rama V (1868–1910), who built the connecting avenue together with a new palace, a modern marble building. In the surrounding area they are all new palaces in the modern style. The original plan in the 1900s was that the two sides of this long street would be lined with buildings in the modern royal style. But the project was not realized. The People's Party then modified the project with buildings along the boulevard in the style they preferred, including the fascist style of the 1920s and 1930s, which in their view, before WWII, represented modernity. The major figure behind the foundation of the art school in Thailand, glorified as a kind of father of modern art in the country, was an Italian, Corrado Feroci. He wasn't particularly famous in Italy when he was hired in Bangkok to establish the art college that would become the fine arts university, Silpakorn University. He designed and created many monuments including the Democracy Monument, a huge memorial at the midpoint of the royal boulevard, to commemorate the 1932 revolution. So you could say that the Thai democracy monument for the revolutionaries who overthrew the absolute monarchy was built under a fascist artistic influence. Full of ironies!

Many buildings of the People's Party have become targets of the royalist conservatives for demolition. Various reasons were always given. But the royalist anti-democratic actions since the 2006 coup helped people become aware of the true nature of the royalist project.

At one corner of the Royal Avenue, there used to be a very famous movie theater built around the 1940s. But it was in front, and blocked the view of a classical temple built by King Rama III (1824–51). In the 1980s, the movie theater was demolished to clear the view of the royal monastery. At the time I didn't realize it was a royalist project. But after 2006, those kinds of demolition projects intensified. Three or four huge buildings of the People's Party with rich symbolism of the revolution against absolute monarchy were demolished, including the judiciary complex that was replaced by buildings in the royal modern style. The public never got an honest reason: "It's hard to maintain. It's not beautiful. We are going to build a new one in a beautiful Thai style with a traditional rooftop," etc. Architecture and art historians protested, but the government didn't listen. In fact, the royalists did the exact opposite. Since the present king came to the throne in 2016, the palace has begun to reclaim those lands and buildings and made them crown properties, including the only public zoo in Bangkok and the parliament halls. Several major streets were made part of the royal complex, not for public use any more. Places that were founded and named after leaders of the 1932 revolution were either demolished, remade, or at the least renamed.

Another interesting case was the monument to commemorate the victory over the counter revolutionary coup in 1933. One year after the end of absolute monarchy, a civil war was instigated by the monarchists. Thousands of soldiers clashed on the outskirts of Bangkok—which today is an area inside the city, and the rebellion was quelled. The People's Party built a monument at the site of the battle to commemorate the sacrifice. Over time, this place evolved from being just a huge isolated field with a monument, becoming a dense business and residential area (and one with the worst traffic problem in Bangkok). So, in the late 1990s, the government relocated the monument to a nearby location for the expansion of traffic lanes, and in 2010 it was proposed to remove it to make way for an elevated road. After protests by scholars and the public, since it was registered as a historical site, the removal was delayed. However, in December 2018, the monument disappeared without notice. Ever since, nobody knows where it is. The government agency in charge of historical sites refuses to get involved, mysteriously saying that the removal was beyond their authority.

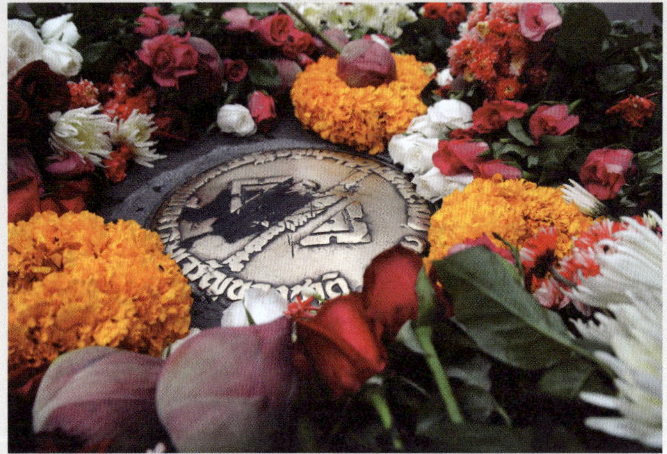

FIG 6 A plaque that was embedded in front of Bangkok's Ananta Samakhom Throne Hall was occasionally decorated with flowers by activists. It read: "Here on June 24, 1932, at dawn, the People's Party proclaimed a constitution for the country's advancement." Photo courtesy Nick Nostitz.

Now, more context on the plaque of People's Ground. Shortly after the 1932 revolution, the leader of the People's Party stood among the public and his supporters to read their first announcement. "At this place, six o'clock in the morning of June 24, 1932, people declared the end of absolute monarchy. And the People's Party was established in the new regime under six principles ... (1, 2, 3, 4, 5, 6). Thailand will be forever prosperous, etc ...." At the place where he read this declaration, the People's Party made a little plaque, about a foot in diameter, and installed it on the ground. It was there for decades, including the period when the memory of the People's Party faded away and people did not care much about that historic event anymore. If you know the equestrian monument of King Rama V on horseback in Bangkok, the plaque was beside that monument, not because they wanted to celebrate the monarch, but because on the day of the revolution in 1932, the revolutionaries put the high royals in the marble palace behind the monument, locking them up, and declaring the revolution a success in front of that palace. But the People's Party didn't remove the equestrian monument. They just put a little plaque next to it. For decades, as the Bangkok traffic became terrible, cars ran over the plaque every day, as it sat in the middle of a main street. Most people didn't know it was there until after 2006, so, ironically, it was thanks to the coup that it emerged from neglect. The plaque thus became a thorn on the side for the royalists. Then one night, in April 2017, it was removed from the ground. In its place a new plaque was installed, newly made and still shining in its golden color. The inscription on it says something like: "People with happy face live in this kingdom with prosperity and happiness blah, blah, blah."

We can't say the royalists lack a sense of humor, even if they were serious in what they did. The general reaction was fury at the loss of the original plaque. At the same time, people greeted the new plaque with humor—like a hilarious meme. You can talk to anyone in Thailand about "the happy face plaque" and people would know what you mean. The fact remains, however, that the plaque was stolen. It was a crime. All relevant government agencies were evasive about what they would do. Some bluntly refused to get involved, mysteriously saying something like: "We can't say anything about this." There seemed to be something or someone at play that could not be mentioned. Their responses were in coded language, making the public realize that what happened went all the way up through the ranks of authority. The news about the incident in the mainstream media suddenly stopped. Officially, the incident of vanishing plaque didn't exist, it never took place. After the loss of the plaque, there was a huge project announced by the new king to turn the whole area of the original plaque into a flower garden as part of the new palace ground. Despite its disappearance, the plaque remains a thorn in their side. It gained more fame, becoming a meme, commodified as a sticker, a fridge magnet, a key chain, a clock face, a saucer, and more. Stories of the revolution are thus reiterated many times, both in print and online.

CC

The happy face of the people is now covered as well?

TW

Yes, that's gone too, underneath the garden. It didn't work, except for being a subject of ridicule. Today the spot has become part of the palace ground, inaccessible to the public.

Now, the whole hour we've talked so far was just covering context. Let's say it is political context and even a bit of art historical context as a preface to the 2020 attempt to establish a new plaque and make the whole Royal Ground in front of the Grand Palace public ground. As mentioned earlier, many significant political gatherings happened there, as well as the weekend market and the playground for kids. So, in practice it had been a public place for decades. Now, on that night of September 23, 2020, when protesters installed the new plaque, they performed a ritual. They knew that they couldn't stage a Buddhist ritual as it is the official religion. So, they made it look more magical and Hindu-like. In Thailand, Hinduism is perceived as more of a code for magic, superstition, and vernacular forms of the sacred; it is different from

Hinduism in India, or even Singapore or Malaysia. The people who installed it wore white and chanted in made-up words that sounded like Sanskrit, but it wasn't Sanskrit. The general public who participated in the ritual remained silent, thinking perhaps that it was real. And it took the government officials and conservative intellectuals much effort to debunk it as a fake ritual. Finally, the person who performed the ritual admitted that it was fake and that he didn't even know what he said. Of course, that plaque was then removed within twenty-four hours by the police, but it was already established in people's minds that, yes, a battle for that place did occur. I find the role of humor to be very powerful here. This kind of combination of elements is a high point in my view—the way they made fun of the power play and cover-up. In this case the protesters didn't even try to make their own event look sacred or powerful, they just made fun of themselves, and they made fun of other people too. They didn't care too much.

In the US, I love night-time talk shows (Comedy Central, etc.) because the comedians there are politicized. Non-political comedy, like The Three Stooges, etc., just smashing each other, for example, has gone, or is at least marginalized. Even the stand-up comedians in small theaters in the US today must involve political satire, or social satire at least. The big ones on TV right now still include some dirty jokes, but it is mainly political and social satire. And I used to compare this to Thailand because political satire and social satire almost didn't exist in Thailand, where comedians and jokes were more about just smashing people, slapstick, and telling dirty jokes. In Thailand in previous decades, we've included a lot of music and jokes through skits. But in recent Thai protests, there were plenty of humorous speeches. The guy who wore white and chanted in fake Sanskrit often gave an entirely satirical performance. After that event in September 2020, he became famous and started giving public speeches in front of thousands of people at every protest; he offers political and social satires as entire speeches, like an American stand-up comedian in a theater or late-night TV show.

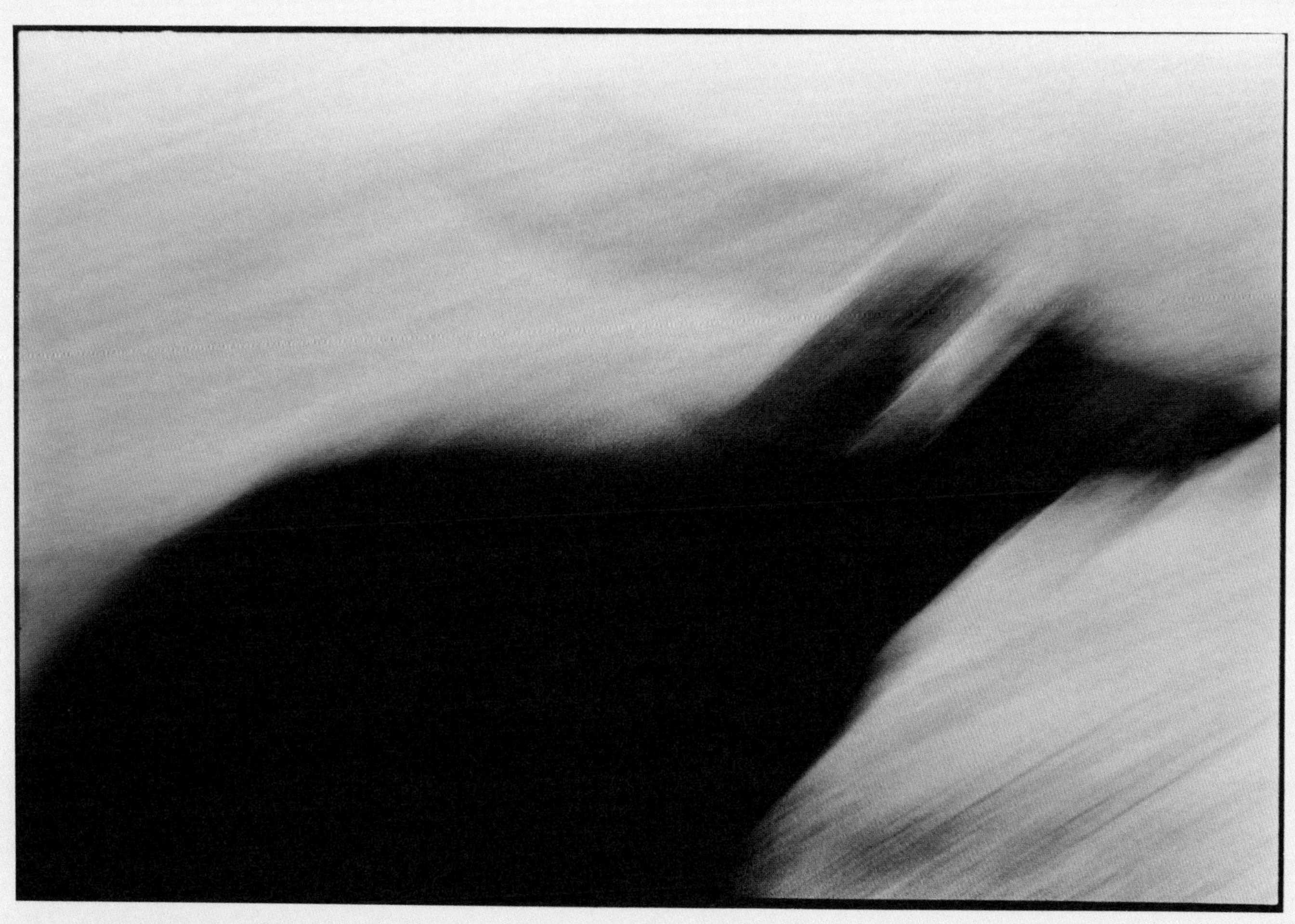

FIG 7 Liam Morgan, *Game 1–3*. 2015.
Image courtesy the artist.

While some of the protests mainly featured speakers, there have been several others called Mob Fests (in Thai, "mob" is not a bad term because it means something like "public protest" without having any gangster connotations). Whenever there is a Mob Fest you get dozens of small music bands, theater groups, parades, etc. It's like a carnival! And they have had these events three or four times in the past year or so. LGBT groups are included and featured prominently too. There are various performances and speeches, but with satire and lots of jokes against the government and royals. This was the tone of an event in July 2020 when a protest leader pronounced that, in his view, the monarchy is the key political problem. The speech was serious, explaining point by point why the monarchy is a problem, such as endorsing the coup, protecting the

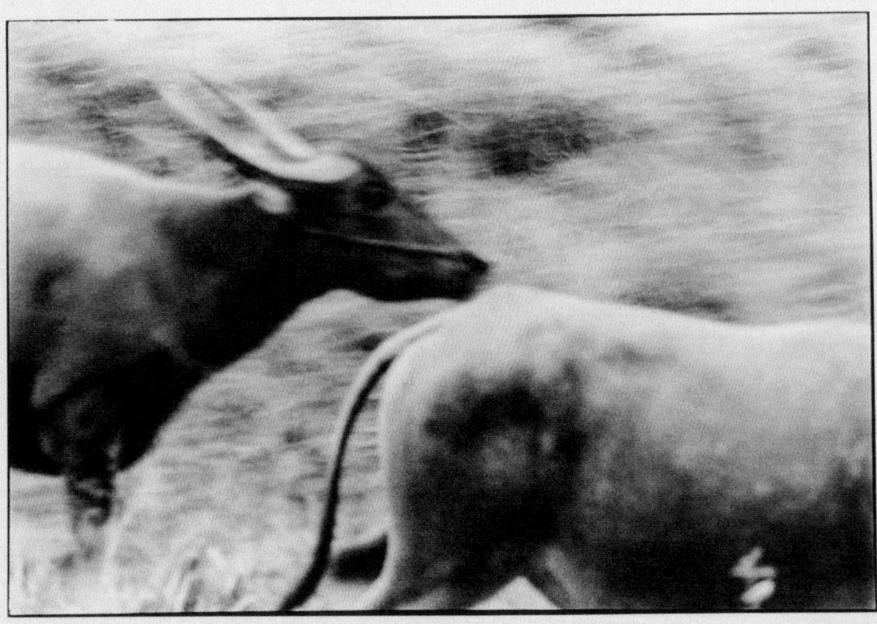

FIG 8 Liam Morgan, *Game 1–12*. 2015. Image courtesy the artist.

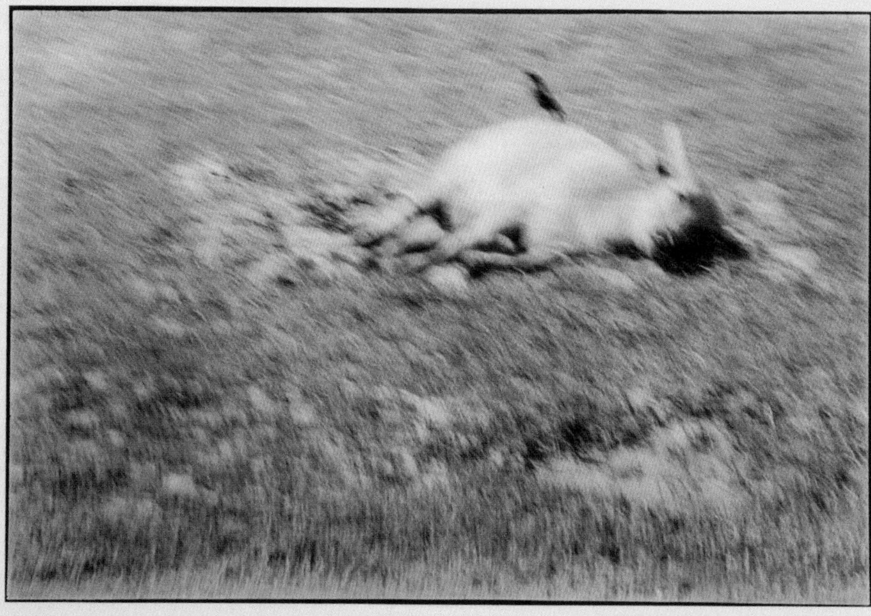

FIG 9 Liam Morgan, *Game 1–22*. 2015. Image courtesy the artist.

coup leaders, and so on. But the event was called the Harry Potter Gathering because it was carnival-like. The leader who made such a speech is a lawyer named Anon Nampa. He wore the Harry Potter costume, held a wand, and read the proclamation explaining how the monarchy is a problem of the country. (He was later charged and jailed for *lèse-majesté* for his action in that event.) At that moment, the gathering wasn't big, maybe only a hundred people at one corner of a street, but, not long afterwards, on August 10, the gathering at Thammasat University of 50–60,000 people made forceful arguments about how they wanted the monarchy to be reformed. Those events led up to the September 20 plaque event. The humor they employed on that day really made the authorities scramble. They tried to say that the burying of the new plaque at the Royal Ground was illegitimate because it wasn't a real ritual. But nobody cared that it wasn't a real ritual. People knew that, but they also knew that the action was very meaningful.

Humor is powerful. Even though protests always have a serious point to make, humor really has the power to make them more subversive. It is less confrontational, but more subversive in meaning: it's the carnivalesque. Nonetheless, the reason the protest movement has lost its playful spirit lately is that most of its leaders are now in jail, denied bail, or got bail on conditions that they have to end their political activities. Even one web designer who made lots of fun of the authorities online has been put in jail. It's too serious now. And maybe the authorities are "right," because the movement was too subversive for them. Perhaps academic language like mine is less radical. Maybe the authorities aren't stupid in how seriously they take subversive humor.

CC & IG

In the 1980s Soviet Union and Eastern Bloc, where of course there was much humor about the regime and communism and the West etc., there was an idea among people that these jokes were actually created by the secret services as a way to give the people a space to express discontent without overthrowing the regime. There were all these conspiracy theories that jokes about communism were actually created by the KGB.

TW

I don't know much about the Soviet Union but, yes, I know some Soviet jokes. It's hard to trace the origins and creators of humor. I don't know if any of them were put in jail. In the Thai case, in a period of less than two years they have mostly been put in jail. But it doesn't mean those jokes have stopped because it's so hard to trace the origin of a joke. Multiple people are involved. Often humor is an initial reaction to something the regime does and then serious protest action comes later. Listening to you talking about the Soviet Union, I think the way Thais are using humor now is so subversive partly because people can't speak and criticize the monarchy in normal language—they actually have to turn to humor to accurately express what is happening, and hopefully evade the police. Have they done so successfully? It looks like they haven't, but yet it also looks like they're successful in sabotaging and undermining the official meanings of certain things. People make jokes about the monarchy all the time these days without mentioning their names, for example.

I find it interesting culturally that nowadays when someone ridicules the Democracy Monument for its fascist art built by fascist artists, many people defend the monument, not because it's beautiful but because it represents anti-monarchist history. It embodies a meaningful memory. These defenders of the legacies of the People's Party were at the fore when the public theater was demolished in the 1980s. Some art historians have been protesting since then, and it is they who kept looking at the different monuments by the People's Party that had been removed, including small things that don't necessarily have artistic value, like the names of schools, bridges, and military camps from the time of the People's Party. I'm not sure if this is the reason why art historians have come to the fore now. It's definitely one of the reasons, for sure. They have to write more to justify their protest, to disagree with what the government has been doing. They have to explain the history of such-and-such building, of such-and-such name, the history of places.

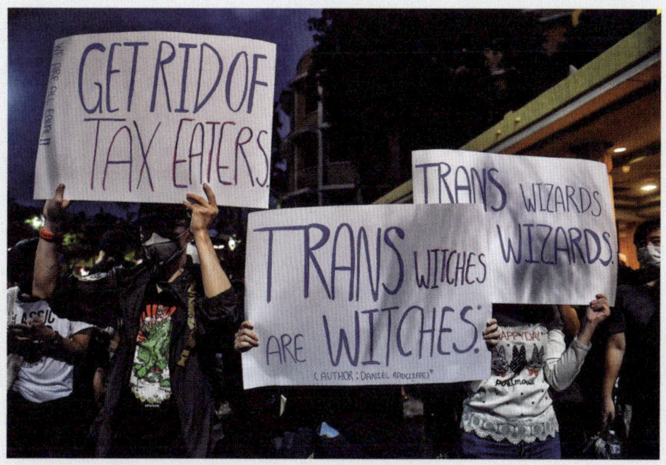

FIG 10 Protesters hold signs in support of transgender rights during a Harry Potter-themed anti-government rally at the Democracy Monument in Bangkok on August 3, 2020. Photo: Lillian Suwanrumpha / AFP via Getty Images.

Artists have become politicized too, on both sides, although the anti-government, anti-royalist side has been more vocal, even if the majority remains conservative, with the establishment. Musical bands, visual artists, and art spaces have emerged on the anti-establishment side in a big wave in the past few years. This is phenomenal. There may be people writing about architecture and the attempt to erase memory, as mentioned, but are there writings in Thai about the rising interest in political art and how artists have become politicized yet? I don't think so.

Right now, I mean, even within the last week, art students at Chiang Mai University were on the news. Usually, an art student does a senior thesis and it is supposed to be on display in the gallery of the university. But because many of them became so politicized, the dean of the art faculty shut down the gallery and didn't allow the seniors to display their work. They can't graduate if they don't have their work on display in the gallery. The chancellor agreed with the shutting down of the gallery to prevent those seniors' works to be displayed. This followed a previous exhibit of political art in which the dean also ordered the taking down of the works that students painstakingly put together to show their support of the protest movement in artistic form. The dean ordered them taken down, destroyed, and put in the trash. The dean's order created an uproar that had not quieted down; then last week, it happened again. They shut the gallery, closed the gate, put a chain around it. Then a few faculty members and students cut the chain, opened the door, and set up their works again in the gallery. They gave a name to their resistant action in English: "Occupy Art Gallery." It represents the larger situation, the broader cultural atmosphere. Somehow artists, as well as art historians, have become much more active than any time in the past in Thailand. So why is one of the major political battlefronts now the arena of art and art history in a way that it wasn't previously?

CC & IG

Another question is, how does Thailand place itself in the current context of decolonization and reclaiming Indigenous identities? Considering its own mythology as the only country that has never been colonized in Southeast Asia and a country that has based much of its self-image and symbols of identification on Indigenous heritage, how can we understand the conservative manipulation of heritage in Thailand in this era when the reclamation of heritage is the site of progressive battles in so many other contexts?

TW

Even though Thailand has never been formally colonized, many people have been arguing for decades that it is semi-colonial in various ways. Not semi-colonial in the sense of being neo-colonized. Semi-colonial in that it was allowed to survive. We are allowed to survive, we are even created and contributed to in significant ways by colonial forces. Partly because Thailand—or rather Siam's elites—collaborated to such an extent that the British didn't have to colonize it. And partly because having Thailand as a buffer benefitted the colonial powers at the time. Having a collaborative local elite in the location where they needed a buffer between the French and the British was a benefit to every side. Michael Hertzfeld wrote an article about Thailand as a "cryptocolony," in the sense that it doesn't have to be colonized to have certain characteristics of a culture that claims to be higher, superior, more civilized, although more than whom, I'm not sure—maybe more than the neighbors who are colonized. So, let's say Thais want to be on a par with the West. Whether or not the West recognizes this doesn't matter because this line of thought is for domestic consumption. The main thing is for local people to believe that we are as civilized as others, the belief that Thailand is great, culturally speaking, and Thailand has always portrayed itself in such a way. So that fits well with the nationalism of later times. Thailand has long been very nationalistic, but there are different kinds of nationalism: since the downfall of the People's Party and the rise of the monarchy, this has taken the shape of "royal nationalism." In some periods, like in World War II under the People's Party, it was more of a fascist kind of nationalism.But in Thailand it was mainly royal nationalism, based on the belief in the monarch as a hero, leader, and the main reason for the glory of the nation. Nationalism and royalism in Thailand are inextricable.

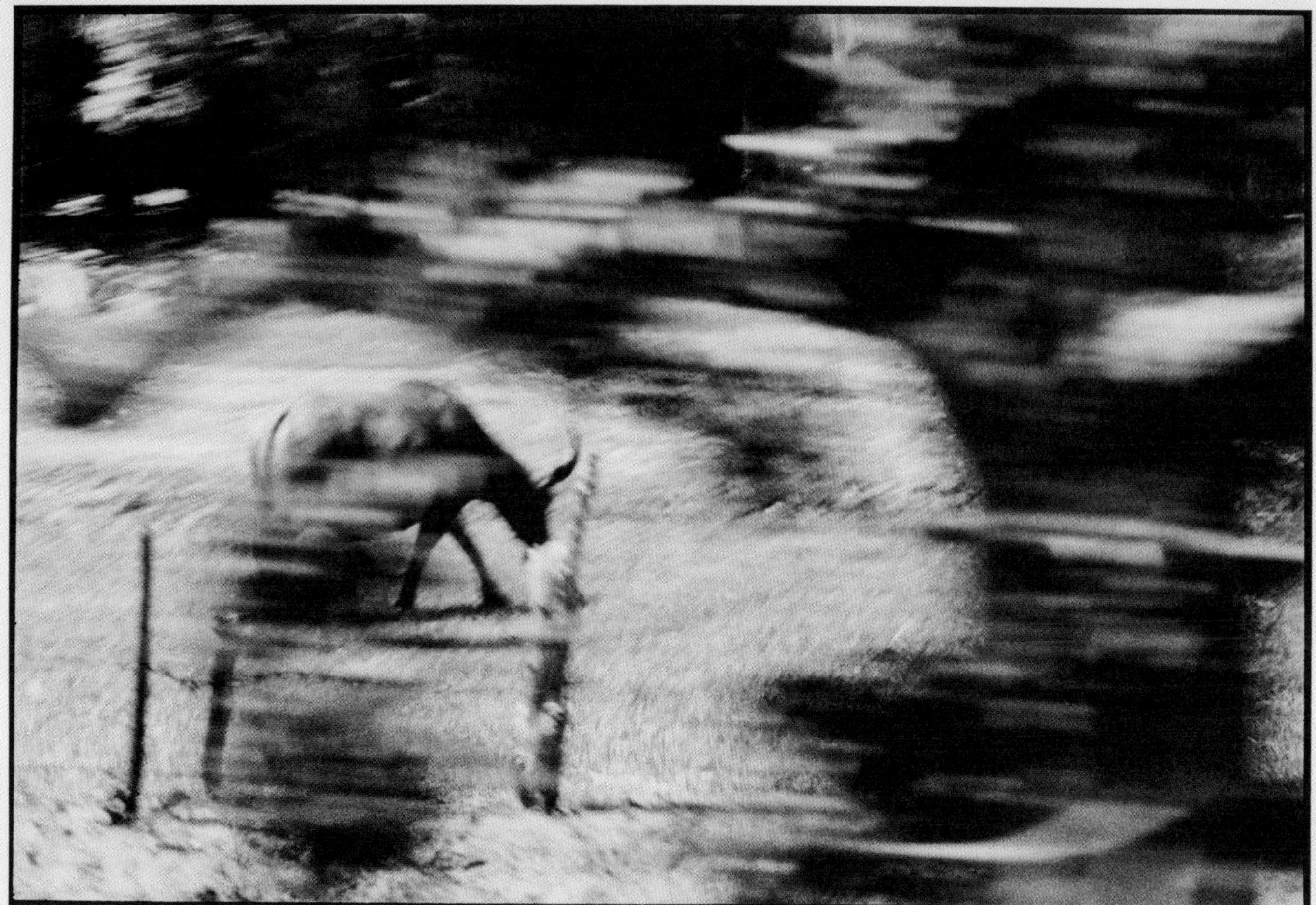

FIG 11 Liam Morgan, *Game 1–23*. 2015.
Image courtesy the artist.

With regards to heritage at this time in Thailand, in my opinion there is a kind of double politics because of the condition of a semi-colony or cryptocolony, through which people try to reclaim the civilized, the advanced, the superiority of Thai culture. I agree that on one hand there's a legacy of colonialism that we have to fight yet things may not be simple or straightforward, and can also play out problematically within the domestic conditions of many countries. We can't just say that we're against colonialism, thus sympathizing with local powers who are oppressors of their people. Scholars have taken the "local view" for granted, often not asking whether they are the ruling power. In Thai studies, even in English, a lot of work done in previous generations was pretty conservative and royalist because the scholarship took the ruling elites' view for granted as the "local view," as opposed to the colonial or Western one. In my generation, we are aware that the ruling class's views don't represent the ruled.

The fight for heritage is happening against such a background of domestic power relations. It's true that a lot of Thais, including anti-royalist, anti-government people, would welcome that kind of decolonial fight to reclaim heritage. I understand that too, because people who are against royalism aren't necessarily anti-nationalism. Most of them love the nation and are patriotic too. Many are even nationalistic. I prefer to remain on the sideline of the reclaiming of cultural heritage, since they could (not always) be part of the nationalistic and royalist promotion. If I'm not involved, it's not because I disagree, but because I don't want to keep telling people to be careful about the nationalistic element, or careful about the royal nationalistic forces that will try to hijack it, and so on.

October 2021

Raffles Will Disappear: The 2019 Bicentennial in Singapore and its Counter-discourses

HONG LYSA

On January 1, 2018 the Prime Minister of Singapore announced that in the next year the country would commemorate the bicentenary of the arrival of Thomas Stamford Raffles to Singapore, the advent of the island as a British colony.

An Incidental Preamble

Following the announcement, an academic workshop, "Reassessing 1819 in Singapore History," was held in early March 2018.

I presented a paper, "The Public Life of History in Singapore: 1819 and the Exceptional Colony," which highlighted the long-forgotten celebration of the 1969 150th anniversary of the island as a British colony and the centrality of Thomas Stamford Raffles in the historical narrative of post-independence Singapore. Six papers out of the nineteen presented either had Raffles' name in their titles, or otherwise examined his legacy as a colonizer.

At some point in the proceedings, one of the organizers observed that he had hoped that Raffles would not have featured in the workshop at all. We should move beyond personalities towards analyzing larger historical forces at work, such as the nature of colonialism.

In other words, we should let go of Raffles.

This exhortation would certainly be most salutary if not for the fact that the workshop itself was organized on account of the impending Bicentennial.

The Not Quite Disappearing Statue/s

On January 3, 2019, the front page of the "Home" section of *The Straits Times*, the paper of record, was headlined, "Raffles does a 'disappearing' act in North Boat Quay."[1] The White statue standing by the Singapore River, which has graced the cover of many a history book, tourist guide, and brochure, had been painted over on one side so that it blended into the distant building in the background and seemed to disappear when viewed from marked vantage points.

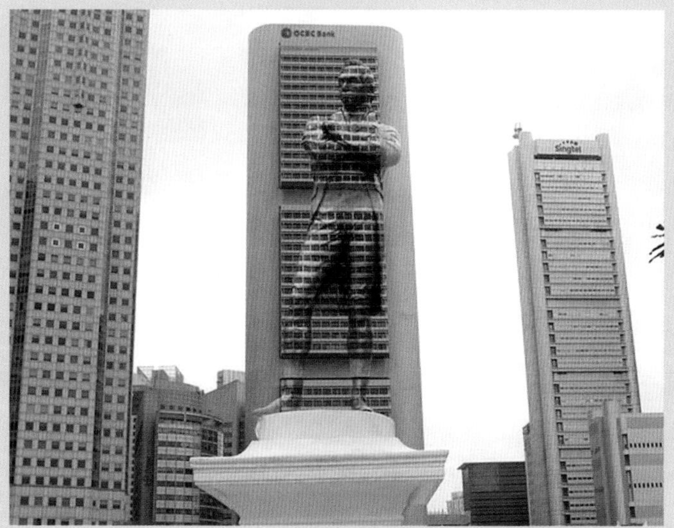

FIG 1 Teng Kai Wei, *Raffles' "Disappearance, (roman)"* 2018. Intervention to the 1972 polymarble replica of Thomas Woolner's 1887 Raffles statue. Image courtesy Najeer Yusof. Image first published in *TODAY*.

The Straits Times report of the "disappearing" statue appeared on the day that the artwork wrought on it would be removed. The no-longer White Raffles had been unveiled only days earlier.

---

1 Vanessa Liu, "Raffles does a 'disappearing' act in North Boat Quay," *The Straits Times*, January 3, 2019.

With a quick clean up, White Raffles resurfaced the next day, in the company of four visually matching companions: Sang Nila Utama, the putative founder of Singapura in 1299; Munshi Abdullah Abu Kadir, Raffles' scribe; and the wealthy and philanthropic Tan Tock Seng and Naraina Pillai. The three contemporaries of Raffles were from Melaka and arrived in Singapore in 1819. The five of them formed "The Arrivals."

After less than a week, the companions "disappeared." They were unmoored from Raffles, and each was consigned to stand by itself along the Singapore River. They were removed at the end of the year.

White Raffles was restored to its pristine and solo state in less than two weeks.

The studiously quirky "pop-up" teasers to flag the Bicentennial year were undoubtedly designed to draw the curiosity of the Twitter and Instagram generation to the White Raffles statue. Mainstream media readers, not "getting the picture" until the very last minute, would have added a buzz to what looked like iconoclasms to the smart set of younger Singaporeans.

The Bicentennial was the national celebration of a sophisticated financial and technological global economy, a cosmopolitan society in the international cultural and lifestyle circuits whose origins in the state-endorsed narrative was reaffirmed as being 1819.

For a sovereign nation to commemorate its foundation as a colony would appear to go against the grain of how former colonies narrate their history. The Bicentennial would make sense only with an examination of the historical specificities of the nature of Singapore as a colony; its anti-colonial phase; the brief merger as a component state of the Federation of Malaysia, and the dramatic Separation which brought sovereignty unexpectedly. Following that, the People's Action Party (PAP) government ditched its rhetoric of being anti-colonial and of the impossibility of the small island to exist as an independent political entity.

Colonial Statuaries in India: From the Pinnacle of Power to the Graveyard

As with other former exploitation colonies, Singapore has had to deal with its colonial statuaries with the end of colonial rule. A brief sketch of the post-independence vicissitudes of the effigies of white men of power in postcolonial India would lend perspective to the processes in other former British colonies in Asia that remain members of the British Commonwealth.

The jewel in the imperial crown, British India populated the public spaces of its key administrative centers with oversized governor generals, military generals, viceroys, and monarchs in bronze, copper, or marble. The earliest was installed in Madras in 1800. The Indian nationalist movement spanning six decades culminated in independence through constitutional transfer of power in 1947. Prime Minister Jawaharlal Nehru, last jailed from 1942 to 1945, rejected active imperial iconoclasm, unlike in Indonesia, where statues of Dutch governor generals were torn down when the country won its war of independence in 1945.

However, with the centenary of the event that imperialists have referred to as the 1857 Sepoy Mutiny, which anticolonialists considered the first Indian War of Independence, radical socialist and Hindu nationalist parties demanded that the early heroes replace former colonial conquerors on pedestals in public spaces. By 1970 almost no British imperial statuary in North India remained where they had stood.[2]

2 Paul M. McGarr, "'The Viceroys are Disappearing from the Roundabouts in Delhi': British symbols of power in post-colonial India," *Modern Asian Studies*, vol. 49, issue 3 (May 2015), https://www.cambridge.org/core/journals/modern-asian-studies/article/viceroys-are-disappearing-from-the-roundabouts-in-delhi-british-symbols-of-power-in-postcolonial-india/5CAFC2200F5D47809B0B327793F55B1F.

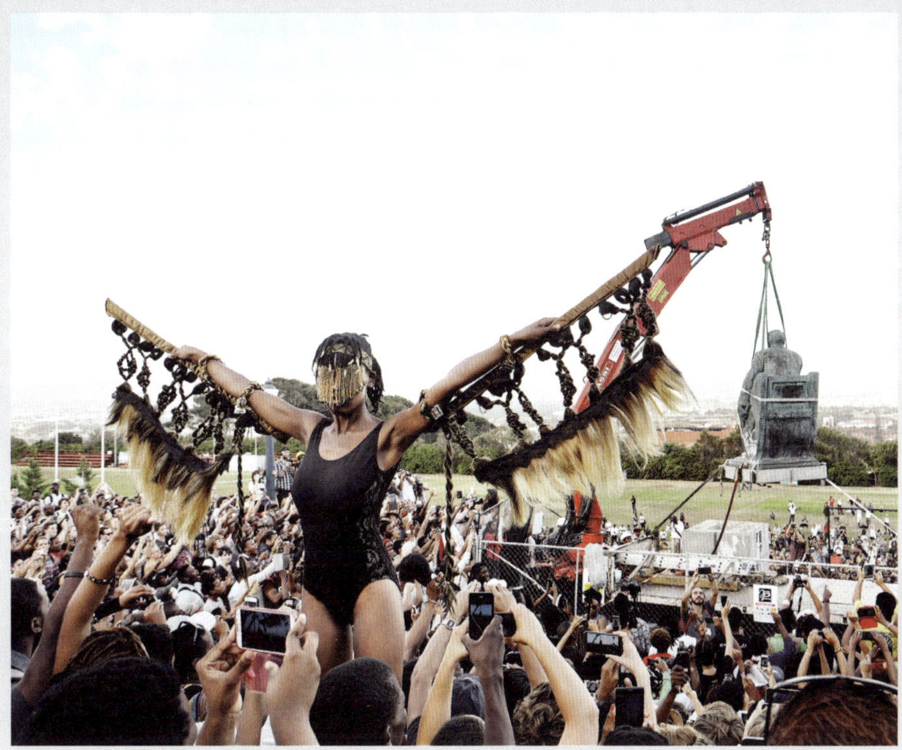

FIG 2 Sethembile Msezane, *Chapungu—The Day Rhodes Fell*, 2015, University of Cape Town, South Africa.

In 2019, a British researcher referencing the 2015 removal of the statue of Cecil Rhodes in the University of Cape Town, South Africa, and subsequently others in the United States and in Britain itself, wrote about "a graveyard" of imperial statues at Coronation Park, the venue of the Delhi Durbars, where Queen Victoria's 1877 proclamation as Empress of India, the 1903 accession of King Edward VII, and the 1911 coronation of King George V as Emperor of India, were held. The statues had been forgotten and were in a dilapidated condition, remnants of an era which no longer had relevance or potency. [3]

---

3 Tom Wilkinson, "Coronation Park and the Forgotten Statues of the British Raj," June 20, 2019, published in LSE International History Blog, https://blogs.lse.ac.uk/lseih/2019/06/20/coronation-park-and-the-forgotten-statues-of-the-british-raj/.

While Nehru and his successors had to contend with countervailing ideologies and political parties, including on the fate of colonial statuaries, Singapore has been ruled by the PAP since 1959. In 1969, the illiberal state pronounced Raffles as the nation's founder in 1819, which was essentially reiterated in 2019 by the Prime Minister, the country's third in sixty years.

By the same token, anti-colonial historical figures were not an option in Singapore. Before the Second World War, the majority population comprised sojourners from China seeking economic betterment in the British trading port. Anti-colonial local nationalist anti-colonial fervor developed only after the Second World War. Entangled in the Cold War, the movement and its leaders were persecuted as "communists" by the colonial rulers in collaboration with its PAP successor.

Not only was Raffles secure on his pedestal, a duplicate of his bronze statue erected in 1877 to celebrate Queen Victoria's Jubilee was produced in 1972 with its material, color, and height modified to suit the sensibilities of the newly independent nation.

The 150th Anniversary

The logic of Singapore celebrating its birth as a British colony in 1969 and 2019 resides in the way the PAP government has explained how it came to inherit the mandate of the colonial rulers. The celebration of the 150th anniversary of Raffles' landing was a bid to reconnect with British colonial rule, following the country's highly acrimonious and short-lived period (September 16, 1963–August 9, 1965) as a state in the federation of Malaysia.

Brief as the period was, Merger and Separation has defined the nature of Singapore's existence. Merger was a lifeline that the British threw to the precarious PAP government facing likely defeat in the general election in 1963 by its expelled left-wing party members who then formed the Barisan Sosialis. Lee had presented himself as an anti-colonial leader and the PAP won the 1959 election on that platform. Once in power, however, he worked directly against the left, with British support. Merger would hand control of Singapore's internal security to the conservative federal government. The mass arrests carried out on February 2, 1963, in the name of the Internal Security Council comprising representatives of the British, Singapore, and Federation of Malaya governments, crippled the Barisan. The mopping-up arrests under the Internal Security Act after the 1963 election, which saw five victorious opposition candidates, among others, on the list to be put away, was executed in the name of the Malaysian government.

With Merger thus having relieved the pressure from the left wing on the island, the PAP found itself as a minor opposition party in the federal legislature. Its effort to win over the disadvantaged segments as a wedge into federal politics drew the wrath of the extreme right-wing Malay component of the race-based ruling coalition. Both sides weaponized "race"—in Lee's terms, Malay superiority versus a "Malaysian Malaysia," which in effect was centered on the Chinese population. The Malaysian Prime Minister decided on Separation to avoid the eruption of riots, with the heightened animosities fueled by both sides.[4] Singapore's merger with Malaysia, however, has stamped the racialization of politics as the hallmark of politics on both sides of the causeway. In Malaysia this has taken the form of Malay domination as the "sons of the soil," while in "multiethnic" Singapore, the colonial-derived categorization of its population into Chinese, Malays, Indians, and Others, right down to the proportion of each, continues to be maintained.

The 150th anniversary gave Lee the opportunity to excise the nightmare that was the twenty-three months in Malaysia, and to reconnect with the colonial past in its historical narrative, economic policies, and racialized governmentality.

The year-long celebrations commenced with the launch of *The First 150 Years of Singapore*, commissioned by the International Chamber of Commerce. It began thus:

---

4 Poh Soo Kai, *Living in a Time of Deception* (Singapore: Function 8 and Pusat Sejarah Rakyat, 2016), 217–319.

> The first one hundred and fifty years of Singapore open and close under the aegis of a great man: Raffles, a beacon of almost blinding light at the beginning, pointing the way; Lee Kuan Yew, successor in a world not even Raffles, for all his vision, could have recognized today [...] Raffles and Lee Kuan Yew, as we shall see, have much in common, not only in themselves, but in their stars.[5]

Lee for his part acknowledged the contributions of, "our founder, Sir Stamford Raffles, and [...] those who came after him. Without them, modern Singapore would not have been the same." He praised the business acumen and regional networks of the Chinese merchants for the success of the British trading houses and disparaged Malay culture and society as backward, feudal, and oppressive.[6] The trauma of the failure of Malaysia was not disguised. At the same time, the PAP crafted its myth of origins—in its initial years as government it was so anti-colonial that the statue of Raffles was earmarked for removal, escaping that fate narrowly. However, by 1969, the party had passed that stage and "only Raffles remains."[7]

The White Raffles polymarble statue, molded from a plaster cast of the 1887 statue, was installed in 1972 by the Singapore Tourist Promotion Board. While the bronze original in front of the Victoria Memorial Hall exuded grim imperial might, White Raffles is taller than the original by two meters, an iconic postcolonial statue projecting a lofty and modern image of aspirational goals.[8]

---

5 Donald Moore and Joanna Moore, *The First 150 Years of Singapore* (Singapore: Donald Moore Press, 1969), 1.

6 "More than a place on the map," *The Straits Times*, February 7, 1969.

7 "Raffles: How he nearly came off his Empress Place pedestal," *The Straits Times*, August 7, 1969.

8 "Marble replica to mark landing of Raffles," *The Straits Times*, July 30, 1971.

The Bicentennial

While the 150th anniversary programme was a regimented affair, the Bicentennial was a massive public relations exercise to generate a collective effervescence. "Complexity," "nuances," and "multi-layered" were the trending Bicentennial-speak. *The Straits Times* headline announcing White Raffles' "disappearing act" explained that the idea was to start a conversation about whether Singapore history was just about one man and one date.[9]

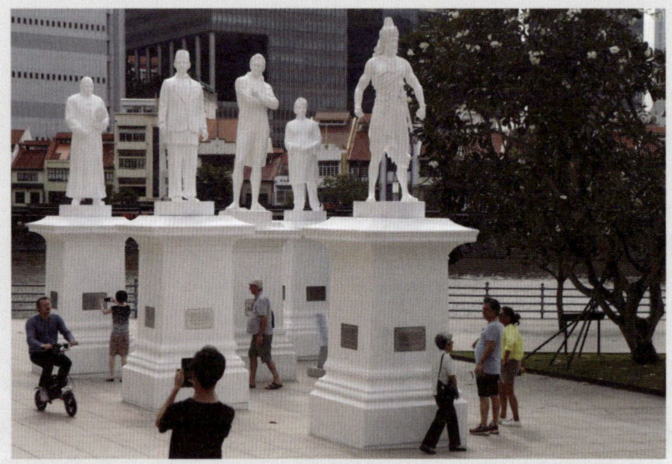

FIG 3 ***The Arrivals:*** **Statues of Sang Nila Utama, Tan Tock Seng, Munshi Abdullah, and Naraina Pillai, placed temporarily beside the statue of Sir Stamford Raffles along Singapore River on January 4, 2019, as part of the Singapore Bicentennial celebrations. Image courtesy Najeer Yusof, first published in *TODAY*.**

However, far from White Raffles "disappearing," artist Tang Kai Wei, a specialist in public sculptures, created an optical illusion where the image of the statue was projected against the full height of the OCBC Bank building in the background—the bank being the oldest existing that was set up by the Chinese in Singapore. The newspaper reported a thirty-four-year-old visitor to

9 Vanessa Liu, "Raffles does a 'disappearing' act in North Boat Quay," *The Straits Times*, January 3, 2019.

the site remarking, "Did they remove the statue and replace it with a hologram? [...] It's actually quite cool."

A veteran cosmopolitan who recently became a Singapore citizen also found the "disappearing" White Raffles to be a "brilliant" trick of artistic cunning and was suitably impressed: "Fifty years ago, who in Singapore would have the insolent irreverence to 'disappear' Sir Stamford Raffles?" The well-educated, well-traveled young Singaporeans were the product of a post-1965 "bold new Singapore."[10] Taking Bicentennial history at face value, the cosmopolitan New Singaporean found herself at home.

The "Arrivals" of the Chinese, Malay, and Indian polymarble companions that surrounded White Raffles were meant to stimulate, or more accurately to "simulate," a related meaningful conversation. It was a "reminder" that Raffles was not the only one to "arrive."[11] Rather, 1819 was also a significant year for other arrivals whose communities brought diversity and plurality to the island.[12]

The "surprise" element in the "Arrivals" was the figure who arrived way before 1819. Sang Nila Utama, hitherto a mythical character in the school textbooks, was validated by the Bicentennial history as the Palembang prince who arrived in 1299 and founded the Singapura kingdom. The five were fellow migrant arrivals, albeit 700 years apart. However, under the sign of Raffles and the concomitant "from fishing village to metropolis" trope, the colonial pecking order, with the majority Chinese under their wealthy philanthropic leaders being at the top of the non-white heap, was reinforced. The Malays, now made "migrants," were evidently less endowed with the industry and economic acumen than those from further afield.

---

10 Meira Chand, "What Singapore's bicentennial means to this new immigrant," *The Straits Times*, September 1, 2019, originally in *Cultural Connections*, July 4, 2019.

11 Sai Siew Min observed that "simulation" worked well in this sentence.

12 Janice Lim, "Arrival in 1819 was major criterion in selecting new statues: Bicentennial Office," *TODAY*, January 11, 2011. https://www.todayonline.com/singapore/arrival-1819-was-major-criterion-selecting-statues-be-added-besides-raffles-sbo.

While much was made by the organizers of the official revisionism of Bicentennial history as manifested in the *longue dureé* of Singapore's past, the Prime Minister's speech at the launch of the Singapore Bicentennial was straight to the point. While it was recognized that Raffles did not "discover" Singapore any more than Columbus did America,

> Without 1819, we would not have had 1965, and we would certainly not have celebrated the success of SG50. 1819 made these possible. This is why the Singapore Bicentennial is worth commemorating.

The "Fall" movements

The Singapore Bicentennial Office under the Prime Minister's Office would have been fully cognizant of the reverberations across continents of the "Rhodes Must Fall" movement in the University of Cape Town, South Africa, in 2015, when it fiddled around with White Raffles. The initial hype surrounding the statue highlighted how far apart Singapore was from the intensity and urgency of #RhodesMustFall.

There are certainly grounds for stating, as the Singapore Prime Minister did in his 2021 National Day rally speech, that Singapore's circumstances and context are completely different from the Black Lives Matter movement in the United States, or the violence between Israel and the Palestinians in Gaza. Nevertheless, there were certainly shared historical forces, particularly the underlying colonialism and race relations, in these developments of global concern that related to Singapore. Singaporeans who critiqued the Bicentennial in fact did draw on the #RhodesMustFall.

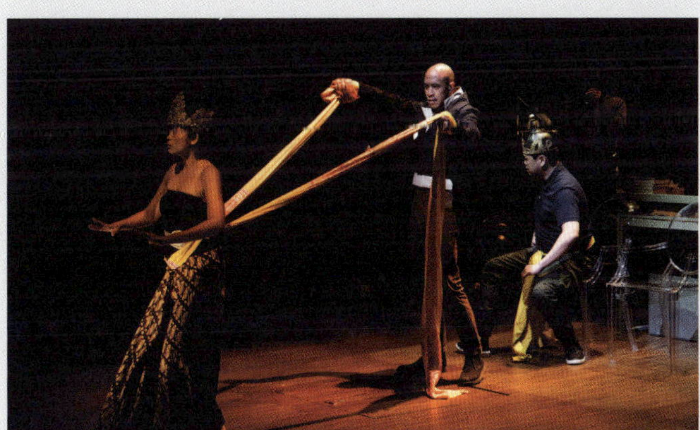

FIG 4 The 2019 theatre production of *Merdeka*/獨立/சுதந்திரம் by Alfian Sa'at and Neo Hai Bin reenacts key events in Singapore's history, including Stamford Raffles' callous treatment of Sultan Husain Shah in Singapore and the royal family in Yogyakarta. Copyright Wild Rice.

The protests by Black students at the University of Cape Town that brought down the statue of Cecil Rhodes on campus commenced on March 9, 2015. The British colonial politician (1853–1902) epitomized racism against Black Africans whose lands were expropriated and who were disenfranchised. He dominated the world diamond market centered in South Africa. #RhodesMustFall rejected the post-Aparthied nonracial "rainbow nation" and neoliberal democracy of the Nelson Mandela era which perpetuated the marginalization of the Blacks, and the university as a white colonial institution. It demanded decolonial education—Africanist positioning in the university's student admission, staff employment, and curriculum. Succumbing to intense pressure, the university's senate approved the removal of the Rhodes statue.[13]

#RhodesMustFall was the inspiration for Alfian Sa'at's *Merdeka* / 獨立 / சுதந்திரம் Bicentennial play which asked: Why celebrate the beginning of colonialism rather than its end? Has Singapore gained independence without truly undergoing a process of decolonization? And if Raffles must fall, what will he take down with him?

Six early-career Singaporeans are the only ones left in the reading group "Raffles Must Fall." At odds with one another, they finally agree that each of them should present their research on a forgotten historical event of their choice. From cast members and seasoned theater goers to school students who professed to dislike history classes, the response to *Merdeka* / 獨立 / சுதந்திரம் was: "Why haven't we heard these stories before?"

---

13 Zethu Matebeni, "#RhodesMustFall—It was Never Just About the Statue," Heinrich Böll Stiftung Capetown, February 19, 2018. https://za.boell.org/en/2018/02/19/rhodesmustfall-it-was-never-just-about-statue.

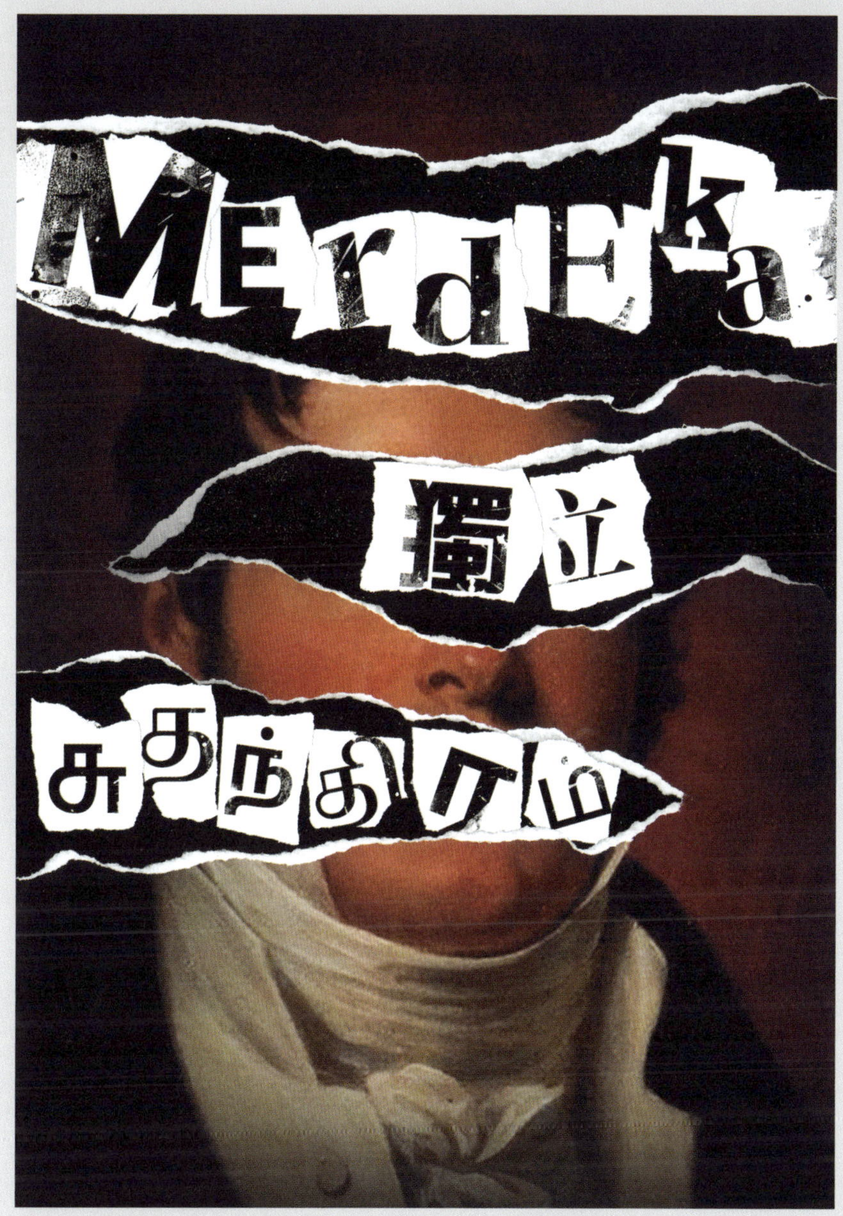

FIG 5 Poster for *Merdeka*/獨立/ சுதந்திரம், directed by Alfian Sa'at and Neo Hai Bin, October 10–November 2, 2019, The Ngee Ann Kongsi Theatre. Courtesy Wild Rice.

With the greater liberty that playwrights have than historians in crafting their narratives, Alfian productively took creative license with his textual sources. As he explained by way of illustration, a line in the records mentions that Sultan Hussein Mu'azzam Shah took three months to sign the treaty ceding the whole of

Singapore to the British in 1824. The conventional understanding in British portrayals, as well as post-1965 critical Malay literary works, was that the sultan was a greedy and dissolute person. The playwright extrapolated that Sultan Hussein could have been pressured by gunboat diplomacy. An actor counts out: one month, two months, three months, prompting the audience to note the prolonged delay. Sultan Hussein did not simply grab at the lucrative deal. The possibility of this offers a kind of liberation, or dignity, to a Malay person pursuing history.[14]

Merdeka / 獨立 / சுதந்திரம் pushed towards decolonial history. Foregrounding the official non-English Singapore languages (Malay [the national language], Chinese, and Tamil) in the play's title as a commitment to multilingualism served a similar purpose.[15] In the final scene, the "RafflesMustFall" reading group has to decide on their next course of action. They are not ready to agitate for the Fall of the Raffles statues. Their concern that their jobs would be at stake aside, they realize that, "Part One was when we got rid of our colonial masters. Part Two is when we begin the real work: decolonizing our minds, our systems, our statues."

Raffles Renounced: Raffles Will Disappear

Merdeka / 獨立 / சுதந்திரம் was followed by *Raffles Renounced: Towards a Merdeka History* (2021), a collection of essays by theater practitioners, artists, and academics, offered as a constant companion volume to the Bicentennial story. The book dissects Singapore's "predicament of independence"—the peculiar postcolonial in which where its history was pivoted not on freedom from colonial rule, but the post-Separation return of the imperialist nexus that would guarantee protection from the hostile Malay world.[16]

14 "What is Merdeka History?," *Raffles Renounced webinar transcript*, March 2, 2021. https://www.ethosbooks.com.sg/blogs/news/what-is-a-merdeka-history.

15 Alfian Sa'at, Faris Joraimi, and Sai Siew Min ed., *Raffles Renounced: Towards a Medeka History* (Singapore: Ethos Books, 2021), 17.

16 Sa'at et al., *Raffles Renounced*, 13.

The essay that deals most unflinchingly with the Raffles statues cites the resolution of the characters in *Merdeka* / 獨立 / சுதந்திரம் on the need to start with decolonizing the mind. Historian Faris Joraimi flagged the danger of ethno-nationalists clinging to Sang Nila Utama as the basis to "revive" the putative golden age of the precolonial Malay nation. Such nativism stemmed from colonial notions of race. According to him, decolonizing the system would hence involve rejecting the rigid and essentialized racial identities overseen by the postcolonial state. The cosmopolitanism and cultural expansiveness of the port-polities in the precolonial Malay world had encouraged the organic evolution of creole cultures. Malayness provided a shared basis for intercultural interaction in this region for centuries, as it did in Singapore's postwar left-wing politics.

The blueprint of the author, a scholar in his mid-twenties, envisages a ceremonial removal of the Raffles statues as a solemn act of renunciation, a powerful moment for the nation to reflect on what it means to no longer be beholden to the colonial narratives.[17]

Raffles *Will* disappear.

---

17 Faris Joraimi, "Finding Merdeka in a World of Statues: Singapore's Colonial Pageant Remade and Unmade," in *Raffles Renounced: Towards a Merdeka History*, ed. Alfian Sa'at, Faris Joraimi, and Sai Siew Min (Singapore: Ethos Books, 2021), 138–43. An abridged version, "Redoing and Undoing the Colonial Pageant: Dialogues with the Raffles Statues," is published in the e-journal *s/pores: New directions in Singapore studies*, no. 20 (September 2021). It should be read together with Sai Siew Min, "Updating the Narrative: a Dialogue Between the Former Coloniser and Colonised," https://s-pores.com/.

FRANK TANG

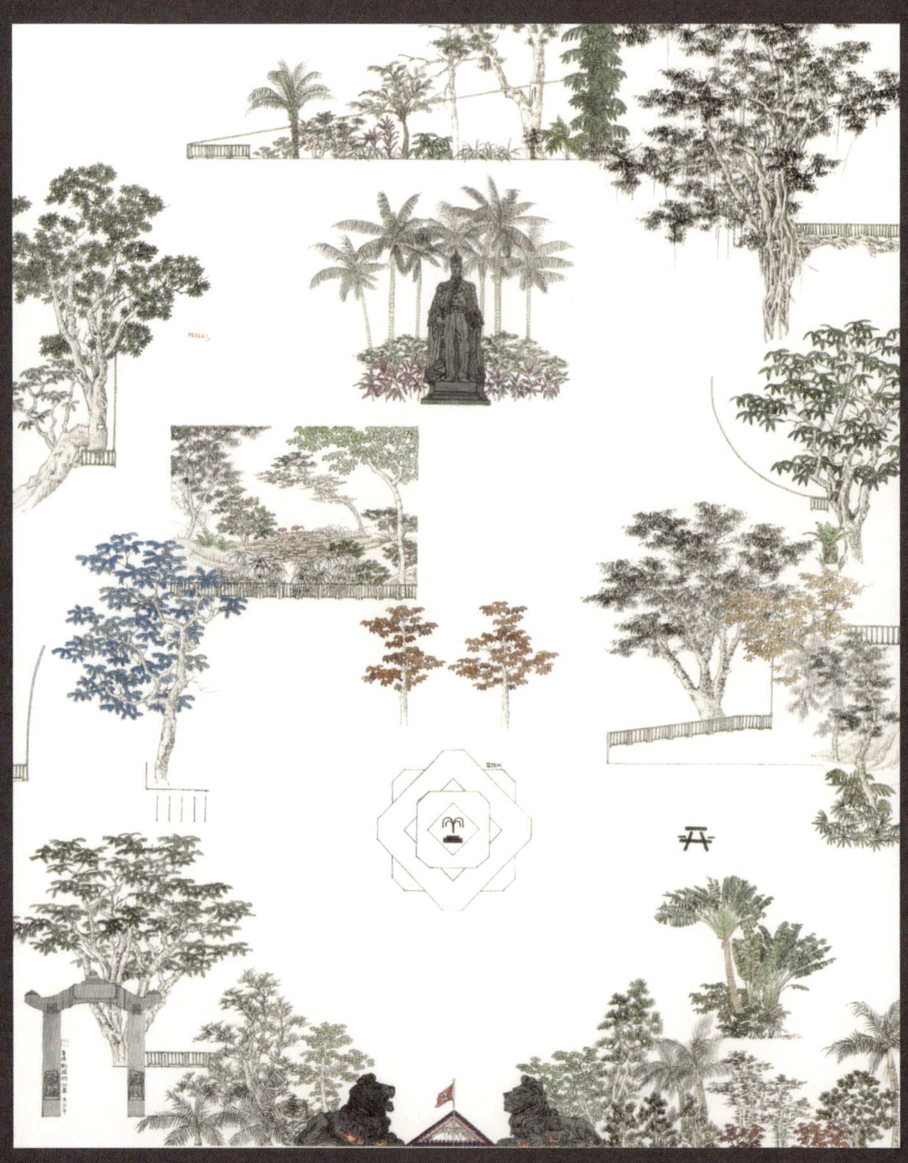

LEFT
Hong Kong Zoological and Botanical Gardens, 2020. Ink and color on paper.

RIGHT
Victoria Park, 2021. Ink and color on paper.

NEXT PAGE
Victoria Park (details), 2021. Ink and color on paper.

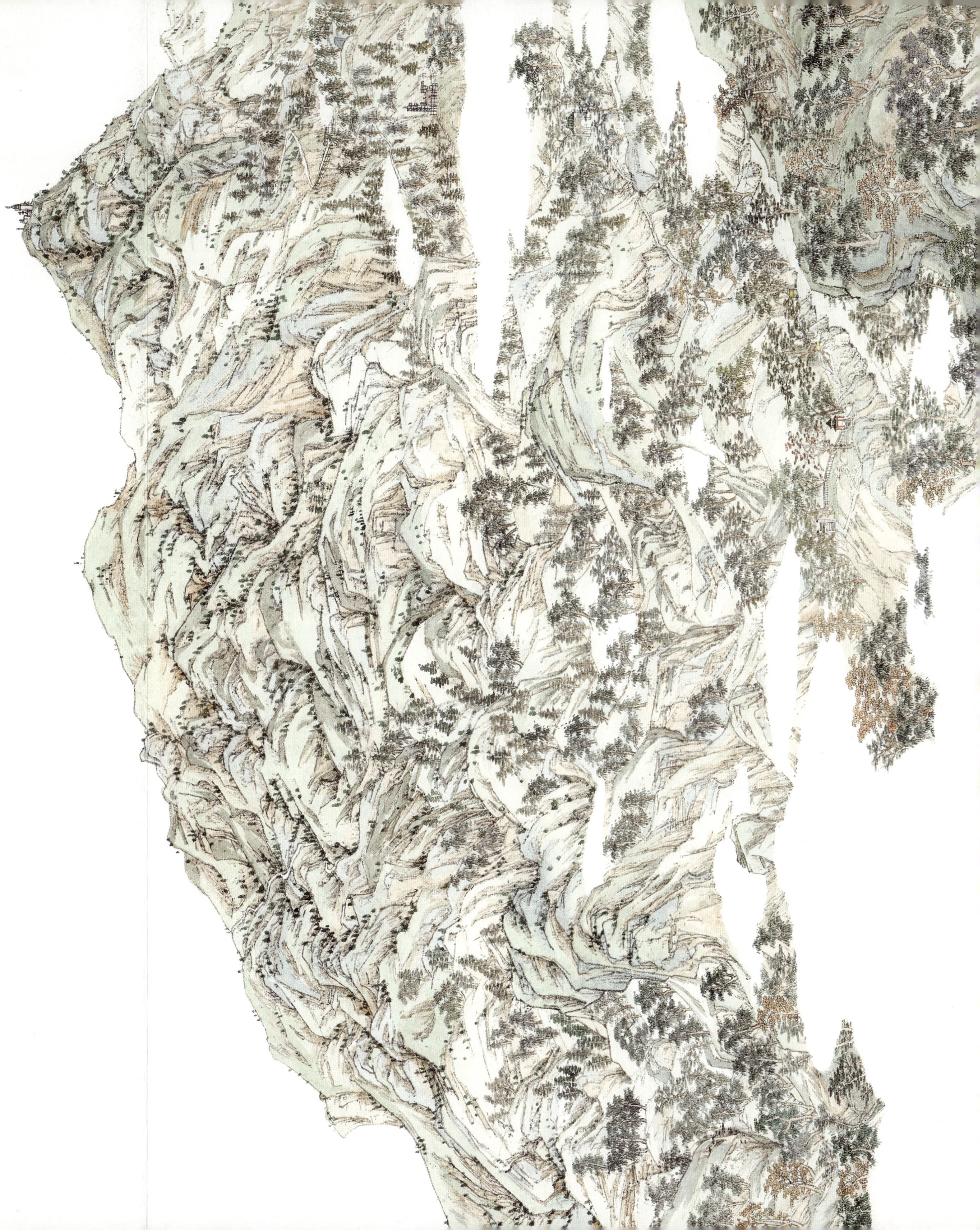

Zhongshan Park, 2022. Ink and color on paper.

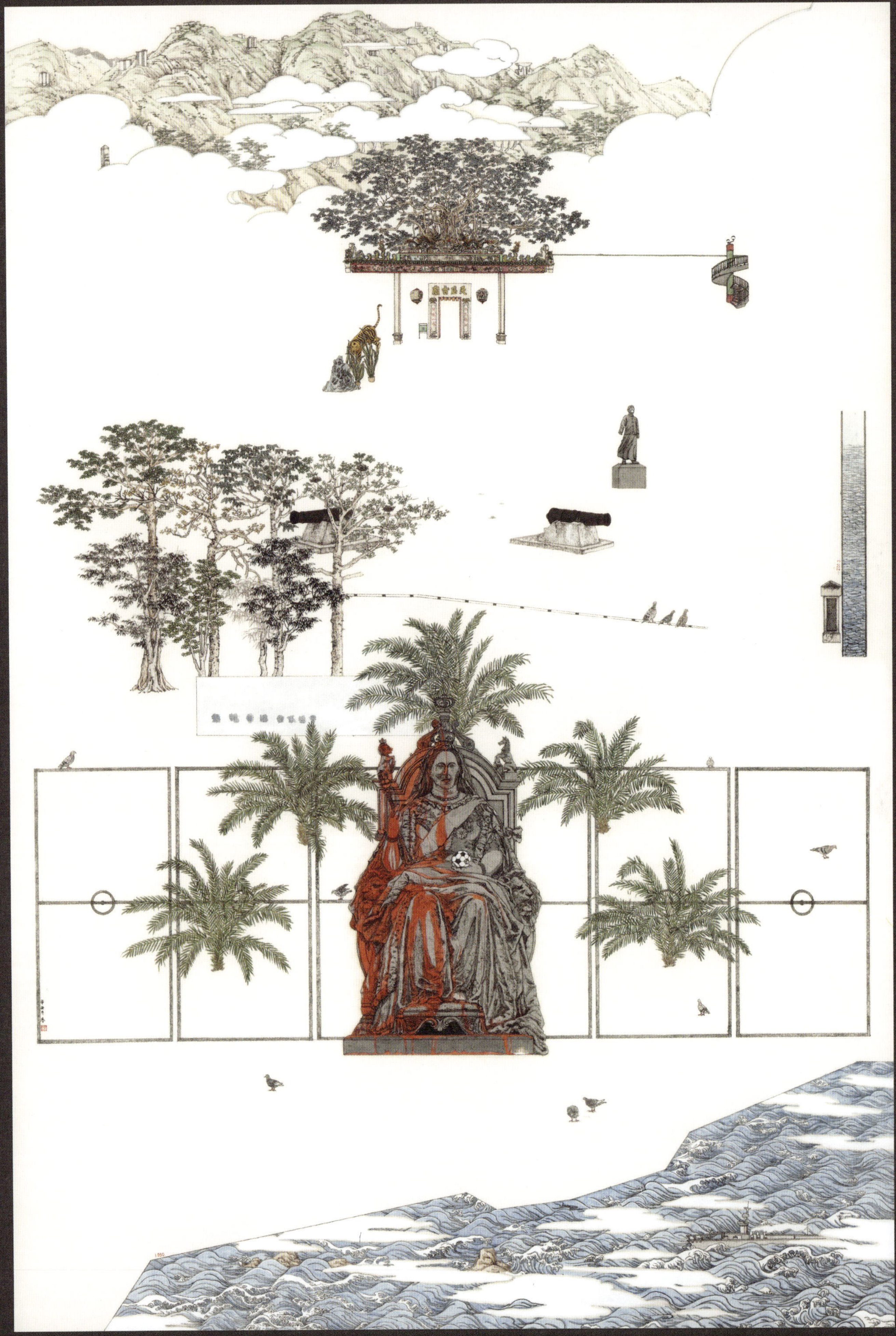

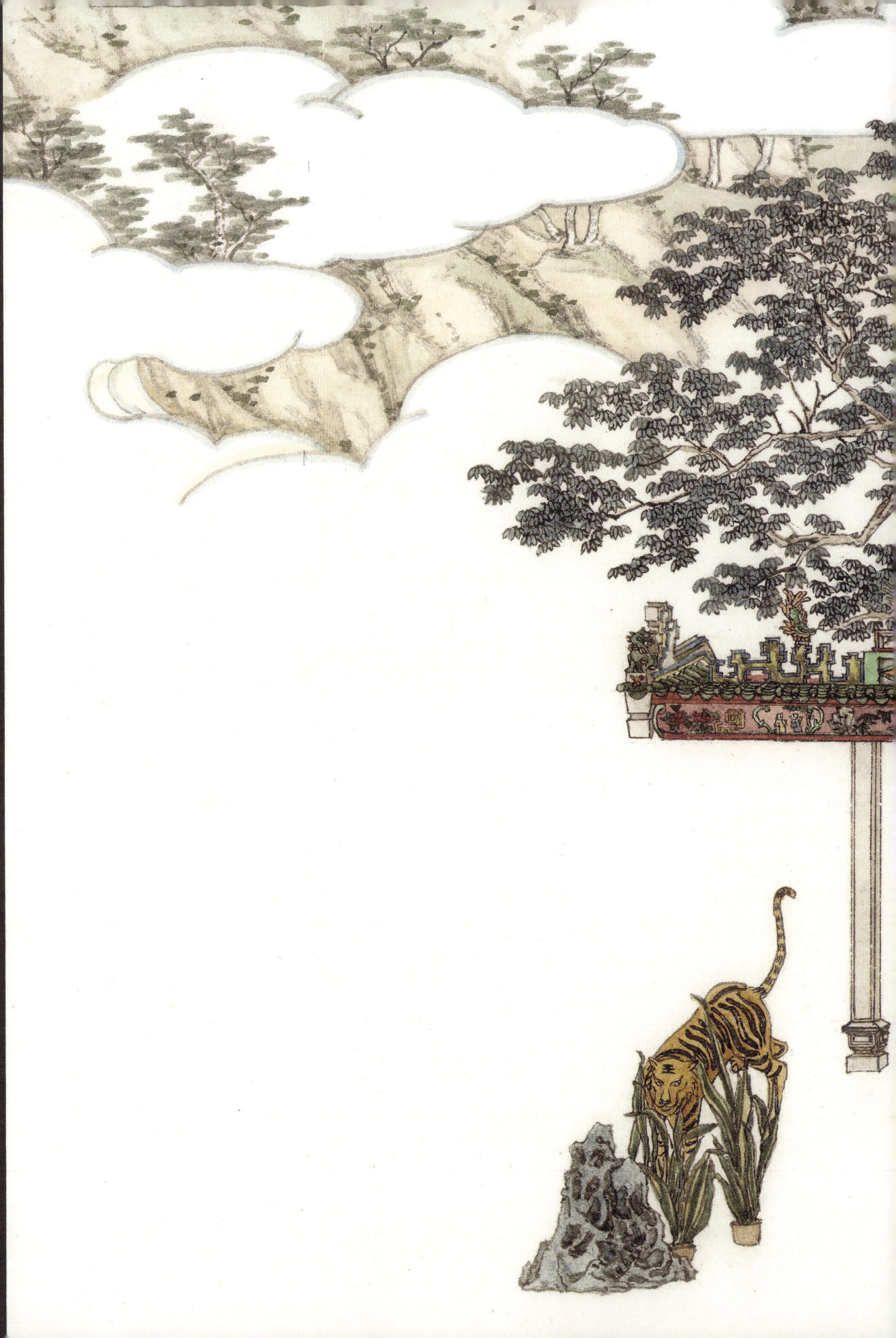

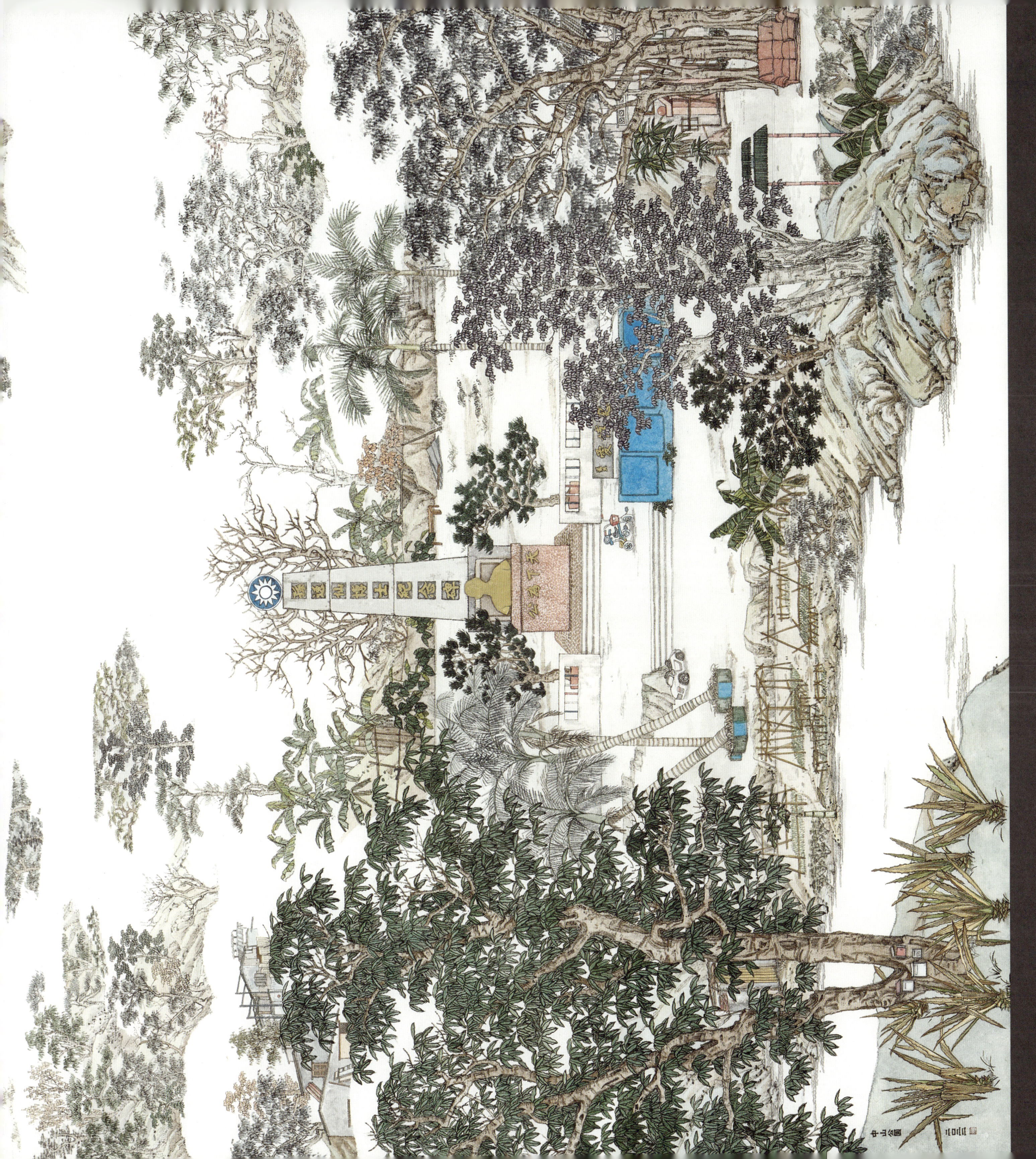

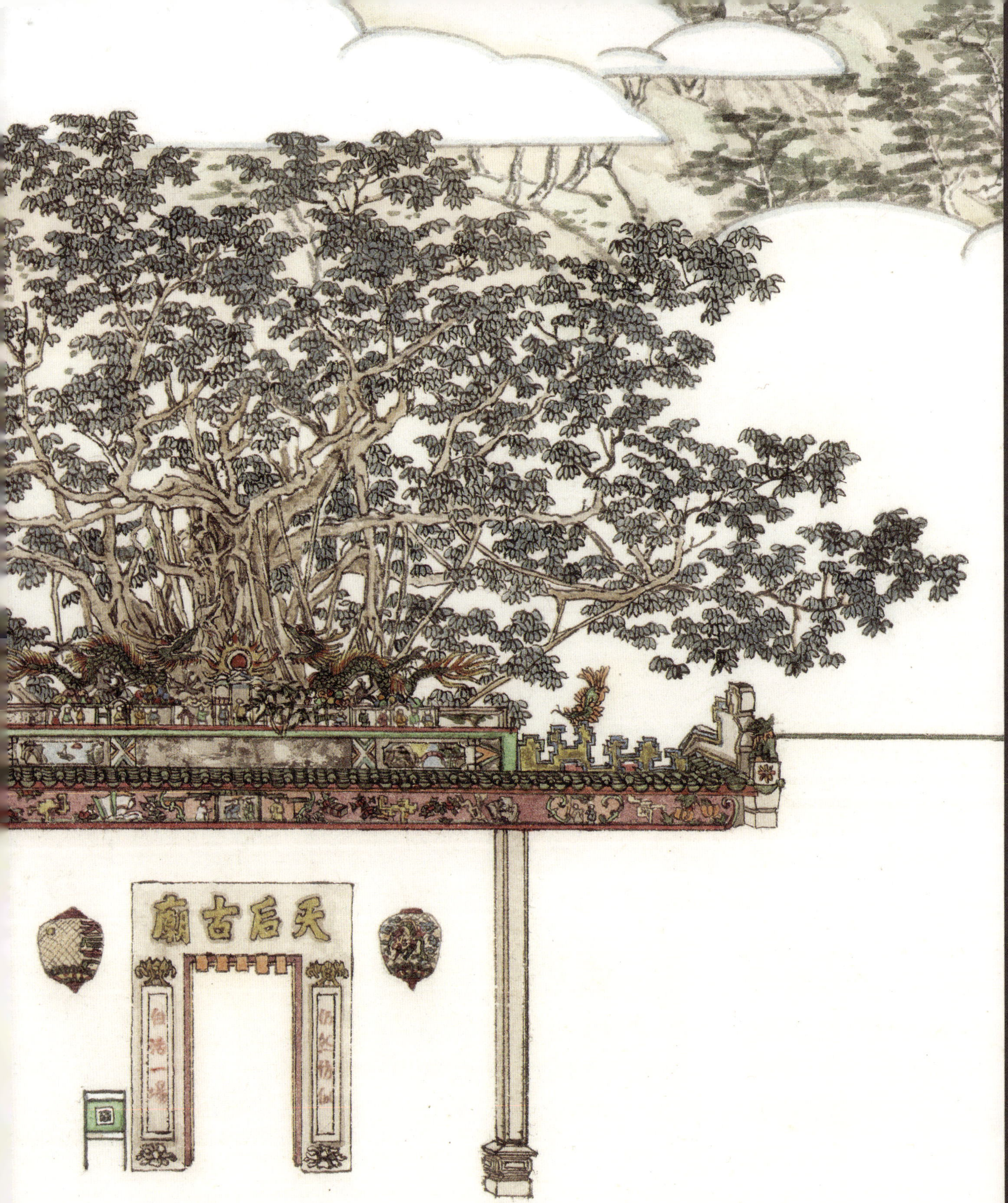

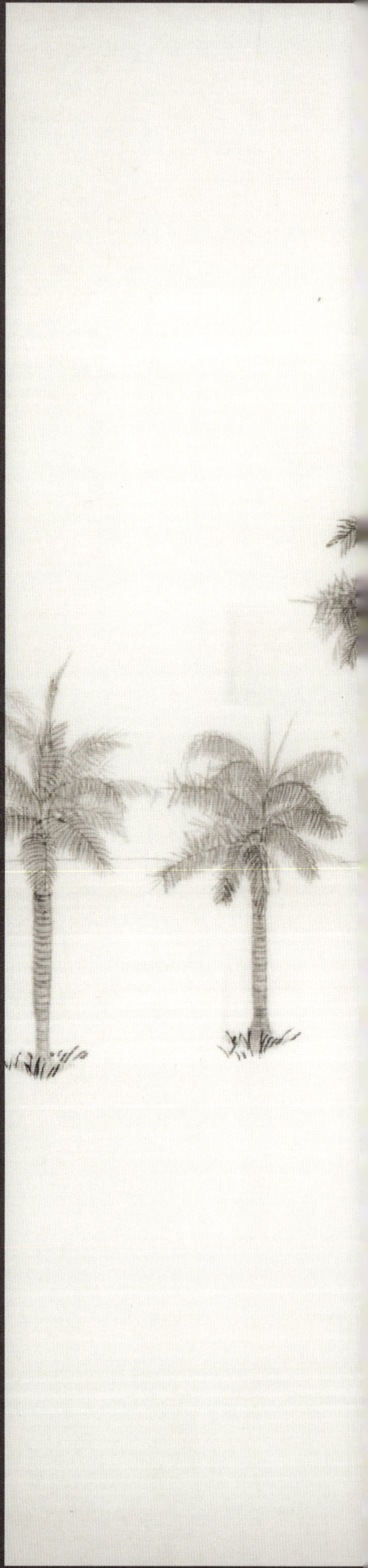

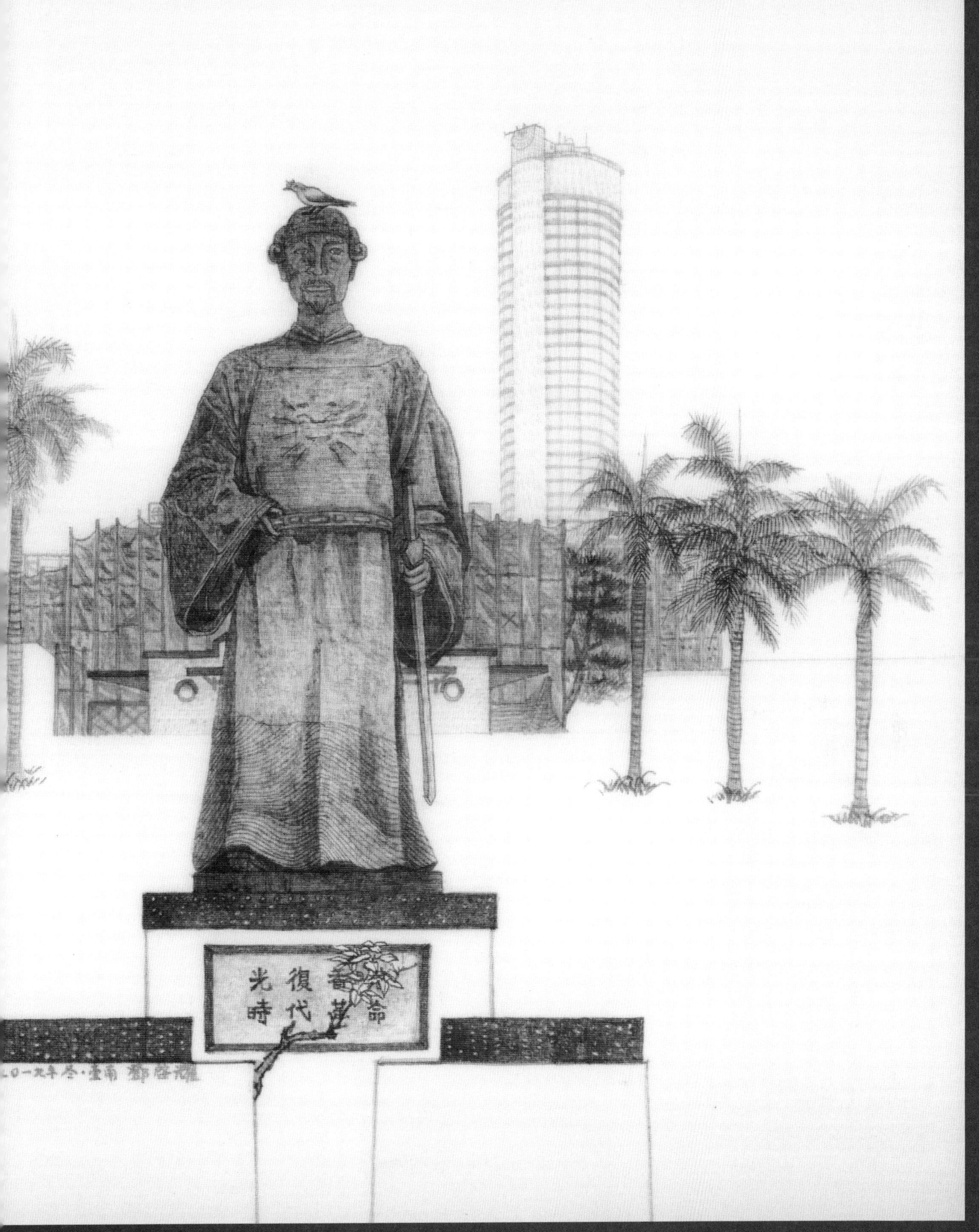
光復香
時代革命
〇一九年冬・臺南

The Impulse to Turn

208

CAROL YINGHUA LU

To consider the idea of heritage in the Chinese context of its post-1949 history, we must return to the end of the nineteenth century and the beginning of the twentieth. Notably, the late Qing dynasty (1840–1912) and early Republic of China (1912–28) ushered in unprecedented transformations for this nation with a long history. An outstanding feature was the violent and frequent change caused by the introduction and impact of Western ideas and scholarship, and the other significant feature accompanying this was the interruption of tradition. In practice though, there were actually many more aspects that were unchanging at that time. The disruptions of traditions were not always complete disruptions either, with many implicit or explicit inheritances. As such, Chinese historian Professor Luo Zhitian has pointed out that it can be said that the interweaving of rupture and continuity is clearly reflected in the interpenetration of multiple different points of departure in the characteristics of modern China.[1]

The paradoxical and conflicting understandings and perceptions of tradition, similarly those of heritage and history, from this turbulent historical juncture, can be extended to the entirety of the twentieth century, as well as to the present. The severe crisis of survival at the turn of the twentieth century compelled Chinese thinkers, intellectuals, and political leaders to consider tradition, the past, and its heritage as an embodiment of corrupt and failed politics, as well as social etiquette, which were signs of backwardness and thus an obstacle to development and baggage to discard. In the May Fourth Movement, the radical aspiration to cut oneself off from Chinese traditions was a dominant trend of thinking. In the following decades, the radical revolutionary culture continuously shapes both national ideology and everyday practice.

With such anti-traditionalist conviction, new and old were not only associated with positive and negative values but projected with different meanings in terms of time and place. In the sense of time, the past was the old and the future the new. In terms of place, the local was the old and the west was the new. In other words, the old and the new in the sense of locality were synonymous with China and the West. To downplay the tension between such dichotomy as a result of equating the old and the new with China and the West, a new conception of space was introduced, which was the world. The world was to signify the new future, while China stayed symbolic of the old past. In such a conception of space, the world was roughly interchangeable with Western Europe and North America, not necessarily including China. Yet, if China would break free from the bygone past, and identify itself with the growing world, it stood a chance of becoming a part of this imaginary future world.

The imaginary complete dichotomy between China and the West, the old and the new, led to the negation of Chinese traditions as a holistic system. Old culture, old politics, and old ethical views were all one. The rejection of the old became an issue of political standing, and had to be upheld with full conviction and no gray areas or ambiguity. As Lu Xun quoted Ibsen saying, "All or nothing," in articulating the absolute opposition between the modern and the traditional, the world and China.

The radicality of the May Fourth Movement emerged from a critical moment of crisis that made thorough reform of the country a necessity for survival at the time. It started with intellectual revolution and evolved into political and social revolution. Yet in the following decades, especially after 1949, the politics of radical revolutions that demanded constant purification of thoughts and spiritual values infiltrated into every aspect of society, falling into the trap of infinite revolutions and denials of continuity in terms of historical relevance. What was even worse, revolutions in intellectual and spiritual realms were orchestrated by political means, which led to disastrous consequences as we have witnessed in twentieth-century Chinese history. In its propaganda the Communist Party of China consciously stressed the connection between the May Fourth Movement and its anti-traditional orientations, and internalized the drastic anti-traditionalist approach to what was considered the old in every aspect of culture. The reform of Chinese ink painting after the founding of the People's Republic of China was one such example.

1 Luo Zhitian, "Self-introduction," in *Inheritance Within Rupture: Culture and Scholarship in Early Twentieth-Century China* (Beijing: Zonghua Book Company, 2012), 1.

After 1949, ink painting on silk or paper—part of a thousand-year-old Chinese tradition—was viewed by Chinese Communist theorists as a remnant of feudal China. Chinese ink painting had to actively reform itself and prove its relevance to the revolution. Many painters devoted themselves to painting new New Year pictures (*Xinnianhua* 新年畫), continuing the ideology of making art for the masses that had been established in Yan'an (base for the Chinese Communist Party from 1935 to 1947) and which drew on a longstanding folk tradition.

On August 10, 1949, the Beijing New Chinese Painting Research Society (*Beijing xinguohua yanjiuhui* 北京新國畫研究會) was established at a meeting attended by more than 150 artists in Beijing. This move helped orgnize Chinese ink painters, who had previously valued more solitary identities, into a formal organization.[2] A series of discussions on reforming Chinese ink paintings was initiated in the newspaper *People's Daily* (*Renmin ribao* 《人民日報》) in 1949, and was then carried on in the journal *People's Art* (*Renmin meishu* 《人民美術》) in 1950 by artists and art cadres including Jiang Feng (江豐 1910–82), woodcut artist and then Vice Chairman of the China Artists Association (CAA), Li Hua (李樺 1907–94), woodcut artist and professor at the Central Academy of Fine Arts (CAFA), and Li Keran (李可染 1907–89), ink painter and CAFA professor, all of whom

2 *Beijing's Painting History* (Beijing Fine Art Academy), 209–10.

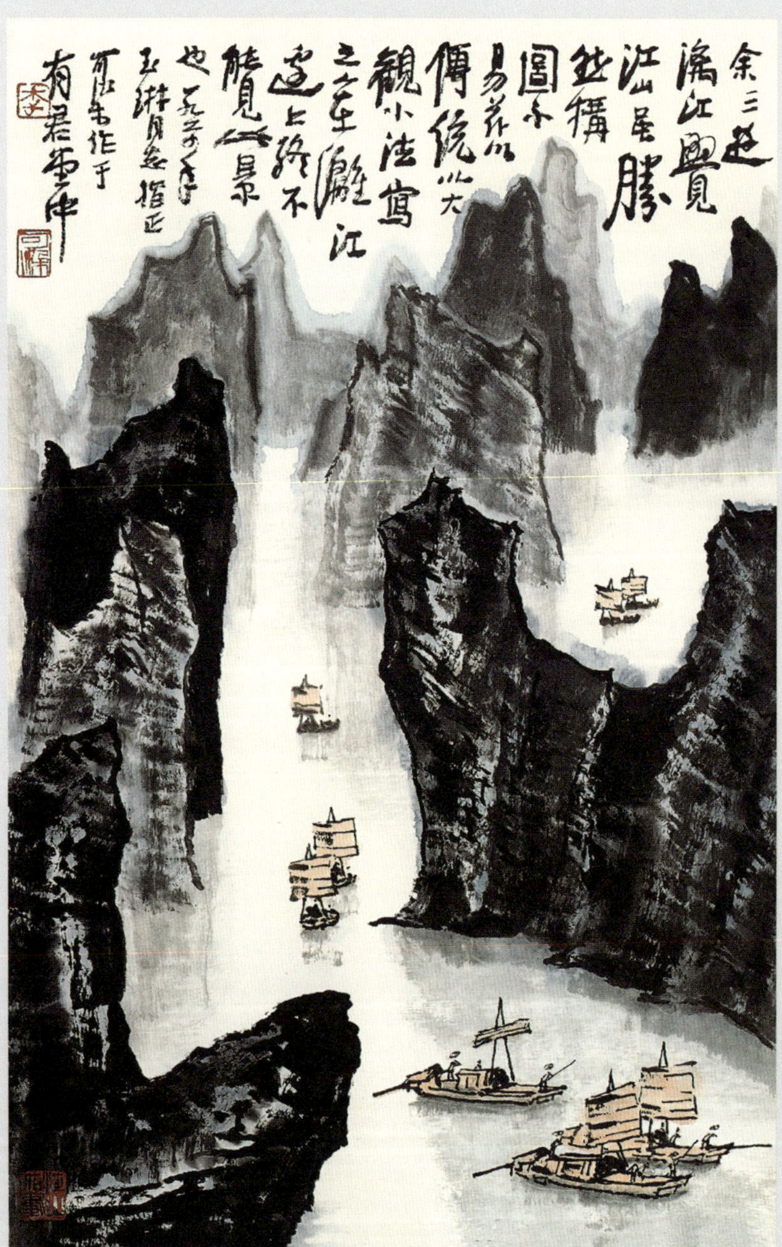

FIG 1 Li Keran, *Li River's Scenery*, 1964. Ink on paper, 66 × 44 cm.

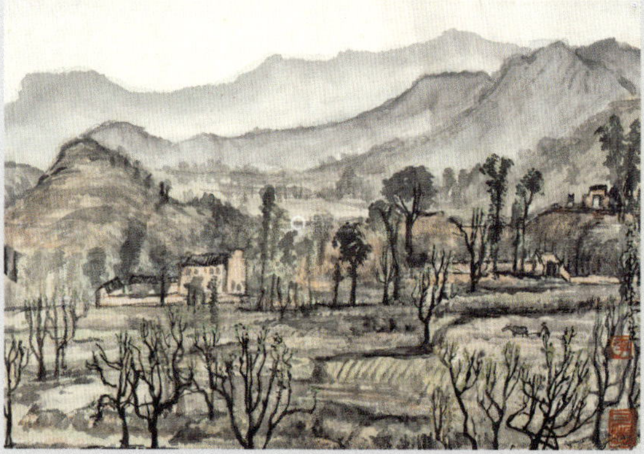

FIG 2 Li Keran, ***Plein Air Sketching In the Countryside (Xiangcun xiesheng*** 鄉村寫生), 1954. Ink and color on paper.

addressed the subject of reforming Chinese ink painting.[3] The central issue was how painters would represent Socialism in Chinese ink painting, and how they would acknowledge the primacy of the CCP's definition of Realism. This was a considerable and fundamental transformation for Chinese ink painting, the earlier development of which had been based on the tradition of emulation, with apprentices strictly copying the works of masters until they completely internalized their examples.

By the 1950s, Chinese ink painters had to alter their landscape paintings to depict nation-building and industrialization by incorporating imagery of factories, railroads, telephone poles, and new Socialist villages into their art. While oil paintings depicted the masses, Chinese ink paintings would also serve the revolution. Consequently, Chinese ink painters commonly embraced *plein air* sketching practice, traveling to famous sites such as the Yellow Mountain (*Huangshan* 黄山) and the Yellow River (*Huanghe* 黄河), as well as to collective farms, major construction sites, and factories, to paint from life.[4] In 1954, artists Li Keran, Zhang Ding (張仃 1917–2010) and Luo Ming (羅銘 1917–2007) took a three-month trip traveling through Wuxi, Suzhou, Shanghai, Tai Lake (太湖), and Hangzhou, along the Fu Chun River (富春江), to Shaoxing and Huangshan, making ink paintings depicting modern Socialist landscapes.[5] As economic construction and industrialization developed further around the country, more Chinese brush-and-ink painters traveled into rural areas to document industrialization and Socialist transformation.

3 Jiang Feng, "Guohua gaizao diyibu" 國畫改造第一步 (The First Step of Reforming Chinese Ink Paintings), *Renmin ribao (People's Daily)*, May 25, 1949, 2. Li Keran, "Tan zhongguohua de gaizao" 談中華美術的改造 (On the Reform of Chinese Ink Paintings), *Renmin meishu (People's Art)*, no. 1, 1950: 35–38. Li Hua, "Gaizao Zhongguohua de jiben wenti" 改造中國畫的基本問題 (The Basics Issues in Reforming Chinese Ink Paintings), *People's Art*, no. 1, 1950: 24.

4 *Beijing's Painting History* (Beijing Fine Art Academy), 242–43.

5 鄒躍進 Zou Yuejin, *A History of Chinese Fine Arts 1949–2000*, 49–53.

In contrast to the swift adaptations of Chinese landscape and figure painters, bird-and-flower painting (*huaniaohua* 花鳥畫) was regarded as irrevocably "feudal" and was given no chance to reform itself.[6] Official reservations about the value of landscape painting, as well as bird-and-flower painting, were voiced as early as the second meeting of the first committee of the CAA in May 1955.[7] Landscape and bird-and-flower were considered lesser genres, unable to reflect Socialist reality and its struggles; they were even dismissed as distractions.

The onset of the Anti-Rightist Movement in 1957 set in motion a series of events that would have a profound effect on ink painters. The initial criticisms of art and artists in 1957 escalated. It was followed by the emergence of the Great Leap Forward (*Dayuejin* 大躍進) in art.[8] This radical campaign called on the masses to participate in artistic creation. On one hand, artists were directed to produce many more artworks and make them affordable to everyone; on the other hand, they were directed to go to villages to live as one with the masses, producing art to celebrate proletarian enthusiasm. As a result, many villagers were engaged in painting murals and propaganda paintings of invented events and scenes. The most frequently painted scenes celebrated extraordinary agricultural achievements. Both professional artists and local villagers participated in the campaigns.[9] Politics was the priority, and in particular the principle of "learning from workers and farmers."[10]

6 Historically, there are three genres in Chinese ink painting: landscape, bird-and-flower, and figures. As a traditional genre of Chinese ink painting, bird-and-flower painting covers a wide range of natural subjects including flowers and plants, fish, insects, birds, and pets such as cats and dogs. Flower paintings, previously associated with Buddhist art, came into its own as a separate branch of painting during the Five Dynasties (907–960). For more details on the political and social reception of landscape, bird-and-flower, and figure paintings, see Amy Jane Barnes, "Imagining China: The Birth and Consolidation of British Visions of China," in *Museum Representations of Maoist China: From Cultural Revolution to Commie Kitsch* (London: Routledge, 2016), 38.

7 *Beijing's Painting History*, 242–43.

8 The Great Leap Forward was initially an economic and social campaign led by Mao Zedong from 1958 to 1962. Confident about the country's development, Mao believed that such a campaign could rapidly transform the country from an agrarian economy into a Socialist society through rapid industrialization and collectivization. It led to extreme and irrational actions in all walks of life.

9 *Beijing's Painting History*, 278–83.

10 *Beijing's Painting History*, 317.

The existence of bird-and-flower painting was called into question again in the middle of the Great Leap Forward. Towards the end of 1958, comments were again made about the irrelevance of Chinese landscape paintings and bird-and-flower paintings, and it was clear that they were to be reformed. But there would be a remarkable reversal of thinking in the wake of the Sino-Soviet split (1956–66), which cast a shadow over the popularity of Socialist Realism in China. With the departure of Soviet experts and the snowballing of tensions with the Soviet Union, the status of Chinese ink painting rose again, alongside renewed discussion about national forms. In mid-April, 1959, Zhou Enlai delivered an address to the National People's Congress, marked by its widely noted "curiously contradictory overtones."[11] In his speech, variety in artistic expression seemed to be encouraged: "just as we need history painting," he said, "we also need bird-and-flower and landscape painting." Such suggestions were immediately interpreted literally, with artists returning to these subjects. He Rong, an editor at *Art* (*Meishu*《美術》) magazine, wrote a series of four essays published in 1959 in defense of bird-and flower painting. In these essays, he evoked the spirit of the Hundred Flowers Campaign (*baihuaqifang* 百花齊放) to argue for the usefulness of Chinese landscape and bird-and-flower painting in serving the masses.[12]

11 Zhou Enlai, "Guanyu wenhua yishu gongzuo liangtiaotui zoulu de wenti" 關於文化藝術工作兩條腿走路的問題 ("On the Issue of Taking Two Approaches in the Work of Art and Culture"). This speech was delivered to a group of practitioners of art and culture in Beijing on May 3, 1959.

12 Trained as an art historian, in 1953 he became a secretary of the Secretariat of the CAA and deputy director of the editorial department of *Art* magazine. See *Beijing's Painting History*, 300–1.

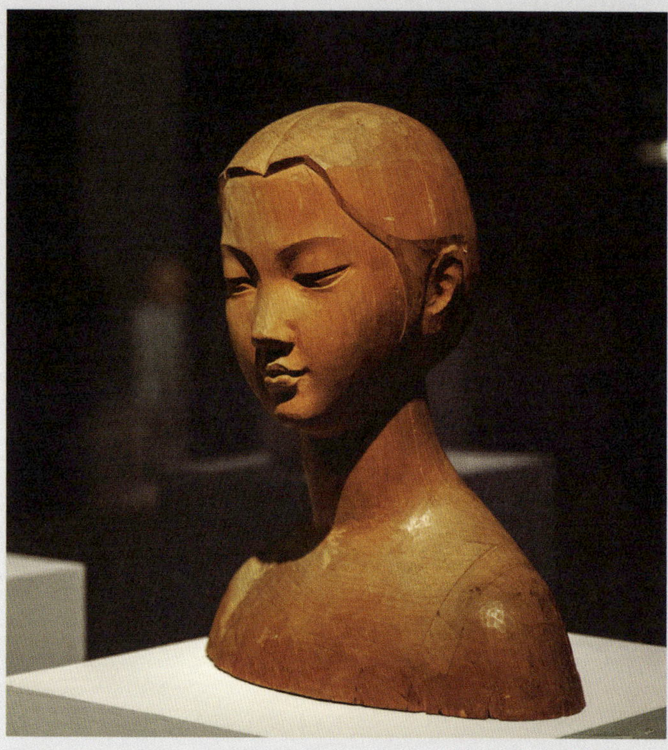

FIG 3 Liu Huanzhang, *Young Girl*, 1961. Sculpture, wood. Photo: Fan Xin.

While He Rong recognized that artworks were an instrument to provide the working people with a Socialist and Communist education, he firmly stood by the idea of maintaining diversity across artistic themes and genres, and thus affirmed the legitimacy of bird-and-flower and landscape paintings. He wrote that the function of art wasn't as direct as political slogans or political arguments. Not only was art unable to be either, it was not necessary. Otherwise, he stated we only need political slogans or arguments, and not art. It is within this context that he offered the slogan, "Peony Is Good, So Is Clove."[13] He Rong's four essays were part of an ongoing discussion on the reform and adaptation of Chinese ink painting, so that it would be understood to be compatible with the ideological frame-work of the PRC. The debate involved many artists and theoreticians of differing opinions and practices. He Rong's justification of bird-and-flower painting was in essence an argument about artistic autonomy and diversity.

13 He Rong, "Peony Is Good, So Is Clove," *Art*, no. 7 (July 1959): 8–11.

In 1959, the CCP became aware of the problems caused by the Great Leap Forward, and started rectifying its 1958 left-leaning thinking. Echoing such correction of political errors, the literature and art worlds started correcting 1958's deviations in the early 1960s, retreating from a radical position. In the early 1960s, a comprehensive "adjustment" in "retreat" was made compulsory. The state's control of social life and the cultural field weakened. Under such circumstances, the demand for diversity in art and literature was made once again, and the creative rules and regulations putting subject first and artistry in service of ideology were criticized. Artists seized the opportunity and gained nourishment and artistic resources in Chinese traditional and folk art, as well as humanist-inspired European classical art and twentieth-century modernist art. Within this short window of time, many artists visited and learned from China's great artistic past. For example, from 1960 to 1961, Beijing-based sculptor Liu Huanzhang and his colleagues were free to visit the Maiji Mountain grottos, later also surveying and making copies in the Dunhuang, Yungang, and Longmen grottos. Bringing along mud during their journeys, they made copies of Buddha heads on the spot. Maiji Mountain's Six Dynasties and Tang Dynasty sculptures were in a state of particularly complete preservation. During his surveys, Liu Huanzhang discovered that Six Dynasties Bodhisattva carvings were very reserved and peaceful, with a clear Buddhist temperament. This experience had a great effect on him. After his return, he drew from Chinese traditional Buddhist sculptures' modeling technique and made a series of wood and stone work, in particular works with female subject matter.

In the formative years of the PRC in the 1950s through the early 1960s, this discussion around the reform of brush-and ink painting, along with discussions on the nationalizing of oil painting, and the reevaluation of Impressionism, played a central role in artistic discourses of this period. While the threads of thought that each seemed to be concerned with were the formal aspects of artistic practice, the discussions were far more than purely stylistic in nature, for the emergence of such discussions was the result of artists and theoreticians responding to the new political and ideological dynamic. Even so, artistic producers were warned against "formalism" (*xingshizhuyi 形式主義*). Such cautions represented the continuation of the cultural directives that had typified the situation in the Soviet Union in the 1930s and 1940s.[14] The politicization of art was a gradual process initiated by the CCP, and implemented by artists who had been integrated into the official bureaucratic structure of the CCP and theoreticians who acted as both specialists and bureaucrats in a centralized system of art.

More importantly, these discussions reveal to us some of the primary artistic concerns of artists and theoreticians at the time, and their tangled commitments to the nation and to the Party. Since 1949, Communist artists had actively participated in the project of nation-building under the new regime. To adapt ideologically and artistically was an integral part of such a commitment. While they were concerned about the development and diversity of a national style, their thinking was essentially contained by the ideological boundaries set by the Party. These discussions were part of the process through which artists and writers developed a discourse within such boundaries. In the process, they increasingly implicated themselves in the same political movement that was working towards curtailing their artistic autonomy. They were part of the government's system of control.

Soon, the eruption of the Cultural Revolution presented ultimate tests to artists and intellectuals who were formulating their relationship with the state. In the turbulent years from 1966 to 1968, what remained of old religious practices, old superstitions, old festivals, old social practices, and old ways of dress were violently attacked and suppressed. Visual evidences of old things were wrecked, and there was an orgy of burning of old books and smashing of old art objects, all under the Smashing Four Olds campaign (*Posijiu 破四舊*). Young Red Guards invaded homes and shattered family altars that denoted continued Confucian reverence for generations of forebears. The few temples, mosques, and churches still used for religious purposes were closed and put to secular use. This was an escalation and extreme form of the anti-traditionalist mindset emerging from the May Fourth Movement. It was also a manifestation of the infinite revolution embedded within the historical course of China since the beginning of the twentieth century.

14 See Hong Zicheng, "Yu 'chouchong' you guan: Mayakefusiji, and Tian Han, Meng Jinghui" 與「臭蟲」有關：馬亞克夫斯基，與田漢，孟京輝 (On The Bedbug: Vladimir Mayakovsky, and Tian Han, Meng Jinghui) (unpublished manuscript, May 2019), 11.

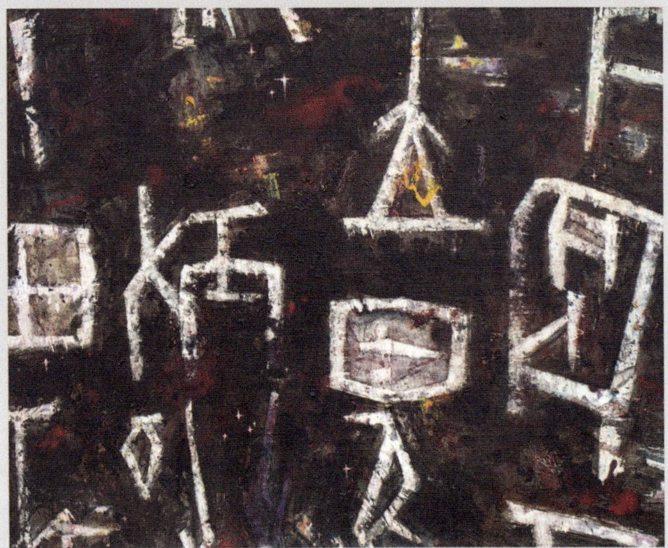

FIG 4 Li Xiushi. *Oracle Reverie*, 1986. Oil painting, 73 × 91 cm. Courtesy of the artist.

The stigmatization and suppression of the old extended to Chinese artistic traditions. It wasn't until the end of the Cultural Revolution that the space was loosened up again for artistic freedom, including the freedom to engage with the past. Amid waves of Intellectual Emancipation, freedom of artistic expression implied for some artists the idea of "formal emancipation." In the wake of the Third Plenary Session of the eleventh Central Committee of the Communist Party in 1978, the issue of form was heatedly debated in the art circle. Artists wanted to unshackle form from a serving and subordinate relationship to subject matter, to be able to experiment with complex aesthetics.

From 1979 to 1981, artist Wu Guanzhong 吳冠中 published multiple articles in the magazine *Art* discussing formal beauty and abstract beauty. Thereafter, the formal beauty of second nature weighed increasingly heavily in art practices. Second nature designates man's transformation and representation of untouched first nature. During Reform and Opening-Up, artists took in modern art from the West on one hand, and turned to historical cultures, heritage, and their native land on the other. Qin-dynasty bricks, Han-dynasty roof-end tiles, Dunhuang murals, and stone carvings of the Huo Qubing Tombs 霍去病墓, trails of admirers made pilgrimages to the native land of beauty, by way of which they sought deep in themselves the nation's creative roots. They created novel composites which expressed the cultures of ancient China through forms developed in Western paintings: Paul Klee's symbols and ancient inscriptions on shells, pottery cultures appearing in fantastic dreams, photo-realist prairie herders, Taichi and Mondrian, Bagua, etc. In such ways, artists rediscovered the lost traditions. Zen Buddhism and mysticism also found a place in the thinking processes of the artists and the visual materials they used. This constituted an artistic phenomenon described by Chinese art historians of the time as "sketching from second nature" (*Xiesheng dier ziran*寫生第二自然).

By now, I have sketched out a trajectory of the negation and resurrection of past artistic traditions in various stages of Chinese contemporary art history since 1949. As such, within the political history of the twentieth century, the reevaluation of heritage and reinvention of tradition has surfaced time and again, but always as a politicized discourse much more than a cultural concern. Such a field of debates and differences in opinions is underlined either by the need for ideological cleansing, the agenda of nation building, the grand narrative of nationalism, or by the desire of intellectuals and artists to regain a certain degree of autonomy.

According to Gao Hua (高華 1954–2011), the late historian of CCP and twentieth-century China, two narrative models have occupied a defining position in modern Chinese history: the revolutionary narrative (*geming xushi* 革命敘事) and the modernization narrative (*xiandaihua xushi* 現代化敘事). Gao made a profound yet simple analysis of the roots and lasting impact of these narratives:

> The so-called revolutionary narrative arose from the 1920s to 1940s and is the revolutionary history of the left. Various 'organic' or 'organized' new intellectuals such as Qu Qiubai (瞿秋白 1899–1935), Zhang Wentian (張聞天1900–1976) and He Ganzhi (何干之 1906–1969) imported a series of concepts and categories from new leftist theories in the Soviet Union and Japan, constructing a system for leftist forces to apply to understanding the reality, past and future of China, with the core theme being the legitimacy and inevitability of revolution in China.[15]

15 Gao Hua, "Xushi shijiao de duoyangxing yu dangdaishi yanjiu: Yi wushi niandai lishi yanjiu weili" 敘事失焦的多樣性與當代史研究：以五十年代和歷史研究為例 (Diversity of Narrative Perspectives and Contemporary Historical Research: the Case of Historical Research on the 1950s), in *Geming Niandai* 革命年代 *(Revolutionary Age)*, (Guangzhou: Guangdong People's Publishing House, 2010), 289. All translations in this essay are by the author unless otherwise stated.

Gao suggested that because the "revolutionary narrative" was rooted in an era of revolutionary struggle, it was marked by strong tones of political mobilization. Socialist Realism was a visual language and carried the inner logic of the revolutionary narrative. Beginning in the mid-1950s, the revolutionary narrative began to slide into ossification and dogmatism. The revolutionary narrative was also underlined by an excessive pursuit of a grand narrative, insisting upon a fixed sense of an inflexible mission before engaging in research and discussion:

> Guided by authoritative descriptions or authoritative documents, it selectively cut-and-pasted historical material in order to affirm a certain authoritative description, simplifying the complex processes of history into an explanation of 'inevitability' while covering over many rich and fresh historical layers.[16]

The other main narrative model, according to Gao, was a narrative centered on the early 1980s as an exceptional moment. According to this model, the discursive frame of contemporary art emerged in the 1980s with the introduction of Western modern art movements, discourses, and theories. Under their impact, art criticism and historical discourse in China adopted Western terminologies and frames to account for contemporary art practices in China. This Western influence, as Gao well knew, had its roots long before, in the May Fourth Movement at the beginning of the twentieth century. This had set in motion new but still hierarchical structures of knowledge. Accordingly, the West was more modern; it was superior and advanced, the model to emulate.

In the past decade, especially in recent years, we have witnessed a drastic reverse of the modernization narrative, in the resurgence of nationalist pride as a dominant phenomenon. The Generation Z, those born between 1995 and 2005, are even considered the generation of nationalists. In practice, such discourses are usually based on generalization and abstraction of the past and selected facts, often out of context, and are in fact a de-historicized understanding of history, as I have demonstrated through Gao's analysis.

Once again, the field of discussing traditions and histories becomes a battlefield of some kind. In recent years, quite a number of conscientious scholars in literature, history, film, and art are working in these respective fields quietly but firmly to counter and subvert such grand and political claims of heritage with the convincing rediscovery and close analysis of detailed historical facts, in order to expand a narrow understanding of the past constructed by the government and mass media. For example, through her research on history and the memory of people in Chinese films since the 1940s, Professor Dai Jinhua 戴錦華, an eminent film historian and cultural theorist at Peking University, looks at how certain films give voices to the people, as opposed to the history told in political discourse and textbooks. Historian Luo Xin 羅新 has researched and is writing about the record of female servants in Northern Wei (386–534) royal palaces in rubbings of monuments from that period so that we can develop our perception of a history that can accommodate everyone, as opposed to a historical record comprised solely of emperors and heroes. At the Inside-Out Art Museum (IOAM), we have been carrying out relentless research into the history of Chinese contemporary art since 1949, analyzing specific years, artistic figures and events, to bring more nuances and historical facts, as opposed to the grand and avant-garde narratives of evolution circulated over and over again. For many of us, the sojourn to the past is the means to the present. The ultimate goal is to loosen or even tamper with the official historical narratives. The more intrinsic motivation is to drag the power of memory and speech into one's own hands. As an exhibition title we organized in 2020 at the IOAM suggested, it's an impulse to turn.

16 Gao, "Diversity of Narrative Perspectives," 289.

Three Plays of Shanshui Memory

216

XIAOXUAN LU &
BO WANG

On September 20, 2018, the last day of the September 2018 inter-Korean summit, South Korean president Moon Jae-in and North Korean leader Kim Jong Un visited a volcanic mountain that straddles the border between North Korea and China. The photo of Moon and Kim, alongside their spouses in front of the crater lake, was a hit on social media FIG 1. In another photo, Moon was captured enthusiastically filling a plastic bottle with water from the lake FIG 2.

This article focuses on the landscape, or shanshui (meaning 山水 "mountain and water" in Chinese) in the background of the photographs mentioned above. In North Korea and South Korea, this mountain is known as Mount Baekdu (백두산 Baekdusan in Korean), which means "White Head Mountain." In China it is known as Mountain Changbai (長白山 Changbaishan in Chinese), meaning "Perpetually White Mountain." Mount Changbai/Baekdu is an active volcano and is the highest mountain in the area of Northeast China and the Korean Peninsula. At its caldera is the Heaven Lake (C. *Tianchi*, K. *Cheonji*), situated 2,744 meters above sea level. This mountain has been characterized by territorial ambiguity and geopolitical contestation for centuries. Its venerable status as a "holy mountain" emerged in the seventeenth century in China and the early eighteenth century in Korea FIG 3.

After conquering China in 1644, Manchu rulers enclosed their homeland Manchuria and converted it into a preserved territory insulated from the Han Chinese and other Tungus tribes. The Policy of Banned Manchuria (C. *fengjin zhengce* 封禁政策, meaning "seal and prohibit policy") was as much a strategic decision to monopolize lucrative local products like ginseng and sable, as it was a symbolic move to romanticize a Manchu identity for political legitimacy. Mount Changbai, the declared birthplace of the Manchu ruling families, where "the dragon rises" (C. *longxing zhidi* 龍興之地), was endowed with sacred status. The Qing Emperor Kangxi ennobled Mount Changbai as the royal ancestral mountain of the Manchu homeland in 1677, thereby dignifying it with the same ritual and ceremonial status as that of the five sacred mountains (C. *wuyue* 五嶽) of the Chinese Central Plains. Mount Changbai's sacredness as the origin of all mountains in Northern China, as Emperor Kangxi claimed, validated the rule of the Manchu over China as a heavenly mandate.

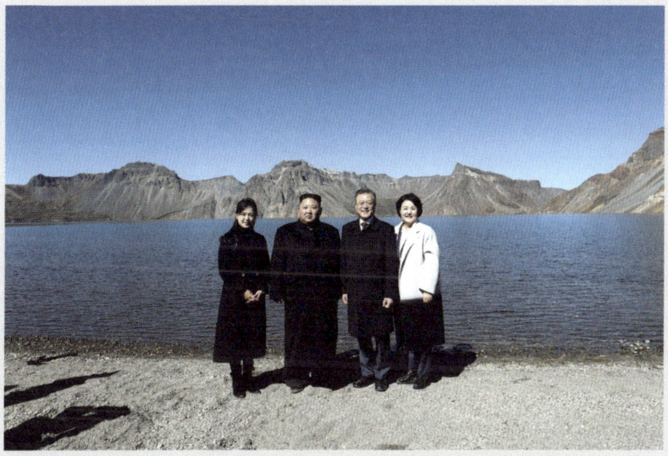

FIG 1 North Korean leader Kim Jong Un (2nd L) and his wife Ri Sol Ju (L) pose with South Korean President Moon Jae-in (2nd R) and his wife Kim Jung-sook (R) at the lakeside on the top of Mount Paektu on September 20, 2018. Image courtesy Pool/ Getty Image News via Getty Images.

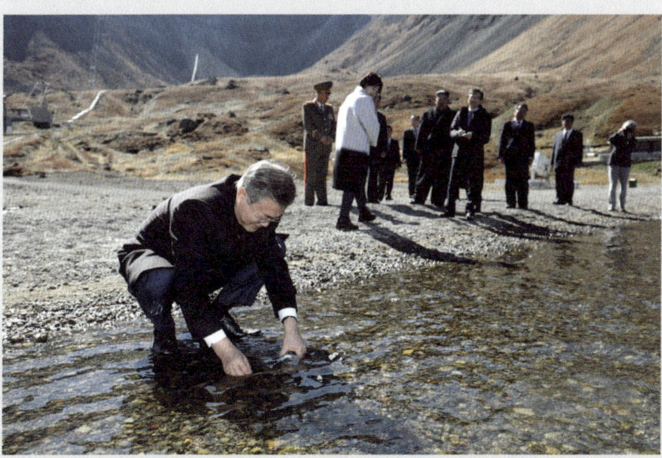

FIG 2 South Korean President Moon Jae-in fills a plastic bottle with water from the Heaven Lake of Mt. Paektu, North Korea, September 20, 2018. Image courtesy Pyeongyang Press Corps / Pool via Reuters.

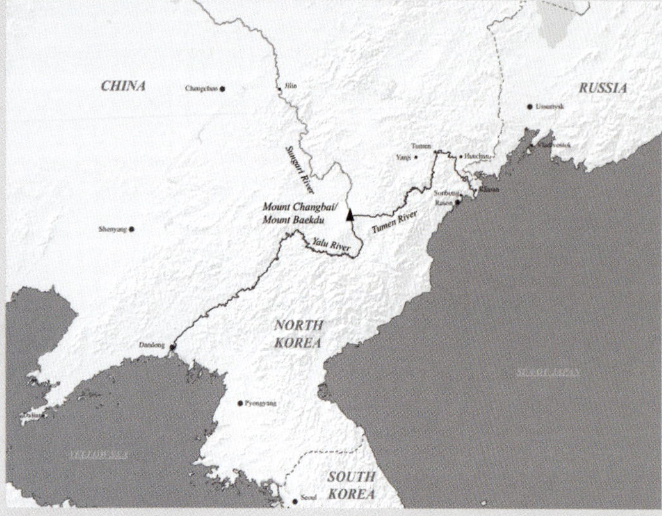

FIG 3 Mount Changbai / Baektu and the Sino-Korean borderland. Map by the author.

In the early eighteenth century, the Joseon government of Korea also promoted the idea that Mount Baekdu was both the progenitor of Korean mountains and rivers, and the birthplace of the ruling family FIG 4. The Korean peninsula is known for being particularly mountainous, which has lent the mountains inherent cultural meanings in spiritual practices and mythologies throughout history. For instance, in the myth of Dangun, the founding king of Gojoseon, Heavenly Princess Hwanung descended from the heavens onto Mount Baekdu and brought to people agriculture and medicine. Hwanung later married Ungyo ("bear woman"), who gave birth to Dangun, the first king of Korea, underneath a sandalwood tree on Mount Baekdu. After ruling the first Korean kingdom of Gojoseon for 1,500 years, Dangun retreated to the mountains and became a mountain god. In earlier versions of the mythology it was at Mount Taebaek that Dangun was born. However, the location was moved to Mount Baekdu given the mountain's increasing significance in the eighteenth century. King Yeongjo of Joseon included Mount Baekdu in the state rites of mountain worship, which linked the legitimacy of his rule with the ancestral origin of Korean landscapes.

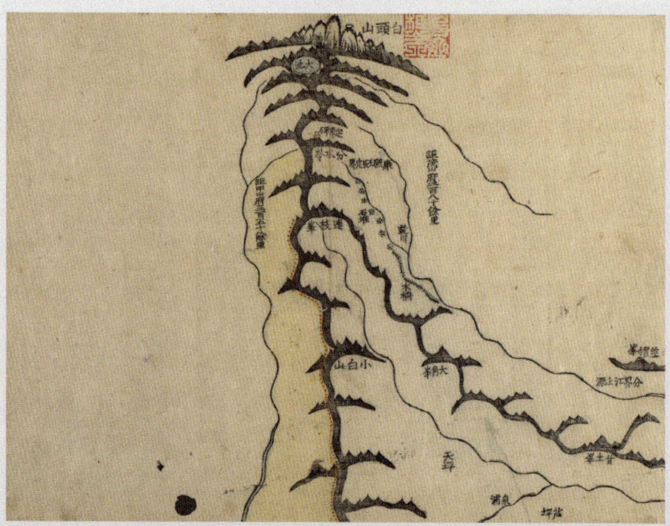

FIG 4 1712 demarcation stele shown on the mid-nineteenth-century Korean map, "Atlas of the Great East" (K. *Taedong yŏjido*). Image courtesy Harvard-Yenching Library.

The two rivers that stream down from the mountain, namely Yalu/Amnok River to the west and the Tumen/Tuman River to the east, have been traditionally regarded as the natural Sino–Korean border. However, the upper reaches of the two rivers remained an unappropriated territory between the two states because of the impregnable topography and complicated river system. In 1712, a joint inspection between Qing officials and Joseon officials was conducted to trace the exact upstream location of the two rivers. A demarcation stele was eventually installed approximately five kilometers southeast of the mountain summit.

> Baekdusan is the progenitor of all eastern mountains, [...] although half of it is foreign land, the other half belongs to our dynasty.
>
> — Han Ikmo, Second State Council of Joseon[1]

1 Nianshen Song, "Imagined Territory: Paektusan in Late Chosŏn Maps and Writings," *Studies in the History of Gardens & Designed Landscapes* 37, no. 2 (April 3, 2017): 167, https://doi.org/10.1080/14601176.2016.1177298.

The 1712 demarcation led to significant contradictions and consequences. From a geomancy point of view, Mount Baekdu was "the progenitor of Korean mountains." However, the 1712 demarcation placed the sacred ancestral mountain outside Korean territory.

The relationship between territorial sovereignties and the myths of national origins were complicated by the mismatch between geomancy and geography.[2] The anomaly of Mount Baekdu as an ancestral mountain of Korea outside the Korean territory lasted until the mid-twentieth century. During the deterioration of Sino-Soviet relations in the late 1950s, China made a significant territorial concession to consolidate support from North Korea. A Sino-North Korean Border Treaty was signed in 1962, which realigned the Sino-Korean border northwards to cut through the middle of Heaven Lake. It was only then that the summit of Mount Changbai/Baekdu became the official border mark between China and North Korea FIG 5. However, the 1962 border treaty compounded modern equivocal discrepancies concerning the relationship among the territorial sovereignties and cultural domains of China, North Korea, and South Korea.

2 Nianshen Song, "Making Borders," in *Modern East Asia: The Tumen River Demarcation, 1881–1919* (Cambridge: Cambridge University Press, 2018), 56.

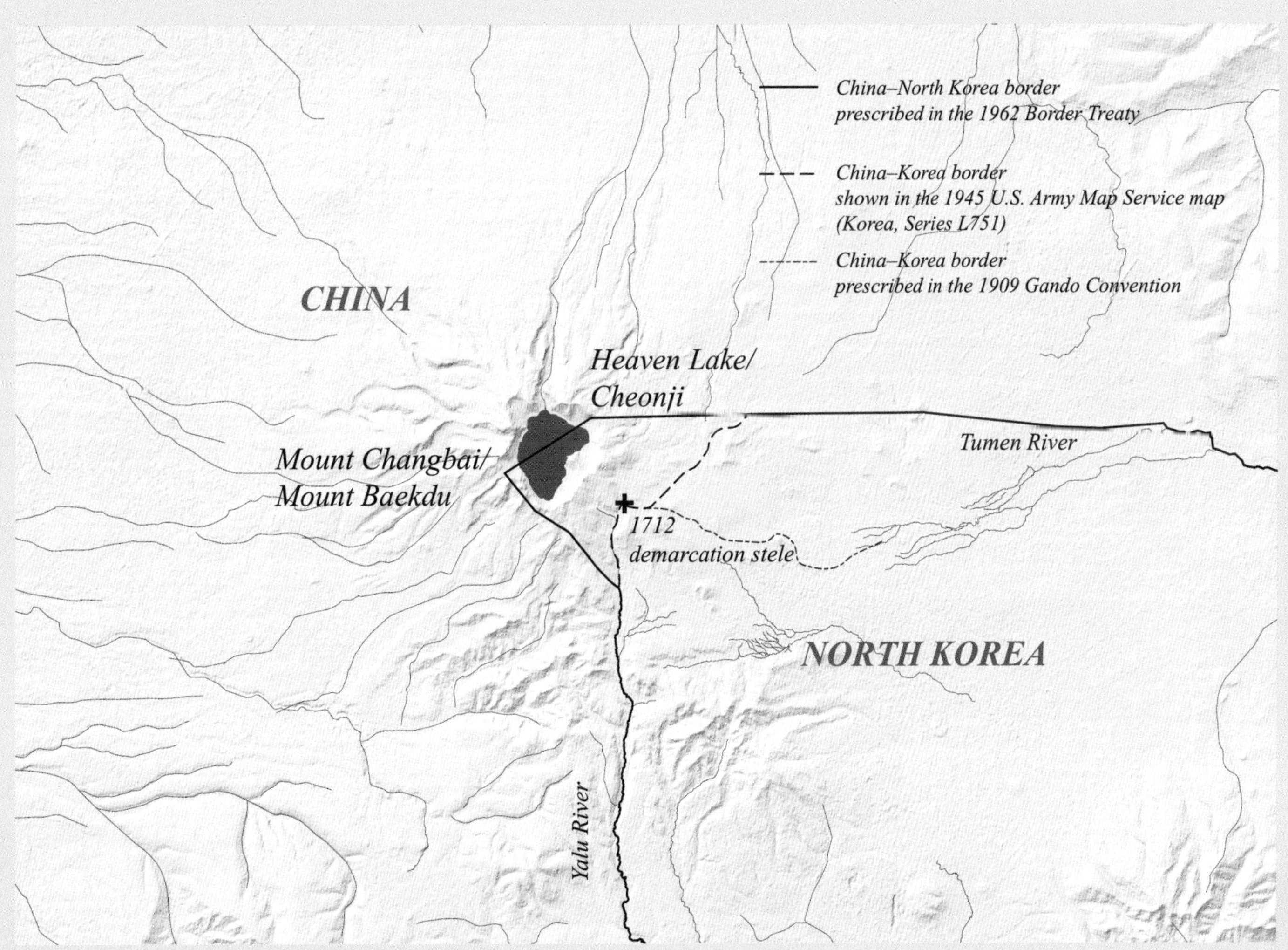

FIG 5 Locations of Heaven Lake, the 1712 demarcation stele, and the borders between China and Korea in 1909, 1945, and 1962. Map by the author.

> Until that day when the waters of the East Sea
> run dry and Mount Baekdusan is worn away,
> God protect and preserve our nation.
>
> — South Korean National Anthem, 1948 [3]

> In the spirit of Mount Baekdu,
> With love of toil that shall never die,
> With will of iron fostered by the truth,
> We'll lead the whole world by and by.
>
> — North Korean National Anthem, 1946 [4]

For nearly four decades after the Korean War in the early 1950s, people from capitalist South Korea were unable to visit Mount Changbai/Baekdu until China and South Korea formally established diplomatic relations in 1992. Mount Changbai/Baekdu has a deep cultural and political significance to South Korean nationalists because of their long overdue opportunity to visit the birthplace of their nation and the reality of division by a war that only ceased but never ended. The fact that South Koreans can only access Heaven Lake and the summit of their ancestral mountain from Chinese territory puts them in an awkward position because their cultural identity is so often wedded with territorial sovereignty in the modern era of nation-states. South Korean tourists visiting Mount Changbai/Baekdu were seen ostentatiously waving national flags and loudly singing their national anthems before heading back home with bottles of water filled from streams in the mountain FIG 6. In 2010, the Chinese local authority imposed a strict ban on any act of nationalist expression that could provoke North Korean border guards nearby and offend visiting Han Chinese and ethnically Korean Chinese.

The increasing number of tourists, particularly those from South Korea, helped stimulate the rapid development of tourism in China's Jilin province, which had been experiencing a crisis of its heavy industry since the launch of China's reform and opening up in the early 1980s. According to the records of the Jilin provincial government, almost half of foreign visitors to Mount Changbai in 2016 were South Korean tourists.[5] Although the Chinese local government banned South Koreans from performing obtrusive acts of worship in Mount Changbai/Baekdu, divertissements are increasingly made available to South Korean visitors on the quest to connect with their roots. A hot spring therapy is a welcome and customary way to top off a tiring day of climbing and paying respects to the mountain. Over the past decade, numerous luxurious hot spring spas with outdoor soaking pools have been built on the northern mountain slopes, which are favored by South Korean tourist groups FIG 7. Immersing oneself in the magical waters of the Changbai/Baekdu volcano is less overtly patriotic, and a more modern consumerist way of connecting physically with the landscape and its cultural connotations.

3 "The National Anthem–Aegukga" (n.d.), https://www.mois.go.kr/eng/sub/a03/nationalSymbol_2/screen.do.

4 "조선민주주의인민공화국의 상징" (2021), https://dprktoday.com/policy/178.

5 Changbai Mountain Management Committee. "長白山景區旅遊人數統計" (2017), http://changbaishan.gov.cn/shjj/tjxx/201701/t20170110_51580.html.

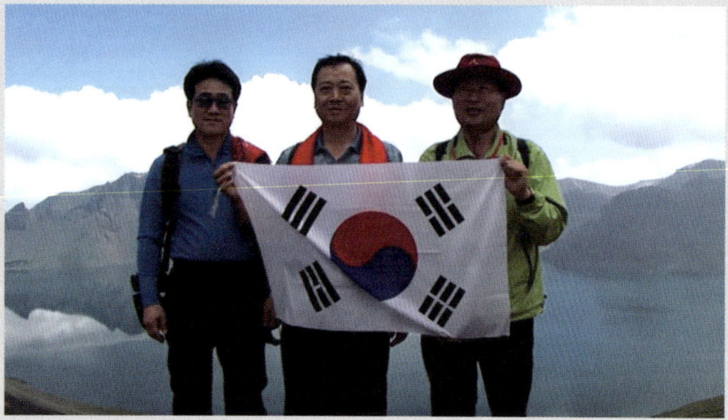

FIG 6 South Korean tourists displaying national flags inside Changbaishan. Source: https://www.youtube.com/watch?v=L59PRv-bNjk (accessed August 24, 2021).

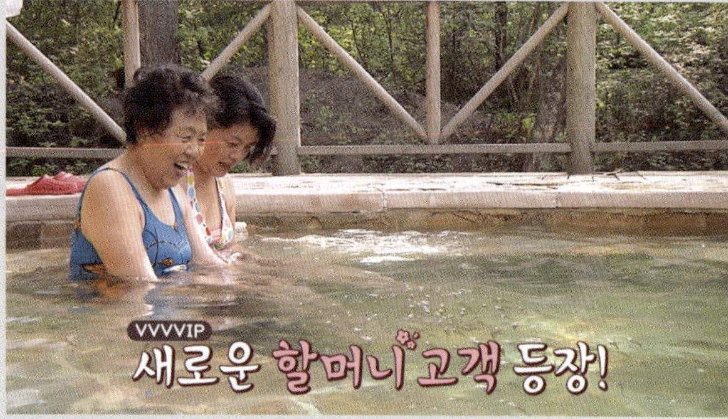

FIG 7 South Korean tourists enjoying Mount Changbai / Baektu hot spring. Source: https://www.youtube.com/watch?v=hpvRlLYtdK4 (accessed August 24, 2021).

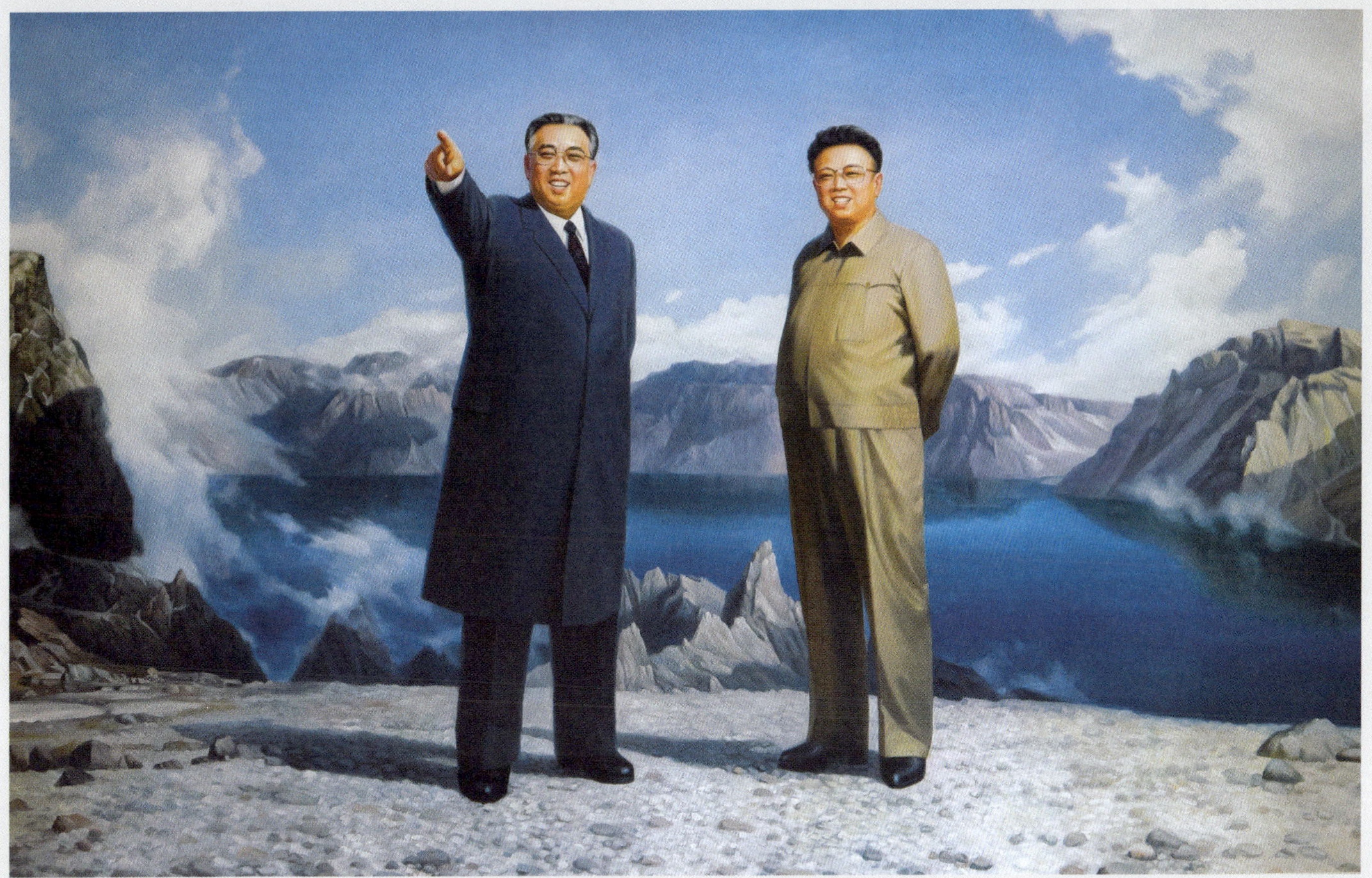

FIG 8 Kim Il-sung and his son Kim Jong-il depicted atop Mount Baekdu. Image courtesty North Korea Picture Library / Alamy Stock Photo.

For North Koreans, the mountain and rivers in the northern border not only connect with ancient mythical origins, but are also a key source of present-day political legitimacy. The landscape of Mount Baekdu is the pivotal space of struggle in the narrative of resistance against Japanese occupation, and lends an almost spiritual dimension to the national struggle. Similar to other like-minded nationalists of his time, a young Kim Il-sung fled north from the harsh Japanese rule in the 1920s. By crossing the Yalu/Amnok River, they entered Manchuria, a liminal space between China, Japan, and the Soviet Union that helped to incubate the anti-Japanese forces and the future political elites of North Korea. The guerilla forces of Korean exiles in Manchuria led by Kim Il-sung were later known as the "Baektusan Generals." Kim Il-sung developed from a young nationalist in exile into a mature revolutionary hero in this ancestral landscape of Mount Baekdu. When they crossed back over Tumen/Tuman River from Manchuria, Kim Il-sung and his guerilla comrades harassed and combatted the Japanese **FIG 8**.

Robert Winstanley-Chesters pointed out the influence of Christian theology in North Korean hagiography, and how the notion of river crossing and return echoes in stories of exodus. The connection, Winstanley-Chesters suggested, might be attributed to the fact that Pyongyang was once populated by Catholics to such an extent that it was even called the "Rome of Asia" at the beginning of the twentieth century.[6] At present, the mountain and water are a space for commemoration. Kim Il-sung's famous crossing in January 1925 through the frozen Yalu/Amnok River has been celebrated in its anniversaries as the beginning of a journey for national liberation.[7] In January 2015, on the occasion of the ninetieth anniversary of the crossing, hundreds of students followed Kim Il-sung's 250-mile journey on foot, traveling from his native village to the crossing point at the Yalu/Amnok River. The act of crossing the river was commemorated in the form of reenactment, but without an actual crossing **FIG 9**.

6 Interview with Robert Winstanley-Chesters, interviewed by Xiaoxuan Lu, October 20, 2019.

7 Robert Winstanley-Chesters, "Charisma in a Watery Frame: North Korean Narrative Topographies and the Tumen River," *Asian Perspective* 40, no. 3 (2016): 393–414, https://doi.org/10.1353/apr.2016.0018.

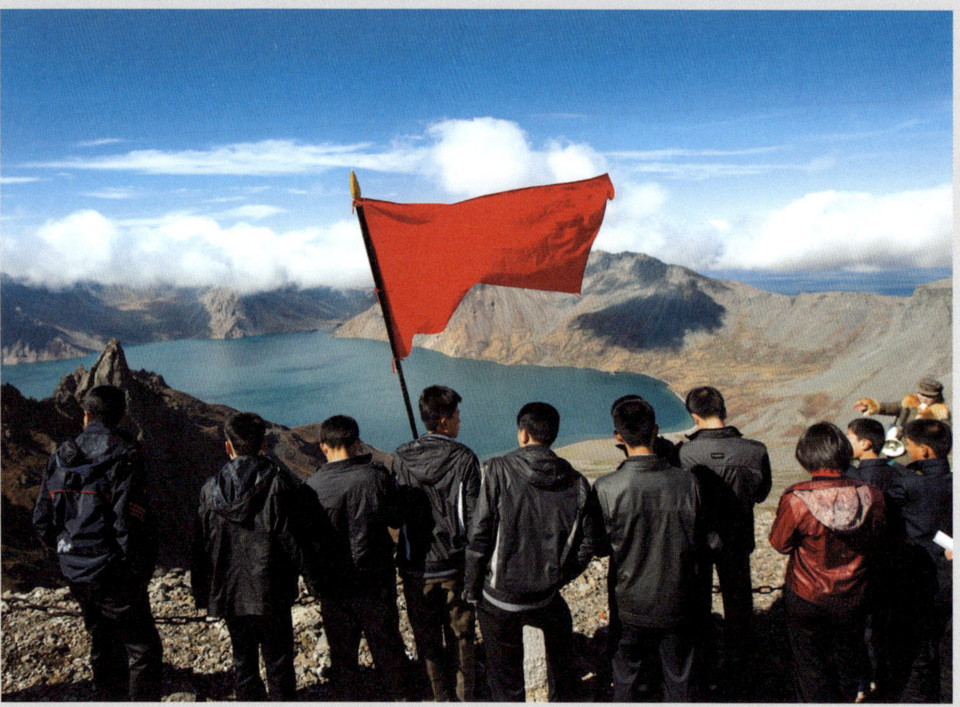

FIG 9 Schoolchildren marching off on the 250-mile pilgrimage for National Liberation, 2015. Image courtesy Eric Lafforgue / agefotostock.

The aura of the landscape as an ancestral origin and a sacred site of national independence converged into the legitimacy of the Kim family succession. According to his official biography, Kim Jong-il, the son of Kim Il-sung, was born in a secret military camp beneath Mount Baekdu in 1941, in the midst of an anti-Japanese war. However, Soviet records show that he was born in Vyatskoye near Khabarovsk, or in Voroshilov near Nikolsk in the Soviet Union.[8] The symbolism of the convergence of Mount Baekdu and the lineage of the Kim family cannot be underestimated, and this significance goes beyond the symbolic. In 2013, the term "Baekdu Bloodline" was edited into the official ideological doctrine, "Ten Principles for the Establishment of a Monolithic Ideological System," which stated that the party and revolution should be "eternally" carried by the "Baekdu Bloodline."[9]

8 Christopher Richardson, "Hagiography of the Kims and the Childhood of Saints," *Change and Continuity in North Korean Politics*, ed. Adam Cathcart, Robert Winstanley-Chesters, and Christopher Green, 2018, http://www.vlebooks.com/vleweb/product/openreader?id=none&isbn=9781134811045.

9 "The Twisted Logic of the N. Korean Regime," *The Chosun Ilbo*, August 13, 2013, http://english.chosun.com/site/data/html_dir/2013/08/13/2013081301558.html.

Act 2: Patriot and Technocrat

The comprehension of borders as a performative and complex process allows a pluralist interpretation of the relationship between sovereignty and globalization, and the notion of bordering permits a more nuanced reading of the intersections between "regimes of sovereignty" and "modes of spatiality."[10] According to to Matthew Sparke, bordering reveals the "discontinuity between the repeated, often reactive, rearticulations of the territorialized nation-state on the one hand, and the neoliberal transnationalizing of the state on the other."[11] It is often believed that today the cultural and political implications of borderland, like the mountains and waters of Mount Changbai/Baekdu, have given way to interests to extract and commodify natural resources, driven by cosmopolitan consumerism that traverses borders. However, a 2015 incident reminded us how an intricate hydrographic system intertwines and overlaps with a dynamic cultural-political-economic context, how the mountain and water could remain an important source of cultural identity and political imagination, and how the seemingly indisputable Sino-Korean border can still be challenged.

10 John Agnew, *Globalization and Sovereignty: Beyond the Territorial Trap* (Lanham: Rowman & Littlefield, 2017), 38.

11 Matthew Sparke, *In the Space of Theory: Postfoundational Geographies of the Nation-State* (Minneapolis, MN: University of Minnesota Press, 2005), 164.

In 2011, South Korea's largest processed food manufacturer Nongshim announced the establishment of its mineral water production plant in Antu County, Jilin province, at the foothill of Mount Changbai/Baekdu. The establishment of a large South Korean industrial facility marked a successful case for Antu County's efforts to attract overseas investments using its natural resources. For Nongshim, the setting up of the mineral water bottling plant in China was a strategic decision in response to an unprecedented crisis in the domestic market. Since 1998, Nongshim had monopolized the sales of Samdasoo, the mineral water brand that had dominated the South Korean market. Samdasoo was extracted from Mount Halla, a volcano in Jeju Island and the highest mountain in South Korea FIG 10. In 2011, however, Jeju Province Development Corporation, the producer of Samdasoo, decided to cancel their contract with Nongshim and chose Kwang Dong Pharmaceutical as their new sales partner.

Nongshim needed to conjure up a new water product in order to reclaim its market share after losing its long-established mineral water brand. What could compete with "the only volcano bedrock water in South Korea," extracted from the highest mountain in the country?[12] There could be no better choice than the waters from Mount Baekdu, the highest mountain in the Korean Peninsula and the place of origin of the Korean people. In traditional Korean geography, the concept of Baekdu-Daegan gives rise to the geomantic interpretation of the mountain system in Korea. Mount Baekdu and Mount Halla are situated at the northern and southern ends, respectively, of Baekdu-Daegan. This mountain system is known as the "spine of Korea," which runs through the length of the Korean Peninsula with a rigid crest line that blocks water from flowing through. Mount Baekdu is referred to as the "grandfather" and Mount Halla as the "grandmother" of Korean mountains.

12 Jeju Province Development Corporation, "The Birth of Samdasoo," https://www.jpdc.co.kr/samdasoo/eng/birth.htm.

At that time, the company may also have been inspired by South Korean tourists' desire to bring water back home from Mount Changbai/Baekdu during their visit to the China side of the mountain. Baeksansoo is the new brand for Nongshim's water extracted from Mount Baekdu, which draws heavily on the cultural imaginations that link the water source to the ancestry of Korea FIG 11. According to the official website of Nongshim, the name Baeksansoo deploys the ancient name of Mount Baekdu—"Baeksan." This name was first used in the seminal geographic work "Critical Waters in the Great Eastern State" (K. *Daedong sugyeong* 대동수경) by Dasan Jeong Yak-yong, one of the greatest thinkers of the eighteenth century in the late Joseon period.[13] Prior to 2015, the overwhelming majority of Baeksansoo was exported to South Korea rather than being sold or consumed in China, its country of origin. However, a 2014 safety scandal involving China's monopolist domestic bottled water brand Nongfu Spring opened up opportunities for Baeksansoo to enter the Chinese market.

13 Nongshim, "GLOBAL NONGSHIM," http://eng.nongshim.com/brand/main/index.

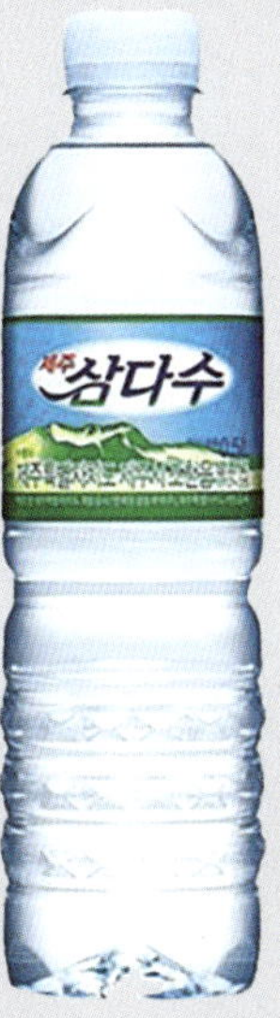

FIG 10 Product image of Samdasoo, showing image of Mount Halla on the bottle label.

If Nongshim's extraction of natural mineral water from China for its domestic market can be seen as a process of de-bordering, the marketing of Baeksansoo in China since 2015 can be interpreted as a process of re-bordering. Initially, the marketing of Baeksansoo in China encountered backlashes. Antu County was accused of selling Mount Changbai to South Korea and issues of ceding the territory to North Korea in 1962 were brought up again in online forums. Chinese bloggers claimed Mount Changbai has always been a Chinese mountain. They posted videos and photographs of South Korean tourists on Mount Changbai waving the South Korean national flags and singing their national anthems, linking the extraction of the mineral water by a foreign brand to a feeling of territory loss.

To prevent further escalation of resentment from Chinese consumers, Nongshim emphasized its longer history of mineral water production compared with other Asian beverage companies and portrayed itself as an international company of Korean origin rather than a domestic one. Most importantly, Nongshim toned down the cultural narrative attached to marketing Baeksansoo in South Korea, and promoted a technological and cosmopolitan narrative tailored for the Chinese market. Baeksansoo is reframed as a collaboration between the Antu County government and Nongshim, where world-class technology meets a natural mineral water source of top quality. Nongshim highlighted its use of best packaging and bottling technologies for Baeksansoo (machines made by Krones AG from Germany), along with their previous success in global markets,

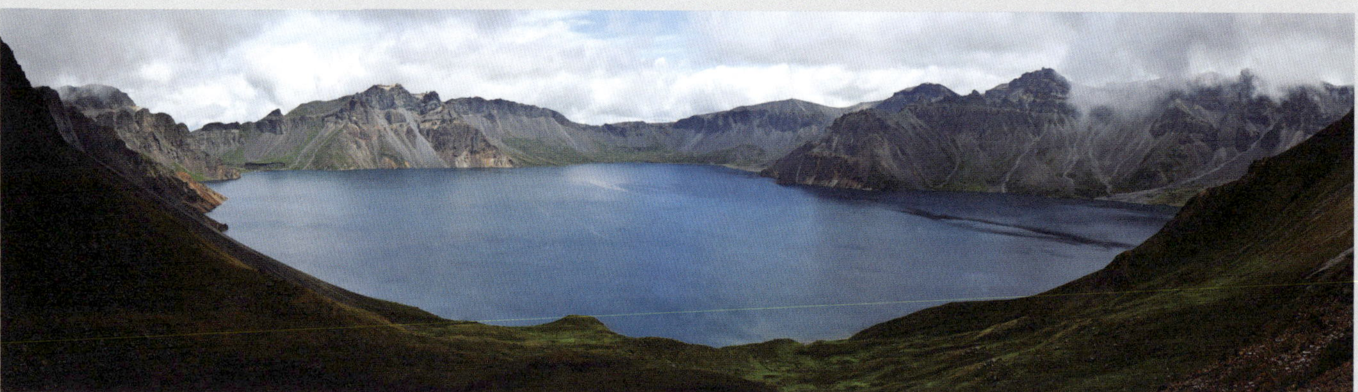

FIG 11 Heaven Lake on Mount Baekdu straddles the border between China and North Korea. Image courtesy Junpyo Lee via Getty Images.

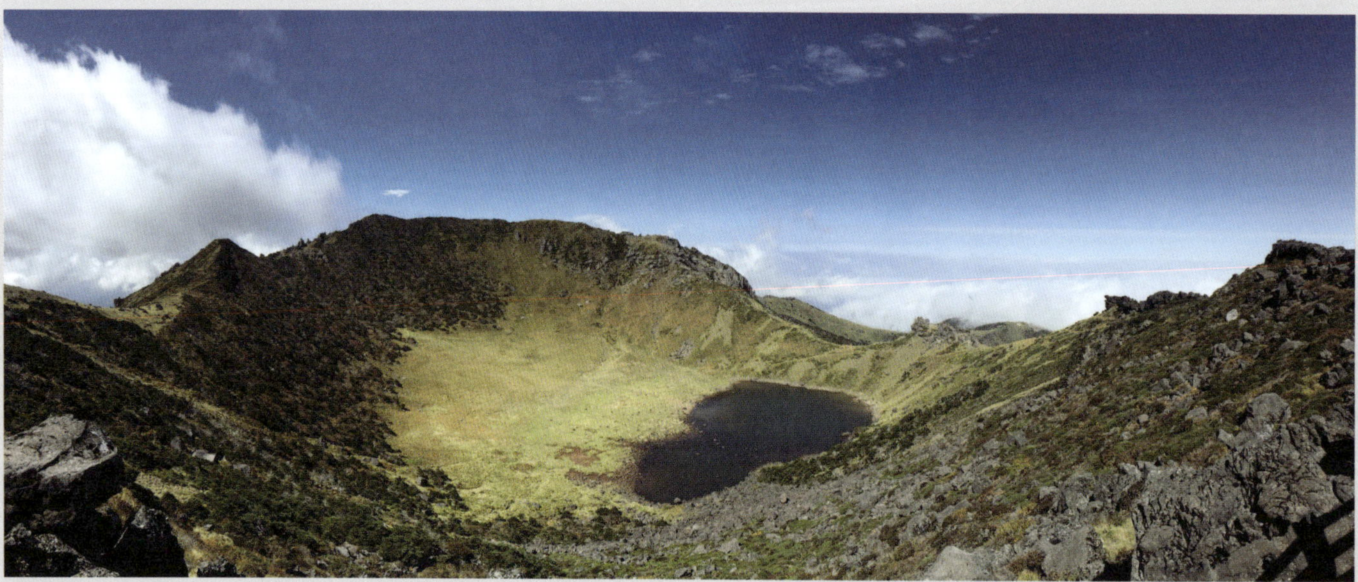

FIG 12 Baengnokdam Lake on Mount Halla in Jeju island, South Korea. Image courtesy etude4/Imazins via Getty Images.

including South Korea, Japan, and Hong Kong, to promote the impression that its product is internationally recognized FIG 12. By stating that "the smart Baeksansoo Factory in Mount Baekdu offers healthier water for the citizens of the globe," Nongshim skillfully refocused the narrative onto corporate responsibility and global vision.[14]

Act 3: Football and Alien

A number of Chinese mineral water producers followed suit after Nongshim's launch of water production plants in Antu County in 2011. Antu County became the largest mineral water bottling base in the world with the completion of Evergrande's water bottling plants in 2013. Evergrande was a newcomer in the bottled water industry. Headquartered in Guangzhou in southern China, Evergrande was the second largest property developer in China as of 2014, having made its fortune by selling apartments to middle- and upper-middle-class buyers since the mid-1990s. The business diversification strategy of the company, which was launched in early 2010, aimed to expand its investments into new territories, such as education, tourism, sports, medical care, entertainment, and consumer packaged goods including packaged foods and beverages. Evergrande Spring (C. *hengda bingquan* 恆大冰泉), the new product of the corporation, was launched within this context.

14 Nongshim, Nongshim Promotion Film, video, 2015, http://eng.nongshim.com/pr/promotion.html.

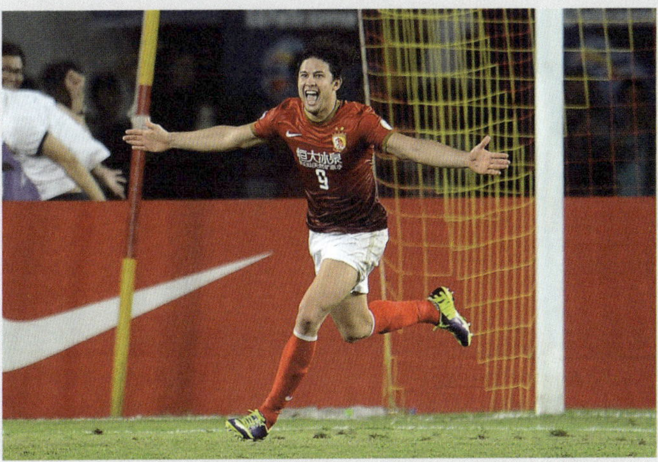

FIG 13 Elkeson de Oliveira Cardoso, later known as Ai Kesen, scored for Guangzhou Evergrande at the Asian Championship final against FC Seoul, November 9, 2013. The sponsorship on his chest displayed "Evergrande Spring, Natural Mineral Water from Mount Changbai." Born in Brazil, Elkeson was naturalized in 2019 and became the first player who ever played for China without Chinese ancestry. Image courtesy (Thananuwat Srirasant / Getty Images Sport) via Getty Images.

The inauguration of Evergrande Spring could not have been made more nationalistic. On November 9, 2013, the second leg of the Asian Football Championship finals kicked off at Tianhe Stadium in Guangzhou. The final game was a match between K-league champion FC Seoul, and Chinese champion Guangzhou Evergrande, which was owned by Evergrande Corporation. The event marked the first time a Chinese club entered the Asian Championship finals since the start of the millennium. Under such historical significance, and given China's perennial Korea-phobia in football, the match was tinted with a heavy, arduous, and suffocating nationalist atmosphere. Before the game started, Evergrande decided to drop the previous corporate sponsorship printed on the chest of their jerseys, and replaced it with a promotion of their brand-new water product, the Evergrande Spring FIG 13. The appearance of a Chinese team in the finals of a continental tournament was a huge stimulus for Chinese football after more than ten years of recession. More than 120 million people watched the game live.[15] After a stressful ninety minutes, the game ended 1-1. Guangzhou Evergrande managed to keep the champion trophy from the visiting rival Korean team on advantage in away goals.

15 Zhe Li, "亞冠決賽吸引1.2億觀眾收看世界盃奧運外10年最高," November 14, 2013, http://sports.sina.com.cn/j/2013-11-14/22366884568.shtml.

If the choice to launch Evergrande Spring in a football game against the South Korean team inevitably drew heavily nationalist sentiments, the branding messages that followed were more nuanced and implicit. For a long time, Chinese food manufacturing brands have been haunted by a series of safety scandals from dominant domestic brands such as that of Mengniu Dairy in 2008 and Nongfu Spring in 2013. Thus, Chinese consumers are deeply concerned about the safety of domestic food brands. In May 2014, Evergrande Spring held a ceremony to sign cooperation agreements with distributors from thirteen European countries at the Great Hall of People in Beijing. This high-profile ceremony paired within the brand the dilemmas of international and local, and modern and pristine. On the one hand, the partnerships with European distributors indicated that the quality of the Evergrande Spring was on a par with international standards, thus setting itself apart from other domestic brands. On the other hand, to rebuild the confidence of Chinese consumers, Mount Changbai was promoted as a pristine landscape and "one of the three golden water sources in the world" together with the European Alps and the Russian Caucasus.

To promote its water brand in mainland China, Evergrande commissioned a multi-million-dollar advertisement in summer 2014. Situated within the corporation's broader diversification plan, the advertisement reflected Evergrande's effort to link entertainment with its rapid turnover consumer goods interests. Around this time, the Korean drama *My Love from the Star* (2013) met unprecedented success in China and received more than 2.7 billion views on Chinese online platform iQiyi alone. *My Love from the Star* was a love story between an alien, played by Kim Soo-hyun, and his human female neighbor, played by Jun Ji-hyun. Kim and Jun were sought after by mass-market advertising agencies in China and the duo were paid 1 billion Korean Won (8.9 million USD) to appear in the Evergrande Spring commercial. However, this high-cost commercial, which was supposedly culturally neutral and apolitical, was met with ferocious political reactions from South Korea. South Korean nationalists raged over the two top K-pop stars, who were supposed to be ambassadors of Korean culture, appearing in a commercial that calls the Korean ancestral mountain Mount Changbai instead of Mount Baekdu.

Kim and Jun temporarily backed out of the deal in June 2014, but later decided to continue with the advertisement because revoking their contracts with Evergrande Spring could potentially result in penalties amounting to tens of millions of Korean Won. In one of the Evergrande commercials, the next-door alien lover Kim Soo-hyun was seen demonstrating how to use the Evergrande Spring for drinking, cooking rice, and making tea. "If you like me, drink Evergrande Spring," Kim called on his fans. This water brand catapulted the influence of the super idol, whose innocuous soft masculinity easily permeates boundaries in East Asia. The 2014 incident demonstrated that the contemporary border between China and Korea is by no means less contested than that between Qing and Joseon in the seventeenth century, even though it is sometimes rendered invisible by the influx of international capital into the borderland. The slowdowns or blockages in the seemingly inexorable flow of commodification remind us that Mount Changbai/Baekdu is not only a physical entity powered by nature but also a biography, a romance animated by our tangled love affairs with imperialism, communism, capitalism, neocolonialism, nationalism, and now our desperate, helpless infatuation with consumerism.

Acknowledgement

The authors would like to thank Dr. Robert Winstanley-Chesters from the University of Leeds and Prof. Nianshen Song from Tsinghua University, whose insight and knowledge into the subject matter steered us through this research. An earlier version of this article titled "My Love from the Mountain: Contingent Bordering Processes at Mount Changbai/Baekdu" was published in *Area* in March 2021 (DOI: 10.1111/area.12706).

References

Agnew, John. *Globalization and Sovereignty: Beyond the Territorial Trap*. Lanham: Rowman & Littlefield, 2017.

Changbai Mountain Management Committee. "長白山景區旅遊人數統計," January 10, 2017. http://changbaishan.gov.cn/shjj/tjxx/201701/t20170110_51580.html.

Jeju Province Development Corporation. "The Birth of Samdasoo," https://www.jpdc.co.kr/samdasoo/eng/birth.htm.

Li, Zhe. "亞冠决賽吸引1.2億觀眾收看世界盃奥運外10年最高," November 14, 2013. http://sports.sina.com.cn/j/2013-11-14/22366884568.shtml.

Nongshim. "GLOBAL NONGSHIM". http://eng.nongshim.com/brand/main/index.

Nongshim. Nongshim Promotion Film. Video, 2015. http://eng.nongshim.com/pr/promotion.html.

Richardson, Christopher. "Hagiography of the Kims and the Childhood of Saints." *Change and Continuity in North Korean Politics*, edited by Adam Cathcart, Robert Winstanley-Chesters, and Christopher Green, 2018. http://www.vlebooks.com/vleweb/product/openreader?id=none&isbn=9781134811045.

Song, Nianshen. "Imagined Territory: Paektusan in Late Chosŏn Maps and Writings." *Studies in the History of Gardens & Designed Landscapes* 37, no. 2 (April 3, 2017): 157–73. https://doi.org/10.1080/14601176.2016.1177298.

Song, Nianshen. *Making Borders in Modern East Asia: The Tumen River Demarcation*, 1881–1919. Cambridge: Cambridge University Press, 2018.

Sparke, Matthew. *In the Space of Theory: Postfoundational Geographies of the Nation-State*. Minneapolis, MN: University of Minnesota Press, 2005.

The Chosun Ilbo. "The Twisted Logic of the N.Korean Regime," August 13, 2013. http://english.chosun.com/site/data/html_dir/2013/08/13/2013081301558.html.

The Chosun Ilbo. "Kim Soo-hyun and Jeon Ji-hyun Were Used in China's 'Northeast Project'?" June 20, 2014. https://biz.chosun.com/site/data/html_dir/2014/06/20/2014062003047.html.

The National Anthem–Aegukga (n.d.). https://www.mois.go.kr/eng/sub/a03/nationalSymbol_2/screen.do.

Winstanley-Chesters, Robert. "Charisma in a Watery Frame: North Korean Narrative Topographies and the Tumen River." *ASIAN PERSPECTIVE* 40, no. 3 (2016): 393–414. https://doi.org/10.1353/apr.2016.0018.

조선민주주의인민공화국의 상징 (2021), https://dprktoday.com/policy/178.

Elusive Inventories: on the Collection of Jane Ryan and William Saunders

228

PIO ABAD

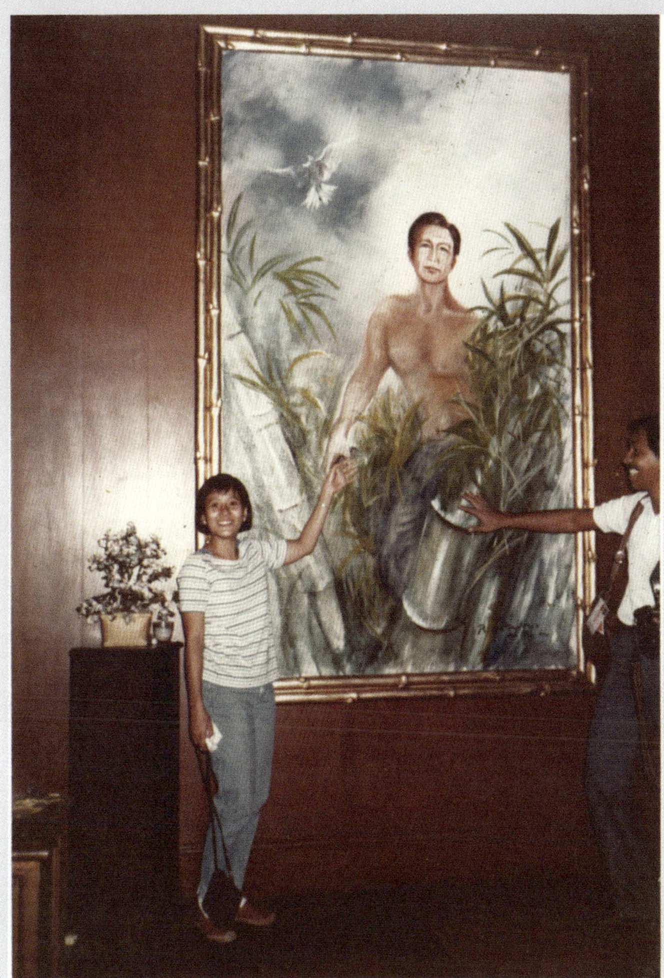

FIG 1 *Untitled (25 February 1986)*, 2011. Framed inkjet print on Hahnemuhle pearl paper.

The Collection of Jane Ryan and William Saunders is an ongoing project that I started in 2012. It focuses on the role that a collection of artefacts has played in the recent history of the Philippines, specifically on the cultural legacy of Ferdinand and Imelda Marcos, who ruled the country as a conjugal dictatorship—under what they preferred to call constitutional authoritarianism, which I prefer to call a "plunderocracy"—from 1965 to 1986.

I started working on *The Collection of Jane Ryan and William Saunders* shortly after the events of the so-called Arab Spring, the wave of anti-government protests that began with a fruit seller self-immolating in the Tunisian town of Sid Bouzid before spreading throughout the Middle East, demanding an end to tyranny and corruption and bringing down long-established autocracies in Tunisia, Egypt, and Libya. In October that year, images of triumphant revolutionaries flashing peace signs astride Muammar Qaddafi's gilt mermaid sofa and footage of the Libyan dictator's brutalized corpse, stripped of his brocade robes, lying unceremoniously in a shopping center cold storage, pointed to the growing consensus that the age of the flamboyant despot was over and that the rest of the world was moving towards a more democratic direction powered by the organizing capacity of social media.

The events of the past ten years have only confirmed the truism that at the end of every revolution, you find yourself right back where you started. Seif al-Islam Qaddafi, the second son and heir apparent, recently emerged from captivity to give an interview to the *New York Times* and announced that he was preparing for a political comeback, having convinced his captors to join his side.[1] In July 2020, it was revealed that Ferdinand "Bongbong" Marcos Jr. had asked the political data company Cambridge Analytica to help in rebranding the family name, part of a concerted social media campaign to erase historical facts and build an army of online trolls to harass critics, in preparation for his ultimately triumphant presidential campaign.[2] In May 2022, Marcos Jr. was elected president of the Philippines with an overwhelming majority of 31 million votes.

1 Robert F. Worth, "Qaddafi's Son is Alive. And He Wants to Take Libya Back," *New York Times*, July 30, 2021, https://www.nytimes.com/2021/07/30/magazine/qaddafi-libya.html. Accessed October 18, 2021.

2 Sofia Tomacruz, "Bongbong Marcos asked Cambridge Analytica to Rebrand Family Image," Rappler, July 15, 2020, https://www.rappler.com/nation/bongbong-marcos-cambridge-analytica-rebrand-family-image. Accessed October 18, 2021.

When I first exhibited the project in 2014, the current unravelling of democratic institutions and historical certainties seemed inconceivable. The scourge of populism that gave rise to Trump, Brexit, Duterte, and Bongbong was not yet part of the political landscape. The phrase "fake news" was not yet uttered in the vernacular. Since then, every invitation to present the work has been an opportunity to reevaluate this project through collapsing political paradigms and to rearticulate its urgency amidst this global resurgence of toxic political fantasy.

The Collection of Jane Ryan and William Saunders is an examination of the fantasies wielded by the Marcoses that continue to shape cultural and political narratives, and a subsequent disavowal of these fantasies by excavating silenced histories, devising actions, and remaking an inventory of objects tainted by the regime's corruption.

The project began with the discovery of a family photograph. The painting in the photo depicts Ferdinand Marcos as the mythical figure Malakas. According to Philippine creationist mythology, Malakas (The Strong) and Maganda (The Beautiful) were the first Filipinos, who entered the world fully formed when a magical bird split a single stalk of bamboo in half, revealing the pair cradled inside. These images of the couple were fed into the propa-ganda machine and proliferated as murals, paintings, and sculptures throughout the city. In assuming the personas of Malakas and Maganda, the Marcoses sought to mythologize and present themselves as the center of cultural and political renewal in the Philippines. The official slogan of the dicta-torship was "Make this nation great again."

The image of the couple emerging nude from a bamboo stalk became the iconographic representation of the regime amidst its proclamations of postcolonial self realization. An irony given that Marcos was largely enabled by Western democracies wary of the rising tide of communism in Southeast Asia. On a visit to Manila in 1984, then-Vice President George H.W. Bush raised a toast to Ferdinand Marcos for "his adherence to democratic principles," shortly after a farcical election marred by widespread fraud and a year after the assassination of opposition leader Ninoy Aquino.[3] This was an American policy towards the dictatorship that transcended presidencies. Richard Nixon consented to his declaration of martial law in 1972, shutting down congress, arresting opponents, and suspending all civil rights. Marcos became adept at using the American military bases in Subic and Clark, key strategic military positions in the American Vietnam War and ensuing Cold War, as bargaining chips to ensure that every American president, from Lyndon B. Johnson to Ronald Reagan, always turned a blind eye.

Fortunately, at least for one historical moment, Filipino agency overtook imperial expediency. On February 25, 1986, the Marcoses were forced out of office after two million Filipino civilians took to the streets in a non-violent uprising known as the EDSA Revolution.

This photograph was taken by my mother that evening, a few hours after Ferdinand and Imelda Marcos fled Malacañang Palace and boarded one of Ronald Reagan's helicopters for a reluctant, yet still luxurious, Honolulu exile. My mother and my father, the person happily posing in the photo, were part of the first wave of protesters to enter their private chambers. A few years before, they were both arrested and detained for their roles in establishing the social democratic movement that would eventually be crucial in toppling the dictatorship. They would later be involved in the country's difficult and increasingly disheartening transition to democracy after twenty years of authoritarian rule, a national project currently in tatters.

3 Stanley Karnow, *In Our Image: America's Empire in the Philippines* (New York, NY: Random House, 1989), 5.

This photo is one of the earliest documentations of that exact moment when the public façade of Malakas and Maganda collapsed and the people they had been oppressing suddenly had access to the sordid private life behind these misrepresentations. The Marcoses' modernist myth came at the cost of 3,240 lives, the torture of 34,000 more, and the systematic ransacking of the national treasury, one of the largest thefts in history that exploited the then-nascent neoliberal system of offshore havens and shell companies.

Jane Ryan and William Saunders were the false identities used by Imelda and Ferdinand Marcos to deposit $950,000 into four Swiss bank accounts at Credit Suisse in Zurich on March 20, 1968. It was through this account, and many others that followed, that the couple purchased art and property, among them 40 Wall Street (now known as the Trump Building), donated a million dollars to each of Richard Nixon's presidential campaigns, and transformed foreign aid into private wealth. By the time they left office, investigators estimated their wealth to be about ten billion US dollars. The annual salary of the Philippine president at that time was P100,000, roughly US$4,700.

The Collection of Jane Ryan and William Saunders begins with these fictional portraits of the collectors. Shortly after the revolution, the portraits of Ferdinand Marcos as Malakas and Imelda as Maganda, made by an artist named Evan Cosayco, were moved from the presidential bedrooms and placed on display at the Malacañang Palace Museum where they remained for a number of years. However, when I visited in 2010, I was surprised to find that they were no longer available. So I decided that the best way for me to see them again was to get them remade. This process of remembering through remaking then became key in rendering this collection visible.

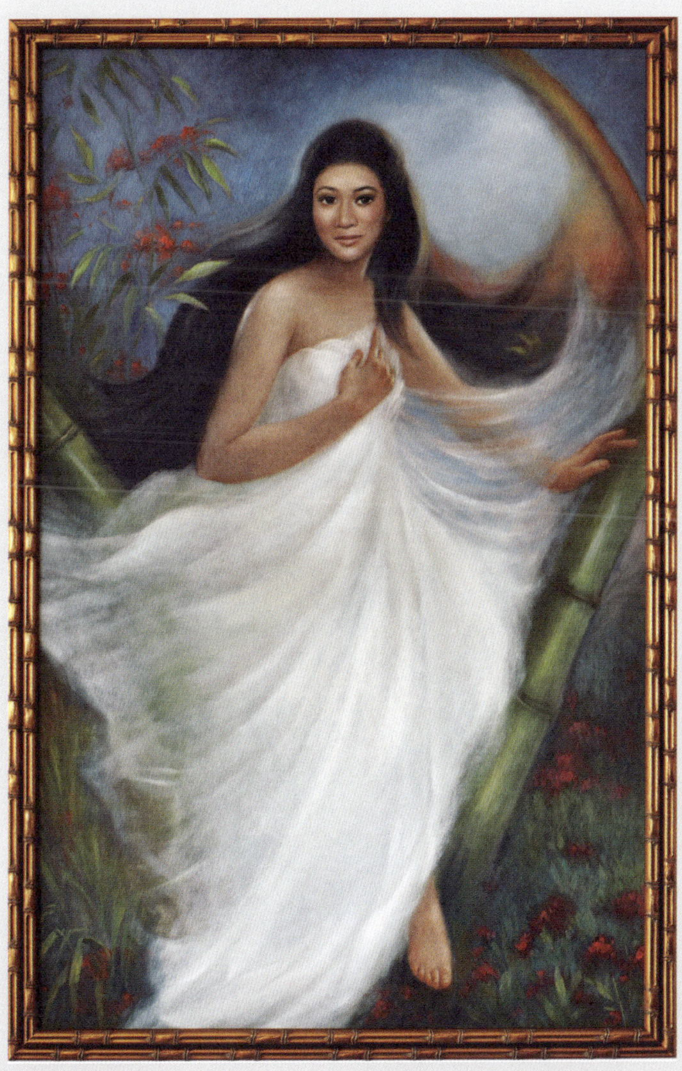

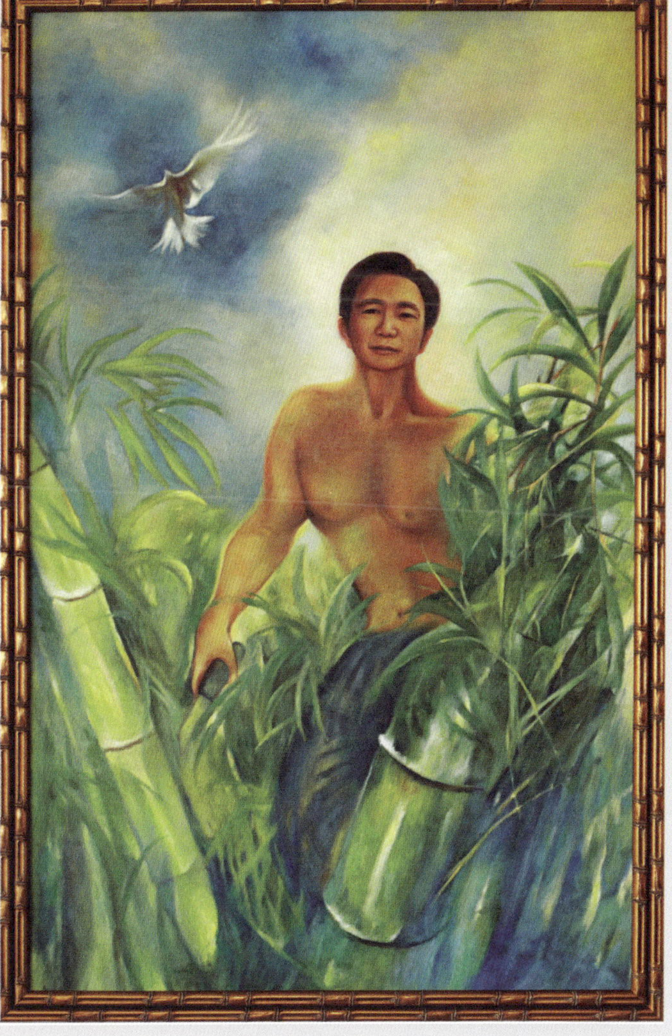

FIG 2 *Imelda as Maganda & Ferdinand as Malakas*, 2014–16. Black paint on digitally printed canvas and faux gold bamboo frame, framed inkjet print on Hahnemuhle pearl paper, and video in white aluminium frame.

On November 18, 2016, the Philippine Supreme Court allowed for the corpse of Ferdinand Marcos to be buried in the National Heroes Cemetery, in a way completing the symbolic restitution that the Marcoses have sought since their temporary defeat. At that time, the Malakas and Maganda replica paintings were on display at the Museum of Contemporary Art and Design in Manila, and I asked that they be painted over, an intervention that seemed the only possible response, an act of protest and an act of despair.

The events of the past few years have changed the photograph entirely, from an image of euphoric revolutionary victory to evidence of political failure. For all my parents' idealism and sacrifice, it is painful to confront the reality that the Marcoses and their adept mythologizing never really went away—that a blatantly corrupt regime, once overwhelmingly rejected, has gained absolution, even fealty, in such a short amount of time.

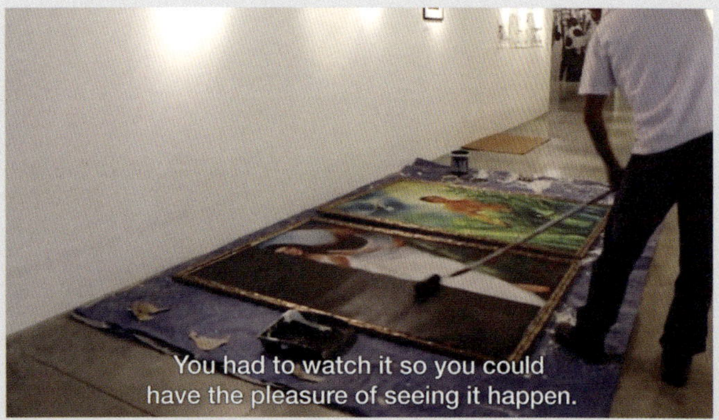

FIG 3 *Imelda as Maganda & Ferdinand as Malakas*, 2014–16. Black paint on digitally printed canvas and faux gold bamboo frame, framed inkjet print on Hahnemuhle pearl paper, and video in white aluminium frame.

A particular childhood memory has been very important in trying to understand how this has happened. As a six-year-old, my first memory of a museum was irrevocably tied to the fall of the regime. For a number of years after the revolution, the basement of the Malacañang Palace was turned into a provisional museum—a hastily constructed display of personal effects that has become a post-revolutionary trope in freshly liberated autocracies. I vividly remember walking through rows and rows of mahogany shelves and table tops, each one spilling over with things: clothing, ornaments, perfume bottles, bulletproof bras and, yes, the infamous pairs of shoes.

Unfortunately, along with the fragile democracy came the failure to institutionalize the collective acts of remembering that these displays were meant to encourage. By 1990, the political compromises of the new government, the blatant refusal of other governments to aid any substantial efforts to recover the Marcos' loot lest their own complicity be called out, and the convenient shifts in allegiances by many of Marcoses' cronies, meant that by the time this museum was packed away, the clam of an exhausted and disillusioned public for accountability seemed to have gone with it. Thirty-six years later, no one from the regime, much less the family, has been persecuted and accounts of its corruption and violence remain absent from school textbooks and historical curricula, making it too easy for collective memory to be transformed into partisan fictions.

Reconstructing the collection has been a defiant attempt to achieve some kind of accountability by insisting on the inventory as a strategy for transparency and resistance. The scale of the Marcoses' loot is so vast and so astonishing in range that it is often only referred to in collective terms—loot, plunder, ill-gotten wealth. So much so that over time, it has assumed, in its status as a collective noun, an almost abstract singularity—a single object then easier to disregard, to trivialize or contain within one of Imelda's stilettos. One of the main reasons behind this project was to disentangle this "loot" from that collective singularity, laying out individual objects almost forensically to confront the public with its unwieldy scale and its terrifying range—although what exactly that scale and range were remains unclear.

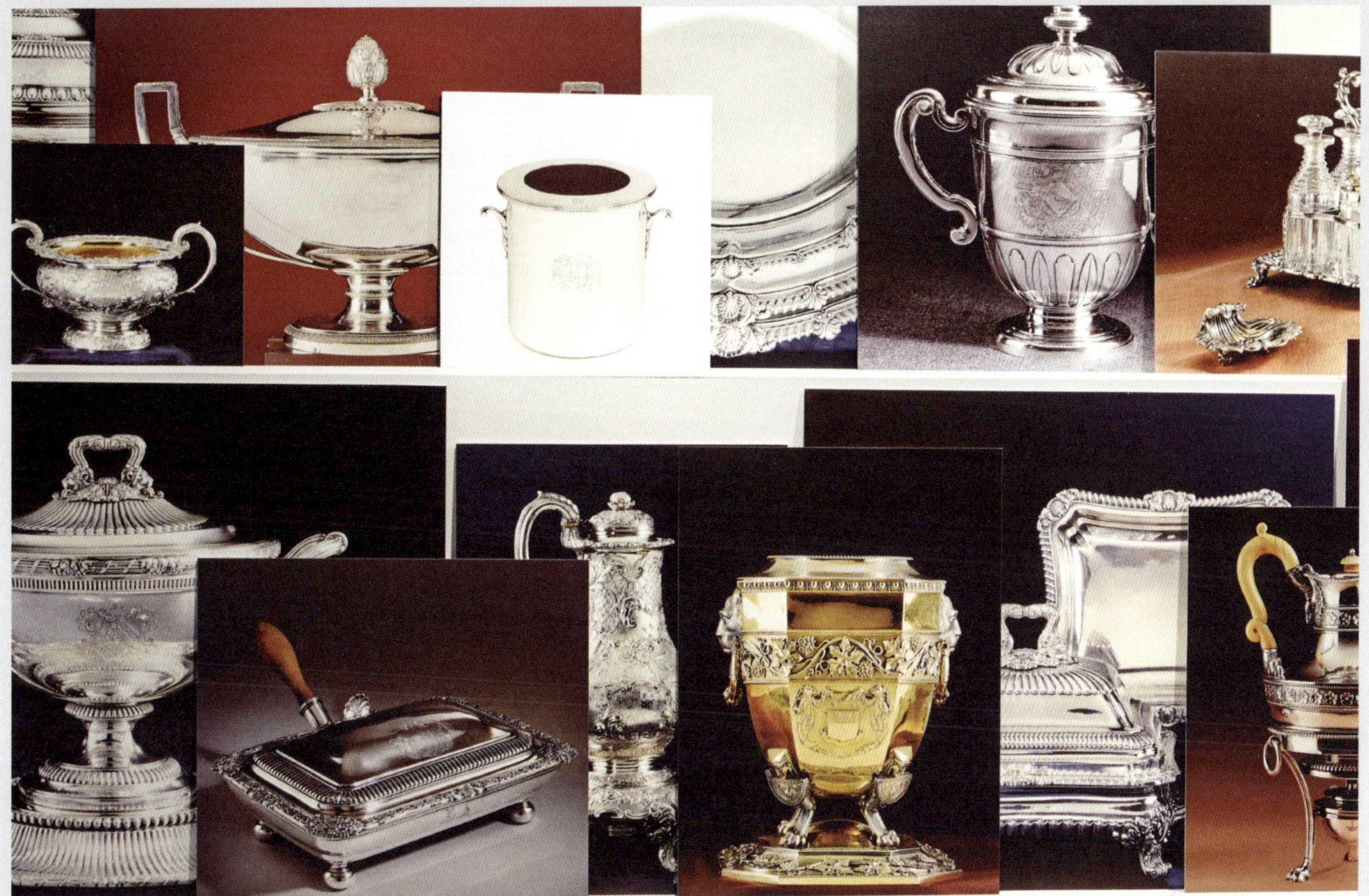

FIG 4 ***The Collection of Jane Ryan & William Saunders*** (detail). Forty pieces of silverware sequestered from Ferdinand and Imelda Marcos and sold by Christie's on behalf of the Philippine Commission on Good Government. Archival inkjet print on Epson semi-gloss paper, mounted on dibond. 2014. Photo: Matthew Booth.

Initially, it was difficult to piece this collection together, as it had obviously never been available to the public. What has been recovered of the so-called Marcos Collection is a seemingly arbitrary assortment of Old Masters, Georgian silverware, and a large collection of Grandma Moses paintings sequestered by the government, some hidden away in storage, a few displayed in government offices, and most auctioned off. Thirty years on, a huge number of works of art remain unaccounted for, their existence proven only by pale patches and brass plaques on the walls where they used to be displayed. Among them, the *Madonna and Child* by Michelangelo, the *Marquesa de Santa Cruz* by Goya, a couple of Monets, two Braques, a Pissarro, and a Manet.

Just recently, Imelda's former assistant, Vilma Bautista, was sentenced by the Manhattan Supreme Court to six years in prison for selling a stolen Monet painting for US$32 million that legally belonged to the Philippine government.

The solution to finding this invisible collection came about purely by chance when I came across a pair of Christie's catalogs from two auctions in 1991. The sales were dubbed "Magnificent Silver and Important Old Master Paintings, sold on behalf of the Republic of the Philippines, through the Presidential Commission on Good Government," the Philippine agency tasked with seque stering and liquidating the Marcoses' ill-gotten wealth.

On January 10, 1991, this hoard of magnificent silverware broke the record for the sale of silver at a Christie's auction in New York City. Seventy-eight lots—an assortment of wine coolers, platters, tureens, candlesticks, and dinner plates from the Regency era and Queen Anne period—sold for US$4,451,350. It was the largest auction of silverware from a single collection at the time.

The following day, seventy-eight Renaissance paintings from the Marcos Collection sold for a total of US$15.4 million. An early painting by the Italian master Raphael, *Saint Catherine of Alexandria*, which dates from 1503, sold for US$1.65 million. El Greco's *Coronation of the Virgin*, painted in 1603, sold for US$2.1 million. Titian's *Portrait of Giulio Romano*, from about 1536, was bought for US$1.1 million. Surprisingly, the bidders were undeterred by the disclaimer printed on every page of the catalog stating that the Christie's warranty of authenticity did not apply to works executed before 1870.

The images in these catalogs became the basis for the first presentation of *The Collection of Jane Ryan and William Saunders* at Gasworks in 2014. I showed it as an installation that assumed the classical guise of a European museum. A performance of first world civility amidst evidence of third world criminality.

I was interested in anchoring the exhibition to the auction for a number of reasons: for one, the Christie's catalog provides the most thorough visual accounting of the Marcos collection that even the Presidential Commission on Good Government (PCGG) used it as a main point of reference. Another reason was the 1991 timing of the event itself, taking place in between two defining, if unfortunate, episodes.

A few months prior to the auction, Imelda was indicted by the Federal Court in New York City for fraud and racketeering charges. Her tearful performance as a naïve widow during the trial was sensational; she presented herself as nothing more than a well-loved wife, lavished with expensive presents by a devoted husband. She repeatedly broke down in tears as the prosecution presented mounting evidence of bank transactions and shell companies that allowed her to use the Philippine treasury as a personal piggy bank. At one point, Imelda collapsed in the middle of the trial and was later strapped to a portable blood pressure monitor, which would gurgle loudly every time her blood pressure rose.

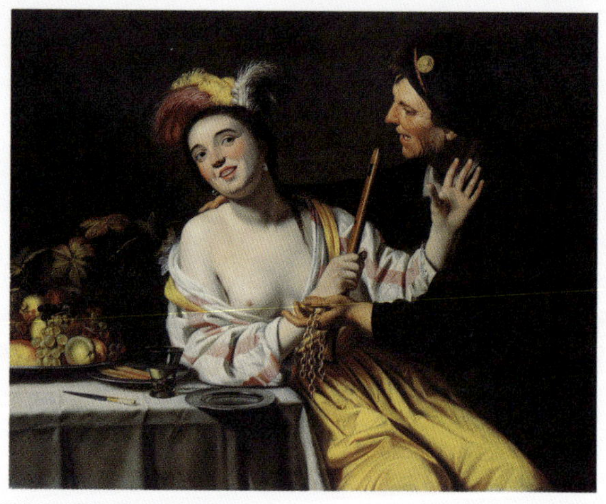

A Crash in the Limo Lane: Kashoggi's Fall
Vanity Fair, Dominick Dunne, September 1989

Lavish villas, perfumed houris, costume balls, fabulous deals with foreign powers and Oriental potentates—Adnan Khashoggi's life was an eighties remake of The Thousand and One Nights. The rumours started during the Iran-contra scandal, and the Saudi arms dealer once touted as the richest man in the world had to resort to such inconvenient economies as selling his famous yacht to Donald Trump. Now, after three months in a Swiss jail, he's been extradited to the U.S. on charges of mail fraud and obstruction of justice.

Now, reportedly broke, or broke by the standards of people with great wealth—his yacht gone, his planes gone, his dozen houses gone, or going, and his reputation in smithereens—he has recently spent three months pacing restlessly in a six-by-eight-foot prison cell in Bern, Switzerland. True, he dined there on gourmet food from the Schweizerhof Hotel, but he also had to clean his own cell and toilet as a small army of international lawyers fought to prevent his extradition to the United. Finally, Khashoggi dropped his efforts to avoid extradition when the Swiss ruled that he would face prosecution only for obstruction of justice and mail fraud, not for the more serious charges of racketeering and conspiracy. On July 19, accompanied by Swiss law-enforcement agents, he arrived in New York from Geneva first-class on a Swissair flight, handcuffed like a common criminal but dressed in an olive-drab safari suit with gold buttons and epaulets.

Allegedly, he helped his friends Ferdinand and Imelda Marcos plunder the Philippines of some $160 million by fronting for them in illegal real-estate deals. When United States authorities attempted to return some of the Marcos booty to the new Philippine government, they discovered that the ownership of four large commercial buildings in New York City—the Crown Building at 730 Fifth Avenue, the Herald Center at 1 Herald Square, 40 Wall Street, and 200 Madison Avenue—had passed to Adnan Khashoggi. In addition, more than thirty paintings, valued at $200 million, that Imelda Marcos had allegedly purloined from the Metropolitan Museum of Manila, including works by Rubens, El Greco, Picasso, and Degas, were being stored by Khashoggi for the Marcoses, but it turned out that the pictures had been sold to Khashoggi as part of a cover-up. The art treasures were first hidden on his yacht and then moved to his penthouse in Cannes. The penthouse was raided by the French police in a search for the pictures in April 1987, but it is believed that Khashoggi had been tipped off. He turned over nine of the paintings to the police, claiming to have sold the others to a Panamanian company, but investigators believe that he sold the pictures back to himself. The rest of the loot is thought to be in Athens. If he is found guilty, such charges could get him up to ten years in an American slammer.

FIG 5-6 ***The Collection of Jane Ryan & William Saunders*, 2014—ongoing. Postcard reproductions of Old Master paintings sequestered from Ferdinand and Imelda Marcos and sold by Christie's on behalf of the Philippine Commission on Good Government (PCGG). 98 sets, unlimited copies.**

Unfortunately, her performance also proved convincing. After a four-month trial, Imelda Marcos was acquitted of all charges. True to form, American expediency found a way to aid Philippine impunity. The jury decided that the late Ferdinand Marcos looted the Philippine treasury without the explicit knowledge of his wife, despite her previous roles as Minister of Human Settlements and Governor of Manila. Immediately after the verdict, she headed to St. Patrick's Cathedral and proceeded to creep down the entire aisle to the altar on her knees. After the acquittal, there were no longer any legal impediments to bar Imelda's return to the Philippines.

On November 4, 1991, an unrepentant Imelda returned home along with two of her children. The 2016 presidential elections saw the return of the strongman in Philippine politics in the form of Rodrigo Duterte. In November of that same year, the newly installed Duterte fulfilled a personal promise to the Marcoses by allowing the body of the dictator Ferdinand to be interred at the National Heroes Cemetery. The stage was set for the return of the Marcoses to power, which culminated in Bongbong Marcos's landslide presidential victory—his vice president is Sara Duterte, the eldest of Rodrigo Duterte's children.

Viewed in the context of these events, the auction, by dispersing the Marcos collection and recirculating it back into the market, also served to launder these objects, silencing the historical narrative they are tainted with. The museum-like installation and extensive texts that accompanied it became a way of reconstituting this collection and reiterating the complicity of these Western objects in a Philippine history of corruption.

In his essay "Total Community Response," Patrick Flores uses the term "democratic gesture" in relation to the development of avant-garde practices in the Philippines during the Marcos regime.[4] Imelda became the self-appointed patroness of the avant-garde, supporting conceptual practices as it served as a sophisticated retort to the more activist inclinations of social realism, and offered no conflict between its aesthetics and the rhetoric of progress of their authoritarianism.

4 Patrick Flores, "Total Community Response: Performing the Avant-Garde as a Democratic Gesture in Manila," *Southeast of Now: Directions in Contemporary and Modern Art in Asia*, no. 1 (March 2017): 13–38.

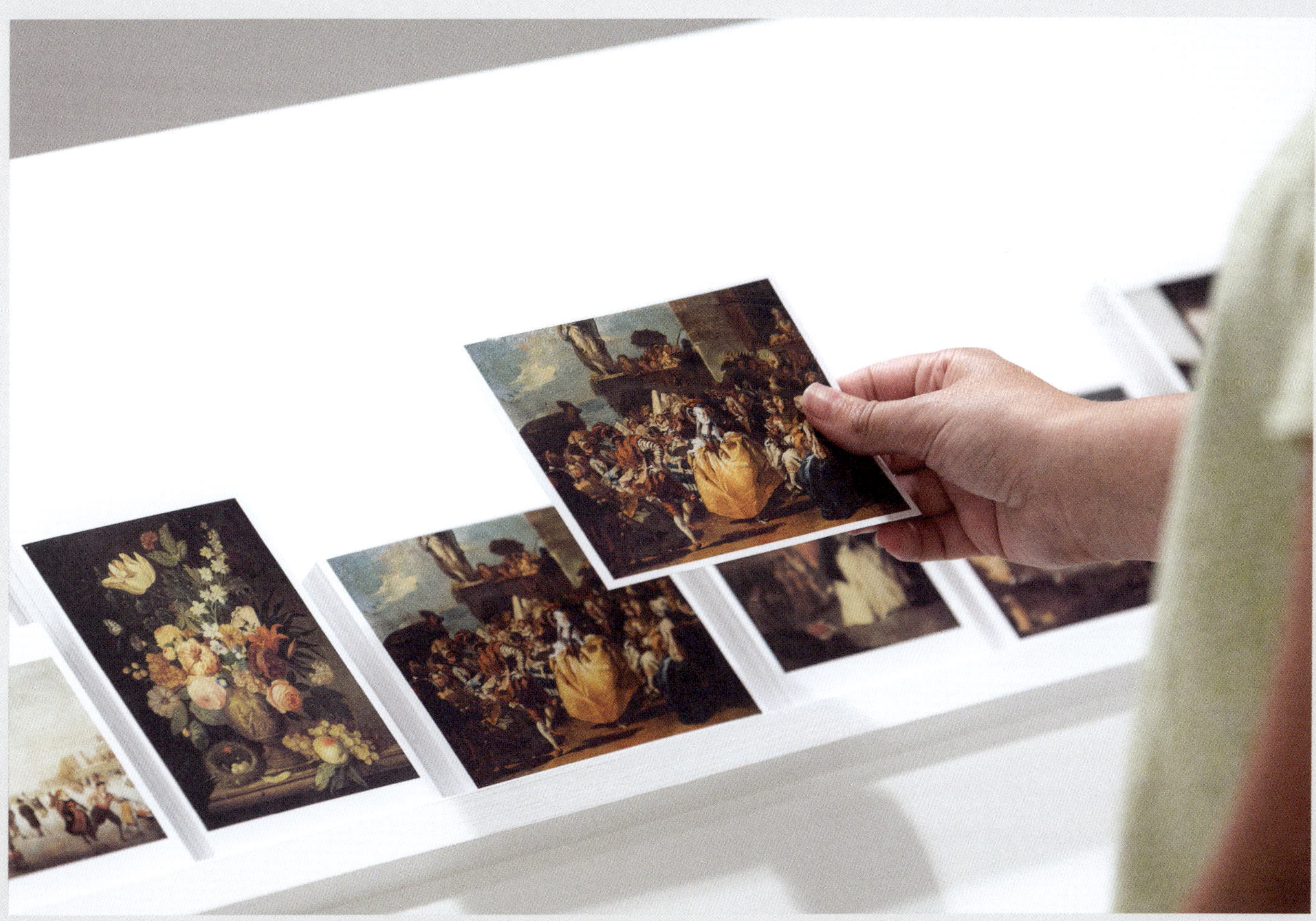

FIG 7 ***The Collection of Jane Ryan & William Saunders*. Installation view, 4A Centre for Contemporary Asian Art, 2016. Photo: Document Photography.**

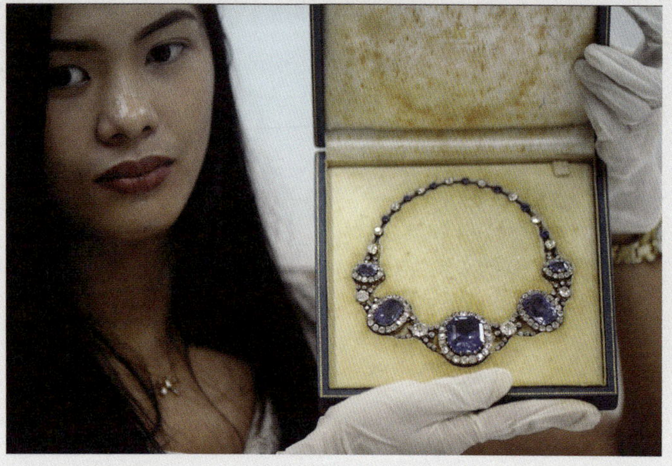

FIG 8 File photo taken on November 27, 2015, shows an official from the Presidential Commission on Good Government (PCGG) holding a piece of jewellery seized by the Philippine government from former first lady Imelda Marcos, at the Central Bank headquarters in Manila. Photo courtesy AFP / NOEL CELIS via Getty Images.

At the center of *The Collection of Jane Ryan and William Saunders* is the dismissal of Imelda's instrumentalization of the "democratic gesture" as part of her self-serving narrative of nation building, replacing it with a series of presentations and actions that could lead to something truly emancipatory.

To quote Flores in the aforementioned essay:

> The term "gesture" is salient. It plays on the state of semblance. A gesture is allusive, maybe even allegorical. Also, a gesture is performance, a moment in theater. Finally, a gesture [...] is pedagogical, a crystallisation of a social arrangement involving social actors.[5]

When I presented the project at the Jorge B. Vargas Museum in Manila, the paintings from Imelda's sequestered collection were printed as postcards laid out on a ten-meter long white plinth spanning the length of the gallery. The idea was to present an installation in an almost forensic fashion—a monumental body of evidence neatly arranged for scrutiny. For most, if not all, of the audience, this served as their first encounter with these objects that have long been reduced to an abstraction. On the back of each postcard are various texts, each painting bearing witness to these fraudulent acts and, in the process, implicating an expansive network of players from the worlds of art and politics.

The public is invited to take ownership of the artworks by getting as many postcards as they want. The democratic gesture is performed as they create their own personal collection of paintings from the postcard reproductions—restoring the collection to their rightful owners, who unknowingly purchased the works but never enjoyed its visual benefits.

The most recent part of this project concerns twenty-four pieces of jewelry from the Hawaii Collection, the horde of fine jewelry found hidden inside disposable diapers and seized by US Customs from the Marcoses at Honolulu Airport when they sought exile in 1986. Shortly after their seizure, the collection was turned over to the PCGG. For three decades, they have languished in the vaults of the Central Bank, hidden from public view, amidst legal challenges from the Marcos family. In February 2016, the PCGG announced that all legal impediments have been cleared for the pieces to go to auction with a planned public exhibition to precede the sale. Along with planning the exhibition, they also valued Imelda's jewelry in terms of the specific costs of national development it would have financed.

In early 2016, I was in initial discussions to find a way of collaborating with the PCGG on some kind of presentation when the victory of Rodrigo Duterte in May 2016 put a stop to these plans. His administration announced plans to begin dismantling the PCGG with its responsibilities being transferred to the Office of the Solicitor General, a position held by a Marcos loyalist.

5 Flores, "Total Community Response," 18.

Not knowing what to do with these high resolution images of the jewelry shared by the PCGG and fully aware of the implications of showing photographs that were not mine, I began a collaboration with my wife and jewelry designer Frances Wadsworth Jones. The role of family has always been central to this project and in this instance this role shifts crucially from being archive to agent. From these single images from the PCGG and scant news footage available online, Frances painstakingly created computer renderings of each piece of jewelry, equal parts forensic reconstruction and creative speculation, which were then printed in white translucent resin and mounted on brass stands. We first exhibited them as part of the Honolulu Biennial in 2019—completing a journey that returns the jewelry to the scene of the Marcos family's temporary defeat. Laid out in a spectral line-up, these items return to Honolulu, not as luxurious accessories but as reconstructions hovering between evidence and effigy, narrating a painful history of impunity. Alongside the pieces are texts lifted from the PCGG project, detailing what Imelda's profligacy has cost the nation. Her pink Golconda diamond could have paid for the construction of two domestic airports. Her diamond, sapphire, and ruby bracelet, pendant, and earrings set could have financed the full immunization of 20,000 children. Her diamond tiara could have sent 2,000 university students to school.

On the day the show opened in Honolulu, the Duterte government announced they are once again considering auctioning the Hawaii Collection. On the proviso that Imelda Marcos herself can be invited to bid for the jewelry.

In the ten years that I have been working on *The Collection of Jane Ryan and William Saunders*, the search for any kind of justice for the crimes of the Marcos dictatorship has proven ever more elusive. As the spaces to present this project outside the Philippines have multiplied over the past few years, the space to realize its aspirations within the Philippines has decreased immeasurably. As these political defeats mount, compounded by personal loss, I find that the emotional labor involved in producing this work has grown, wildly oscillating between despairing that the possibility of democracy in the Philippines is another fantasy, and being bolstered by those who continue to negotiate a space for it in the direst of circumstances. Nonetheless, it's important to persist. We cannot reconcile with the past without litigating for it, and we cannot litigate without any evidence. By ensuring that the details of this collection are continuously presented in the highest resolution, the possibility of accountability and restitution, however diminished and imaginary, will remain.

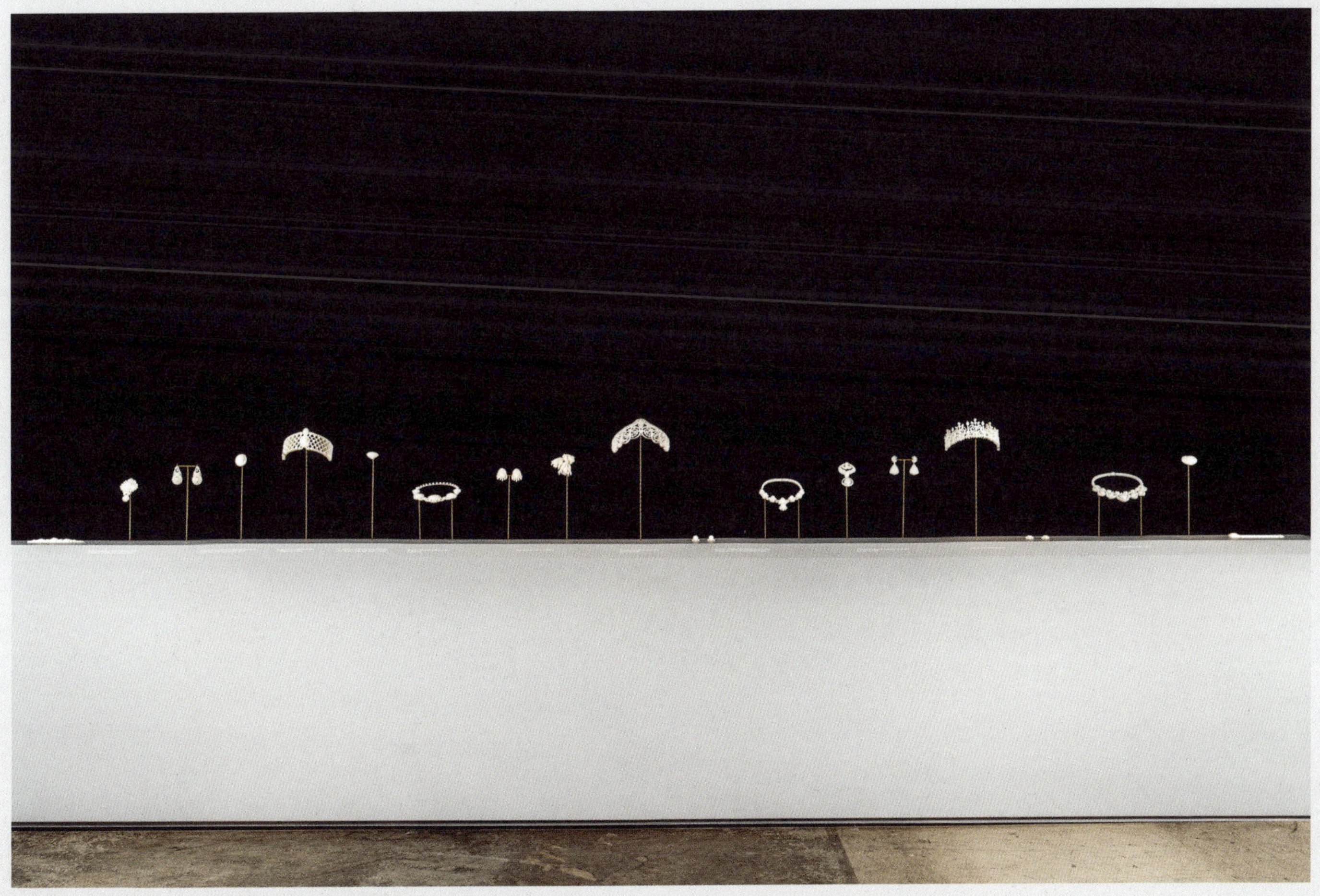

FIG 9 Installation view, *The Collection of Jane Ryan & William Saunders*, 2nd Honolulu Biennial, 2019.

PIO ABAD &
FRANCES WADSWORTH JONES

The treatment of 12,052 tuberculosis patients until their full recovery.

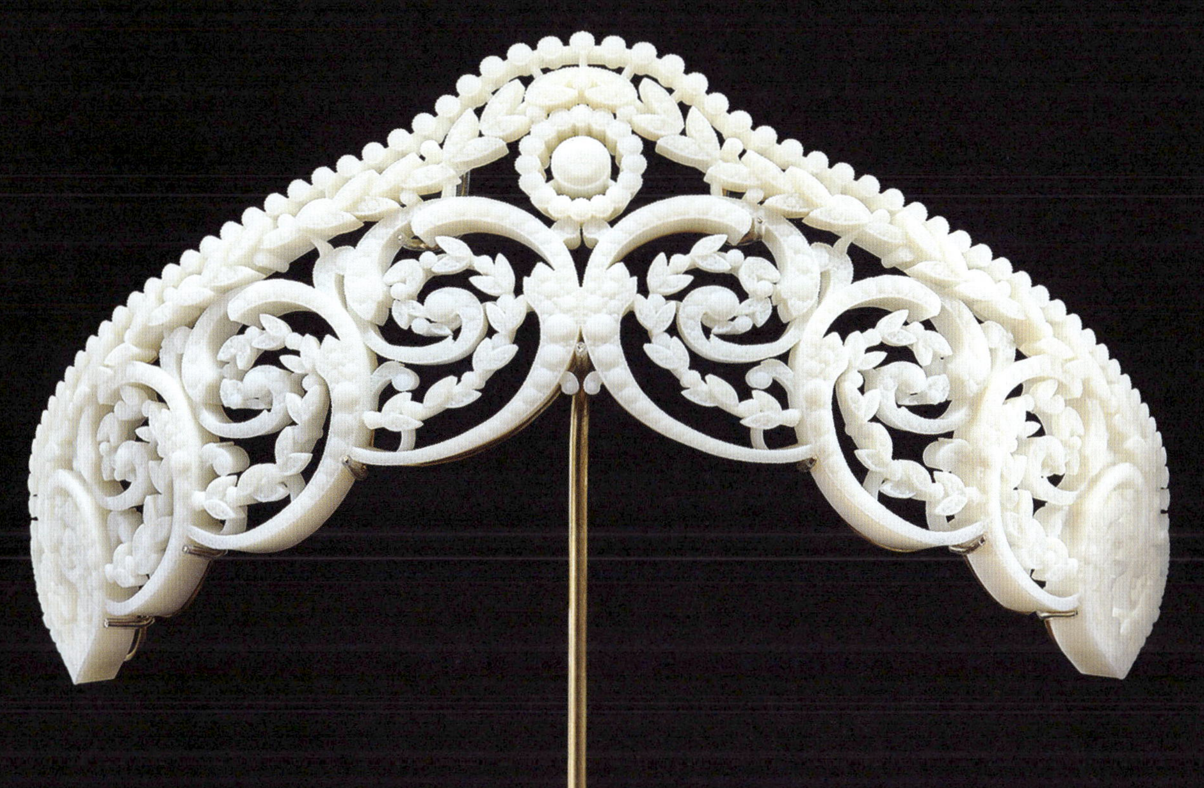

unization of 20,000 children plus 17,600 pneumococcal vaccines to senior citizens and

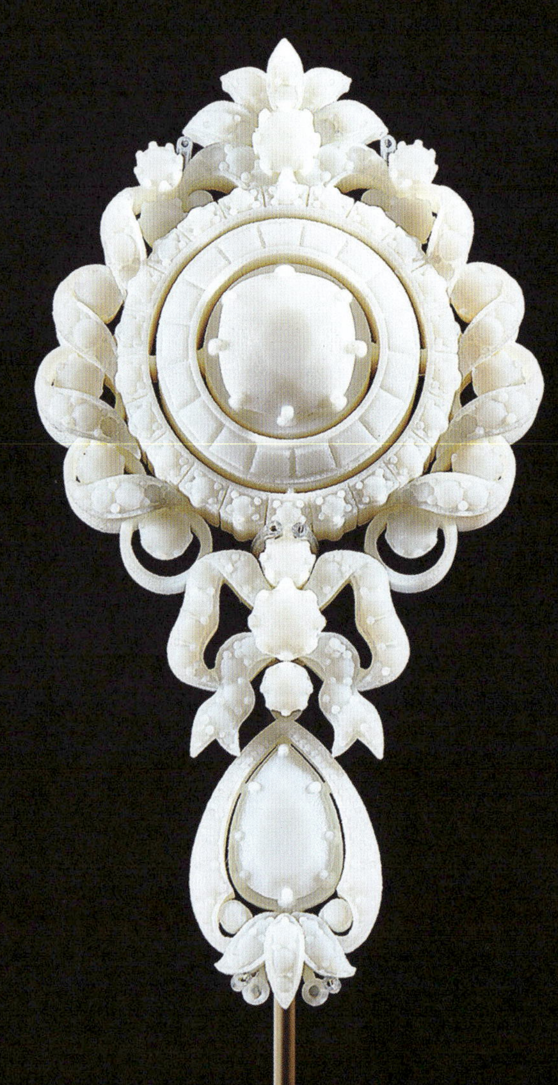

The full imn

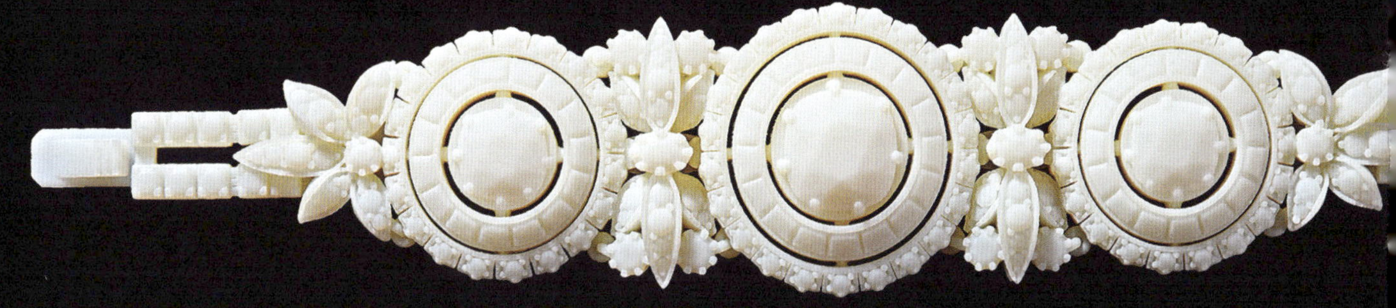

The average annual

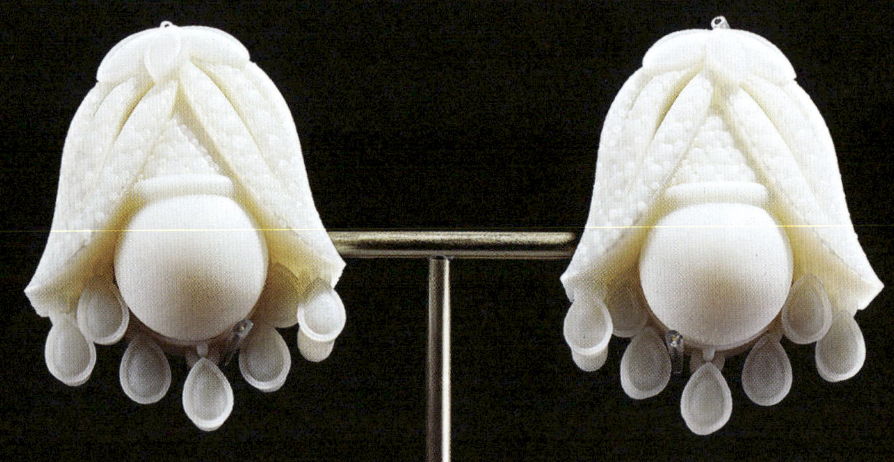

income of 15 Filipinos.

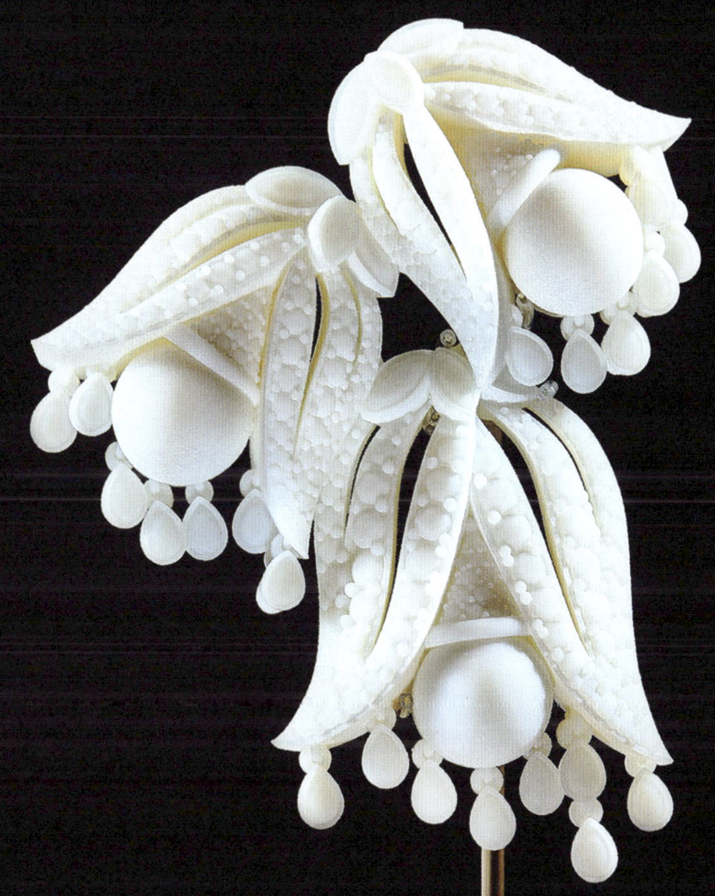

Electricity to approximately 2,252 households in off-grid areas.

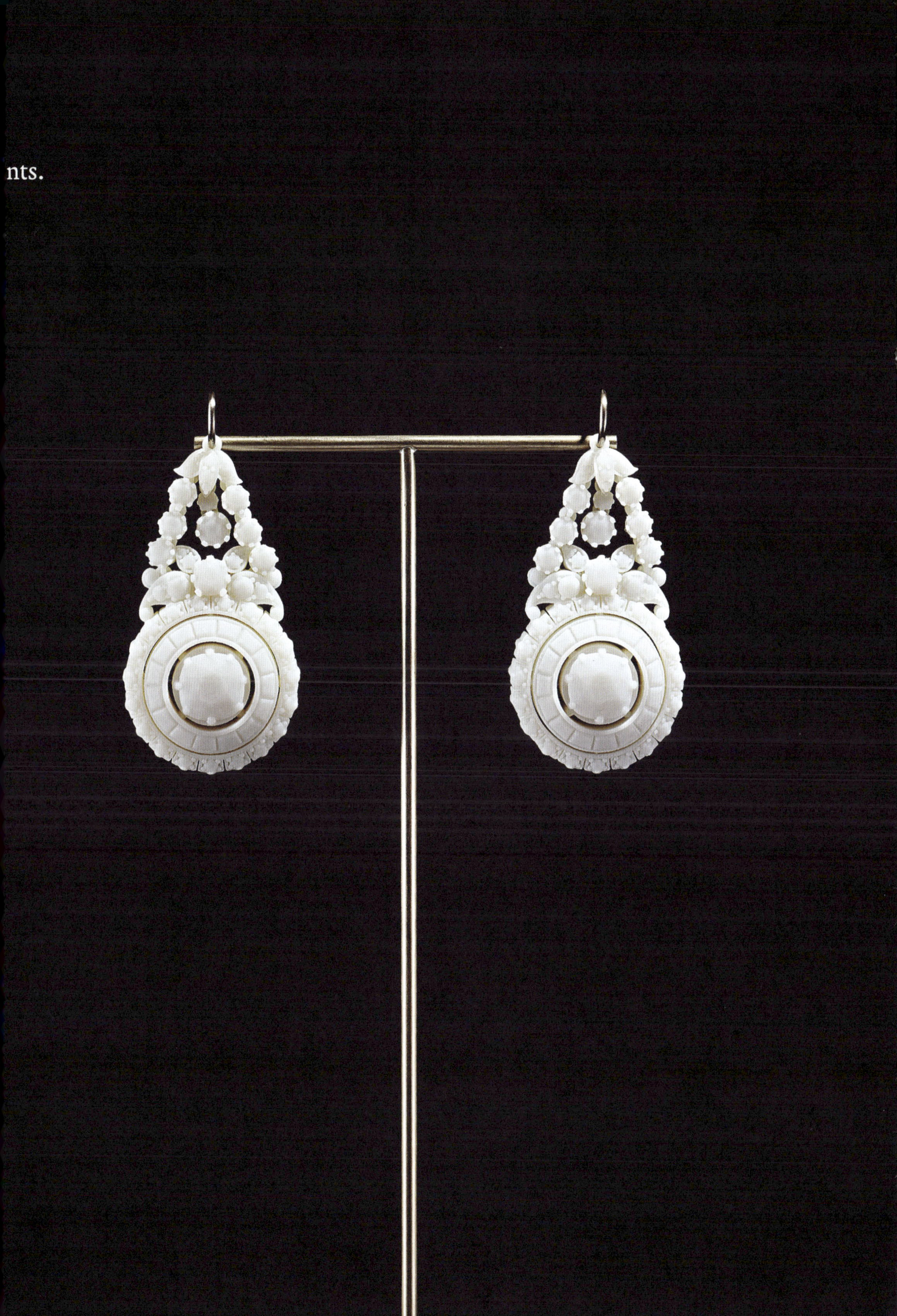

nts.

The combined construction of Bicol International Airport and the renovation of Sanga-Sanga Airport in Tawi Tawi.

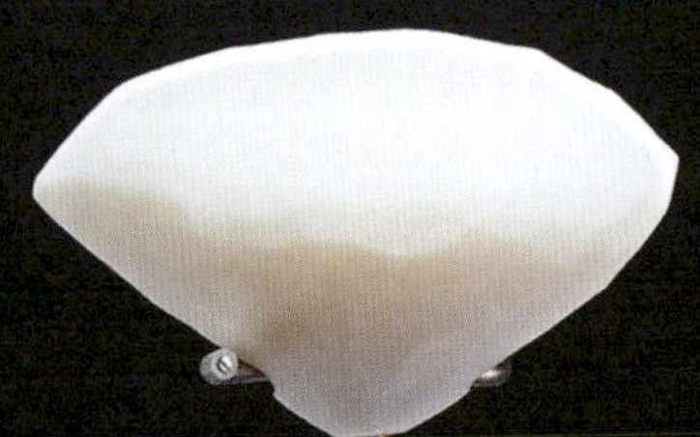

The Collection of Jane Ryan & William Saunders is an ongoing work that reproduces parts of the vast trove of art, antiquities, and jewelry acquired by Ferdinand and Imelda Marcos during their conjugal dictatorship. This iteration consists of 3D printed replicas of the jewelry collection seized by US. Customs when the Marcoses fled to Honolulu in 1986. The jewelry has since remained unseen, locked in legal and political limbo. Using images gathered from news footage and scant documentation, each piece of jewelry has been digitally reconstructed, resulting in 3D-printed resin sculptures that are equal parts forensic reconstruction and creative speculation. They reappear not as luxurious accessories but as a spectral line-up that hovers between evidence and effigy, carrying with it the painful history of a nation.

LAWRENCE ABU HAMDAN

For the Otherwise Unaccounted, 2020
17 A3 Thermographic Prints

In 1997 the psychiatrist and professor at Virginia School of Medicine, Dr. Ian Stevenson published his life's work, *Reincarnation and Biology: The Etiology of Birthmarks*. The book was the result of fieldwork in Asia, Turkey, Lebanon, and across Africa and Alaska, in which he interviewed and investigated claims of reincarnation with particular attention to the correspondence of birthmarks on the reincarnated subject to the circumstances of their death in their previous lives. Stevenson's book is a strange and beautiful mix of narrative literature, forensic analysis, biological data, historiography, theology, and conflicting scientific hypotheses. In focusing on the claim to reincarnation rather than the ethnography of a single people, Stevenson's monolog chronicles a collectivity of people who exist at the threshold of the law and for whom injustices and violence have otherwise escaped the historical record due to colonial subjugation, corruption, rural lawlessness, and legal amnesty. The raised-ink renderings of these birthmarks highlight the ways in which testimony is stored in the body. This work isolates the birthmarks from their bodies, and in this way archives the only surviving remnants of historical erasure, such as forced religious conversions, destruction of language and property, colonial occupation, and territorial annexation.

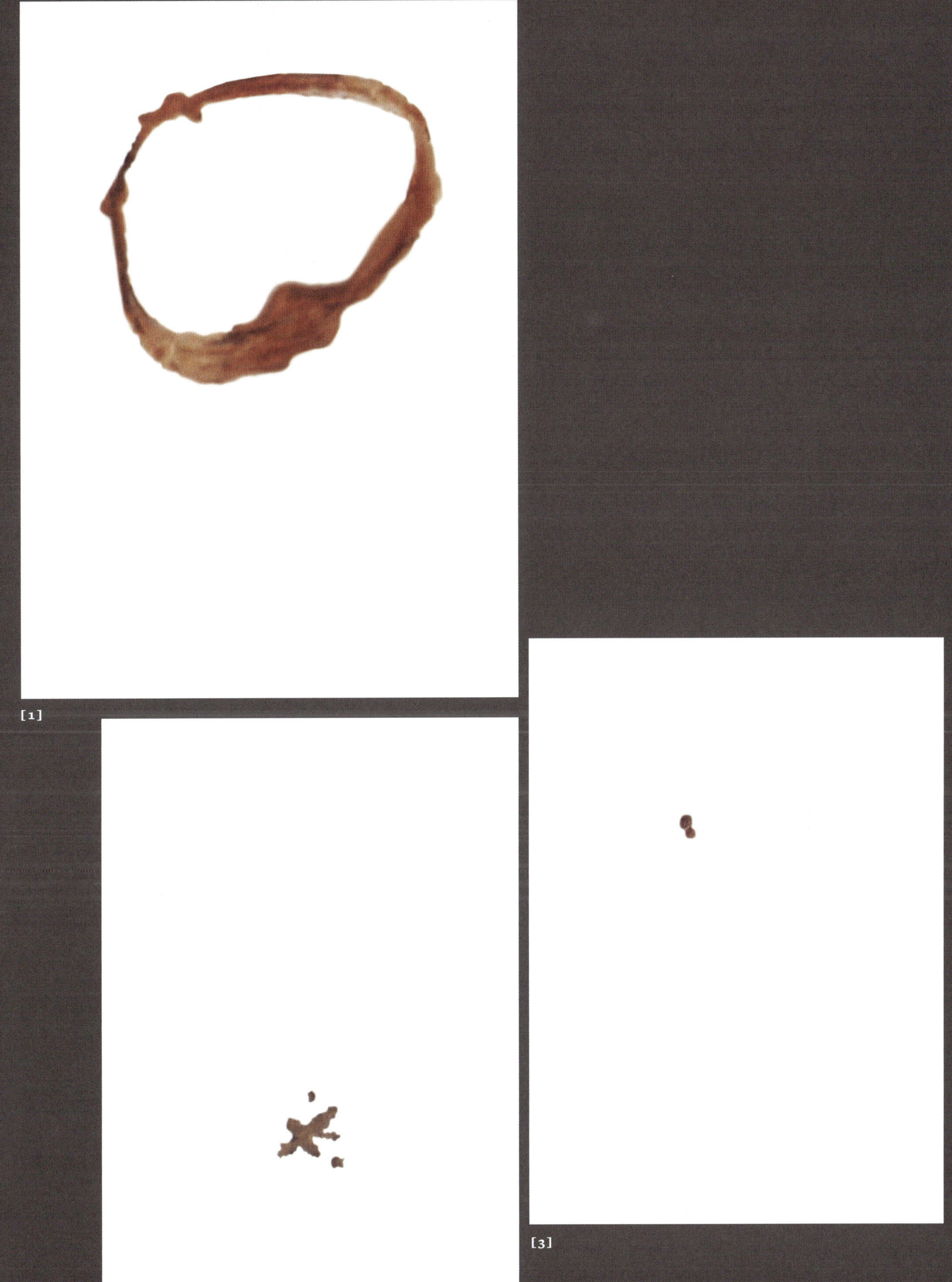

[1]

[2]

[3]

1
Jacinta Agbo, 1980 Enugu, Nigeria

PREVIOUS PERSONALITY
Nsude Agbo 1970
Engu, Nigeria

LOCATION OF BIRTHMARK
Crown

CORROBORATING EVIDENCE
Medical records destroyed

Though it was a little thicker than it should have been, Dr. Ian Stevenson hypothesized that the mark which encircled Jacinta Agbo's crown resembled the incisions of neurosurgery. This corresponded to testimony that Nsude Agbo, of whom Jacinta was the reincarnation, had died in hospital due to a club wound to the head. Whether or not he was operated upon by a neurosurgeon before he passed will remain unknown. The medical records of Nsude, as well as those of the many who died during the Biafran pogroms, went up in flames when the University Hospital in Enugu was bombarded by the Nigerian military and their British artillery in March 1970. Moreover, as Legal Amnesty was given to all crimes committed during the Biafran War, very few testimonies of perpetrators have been heard or verified. Jacinta's memories of her past incarnation have faded over the course of her life. Though she visibly carries the marks of the pogroms, she recalls nothing of the event itself, only that she was a man, and that if she had the means, she would return to being a man.

2
Yvonne Ehrlich, 1953 São Paulo, Brazil

PREVIOUS PERSONALITY
Martha Demmer, 1944
Vienna, Austria

LOCATION OF BIRTHMARK
Neck

CORROBORATING EVIDENCE
Injuries witnessed by
Hermann Demmer

On November 5, 1944, the air raid sirens blasted out over the city of Vienna. Martha Demmer, her sister Leopoldine, and her son Hermann, descended into their building's basement for shelter from the bombing. When the building took a direct hit, the force of the blast threw Martha and her son ten fifteen meters down the basement corridor. After some time, Hermann returned to consciousness, dug with his bare hands through the rubble, and found his mother's lifeless body. The surviving family members fled the US Air Force bombing raids and took refuge, across the planet, in Brazil. Nine years later, Leopoldine's grandchild was born in São Paulo. The birthmark on the nape of her neck was key in the Spiritist diagnosis that she was the reincarnation of her great aunt Martha.

3
U Tinn Sein, 1948 Wundwin, Myanmar

PREVIOUS PERSONALITY
An unknown Japanese soldier

LOCATION OF BIRTHMARK
Chest

CORROBORATING EVIDENCE
No known records

For some misdemeanour, U Tinn Sein's father raised his hand to beat him, but froze in sudden confusion when he heard his son exclaim, "I am going back to Tokyo!" This was the first clear indication that U Tinn Sein was the reincarnation of a soldier from the Japanese occupying forces stationed in Myanmar. Although in his current incarnation, he had never been to Japan, in his previous life, he had never wanted to leave. His past incarnation was threatened with torture if he did not abruptly end his studies and join the Japanese army to fight in Myanmar. U Tinn Sein does not remember his name, but has lucid flashbacks of a low flying British or American plane opening fire on his platoon. As he ran for cover, he was shot in the chest.

[5]

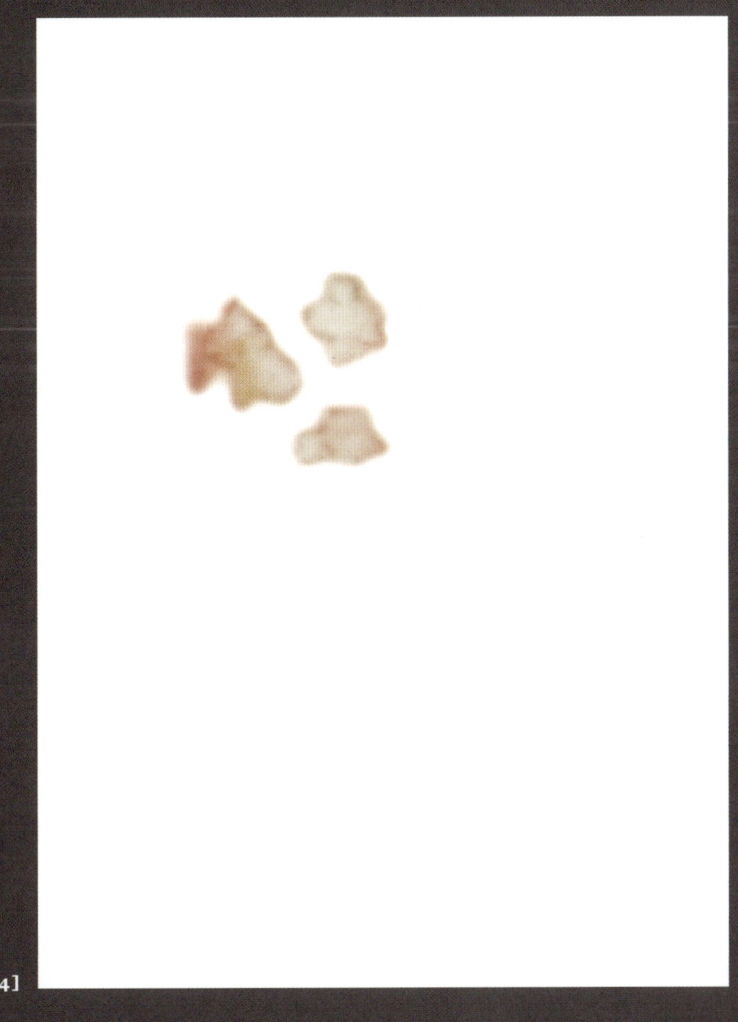

[4]

4

Hanumant Saxena, 1955
Farrukhabad, India

PREVIOUS PERSONALITY
Maha Ram, 1954
Farrukhabad, India

LOCATION OF BIRTHMARK
Chest

CORROBORATING EVIDENCE
Verified in postmortem report

Maha Ram had no known enemies. The reason for his shooting is unknown and is speculated to be a case of mistaken identity. He was shot at close range by a shotgun. The postmortem report showed that the main charge of pellets had hit Maha Ram in the lower chest, and that there was a scattering of shots around the principal wound. The postmortem report includes a sketch of the location of the wounds. This illustration is in almost exact correspondence with Hanumant Saxena's depigmented birthmarks, the child who claimed to be his reincarnation. Saxena was not alone, local judges and officials across the region tasked with attending to the extremely high homicide rate in Farrukhabad, began to observe a common connection between violent deaths and cases of children who claim to have memories inherited from the lost.

5

Tali Sowaid, 1965
Btebyat, Lebanon

PREVIOUS PERSONALITY
Said Abul-Hisn, 1965
Btechney, Lebanon

LOCATION OF BIRTHMARK
Cheeks

CORROBORATING EVIDENCE
Verified by records at
Ras Beirut Hospital

Many people across the Levant have difficulty pronouncing the trilled "R" of "ر", but Tali Sowaid had a very rare speech impediment; he could not adequately lift his tongue to sound the "sh" of the letter "ش". He explained this and the hyper-pigmented birthmark on his cheek as an inherited injury from his past life. Indeed, the postmortem confirms that Said Abul Hisn, who transmigrated to Tali, died in hospital from complications caused by the bullet "which entered the left side of his face, shattered his mandibles, cutting the root of the tongue and damaging the lingual vessels and hypoglossal nerve." From all of Tali's past-life memories, he most lucidly remembers seeing his/Said's cousin, Ramez, come around the corner and indiscriminately fire his shotgun into the village square. While in psychiatric custody, Ramez was asked why he killed Said. He explained that he was in a hallucinatory state, or as he describes, a parallel world. Where people stood, he saw only hyenas.

6

Ma Khin Hsann Oo, 1974
Tatkon, Myanmar

PREVIOUS PERSONALITY
Ma Ahmar Yee, 1974
Kyidaungone, Myanmar

LOCATION OF BIRTHMARK
Extends from the thighs, across the torso, and up to the crown

CORROBORATING EVIDENCE
Medical report states that "tar, dirt, burning oil and hot liquid sugar" covered the bodies

On March 23, 1974, a truck left Tatkon, heading north for Mandalay. It was carrying a heavy load of unrefined sugar and twelve hitchhikers; cloth traders who improvized their seating atop the cargo. At around 2:00 a.m., the nuts of the left rear wheel spun off, the wheel separated, the driver lost control and the truck overturned. The driver and two of the passengers were propelled to safety but the remaining ten were trapped under the truck and the heavy boxes of sugar. When they heard the truck crash, the villagers of Kyidanungone ran to the passengers' aid. To light their way through the darkness of night, they used kerosene torches. Witnesses remembered that the shouts for the villagers to keep their torches away from the flammable scene came too late. Of the ten who died, three children have since returned. Only one of these children had hyper-pigmented birthmarks, which extended from her thighs to the top of her head. The villagers conjectured that these were an index of the splatters of hot molasses that landed on the subject's previous incarnation.

[6.1]

[6.2]

[7]

[8]

[9]

[10]

[11]

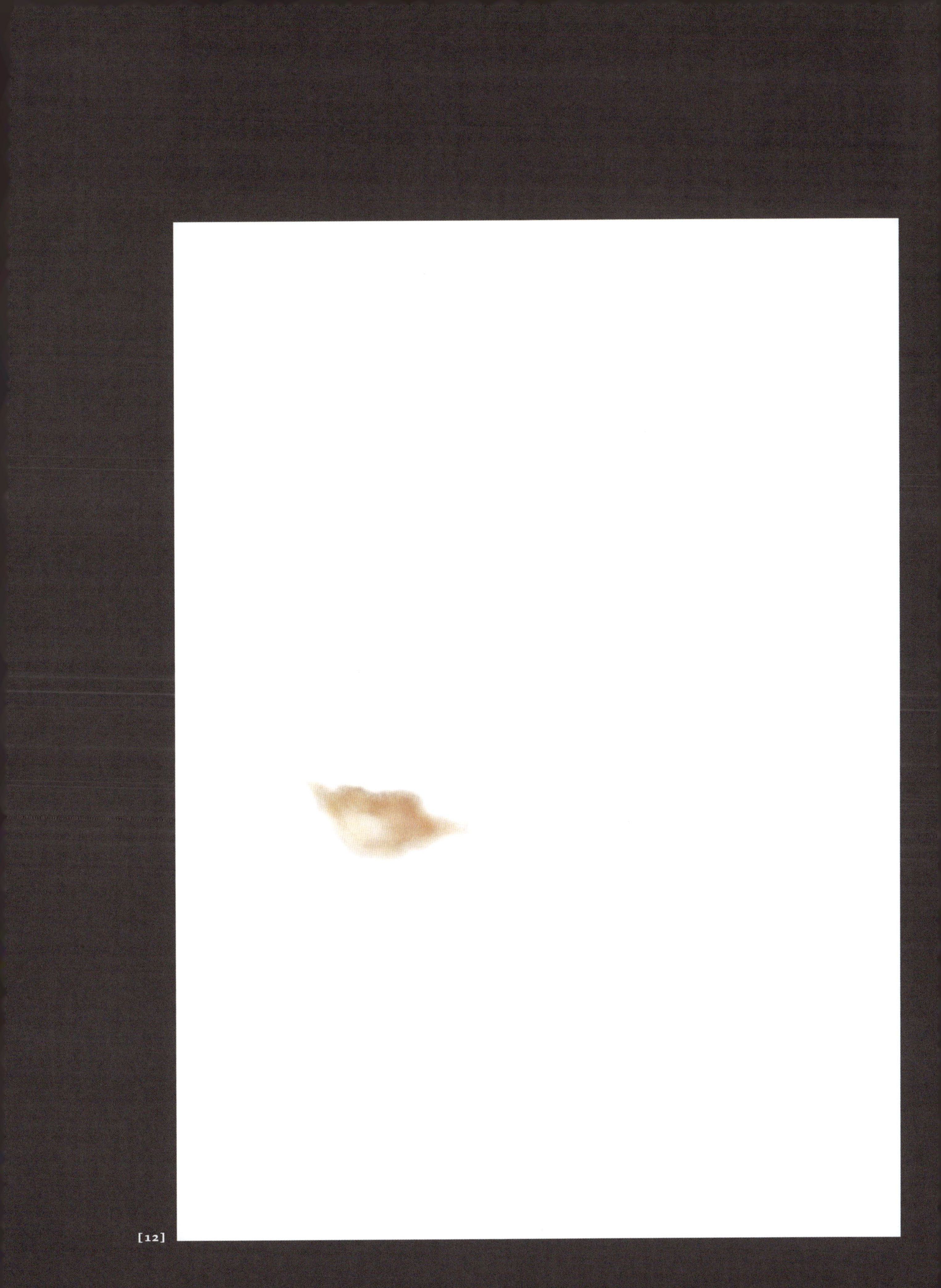

[12]

7

Frank Dudley, 1914
Haines, Alaska

PREVIOUS PERSONALITY
Dadtookuch

LOCATION OF BIRTHMARK
Under Chin

CORROBORATING EVIDENCE
No recourse to law

Frank Dudley's memories of his past life corresponded with his grandmother's cousin, Dadtookuch. His birthmark sits in the place Dadtookuch was shot, when he was ambushed in a Tlingit clan war, during a period of territorial rivalry, which emerged in the wake of the United States' purchase of Alaska from Russia. Dadtookuch's death came just after 1885, the year US laws were implemented, which sought to convert Indigenous communities to Christianity, and outlaw Indigenous protocol and rituals for administering births, deaths, marriages, and crimes. This sudden imposition of one legal system over another, meant that there is neither any form of US death record, nor a Tlingit burial of Dadtookuch. The place of his death, or where his body is buried, is unknown. The only physical record of Dadtookuch's life is now buried with Frank Dudley, and the café au lait birthmark underneath his chin.

8

Charles Porter, 1907
Sitka, Alaska

PREVIOUS PERSONALITY
Chah-Nik-Kooh, 1853
Sitka, Alaska

LOCATION OF BIRTHMARK
Abdomen

CORROBORATING EVIDENCE
No recourse to law

Charles Porter was very young when he was taken to an American Missionary boarding school in Alaska. It is no secret that in these schools Tlingit language and culture were aggressively discouraged. Despite enduring this brutal erasure, Porter managed to retain his past-life memories as a Tlingit warrior who had been stabbed by a spear. When he returned to his village and spoke of this, his parents took him to see a woman in the village who was old enough to have lived prior to first contact with the Europeans. She held a Tlingit battle spear to his birthmark and remarked that the tip corresponded in both size and shape. From the place and shape of the birthmark, she identified him as Chah-Nik-Kooh, a Wrangell warrior, who had been speared to death while leading an unarmed peacemaking mission to the territory of the Sitkas in 1853.

9

B.B. Saxena, 1918
Uttar Pradesh, India

PREVIOUS PERSONALITY
Arthur

LOCATION OF BIRTHMARK
Neck

CORROBORATING EVIDENCE
Unverified

B.B. Saxena was born with an ovoid depigmented macule on his neck. We do not know if the birthmark corresponded to the way in which a British Captain, named Arthur, died in World War I, although this is the person from whom Saxena's memories have been inherited. Whenever he would speak of his life as Arthur, his parents would find ways to stealthily change the course of the conversation. It was embarrassing for them to have a British officer transmigrate into their home at the height of Gandhi's anti-imperial "Quit India" movement.

10

Ma Shwe Yee, 1949
Kyet Mouk, Myanmar

PREVIOUS PERSONALITY
An unknown Japanese soldier

LOCATION OF BIRTHMARK
Chest

CORROBORATING EVIDENCE
No known records

During the period of intense fighting between the Japanese and the British, the villagers of Kyet Mouk, in central Myanmar, fled. When they returned after the Japanese army retreated, they found burial mounds under the mango tree. The tree that was right next to the house in which Ma Shwe Yee was born, with a port-wine stain birthmark on her chest. Before the age of five, Ma Shwe Yee spoke words that her parents did not understand. At first they brushed it off as the babbling of an infant, but slowly they started to hear in her uttering a cadence and phonic palette which they recognized from a time they would rather forget. Her utterances matched the grating indecipherable commands that used to be shouted at them by Japanese soldiers during the period of their military occupation. Ma Shwe Yee was late to speak but when she eventually mastered her mother tongue, she would recurrently recount her last moments as a Japanese infantry soldier. Her memories were hazy but she distinctly remembered locking eyes with her assailant, an "Indian man" wearing British military fatigues, as she felt the bullet enter her chest.

11

Maung Mhat Tin, 1945
Nga-Zun, Myanmar

PREVIOUS PERSONALITY
Maung Aung Su, 1944
Nga-Zun, Myanmar

LOCATION OF BIRTHMARK
Abdomen

CORROBORATING EVIDENCE
No recourse to law

Maung Mhat Tin believed he was the reincarnation of a bullock cart driver from a village, which was eight kilometers away from his place of birth. Maung Aung Su killed the Japanese soldier who had commandeered him to transport rice for the Japanese Army, during their occupation of Burma. When the Japanese threatened to raze his entire village and its inhabitants to the ground, Maung Aung Su turned himself in. He was killed by firing squad. Maung Mhat Tin remembers his last exclamation from his previous life: "Do not blindfold me, if you want to shoot, shoot." It is impossible to verify the birthmark in this incident, as there are no records of the execution, and no known grave for the deceased.

12

Mahmut Ekiçi, 1923
Adana, Turkey

PREVIOUS PERSONALITY
Mahmut Namik , 1921
Adana, Turkey

LOCATION OF BIRTHMARK
Abdomen

CORROBORATING EVIDENCE
A torn shirt

Mahmut Namik was killed in 1921, whilst in service to the Marash militia fighting to liberate Adana from the French occupying forces. After the retreat of the French in 1922, his body was eventually found, buried under a pile of hay in an abandoned barnyard. The family stripped the shirt he was wearing as a "sacred relic" of his life and struggle against the French oppressors. In that same year, a child was born with a birthmark on the left side of his abdomen, which discharged for two months before it fully healed. It took this boy forty-five years to put together the fragmented pieces of his past-life memories, realizing that he was the return of Mahmut Namik. In 1967, he found the family to which his past life belonged. The skeptical younger sister of Namik demanded that Mahmut Ekici wear the shirt in which her brother died. His two-to-three-milimeter deep depigmented birthmark beamed through the place in which the shirt was torn. Stunned, she listened in silence to Namik's past-life testimony; he and another partisan companion had been hiding out in a deserted farm. Whilst searching for a water well, Namik was attacked by two French soldiers, one grappled him, locking his arms and shoulders from behind, while the other from the front, drove a knife into the lower left side of his abdomen.

[13]

[14]

[15]

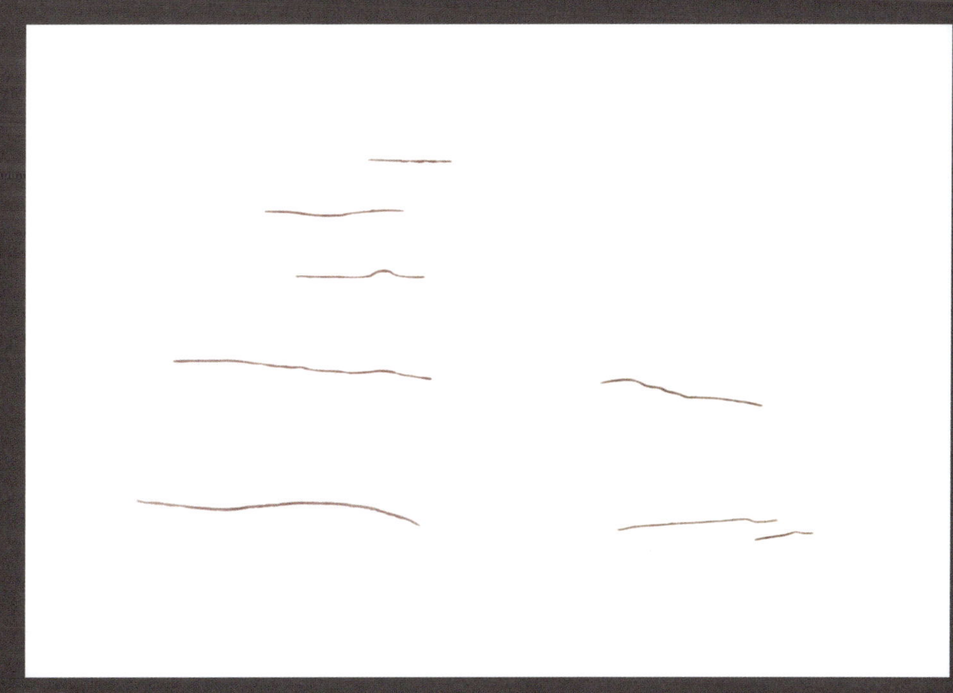

[16]

13

Çemil Fahriçi, 1935
Antakya,Turkey

PREVIOUS PERSONALITY
Çemil Hayik

LOCATION OF BIRTHMARK
Neck and top of head

CORROBORATING EVIDENCE
Multiple witnesses

Çemil Hayik killed the two gendarmes who sexually assaulted his sisters during the French occupation of Turkey's Hatay province. He managed to evade French custody, and for two years maintained a precarious freedom in the mountainous area between the cities of Antakya and Samandag. After frequently ambushing the French and their allies, his location was eventually revealed, and the French surrounded the house in which he had taken refuge. A shootout ensued. Facing the inevitability of his capture, Çemil Hayik put the muzzle of his long rifle gun under his chin, and pulled the trigger with his toe. The body of the bandit was then taken into Antakya and displayed in the courthouse square. When Dahham Fahriçi was two years old, he resolutely refused to be called anything else but Çemil. This persistence, together with his recurring nightmares involving French soldiers, forced his parents to concede to his demands and recognize that he was the return of the famous bandit. For years he thought he possessed just one birthmark on his neck, which corroborated the memories of his past life as the partisan fighter. One day, however, as his sister leaned over him to place a serving spoon on the table at which he sat, she noticed a linear area of hairlessness and pigmentation on the top left side of his head. An account made by one of the French gendarmes who had been present when they found Çemil Hayik's body gave a description of the bullet's exit wound, which confirms the correlation between the bullet's trajectory through the skull and the space between Fahriçi's two birthmarks.

14

Maung Tin Win, 1954
Moenagone, Myanmar

PREVIOUS PERSONALITY
U Thet Tin AKA Napoleon, 1953
Moenagone, Myanmar

LOCATION OF BIRTHMARK
Lower Back

CORROBORATING EVIDENCE
Amnesty decreed for all crimes during the conflict

Napoleon was the leader of a bandit group of Communist defectors in what was then Upper Burma. For terrorizing the regional villages with theft, rape, and murder, Napoleon was wanted by Communist insurgents and within government controlled areas. His capture by one or the other of these groups was inevitable. He held an entire village for ransom in an attempt to negotiate his free passage to China. Knowing that their escape was untenable, one member of Napoleon's crew, hoping to score points with his captors, turned his gun to his leader. As Napoleon fled, he was floored by a shot to the knee, and then another in his stomach. Maung Tin Win only ever spoke of his past life as the famous bandit when he was drunk. From the age of sixteen he would frequently slur that "Napoleon never gave in to anyone!" When his fellow villagers sceptically questioned his tirades, he would brandish the birthmark on his knee as proof of his past life. Maung Tin Win did not, however, have a birthmark on his abdomen where the second and fatal bullet entered Napoleon's body. For this, Maung Tin Win had an answer; on his lower back, a large birthmark in the position of the bullet's exit wound.The bullet that entered one life, exited another.

15

Obike Nwonye, 1973
Obeagwu Ozalla, Nigeria

PREVIOUS PERSONALITY
Nwachime Onya, 1937
Anambra State, Nigeria

LOCATION OF BIRTHMARK
Chest

CORROBORATING EVIDENCE
No recourse to law

In 1937, British Petroleum began oil exploration in the eastern regions of Nigeria. Each probe they tunneled into the earth caused a ripple of local land disputes. Nwachime Onya was shot in the chest, during a conflict arisen over who owned a plot of land which BP flagged for potential extraction. As was the prevalence of such disputes at the time, the information as to who exactly his assailant was has been lost. Though his soul transmigrated thirty-six years later, Obike Nwonye, his new incarnation, does not remember any details that could help implicate a perpetrator. The birthmark on his chest is known as a purpura, and is made up of a series of burst blood vessels under the skin, which create a cluster of purple dots. These dots are consistent with a wound that would have been made by a Dane long-muzzle shotgun, commonly used for hunting across the delta. If we reason backwards, from the birthmark to the presumed corresponding wound, the gun must have been discharged at a distance of two meters, or less. A further deduction can be made, therefore, that due to the proximity of the shooter to Onya, other villagers participating in this fight would have been close enough to clearly identify the killer.

16

Ram Narain Diwedi & Shesh Narain Diwedi, 1964 Farrukhabad,India

PREVIOUS PERSONALITY
Bhimsen Pitamah & Bhism Pitamah, 1964
Uncha Larpur, India

LOCATION OF BIRTHMARK
Abdomen

CORROBORATING EVIDENCE
The police made no arrests.
Inconclusive autopsy

Ram Narain Diwedi and Shesh Narain Diwedi were twins whose past-life memories perfectly conformed with the lives and deaths of twins from a village eighteen kilometers away. Bhimsen and Bhism were owed money from a local landowner who lured them to his town under the pretext of settling their financial dispute. It was a trap. All of the eyewitnesses to the crime were either implicated or cowed into silence. The only witnesses to the event willing to speak are the reincarnated twins, who offer as corroboratory evidence to their testimony the thin linear birthmarks that stretch across both their abdominal regions.

Bringing Conversations on Gender and Sexuality to the National Museum of India

NAMAN P. AHUJA

Designations like a "National Museum" communicate, with a certain onerousness, a responsibility for providing in India's diverse cultural space a representation of the nation and the national. Given that the history of the measures of morality or ethics used to form India's "national" norms on gender and sexuality have been the subject of sustained academic discourse for decades, one wonders what, now, guides or speaks for the diversity of these views in the field of public visual culture? When norms are not explicit, precedents can inform policy on these matters, and museums can play an important part in shaping public discourse. Since understandings of gender and sexuality are caught in the flux of changing attitudes, objects and rituals from times past can be read in ways that make them resonate with current knowledge formation, while still posing questions about the context in which that art was made. This is not new—it is an effective method of communication mobilized by many historians and social reformers. By harnessing it, the museum and the wider discipline of art history in India can be made relevant to the public.

When, and how, can the imperative questions around gender trump the priority given by the museum to the requirement of instilling patriotism or national pride? This involves being open to locating what makes up the nation through the intersection of gender with art, the caste, class, and community of the maker and the viewer, their access to technology and literacy, and a recognition of their contexts—be they war, religion, or any other variable. Museums and the bureaucracy in India, however, have been less than welcoming to such complex narratives. At a press conference in Paris three months before the opening of the exhibition "The Body in Indian Art" in Brussels, I was asked, "And in what way will the exhibition on the Body deal with the atrocities perpetrated on women's bodies in your country?" It was a question that came soon after the city of Delhi had been shaken by the brutal rape of a young woman on a public bus, and which had brought thousands to the streets in protests that demanded an end to violence against women.[1] I welcomed the question from the journalist as it offered the opportunity to speak to the importance of curating and presenting art within a contemporary frame, rather than as objects that merely pointed to a glorious past. I too had addressed similar concerns to those in public office at museums and the government previously. Standing beside the Indian diplomat, who was coordinating the exhibition for the Government of India, I was able to iterate how the exhibition will show art as relevant to the concerns of the moment, rather than distanced from them. The press conference made clear to the commissioners and government agencies present there that ways had to be found to negotiate the curating of an exhibition that reflected current concerns along with the need for officialdom to show the beauty and glory of a distant past.[2]

1 Citations for the nature of Indian rapes (extending to rape analyzed as a crime against humanity or an element of genocide, mass rape in conflict or communal violence, and rape as a tool of caste oppression), the rise of rapes in India, and on the sociology of atrocities against women and legal protection being promulgated as remedies are vast. See: Baxi, Pratiksha. *Public Secrets of Law: Rape Trials in India* (New Delhi: Oxford University Press, 2014). Mehra, Madhu, and Vidyun Sabhaney. *The Rape Law and Constructions of Sexuality* (New Delhi: Partners for Law in Development, 2018). Kannabiran, Kalpana. "Introduction: The Habitations of Violence in India" in *Violence Studies*, ed. Kalpana Kannabiran (New Delhi: Oxford University Press, 2016).

2 In previous papers I have argued for using the objects in a museum to tell narratives of conflict —whether caused by economic necessity, on religious grounds, territoriality, or expressed as gendered violence. A key example studied in those essays was of the decapitated "Mallinatha," portrayed as a female ascetic. See: Naman P. Ahuja, "Conflict: Can Museums Tell Us Why?," *Marg* 71, no. 4 (2020): 26–37; and Naman P. Ahuja, "Discourse on a Label: exposing narratives of violence," in *Historians of Asia on Political Violence*, ed. Anne Cheng and Sanchit Kumar (Paris: Collège de France, 2021), 19–70.

Changes in the contemporary context raise questions that we often look to the past to illuminate. Art history, like many other disciplines, is in a state of constant exploration and inquiry. Museums are spaces where an attempt can be made to address our relationship with the past—to see continuity, as well as to acknowledge the inevitability and necessity for change. Museums are also spaces where one encounters the power of visual communication to express the complexity and beauty of thought as it grows out of particular cultures and contexts. It is not by focusing only on the glories of the past that we find a deeper engagement with it, but rather through a lens that displays both strengths and frailties, and which allows for interpretation and understanding that emerges from the present.

Critically important archaeological evidence and artworks lie neglected in museums for want—not just of better designed galleries, but—of a better designed interpretative framing that's commensurable with the needs of our times and which reflects a more accurate picture of the research that has been done in the past fifty years. This article provides citations from research in the social sciences that can help interpret the types of objects encountered in many museums of South Asia. The enterprise of bringing this kind of research on gender and sexuality to the public was fraught with problems. Why was this so difficult to execute?

Displays of Indian art, I have argued elsewhere, are trapped by limiting proclamations on iconography: whether Hindu, Buddhist, or Jain. Displays that focus on who the gods of India are, what these religions are about, and how endemic these religious ideas are, serve to reinforce the dominant cliché about India being led by religion. Little effort is made to demonstrate how museum objects show shifts and diversity in religion and its practise, record new power structures, or indeed, how they tell a gendered history. A second, equally enduring cliché in museums of historical art is to achieve a dazzling spectacle through the display of courtly art and jewels. Akin to the dazzling effect the ruler had on her or his subjects at court, these displays harness our infinite capacity for being in the thrall of materialism, now used to the museum's benefit as the ticket-selling purveyor of wealth and power, and reinforcing the very old-fashioned expectation of history as a subject that provides a list of kings. Few cultures in the world have managed to serve this up with quite as much aplomb as India with its endless lists of Maharajas and Nawabs who vied with each other for ever-grander jewels and costumes. For the past 150 years, these riches have left museums filled with displays not in India alone, but in England and Europe too. This has stereotyped India as a land of profligate bejeweled wealth. Rarely can one escape a museum gallery where the culture is not epitomized by it. This works in a neat contrast to the general poverty of the country, which serves up the richness of India's spirituality as a panacea alongside. Policy makers, politicians, and their publicists thus remain convinced that the desperately poor will need their recompense in a richness of religion.[3] The wealth displayed in these galleries of course has another public takeaway for the Indian cultural nationalist: the lament about how rich India was before it was looted by rapacious colonialism. A narrative on the concentration of wealth in a small courtly elite ends up being then, not a source of lament for the poverty and casteism that are pre-colonial too, but a nostalgia for lost "national" wealth.

Breaking away from these modes of presenting

3 Bernard Cohn has examined a much larger apparatus within which museological narratives emerged in colonial India. His book explains how historiography, observation and travel, the requirement to survey and enumerate, and surveillance by the state can be seen alongside the drive to create museological narratives. He says, "The power to define the nature of the past and establish priorities in the creation of a monumental record of a civilization, and to propound canons of taste, are among the most significant instrumentalities of rulership." (p.10), Bernard S. Cohn, "Introduction," in *Colonialism and Its Forms of Knowledge: The British in India*, ed. by Bernard S. Cohn (Princeton, NJ: Princeton Univ. Press, 2006), 6–15. His introduction, pp. 6–15, deals with the specific "modalities" he identifies for colonial knowledge formation. The continuing fascination with contemporary Indian art, with Indian design, with Indian craft and tradition, has a long history. This is evident by how Indian craft has been displayed in the west, as well as for Indians themselves. These issues have been analyzed by Saloni Mathur in *India by Design: Colonial History and Cultural Display* (Berkeley: University of California Press, 2007) and Abigail McGowan, *Crafting the Nation in Colonial India* (New York: Palgrave Macmillan, 2009). On the imperatives that guided Indian exhibition and museum making in the 1980s, see Rebecca Brown, *Displaying Time: The Many Temporalities of the Festival of India* (Washington: University of Washington Press, 2017); I have examined the role of orientalism in stereotyping India as a place of spirituality in the western imagination in Naman P. Ahuja and Louise Belfrage, eds. (Mumbai: Marg Publications and Ax:son Johnson Foundation, 2019). On the very need to stereotype the other, see Naman P. Ahuja, "Tropes & Places", in *Influx: Contemporary Art in Asia*, Naman P. Ahuja, Parul Dave Mukherji and Kavita Singh, eds. (New Delhi: Sage, 2013).

Indian culture has not been easy. I curated "The Body in Indian Art and Thought" and co-curated "India and the World" with these concerns in mind.[4] The main subject of each of these exhibitions was stated in their titles. The first exhibition examined Indian art history intersectionally, while the second presented that intersectionality in relation to the globalizing force of art history and the museum. Each of the exhibitions was divided into eight (in the first instance) and nine (in the second) galleries to reflect aspects or themes that made up the narrative. However, each gallery also had an extremely important subtext and sometimes even a counternarrative, which was consciously worked into the storyline. This subtext allowed me to explore ideas that were politically and socially relevant. One consistent subtext in both the shows was to reinterpret, or re-present heritage to nuance a history of erotica, gender, and sexuality through art historical sources. It is important to note that given the diversity of class and caste structures and cultures in South Asia, concerns on gender and sexuality cannot be spoken about in a generalized "Indian" context. The past two or three decades of scholarship in this field have adequately exposed how ideas of morality were reframed and looked at within a nationalist agenda, and even how they were stereotyped in the colonial period.[5] Each age, ours included, resuscitates or selects the objects in museums and narratives in history as evidence for ideas from the past that respond to current exigencies. The following sections of this essay will discuss some of the ways by which this was done.

---

4 "The Body in Indian Art and Thought" was held at the Palais des Beaux Arts in Brussels from October 5, 2013 to January 5, 2014, and subsequently at the National Museum in Delhi from March 14, 2014 to June 7 2014; "India and the World" was held first at the CSMVS in Mumbai from November 11, 2017 to February 18, 2018, and then at the National Museum in Delhi from May 5, 2018 to June 30, 2018. The main books, catalogs, articles, podcasts, and films that deal with them are: Naman P. Ahuja, *The Body in Indian Art and Thought* (Antwerp: Ludion, 2013) and Naman P. Ahuja, *Rupa Pratirupa: The Body in Indian Art* (Delhi: National Museum, 2014), followed by: *Rupa Pratirupa: The Body in Indian Art*, an eight-part documentary series produced by Red Dot Productions for the Indira Gandhi National Centre for the Arts (IGNCA), 2015 (available on DVD).; Naman P. Ahuja and J.D. Hill, *India and the World: A History in Nine Stories*, (Delhi: Penguin, 2017), followed by a podcast on June 15, 2018 by Naman P. Ahuja, "Curating Universal Museums in Non-western Countries," in conversation with Jim Cuno, President, Getty Foundation.

5 A key text on this remains: Kumkum Sangari and Sudesh. Vaid, *Recasting Women: Essays in Colonial History* (New Delhi: Kali for Women, 1989). In the richly layered opening essay, for instance, Uma Chakravarti explains how the histories of Vedic women like Gargi and Maitreyi were consciously revived to show they were learned and educated, just as the histories of women characters in Kalidasa's plays, the romances Nala and Damayanti, or Savitri and Satyabhama, or the biographies of female bhakti poets were also revived. She notes which scholars were engaged in this enterprise and how this was done in order to lend Indian cultural nationalism the moral ground needed to counter colonial politics. It served to give confidence to Indians that, "the degeneration of Hindu civilization and the abject position of Hindu women" was not one "requiring the 'protection' and 'intervention' of the colonial state." (p.35). This was, however, predicated on the revival of an idea of an Aryan woman. Spiritually inclined, her moral rectitude counterbalanced the revival of the other ideal, the valorous Aryan male imbued with martial vigour who could lead a militant cultural nationalism. Not only were these exemplars widely picked up by historians and popular writers, they were used by social reformers for shaping institutions. Importantly, she concludes her study not simply by exposing these biases in the invention of the idea of Indian tradition, but with the provocative question of the many sections of women this 150-year period of social uplift left unaddressed. For an illustrated history of the women's movement in India see Radha Kumar, *The History of Doing: An Illustrated Account of Movements for Women's Rights and Feminism in India, 1800-1990* (Delhi: Zubaan / Kali for Women, 1993) which provides documentation that art historians and curators will find useful.

1. Histories that Reinforce Gender Stereotypes and Histories that Question Them

An extravagant courtly object, such as a shield made of rhinoceros hide from eighteenth-century Udaipur FIG 1A–1C, was displayed as part of a narrative on "courtly culture." Richly painted with pure gold, it served to dazzle the public with its refined brushwork. Art historians usually point out the marvellous *nim qalam* style of painting, the shaded gray and gold evident on this shield, without focusing on the content of the narrative. Instead, the object's accompanying captions and exhibition text were used to bring attention to notions of upper-class (Rajput) masculinity, to the hunting and extermination of many animals in India, and to how this behaviour was made normative through the apparatus of the court.

It shows a day in the life of a maharana divided into eight scenes, the eight *prahara* (or segments) of a single day. The first shows him leaving the palace, four scenes are about his bravery as a hunter and warrior: practicing archery, hunting with a spear, then using a gun from the protection of a *machan*, camouflaged in the forest—hunting tigers and more tigers. Killing animals and taking life with impunity was not just a royal pastime but a royal prerogative and even seen as the upholding of *dharma*. Events can be read differently in different times and spaces. In the past this act was seen as a display of bravery and masculinity, necessary for moral order, whereas today it may be seen as an unnecessarily violent disturbance of the ecological order. In one of the other scenes, the maharana is offered a bathing beauty he encounters in a forest; while in another his piety is referenced, as he passes by a temple, presumably

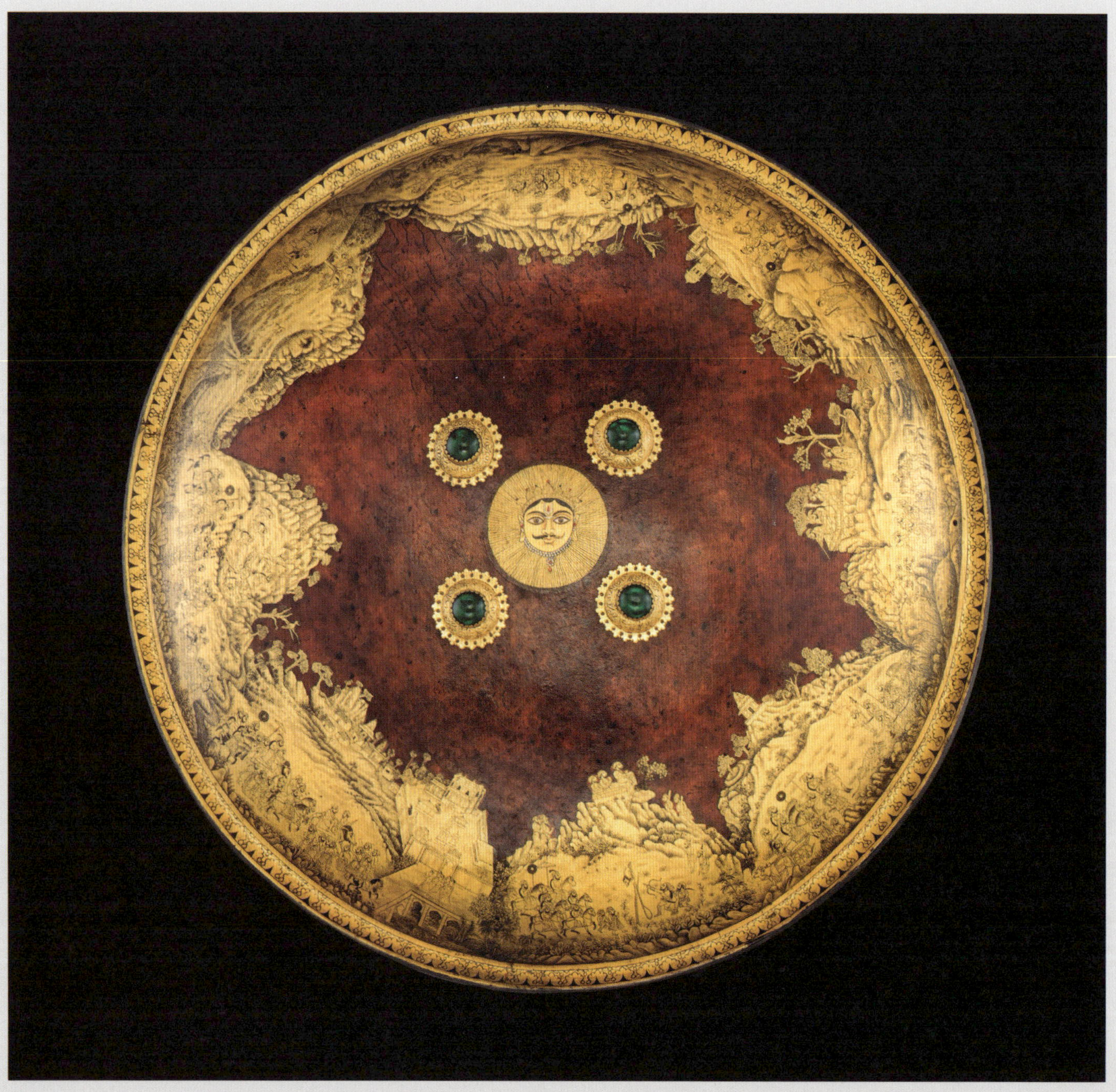

taking its deity's blessings. The last scene shows him coming back home to his fort where his wives have all lined up at the rampart, waiting to receive him. In sum, his depiction adds up to a narrative of male virility, piety, and agency, and the command he holds on a supplicant group of women.[6] The machismo inherent in this narrative is questionable from our feminist perspectives today, just as the very materiality of the object itself can raise questions: it is an object made out of the hide of a rhinoceros—an animal that once roamed across South Asia but is now extinct in most of that region, relegated to a couple of protected forests in Assam and Nepal. Both these matters were put forward to the public in addition to the excellence of the courtly painting.

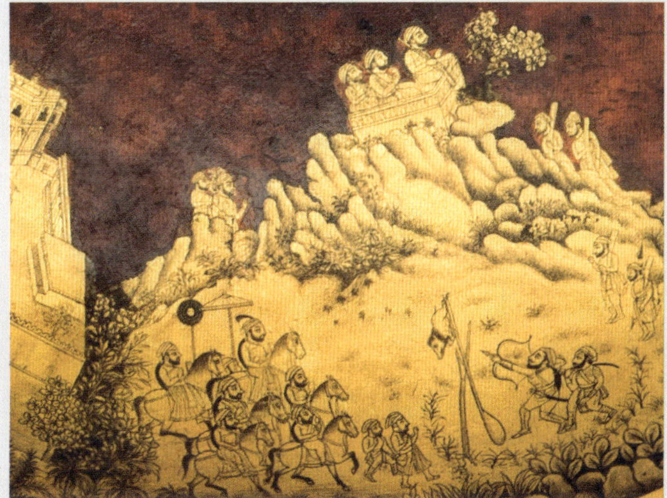

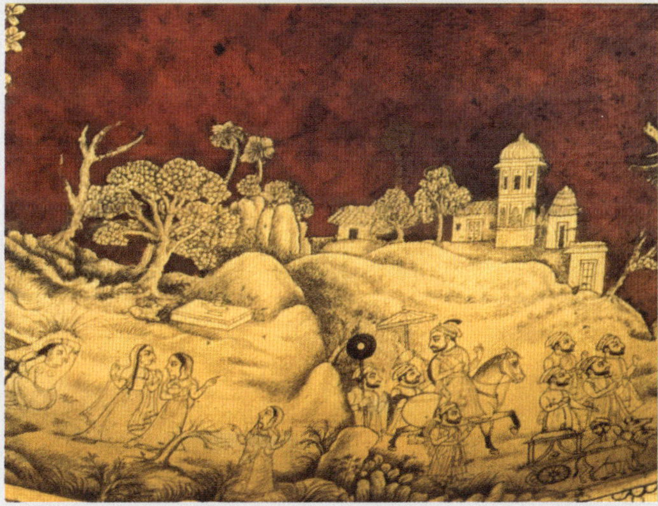

FIG 1A **Used ceremonially, objects such as this painted shield communicate a narrative about the king's valour and virility as well as the capacity to command worship from his wives. Like it, other objects also capture ideals of masculinity as embodied by some sections of pre-colonial society.**

Shield (dhal) of Maharana Sangram Singh II. Rhino hide. Mewar, about AD 1730. Udaipur, Rajasthan, India. Height: 9.7 cm, Diameter: 62.5 cm. National Museum, New Delhi (62.2879). Image courtesy: Naman P. Ahuja, *India and the World: A History in Nine Stories*.

FIG 1B–C **Details of FIG 1A.**

6 Masculinity however, in ancient and medieval Indian art remains under researched. For an essay with comparable contexts see Vishakha Desai, “Reflections on the History and Historiography of Male Sexuality in Early Indian Art,” in *Representing the Body: Gender Issues in Indian Art*, ed. V. Dehejia (Delhi: Kali for women in association with the Book Review Literary Trust, 1997), 42–55. Just as there may have been traditional tropes in India that merged theological and political ideals, a different set of ideals challenged Indian art in colonial times. Art historical presentation in colonial times of the Indian male body as effete was countered by the argument that it was, in fact, yogic and spiritually aware. The decisive impact this had on the history of Indian art and art practice in the early twentieth century has been astutely analyzed by Sugata Ray, “The ‘Effeminate’ Buddha, the Yogic Male Body, and the Ecologies of Art History in Colonial India,” in *Art History* 38, Issue 5 (November 2015): 916–39. Ray analyzes the subject further to contextualize the presentation of the andronynous, demasculinized qualities of the male body as an affirmative, consciously sought ideal that was prevalent at least in the domain of divine imagery.

Written histories have most often focused on the political and ruling classes, and in the past few decades we have seen that the revival of empowering histories of women from one class or caste could not adequately resonate with those of another. Intersectional histories have come to the fore, in which the importance of speaking about the sociocultural, together with the political economy, has become necessary.[7] The same beautifully painted shield, thus, lends itself to two further lines of questioning: did the male *bhil* servants who accompanied this maharana in the painting have the same notions of machismo, or have a retinue of wives waiting for them? Next is the issue of the intended use of the luxurious object: for whom or what was this shield so beautifully painted? Such shields were not intended for actual use in war, but were the type on which gifts would be sent from a princely suitor to the family of his bride-to-be. It could also be sent as a general gift or tribute-bearing tray. Either way, it was to impress the receiver and their family. And given that function, its painted narrative reveals what would have been acceptable codes of gendered behaviour at a different moment in history.

Through its subtext, this shield provided an opportunity to move the narrative away from just a celebration of courtly riches, to questioning the history of those social issues that we, today, want the public to engage with. The compulsions of pluralism force an acknowledgement of intersectional telling of diverse histories: which "Indian" man, and which type of "Indian" woman, does one extrapolate as the Indian voice in a "National" Museum's display —the Bhil or the indologist, the maharana or the environmentalist, or that of the art/cultural historian? The museum can never comprehensively address the diversity of its publics, yet it can, at least, serve to make that public aware of the complexity at hand. How can these concerns be reflected in the way in which the diverse publics can read the objects in museums? Posing the question and making the public examine issues of patronage and ownership alongside artistic style and technique is one step in this direction. However, an engagement with this historiography of the subject also needs to be communicated. Much of the literature on gender studies in India has located the force of colonialism as being the principal agent that radically altered gender roles by introducing binary stereotypes of acceptable patterns of masculinity and femininity, which even the Indian cultural nationalists were found espousing. We have objects that have furthered this view, substantiating it in all sorts of ways; and we can produce evidence that questions not just the chronology of these ideas, but equally the over simplification that has caused such gender stereotyping.

Scholarship has shown that the idea of the valorous aryan man was specifically developed by leading writers and historians of the nineteenth century to strengthen a national movement. This approach was in rebuttal to the colonial charge that the Indian man was effete when compared with the European. This led not just to the noble aryan being celebrated, but also to its merging with ideas of the warrior kshatriya, the martial Rajputs and Sikhs, the valiant Shivaji who led the Marathas, and so on, and whose virtues were extolled in various books in Marathi, Hindi, and Bengali. However, rather than see such versions of masculinity as being only a nineteenth-century revival, one needs to examine objects that celebrate such ideas in earlier,

7 One of the most succinct summaries of the cautions and caveats necessary in writing a gendered history for South Asia is by Janaki Nair, "On the Question of Agency in Indian Feminist Historiography," in *Gender & History*, vol. 6, no. 1 (April 1994): 82–100. She says, "The process of redressing the biases of 'bad history' by discovering women in history, however, soon runs aground on the categories of 'history-as-usual' that are clearly insufficient to analyze gender… feminist historiography cannot be just additive, for if such historiography is already hampered by the nature of the archive, which disproportionately reflects the interests and concerns of the dominant classes, then the search for fresh 'evidence' could obscure the need for a critique of the techniques, and even disciplines, by which patriarchies remain resilient." (p. 84).

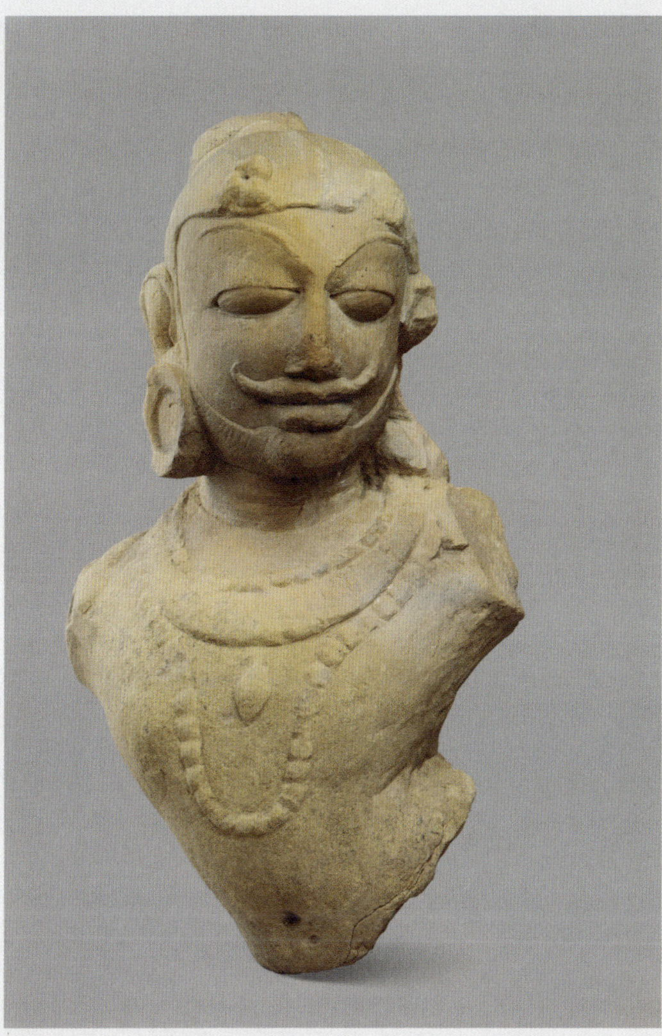

FIG 2 **A Warrior. Sandstone. Jamsot, Kaushambi, Allahabad, Central India. c. 10th–11th centuries. 33 × 19 cm. Allahabad Museum (Acc. No. 1209). Image courtesy: Naman P. Ahuja, *The Body in Indian Art and Thought*.**

pre-colonial times in India.[8] The eighteenth-century gold-painted shield was just one example. The moustachioed male warrior taken from the walls of a twelfth-century temple at Jamsot FIG 2, in the old Bundela territory (in central India) is another, much older example of the type. The idea of the heroic king as one who proclaimed his universal dominion, commanded Vedic sacrifices, sacrificed animals, was shown with a halo displaying his divine effulgence, and often on horseback surrounded by parasol and fly-whisk bearers, as the keeper of religious, moral and sacrificial order, is a very old trope that was reinterpreted in each age in new garb, and mildly altered settings.

---

8 These form a stock of motifs in illustrated manuscripts from the Bundi and Kota region harking back to much older forms of extolling these "heroines" and "heroes" as nāyikas and nāyakas, as personifications of aesthetic virtues on the walls of temples (at Khajuraho, and many other temples, for instance), and even on older early historic monuments at Gandhara, Mathura, and Amaravati. Equally ancient and prolific are their depictions on many small finds of bone, ivory, terracotta, and wood images of the period between the second century BCE and second century CE. These motifs have a long literary and iconographic history in which they have consistently stimulated discussion on matters of gender, fertility, beauty, and virility. Moving forward in history, the same motifs illustrate *rāgamālas*, and are to be found in the literature around *śṛingāra* and *vīra-rasa* in the music traditions of Rajasthan, central India and up, as well as dhrupad, ṭhumrī, and ḳhayāl. The literature on the subject is vast. On the *karpuramañjari* and *śālabhañjikā* motifs see: Devangana Desai's essays,"The Karpuramanjari Motif in Indian Art," in Mevissen, C.W. and Mevissen, Gerd JR eds., *Indology's Pulse: Arts in Context: Essays Presented to Doris Meth Srinivasan in Admiration of her Scholarly Research* (New Delhi: Aryan Books International, 2019); and, Devangana Desai, "Shalabhanjika: Woman-and-tree in art and literature," Professor K.D. Bajpai Memorial Lecture, 19th Session, *IAHC* [Indian Art History Congress], Kanyakumari, October 30, 31, November 1, 2010. On the rasikapriyā and rasamañjarī, see Vishakha N. Desai, "Loves of Rādhā in the 'Rasikapriyā' Verses and Paintings," *Ars Orientalis* 30, Supplement 1, Chāchājī: Professor Walter M. Spink, Felicitation Volume (2000): 83–92;, and Molly Emma Aitken, *The Intelligence of Tradition in Rajput Court Painting* (New Haven: Yale University Press, 2010). To look into the longer history of these tropes in the pedagogy of elite circles in ancient times see Daud Ali, *Courtly Culture and Political Life in Early Medieval India* (Cambridge: Cambridge University Press, 2004), as well as, Sheldon Pollock, *Rasa Reader: Classical Indian Aesthetics* (New York, NY: Columbia University Press, 2016). Some of the examples of how these aesthetic tropes migrated into muslim courts has been provided by A.N.D. Haksar trnsl., Suleiman Charitra by Kalyana Malla (author) (India: Penguin, 2015), as well as his trnsl., *The Courtesan's Keeper:* Samaya Matrika by Kshemendra (author) (India: Penguin, 2014).

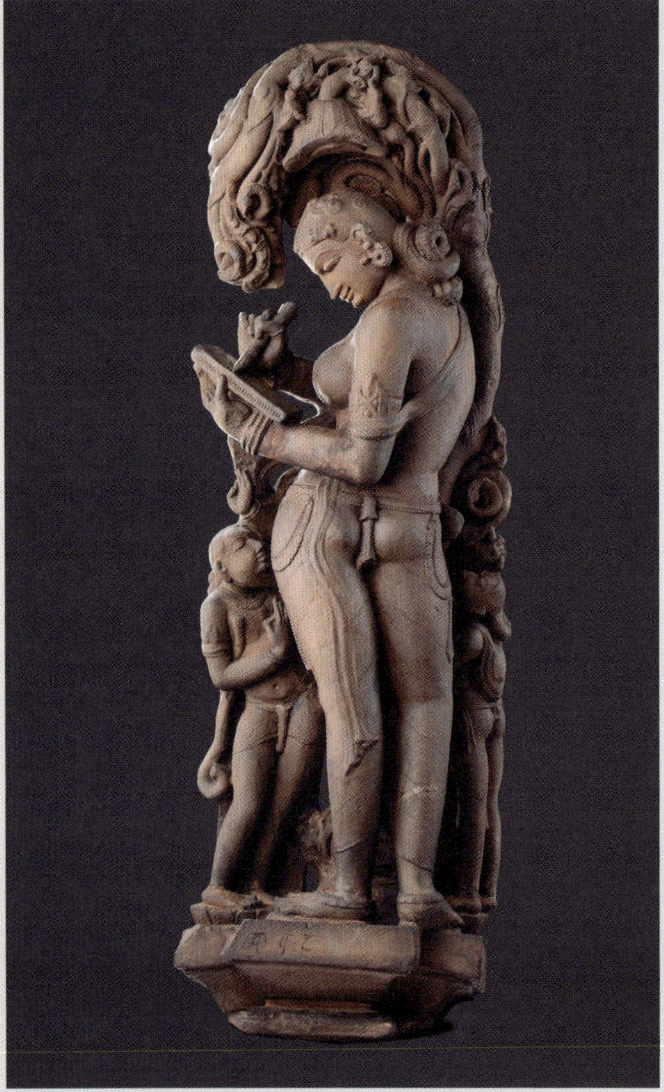

FIG 3A *Surasundari Patralekha*. Sandstone. Khajuraho, Chandela, 10th–11th centuries. Indian Museum, Kolkata. 94 × 30 × 17.5 cm (Acc. No. Br 4/A 26231). Image courtesy: Naman P. Ahuja, *The Body in Indian Art and Thought*.

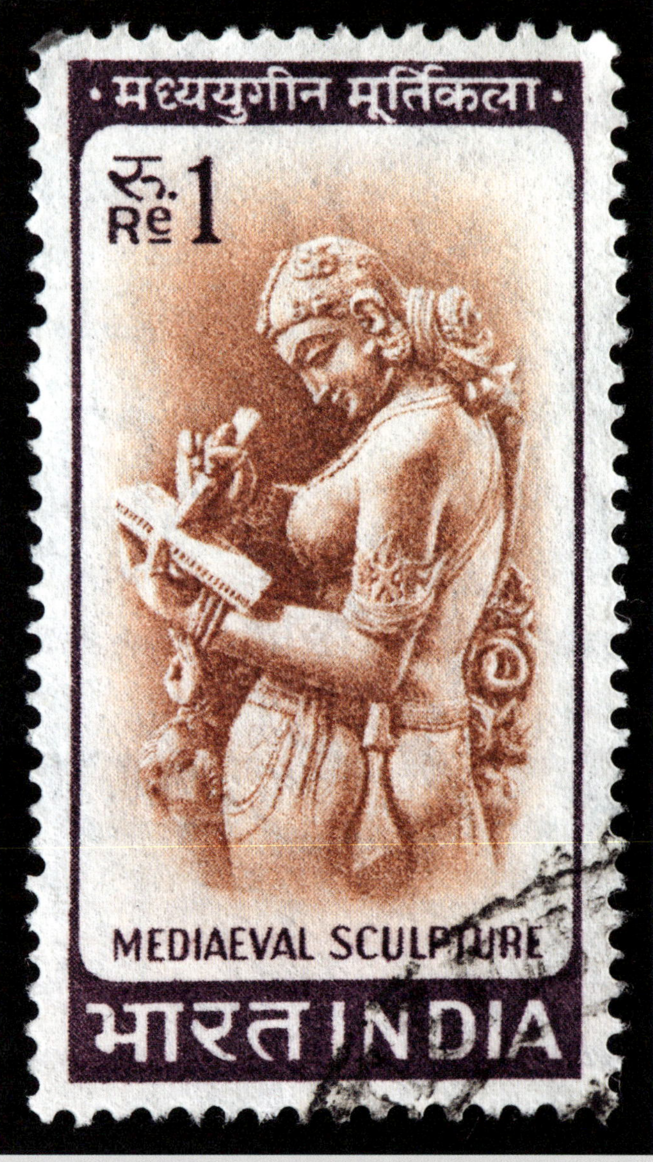

FIG 3B In 1964, an Indian government postage stamp of Patralekha was issued to celebrate women's literacy in a series on medieval Indian sculpture. Image courtesy: Ivan Vdovin / Alamy Stock Photo.

The curling moustache and beard, being one of the more enduring visible markers of masculinity and the valorousness of the warrior-king, are often found sported by the men among images of erotic female sculptures in medieval temples. This is important, because here the sculptures are meant to communicate aesthetic ideals of femininity and masculinity. Jamsot is known for the most extraordinary sculptures of sexually-charged dancing female celestials, some of the best examples of which are in the Allahabad Museum. Striking a pose that deliberately shows off their bodies and ornaments, they can be shown playing musical instruments, or sometimes being teased by a monkey who is disrobing them. Jamsot's temple sculptures can be studied in a context similar to Khajuraho. And Khajuraho's erotic art has provoked hundreds of photographers and writers to comment on ancient and medieval mores on erotica and sexuality, tantra and militant Shaiva ascetical centers, and, indeed the context of warfare and memorialization in which these visions of male bravado and celestial *apsaras* in the heavenly abode of the gods reside. Although rare, such sculptures of bearded and moustachioed male patrons, warriors, or militant ascetics, would be positioned amidst these sculptures of erotically-charged women on the exterior walls of those temples.

One of the three images of *apsaras*, or *surasundaris* from the temple of Khajuraho included in the *Body in Indian Art*, is called the "patra-lekha." The sculpture represents an adorned woman, smiling as she holds up a stylus in her right hand to write on a tablet held in her left FIG 3A. The establishment has a history of approving of this inspirational image as it showed female literacy in ancient India. The Government of India even made postage stamps of her in the 1960s that circulated widely FIG 3B. Fuzzy postage stamps of a small size however, didn't quite allow us to appreciate the details of her body. While the fact that she was literate was a good narrative indeed, it was for the details on her back that I chose this sculpture. Her back is incised with nail marks that have been driven into her flesh by her lover. She has nail marks incised on her back in three areas: both sides of her back, and just under her shoulder FIG 3C-D. And she is not the only *apsara* in Khajuraho who has these nail marks. The more we start looking at them the more we find these marks on the bodies of two dozen (or more) *apsaras* on the walls of temples in Khajuraho: even when the sculptures would have been placed well out of view at the height of twenty or thirty feet. No one could have seen the nail marks. They are thus iconographically mandated communicators of passionate lustful encounters.

What emerges is that this is a woman driven to write in a state of rapture; the sex, then, is a symbol of joy, of strength through union. The romance associated with a mark—a bite or scratch—is extolled in various medieval literary tracts.[9] The temple has many such *surasundaris*, celestial women, seductively scattered in deliberately *déshabillé* poses, putting on their make-up or jewelry. These are acts that would seldom attract other women's attention, who perform them everyday, however modest their means. However, from a gender-perspective, we equally need to acknowledge that what we are looking at on the temple's walls are several beautiful women for the pleasure of men, performing a literary trope created by, and for a patriarchal society that became iconographic. When looking at the temples and sculptures such as those at Khajuraho, the whole temple reveals itself to subscribe to a heterosexual male perspective of a beautifully

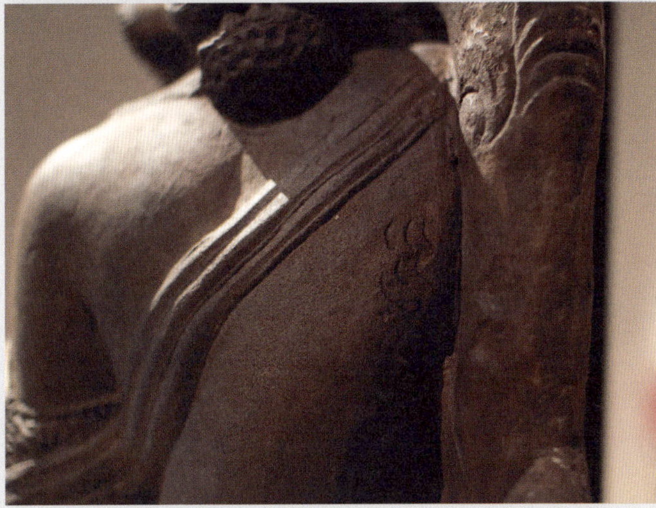

FIG 3C-D Details of the sculpted incisions of nail marks on the back of the sculpture shown as FIG 3. Image courtesy: Naman P. Ahuja, *The Body in Indian Art and Thought*.

9 In fact, in the Kamasutra, book 2, ch. 4 specifically mentions the types of nail marks that can be seen on bodies: what are their shapes, and why must one mark one's lover? Nail marks serve as a memento of the passionate encounter, which occupies the mind long after the encounter itself. This keeps love growing. It also has a particular effect on those who see such marks on another, making them both respect the person who has them as well as find that person desirable. There are eight types of nail marks listed in the text: Achchhuritaka: snapping nail mark, *ardhachandra*: the crescent one, Mandala: the circular mark, Rekha: the linear nail mark, Vyaghranakha: the one that is like a tiger's claw, Mayurapadaka: the peacock's foot, Shashaplutaka: like a jumping hare and Utpalapatrakam: like a lotus petal.

erotic world.[10] The semi-divine *apsaras* whose role is (frequently at the god Indra's disposal) to seduce various earthly men, is not a class of characters that has a male equivalent.[11] While there may be hundreds of ancient and medieval examples of stereotyping sexualized women, there remains a serious lack, both in art-history and in studies of classical literature, of excavating tropes typecasting the erotic male figure. Is this because we haven't looked? Partially, yes, that is true. But there can be no gainsaying the gaze is largely heteronormative and comes from a patriarchal society. How far back can this trope be taken? And can this question itself be posed in our displays of classical art?

There is a long history of Indian discomfiture with depictions of sex, even when it is on the walls of temples. Mahatma Gandhi tried to have the images at Khajuraho covered with cement plaster once, and even the President of the Indian History Congress was embarrassed about this "decadence."[12] This academic and political puritanism has been attributed to colonialism by many, although various other possible reasons for it have also been listed, and should not detain us here. It exists, and it rears its pernicious grip on our institutions and heritage repeatedly. In the year prior to the opening of the exhibition on *The Body in Indian Art*, I was informed that the government would not back an exhibition containing images that display sex openly even though this was meant to be an exhibition on "the body." The European public's expectation, however, was that sex would obviously be shown in the art of the country famous for the Kamasutra and tantra. The international press, as well, was already asking questions on how India was going to address the atrocities meted to its female bodies through the exhibition or museum's narrative, fueled of course by the reportage emerging from India's own vocal media. The gulf between a code of puritanical morality brushing things under the carpet expected by the government versus the enormous advances made in the discussions in other public spheres were already palpable. Time and again, the question of why a culture with such a rich history of psychosexual aesthetics was now unable to discuss this subject openly needs some unpacking.

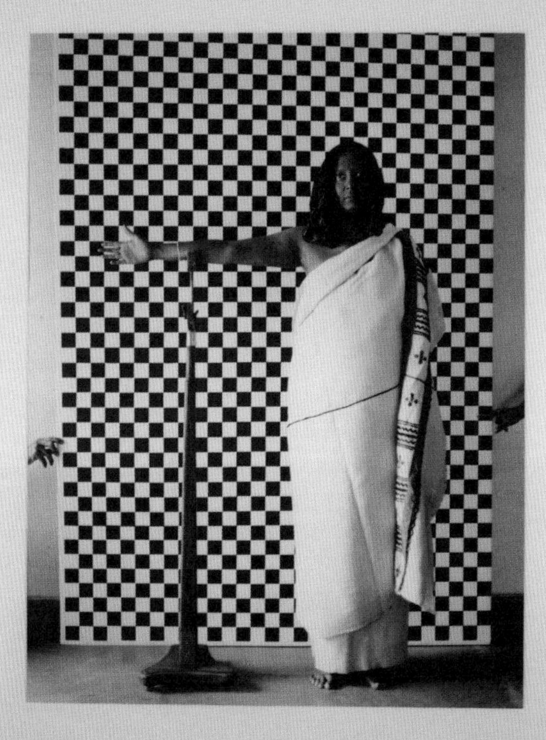

FIG 4 Various knowledge systems have exerted control on the body, including nineteenth-century "science" that sought to regulate along racial lines. Anthropology used the measurement of bodies as the new system of taxonomy. One system of regulation thus replaced another. *Toda*, a photo-performance, is part of a series called "The Ethnographic Series Native Women of South India: Manners & Customs." This photograph references a late 19th-century anthropometric photograph The photograph is a critique of the instrumentalization of colonized bodies. As the artist attempts to reverse the colonial gaze from the position of a post-colonial feminist artist, she is enacting the double consciousness of the "native woman" as well as a "native informer." Pushpamala N. in collaboration with Clare Arni, *Toda* from "The Native Types, Native Women of South India: Manners & Customs," 2000–2004. Sepia-toned silver gelatin print. 70 × 50.8 cm. Collection of Devi Art Foundation. Image courtesy of Devi Art Foundation for *The Body in Indian Art and Thought*.

Various knowledge systems have exerted control on the body, including nineteenth-century "science" that sought to regulate along racial lines: Aryan and non-Aryan was one such divisive classification. Anthropology used the measurement of bodies (and craniums) as the new system

10 In addition to the works of Devangana Desai listed above (supra, note 8), see the classic: *Erotic Sculpture of India: A Socio-cultural Study* (New Delhi: Munshiram Manoharlal, 1985); and, *The Religious Imagery of Khajuraho* (Mumbai: Franco-Indian Research, 1996). One of the first collections of essays to specifically address Indian art from a more contemporary gender perspective can be found in Vidya Dehejia ed., *Representing the Body: Gender Issues in Indian art* (New Delhi: Kali for Women, 1998). This has encouraged others to start developing the theme. For instance, Seema Bawa, *Gods, Men and Women: Gender and Sexuality in Early India* (New Delhi: DK Printworld, 2013).

11 The question that needs to be asked then is why there isn't a similar gender stereotyping of male figures? Indeed, this is imbalanced, because while there are hundreds of these semi-divine beautiful women whose sexual allure is part of their iconography, there are far fewer equivalent sculptures of men or male deities who fit that criterion—at least not as what would qualify as eye candy for women. There are images of attractive gods (Krishna or Bhikshatana may even be written into poetry for their seductiveness) but, they're gods, meant to be worshipped.

12 At his presidential address to the 18th Indian History Congress in Calcutta (now Kolkata) in 1955, K.M. Panikkar said, "[…] another problem that faces the student is the decadence that seems to have overtaken Hindu society between the eighth and the 12th centuries… The Khajuraho and Orissa temples for all their magnificence testify to a degeneration of the Hindu mind." Discussed in Naman P. Ahuja "From the Kama Sutra to Virtual Sex," in *Mint*, August 13, 2010. https://www.livemint.com/Leisure/1l2ElzlQhYlopkii9RIdUK/From-the-Kama-Sutra-to-virtual-sex.html.

of taxonomy, and racially driven theorists were keen to explore whether the various species of Indians could be shown to be sufficiently different in order to justify their subjugation. One older Indian system of caste and race that was used to regulate and control society by a Brahmanically dominant elitism was thus replaced by another—this time it was colonial, white, martial, evangelical, and called itself "scientific." The historiography of these ideas came through in three galleries. Gallery 6, on how a society fashioned its ideal heroes, allowed us to explore the shifts in society's aspirations; Gallery 5 showed examples of how communities fashioned their idea of supernatural gods and who was left out of worshipping them; and Gallery 4 was on ideas of cosmology, which looked at different knowledge systems that defined the place of a person in the cosmos. It was in such a context that a strategic dialogue between the images of two imagined women from different epochs was staged.

Toda, a photo-performance by Pushpamala N., is part of a series called "The Ethnographic Series Native Women of South India: Manners & Customs FIG 4." Formally, the figure stands against a chequerboard grid used to provide a scale against which she is measured. This photograph references a late nineteenth-century anthropometric photograph of an Andaman Islander from the collection of Oriole Henry. By restaging this photograph, we are reminded about the history of the instrumentalization of colonized bodies. However, Pushpamala reminds us also, that criticism equally involves questioning who is looking at whom; was the person being looked at willingly performing an identity for the sake of the onlooker? As the artist attempts to reverse the colonial gaze from the position of a post-colonial feminist artist, she is enacting the double consciousness of the "native woman" as well as a "native informer." Near it was displayed an unusual diagram of the cosmos FIG 5. Inasmuch as the body of the Indian is surrounded by the scientific chequerboard that contains and regulates her in the name of modern science (and a new education system that was brought into play), the older painting shows a chequerboard contained within the body of the person instead. Such diagrams, called *lokapurusha*, wherein the cosmos is shaped like an hourglass (*vajra*), are common in the Jain tradition. The *lokapurusha* images were extremely popular and were made on paper or cloth in both manuscripts and as larger paintings. Rarely, however, as seems to be the case in this particular painting on cloth, does the cosmic person seem like a woman, with specific feminine accoutrements: large earrings and anklets, for instance, are visible in this painting.[13] Empowering though the idea of the person containing the entire macrocosm within their body may seem, ancient science was equally pernicious. It provided legitimacy for regulations on a person's place and station in the inhabitable world. Behaviour deemed ethical would lead to rebirths in higher stations on the chequerboard, while what was judged as inappropriate behaviour could relegate the person to a rebirth in one of the squares in the nether regions. The viewer was thus urged to see similarities in diagrammatical devices, used to show a method of "science" by which human life was to be regulated, for visual communication in ancient, medieval, and now, modern times.

---

13 Piotr Balcerowicz has shown that the idea of the cosmic man in Jainism was much older than the sixteenth century previously thought (overlaid by the purusha, is already described by Śvetāmbara Umāsvāti (c. CE 400–500)), and, importantly, that although the cosmic woman appears less frequently, she does exist: Piotr Balcerowicz "The Body and the Cosmos in Jaina Mythology and Art," *Art, Myths and Visual Culture of South East Asia* (New Delhi: Manohar, 2011), 95.

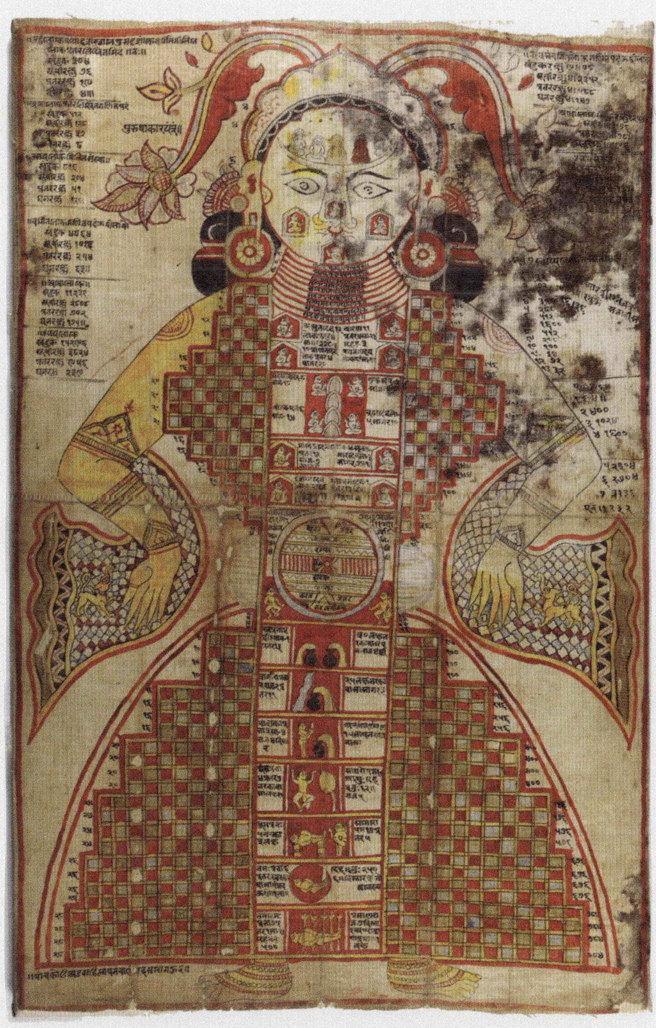

FIG 5 Lokapurusha, *The Cosmic "Man."* Gouache on cloth. Rajasthan, c. eighteenth century. 57 × 38 cm. Ajit Mookerjee Collection, National Museum, Delhi. (Acc. No. 82.575. Image courtesy: Naman P. Ahuja, *The Body in Indian Art and Thought*.

2. Objectification and State Censorship of Narratives

Dialogs between the past and present were used to strategic effect in each of the galleries of the exhibition. Sometimes this served to allow the viewers to compare present views on a subject with the past, and at others it allowed for continuities to be registered, reducing anxieties about the contemporary. The first step was to try and negotiate permission to show images of deities in which different parts of the body were in focus. I tried to get an anatomically explicit depiction of Shiva as the phallus, *linga* from the Bharatpur Museum FIG 6 —it was censored *after* the exhibition's catalog had gone to press. I pleaded for a glorious Lakshmi expressing milk from her breast, an image once placed at the entrance to the National Museum itself, but that too was similarly censored, after an initial assurance that permitted its inclusion in the publication FIG 7. The reason given was that the conservation status of both the images was not good enough to let them travel. This was blatantly untrue as both robust sculptures had been on display in hidden corners of museums for decades, and besides, the conservation studio had more than adequate notice to consolidate the sculptures to make them showworthy. Verbally, however, the then Director of Exhibitions at the National Museum had informed me that I ought to have been more circumspect of India's reputation and selected less sexually overt objects! At any rate, if this was the hesitation with reference to the sexualized anatomy of the great gods Shiva and Lakshmi, how then was one to be able to speak about other more direct sexual experience expressed in Indian art? I cannot detail all the many ways this was navigated, but it may be worth looking at just one example.

Mrinalini Mukherjee's work, *Basanti*, was displayed in a section devoted to the varying ideas of "mother" within a large gallery called "[re]birth" FIG 8A-B. The display explored more than just formal connections in iconography. The sculpture could be read as a magnified inner portion of a flower or a gigantic vulva woven in brown and yellow hemp. Mukherjee's work *Basanti* commanded a gallery filled with *matrikas* (mother goddesses), a Manasa *ghata* (an earthen pot that substitutes for Manasa, the goddess of snakes), disease alleviating deities, entwined mating *naga-mithunas* (copulating serpent deities), and a bold, squatting, vagina-displaying "Lajja Gauri" sculpture from the fourth to sixth centuries CE. This gallery delved into the agency of birth and creation, and how artists had developed new iconographies in each age for the elemental and varying aesthetics of *prakriti* (nature) FIG 9A-B. This prevented us from falling into the all too easy trap of showing an unchanging history. It was obvious that Mukherjee's work was in no way a direct imitation of ancient sculpture—it was not motivated

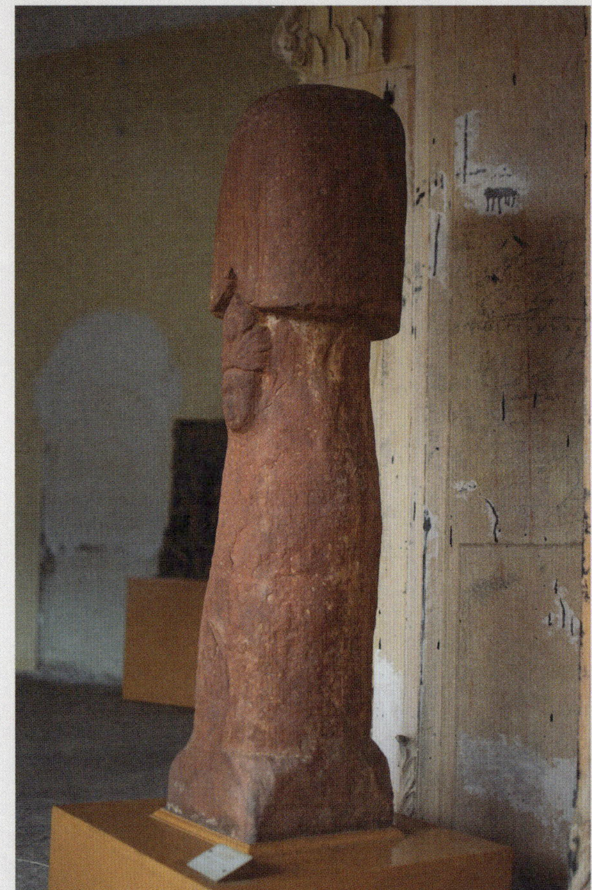

FIG 6 *Ekmukha linga*. Sandstone. Pre-Kushana, 1st century. Aghapura, Rajasthan. Height 152.4 cm, width at base 30.5 cm. Bharatpur Museum, Rajasthan (Acc. No. 52). Image courtesy: Naman P. Ahuja, *The Body in Indian Art and Thought*.

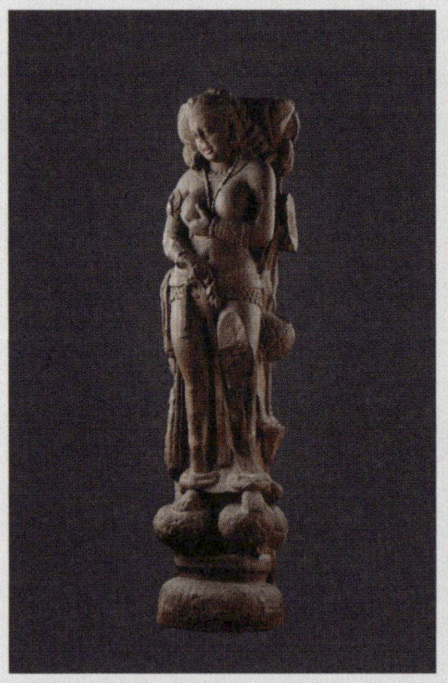

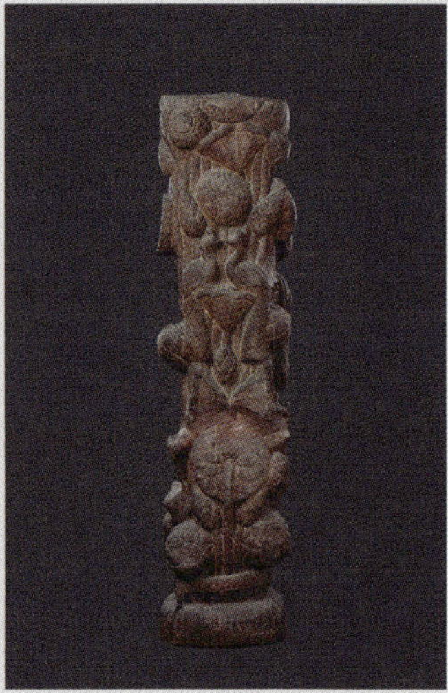

FIG 7A & 7B (REVERSE OF THE SCULPTURE) The change in the location of a sculpture within a museum, such as this famous Lakshmi—once in the National Museum's entrance rotunda, transferred to a nondescript spot in the museum's corridors—seems to be a direct reflection of the embarrassment even classical sculpture now elicits if it is explicit. The smiling Lakshmi presses her breast with one hand while the other holds a branch of fruit on her abdomen that falls, carefully, on her thinly veiled vulva.

Shri Lakshmi (front and reverse views). Red sandstone. Kushan, 2nd century. Mathura region. 123 × 28 × 25 cm. National Museum, Delhi (Acc. No. B.89). Image courtesy: Naman P. Ahuja, *The Body in Indian Art and Thought*.

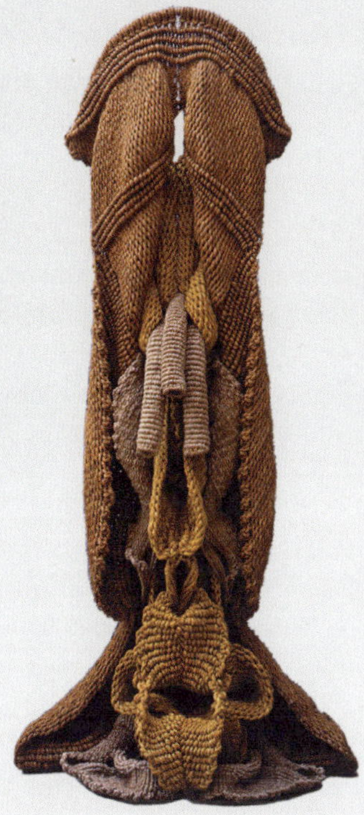

FIG 8A Mukherjee's work amplifies and makes surreal an organic, pliable biological form. "Basanti," she of spring, alludes to the fructifying forces of nature. Mrinalini Mukherjee. *Basanti*, 1993. Dyed hemp, 102 × 125 × 82 cm. Collection NGMA, New Delhi. Image courtesy of the artist for *The Body in Indian Art and Thought*.

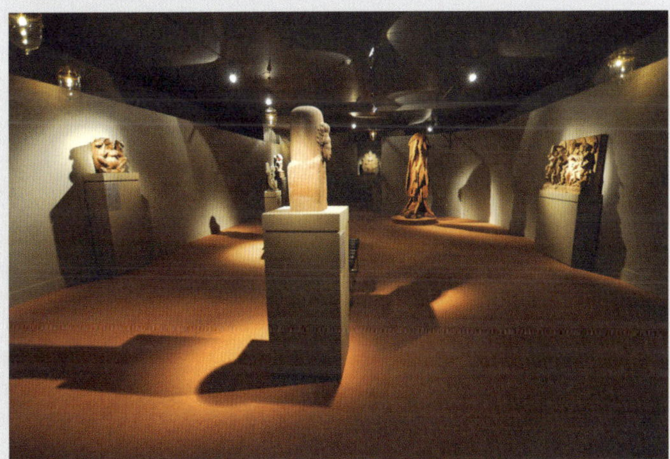

FIG 8B The ovoid gallery in which Mukherjee's vulva-like *Basanti* was displayed had various goddess sculptures along the perimeter and a statue of Shiva in the center, like ancient Yogini temples. One large part of the gallery explored the variety of typifications of the idea of mother, another looked at conception / creation while a third looked at birth itself. Image courtesy of the artist for *The Body in Indian Art and Thought*.

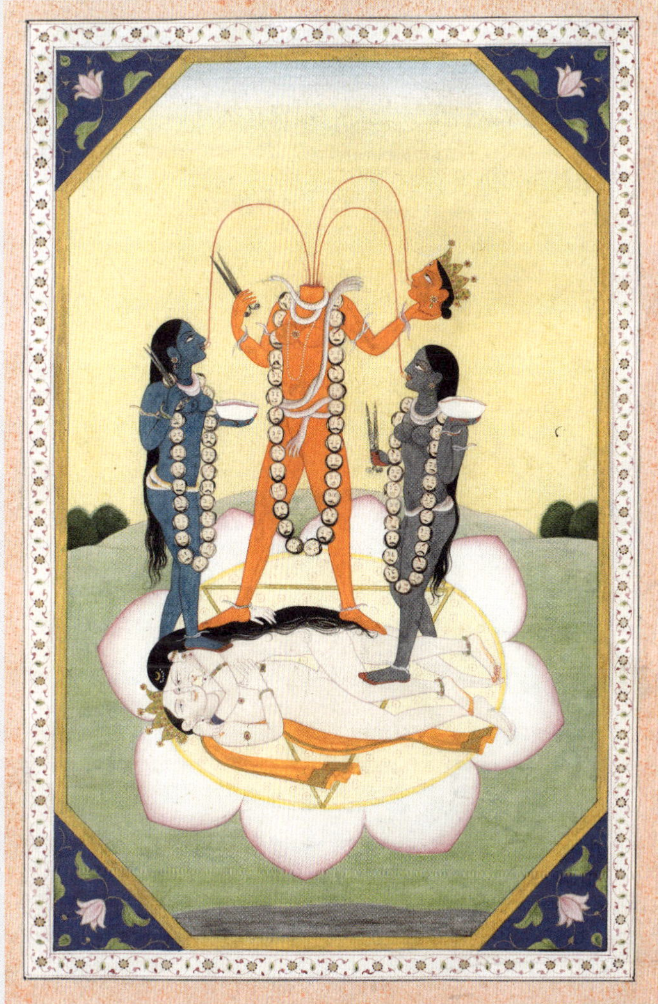

FIG 9A-B India's long history of goddess worship has been the staple on which art history has provided a narrative on the idea of an empowered divine feminine. The variety of goddesses and the different aesthetic functions of these goddesses were explored in the gallery on "[re]birth." The birthing "Lajja Gauri" was placed within eyeshot of the horrifying Chamunda, the snake-goddess Manasa from Bengal was diagonally opposite the disease removing Jyeshta from Tamil Nadu, and so on. These exemplars brought a comparative study of the nature of motherhood to viewers. At various points the public could also reflect on the legacy these iconographies have on the contemporary.

9A *Chinnamastā* (from a Tantric Devī series). Guler, Punjab Hills, c. 1790. Opaque watercolor, gold and silver on paper (formerly published by Arturo Schwarz from the collection of Marcel Duchamp)now in the collection of Shubha and Prahlad Bubbar. Image courtesy: Prahlad Bubbar for *The Body in Indian Art and Thought*.

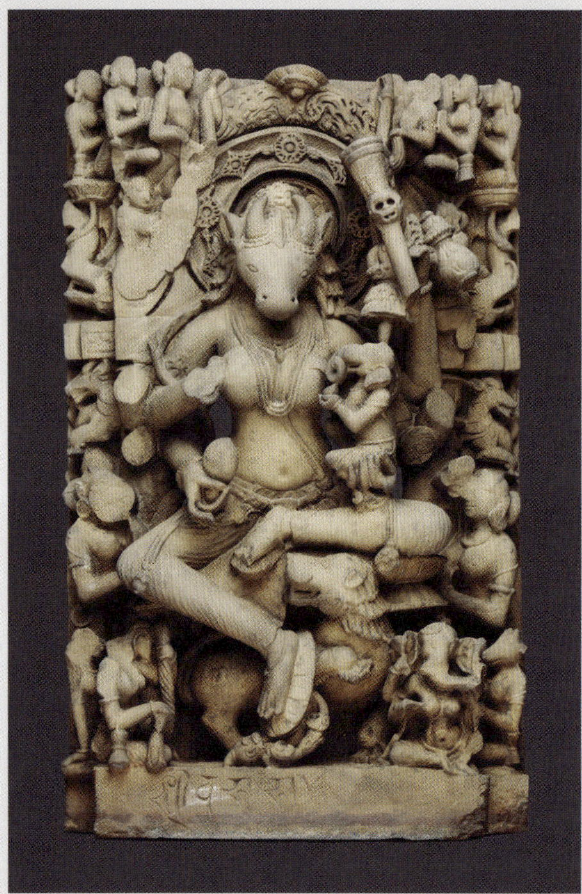

9B ***Vrishabha*****. Chandella, Satna, 10th century. Sandstone 75.5 × 48 cm. Indian Museum, Kolkata (Acc. No: 5494 / A25128). Image courtesy: Naman P. Ahuja, *The Body in Indian Art and Thought*.**

by religiosity, nor did it have the same iconography, yet its vulva-like form captured something of an inspiration from elemental forces, which were canonized and made into religious imagery.[14]

Given that all the objects had been on public display at different times and spaces, the current restrictions brought into focus the notions of "morality" that need to be negotiated to be able to display them "safely" today. The same gallery that displayed the Lajja Gauri and Mukherjee's *Basanti* also contained a central abstract lingam. Unlike the Bharatpur Museum's ancient (pre-Kushan period) *lingam* that had been blocked, perhaps it was the abstraction of this Gupta-period one that allowed it to be displayed, rather like the abstraction in Mrinalini Mukherjee's work. Or perhaps it was the nature of the display that was arranged as a circle to echo the ancient tantric yogini temples, which too are widely interpreted for their vulva-like form with a central shrine to Shiva. Whether abstraction, or direct historical references, the subjects of creation and birth remain powerful contexts within which reproductive genitalia could still be placed on display at the National Museum in 2013.

One cannot, however, assume that the contemporary sculpture was seeking continuity with the history of such form in Indian iconography, and I remain grateful to Mrinalini Mukherjee for coming to the Museum to see the context in which her work was being displayed. Displaying objects from different periods and places together can run the risk of privileging certain kinds of dialogs over the type of historical contextualization we normally see in galleries that are dedicated to a particular time period. Thematization allowed instead a focus on the changes from the past to the present. Historiography, which requires the questioning of assumptions or values inherent in the writings of our forebears that have established how we view the past, and indeed, in turn ourselves, must remain an ongoing exercise as we question the process of our becoming in the present. I began to raise some of these issues in the public walkthroughs and press interviews for *India & the World*. One sculpture that permitted this was the famous "Dancing Girl" of Mohenjodaro, which, for instance, is reproduced in every Indian school child's textbook FIG 10A. Given the ubiquity of this image, it became a good example to use to ask why she has been named the "dancing girl." While there is nothing wrong with the idea that a young girl should be dancing, one also needs to ask if that is really the best title for her?

Dancing girls, in the Indian context, was the term for courtesans in the colonial period when this sculpture was found. The British anglicized the Hindustani word for dance, which is "nāch" and used the term "nautch girls" in much of their writing on Indian culture. This general background apart, there are two main possibilities for why Ernest Mackay named her a "dancing girl." [15] Edgar Degas's ballerinas had become famous in the world's art circles by the time this statuette was discovered in 1926. The Mohenjodaro statuette, made, albeit a few thousand years earlier, does bear an uncanny resemblance in mood and attitude to the famous sequence of Edgar Degas's images in both bronze and as paintings of ballerinas, which had become all the rage of the western modern-art establishment by the 1930s.[16] However, the sculpture also falls into a larger, well-established mindset, in which Indian female figures

14 For a longer discussion of the references Mukherjee drew on for her work, see Naman P. Ahuja "Indian Roots for a Universal Idiom," an essay on the inspirations and influences on the work of the artist Mrinalini Mukherjee in *Mrinalini Mukherjee*, exhb. Cat. (New York, NY: the Metropolitan Museum of Art, 2019).

15 A problem well noted by Jonathan M. Kenoyer in P. Matthiae, Lamberg-Karlovsky, Carl Clifford, *Art of the First Cities: The Third Millennium B.C. from the Mediterranean to the Indus* (New York: Metropolitan Museum of Art, 2003), 391.

16 In 1973, British archaeologist Mortimer Wheeler described the item as his favourite statuette: "There is her little Balochi-style face with pouting lips and insolent look in the eyes. She's about fifteen years old I should think, not more, but she stands there with bangles all the way up her arm and nothing else on. A girl perfectly, for the moment, perfectly confident of herself and the world. There's nothing like her, I think, in the world."

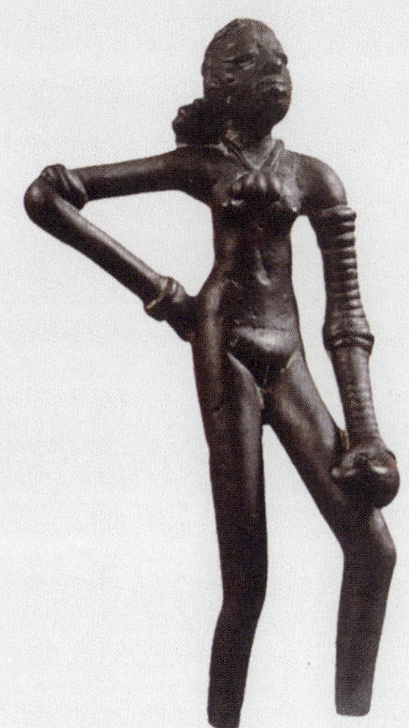

FIG 10A **"Dancing girl" figurine. Bronze. About 2500 BCE. Mohenjodaro, Sindh, Pakistan. 10.5 × 5 × 2.5 cm. National Museum, New Delhi (5721/195). Image courtesy of Naman P. Ahuja, *India & the World: A History in Nine Stories*.**

are either called "apsaras," seductive celestial nymphs, or they're called "devis," who are worshipped as mother goddesses. Rarely is there a space in between for female exemplars, even though portraits of a few prominent historical women do survive.

Rather than open the possibility that this may be a reflection of some historical person, or even a toy or a games-counter, several generations of scholars have continued to celebrate this sculpture as a dancing girl. This was the case even when a revision was suggested by a venerable organization such as the Indian Council of Historical Research a couple of years ago, that she be called the goddess Parvati.[17] Once again, from the "dancing girl," an effort was made to portray her as a goddess. The two paradigms for the reception of this image in the media—of a religiously guided reverence or the lascivious ogling of a youthful nude dancing girl—were both problematic. Demonstrating that these nomenclatures do not have any basis would require more text than the labels in the gallery could carry. Mobilizing conversation in the press and social media was an alternative strategy FIG 10B.[18] One was thus confronted by a double bind: the hesitation in displaying a nude pubescent girl as a "dancing girl" was because its nomenclature may make it seem sexually inappropriate, and on the other hand, bringing a balanced view to examine those sculptures which *are* deemed erotic into a public discourse, as seen with the Khajuraho images, was also foreclosed.

When looked at formalistically, this is a girl whose body is bent toward one side, and in the arm that is akimbo, resting just above her knee is a socket, which has a hole through it. Potentially, then, you could put a stick in it. She clearly held something in that hand: was it a warrior's spear? Or a sweeper's broom? The minute you put any vertical in it, it acts as a counterpoint to the extended elbow on the other side and it creates a certain balance in the figure. Further observation makes us note that her left arm is loaded with bangles while she only has one wristlet and one bangle on her elbow at the right. Everybody who wears bangles knows that they come in the way of working and to keep the working arm free, women tend to shift their bangles to the other arm. Could it then not be that this is a woman who was working rather than dancing? She appears to be somebody who has a capacity for labour. Yet she has been written about in every textbook as the "Dancing Girl." Raising this question in the public has served the benefit of at least allowing it to now be published with the nomenclature of "dancing girl" being put in inverted commas, which perhaps is all the success we can hope for in this case.

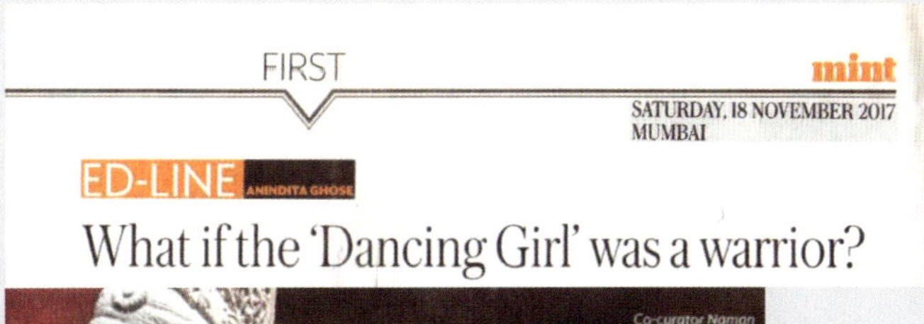

FIRST

mint

SATURDAY, 18 NOVEMBER 2017
MUMBAI

ED-LINE ANINDITA GHOSE

What if the 'Dancing Girl' was a warrior?

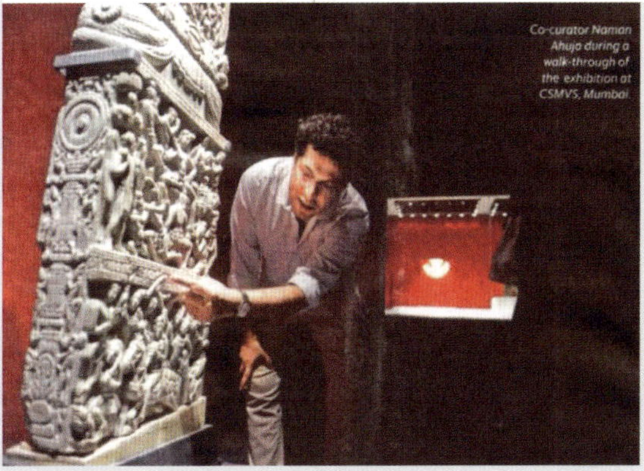

FIG 10B **Curator's interview in a media article, "What if the 'Dancing Girl' was a warrior?" by Anindita Ghose in *Mint*, Saturday, 18 November 2017.**

17 This claim was first made by Thakur Prasad Verma, a retired professor of the Banaras Hindu University in his article, "Vedic Sabhyata Ka Puratatva (Archaeology of Vedic Civilisation)," *Itihaas* (Shodh Patrika), vol. 2, no.1 (Jan-June 2016): 11–46.

18 Anindita Ghose, "What if the 'Dancing Girl' was a Warrior?," in *Mint*, November 17, 2017. https://www.livemint.com/Leisure/SwYaT4ZYGxFPnzBc2yHLTI/What-if-the-Dancing-Girl-was-a-warrior.html.

3. Patriots and Martyrs: Gendered Nationalism

Communicating history through a critical frame is tough when curating an exhibition at a "National Museum." The museum is expected, above all, to impress the public with a sense of national pride in its aesthetic history and, in India, in its religious or spiritual currency. These matters concerning gender had, as I explained above, to be a subtext to its galleries, contained within issues on heroism, birth, asceticism, death, and other such themes. The "Body" exhibition's first gallery opened with a series of memorials to the dead—both men and women FIG 11. This included a series of stone carvings that commemorated sati—the practice of "voluntary" immolation by a woman on her husband's funeral pyre. Sati has typically been thought of as an example of Rajput commemoration of women's valor and fidelity, which is clearly situated within patriarchy. Usually thought of as widely prevalent in parts of northern, central and eastern India only, the Sati stone from the Chennai Museum was deliberately chosen to disturb that inaccuracy and show that the practice in fact existed in South India too FIG 12. For more politically aware viewers, opening the exhibition with memorials to women held significance, while for scholars, the subject of sati is itself a key subject in not just the history of arguments of gender inequity that were used in the history of colonization, but served to form the foundations of gender studies in India.[19] Once curiosity was aroused and the capacity to question history was opened for the public, it became easier to carry on questioning other received ideas as well.

Displaying commemorative sati stones at the entrance, then, served to surprise and even pique the curiosity of the public right at the outset. This placement was used to communicate not merely how widespread the practice was, but also as a strategy to contrast the memorials of these victims of patriarchy with others that may now be construed as evidence of empowered women in history. Contemporaneous memorials to men were usually erected when they had fallen in war. To try and show that women's valor was not dependent only on committing sati, we displayed a sculpture of a female warrior who had also been shown as having laid down her life, committing ritual suicide with a blade at her throat FIG 13. Importantly, this sculpture came from the same time period and broadly the same region as the sati stone.

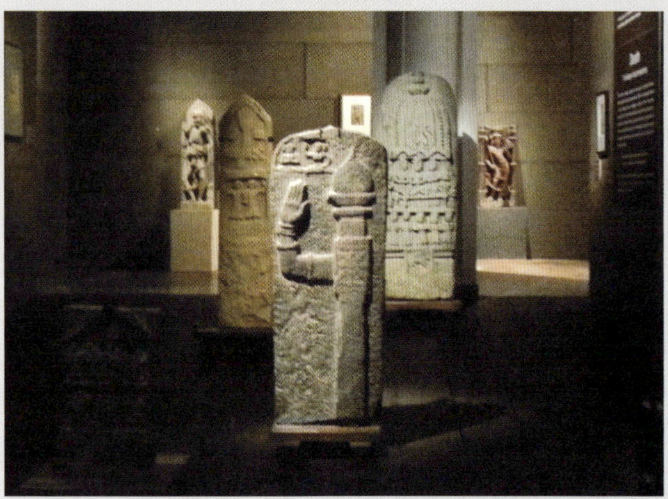

FIG 11 Entrance to the exhibition through memorial stones in the gallery "Death." Image courtesy: Naman P. Ahuja, *The Body in Indian Art and Thought*.

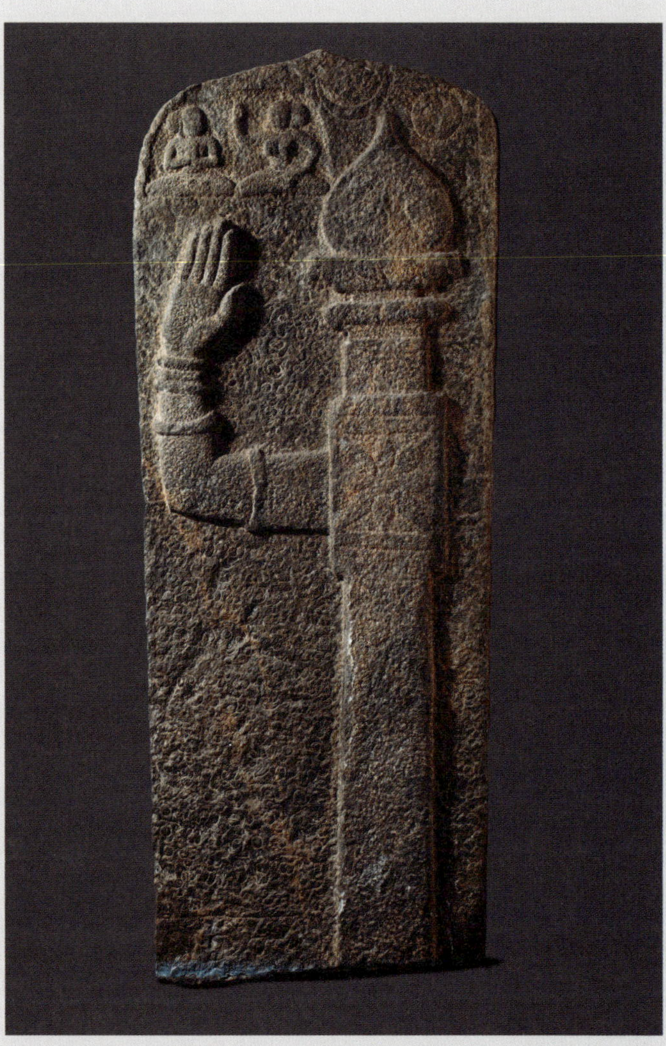

FIG 12 Inscribed satī memorial. Stone. 13th century. Penukonda, Andhra Pradesh, 138 × 55 cm. Government Museum, Chennai (Acc. No. 68 / 37). Image courtesy: Naman P. Ahuja, *The Body in Indian Art and Thought*.

19 Rajeswari Sunder Rajan, *Real and Imagined Women: Gender, Culture and Postcolonialism* (London, New York: Routledge, 1993), 15-33.

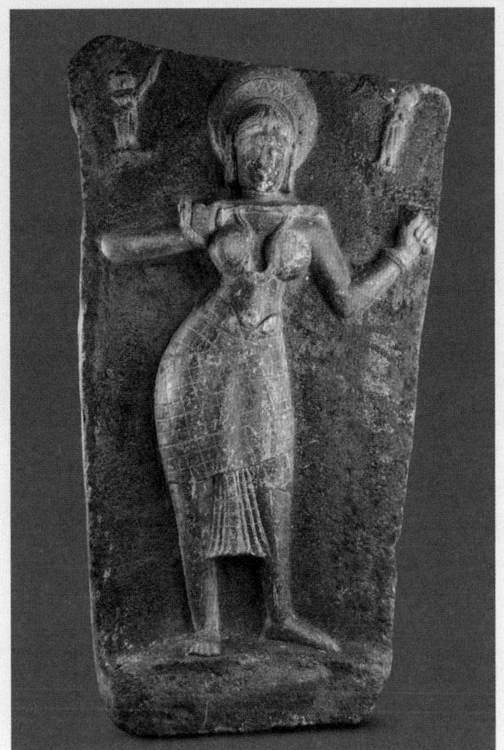

FIG 13 *Virasati* **(memorial to a female warrior). Black basalt. Kakatiya, thirteenth century. Telangana. 112 × 71 × 13 cm. State Archaeology Museum, Hyderabad (Acc. No. HM 88-51). Image courtesy: Naman P. Ahuja, *The Body in Indian Art and Thought*.**

Representations of women warriors are rare, although a few figures are known in history. A statue that came from the region and period of the reign of Rudramma Devi, the thirteenth-century Kakatiya queen who went to battle in Telangana, allowed, at first glance (in contrast to the sati stone beside it) to see that women had agency as well. They were brave soldiers, and society acknowledged them for it, besides acknowledging their "courage" when they committed sati to be united with their husbands in death. Any celebration of that supposed marker of gender equality, however, was soon dispelled as the visitors scrutinized the sculpture further.

The uppermost corners of the sculpture have images of women attendants, the conventional way of showing celestial *apsaras* that are invariably also shown waiting for male soldiers in heaven. Why aren't there male attendants for a sculpture of a female martyr? Was it that as a woman she isn't allowed to have men waiting upon her, even in heaven? Was it that servitude for personal comfort was a role only performed by women—where male and female roles are once again defined through relationships of master and servant through patriarchal mindsets? Marriages, in the Hindu tradition are commonly thought of as being ordained for seven rebirths—how then, would such a patriarchal society permit attractive manservants waiting upon the female hero when she ascended to her heaven? Men, on the other hand, did not suffer the same diktat, and were invariably shown with celestial damsels serving their needs in heaven.[20] If the National Museum's gold-painted shield had provoked a bevy of questions on pre-Modern Rajput society, this object certainly opened similar ones in Telangana's history: which type of woman is able to be commemorated thus? A common woman or someone who comes from a place of privilege? Is it a society that forces servitude on the female gender? Again, this allows the public to raise questions on the many spaces from which discrimination happens—race, class, gender, caste, etc. Sculptures or paintings of brave women from history who have displayed physical strength cannot always be assumed as possessing agency or autonomy.

These questions, and others, were posed in the many interviews, public conferences, and television programmes that accompanied and followed the show in an effort to build up a public habit of participating in questioning history and learning to read artefacts. Again, these memorials to martyrs, whether male or female, also served to make a second, equally large political point: that both martyrdom and wars were religiously sanctioned in Hinduism as they had been with the Knights Templar in the same period, and just as wars and martyrdom were legitimized in the Islamic tradition of *jihad*. Indeed even the traditions of martial arts that have been connected to monks who worked in the service of kings springs from a similar history of militant traditions within religion that was reinforced later in the exhibition in the text that accompanied the galleries on Asceticism. In each culture, the politicization of the "soldier-saint" in religions comes from shifting a philosophy of meditation to a militaristic defense of one's beliefs and discipline. Here, however, at the very entrance of the show, the provocation was simply to ask the public to notice that the Hindu memorials and mythic epics, like the Mahabharata, also promise celestial beauties, *apsaras*, to slain warriors in heaven, like the *jihadis*, who were rewarded with *hoor-paris* in their heavenly paradise.

---

20 For a more complete review of the variety of hero stones and concomitant attitudes to the heroic dead, see *Memorial Stones: a Study of their Origin, Significance and Variety*, eds S. Settar and G.D. Sontheimer (Heidelberg and New Delhi: South Asia Institute, University of Heidelberg, 1982). On the gendered reading of hero stones, see: Julia Leslie, *Roles and Rituals for Hindu Women* (Delhi: Motilal Banarsidass Publishers, 1992); Romila Thapar, "Death and the Hero" in *Cultural Pasts: Essays in Early Indian History*, (New York: Oxford University Press, 2000). Lindsey Harlan, *The Goddesses Henchmen: Gender in Indian Hero Worship*, (New York: Oxford University Press, 2003); Melia Belli Bose, *Royal Umbrellas of Stone: Memory, Political Propaganda, and Public Identity in Rajput Funerary Architecture*, (Leiden: Brill, 2015).

In their time, these public memorials served an important function in normalizing *sati*, or warfare. Children would be taken along to hear folk songs of their ancestors' valor and communities performed rituals to commemorate their sacrifice. The activities around such memorials served to make the values they espoused into social aspirations. Today, museums need to display the very same objects with a completely different intention: not of celebration, but to show how we have changed: our arrival at the present moment comes through a history of questioning of attitudes and systems that existed in the past.[21] This intention often sits in an uncomfortable relation with the museum's need to connect people with their history and national identity—which is often validated through the representation of a glorious history and tradition. The requirement for raising sentiments of patriotism or nationalism also relies on invoking a heroic historical or mythic past.

To locate powerful models for women in Indian history, one can go further back into some mythic past to try and find examples there. This has been done in the field of anthropology and psychology when they have drawn on iconographic models. There is no gainsaying that Lakshmi, Sita, and Savitri served as models for wives, that Vishnu was a model for kingship, Hanuman for youthful valor and so on. But in general, the application of these archetypes must be done with care to demonstrate how mythic figures have influenced social behavior in particular ways in each historical epoch, lest we fall into the trap of imagining eternal tropes for "Hindu Civilization."

A work by Sheela Gowda called *Draupadi's Vow* FIG 14A-B was exhibited in *The Body in Indian Art*. Long, flowing hair may normally be associated with beauty, but tinged here with red, it had a specific cultural connotation. Draupadi, the wife of the Pandava brothers, heroes of the Mahabharata epic, vowed she would only be avenged when she could wash her hair in the blood of those who had defiled her. Her vendetta makes for a violent archetype of heroism for women, as compelling as those of the warring men in the epic.

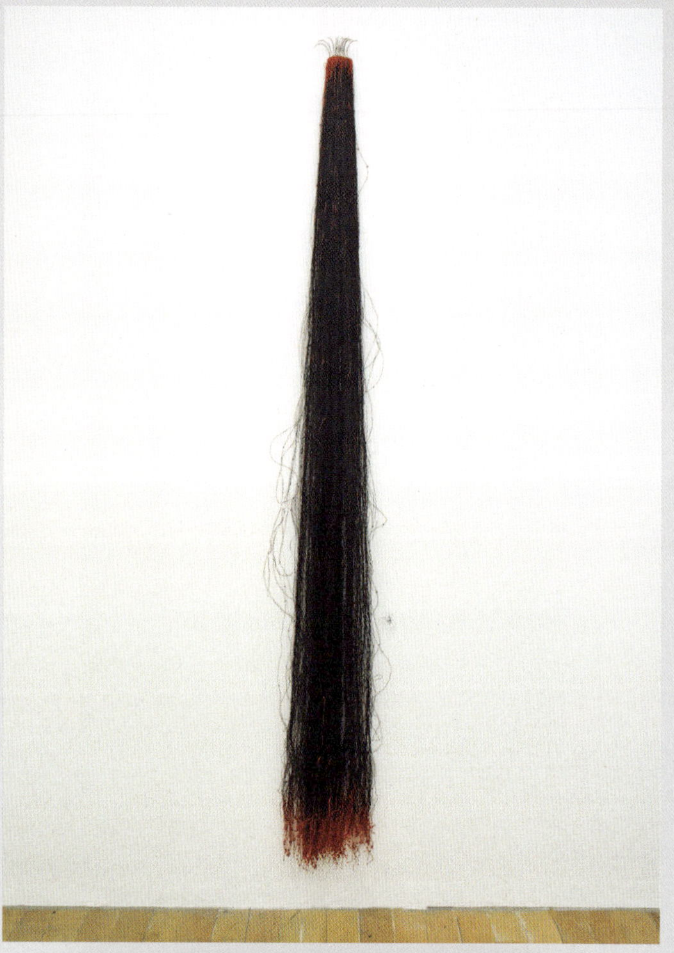

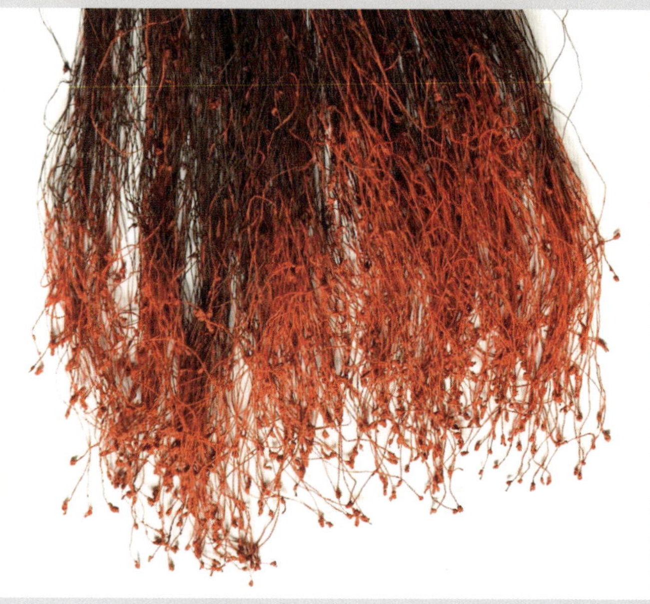

FIG 14A-B Gowda's use of common materials brings the epic into the everyday.

Sheela Gowda. *Draupadī's Vow*, 1997. Threads and metal hooks. 195.5 × 15.2 × 10 cm. Collection of Devi Art Foundation. Image courtesy of the artist and Devi Art Foundation for *The Body in Indian Art and Thought*.

21 For a key text to explain the fast changing nature of epistemology in relation to gender, see Sandra Harding, "The Instability of the Analytical Categories of Feminist Theory," *Signs: Journal of Women in Culture and Society*, vol. 11, no. 4 (1986): 645–64. Also see, Rajeswari Sunder Rajan, "Introduction" in Rajeswari Sunder Rajan ed. *Signposts: Gender issues in Post-independence India* (New Brunswick: Rutgers University Press, 2001), 1-16. More recently, a summary of the many shifts in the field of the representation of sexuality and what has led to it is available in Nivedita Menon ed. *Sexualities*, (New Delhi: Women Unlimited an associate of Kali for Women, 2007).

Draupadi has been invoked by artists and writers time and again for such purposes, and archetypes embedded in the collective subconscious have been strategically invoked for political purposes in India at times when there was a requirement to combat rape, empower women, and even to rouse patriotism.[22] During India's freedom movement, a large number of mass-produced popular prints were circulated, each of which personified India as a goddess. Bountiful and graceful like Lakshmi sometimes, shown as the warrior goddess Durga at another, and famously, as a *sadhavi* or ascetic for Abanindranath Tagore, each artist has tried to rouse public imagination and patriotism by imaging the motherland through a female archetype FIG 15A–C.[23] It was in this context of extending the themes of the iconographies of heroic death and martyrdom, that popular posters from the 1920s to 1940s were shown FIG 15D, some of which picked up on the very same type of imagery the visitor had seen on medieval sculptures. A case in point is the print that shows Subhas Chandra Bose, the leader of the Indian National Army, offering his head to the mother goddess India (Bharat Mata), just like the iconographic strategy of memorial sculptures of medieval warriors FIG 15E. "National" museums, funded and maintained by governments, especially right-wing ones, become a difficult space in which the past can be questioned. Yet using the opportunity to show how visual culture is mobilized for propaganda, even if that propaganda was issued by a rival political group, allowed the public to become more active participants in the process of what historians do and how images play their part in shaping society.

22 Rajeswari Sunder Rajan, "The Story of Draupadi's Disrobing: Meanings for Our Times" in Rajeswari Sunder Rajan eds., *Signposts: Gender issues in post-independence India* (New Brunswick, NJ: Rutgers University Press, 2001),332-359.

23 Sumathi Ramaswamy, *Goddess and the Nation: Mapping Mother India* (New Delhi: Zubaan, 2014) and Jain, Kajri, *Gods in the Bazaar: The Economies of Indian Calendar Art* (Durham: Duke University Press, 2007), and Christopher Pinney, *Photos of the Gods: the Printed Image and Political Struggle in India* (New Delhi, New York: Oxford University Press, 2004).

4. Displaying Same-sex Love in the National Museum

From 2013–14, when the exhibition *The Body in Indian Art and Thought* was on display, was a time when Section 377, which criminalized homosexuality in India, had not yet been struck down. Homosexuality was looked upon as being against Indian tradition, and while one could look at various contemporary artworks that questioned that narrative, they were not necessarily going to demonstrate the existence of same-sex love in Indian history. I wanted to be able to place contemporary artworks in the exhibition to show strains of how that tradition has been inherited and adapted, as well as how that tradition has been questioned by the contemporary voice.

Art history also needed to catch up with the efforts being made in literature and history, to complement the longer histories of same-sex love in India published over the past two or three decades. Pairing some of the poetic verses of religious leaders and some of their followers with their portraits in a gallery on "Asceticism" provided a solution. Eroticism has frequently been directed toward the divine, but its overtly homoerotic nature has not really been brought out as a feature in the public sphere to explain the long-standing acceptability of homoeroticism.[24] Dara Shikoh's description of his initiation under the mystic Mulla Mir of the electric energy that passed when the sage rubbed his bare chest against his own, or the famous *bhakti* saint Manikkavacakar's poems that claim how "giddy" he felt when he looked, with longing, at Shiva's lips, body, and feet, for instance, were strategically placed on the gallery walls near appropriate artwork FIG 16A–B. Eroticism, then, was being included within the wider habitus of religious establishments, as well as in the cultivation of asceticism.

24 The subject of desire within which exists also homoerotic desire, in ascetical or religious contexts, is dealt with at greater length in Naman P. Ahuja, *The Body in Indian Art and Thought* (Antwerp: Ludion, 2013), 277–84. For the Hindu context, see: Karen Pechilis Prentiss, *The Embodiment of Bhakti* (Oxford and New York: Oxford University Press, 1999); Vidya Dehejia, *Slaves of the Lord: The Path of the Tamil Saints* (Delhi: Munshiram Manoharlal, 1988, reprinted 2002), 16, 89, 91. Norman Cutler, *Songs of Experience: The Poetics of Tamil Devotion* (Bloomington: Indiana University Press, 1987). On other legal and ritual texts see Kumkum Roy, *The Power of Gender—the Gender of Power: Explorations in Early Indian History* (New Delhi, Oxford University Press, 2010). Much has been written about male-male desire in Islam through the valorization of youthful beauty, which has, in turn, had a tremendous impact on theories of gender and sexuality in contemporary scholarship. Najmabadi's case study on Iran is equally applicable in the north Indian context, see Afsaneh Najmabadi, *Women with Mustaches and Men without Beards: Gender and Sexual Anxieties of Iranian Modernity* (Berkeley: University of California Press, 2005). For a succinct understanding of homoeroticism in South Asian Sufi poetry, especially within the personal and political context of current discourse regarding same-sex love in the region, see Ruth Vanita and Saleem Kidwai eds., *Same Sex Love in India: Readings from Literature and History* (New York and London: St. Martin's Press, 2000), 107–25.

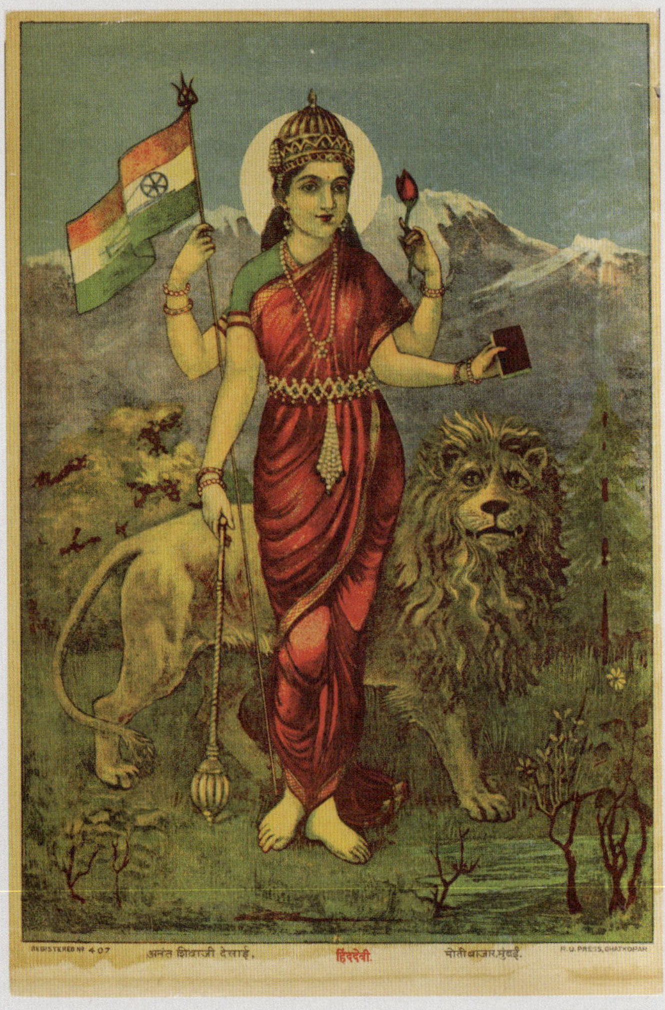

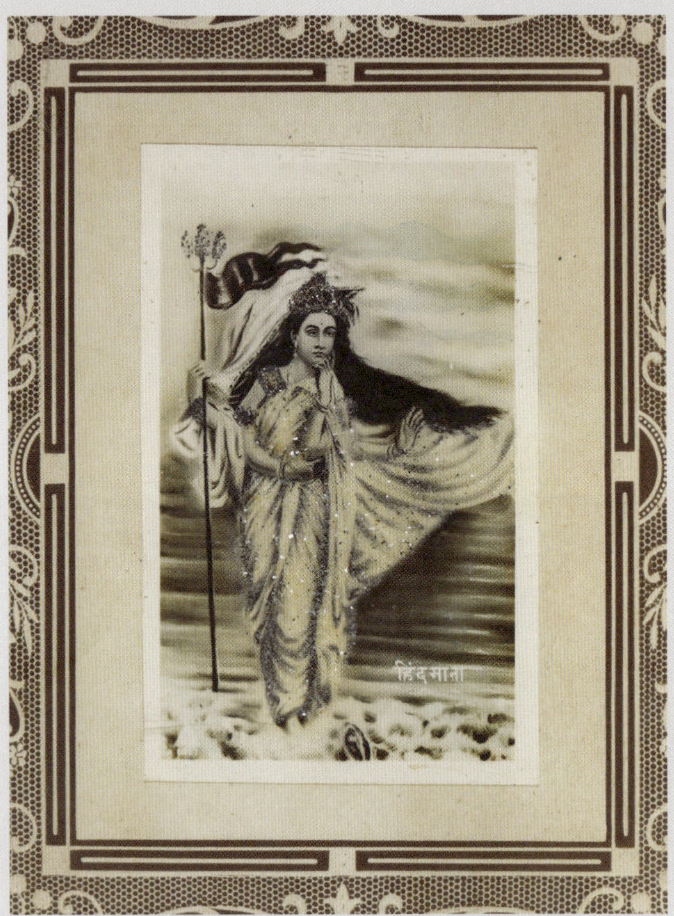

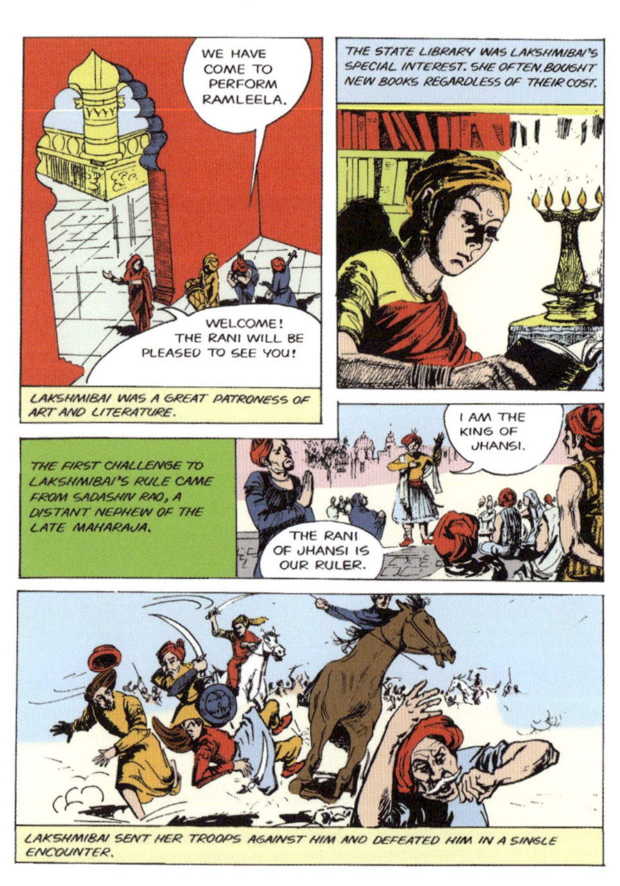

FIG 15A Anant Shivaji Desai Oleograph, *Hind Devī (Bhāratamātā)*. 38 × 25 cm. Moti Bazar, Mumbai R.U. Press, Ghatkopar. Collection of Priya Paul.

FIG 15B *Hind Mata*. Black and white painted photograph embellishedand glued onto decorative mount, 28.4 × 23.4 cm. Collection of Priya Paul.

FIG 15C Page from the comic book *Rani of Jhansi*, Amar Chitra Katha, vol. 539, Published on January 1 1974, by Amar Chitra Katha Pvt. Ltd.

Protecting the motherland, personifying India as a mother, a woman ascetic, a benign bountiful goddess, or a powerful Durga-like protectress was promoted through popular posters through the Indian Independence movement. Displaying these posters near historic images allowed the viewer to make the connection on how propaganda uses socially embedded visual imagery. Popularising Indian history and mythology continued well into the late twentieth century, and the Amar Chitra Katha comic books played an important part in this. Several stories of women heroes were revived, and their imagery was contrasted with those of male heroes in the exhibition through the scenography, as well as by creating a small reading-room between Galleries 6 and 7 where children and adults could take a pause to browse through these popular comic books. Again, their narrative and imagery were now placed within a historical context which provoked conversation in the public on how "tradition" is repackaged and why.

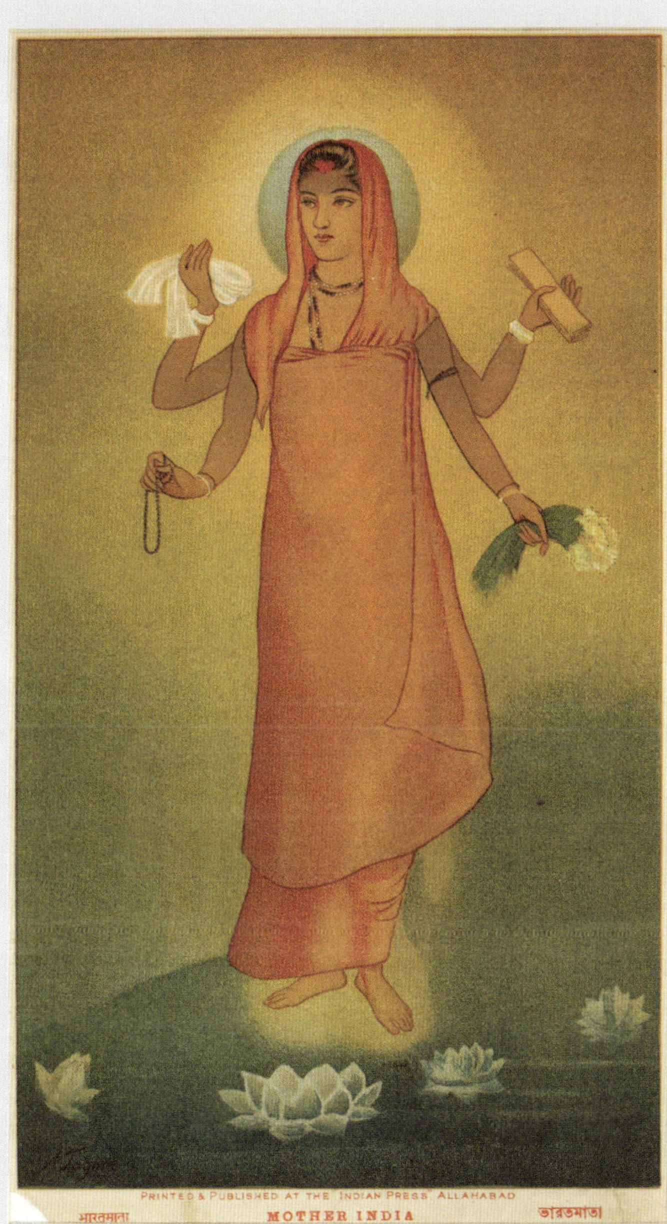

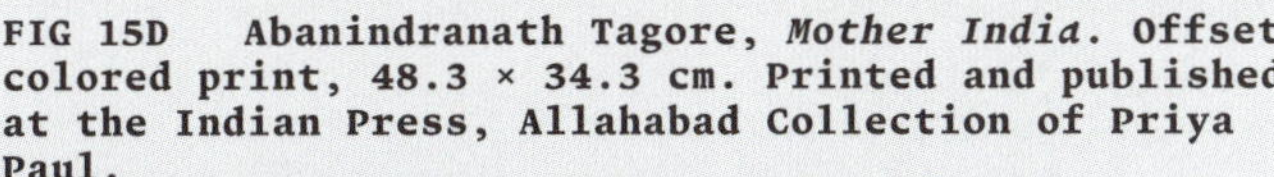

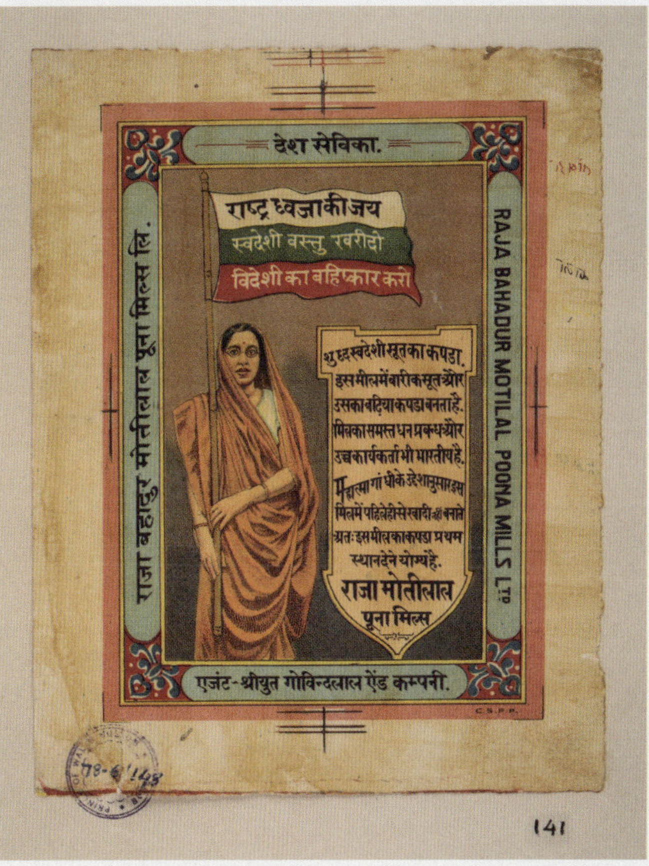

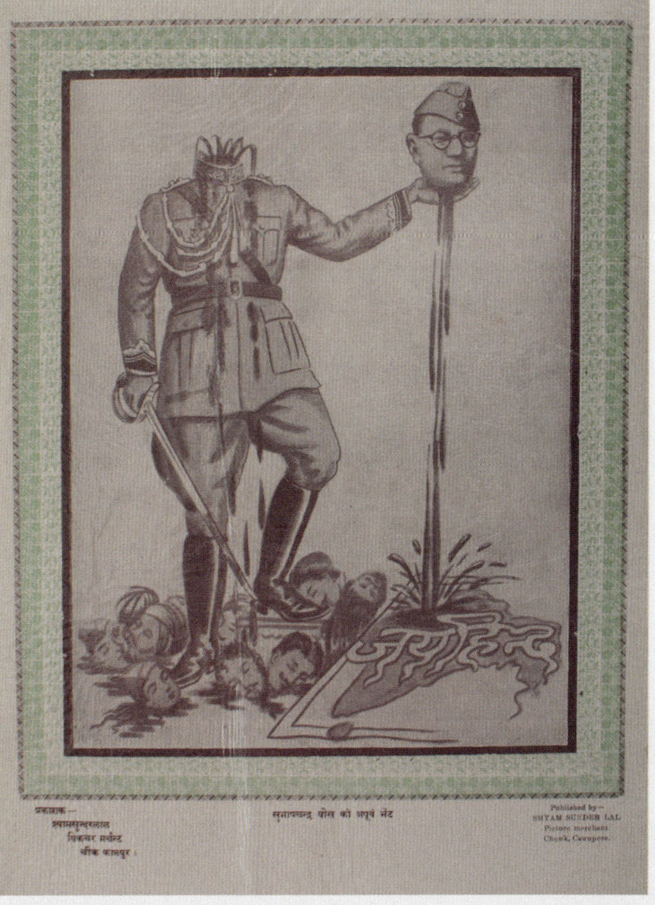

FIG 15D Abanindranath Tagore, *Mother India*. Offset colored print, 48.3 × 34.3 cm. Printed and published at the Indian Press, Allahabad Collection of Priya Paul.

FIG 15E Desh sevika, textile mill label. Paper. AD 1925–40. Raja Bahadur Motilal Poona Mills Ltd. Height: 16 cm, Width: 12 cm. CSMVS, Mumbai (78.6 / 148). Image courtesy: Naman P. Ahuja, *India & the World: A History in Nine Stories*.

FIG 15F *Subhas Chandra Bose's Remarkable Offering*. Offset Print. "Published by Shyam Sunder Lal, Picture Merchant, Chowk, Cawnpore." c. 1940s.

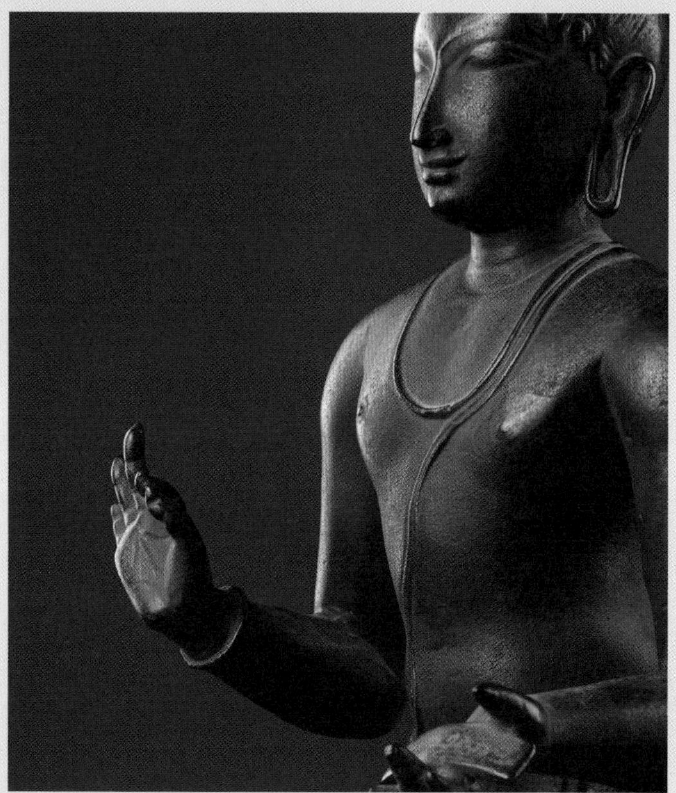

FIG 16B *Manikkavacakar* (detail).

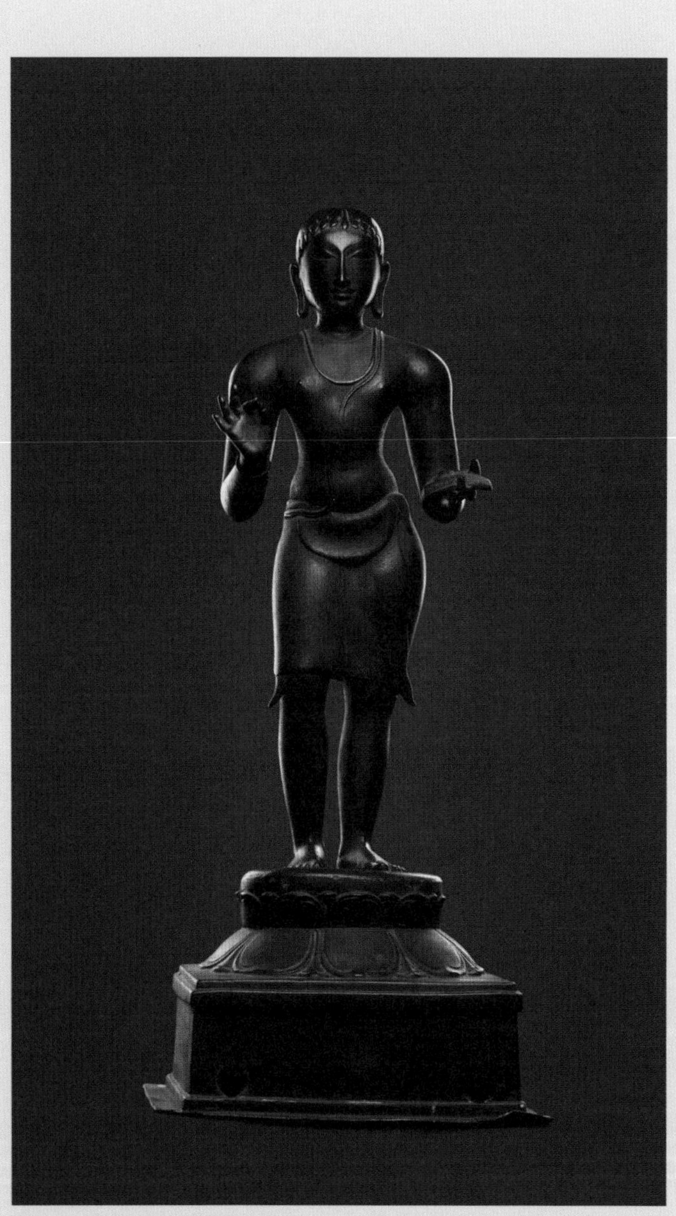

FIG 16A *Manikkavacakar*. Bronze. Chola, tenth century. Tamil Nadu. 50.2 × 21.8 × 20.8 cm. National Museum, Delhi (Acc. No. 57.16 / 3). Image courtesy: Naman P. Ahuja, *The Body in Indian Art and Thought*.

Religious performances in the service of god include rich traditions of music, theater, and dance. In each, the spaces play on the erotic emotion, and this needs careful cultural education from an early age. Religious establishments also serve as pedagogical centers within which an understanding of the body and gender normativity are taught along with literature and music. The phenomenon is widespread, but again, one example may suffice. In a prominently displayed video piece, we extracted a portion of Gulbahar Singh's film about the Gotipua dancers of Odisha FIG 17. It demonstrated the cultivation of boys to perform as women, and who revert into conventionally "masculine" boys when out of costume. The filmmaker had clearly highlighted this aspect through his cinematography. References to studies on using cross-dressed boys as women in performance traditions are aplenty. This has been understood both as symptomatic of a patriarchal society that prohibited girls from being on stage, and through the lens of queerness and the homosociality of men. In the former, men describe and enact feminine behavior which serves to define and circumscribe womanhood from the perspective of men. Both types of citation brought a gendered discourse through traditional Indian culture to public attention.[25]

25 One of the key texts to deal with this issue in a comparative manner is by Judith Lynne Hanna, *Dance, Sex and Gender: Signs of Identity, Dominance, Defiance and Desire* (Chicago, IL: University of Chicago Press, 1988); more specifically, Arunima Banerji, *Dancing Odissi: Paratropic Performances of Gender and State* (Calcutta: Seagull Books, 2019).

This film played in the same gallery where a painting from c. 1780 in which Radha and Krishna are seen dressed in each other's clothes FIG 19, pointing to the use of cross-dressing to generate meaning from earlier times. The varied nature of love, its many moods and shades, are often expressed via the images of Radha, and Krishna. Amongst them was positioned one that showed Krishna veiled and wearing a red skirt and blouse just as his lover, Radha has donned Krishna's robe and peacock feather crown. The transference is not just outwardly cross-dressing, however. The dark-skinned Krishna becomes the shy Radha with entreating eyes, even as she takes his arm and draws aside his veil—both caressing and confident, embodying Krishna—the seducer and initiator of the act of love. The body is an important metaphor in Indian art. Here it shows how love can make a person lose themselves completely to the other, such that one's body is no longer one's own but another's.

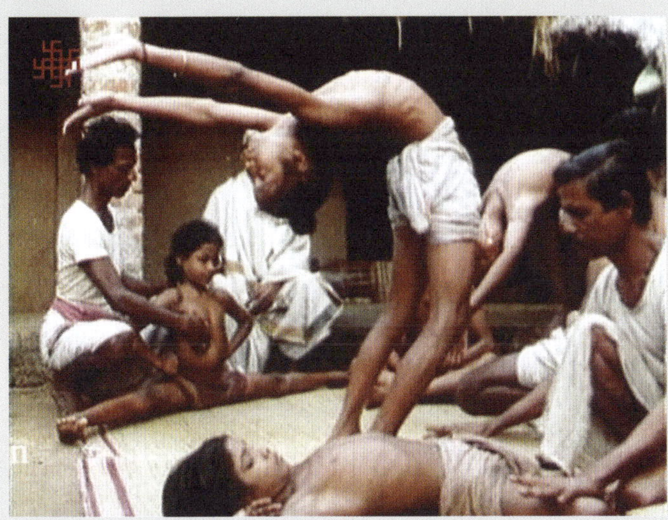

FIG 17 *Gotipua*. A Film by Gulbahar Singh. Courtesy Indira Gandhi National Centre for Arts (IGNCA), Delhi.

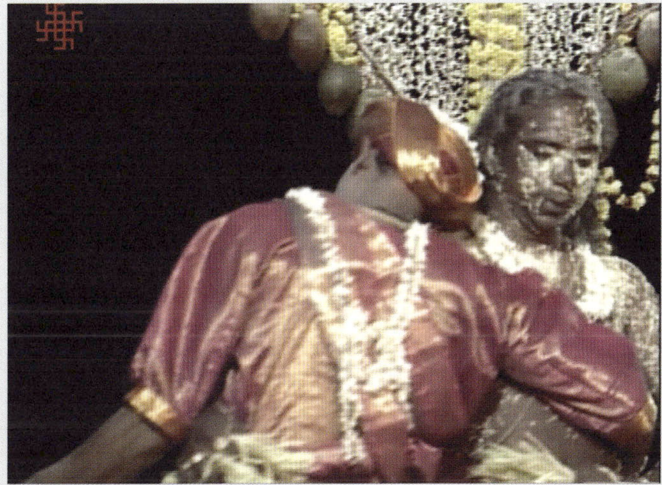

FIG 18 *Nagamandala*. A Film by Shivprasad. Courtesy Indira Gandhi National Centre for Arts (IGNCA), Delhi.

I attempted to take the matter forward in the gallery on (re)birth. Creation, when commonly used as referring to reproduction, often provides the argument used against the moral or religious sanction of same-sex love. Yet it is precisely in celebrations of creation and for the sake of fertility that same-sex love is captured in traditional Indian rituals. Whereas the presence of *hijras* at weddings is commonplace, I elected to show a lesser-known ritual such as the Nagamandala from Karnataka FIG 18 that showed a same-sex environment. The video was extracted from a film by Shivprasad and showed men who cross-dressed and embraced each other as symbols of fertility like ser-pents. If the hirsute Rajput—who thought being a warrior carved in stone or painted in gold using a rhino-hide shield would hold allure for his wife-to-be—formed one stereotype, in this video we see two other forms of masculinity in a ritual context. The first makes it possible for two men to enact their tender erotic embrace for the fulfilment of society's need for fertility, prosperity, and progeny. And second, the presence of a cross-dressed man in this fertility ritual may be on account of a society where it would be unsafe (and hence inappropriate) for a woman to perform such a ritual with a man publicly. The nature of womanhood is perceived in (and through) a cross-dressed man. In each of the examples above, whereas the homosocial environment may have been impelled by a loss of women's space publicly, its varied and widespread nature also claims a place of its own.

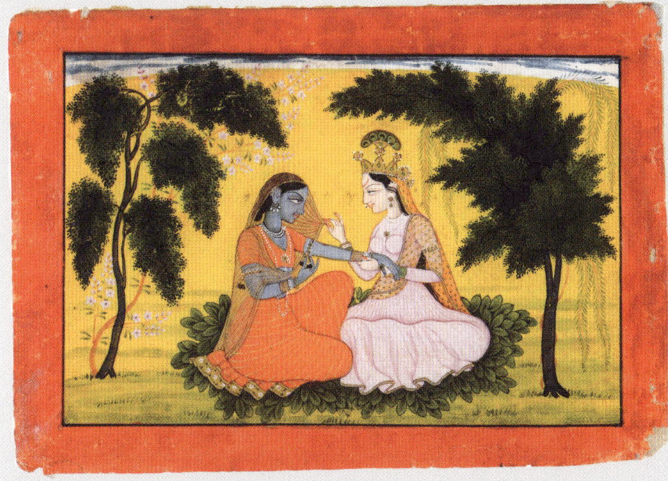

FIG 19 Radha removing the veil from Krishna's face, each dressed in the other's clothes. Gouache on paper. Guler / Kangra, c. 1780. 9.3 × 13.8 cm. Chandigarh Museum and Art Gallery (Acc. No. I–124, M47.9.53). Image courtesy: Naman P. Ahuja, *The Body in Indian Art and Thought*.

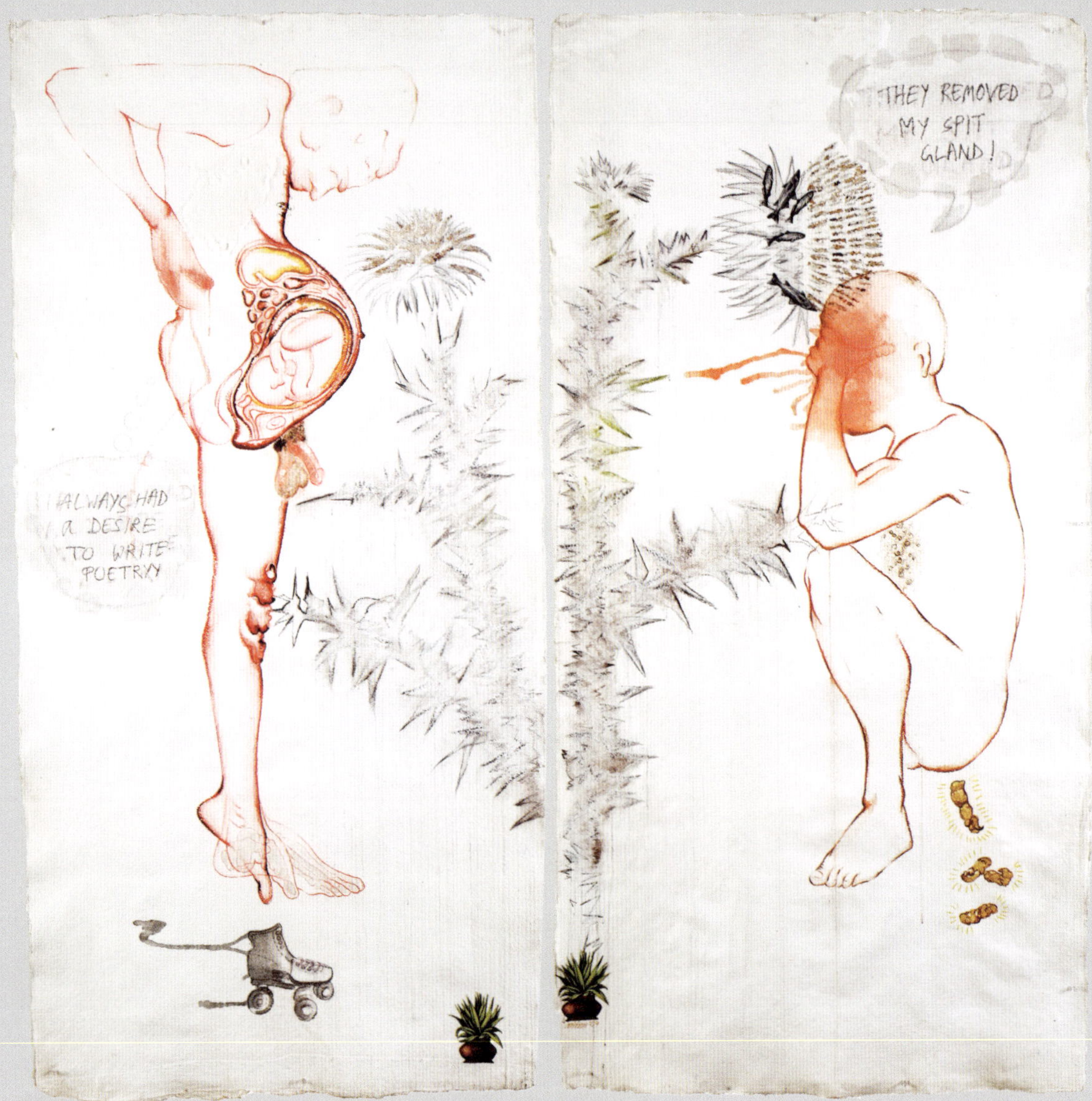

FIG 20 Mithu Sen, *You Owe Me*, from the series "BLACK CANDY (iforgotmypenisathome)." Diptych, 2009–10. Watercolor and mixed media on paper. Gallery Chemould, Prescott Road, Mumbai. Image courtesy the artist for *The Body in Indian Art and Thought*.

Regrettably, the effort to bring in relevant narratives even through the mode of pairing modern and ancient works, or by using artwork to pose questions, would not always work in the context of a state-sponsored public exhibition. Of the various works that were censored was a diptych by the artist Mithu Sen FIG 20. The work came from an exhibition called "Black Candy: Iforgotmypenisathome," which was shown by Gallery Chemould in Mumbai, and by the School of Arts and Aesthetics at JNU in 2010. Sen even won the Skoda prize for contemporary art for this exhibition that year, so it was certainly a body of work in the public eye and an exhibition that had been reported by the media. Opening with a homage to the artist Bhupen Khakar the exhibition dealt with male desire and the secrecy around it, primarily in the context of homosexuality as perceived by a woman. The artist wished to use the exhibition to focus on the pain Indian men endure because of their society's expectations of marriage, children, and hetero-normativity, while still dealing with childlessness. I selected a diptych called *You Owe Me* for the gallery on [re]birth. Sen's diptych showed a drawing of a pregnant man, which, given the disbarred nature of the fantasy, was placed in the part of the gallery that dealt with mythical stories of miraculous births and divine conceptions. The ICCR (Indian Council for Cultural Relations), however, questioned whether the work should be shown in the exhibition at all. In my negotiation with them, I quoted verses from the Vedas that mentioned the pregnant male, and, consequently, I was permitted to show the diptych's left half. The right half, however, which showed a man defecating turds made of gold, was not given permission to be shown. Even the left side was shown only in Brussels, while no part of the work was shown when it came to the National Museum in Delhi. Unlike Mrinalini Mukherjee's abstraction which was accepted in one gallery, Mithu Sen's insouciant work was too narrative and remained blocked. The discussions and experience signposted, with

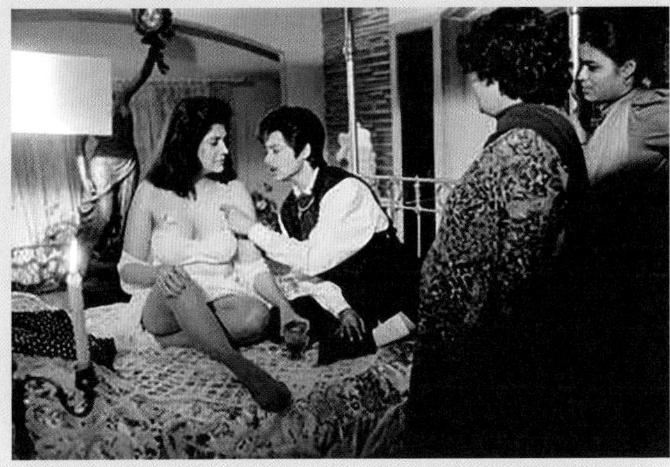

FIG 21 Dayanita Singh, *Saroj Khan, choreographer* (from the "Untitled Masterji" series). Photographed 1993, printed 2013. 91.5 × 136 cm. Image courtesy the artist for *The Body in Indian Art and Thought*.

clarity, the massive discomfort in showing anything to do with explicit bodily functions: homosexuality, defecation, expressing milk, anatomically-correct phallic antiquities—all elicit discomfort in the National Museum, which is regarded as a temple to both "Indian tradition" and the tradition of Indian bureaucracy! It was the latter that helped me come up with a better defense for showing a work by the contemporary photographer Dayanita Singh.

Singh artfully observed Bollywood's famous choreographer Saroj Khan at work for a series called "Masterji." In the early 1990s, Saroj Khan was the catalyst that led to the change in the representation of the erotic female in Indian cinema. Her landmark choreographies invested the heroine with an overt seductiveness that was previously the preserve of the "vamp." In consultation with Singh, I selected a frame she had composed at work on the set of a film that was never released. The film was an Indian adaptation of Hollywood's famous *Basic Instinct,* and the still from its set showed Rekha, India's glamorous star, cross-dressed as a man, examining the actress Asha Sachdev on a bed, while "Masterji" Saroj Khan stands, along with her assistant, in profile. She commands a space where the aesthetics of the female body are being orche-strated FIG 21. Unlike Mithu Sen's work, I was able to provide documentation to demonstrate that Dayanita Singh's Masterji series had already been shown at the NGMA (National Gallery of Modern Art), providing a necessary precedent for the National Museum to not block its display.[26] The same was the case with Mrinalini Mukherjee's *Basanti*, which also came from the collection of the NGMA. Is it, then, that the government-sponsored NGMA's curators and director are given greater rights to show and collect works that reflect contemporary understandings of the body and sexuality, while the National Museum must, *ipso facto*, uphold a more constraining idea of tradition?

Conclusion

The empowerment of women was a significant concern of the education systems of the late nineteenth and entire twentieth century. Active policies were created to pursue the necessary social change in the body politic. This received a major fillip in the run up to Indian independence. While historians began to find exemplary women heroes from the past with which to inspire a new generation—Rudramma Devi, Sembian Mahadevi, Razia Sultan, and Rani Lakshmibai, for instance—the museum sector was not always able to keep pace and find adequate heroes and stories to bring such narratives to the public. Meanwhile, significant critiques

26 This work offers the opportunity to show how "cross-dressing" was used to generate meaning metaphorically to signify "union" etc. in earlier contexts. Also, when it comes to females cross-dressing, it is not seen as a threat to masculinity. The same would not be the case with male cross-dressing in the current context. Therefore these issues have to be seen in multiple ways: transvestism, drag, but also in the long history of sakhi-bhava in bhakti poetry that seeks to establish divine union through erotic fervor. They must also be read as ways in which female agency is recorded within a Vaiṣṇava society. Tracy Coleman explores these ideas in two studies: "Radha: Lover and Beloved of Krishna" in Mandakranta Bose (ed.) *The Oxford History of Hinduism: The Goddess* (Oxford: Oxford University Press, 2018) (online edn, Oxford Academic, July 19, 2018), https://doi.org/10.1093/oso/9780198767022.003.0007, 116–46; and "Viraha Bhakti and Strīdharma: Re-reading the story of Kṛṣṇa and the Gopīs in Harivaṃśa and the Bhāgavata Purāṇa," *Journal of the American Oriental Society* (2010): 385–412. The bearing of these ideas on paintings themselves has been initiated in a few studies, among them: Molly Emma Aitken, "Spectatorship and Femininity In Kangra Style Painting," in *Representing the Body: Gender Issues in Indian Art*, ed. V. Dehejia (*Delhi: Kali for women in association with the Book Review Literary Trust*, 1997), 82–101; and Annapurna Garimella, "My Heart Values His Vulgar Ways: A Handmaid's Tale-Sakhis, Love and Devotion, and Poetry in Rajput Painting," in *Love in Asian Art and Culture*, Arthur M. Sackler Gallery of Art, (Washington DC: Smithsonian, 1998), 77–101.

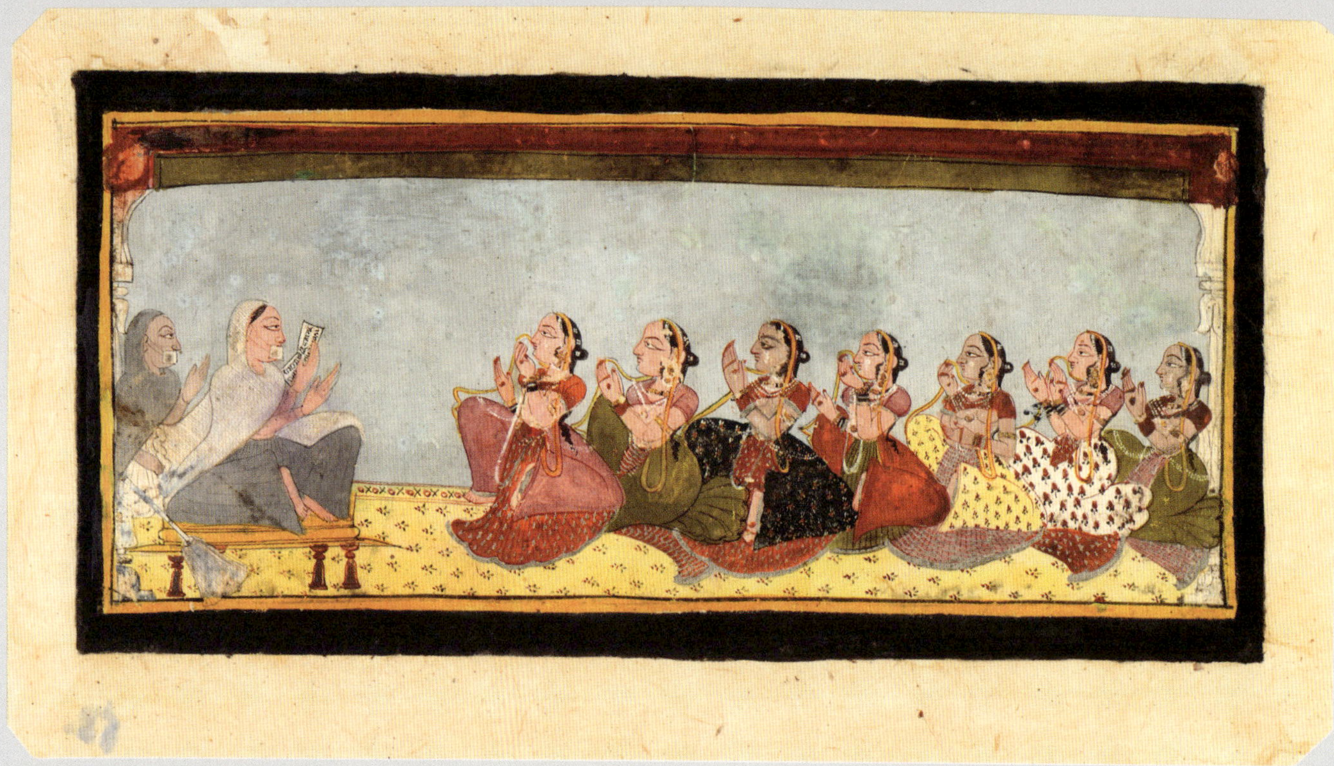

FIG 22 *Jain women ascetics*. Gouache on paper. Early nineteenth century. Jodhpur, Rajasthan. 24.5 × 11.5 cm. Salar Jung Museum, Hyderabad (Acc. No. 63–46). Image courtesy Naman P. Ahuja, *The Body in Indian Art and Thought*.

emerged on how the narratives that were selected previously did not reflect all types of Indians. Multiple "waves" of feminist studies had passed and the museum had a lot of catching up to do. Neither have current art historical issues of the male gaze implicit in the creation of classical art been made explicit in the museum. Female patronage, too, is not a matter discussed in the current galleries. And the complex and rapidly changing terrain of gender studies and sexualities seldom find anchoring in South Asian museums, which continue to focus on jewelry, the decorative arts, iconography, and religion.[27]

Even the words "sex," body," and "sexuality" tend to be closely understood in relation to morality today, and we have seen above that bringing narratives around them to the museum was not always straightforward. The exibited works were not gratuitous or titillating displays of sex. Instead, they generated meaning (whether ritual meaning or otherwise) within larger narratives of histories of warfare, caste, religion, and literature. It is the contemporary context (time and space)/codes of morality, that make objections to public displays of these objects and thus the histories that come with them. However, it is also the contemporary context that makes it relevant to bring these issues to the public, and in this article I have tried to show both the sort of research and thinking by which this was driven, and how, practically, this was translated into displays without letting the museums concerned feel compromised.

We have seen above that not all institutions run by the state have the same conservatism: documentary films sponsored by the IGNCA and artwork from the NGMA that contained subject matter that was much more directly about sex or body parts could be shown, while the National Museum's own ancient Lakshmi or the giant lingam of Shiva from Bharatpur could not. Contained in both inactivity and colonially-defined notions of censorship and morality, the Museum is unable to make itself relevant to contemporary issues. The subjects on which this paper has touched have vast and growing bibliographies, yet the Museum has not been able to keep pace with these urgent advances in the rest of the social sciences, or for that matter with the concerns reflected in the changing laws. Social sciences apart, even changes within the discipline of art history reflected in the nature of the enormous shifts made in modern and contemporary art galleries, as well as texts on pre-modern art, do not find curatorial display in India's museums of historical art.

27 The dilemmas the history museum faces in South Asia are different from the ones seen in the field of politics of crafts and design, or those faced by the galleries and museums of modern art. In each of these arenas, there is a different history of gender politics in terms of both representation of women in what is depicted, as well as being contributors to the economy where women are part of the workforce. While the space for women in modern art has far too substantial a bibliography to summarize, for the nature of women's association with the Indian craft sector, see: Abigail McGowan, "Mothers and Godmothers of Crafts: Female Leadership and the Imagination of India as a Crafts Nation, 1947–67," in *South Asia: Journal of South Asian Studies*, Vol. 44, no. 2 (April 2021), DOI: 10.1080/00856401.2021.1876589.

The manipulation, for contemporary political purposes, of history and the construction of what the public regards as its tradition, has a significant history in South Asia. A museum always plays its part in fostering these narratives; and when it is silent on certain issues, which have long disciplinary histories, it can only be seen as a deliberate action. As this essay has shown, there are several other case studies to serve the intention of opening up the ideas of "tradition," history, and myth, to enable national institutions in their effort to start displaying narratives that are required for our times. A responsible manner in which to do this is imperative lest Indian culture find itself relevant only in the hands of those who can interpret it as a means to enforce their conservative and oppressive agendas. Certainly, the instances provided in this essay for those types of examples blocked or censored signal what institutions need to reconsider. Equally, the many ways in which diverse narratives on gender and sexuality were contextualized and displayed also serve as an example of not just what is possible, but also how it can be done.

Histories apart, a curator also needs to put things across visually. This essay has shown some examples of the practical curatorial strategies involved in looking at art, which opens up its communication of aesthetics, materiality, form, line, and color to enable histories in its own language; and looking at larger cultural history narratives to imbue the objects in history museums with richer subtexts and sometimes even counter-narratives. This allowed history to be seen with some amount of (what should be regarded as) healthy suspicion, and turned the exhibition process dialogic; in this case, taking the museum staff's research and didacticism to arenas of gender studies and sexualities that complement the writing in those disciplines. Administrative officers' and funders' anxieties about the museum deviating from instilling national pride were allayed by the success of the exhibitions discussed. They also came to see that this kind of informed public conversation is a process; one that robs the curator of completing their "job" with authorial command at the moment the exhibition is inaugurated, and expands the museum's function to actively participate in using the objects to have conversations with the viewing public for months afterwards. The research this generates feeds back to the museum and press (including social media), and that turns the writing of history into a participatory process.

As I come to conclude my own (limited) post-mortem of writing histories of sexualities and gender in my curatorial work, I would like to remember that we've looked at the subject of writing itself many times in this essay. "Patralekha" from Khajuraho was driven to write for reasons of rapturous longing, while her sculptors and patrons left a testimony in stone to let us know that writing in such contexts was divine. Thorughout this essay, we have also looked at the many types of writing that have been conducted on the rapidly advancing subjects of gender and sexuality in modern times, and what has driven the requirement to write it: the forces of development, nationalism, democracy, and so on. I'd like to end this essay with a charming and modest little painting that shows Jain women being taught in their own educational institutions FIG 22. Their curriculum may have been circum-scribed by patriarchal forces in their time, but it is important to remind the public that spaces for women's education, as well as habitats with diverse social norms, have existed in India for centuries. There are histories, rituals, songs, and traditions of a variety of norms on gender. There are even temples that religiously sanction communities of people of different genders and sexual orientation. Writing and presenting how these views shape the idea of tradition and society allow for strengthening of history, just as they do, on occasion, allow us to question history. This latter feature makes the public an active participant in shaping and thinking about their role in society via the objects in their "national" museum.

Acknowledgements

I would like to acknowledge the gift of the time Uma Chakravarti, Gita Sahgal, Belinder Dhanoa, Nivedita Menon, and Urmimala Sarkar—friends and colleagues—have spared to offer me their guidance. Belinder and Gita have discussed these issues with me for years from multiple perspectives. Nivedita Menon and I shared the stage on a sunny afternoon at the Kasauli Literature Festival for a lively public conversation on some of these issues in 2019, which she kindly followed up recently with some pertinent readings. And Uma Chakravarti's guidance has benefited many scholars over many years of committed service to our fields. My thanks to them all.

Despite all the objects that may have been blocked, many narratives were permitted thanks to the sensitivity of certain members of the bureaucracy and official commissioners of these exhibitions. I owe many of them my thanks but would particularly like to mention Venu Vasudevan and Anita Nayar.

All the images that accompany this essay, unless otherwise indicated, are from the exhibitions "The Body in Indian Art" and "Thought and India & the World." Most of the photographs for "The Body in Indian Art" were taken by Bandeep Singh. They are exceptional in the sensitivity shown for the subject matter and I cherish his work. All rights for their use in the contexts of discussions on these exhibitions rest with Naman P. Ahuja.

And finally, I would like to thank Cosmin and Inti, and everyone at Para Site for the invitation to present these ideas in Hong Kong in 2018.

The Museo del Barro: Another Way to Understand Patrimony

LIA COLOMBINO

Translated by Tony Beckwith

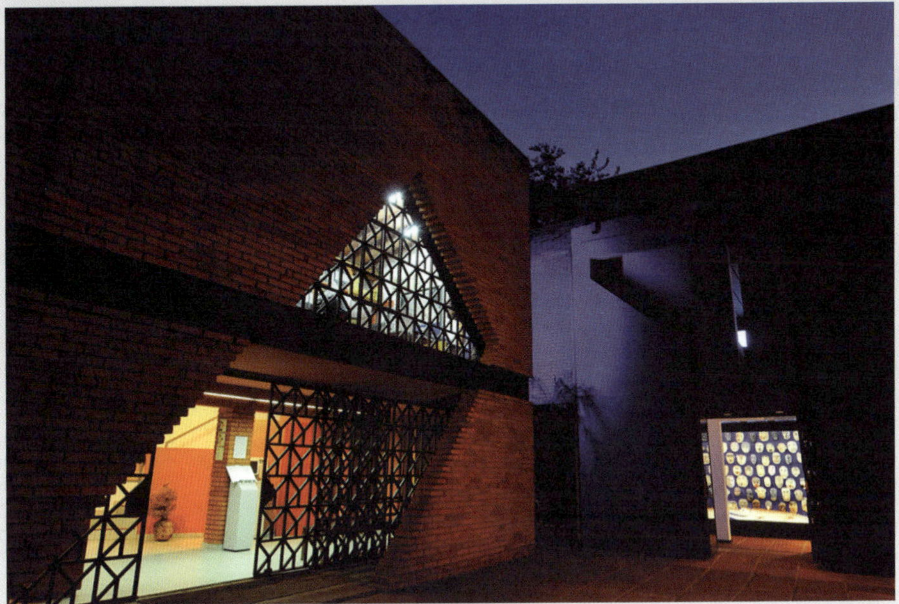

FIG 1 Visual Arts Center / Museo del Barro, Asunción, Paraguay. Interior facade. Photograph: Fernando Allen. Documentation and Research Department (DDI) – Centro de Artes Visuales / Museo del Barro.

The Museo del Barro, as the Centro de Artes Visuales in Asunción, Paraguay, is known, houses collections of *arte popular*[1] and "ethnic art,"[2] as well as several expressions from Paraguay and Iberoamerica of what the museum calls "urban art," meaning art production that is more closely related to Western art.

Upon entering the Museo del Barro, visitors become immersed in an assortment of images that are not particularly well-organized; nor are they methodically categorized or systematically classified in the manner usually associated with this sort of institution.[3] Visitors may come across a collection of traditional masks, Franciscan and Jesuit religious images, ceremonial costumes, or a selection of Latin American and Paraguayan art (based on Western tradition). Temporary exhibits can vary, ranging from an event featuring the works of an emerging artist to a comprehensive presentation of different approaches, to portrait painting in Paraguay in the nineteenth century, or a collection of recent *ao po'i* works made using a formerly Indigenous weaving method that produces cloth with a pattern referencing colonial shirtmaking. Keeping that range in mind, the Museo del Barro embraces the ambiguity of being a museum even though the word "museum", in this particular case, is not entirely applicable. It seeks to shift the parameters of the concept associated with the word in order to challenge it and make it porous. This is an art museum, in which the definition of art has also been shifted in an attempt to include, as Ticio Escobar would say, "the beauty of others."

1 Across Latin America, *arte popular* is the term referred to artistic vocabularies stemming from artisanal materialities and temporalities that embody the complex processes of colonialism and post-colonialism. It is distinct from Western Pop culture which engenders from industrialized consumption, mass media, and today's digital platforms.

2 According to information provided by the NGO Tierra Viva, ethnic groups in Paraguay are divided into five linguistic families, one of which is Guaraní. These include the Paĩ Tavyterã with 15,494 inhabitants, the Aché with 1,884, the Avá with 17,921, the Mbyá with 20,546, the Ñandeva with 2,470, and the Western Guaraní with 3,587. The Matako Mataguayo linguistic family includes the Nivaclé with 14,768 inhabitants, the Manjui or Lumnana with 582, and the Maká with 1,888. The Zamuco family includes the Ayoreo with 2,461 inhabitants, the Ybytoso with 1,915, and the Tomáraho with 152. The Maskov family includes the Toba Maskoy with 2,072 inhabitants, the Enlhet Norte with 8,167, the Guaná with 393, the Angaité with 5,992, and the Sanapaná with 2,866. The Guaicurú family includes the Qom with 1,939 inhabitants (Tierra Viva, 2021).

3 The *arte popular* (vernacular art) collection was started with a set of ceramic pieces. The collection as a whole came to be known as the Museo del Barro (Museum of Clay or Pottery), inspired by Josefina Plá's observation that "clay is the material with which dreams are created."

Introduction to a Brief History: the Museo del Barro or the Expression of Difference

The Centro de Artes Visuales / Museo del Barro is the result of a number of initiatives over the course of more than forty years of work. It is unique for having been created and managed by artists, anthropologists, and art critics who originally started it as a place where they could develop their practices beyond the oversight of the State and in opposition to its policies. It should be remembered that Paraguay was under the Alfredo Stroessner military dictatorship from 1954 to 1989.

The collections that make up the Centro de Artes Visuales (what is known as the Museo del Barro (Museum of Clay or Pottery), Museo de Arte Indígena (Museum of Indigenous Art), and Museo Paraguayo de Arte Contemporáneo (Paraguayan Museum of Contemporary Art) were created separately; subsequent circumstances drew them together under one roof and combined them into a single entity. The roots of the museum can be traced back to the Colección Circulante (Traveling Collection) that was started by the artists Olga Blinder and Carlos Colombino in 1972. That collection, which consisted mainly of prints, had no home of its own and was transported to a different venue for each new exhibition.

In 1980, while its permanent home was being built, the Museo del Barro opened in a small house. The artists Osvaldo Salerno, Ysanne Gayet, and Carlos Colombino worked on this project dedicated solely to popular art (*arte popular*) and Indigenous art. The critic Ticio Escobar joined them at a later date. The group had been interested in popular art and Indigenous art for some time, which had been instated to this group via the writer and artist Josefina Plá.[4] Finally, in 1984, the group opened the first room of what would become the building complex that would house the collections of "Arte Popular" (Museo del Barro), "Ethnic Art" (Museo de Arte Indígena), and various examples of Paraguayan and Ibero-American "Urban Art" (Museo Paraguayo de Arte Contemporáneo).

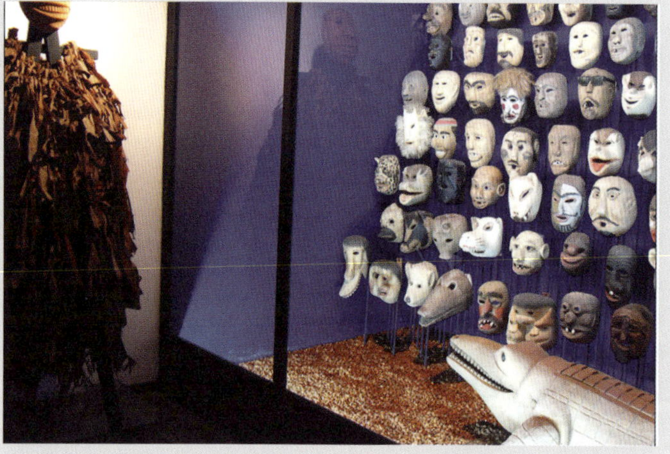

FIG 2 Showcase of popular masks. Festivity of Kamba Ra'anga, community of Ita Guasu, Altos, Paraguay. Photograph: Fernando Allen. Documentation and Research Department (DDI) – Centro de Artes Visuales / Museo del Barro.

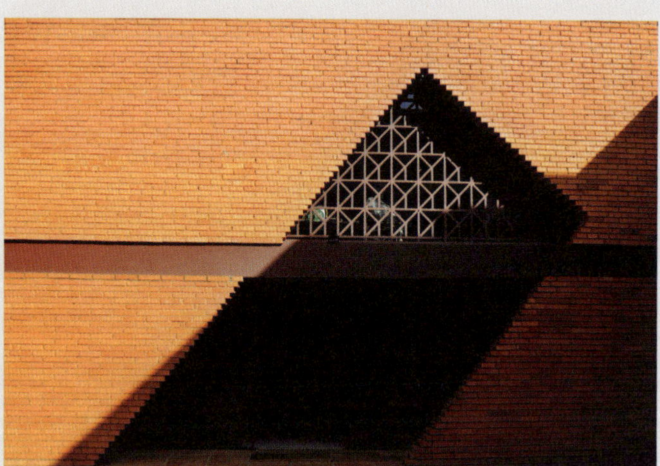

FIG 3 Visual Arts Center / Museo del Barro, Asunción, Paraguay. Interior facade. Photograph: Fernando Allen. Documentation and Research Department (DDI) – Centro de Artes Visuales / Museo del Barro.

4 When we talk about Indigenous art and vernacular *arte popular*, we are referring to the members of subordinate groups that have no voice in the policies that affect their lives; any impact they manage to have on those policies is a result of pressure or long-term struggles. They have no political representation. Also, when speaking of Indigenous and vernacular art, we are talking about community rather than individual practices and, even when they are individual, they are still part of a community practice.

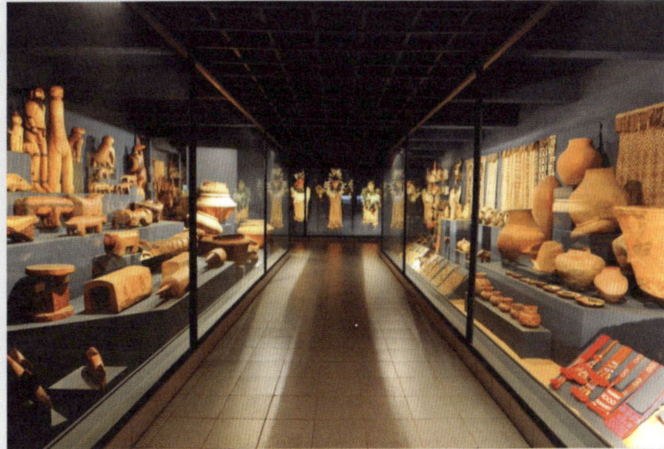

FIG 4 Room of the Museum of Indigenous Art of the Centro de Artes Visuales / Museo del Barro. The collection contains more than 2,000 pieces of the aesthetic-poetic production of the Indigenous communities of Paraguay. Photograph: Fernando Allen. Documentation and Research Department (DDI) – Centro de Artes Visuales / Museo del Barro.

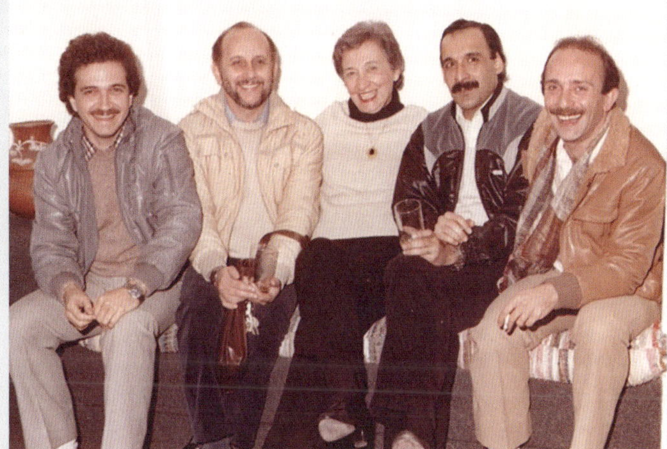

FIG 5 Osvaldo Salerno, Carlos Colombino, Olga Blinder, Ticio Escobar, and Ricardo Migliorisi. The team that served as the foundation for the creation and continuity of the CAV / Museo del Barro project. Documentation and Research Department (DDI) – Centro de Artes Visuales / Museo del Barro.

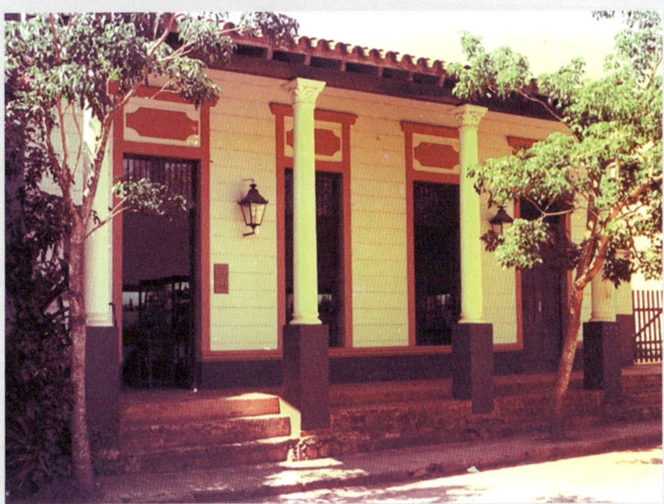

FIG 6 First site of the collection of archaeological and popular ceramics. San Lorenzo, c.1980. Documentation and Research Department (DDI) – Centro de Artes Visuales / Museo del Barro.

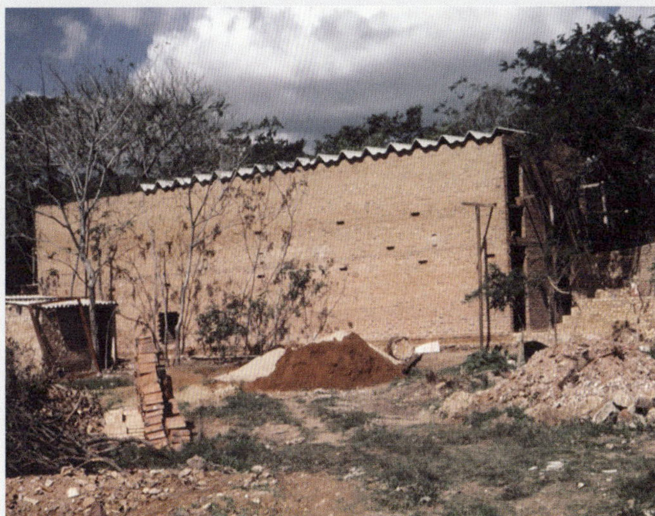

FIG 7 Construction of the first room on the current site where the museum is located in Asunción. It will later become the Josefina Plá room. c. Documentation and Research Department (DDI) – Centro de Artes Visuales / Museo del Barro.

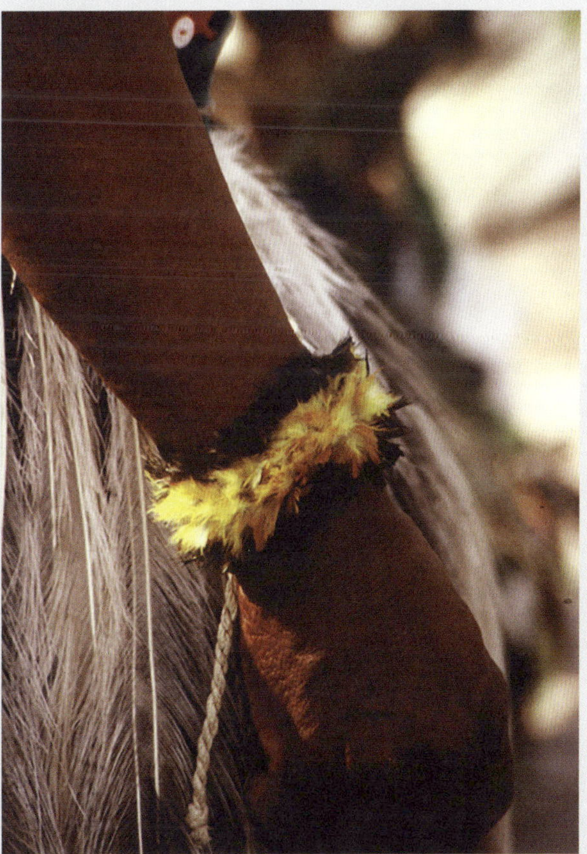

FIG 8 Ishir tomaraho man with ceremonial bracelet made of feathers and vegetable fiber. Community of María Elena, Alto Paraguay, Chaco, c.2002. Photograph: Nicolás Richard. Documentation and Research Department (DDI) – Centro de Artes Visuales / Museo del Barro.

Since then, the museum's exhibitions have sought to ensure that *arte popular* and Indigenous art are presented as equals of Western art vocabularies. The museum wants these works to be compared and to engage in a dialog in a spirit of respect for differences, seeking to refute the official myth that reduces *arte popular* and Indigenous symbolic production to categories such as "folklore," "native," and "vernacular"—"our very own" art. In other words, to trivialized versions of that production, purged of the nuances and opacities of something different.

When Ticio Escobar, who has given a great deal of systematic thought to Paraguayan art from that triple perspective, wrote *La Belleza de los Otros* (The Beauty of Others) (1994), he included the foundational story told in the book, "El brazalete de Túkule" (Túkule's Bracelet). Túkule, a powerful Ishir shaman, was very carefully making a bracelet, known as *oikakar*, using a net woven from vegetable fiber taken from bromeliads, to which he was tying small and large feathers one by one. When Ticio asked him why he was adding a string of multicolored feathers to what seemed to be already finished he replied, "To make it even more beautiful." The bracelet, whose functions are ceremonial, shamanic, and ritualistic, should also sparkle and catch our eye.

The bearer of the language of difference, embraced initially at an intuitive level — practice came first, followed by theory — and then wholeheartedly, the Museo del Barro's path became clear as it unfolded. Its component parts gradually coalesced until they were all fused together (though they were never entirely fused) in one place (actually, in two: a physical place and a place of words).

Paraguayan art, in its various forms of expression, sought to establish, at the Museo del Barro, a space where we could see ourselves from many different perspectives, questioning the "we" that, in Paraguay, represents our dual identity (at least two, as our language so clearly expresses). In Guaraní, the language spoken by most Paraguayans, there are two ways to say "we" — one is inclusive (*ñande*) and the other is exclusive (*ore*). These two ways to say "we" provide an alternative approach to understanding identity. While the country's official culture tries in various different ways to present a single unified "Paraguayan self," our language makes it clear that there is no such thing.

Heritage

It is one thing to speak of inheritance, and another to speak of patrimony, patrimonial, or patrimonialization. I would like to take this opportunity to discuss the processes involved in patrimonialization, to identify what part of our inheritance, what we inherit from earlier times, can or cannot be considered patrimony. This is a mostly political process that, in Paraguay at least, was appropriated by the nationalist agenda and came to be associated with the issue of identities of monolithic entities. The Museo del Barro hosts another way to understand patrimony via the creation of another repertoire that, at the time, could find no faces in which to recognize itself. One of the founders of the museum, Carlos Colombino, said: "Planning a space in which to house people as well as artworks was one of many possible strategies. This encouraged a certain sense of resistance. To believe that we were the essential components of the community and that we had to create a different image of Paraguay, one that we wanted to invent. In time, that sense of community expanded, the circle grew larger ..."

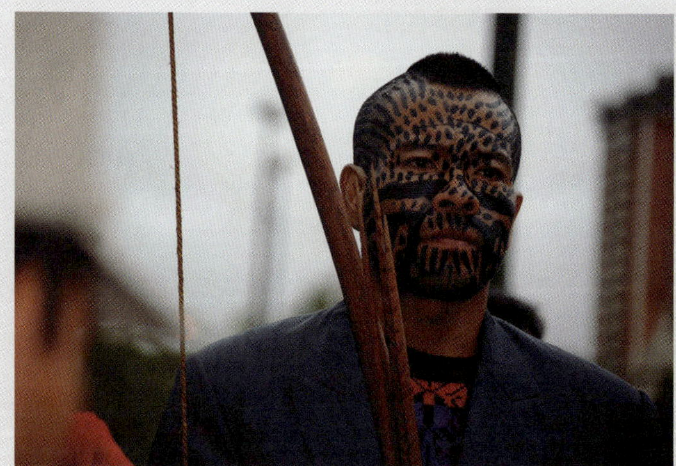

FIG 9 Ache man demonstrating for his ancestral lands in Asunción. He carries a bow and arrow and wears warlike face paint and a Western dress jacket. Photograph: Tide Escobar. Documentation and Research Department (DDI) – Centro de Artes Visuales / Museo del Barro.

The Written Version

The idea of bringing together the artistic production of the various peoples of Paraguay so that they could engage in a dialog arose from a random sequence of events. As Ticio Escobar set about writing *Una interpretación de las artes visuales en el Paraguay* (An Interpretation of the Visual Arts of Paraguay) (published in two volumes, in 1982 and 1984), he grappled with the problem of how to express those differences and find a place for them in a history that denied their existence. In his book, *El mito del arte y el mito del pueblo* (The Myth of Art and the Myth of the People) (1986), Escobar suggested that *arte popular* and Indigenous art were on an equal footing with, and should be seen as equal to, the more "highbrow" forms of art. He thus laid the groundwork for a deeper discussion about modernity and a conversation about Western culture and *arte popular* in which they are not set against each other in a binary confrontation but presented in terms of an issue that problematizes and defines relationships. Escobar's book encapsulates the goals of the CAV / Museo del Barro, stepping away from art theory in order to explore culture theory with all its political implications, including the debate over hegemonic control of the symbolic capital of a territory that has become a nation.

That book, which is at the core of the Museo del Barro's practice, formed the theoretical basis of the questions that ran parallel to its evolution. The concept of art that Escobar describes and that, by extension, is presented at the museum—*the manipulation of tangible forms that disrupt our understanding*—creates an opportunity to introduce the concept of popular art into the narrative of another history of art and begin to dispel Eurocentric approaches. These ideas are related to the autonomy of art and the concept of contemporaneity and uniqueness, to mention just a few.

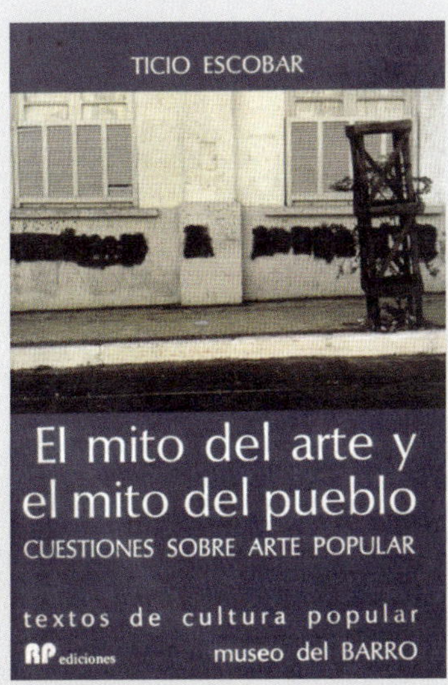

FIG 10 Cover of the first edition of the book *El mito del Arte y el mito del pueblo* by Ticio Escobar. The cover was designed by Osvaldo Salerno for the CAV / Museo del Barro publications project in 1986.

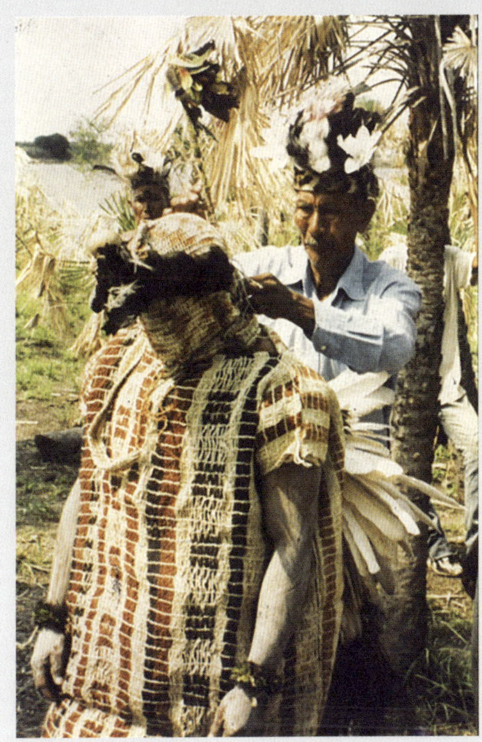

FIG 11 Tamusía, ishir shaman tomaraho in the ritual circle of the Debylyby. Community of María Elena, Alto Paraguay, Chaco, c. 2002. Photograph: Nicolás Richard. Documentation and Research Department (DDI) – Centro de Artes Visuales / Museo del Barro.

Art for Indigenous and Peasant Communities

One of the major debates concerning the use of the word "art" to refer to the aesthetic-poetic production of non-Western cultures hinges on a concrete fact. These cultures do not use that word to refer to the production of tangible forms and, on the whole, do not see their production as works of art.

Art history, however, has never hesitated to use the category when it believes that this or that production relates to its own past—as is the case with Egyptian art or cave art. Yet peasant and Indigenous cultural expressions appeal to the senses when they attempt to represent the world in which they live. According to Escobar, certain cultural moments are counted and recorded, producing taut configurations that are the equivalent of what the West understands as art.

Particular Features

Indigenous and *arte popular* are both endowed with particular features that distinguish them from modern art or what is referred to as contemporary art.

Neither popular art nor Indigenous art have felt the need to claim an autonomy that separates them from a form of worship. They have maintained a close relationship with such devotion and, in some cases, artistic expression is closely related to the performance of a ritual. The inherent poetry of an object is inextricably intertwined with the act of worship and with everyday life. In this regard, advocates of Indigenous or *arte popular* reject the idea that, to be considered art, a work must have no function.

The concept of originality is also disputed, since these cultures, on the whole, work with traditions that have been handed down from earlier times, expressing new meanings and forging new ways to shape forms that differ from the approaches taken by "highbrow" art. I always say that Western art is very traditional, and so is modern art; for something to be considered modern it must have broken with a previous tradition, and that is its own tradition. Authorship has never been an important issue in Indigenous art or *arte popular* in Paraguay, although that is changing with time and many ceramicists and wood carvers now sign their work.

While these particular features or characteristics distance *arte popular* and Indigenous art from the concept of art inherited from the West, their forms and dense meanings are influenced by the living and working conditions in the communities in which they are produced; that is why the existence of these alternative approaches to art also challenges the usual concept of contemporary art and instead relies on an alternative contemporaneity that is more directly relevant to each of these different realities.

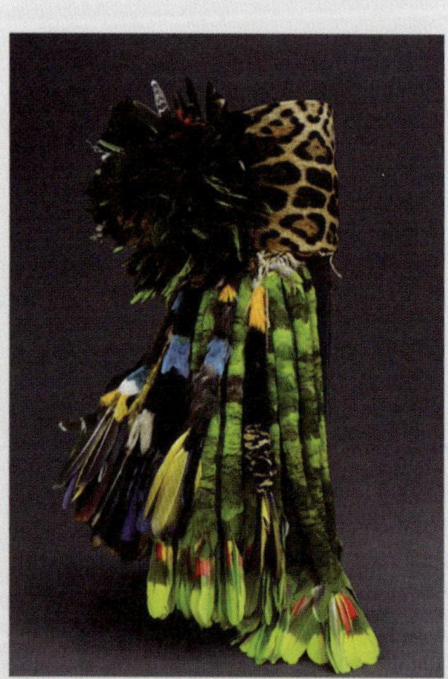

FIG 12 Ayói. Traditional Ayoreo cap made of feline fur with a cover made of feathered shafts. Collection of the Museum of Indigenous Art of the CAV / Mdb. Photograph: Marcial Barni.

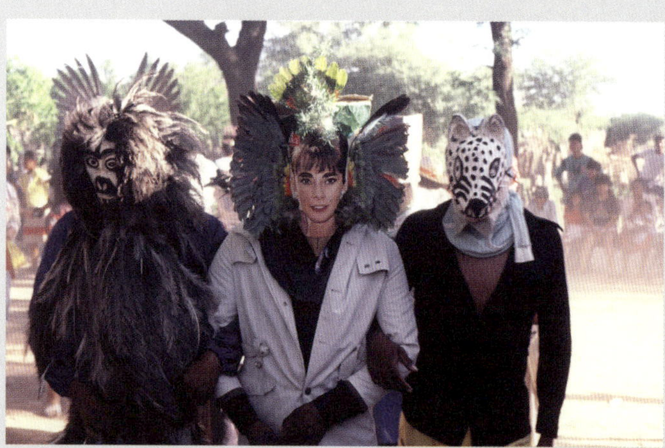

FIG 13 Festivity of the Arete Guasu, Santa Teresita, Boquerón, Chaco, c. 1993. The festivity corresponds to the Guarani Chaco culture in which masks have been borrowed from the Chané culture. Photograph: Ticio Escobar. Documentation and Research Department (DDI) – Centro de Artes Visuales / Museo del Barro.

Which Contemporary Art?

The term "contemporary art" is something else I would like to question. In Paraguay, "contemporary art" means a current, urban artistic practice—a Western or Westernized practice, if you will, to confuse things even more.

At the present time, when we are already skeptical of a totalizing, conclusive narrative, I do not think we can continue to use the term "contemporary art" to refer to the art produced in these categories. Furthermore, to question this notion means accepting that there are other present times that are not mutually interchangeable. Present times which experiment with other names for themselves and bypass definitions, that allow the possibility for contagion.

By this I mean that *arte popular* can be considered contemporary as long as the word "contemporary" is used to refer to a time in which differences can coexist, embracing distinct approaches to the process of giving meaning to or imagining other times, and perhaps challenging them.

The Boundaries

In everything the Museo del Barro has done—which, in many cases, has transcended the parameters usually associated with a museum—it has sought to soften the boundaries that jealously guard certain academic categories. This approach has led the Museo del Barro to explore other ways to be involved in the milieu in which it operates. This explains why the viability of Indigenous and *arte popular* relies on the flexibility of those boundaries, seeking to undermine the certainties of established fields of knowledge and move what appears to be set in stone so that the prism through which we see reality can shift and reveal what was out of sight, allowing the unseen to appear. Indigenous artists and *artistas populares* have their own ways of expressing their own personal reality to address the open wound inflicted by the Western view of the history of art. Ticio Escobar's reading, documented at the Museo del Barro, shows these other processes and helps us keep moving those boundaries that have been static for perhaps too long.

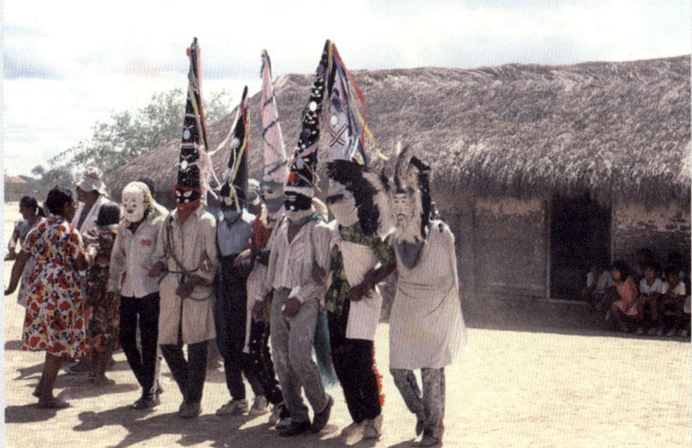

FIG 14 Festivity of the Arete Guasu, Santa Teresita, Boquerón, Chaco, c. 1993. The apyte puku are long-hooded masks that the Guarani youth wear and with which they appear at the feast. Photograph: Ticio Escobar. Documentation and Research Department (DDI) – Centro de Artes Visuales / Museo del Barro.

Dialogs

The Museo del Barro influenced art that is currently being produced, so I am going to present three examples in which the places where the works were made intersect and engage in a dialog. I will discuss three coincidental case studies: the work of Fredi Casco, Julia Isídrez, and Marcos Benítez. Certain ideas, which emerged in several places in the Americas at about the same time, prompted many artists to become quasi-anthropologists who were rigorous researchers and read beyond the scope of their very particular views, but not for the purpose of conducting ethnographic studies. I will select aesthetic-poetic practices from different places and let them talk to each other. Let me be clear: this reading does not ignore the idea that there are asymmetries in these intersections. There certainly are. But in those assumed asymmetries one can detect forms of a conspiracy intent on expanding the fields of art and its categories—and onexpanding the potential of *arte popular* and Indigenous art, and its coexistence with so-called "contemporary art." In other words, *arte popular* read from a contemporary art perspective and expressed in terms of the different contemporaneity it represents.

Fredi Casco: Frontiers

Fredi Casco's approach is inspired by his interest in the boundaries that isolate what might be called "high culture" from *cultura popular* and mass culture. He takes an almost revisionist approach to the tradition and power that are part of certain narratives. Casco explores what are often subtle transgressions and adds a certain irony. Casco's first solo exhibition at the Museo del Barro already showed his interest in those other fields. *La carne fluorescente* (Florescent Flesh) was a Polaroid shot of the silhouette of a nineteenth-century *santo de bastidor* (cage doll) lit by the light from the museum cabinets. The cold light from the cabinets shrouded these objects in a sort of fluorescent aura, a blinking light (Escobar), a "cold aura" according to the Spanish theorist José Luis Brea.[5] In the photo series and video installation *Chaco Fantasma* (Ghost Chaco), Casco reflects on certain ideas about otherness and resistance to cultural practices such as the *Chiriguano* ritual of Areté Guasú from the Chaco. In his work, the Chaco region of Paraguay, its landscape, and this ritual, which challenges the idea of this place as flat and barren land, becomes a sort of other, parallel, ghost world. On the threshold of the world, something that hasn't finished happening or hasn't finished not happening. *Areté* is a Guaraní word that can be translated as "fiesta." However, it contains the root "ara," that alludes to "time," and is enriched by the suffix "eté" which means something presumed to be true or something extraordinary. Ordinary time is unable to provide entry to other times that have been left out. The Areté Guasu ceremony splits time in two and imposes a three-day break on the Guaraní Chitiguano community of Santa Teresita in the Paraguayan Chaco. Those days are spent renewing the social contract, reasserting oneself, and settling conflicts. This parenthesis, this interdiction, allows extraordinary things to take place as the days unfold. Indigenous art never adapts to what hegemonic centers call contemporary art, let alone a ritual. Its contemporaneity is counter-presented as a different contemporaneity. We accept as a given that time levels us all, we assume that "contemporary" means similarity and fitting in. Current Indigenous art rattles that certainty, leaving it at a loss for words. Ticio Escobar's anthropological and aesthetic reading of the *Arete Guasu* in the 1980s underscored the invisibility of Indigenous art and contributed to its revival as part of a campaign for restitution and revindication that took place during the 1980s in various parts of Latin America.

5 In his book, *Las auras frías. El culto a la obra de arte en la era posaurática* (Cold Auras. Worshiping Art in the Post-aura Era) (Barcelona: Anagrama, 1999), Brea discusses the transition of the Benjaminian aura, not in terms of loss but of the image of its cooling off.

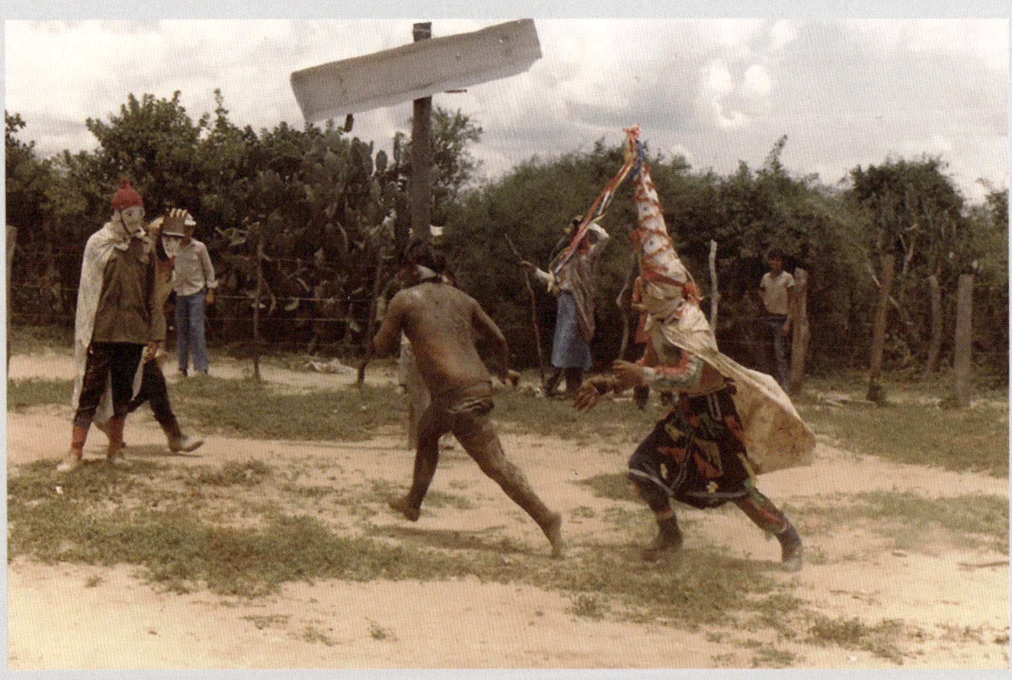

FIG 15 Festivity of the Arete Guasu, Santa Teresita, Boquerón, Chaco, c. 1993. The *cuchi cuchi* (representation of a pig) are people at the party who smear mud on themselves and run at those present to smear them. It is practically the end of the ritual. Photograph: Ticio Escobar. Documentation and Research Department (DDI) – Centro de Artes Visuales / Museo del Barro.

Marcos Benítez: a Perspective

Marcos Benítez began to explore new areas as a result of his involvement in a group of artists called El Aleph that was interested in the question of identity. He took several approaches to *arte popular* from the very particular perspective of his own works. Benítez has recently become interested in basket-weaving *Mbyá*, an Indigenous community of the Tupi Guaraní whose craft is deeply rooted in Amazonian basketry traditions. *Mbyá* basket-makers create delicate geometric and symmetrical patterns by weaving *guembepí* and *takuarembó* natural fibers to reproduce the *mbói jegua*, the decorative markings on snakeskin. In a similar work intended to depict his own face, Benítez portrays himself in a photograph with a moving snake's head.

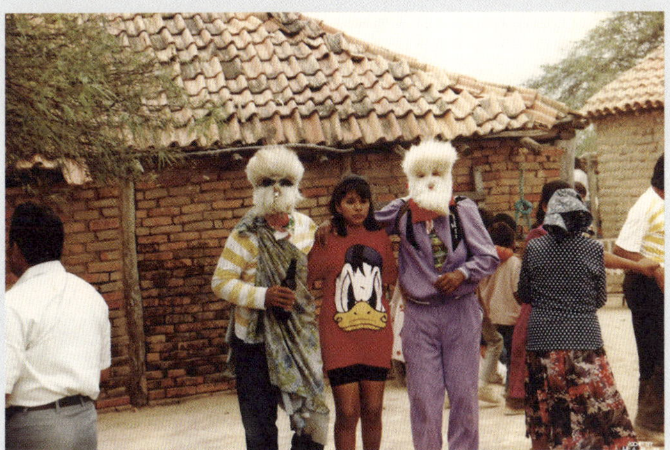

FIG 16 Festivity of the Arete Guasu, Santa Teresita, Boquerón, Chaco, c. 1993. The festivity corresponds to the Guarani Chaco culture in which masks have been borrowed from the Chané culture. Photograph: Ticio Escobar. Documentation and Research Department (DDI) – Centro de Artes Visuales / Museo del Barro.

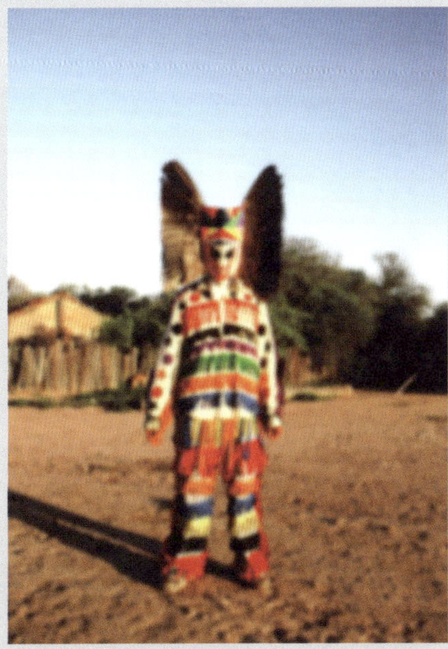

FIG 17 *Chaco Phantom*. Series of photographs by Paraguayan artist Fredi Casco. This series contains misty photographs, alluding to the strangeness of the conjugation between landscape and ritual and their survival. The complete work comprises a four-channel projection. Courtesy of the artist.

Relying on a process of numerical reconstruction (Benítez does not visit a *Mbyá* community to see how they make their baskets), he recognizes the pattern and uses photography to do what these Indigenous craftsmen do with *guembepí* and *takuarembó* natural fibers. He produces a digital photograph in which, thanks to a trompe l'oeil effect, we do not notice the pixels. The snakeskin shows us a handcrafted version of what we do not see: the pixels that create the artist's face.

Julia Isídrez: a Parallel Contemporaneity

From Itá, her native city, her other contemporary being, Julia Isídrez, along with her mother, Juana (now deceased), presents her fierce gesture to the world. It is the same gesture that all the women from whom she is descended have made. A gesture involving hands that encircle the void and protect it with the form that her hand selects. She has learned how to reframe her own forms, taking inspiration from the depths of her own history. With each potent gesture of her hands, Julia removes the folkloristic, romanticized vision bequeathed to her by history and stands beside the beings she has created.

> Ticio Escobar says:
>
> These disturbing sculptures show that, in and of themselves, neither tradition nor modernity offer guarantees or represent threats; what legitimizes the symbols that either of them produce is the truth that nurtures them both. And the truth that Juana Marta and Julia communicate is from an ambiguous time and a disintegrating present. Expressing it completely and clearly takes an intense effort and demands reliable, solid forms, figures that are from the remote past and impervious to the barrier created by our modern threshold.[6]

It should be noted that Isídrez and her mother are the only Paraguayan artists to have shown their work at documenta in Kassel, Germany (2012). The fact that the curator Chus Martínez had some idea, albeit a vague one, about traditional Paraguayan ceramics was the result of over forty years of work trying to break or expand the very boundaries mentioned in this essay.

---

6 Ticio Escobar. *Itá y la aldea global* (Itá and the Global Village), (Asunción, 1998). Digital version of the text supplied by the author.

OLINDA SILVANO

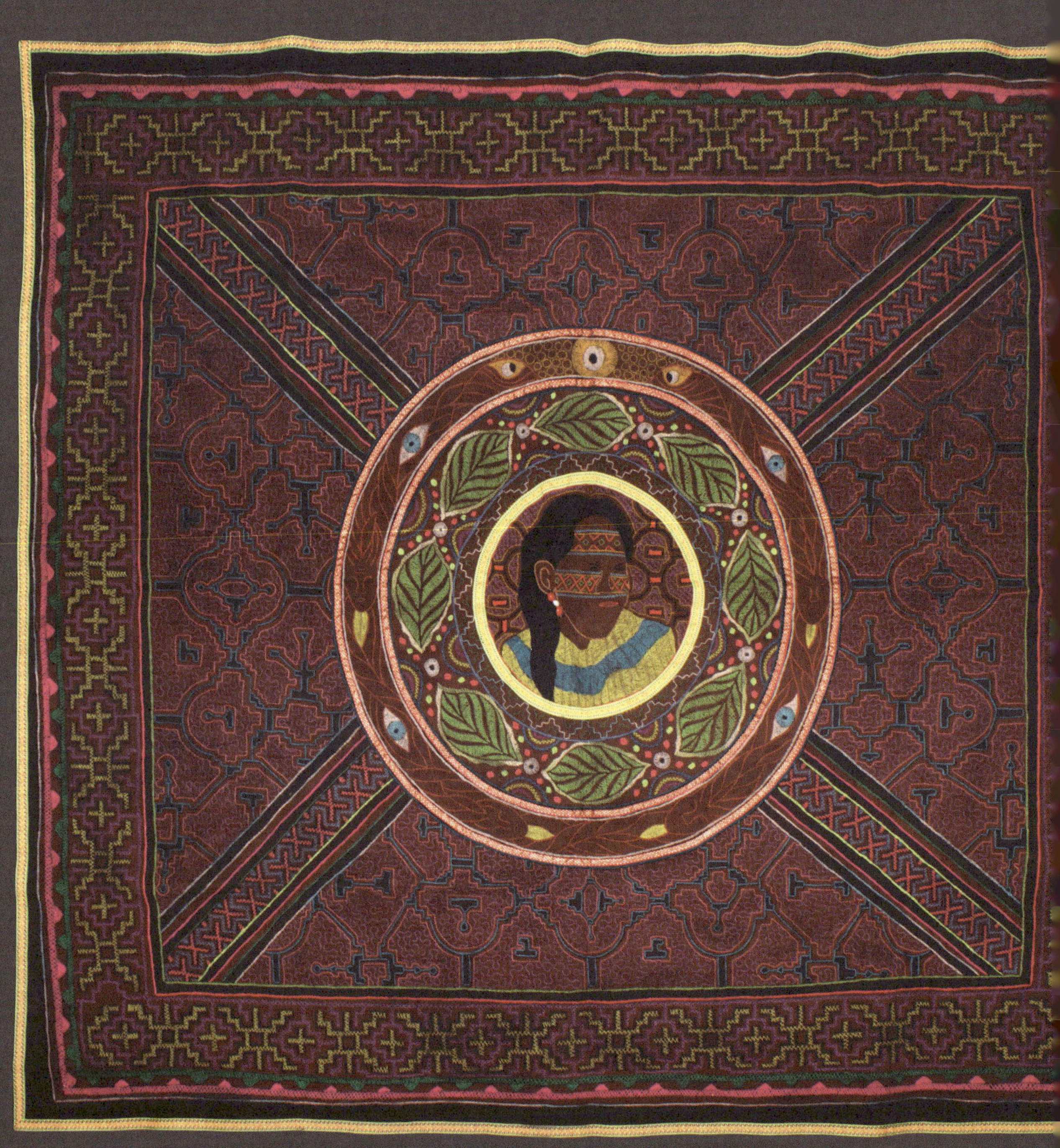

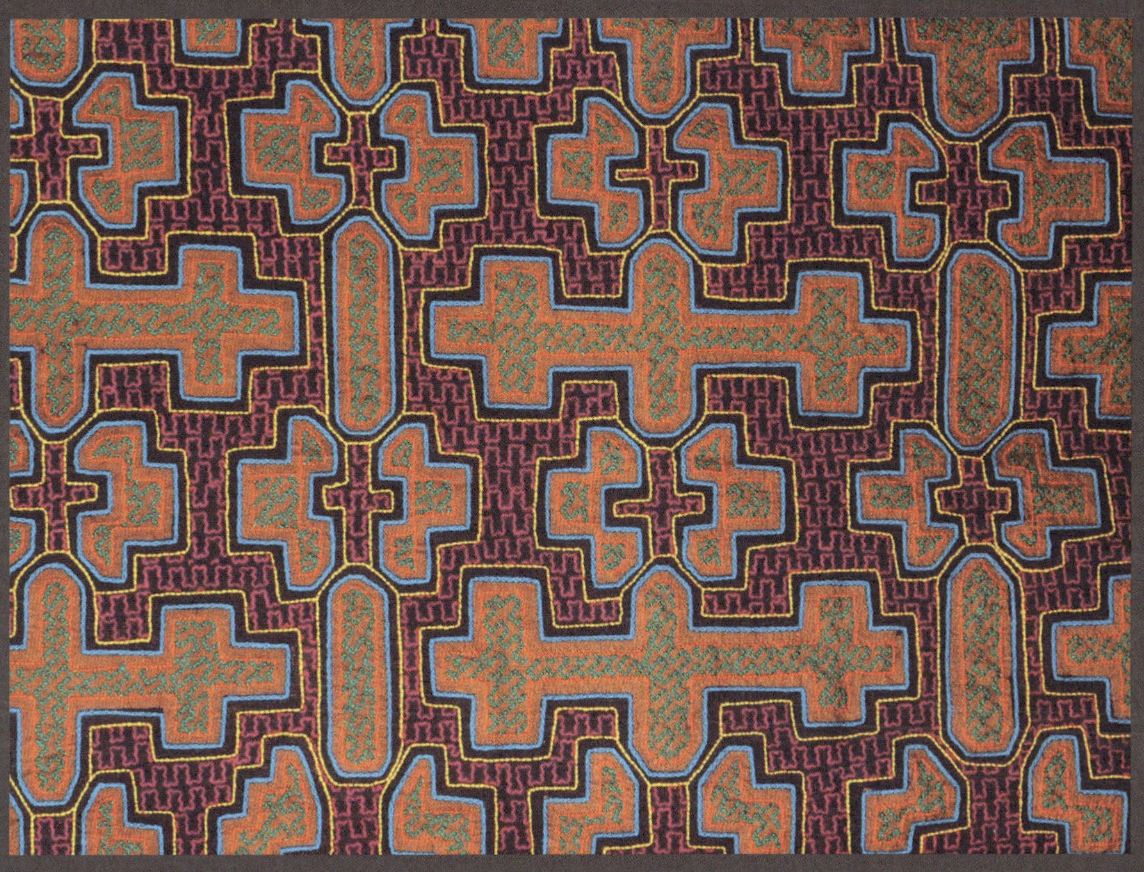

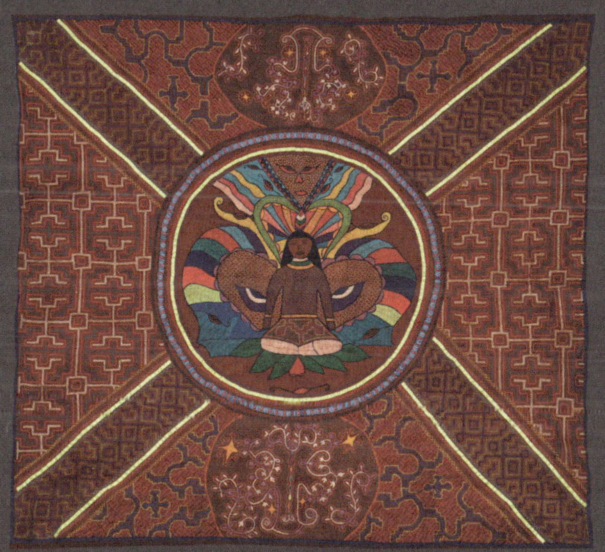

LEFT
El mundo de matico (The World of Matico), 2020. Dyes and embroidery on fabric.

TOP RIGHT
La memoria ancestral (Ancestral Memory), 2018. Xao Quené embroidery, dyed with natural pigments on mahogany and yacushapana bark with "Barra Virgen" from the Jungle's lagoon.

BOTTOM RIGHT
El espiritu de las madres planta (The Spirit of the Mother Plants), 2020. Natural dyes and embroidery on fabric.

NEXT PAGE
El espiritu de las madres planta (The Spirit of the Mother Plants) (details), 2020. Natural dyes and embroidery on fabric.

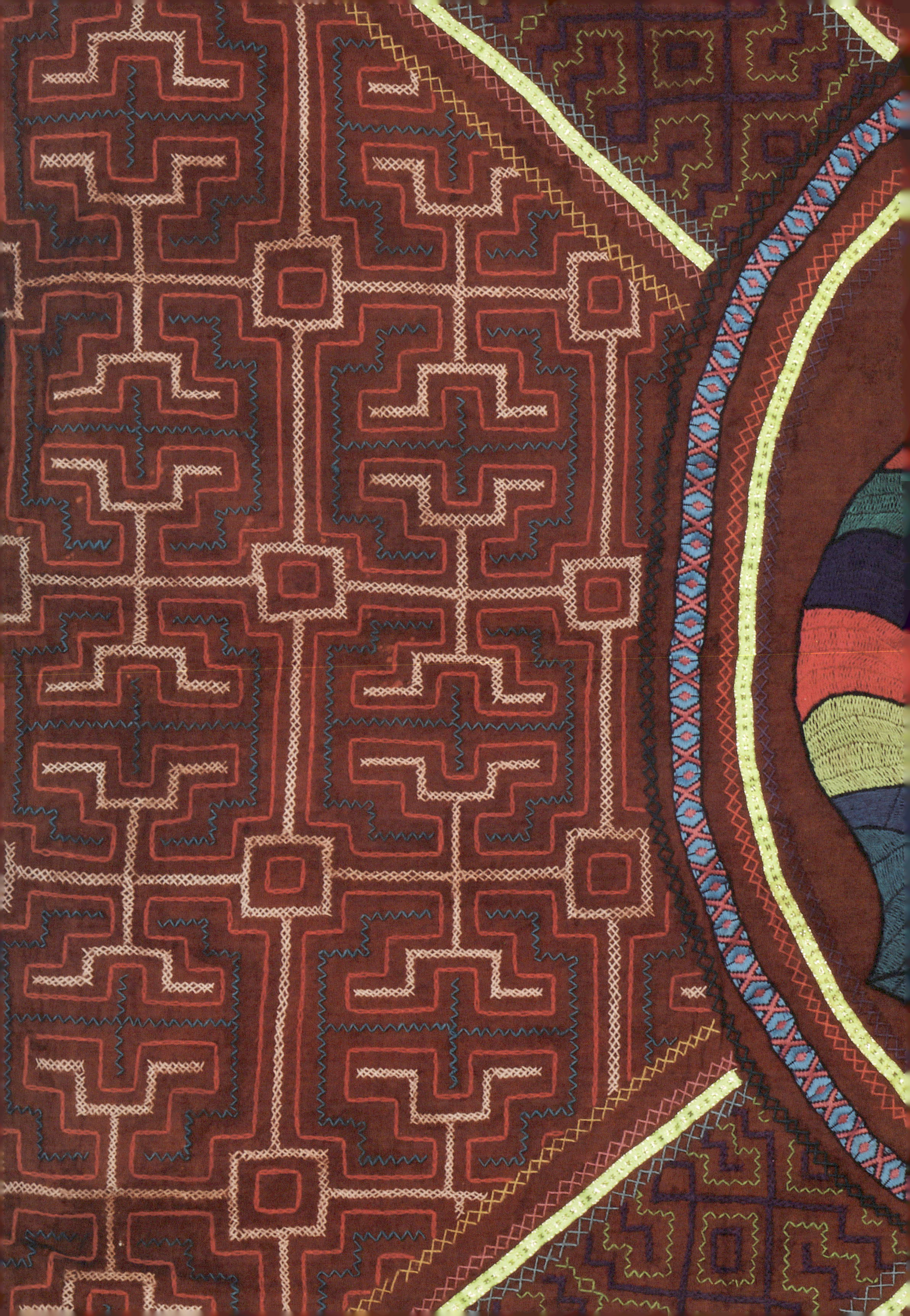

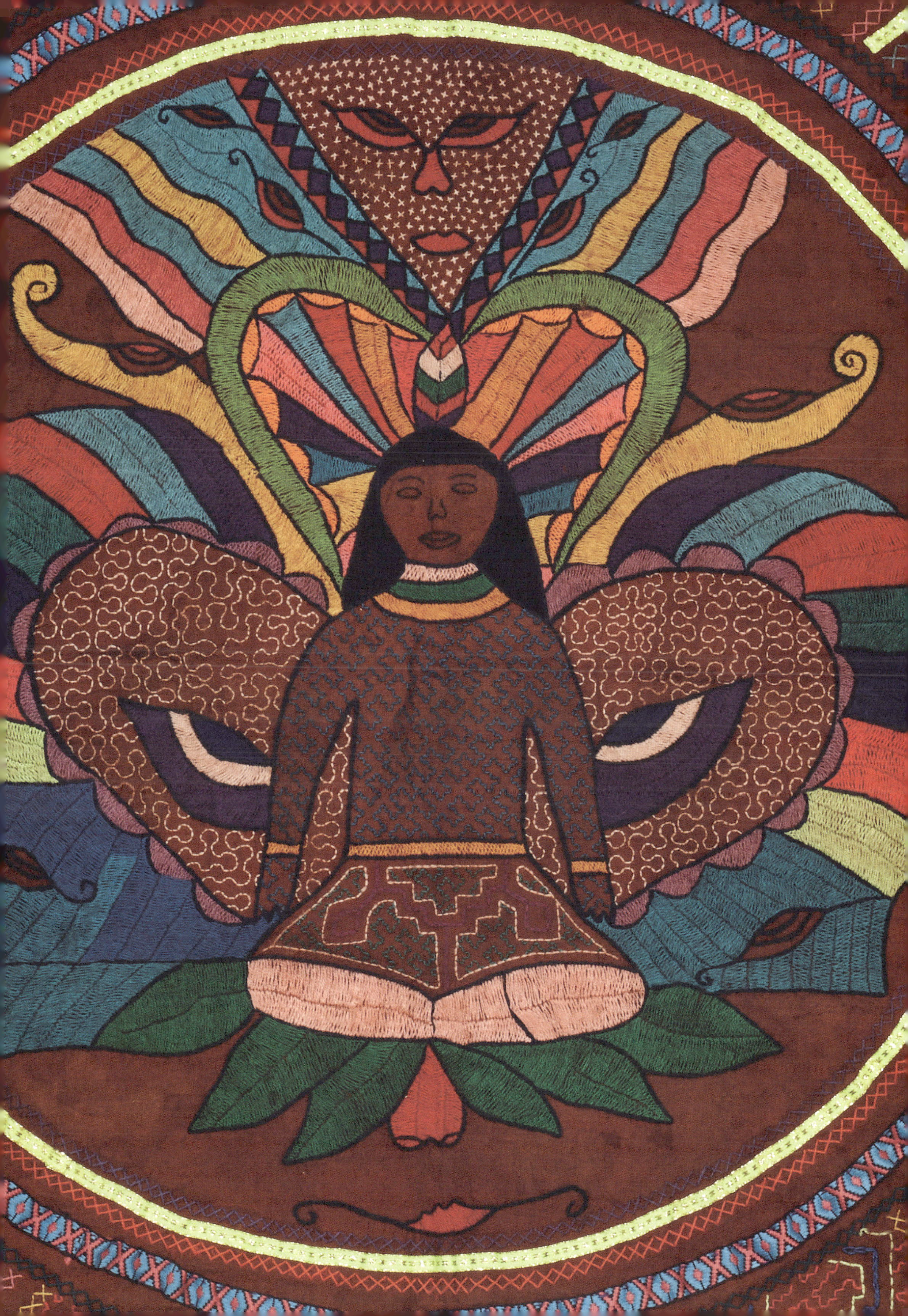

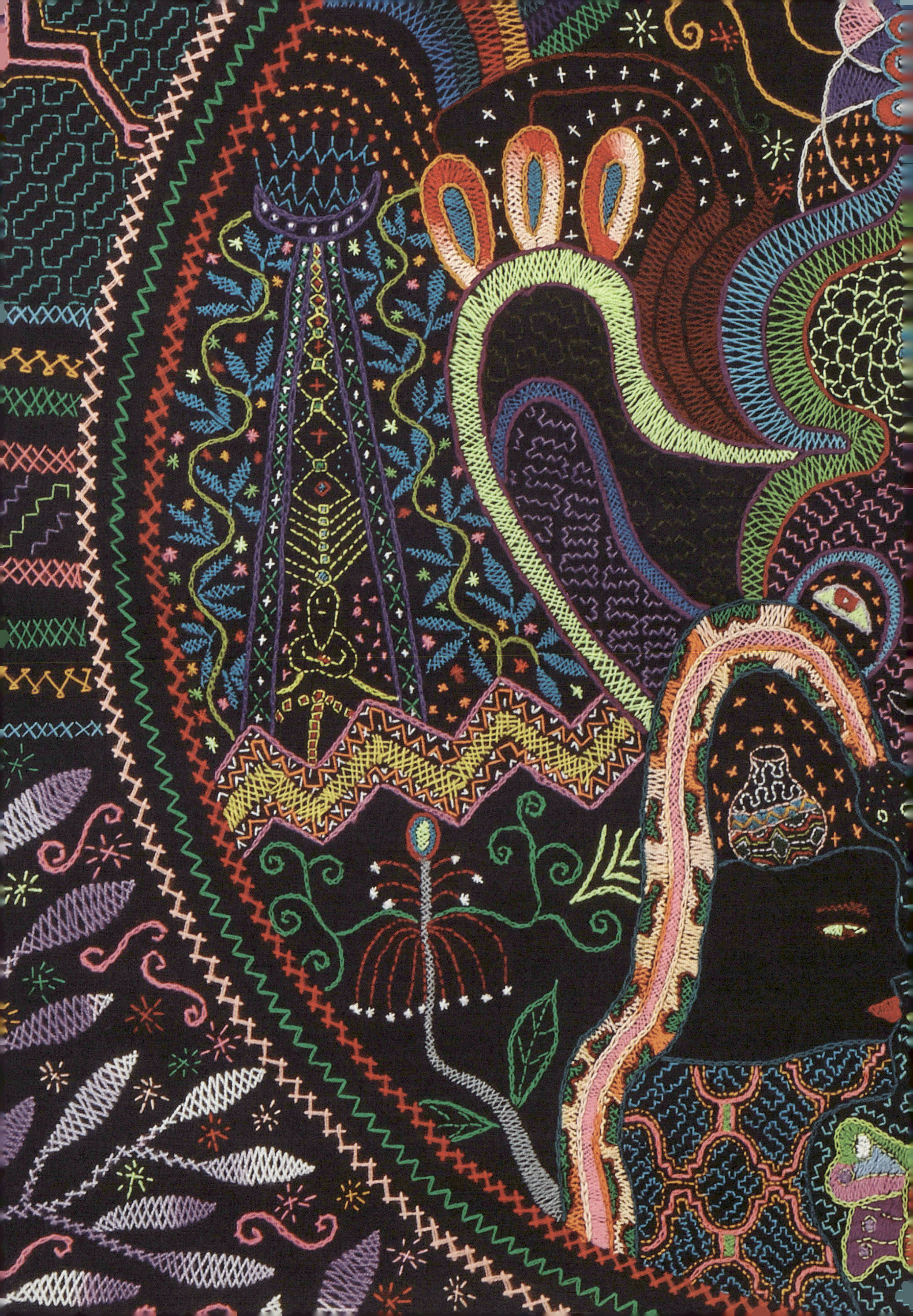

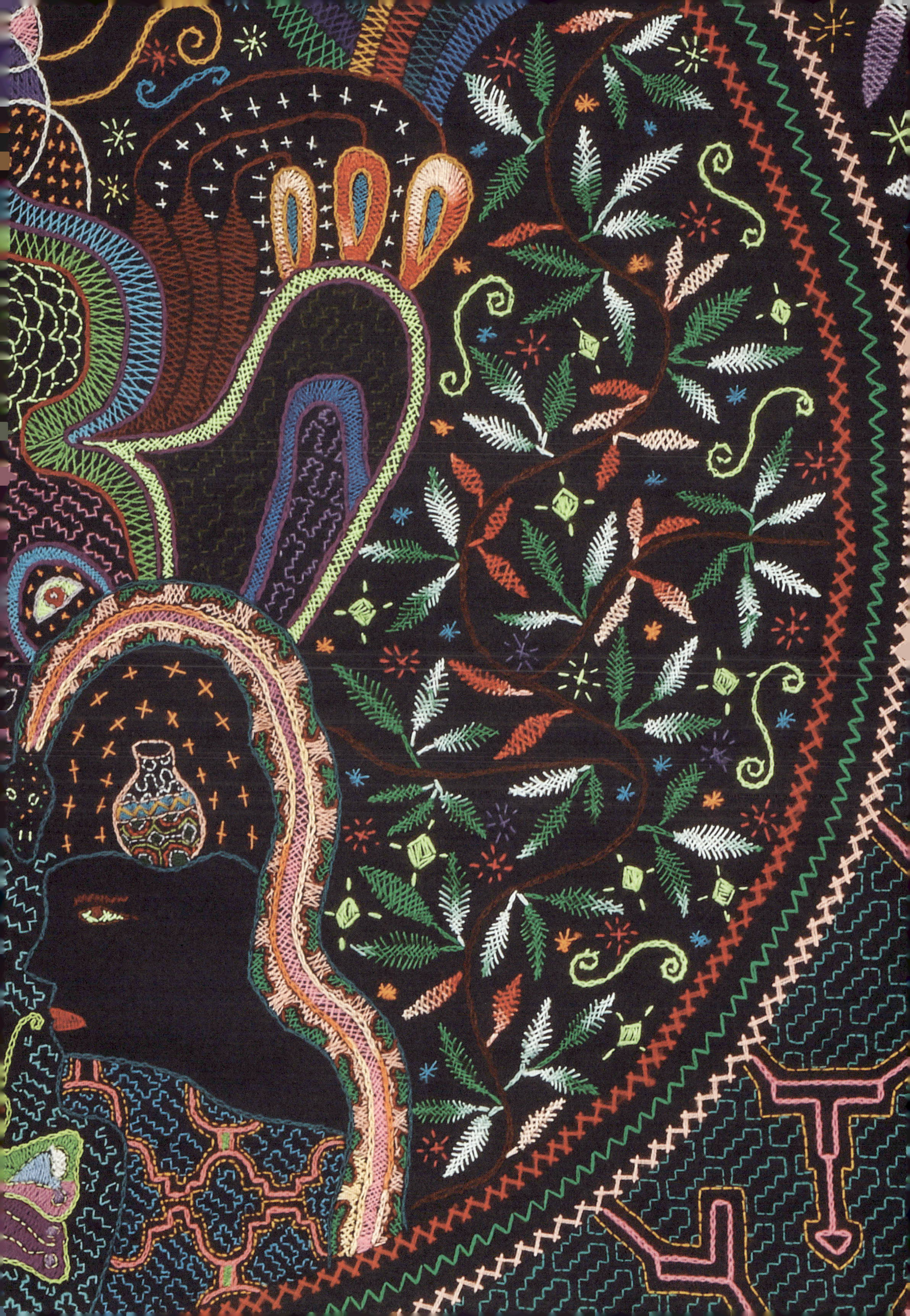

PREVIOUS PAGE
El espíritu de las madres planta (The Spirit of the Mother Plants) (details), 2020. Natural dyes and embroidery on fabric.

TOP
Visión de ayahuasca (Ayahuasca vision), 2020. Natural dyes and embroidery on fabric.

BOTTOM LEFT
El espíritu de las madres planta (The Spirit of the Mother Plants) (detail), 2020. Natural dyes and embroidery on fabric.

BOTTOM RIGHT
Julia Ortiz Elias and Olinda Silvano (Reshinjabe), *Historia de la selva y la ciudad* (History of the Jungle and the City), 2013. Oil, natural dyes, and traditional shipibo. embroidery on tocuyo.

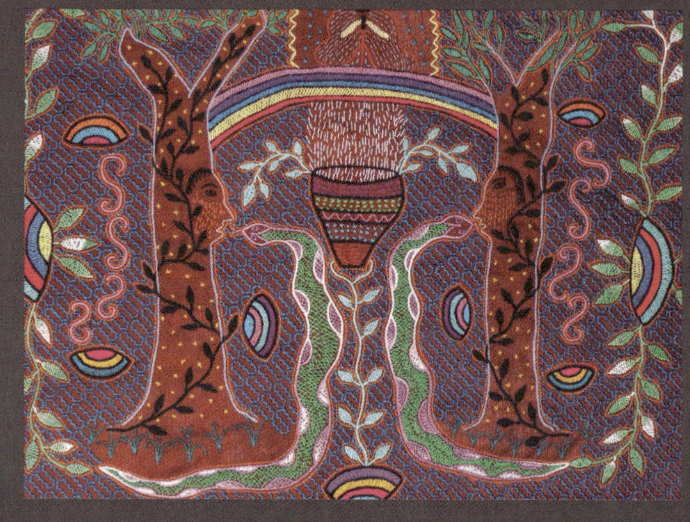

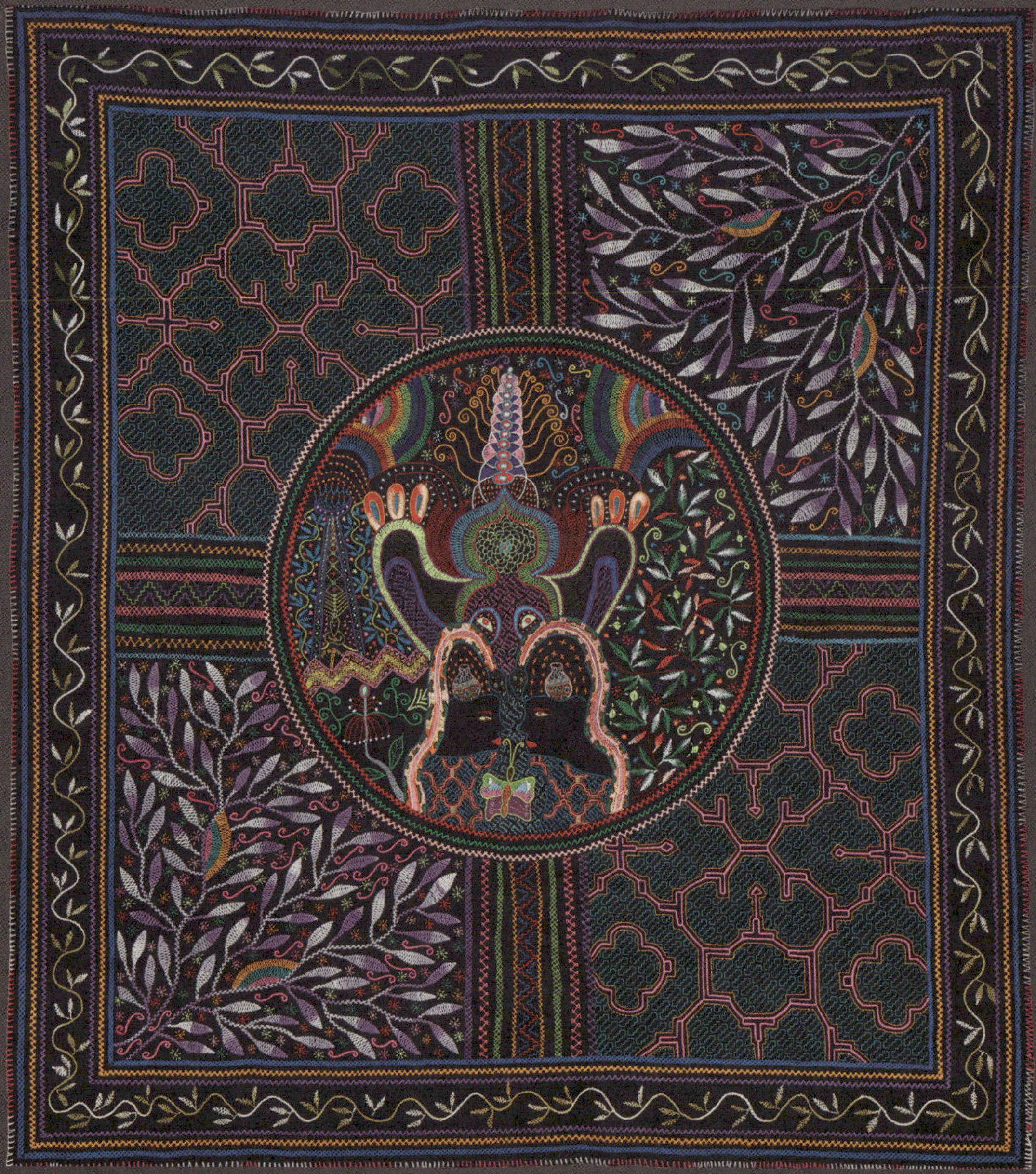

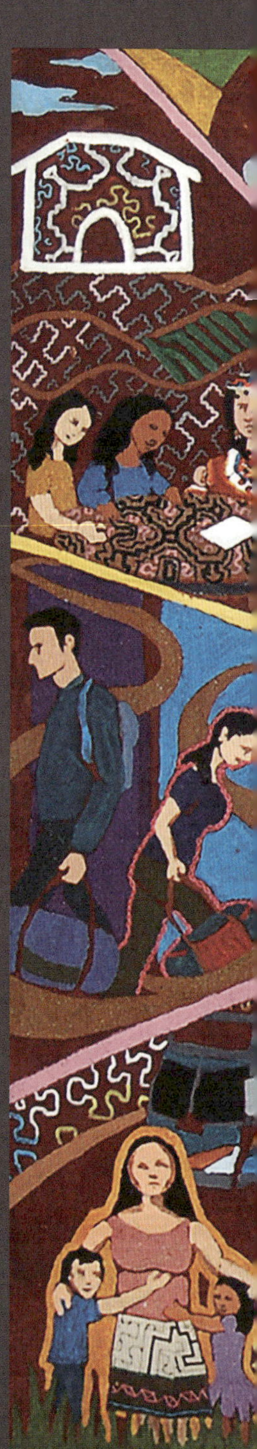

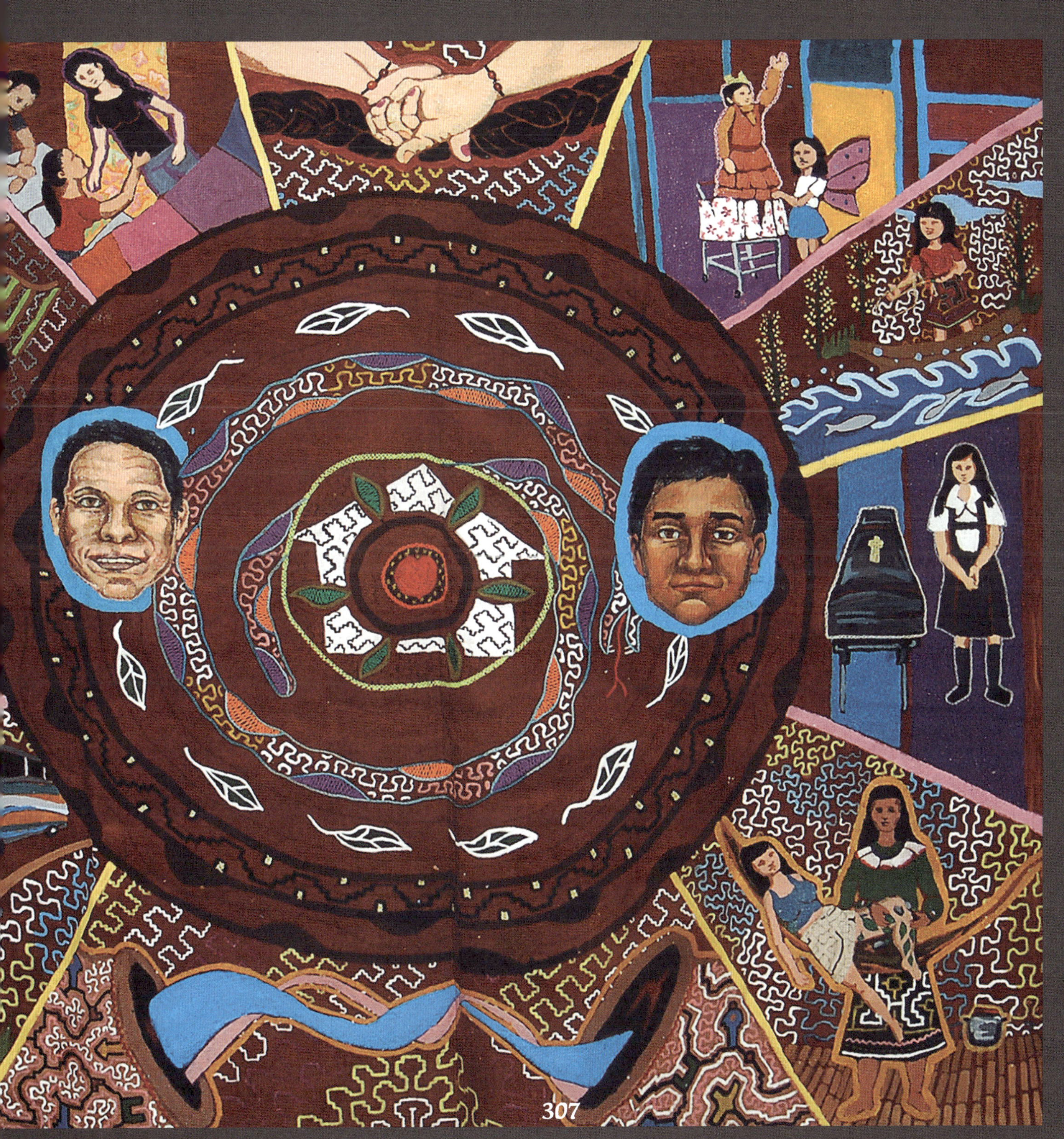

Theater, an Artform that was Going to Change the World

308

VALI MAHLOUJI

> Black milk of daybreak we drink it at sundown
> we drink it at noon in the morning we drink it
> at night
> we drink it and drink it
>
> — Paul Celan [1]

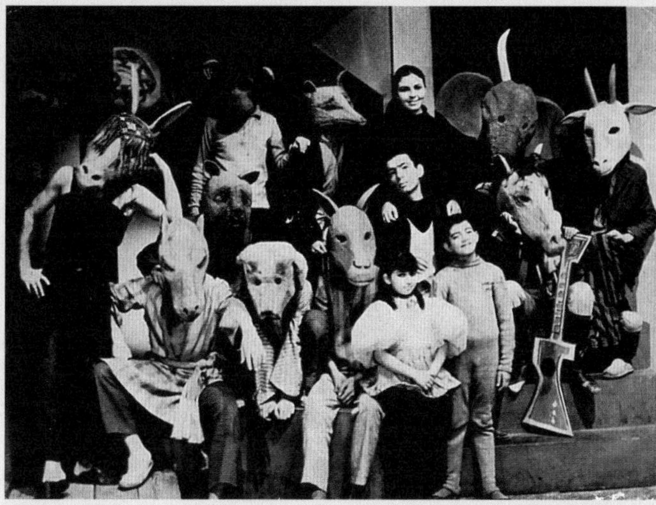

FIG 1 Shahr-e Qesseh (City of Tales): Bijan Mofid (playwright and director) theater troupe in 1968 at the World Premiere, commissioned by the 2nd Festival of Arts. Courtesy of Dariush Hajir and Bijan Mofid Foundation / Vali Mahlouji / Archaeology of the Final Decade.

Introduction

When a small group of like-minded Iranian cultural practitioners got together in 1967, there was a euphoric incorruptible innocence in the air that art, and particularly live art, was going to change the world. There was vigilant wisdom that the new world was ready and overdue for radical new orders and plural historical sensibilities. Heroic acts of courage were called upon from the depths of ancestral wisdoms to annihilate old hegemonies, their monolithic designs, their discriminating conceptions of superiorities, and their injurious deficiencies, which were irreparably contested. The past was inescapably condemned in the interests of a necessary, and hopefully better, novel present. There was hope for a more just world based on a profoundly more polyphonic and democratic reordering. Artists, poets, musicians, dramatists and performers, writers, and critics assembled and convoked with three aims—disrobing, disassembling an unjust and disfiguring past; defining, steering, and conducting the revolutionary discharge; and restoratively aspiring towards new realms where creative realities and utopias could intersect. Their disassembling and dismantling strategies were structured through the forging of new fidelities and alliances, borrowings and exchanges, adaptations and adoptions, looking-ins and looking-outs, essentialisms and universalisms. Those were fundamental to new modes of knowledge and know-how designed for troubling old and defunct foundational orders of society.

One such project, as I have aimed to show, was a pioneering and groundbreaking international festival of performance, *Jašn-e Honar-e Shiraz*, or the Festival of Arts, Shiraz-Persepolis, staged in Iran from 1967 until 1977. Its experimentally radical, exuberant, inventive, and progressive stage ran annually every summer for eleven consecutive years until the advent of political turmoil in Iran. Its longevity was remarkable and exceptional for its type of radical cultural position.

As this essay aims to show, its cultural politics found alliance with only a handful of performance festivals around the world, namely two held in Europe, in Belgrade and Nancy, and two incredibly elevating African festivals that happened in 1966 and 1969 in Dakar and Algiers (First World festival of Negro Arts and Festival panafricain d'Alger respectively). Its meta-theatrical vision and its sophisticatedly meta-political stance made Shiraz-Persepolis one of the most uniquely transformative intercultural experiences, perhaps the most radical multidisciplinary crucible of any commissioning festival in history. Its complex and transcendental politics that aptly penetrated "first world" and "third world" divides and Cold War standoffs, and broke down perceived spatial and temporal borders, has yet to be fully acknowledged.

Shiraz-Persepolis emerged as the brainchild of a close-knit group of progressive Iranian cultural practitioners, led by the visionary Reza Ghotbi; the director of the National Iranian Radio and Television (NIRT), Farrokh Ghaffari, who returned from work at the Cinematheque in Paris; and Khojasteh Kia, who was educated at the Old Vic and led theater research at the NIRT in its initial stage. The festival had the support of the crucially culturally proactive Queen, Shahbanu Farah Pahlavi, as patron. Her emancipated relationship to art and patronage and the open-minded leadership of Reza Ghotbi ensured the festival's relative autonomy from the main state cultural apparatus, and protected its open liberal space across political restrictions and a relatively conservative and challenging national cultural terrain. Many important cultural practitioners were intimately involved with the programming of the festival, including Sheherazade Afshar, Bijan Saffari, Hormoz Farhat, Dariush Safvat, and Fowzieh Majd, among others.

1 Paul Celan, "Death Fugue," *Poems of Paul Celan*, trans. Michael Hamburger (New York, NY: Persea Books, 1988) 61.

The Great Assault

> [It is] always most terrifying, most dangerous
> when elimination and erasure is done
> in the name of the public, or even worse in the
> pretence of the protection of the public good.
>
> — James Baldwin [2]

The Festival of Arts' 1978 iteration was canceled by its board due to security concerns following political unrest. A religious *fatwa* (decree) had already precociously been declared, specifically against the festival, by the rising Islamist leader Ayatollah Khomeini in September 1977. The fatwa singled out the festival as the most decadent among all cultural projects, long before there was any inkling that "Khomeinism" was going to assault the course of Iran's modern history and aspire to brutalize the country's cultural landscape. Stigmatized by the condemnation, the festival became a particular target of religious bigotry and was duly banned following the establishment of the Islamic Republic in 1979. Post-revolution, the institution of the festival was immediately dissolved. The annual events were deemed illegal, un-Islamic. Many of the involved artists never worked again.

It is worth remembering the historical context around the closure of the festival and the intentional erasure of its traces, in the aftermath of the political change of 1979. History has shown us (and is yet to hold accountable) how the consolidation of the Islamic Republic necessitated an unprecedented dimension of terror. The Islamist political takeover unleashed a violent and inexorable dismantling and restructuring of socio-political, legislative, and cultural structures, with enormous human and material casualties. Terror was endemic to the political project, which was intent on securing its own success. It achieved, firstly, the decimation of all political counter-options, and secondly, the transformation of a modern political and judicial system into a theocracy. The theocratic structure that was installed (whereby ultimate authority rests neither with the state nor citizenry but is bestowed upon an unelected religious individual linked to the divine) is undeniably historic regression. Its undemocratic absurdly divine *legitimacy* has no contemporary equivalent—it is the only one of its kind in our current world.

It is clear to any historian that the totalizing system of control and closure which is at play here is fundamentally in keeping with the delusional strategies imposed by any totalitarian catastrophe. It distinctly lacks ingenuity or originality. There is no mystery to the method, nor to the ruin in its wake. The hypocrisy deployed is that of *protecting* people and space. The citizens are to trust that the state's sadism is for *their* benefit. There is one nuance: the Khomeinists' carcinogenic discriminatory self-righteousness justifies its devastating menace, its bloodletting, through religious ideological dogma—*by the will of, and for the greater good of, god.*

Civilizational Withdrawal. Atrophy

To speak of *culture*, the divine-led transmogrification set about to forcibly *re-civilize* society: our new "moral guides" devised a version of evangelization within weeks of taking the reign. An all-encompassing (what I term) *deterritorialization* and *reterritorialization* was systematically aimed at cultural "correction" and control. That transformation was such that culture and the totality of the public sphere could be tyrannically subjugated to ideological state control. Its grandest narrowing of liberties was the enforcement of the veil on *all* women in public. That was first announced on March 7, 1979, on the eve of International Women's Day. The cynicism at the heart of it was intended to break the spirit and remains a deep wound, a profound humiliation.

> A civilization that withdraws into itself
> atrophies.
>
> — Aime Cesaire [3]

2 James Baldwin, interview cited in the film *I am Not Your Negro* (2016), directed by Raoul Peck.

3 Aimé Césaire, *Discourse on Colonialism*, trans. Joan Pinkham (London: Monthly Review Press, 1972). Originally published as *Discours sur le colonialisme* by Editions Presence Africaine, 1955.

The new political order institutionalized an Islamizing "cultural cleansing" (*paksazi-e farhangi*). It replaced our Ministry of Culture with a "Ministry of Culture and Islamic Guidance" (Vezarat-e Farhang va Ershad-e Islami), swapping emancipation and edification with a project of evangelization. The objectives of that modern inquisition have been to enforce cultural homogenization, gender segregation, the censorship of our thought, restriction of our expression, restraint of our aspiration, and regulation of our connection to ourselves and to the world. The outcomes: severance, atrophy, the nihilistic narrowing of *being*, of meaning, of experience, of expression, of love, of *joie*. As though we were colonized by aliens whose pursuit is to sever us from ourselves and to whose self-serving project we must be subordinated. Perhaps it is necessary to qualify "we": we are those ordinary citizens who find ourselves on the margins of Khomeini's delineations of Islamic moralities. The colonial analogy is apt when one observes the system of *(intra-)* cultural dispossession. Khomeinists' populist right-wing agendas aim at *extermination of difference*.[4]

4 See Ervand Abrahamian, *Khomeinism: Essays on the Islamic Republic* (Berkeley, CA: University of California, 1993).

An expanded discussion of the "Islamic cultural revolution," which merits serious study, is not within the remit of this text. However, it is important to remember that its systemic ambush on intellectual and artistic life ultimately failed to silence or quell society's innate drives for emanipation, our cultural openness, adaptability and tolerance, and our ability to negotiate *difference*. The free will of the Iranian phenomenon insists, in spite of terror, on asserting its own complex and variegated picture of the individual and society wherever possible. Art has successfully devised survival tactics and means to circumvent the state-imposed monistic vision of existence.

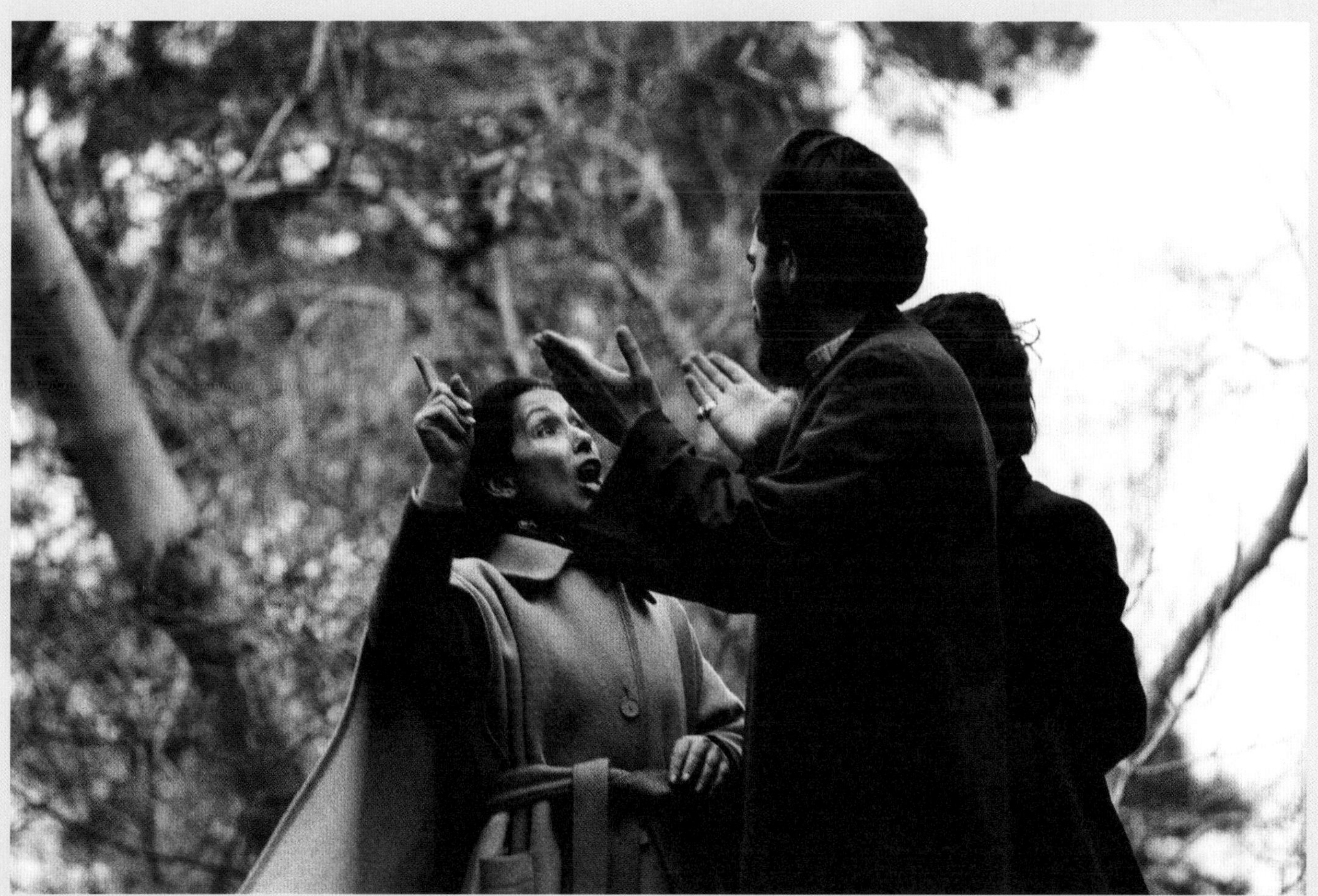

FIG 2 Hengameh Golestan, *Untitled* (Witness '79 series), photograph, March 1979, Anatole France (Neuphle le-Chateau) Street, opposite the USSR (Russian) Embassy, Tehran. © Hengameh Golestan, Courtesy of Vali Mahlouji / Archaeology of the Final Decade.

It is imperative to insist, however: our creativity is *not* enlivened by our harsh existence. That oft-frequented idea is dangerous. Our achievements, our creativities are *not* indebted to oppression. That distorted reading only camouflages, confirms, reinforces fear, an *inability* to stand up to power. It is clear to any free spirit that confronting truth engenders risk, begets unpleasant consequences. It takes great courage to *know* gross abuse, and greater courage to call it out for what it is. But to be asked to contemplate propitiousness in crime? Whitewashing, excusing, glossing over, shrugging off crime, absolving tyranny, in the name of creativity? That would be simply morally, spiritually degrading, hideously demeaning of a people's real-life struggle, humiliating towards the spirit of culture itself. Instead of conceding, of being coerced as an accomplice, we have conscience—to defend our will, our right to dream, to be *different*, open, in contact. Our freedom to *be*.

What Not to let Go

> A civilization that chooses to close its eyes to its most crucial problems is a stricken civilization.
>
> — Aimé Césaire [5]

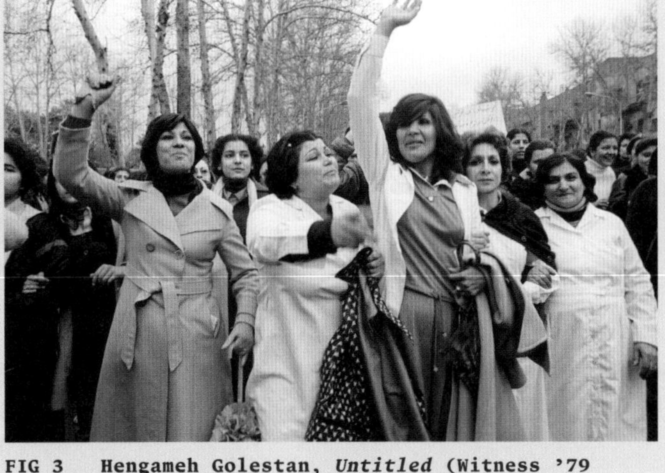

FIG 3 Hengameh Golestan, *Untitled* (Witness '79 series), 1979, Enqelab (Shah Reza) Avenue, outside Tehran University, Tehran. © Hengameh Golestan, courtesy of Vali Mahlouji / Archaeology of the Final Decade.

The purpose of the above polemic is to open a window onto the nature, meaning, and function of culture and heritage in a contemporary space that is under duress, that is administered by fear, where cultural dispossession is experienced internally, intra-culturally. Cultural obstruction is not abstract. It curbs our capacity for expression, limits our experience of existence. Violent amputations, exterminations, vacuums, and evacuations of historical and cultural experience, whether perpetrated by us or by strangers, psychoanalytically speaking, swap containment for alienation. Their *raison d'etre* is to disorientate, to levy an experience of being internally colonized. Life ceases to be safe or pleasurable at home and home becomes a "breeding ground

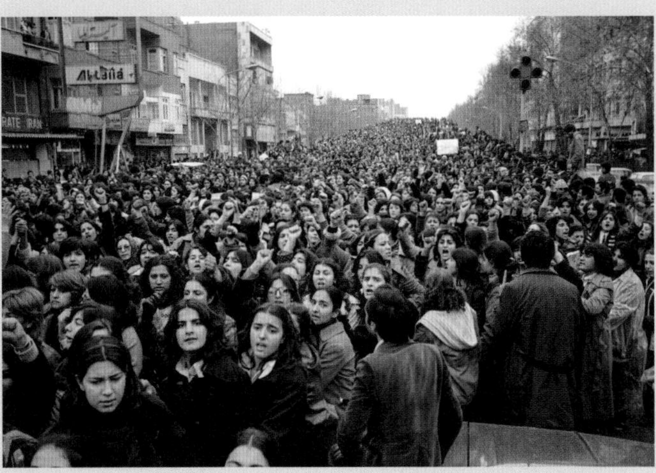

FIG 4 Hengameh Golestan, *Untitled* (Witness '79 series), photograph, March 1979, Shah Reza (Enqelab) Avenue, Hafez Flyover, Tehran. © Hengameh Golestan, courtesy of Vali Mahlouji / Archaeology of the Final Decade.

5 Césaire, *Discourse on Colonialism*.

of every uncertainty of the self," in the Barbadian writer George Lamming's words.[6] The alienating experience of suffering to settle in one's own home is not dissimilar to one of disruptive exile in a foreign land. It too inflicts savage and enduring psychic and historical damage. The annulment, the hollowing out, the *unreadability*, is like what Jacques Derrida calls the "hell of our memory."[7]

When we claim back heritage in such disorienting contexts of dismemberment, we are on a *real* mission. Our claim attains soul and spirit—political charge, historical function, curative meaning—much beyond any mere fetish we may assign to a given desired cultural object. There is no nostalgia or fantasy at play here. Working through (disrupted history) is an antithesis of the trauma which severs us from a relationship to ourselves. Only then, the dreamer is allowed to dream again, a nation to aspire again.

The fraught relationship between heritage, ownership, and assimilation on the one hand, and erasure, amnesia, and threat to cultural health on the other, has been my preoccupation for the past decade. For that purpose, aspects of my curatorial practice involve themselves primarily with issues pertaining to power, radical democracy, conflict, activism, art, and cultural projects that evince social and political commitment. Those subjects/objects of study allow us to penetrate/dislodge historical distortions.

6 George Lamming, quote from Tate Britain, *Life Between Islands*, 2022; *The Emigrants* (London: Michael Joseph, 1954).

7 Jacques Derrida, "Shibboleth for Paul Celan," *Word Traces: Readings of Paul Celan, ed. Aris Fioretos* (Baltimore: Johns Hopkins University Press, 1994), 50.

The Rubble of History

Over the last decade, I committed to an archaeological, forensic excavation of the ruin and traces of the Festival of Arts and published a series of essays on its ideation, lands-cape, and genealogy. I published the first critical evaluations of the festival primarily to address the art historical gap, and the pitifully poor and outright absent critical scholarship.[8] My second objective was to deconstruct the political and cultural condemnations, and the complex areas of polemical contestation that kept its distinct topography, vision, and praxis in obscurity. My mission became one of *restitution* — firstly, to rescue the artefact from history's rubble, and then, to demystify the object as a healthy act of restoration.

As expected, scarcity of original documentary material and voids left by factual blackout following the cultural cleansing reduced critical discourse to crude myth. In that absence, offensive demonizing anti-festival rhetoric has continued to operate with ferocity. It has sometimes ascribed to it superpowers, reaching near-mythological status, with flamboyant histrionics blaming the festival as a cultural trigger even for the 1979 revolution itself.

It quickly became clear that the site of the festival's ruin had the capacity to shift our understanding of not only cultural politics, then and now, but also of rethinking the radical potentialities of culture-writ-large. Delving into its blind spot revealed a rich territory of twentieth century intercultural dialog and hypermodern utopian aspirations. What has been erased is a nexus of the peripheral, the "third world," the dissenting, the unortho-dox, the *counter*cultures, the outsiders offering a precociously profound and sophisticatedly novel postcolonial posturing.

8 Vali Mahlouji, "Perspectives on the Shiraz Arts Festival: A Radical Third World Rewriting," in *Iran Modern*, Fereshteh Daftari, and Layla S. Diba ed. (New Haven, CT: Asia Society Museum / Yale University Press, 2013); also, Vali Mahlouji, The Contested Space: *The Metapolitics of The Festival of Arts, Shiraz-Persepolis, in Unedited History, Iran 1960–2014* (Rome: Musée d'Art Moderne de la ville de Paris, 2014 / MAXXI museo nazionale delle arti del XXI secolo, 2014).

> The need to tell our story to "the rest," to make "the rest" participate in it, had taken on for us, before our liberation and after, the character of an immediate and violent impulse.
>
> — Primo Levi [9]

Before elaborating, it is useful to delineate several clarifications and admissions regarding my militating missions and methodology, ideas, and broader intentions.

I am acutely aware of my own self-identification with the situations that I critically scrutinize. I admit that there is a stringent interplay between my worlds of ideas and cultural interests, and the political urgencies that shape my personal life. The dynamic and symbiotic interplay between the two is integral to my practice. The barbarity inflicted on citizen and society in Iran is also a personal experience. It has deeply shaped my superhistorical militancy. Considering my tight focus of interest, I pursue a stable line of connection: the matrix linking trace, time, and trauma. I place at the center of my attention the complex layered relationships between trace and memory, fragment and whole, ruin and monument. In this regard, my work bears in mind the relational dynamics between memory, fact and discourse, objective truth and narrative or experience.

My method is that of the archaeologist, or that of thepsychoanalyst, simply for the reason that my training and experience has been in those disciplines. My investigations often start from a mark of hidden existence, a footprint of past activity: where we detect traces, marks, tracks, contours, deposits, barely visible vestigial remains, or where there are injuries, omissions, and cavities. Pursuing those evidentiary traces have proved enormously rewarding if and when the trace comes to reveal itself as a container or carrier of "deep memory": as a signifier of something in and of the past that has left behind an indelible imprint on the present. My work is about looking (in the Benjaminian sense) for radical potentials embedded within such sites. It is to release the "working through" potential of the evidentiary traces so that we, the inheritors, may mediate memory away from myth towards experience. As excavator, my approach considers the *ruin-as-monument* as a subterranean repository of precious mnemonic and experiential material. It holds firmly to the belief that reactivation of that micro-ecology of trauma — the release of the repressed — reveals knowledge and meanings, generates intellectual and affective experiences, and sheds light on the macro social and political level in the here and now, and by extension, on the present historic struggles for civil and democratic rights.

Refuting and contaminating the dominant narrative of the oppressor is a prerequisite for freeing up the terrain of the condemned/absented *event-object* for a present-day postmortem. Using a psychoanalytic analogy, my impulse follows the premise that, in Sigmund Freud's words, the repressed is to be commemorated as monument to enhance a healthy relationship to history, to shift from a developmentally-arrested position of *living-with-ghosts*.[10] It is only then that we may reckon with and reflect upon history, the precise nature of justice, the anonymity of death, the violence of erasure. To bear witness. Otherwise, as citizens, we remain complicit observers.

9 Primo Levi, *Survival in Auschwitz*, trans. Stuart Woolf (New York, NY: Collier Books, 1961), 5–6.

10 Sigmund Freud, "The Aetiology of Hysteria," in *The Standard Edition of the Complete Psychological Works of Sigmund Freud, vol. III: Early Psycho-Analytic Publications* (1893–1899), (London: Hogarth Press and the Institute of Psycho-analysis, 1962),192.

> The philosopher, as a necessary man of tomorrow and the day after tomorrow, has always found himself ... in opposition to his today.
>
> — Nietzsche

The Festival of Arts, Shiraz-Persepolis (1967–77), was undoubtedly, in my view, the boldest and most optimistic artistic response to the climate of its time. A triumph of creative vital diversity over antagonistic adversarial antipathy. A head-on incursion into the existential question of the future of culture. Affirmative. Tolerant. Elevating the free, the strong. An advocate of a Nietzschean restlessness towards moderation and restraint. Its temperament that of overcoming stillness and inhibition. Dionysian destructiveness and regeneration, its norm. Revitalization and regeneration of native life and the forms it takes, its intention and practice. Transforming Asian and African cultures through a *utopian* proposition, its mission.

> Psychoanalysis has taught that the dead—a dead parent, for example—can be more alive for us, more powerful, more scary, than the living. It is the question of ghosts.
>
> — Jacques Derrida [11]

It is not surprising, therefore, that the Islamist cultural cleansing stigmatized the Festival of Arts and labeled its genealogies the highest order of *counter-revolutionary decadence.* A festival of such diversity and breadth of criticality, form, and aesthetics, as any critical evaluation would attest, is antithetical to totalitarian politics. Such a festival is a philosophical attitude. Its inquiry is open-ended, philosophical. It is always on the mark of freedom — propelled by euphoric optimism, openness, emancipation, inclusivity. It brings the unknown *other* right inside the city walls. It thrives on a *phyloxenic* curiosity towards the other. It is an open-ended act of courage. It is genetically unpredictable, dangerous. Its ideological bomb could be anywhere.

11 Mitchell Stephens, "Jacques Derrida," *New York Times Magazine* (January 23, 1994).

Deploying the timeworn clichés—counter-revolutionary, decadent, immoral, obscene, blasphemous—the targeting was astute, yet unoriginal. Those malleable accusations are over-deployed across history: applied to individuals, groups, ideas, objects, artefacts, events, even memories. It is hardly surprising that even the ghost of the festival's cultural artefact would instill such enduring concern and fear. Over forty years on from its condemnation, official history keeps it under wraps.

Accordingly, all archives and documents associated with the festival, collated by the National Iranian Radio and Television (NIRT) — the festival's official founder, sponsor and organizer, headed by Reza Ghotbi—were banned. The archives, specifically amassed for public dissemination by the NIRT, were removed from public circulation. The authorities forbade access to any of the festival's trove of audio and video recordings, photographic documentations of rehearsals and performances, its vast array of publica-tions, which included critical research into theater, conferences, annual catalogues with their exten-sive and in-depth artistic contents, playscripts, bulletins published daily during each festival, program note booklets, and posters. To date, the material remains inaccessible and censored.

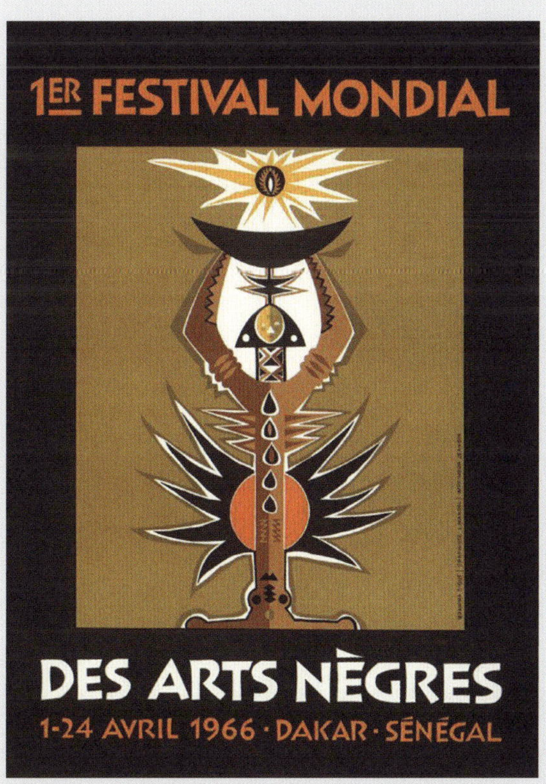

FIG 5 Poster of the First World Festival of Negro Arts, Dakar, Senegal (1966). It was a month-long celebration of African culture, poetry, sculpture, painting, music, cinema, theatre, fashion, architecture, design and dance from artists and performers of Africa and the African diaspora.

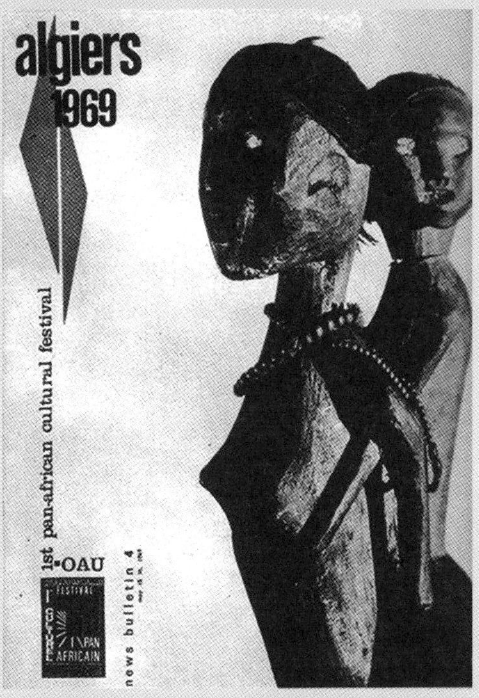

FIG 6 Poster of Festival panafricain d'Alger, (1969). It was one of the great cultural manifestations of Pan-Africanism in the twentieth century, and it marks a major attempt to collect and bring together artists and intellectuals of the African diaspora.

Breaking Down the Proscenium

> The connotation of courage, which we now feel to be an indispensable
> quality of the hero, is in fact already present in a willingness
> to act and speak at all, to insert one's self into the world
> and begin a story of one's own."
>
> — Hannah Arendt[12]

12 Hannah Arendt, *The Human Condition* (Chicago, IL: The University of Chicago, 1958), 186–87.

Shiraz-Persepolis's politics of festival correlated with only a handful of other performance festivals: the festivals of Belgrade and Nancy via Dakar and Algiers. Collectively, in various measures, those internationalist solidarities dismantled the Eurocentric myth of culture. Each, in their own way, emancipated new and subversive postcolonial cultural mappings. Of those, only the Belgrade International Theatre Festival (BITEF), which was also inaugurated in 1967 like Shiraz-Persepolis, survives the political shifts of the late twentieth century. The university-based Nancy World Theatre Festival opened four years earlier in 1963 but folded in 1988. At Nancy and Belgrade, the politics of society and art defended radical desires to "destroy the myth of culture"[13]—to break down hierarchies of high and low, and geospatial divisions of culture. Belgrade, and especially Nancy, challenged systems of official culture from within the very heart of Europe. Their transnationalism correlated closely with the politics of Shiraz-Persepolis, with the difference that they operated within Europe while the latter operated on the ground outside and beyond Europe. The Senegalese and Algerian festivals, First World Festival of Negro Arts in Dakar (1966), and Festival panafricain d'Alger (1969), shone like stars. They rose as two inspiriting markers of African renaissance. Over two thousand writers, artists, and performers from Africa and the African diaspora participated in the historic Dakar event. They were limited to a single iteration, but they epitomized the spirit and experience of vast swathes of human culture and history, and their legacy leaves an enduring imprint. It was FESTAC World Black and African Festival of Arts and Culture in Lagos, Nigeria, that brought African cultures and diasporas together once again in 1977. A new FESTAC is due to take place in Zanzibar in 2022.

13 Roberta Minnucci, *Poor Art / Arte Povera, Italian Influences, British Responses* (London: Estorick Collection of Modern Art, 2017), referring to Germano Celant's critique in "Untitled," in *Arte Povera*, ed. Eva Madelung (Munich: Kunstverein, 1971), published in English in *Arte Povera. storie e protagonisti / Arte Povera. Histories and protagonists*, 155–62.

> I have been to the mountaintop.
> Only when it is dark, can you see the stars.
>
> — Martin Luther King Jr.[14]

Those were auspicious years (1950s–70s) for freedom-seekers: in 1960 alone, seventeen African nations severed French colonial ties, including Senegal, which beckoned African pride in its historic World Festival of Negro Arts in Dakar only six years later. The era radiated, to borrow from Martin Luther King, "a revolution of values,"[15] and unleashed dreams and aspirations, revolutions and manifestations of change that had art and politics enmeshed and spilling onto the streets. But the roads and ideals to social betterments also met dark and deranged antimonies. Power adjustments were marred with battlefields and witch-hunts, dead-ends, and proxy wars.[16] Decolonization, nevertheless, generated an uninhibited flourishing of new narrative-shifting cultural initiatives in a modern context, a network to which Shiraz-Persepolis also belonged.[17] Their carefully-directed missions harnessed regional and transnational alliances and purposes. They reimagined rekindling millennia-old reciprocities that had been severed by European interventions. Although, it was also the case that emergent and circumscribed *nativisms* occasionally acquiesced into postcolonial dissonances.

> Either we go up together, or we go down together.
>
> — Martin Luther King Jr.[18]

14 "I've Been to the Mountaintop" is the popular title of the last speech delivered by Martin Luther King Jr. on April 3, 1968, at the Mason Temple in Memphis, Tennessee, the day before his assassination. The speech was delivered to the striking sanitation workers of Memphis.

15 Martin Luther King. *Ibid.*

16 The era was marked by post-McCarthyist witch-hunts of intellectuals, divisive dead-ends, and proxy wars of the Cold War, inherited scars of Stalinist genocidal pogroms, deep ravages of the Vietnam War (1955–75), inhumanities of Chairman Mao's Cultural Revolution (1966–76), backlashes against civil rights movements, and the assassinations of Malcolm X in 1965 and Martin Luther King Jr. in 1968. Southern Europe–the home countries of Constantine Cavafis, Federico Garcia Lorca, and Fernando Pessoa–were throttled under the grip of military fascist regimes with various churches in collusion.

17 The Bienal de São Paulo was launched in 1951. The Alexandria International Biennial for Mediterranean Countries was inaugurated in 1955. Tehran held its first Biennial in 1958. Moscow opened its film festival in 1959. Zagreb founded its international contemporary Music Biennial in 1961. The First Biennale of Arab Art was held in Baghdad in 1974.

18 Martin Luther King, op. cit.

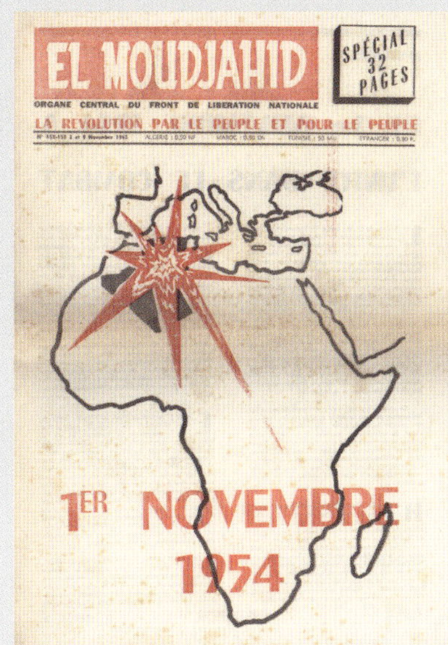

FIG 8 Official Newspaper of the National Liberation Front, El Moudjahid, November 1, 1954. It declares the ensuing Algerian revolution as "The Revolution by the People, for the People." Algeria became the hub of revolutionaries and anti-colonoial progressives from all over the world.

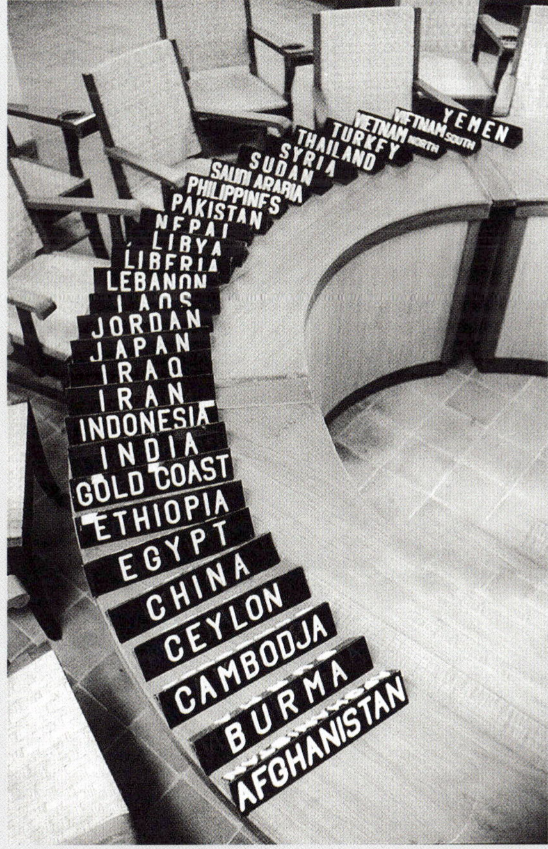

FIG 7 Bandung Conference, April 18-24, 1955, Indonesia. Bandung Conference was the first large-scale Afro-Asian conference organized by Indonesia, Burma, Pakistan, Sri Lanka, and India, with twenty-nine participating countries.

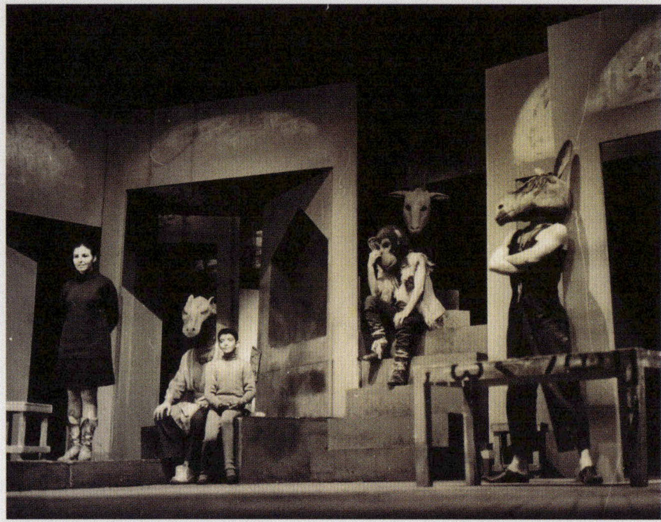

FIG 9 Shahr-e Qesseh (City of Tales): Bijan Mofid (playwright and director) University Hall, 1968. Courtesy of Dariush Hajir and Bijan Mofid Foundation / Vali Mahlouji / Archaeology of the Final Decade.

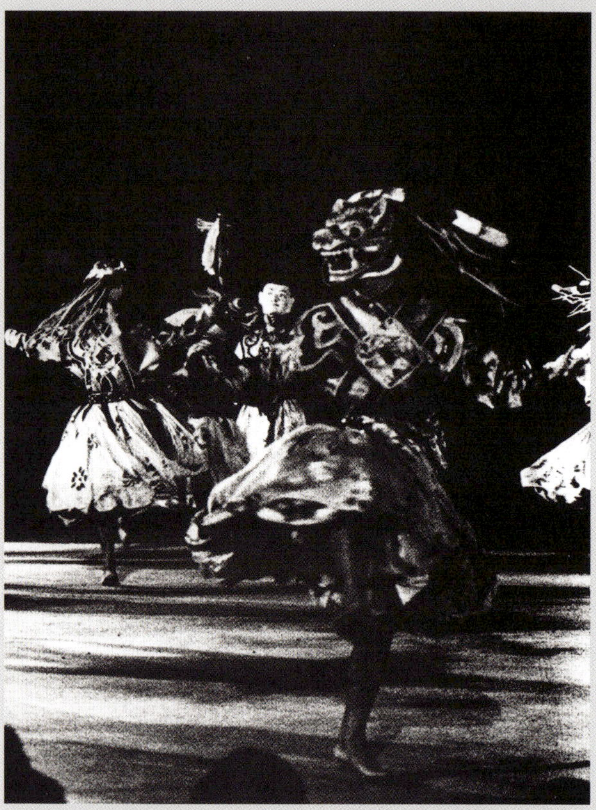

FIG 10 "Chham," Masked Ceremonial Dances of Bhutan: Sacred and magic ancient Buddhist dances: "Dramitse Nga Cham" (Drum Dance of Dramitse); "Shawo Shachi" (Dance of the Stag & the Hounds); "Dri Ging" (Sword Dance); "Nga Ging" (Drum Dance); "Pachham" (Dance of the Heroes); "Pholay Molay" (Dance of the Noblemen & Ladies), Dasho Sithey (director), Jahan-Nama Garden, 1976. Courtesy of Vali Mahlouji / Archaeology of the Final Decade.

Most notably, the Festival panafricain d'Alger of 1969 addressed an internal postcolonial conflict that emerged between *Negritude/Blackness* and *Africanism*. In Algiers, the African continent came together as a unified and cross-pollinating entity with a shared set of struggles and legacies. By 1977, in Lagos the FESTAC festival referred to both "Black" and "African" in its title. For all intents and purposes, though, the earliest of such African festivals—the First World Festival of Negro Arts in 1966—deliberately distinguished between North Africa and Black sub-Saharan Africa. It was masterminded by Léopold Sédar Senghor, independent Senegal's first leader and one of the champions of negritude as a paradigm. The poet Senghor had dedicated decades to the cause, as an active and founding thinker of the emancipatory negritude movement, with the literary giant Aimé Césaire and others such as Alain Leroy Locke. In Dakar, *Blackness* was celebrated gloriously and on an unprecedented scale. Over two thousand artists and performers came together from all around Black Africa and its diasporas, especially the Americas. North Africans were not invited to Senghor's grand celebration of negritude at Dakar. That certainly aggravated unresolved issues and tightened a rift between various postcolonial African impulses and urgencies, which the Algiers and later Lagos festivals consciously addressed.

Cultural Particularism—Unity of Contradictions

Unlike Dakar and Algiers, Shiraz-Persepolis bypassed any affirmation of raciality, ethnocentricity, or regionality. Shiraz-Persepolis came from a somewhat particular political trajectory. Its artistic and political remit was insistently driven by *cultural particularism* but not the delineation of *difference*. There may be a good reason for that: Iran's experience of colonialism was tangential. It certainly suffered major political, economic, and cultural consequences of semicolonial Anglo-Russian exploitations, especially in the nineteenth century, but it was one of only a handful of geographies that never officially fell under colonial rule. It perceived its cultural, linguistic, and ethnic soul and spirit as having escaped, for the most part, intact and unbroken by mainstream disturbances and disorders, and moral indignations of colonial angst and damage.

In contrast, the rhetoric of the festival, as articulated in its publications, returns regularly to its own articulation of universalism, and a dream of unity calling for, in Edward Said's words, "a postcolonial intellectual project" looking to "expand the area of overlapping community between the metropolitan and formerly colonized societies."[19] Their dream of unity rejects any unifying reductivist principle that subsumes world cultures under the rhetoric of a globalized culture. Conversely, by upholding particularism and coexistences across time and space, it focuses on achieving a fertile dialectic between values of permanence and change, eternal and new, in what Marshall Berman refers to as "a contradictory unity, a unity of disunity."[20] Here, the juxtaposition of the anti- and post- colonial were complementary relationally reinforcing or extending a *whole*.

Its ideation and praxis interrogated "the rise of Europe" and insisted on a radical shift towards the *present*. Its cosmopolitan stage protested the European construction of "world civilization." Instead, it determinedly negotiated universal intercultural connectivity, and permeating, circulating encounters of heterogeneous expressions. Its territory belonged to the confrontation of diversities, competing solidarities, proliferating visions. A contested site of an interconnected world, following a liberal praxis of pluralistic accommodation of the *other in the narratives of the same*. It revolted against the impairments of "African enslavement, Latin American conquest, and Asian subjugation."[21] Its stage was close to what Sylvia Wynter calls "Unsettling the Coloniality of Being/Power/Truth/Freedom"[22] —in essence, an equalizing call for what Homi Bhabha would name a "third world re-writing."[23] It shifted the center of gravity towards the (re-emerging) *other*, intent on annulling colonialism as a system of exploitation or articulation of cultural dominance. The annulment, the bypassing, was done not through the binaries of *us* and *them*, but through the realization of a juxtapositional universality (temporal, spatial, and political) and an idealistic dream of a *utopian unity of disunities*. With a bold and optimistic drive, the directors of the festival reimagined an open universal arena for permeability, circulation, and mutual cross-cultural

19 Edward Said, "Intellectuals in the Post-Colonial World," in *Salgamundi*, no. 70/71 (New York, NY: Skidmore College, 1986), 46.

20 Marshall Berman, *All that is Solid Melts into Air: The Experience of Modernity* (New York, NY: Simon and Schuster, 1982), 23.

21 Sylvia Wynter, "Unsettling the Coloniality of Being/Power/Truth/Freedom: Towards the Human, After Man, Its Overrepresentation—An Argument," *The New Centennial Review*, vol. 3, no. 3, "Coloniality's Persistence" (Fall 2003): 263.

22 Ibid., 257–33.

23 Homi Bhabha, The Location of Culture (London: Routledge, 1994), 2.

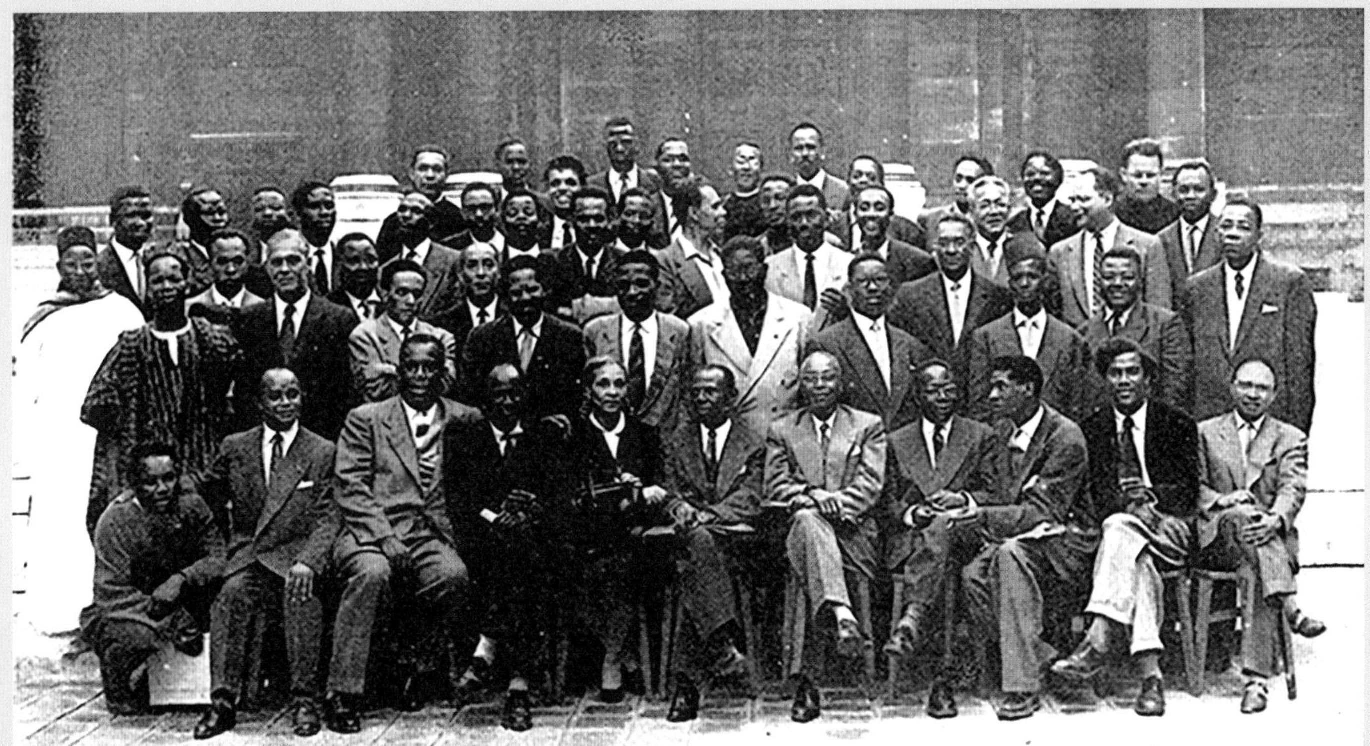

FIG 11 First Congress of Black Writers and Artists, Paris, 1956.

exchange. They self-consciously set out to map coexisting heterogeneous truths within a modern discourse providing meaning to possibilities of disjointed, dispersed, and interchangeable points of view across constructs of "first" and "third" worlds: archaic/traditional/contemporary. It was the most powerfully germinal (predating the seminal Havana Biennials of 1986 and 1989 by two decades), inventive, and enduring project of its kind to triumph in that mission—at least for the limited duration of its lifespan. Shiraz-Persepolis was uniquely successful in realizing that sophisticated aspiration and actualizing a utopian model for *unified coexistences of being* from within the "third" world. For a couple of intense weeks every year, for eleven years, it was the only enterprise for alterity of its kind and scale in the world—unlike Belgrade and Nancy, it was incubated in and projected from the dissenting so-called "periphery."

Otherness in Sameness—Sameness in Otherness

Shiraz-Persepolis' *euphoria of togetherness* was by no means a unique vision. In fact, a tour of writings of the time, especially of African thinkers, reminds us of as much about radical *otherness* as it does about the dream of *otherness in sameness* or *sameness in otherness*. To quote Aimé Césaire, for example:

> I have a different idea of a universal.
> It is of a universal rich with all that is particular,
> rich with all the particulars there are,
> the deepening of each particular, the
> coexistence of them all.
>
> ... and no race possesses the monopoly of
> beauty, of intelligence, of force.
> And there is a place for all at the rendezvous
> of victory.
>
> — Aimé Césaire[24]

From their own vantage point, the directors of Shiraz-Persepolis seized the moment to intervene at the intersection of "modernism," art, and revolution. They clearly believed that in the aftermath of the collapse of European hegemonies, a fluid artistic exchange was possible across geo-graphies, histories, and forms in ways and on a scale that had never been possible before. They acted on the conviction that such inter-geopolitical and inter-historical dialog are necessary for human emancipation and for realizing a progressive postcolonial coexistence.

24 Aimé Césaire, *Return to My Native Land*. (Harmondsworth: Penguin, 1969), 85.

The Imperative to Remain Awake

> "Eternal streams flow out of the One.
> You and I are nothing in it, nameless.
> Lalon says: If only I knew 'me,'
> all riddles would be solved!"
>
> — Lalon Fakir[25]

25 Lalon Fakir (1772-1890) was a Bengali Baul saint, songwriter, and social reformer who rejected "all distinctions of caste and creed," resonating with the notion of a universalist utopia and inspiring many twentieth-century poets and thinkers.

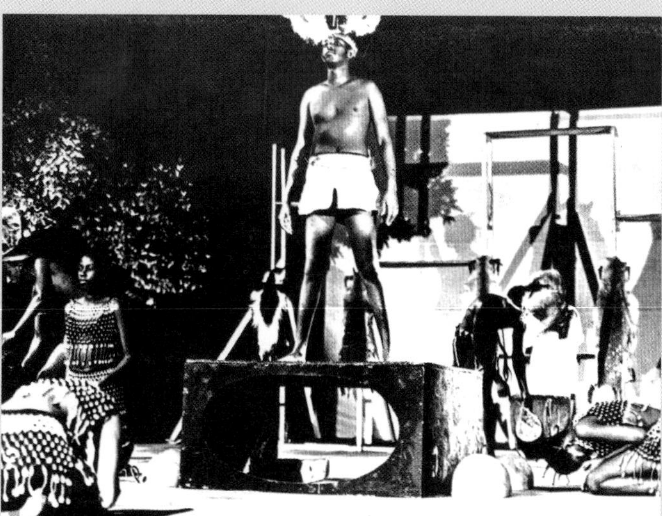

FIG 12 Renga Moi, Robert Serumaga (playwright and director), African dance-drama, National Theater of Uganda, Saray-e Moshir, 1975. Courtesy of Vali Mahlouji / Archaeology of the Final Decade.

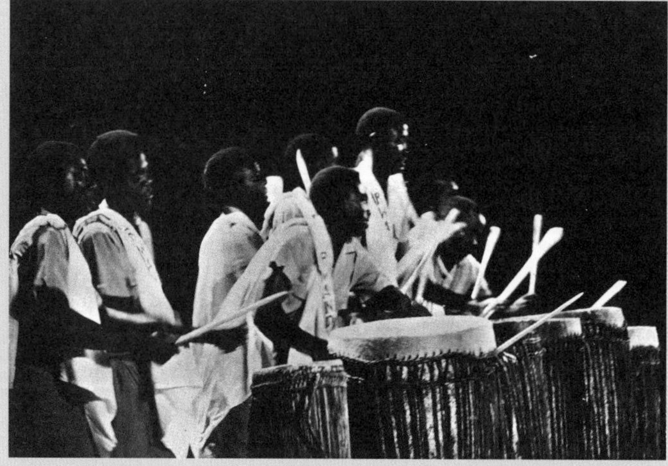

FIG 13 Rwanda Drum Ensemble, Open-Air Theater, 1969. Courtesy of Vali Mahlouji / Archaeology of the Final Decade.

If the "ethnic other" were to take the lead, to realize the dream of a new world order, then it was imperative for its civilizations to be awake. Without unlocking the potential of its Indigeneity, unleashing the power of its ethnic ingenuity, and encouraging an intellectual and cultural return to its "authentic self," then the mission of advancing contemporary reality would not be realized.[26] The regenerative liberation of its compressed forces, the free explosion of its soul, would sever the colonial experience once and for all. That was the shared sentiment and belief.

26 At Shiraz-Persepolis, over one-fifth of all performances across the eleven years were solely dedicated to Iranian classical, traditional, folk, and contemporary compositions. The largest number of foreign artists to perform hailed from the Indian subcontinent. The festival is credited for creating modern Iranian audiences for musical forms that were otherwise geographically or culturally sidelined. Iranian musicians shared the stage with the likes of Bismillah Khan, Vilayat Khan, *mizmar* players of the Nile Valley, Munir Bashir, Iannis Xenakis, Bruno Maderna, John Cage, Max Roach, Abbey Lincoln, Tran Van Khe, and Krzysztof Penderecki. Critical evaluations of local modes encompassed a wide archaic/contemporary genealogical spectrum of performance, ranging from indigenous Iranian *ta'zieh* ritual performances and *commedia dell'arte* style *ru-howzi* chamber pieces in 1967, to the promotion of a new wave of culturally unconventional contemporary theatrical expressions, which saw the premiering of two seminal pieces in 1968—Abbas Nalbandian's *Pazhouheshi (Research …)* and Bijan Mofid's *Shahr-e Qesseh (City of Tales)*.

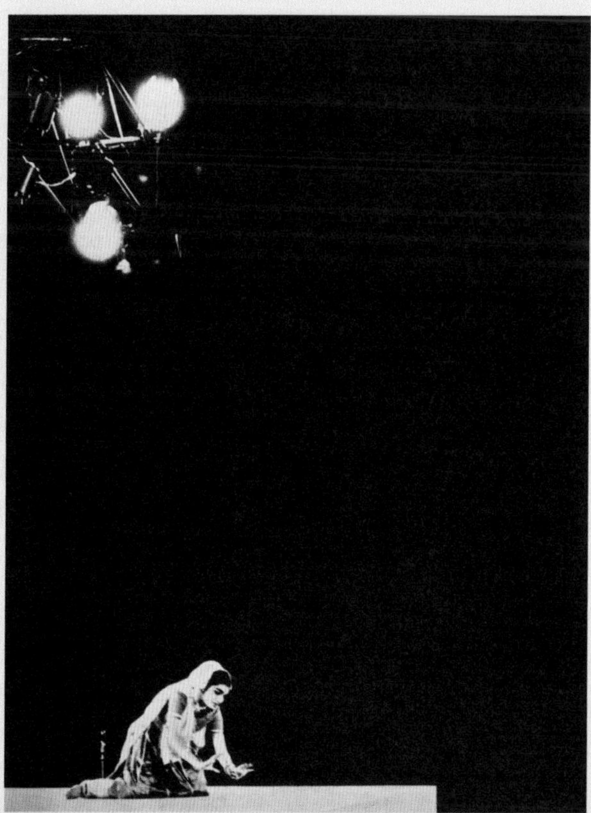

FIG 14 Kathak, Classical Indian Dance, Uma Sharma (performer), Open-Air Theater, 1969. Courtesy of Vali Mahlouji / Archaeology of the Final Decade.

Origins and the Eternal Return

Their "return to the self" opposed the Heideggerian notion of horizontal time. They embraced, conversely, cyclical and vertical models of time as more authentic temporal structures.[27] Those alternative philosophies of time, which have ancient roots in Asian thought, accommodate concurrences of ancestral and modern and the simultaneity of opposites. Vertical time holds the past, present, and future on the same time plain. Iranian philosopher Daryush Shayegan often returned to the notion of the "kaleidoscopic vision" to explain the parallel concurrence of old and new.[28] Shayegan elaborates on the coexistence of an intoxicating quest for the archaic with a driving desire for all that is modern.[29] The model embraces simultaneous infatuations with constancy/change, eternal/new. Those Asian thoughts have long exerted influence on Europe. In *Thus Spoke Zarathustra*, Friedrich Nietzsche elaborates on the concept of "eternal return"—all energy and existence within the universe is eternal and constantly recurring.[30] Through the same interchange of ideas, many European philosophers, from Winckelmann and Schiller to Goethe and Nietzsche, declare sympathy for the archaics "as a possible source of direction for moderns."[31]

27 Kuki Shūzō (1888–1941) was a Japanese philosopher who theorized the Oriental notion of time (cyclical time) as a way of escaping inauthentic temporal models. He further discussed the intellectual negation of time, found in "nirvana," associated with Buddhism, and the voluntarist innate rejection of time as "bushido," which follows an unconcern with temporal structures.

28 Daryush Shayegan, "Le Miroir de L'Ame d'un Peuple," *Le Regard Persan* (Paris: Espace Electra, Les Musées de la Ville de Paris, 2001).

29 Shayegan, "Le Miroir."

30 *Thus Spoke Zarathustra*, trans. Adrian del Caro, ed. Robert Pippin (Cambridge: Cambridge University Press, 2006).

31 Adrian del Caro, "Dionysian Classicism, or Nietzsche's Appropriation of an Aesthetic Norm," *Journal of the History of Ideas*, vol. 50, no. 4 (October–December 1989): 589–605.

> Pass from matter to spirit. Matter is diversity; spirit is light, life and unity.
>
> — Mohammad Iqbal [32]

By its third iteration, the curation instrumentalized a distinct strategy to put non-European and European traditions on the map as valid and equal. It consciously designed programmes to tap into repositories where non-European expressions were highly developed. That was actualized in 1969 around percussion. Percussive forms were identified as the oldest and most basic of instrumental types, indigenous to all cultures. Rhythm, as the most fundamental ingredient to all music, signified a return to basic elemental instinctual drives. The festival insisted on an unrelenting and dynamic progression, constituting an international sonic narrative—one that specifically emphasized the skill and sophistication of Asian and African percussives. Its articulation of unification and universalism through sound allowed for fluid programming, opening with Balinese *gamelan Gong Kebyar*, and closing with Iannis Xenakis' *Persephassa*, a site-specific composition in the ruins of Persepolis. Uma Sharma dancing Indian *kathak*, Max Roach and Abbey Lincoln, Brazilian Percussion Ensemble, and Rwanda Drum Ensemble (which made its world debut) were all amongst the performers. Iranian *tombak* by Hossein Tehran and *santur* by Faramarz Payvar shared a stage with Chien-Tai Chen playing Chinese yangqin.

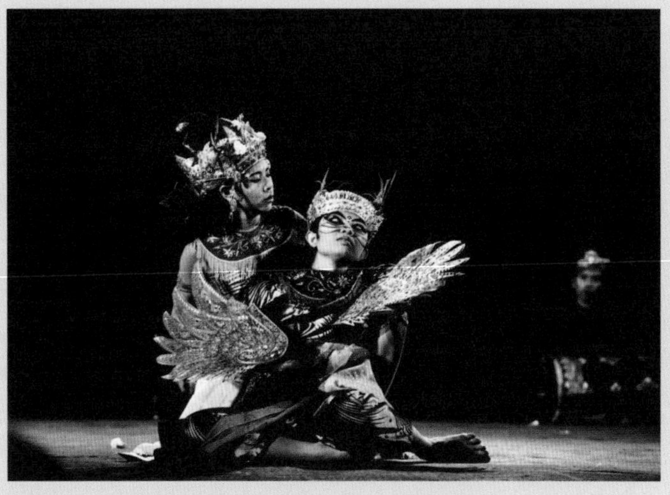

> It is necessary to recover the primeval force. [33]
>
> For many people ... in modern life, it is something organic and natural, to look for the original, for the first, for the primary, for the true, which has no practical utilization... but is a completely other proposal.
>
> — Jerzy Grotowski [34]

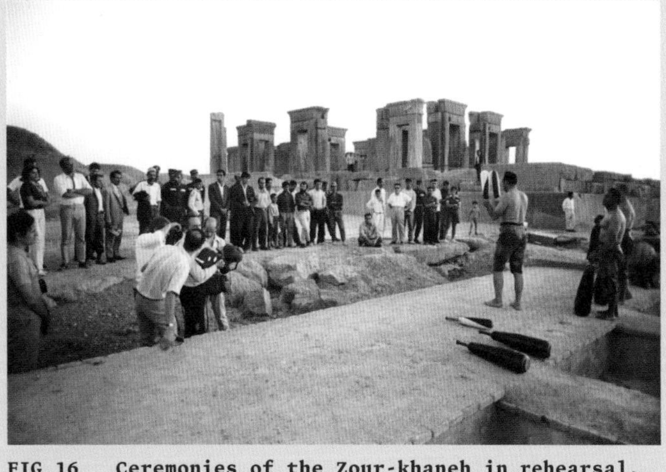

FIG 15 Balinese Gamelan and traditional dances: Legong Keraton and Tari Topeng Masked Dancers, Open Air Theater, 1969. Courtesy of Vali Mahlouji / Archaeology of the Final Decade / Photograph Malie Letrange.

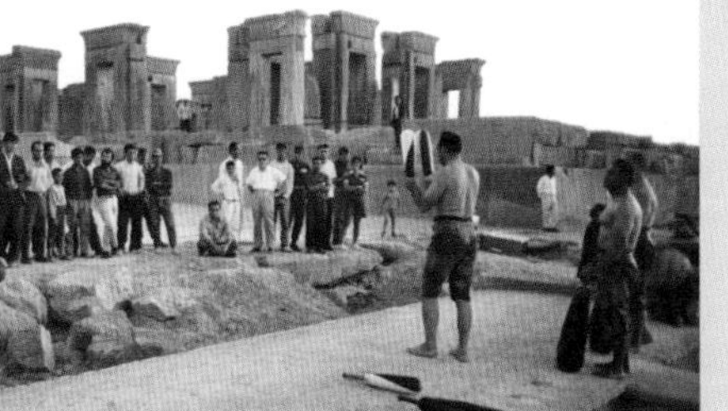

FIG 16 Ceremonies of the Zour-khaneh in rehearsal, Persepolis, 1969. Courtesy of Archaeology of the Final Decade / Photo Malie Letrange.

32 Mohammad Iqbal, *Discourses of Iqbal*, 1st ed. (Lahore, Sh. Ghulam Ali: 1979).

33 Tadeusz Kantor (1915–90), Polish theater director renowned for revolutionary theatrical performances, and the founder of "Cricot 2" theater company.

34 Jerzy Grotowski in *Quien Es Grotowski*, a documentary directed by Mercedes Gregory, 1980.

The years between 1969 and 1974 represent a very high point of experimentation with meta-theatrical preternatural investigations, with programmes around *Theatre and Ritual*, and themes of *Third World Theatre* and *Contemporary Theatre from Traditional Societies*. By design and by default, consciously and circumstantially, the festival became the principal bedrock and pioneering launch pad for novel opportunities for performers to supplant conventional definitions of modern and traditional, native and alien.

> "Ritual theater" was the theme of the Fourth Festival—an appropriate choice since Asia still remains a rich storehouse of ritual and ceremony and after a long period of lack of interest, the West is once again rediscovering its roots in Asian arts. Shiraz was the ideal meeting place for the purpose.
>
> — Eighth Festival of Arts,
> Shiraz-Persepolis Program[35]

The festival dedicated itself to revitalising interest in the archaic core of drama and the roots of music and performance—to the revelation of common sources and universal pools, and to insight into the unconscious world of the collective. The performative—represented by the ritual, ecstatic, epiphanic, cathartic, "primitive"—was pitched to supplant the textual as a deliberate retraction from the European tradition towards a purer emotional, but non-sentimental, core of drama. Once text is bypassed as the carrier of symbolic meaning, the audience may transcend the need for rational discourse and arrive at alternate modes of consciousness.[36]

> A real theatrical experience shakes the calm of the senses, liberates the compressed unconscious and drives towards a kind of potential revolt ...
>
> — Antonin Artaud[37]

Experiments into alternate modes of consciousness produced a seminal transnational site-specific commission in 1971 called *Orghast*, of which the British poet Ted Hughes said:

> The point was to create a precise but open and inviting language, inviting to a lost world we wanted to explore. Music is one such language—mathematically precise, but completely mysterious and open, giving access to a deeper world, closed to direct analysis [...] If you imagine music buried in the earth for a few thousand years, decayed back to its sources, not the perfectly structured thing we know as music, then that is what we tried to unearth. A language belonging below the levels where differences appear, close to the inner life of what we've chosen as our material, but expressive to all people, powerfully, truly, precisely."
>
> — Ted Hughes[38]

> In art, man reveals *himself* and not his objects.[39]

> To the ancestors, only when the spiritual part of man was awakened had art served its basic purpose. For in his cosmic dance in space and time man is forever seeking to unravel the secrets and the infinite and silent world of the spirit, a world that is forever beckoning him."
>
> — William Greaves[40]

---

35 Original catalogue of the Festival of Arts, Shiraz-Persepolis, 1974, Archaeology of the Final Decade Archives.

36 Under the theme of *Theatre and Ritual* in 1970, a wide range of expressions included: influential Polish creator Jerzy Grotowski with Calderon's *The Constant Prince*; an adaptation of Gorgani's Persian verse *Vis-o-Ramin*, by Mahin Tajadod and director Arby Ovanessian; le Ballet National du Sénégal on its first visit to Asia; Jean Genet's *Les Bonnes* by director Victor Garcia and Compañia Núria Espert; *Fire*, by Bread & Puppet Theatre, directed by Peter Schumann; Iranian ritual performance *ta'zieh* of *Moslem ibn Aqeel*; classical sitar by Ravi Shankar; and classical Indian dance by Yamini Krishnamurti.

37 Antonin Artaud was a French radical dramatist, poet, essayist, actor, and theater director, who strove to "liberate the human subconscious and reveal man to himself."

38 Ted Hughes quoted in *Albert Hunt and Geoffrey Reeves*, Peter Brook, *Directors in Perspective* (Cambridge: Cambridge University Press, 1995), 157.

39 Borrowed from Rabindranath Tagore (https://quotepark.com/authors/rabindranath-tagore/?page=6).

40 Narration from the film *First World Festival of Negro Arts* by African-American filmmaker William Greaves, which was officially commissioned to document the Dakar festival, Spring 1966.

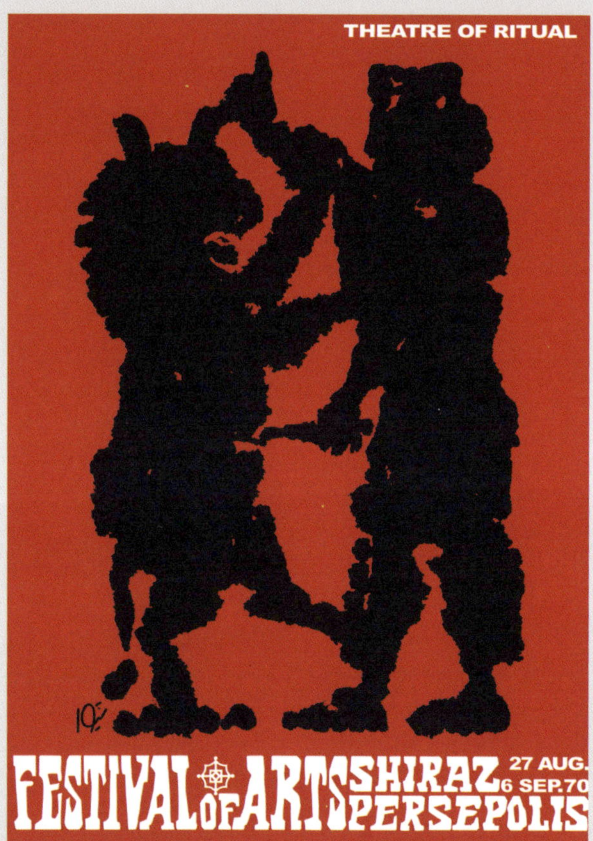

FIG 17 Poster of the Fourth Festival of Arts, Shiraz-Perseolis, 1970, designed by Ghobad Shiva. Courtesy of Vali Mahlouji / Archaeology of the Final Decade / Ghobad Shiva.

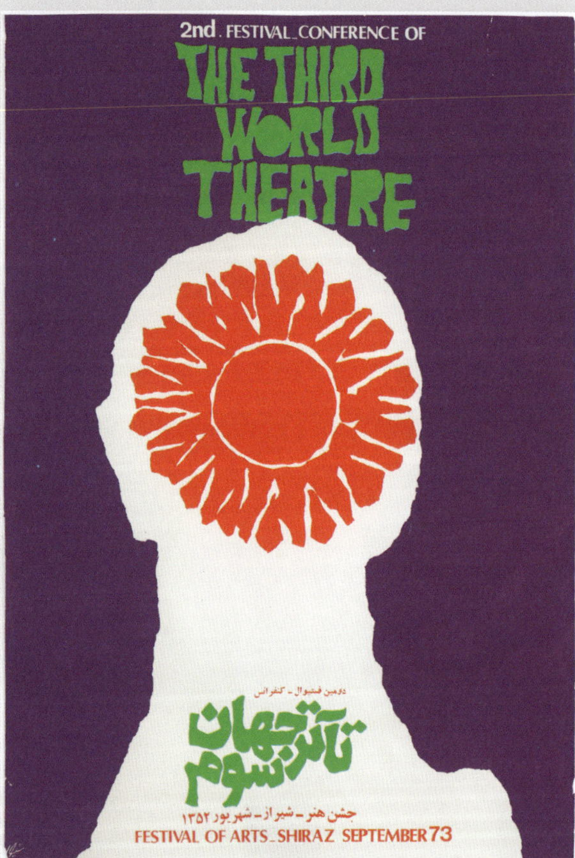

FIG 18 Poster of the Third World Theatre—2nd World Festival and Conference, 1973, designed by Ghobad Shiva. Commissioned by 7th Festival of Arts, Shiraz-Persepolis. Courtesy of Vali Mahlouji / Archaeology of the Final Decade / Ghobad Shiva.

Shifting contemporary cultural reality was exercised through cyclical confrontations and self-confrontations. Over its span of eleven years, the curation integrated an impressive constellation of diverse expressions.[41] With insightful knowledge into the archaic appeal of *revelations of beauty through the wisdoms of the ancestors* as dreamt by the dreamer Aimé Césaire, the directors cunningly co-opted a natural ally in the internationally fluid neo-avant-garde, who explicitly venerated the "third world" as the force behind the revolution. They engaged artists and performers crossing over from both sides of the European iron curtain and the American spheres who were keen to shed the constrictions of their own traditions, and in doing so, would

41 Japanese Noh (making its first appearance outside Japan), numerous Indian *kathakali* performances, Tadeusz Kantor, Jerzy Grotowski, Joseph Chaikin, Andrei Serban, Shuji Terayama, Ravi Shankar and classical Indian dance by Yamini Krishnamurti, Olivier Messiaen, Tran Van Khe & Tran Quang Hai Duo and Tran Van Khe (from war-torn Vietnam), composers John Cage and Karlheinz Stockhausen (who had a retrospective in 1972), Bismillah Khan, Vilayat Khan, *mizmar* players of the Nile Valley, Munir Bashir, Bread and Fire, controversial Squat Theatre from Hungary, Polish Teatr STU with a world premiére, and Núria Espert (who remarked in her interview to the author that she found relative freedom in Shiraz from the dictatorial constraints of Francoist Spain), Robert Serumaga staged the Ugandan contemporary dance-drama *Renga Moi*, which returned to the legend of *Acoli*. Le Ballet National du Sénégal participated with traditional dances and music in the fourth Festival in 1970, followed by L'Ensemble Lyrique du Senegal in 1976. Sardono Kusumo presented Indonesian dance-drama *Kechak* with the people of the village of Teges. Duro Ladipo's famous opera *Oba Ko So*, a dramatization of the Nigerian Yoruba story of *Shango*, the King of Thunder, was staged in 1973. Site-specific commissions were a particular contribution of Shiraz-Persepolis to the international performance arts, including works by Iannis Xenakis, Bruno Maderna, Peter Brook, Kerala Kalamandalam Kathakali Troupe, Merce Cunningham, Robert Wilson (with his early epic *KA MOUNTAIN AND GUARDenia Terrace*, which ran continuously for seven days and nights in the landscape), and Maurice Béjart. Many seminal experimental works were commissioned, at a time when most of the artists (from both "south" and "north") remained marginal in their own countries. Iranian artists such as, to name a few, Arby Ovanessian, Bijan Mofid, Parviz Sayyad, Mohammad Bagher Ghaffari, and Sussan Taslimi communed with the broadest spectrum of creators. New Iranian cinema by the likes of filmmakers Parviz Kimiavi, Nasser Taghvai, Fereydoon Rahnema and Dariush Mehrjui gained visibility alongside auteurs, such as, Yasujiro Ozu, Ingmar Bergman, Luis Bunuel, Sergei Paradjanov, Pier Paolo Pasolini, Satyajit Ray, and Marguerite Duras, to name a few.

turn to Asia and Africa for inspiration just as the early modernists had done at the turn if the previous century.[42] Various tenets of Zen Buddhist, Taoist, Sufi, and Hindu thought were influential on avant-garde practice.

> With the recent involvement of the Third World, a new perspective has been opened ... World theater seems even closer to achieving the goals set by the visionary Artau [...] An important trend of the avant-garde is devoted to developing this kind of expression for an intercultural audience.
>
> — Eighth Festival of Arts, Shiraz-Persepolis Program[43]

The curation consolidated a nexus for *modernizing nativists* mingling with *ritualizing modernists*. It underscored the reverse transmission of knowledge from the "periphery" to the "center," highlighting the depth and continuity of Asian philosophical influence on European and American modernist movements.

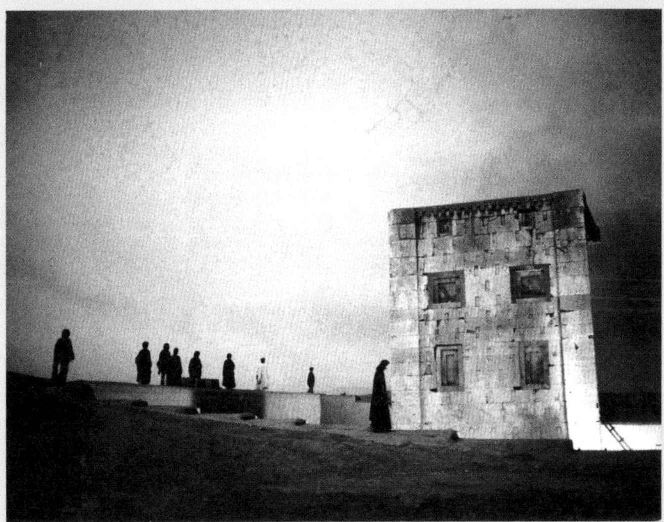

FIG 20 ***Orghast Part II*, Ted Hughes, Mahin Tajaddod (playwrights), Peter Brook, Arby Ovanessian, Geoffrey Reeves, Andrei Serban (directors), Naqsh-e Rostam, 1971. International Centre for Theater Research, commissioned by the Festival and the French Ministry of Culture, with the participation of the Ford and Gulbenkian Foundations and UNESCO. World Premiere commissioned by the Festival of Arts. Courtesy of Vali Mahlouji / Archaeology of the Final Decade.**

42 In 1972, the festival recruited several distinctive European and American experimental practitioners into proximity with the Asian traditions to which they were indebted. John Cage had studied with Daisetz Teitaro Suzuki, a theologian of Zen Buddhism. Merce Cunningham drew inspiration from *I Ching (Book of Change)* to explore notions of chance and indeterminacy. Karlheinz Stockhausen's compositions aimed at reaching a state of inner asceticism and spirituality, correlating with philosophies of Hinduism. Richard Wilhelm (1873–1930) lived for twenty-five years in China and translated Lao-tze's *Tao Te Ching* and *I Ching* in 1925. His translations influenced European/American thinkers, philosophers, and artists.

43 Original catalogue of the Festival of Arts, Shiraz-Persepolis, 1974, Archaeology of the Final Decade Archives.

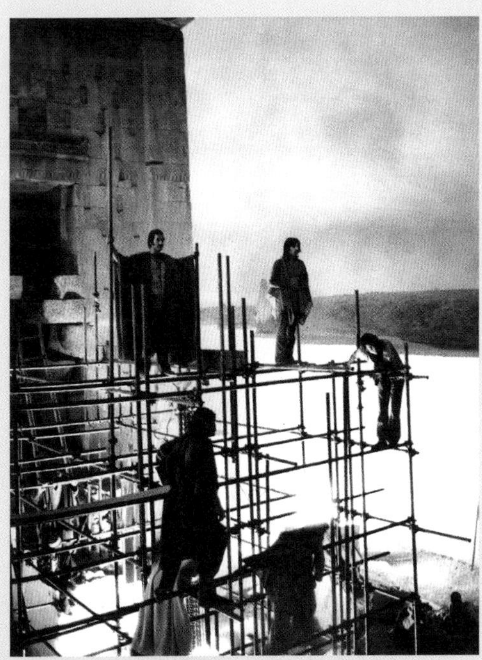

FIG 19 ***Orghast Part II*, Ted Hughes, Mahin Tajaddod (playwrights), Peter Brook, Arby Ovanessian, Geoffrey Reeves, Andrei Serban (directors), Naqsh-e Rostam, 1971. International Centre for Theatre Research, commissioned by the Festival and the French Ministry of Culture, with the participation of the Ford and Gulbenkian Foundations and UNESCO. World Premiere commissioned by the Festival of Arts. Courtesy of Vali Mahlouji / Archaeology of the Final Decade.**

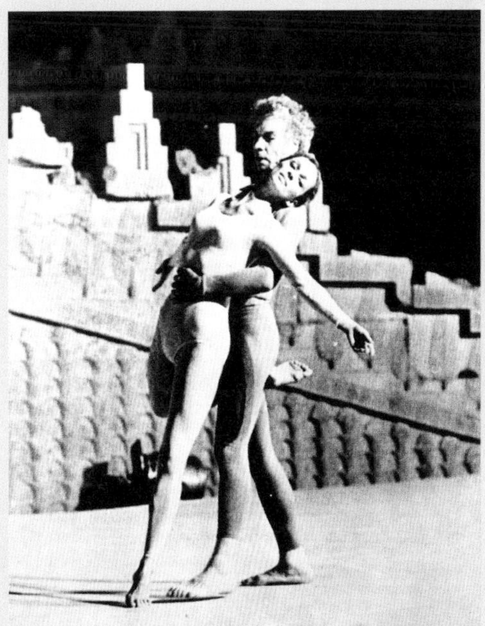

FIG 21 ***Persepolis Event*, The Merce Cunningham Dance Company, Persepolis, 1972, World Premiere. Courtesy of The Merce Cunningham Trust / Vali Mahlouji / Archaeology of the Final Decade.**

Theater as Rebellion

The rebellious philosophical outlook stirred controversy and contestation. These were detrimentally heightened by the fact that at Shiraz- Persepolis, the artwork itself was not only inherently potentially subversive, but also not insulated within institutional walls, safeguarded. The festival set out to break down the proscenium, deconstruct the draconian concept of gallery as temple, artist as prophet, and art as relic or a means in itself. Its transcendental realm intuited to actively shift reality and was more immediately, intimately linked to life and the landscape, as performance is. By its own admission, the festival had boldly set out to challenge, not conform.

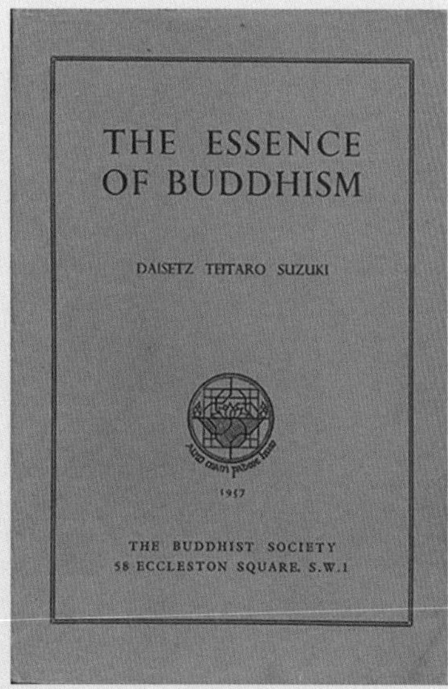

FIG 22 Daisetz Teitaro Suzuki, *The Essence of Buddhism* (London: The Buddhist Society, 1957). Suzuki was an influential Zen and Shin master, and a translator of Sanskrit texts whose writings were studied extensively in Europe and North America.

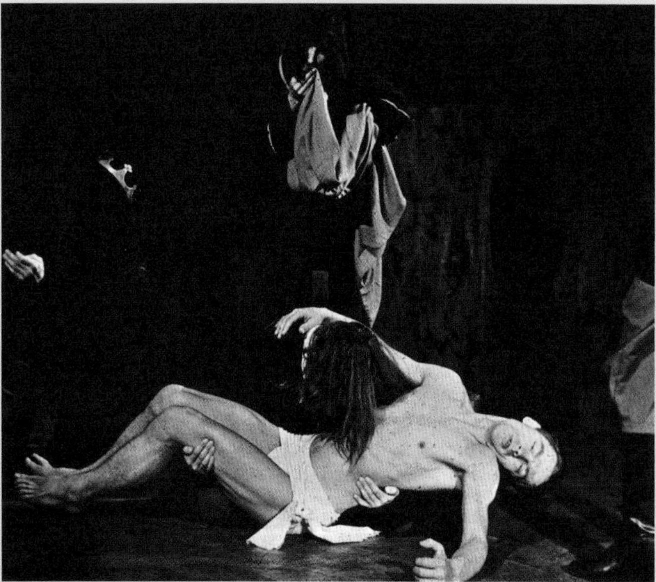

FIG 23 *The Constant Prince*, Calderon (playwright), Jerzy Grotowski, (director), The Laboratory Theater, Delgosha Pavilion, 1970. Courtesy of Vali Mahlouji / Archaeology of the Final Decade.

> The Sixth Festival was considered by many to be the most "difficult" to date. [...] There was little appeal to "popular" taste, a sure sign that Festival organizers now knew what they wanted and were prepared to present it regardless of critical comment, which was not slow in coming. The controversy that boiled over in normally placid Shiraz was rightly considered part of what the Festival is all about, and as a welcome stimulus to artistic creativity and art criticism in Iran.
>
> — Sixth Festival of Arts Program[44]

"We are our own liberators."[45]

Considering its revolutionizing stance, it is not accidental that the Festival of Arts became the biggest casualty of the Iranian religious "cultural cleansing." It was already contentious during its run, *a temporary autonomous zone* ahead of the conventional realities of its time.[46] Too liberal. Too unpredictable. Uncensored. Uncontained. Its philosophical enquiry into the *euphoria of togetherness* shines irredeemably antithetical to the catastrophic notion of a *clash of civilizations* perpetuated by the current regime. The Shiraz-Persepolis stage was a permanent philosophical workshop. Audaciously free. A germinal project of discovery and rediscovery of the self. A cultivator of re-awakenings. An open enquiry into the essential questions of *being*. It still stands at the forefront of "third world" radical imagination today and marks a triumphant pinnacle, an important chapter from our radical histories of the twentieth century. Its multivalent pluralistic praxis remains a forerunner of cross-historical and interwoven aspirations of art and anti-colonial struggle in the 1960s and 1970s. Many of those refinements, like the festival's own stage, were dealt a hard blow by the rise of an antagonistic new world order, concocted simultaneously by neoliberal global agendas and neo-religious/right-wing populist evangelicalisms. Like those dreams, the festival became a target, demonized,

44 Original catalogue of the Festival of Arts, Shiraz-Persepolis, 1972, Archaeology of the Final Decade Archives.

45 Borrowed from Jalil A. Muntaqim, *We Are Our Own Liberators: Selected Prison Writings* (Oakland, CA: PM Press, 2010).

46 "Temporary autonomous zone" as used here is an expression coined by Hakim Bey (alias Peter Lamborn Wilson), the poet and critic who wrote a book of the same name. Wilson paid numerous visits to the Festival and produced different texts on the content of the projects. He went on to be employed by Seyyed Hossein Nasr at the Imperial Iranian Academy of Philosophy until 1978. For him, the temporary autonomous zone is a new territory on the boundary line of established regions, its focus on the moment being beyond any structured system that fuels individual creativity.

demolished, erased, replaced by the temporary artificial success of lesser and tendentious ideas.

"[...] we must redefine ourselves and our lives, in our own terms."[47]

The first that time my excavated and archived historical materials of the Festival of Arts, Shiraz-Persepolis were exhibited was in my exhibition at the Musée d'Art Moderne de la Ville de Paris.[48] The cultural attaché of the Islamic Republic of Iran in Paris, who was invited for a special preview by the museum, stopped, looked through the documentary moving and still images, books, pamphlets, and captions.

He turned to me in Persian, "How did this material get here?"

I replied, "Years of deep research."

He cautiously replied, "It is part of history after all."

The museum's director swiftly diverted him and the Iranian embassy's diplomatic corps via another route so that they would not encounter the second section of my archaeology of erased histories. The second section documented the burning of the old red-light district of Tehran, which was set alight in 1979 in an act of Islamic purification three days before the arrival of the populist religious leader Khomeini to Iran.[49]

47 Max Roach, full quote: "My point is that we much decolonize our minds and rename and redefine ourselves[…] In all respects, culturally, politically, socially, we must redefine ourselves and our lives, in our own terms." Cited https://www.inspirationalstories.com/quotes/t/max-roach/; and https://www.azquotes.com/quote/1241888.

48 Vali Mahlouji, "The Contested Space: The Metapolitics of The Festival of Arts, Shiraz-Persepolis, Archaeology of the Final Decade," at Musée d'Art Moderne de la Ville de Paris, 2014, part of *Unedited History: Iran 1960–2014*, co-curated by Catherine David, Vali Mahlouji, Odile Burlureux, Morad Montazami, and Narmine Sadegh.

49 Vali Mahlouji, "Recreating the Citadel: The Intimate Politics of the Marginal," Archaeology of the Final Decade at Musée d'Art Moderne de la Ville de Paris, 2014, part of *Unedited History: Iran 1960–2014*, co-curated by Catherine David, Vali Mahlouji, Odile Burlureux, Morad Montazami, Narmine Sadegh.

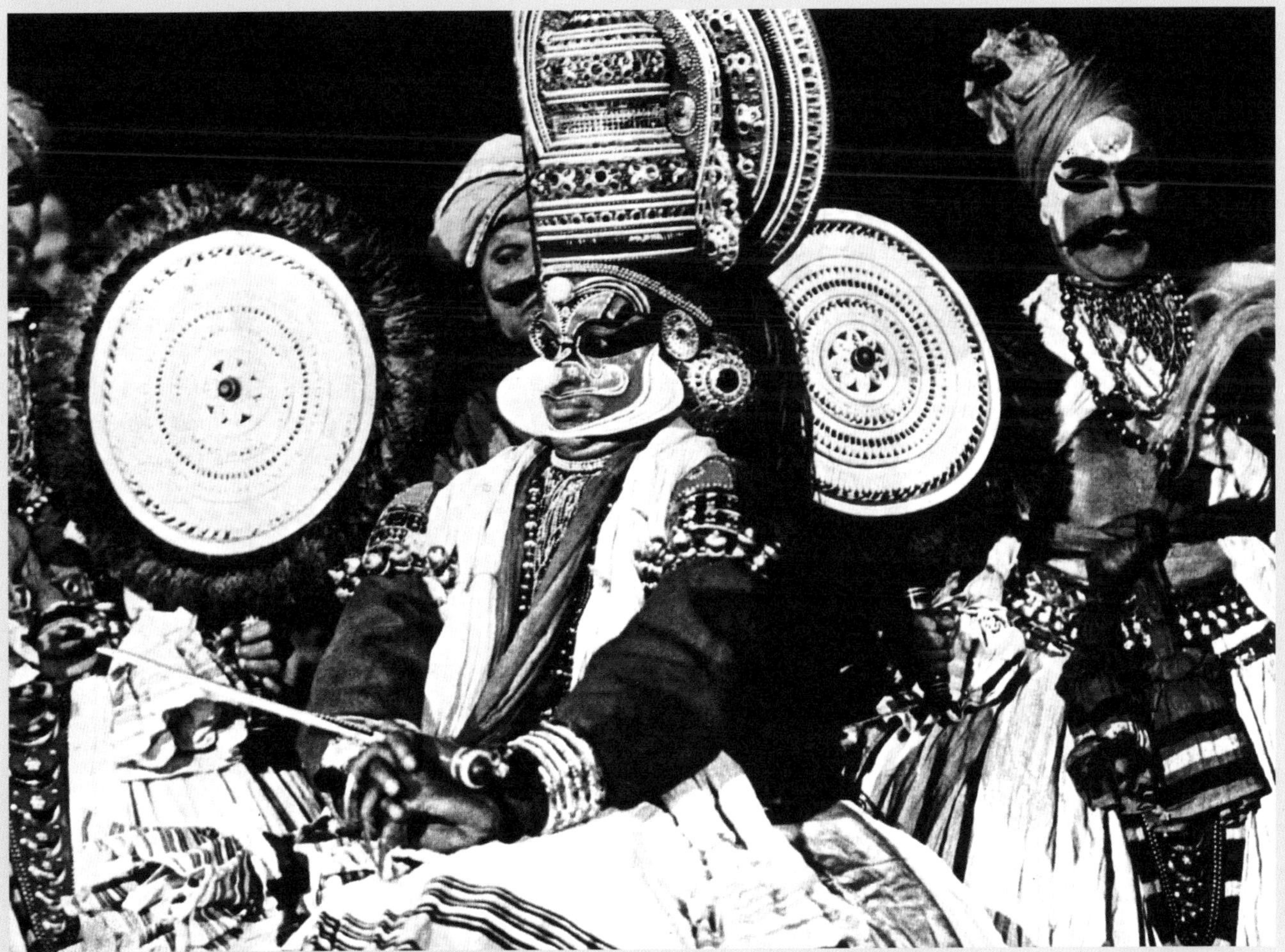

FIG 24 Kathakali: "Rostam & Sohrab," Kerala Kalamandalam Kathakali Troupe, Persepolis, 1972, Festival commission. Courtesy of Vali Mahlouji / Archaeology of the Final Decade.

That epic act was the initiation of the reign of terror. As if the heinous crime of torching (no account was made of the numbers of charred bodies) were not enough, Khomeini's newly-established Islamic revolutionary courts first, cunningly, targeted the most vulnerable marginalized, stigmatized citizens of Tehran: the sex-workers from that poverty-stricken ghetto. Three women associated with the sex district became the first women to be executed for *immoral* sins in an act of divine retribution. Auspiciously for the diplomats, the museum *protected* them from the gaze of the unnamed sex-workers of the ghetto staring out at them in my exhibition.[50] The women's experience was annulled; the portraits were robbed of their power. Perhaps

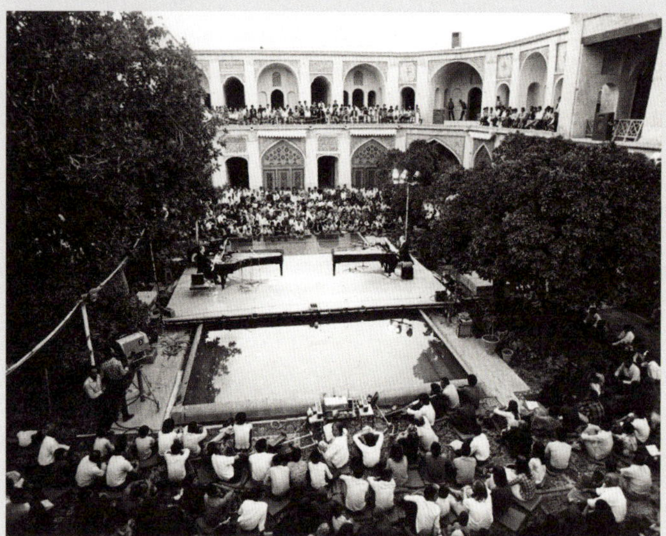

FIG 25 ***Mantra for two Pianos*****, Karlheinz Stockhausen (composer), Alfons Kontarsky, Aloys Kontarsky (pianists), Saray-e Moshir, 1972. Courtesy of Stockhausen-Stiftung für Musik / Vali Mahlouji / Archaeology of the Final Decade.**

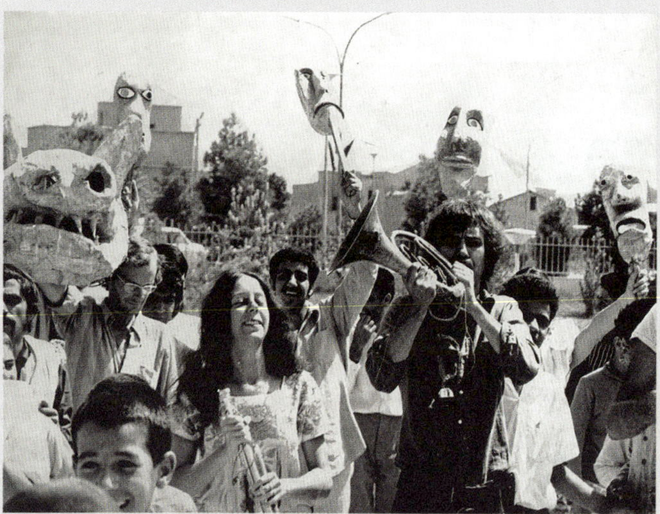

FIG 26 ***King's Story*****, Peter Schumann (creator and director), Bread & Puppet Theater, Shiraz, 1970. Courtesy of Vali Mahlouji / Archaeology of the Final Decade.**

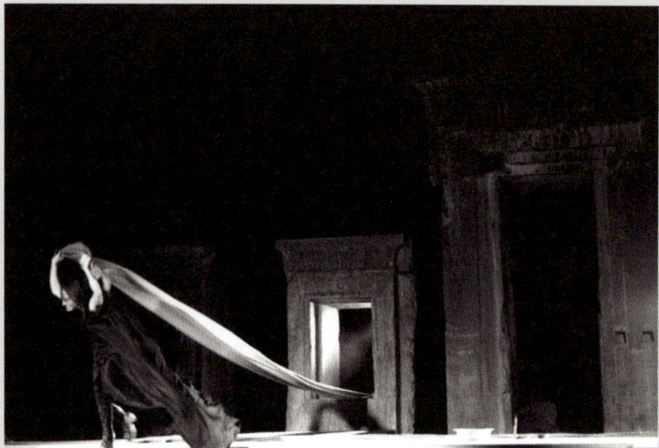

FIG 27 ***Caligula*****, Albert Camus (playwright), Arby Ovanessian (director), Kargah-e Namayesh, Persepolis, 1974. Courtesy of Vali Mahlouji / Archaeology of the Final Decade / Photo Mehdi Khonsari.**

50 The exhibition included Kaveh Golestan's portraits of sex workers in Tehran's red light ghetto, Shahr-e No. See https://archaeologyofthefinaldecade.com/re-creating-citadel/. The series of portraits entitled *Prostitute* dates from 1975–77 and formed part of my curated exhibiton "Recreating the Citadel: The Intimate Politics of the Marginal," Archaeology of the Final Decade at Musée d'Art Moderne de la Ville de Paris, 2014, part of *Unedited History: Iran 1960–2014*, co-curated by Catherine David, Odile Burlureux, Vali Mahlouji, Morad Montazami, Narmine Sadegh.

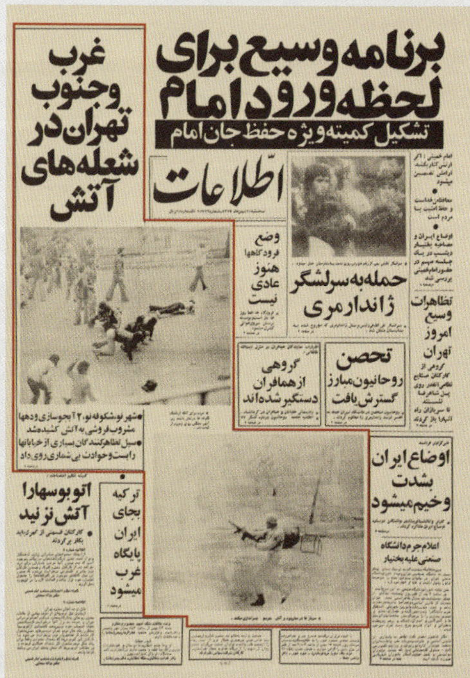

برنامه وسیع برای لحظه ورود امام

تشکیل کمیته ویژه حفظ جان امام

اطلاعات

غرب وجنوب تهران در شعله های آتش

وضع فرودگاهها هنوز عادی نیست

حمله به سرلشگر ژاندارمری

تحصن روحانیون مبارز گسترش یافت

گروهی از همافران دستگیر شده اند

تظاهرات وسیع امروز تهران

اوضاع ایران بشدت وخیم میشود

اتوبوسهارا آتش نزنید

ترکیه بجای ایران پایگاه غرب میشود

FIG 28 **Daily Newspaper** ***Ettela'at*****, Tuesday 10 Bahman 1357 / January 30, 1979, front page. The article, "West and South of Tehran in Flames of Fire" (marked in red) refers to the fire that burnt down the red-light district in 1979. The main headline to the right reads: "Vast Preparations for the Moment of the Imam's (Khomeini) Arrival." Courtesy Archaeology of the Final Decade.**

the diplomats' exposure to new-found knowledge, to the enlivening aesthetic and political proclivities of the festival, which were exploded across the walls and vitrines, was already too much of a culture shock, or too calamitous, injurious to their fragile biases. The director of the museum later apologized to me for his act of cowardice: "I did it to *protect* you," he said. That was certainly not to be my last abject experience of that recurrent erasure of heritage, either within or without Iran.

Ought we not to leave
The free-born mind of man still ever free?
Since vain is the attempt to force belief
With the severest instrument of death?

The raptur'd soul defies the sword,
Secure of virtue's claim,
And trusting Heav'n's unerring word,
Enjoys the circling flame.
No engine can a tyrant find,
To storm the truth-supported mind.
The raptur'd sou …

— Didymus, Händel opera *Theodora*[51]

51 Thomas Morell, libretto of *Theodora*, an oratorio composed by Georg Friedrich Händel and sung by the character Didymus, a Roman soldier (alto), 1750.

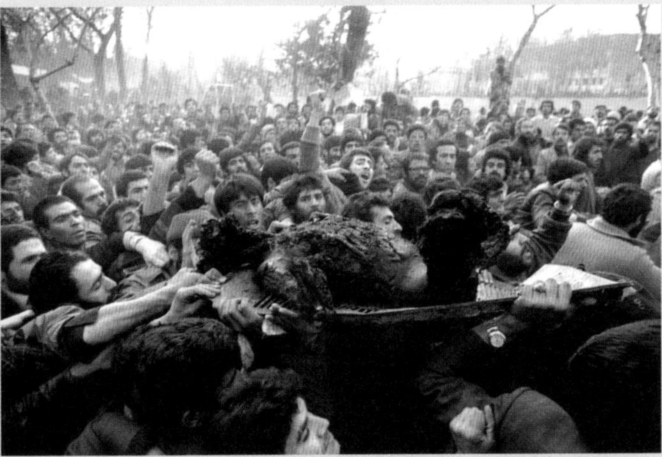

FIG 29 Tehran, January 1979. A revolutionary mob exhibits the burned body of a presumed prostitute as evidence of the atrocity of the Shah's regime. The mob had just set fire to the "red light" district in "Islamic Purifying Fire." © and courtesy Abbas / Magnum Photo.

RADY NGET

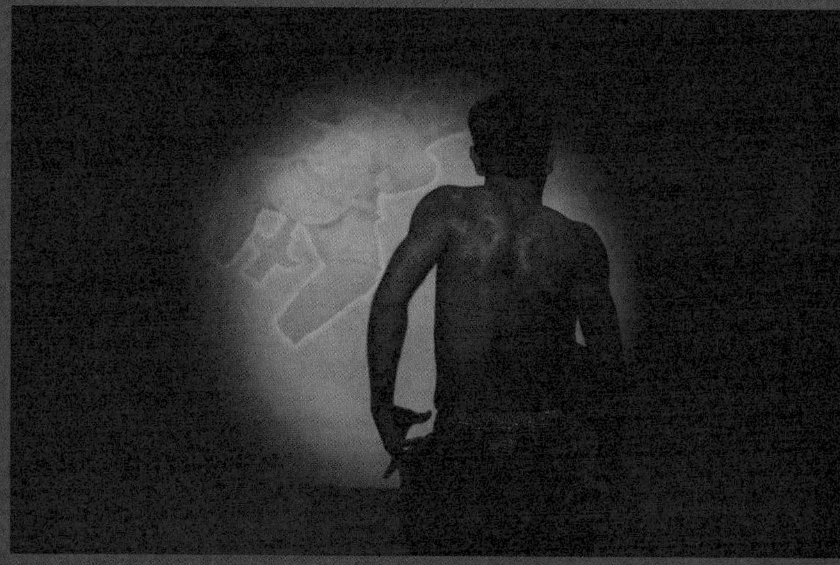

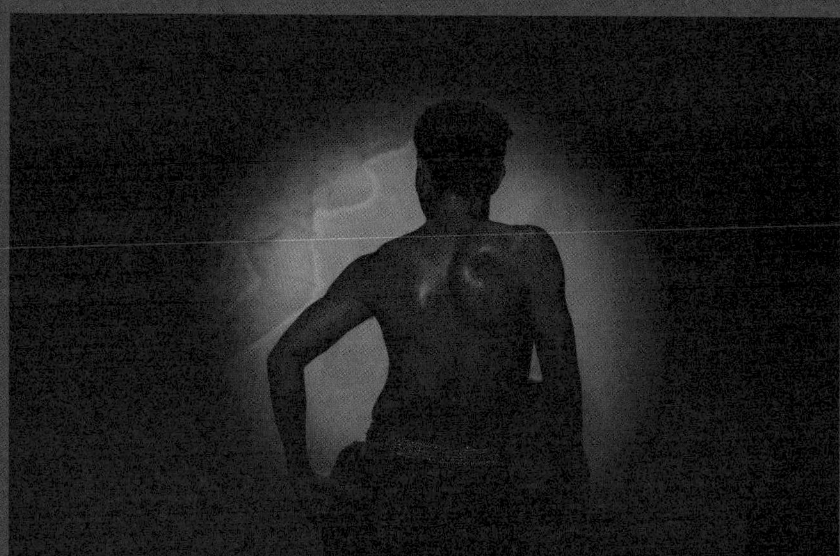

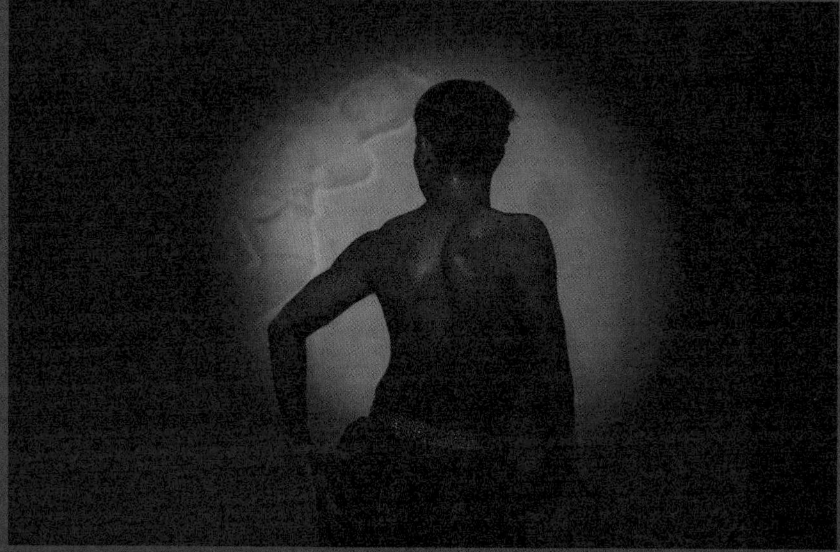

Soul of My Identity, 2021

Soul of My Identity is about the human pursuit of cultural heritage, especially intangible heritage, sculptures that have been lost since ancient times and colonial times. These intangible heritages are part of the connection and fulfillment of the lost in the past. These two cultural heritages are very important because these are the soul of the national identity that cannot be lost.

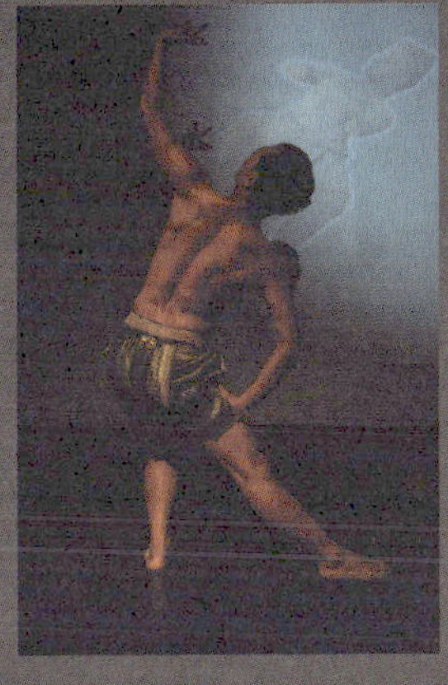

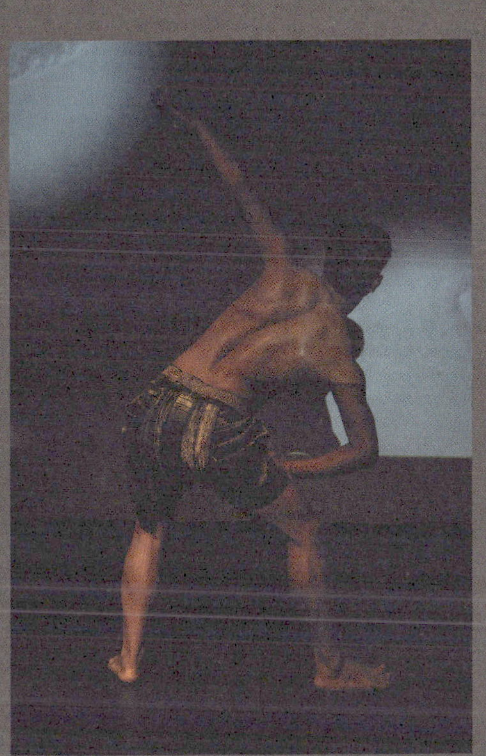

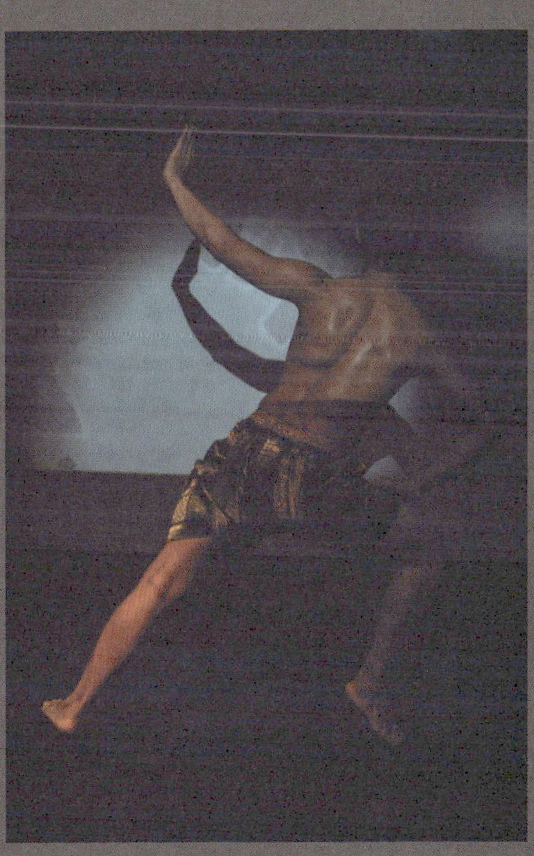

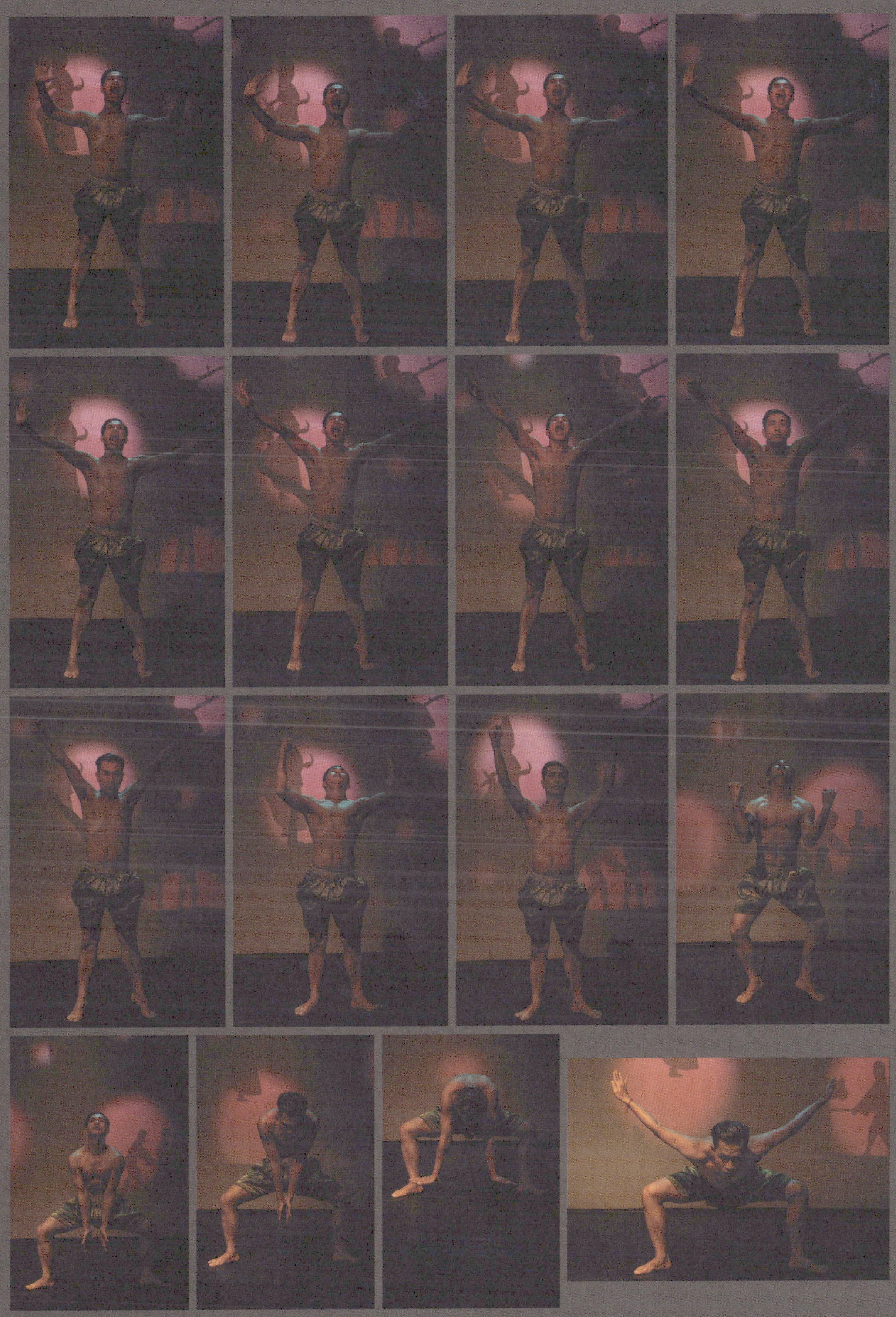

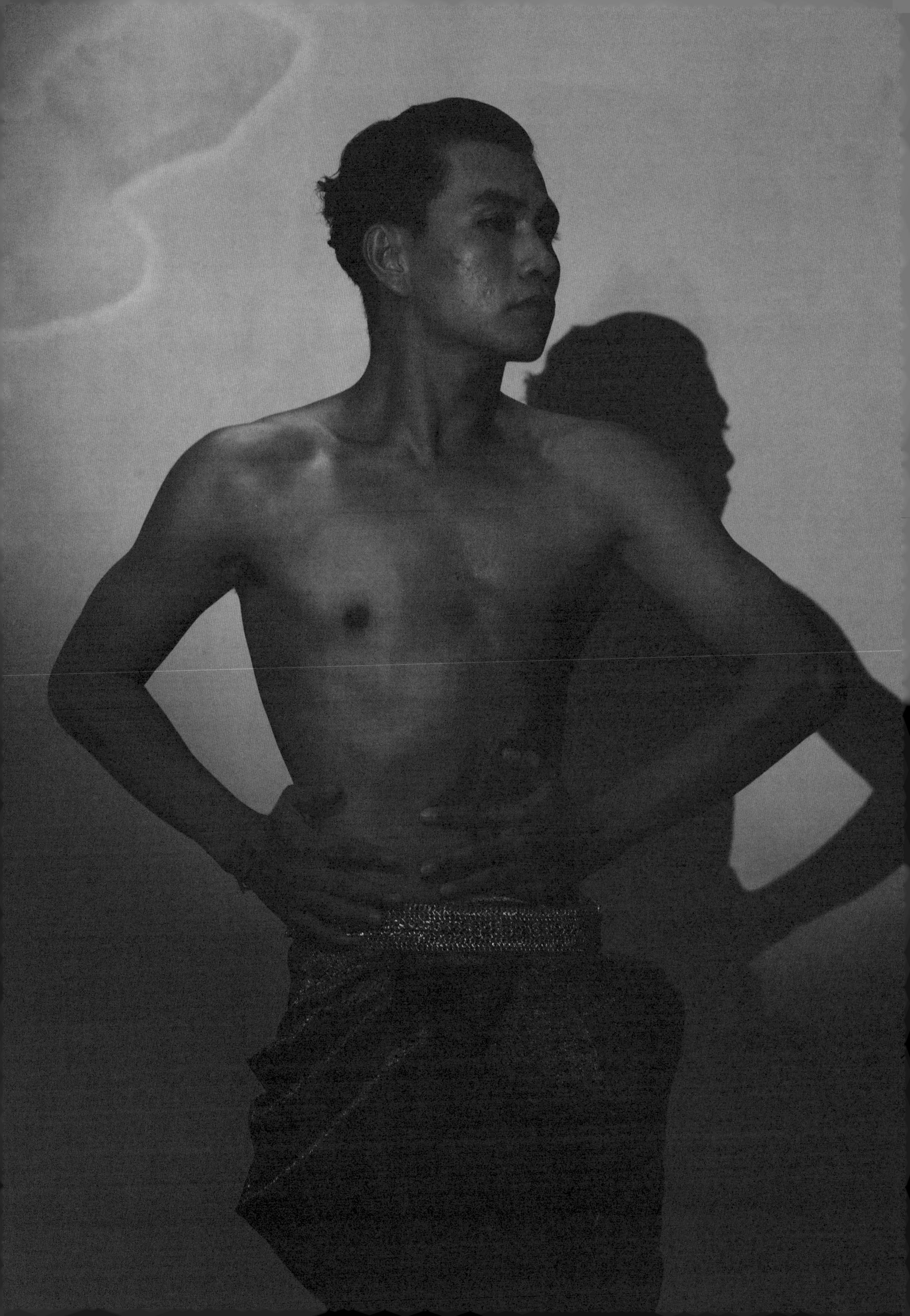

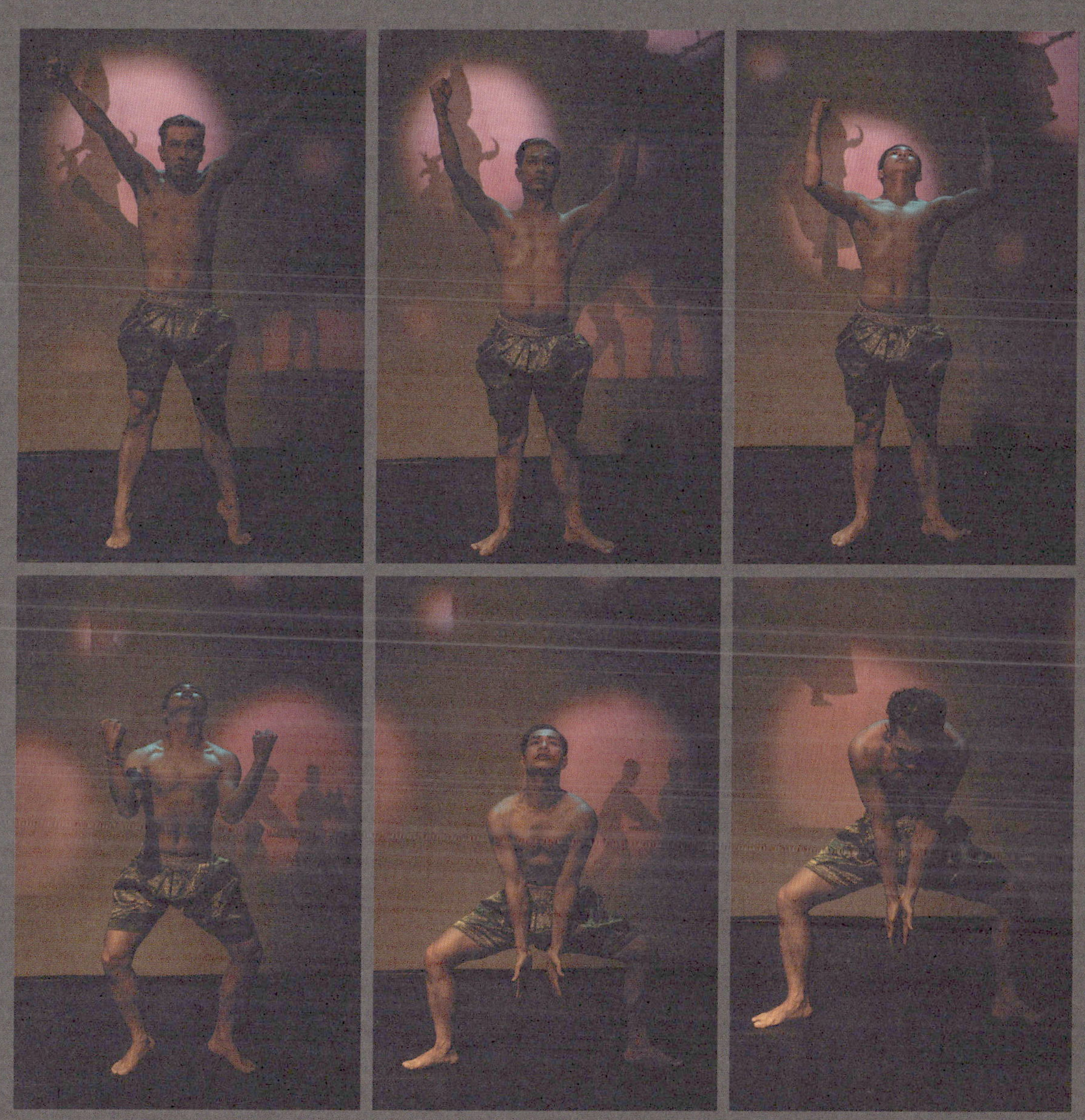

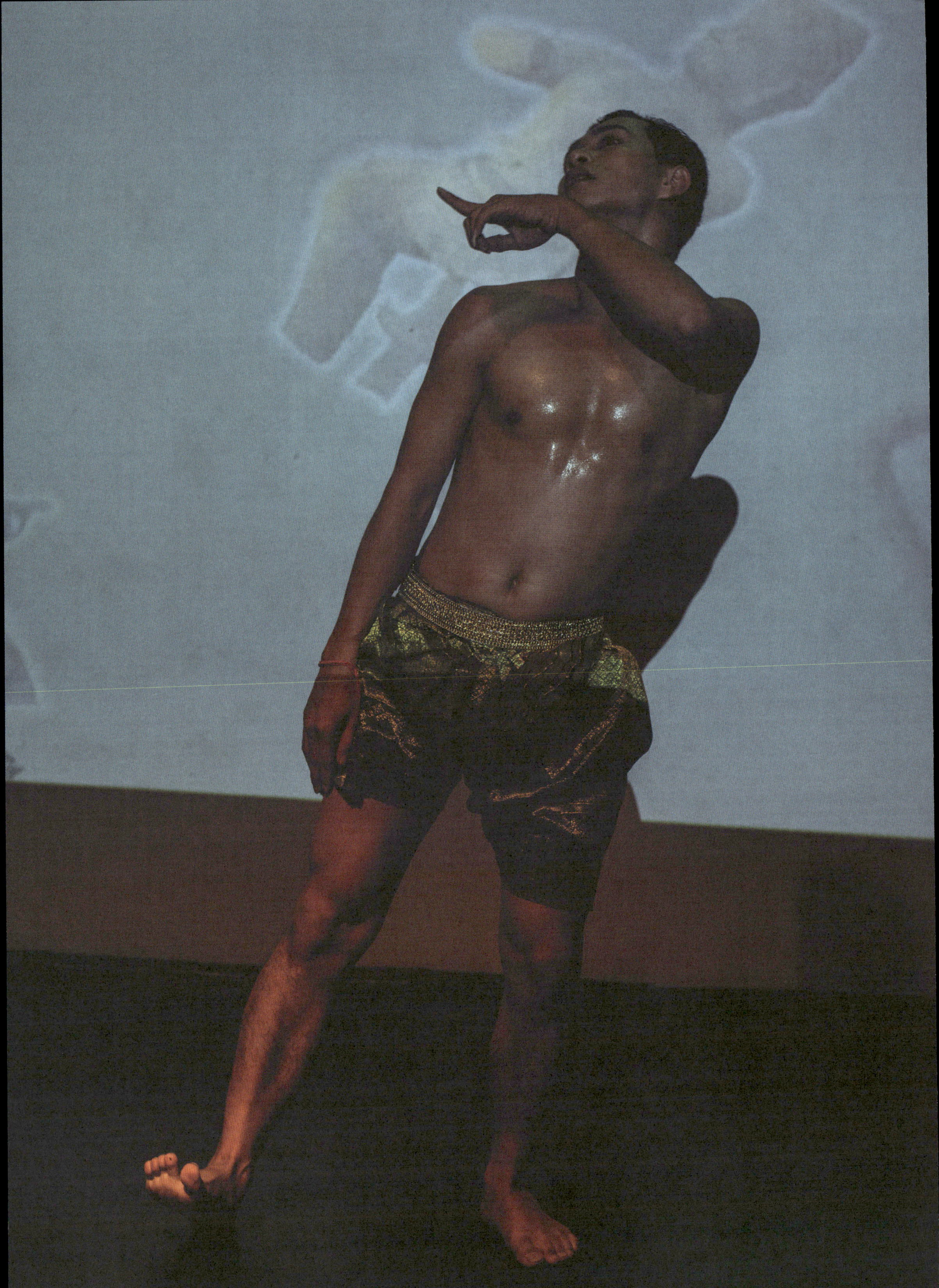

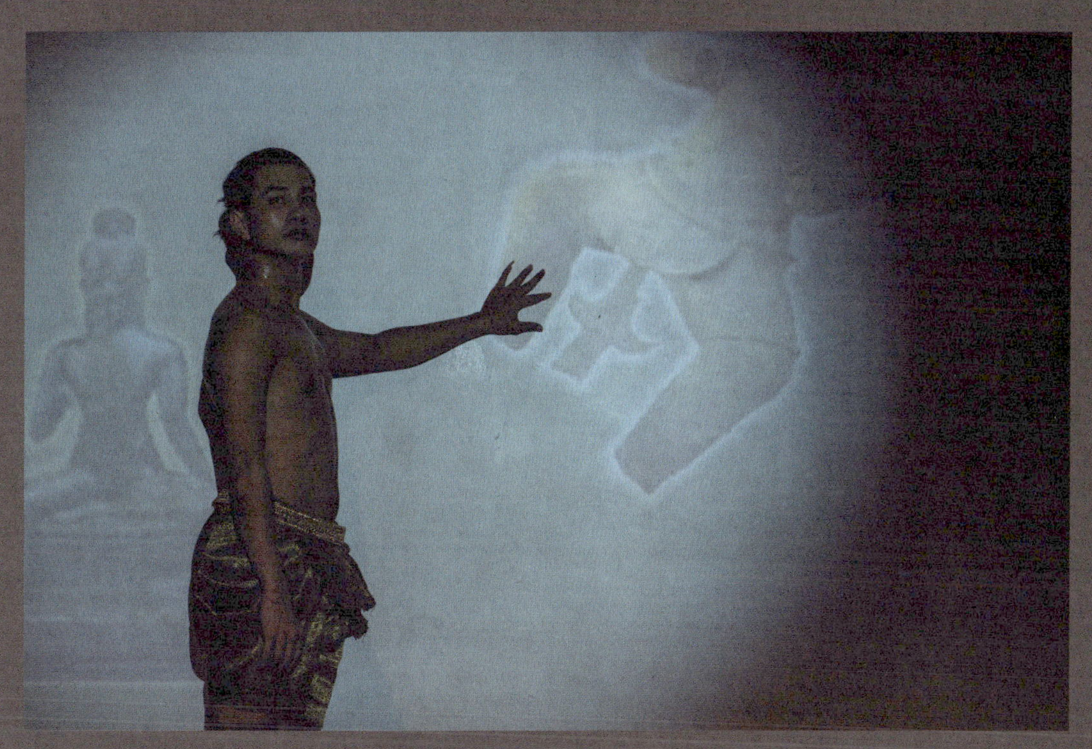

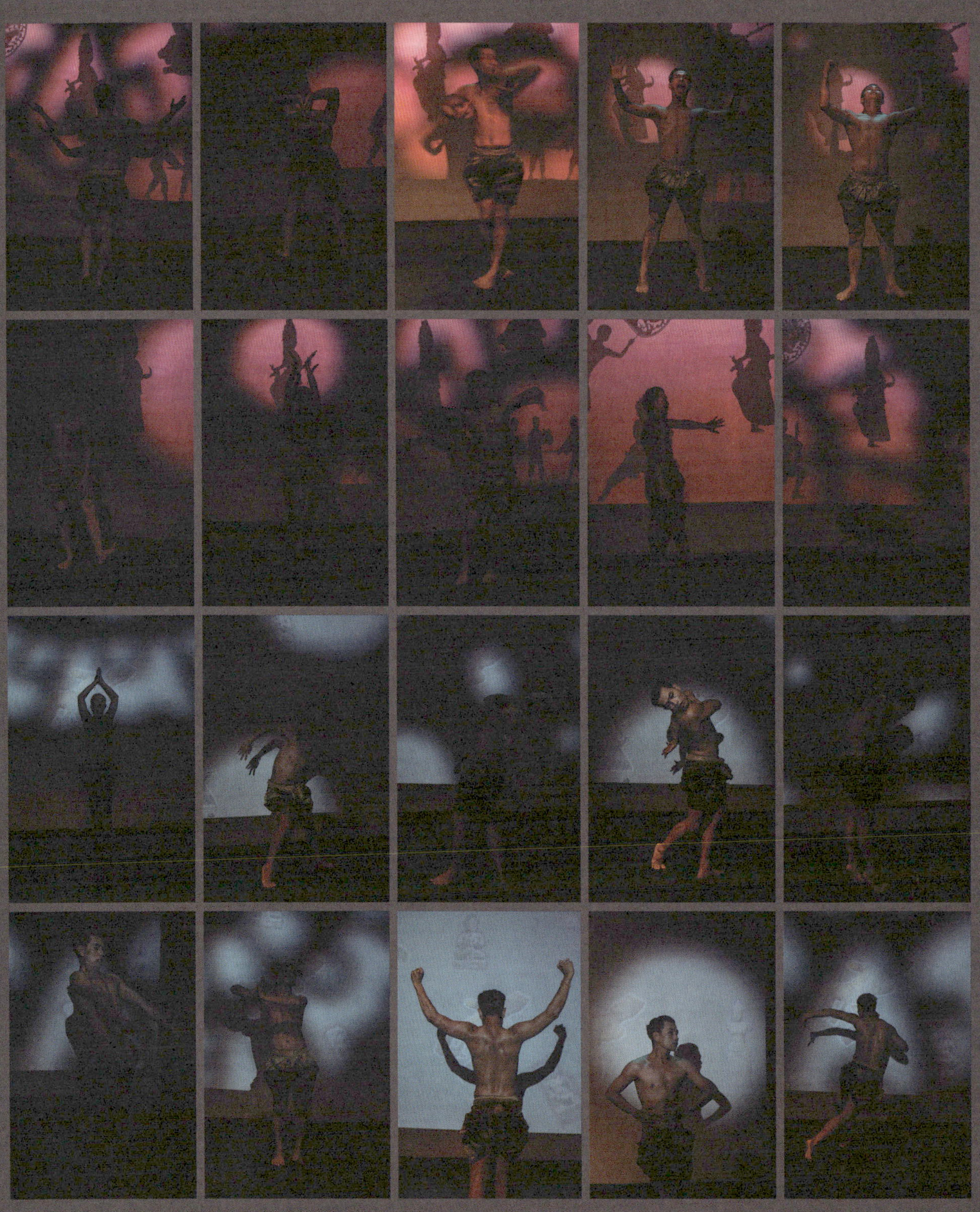

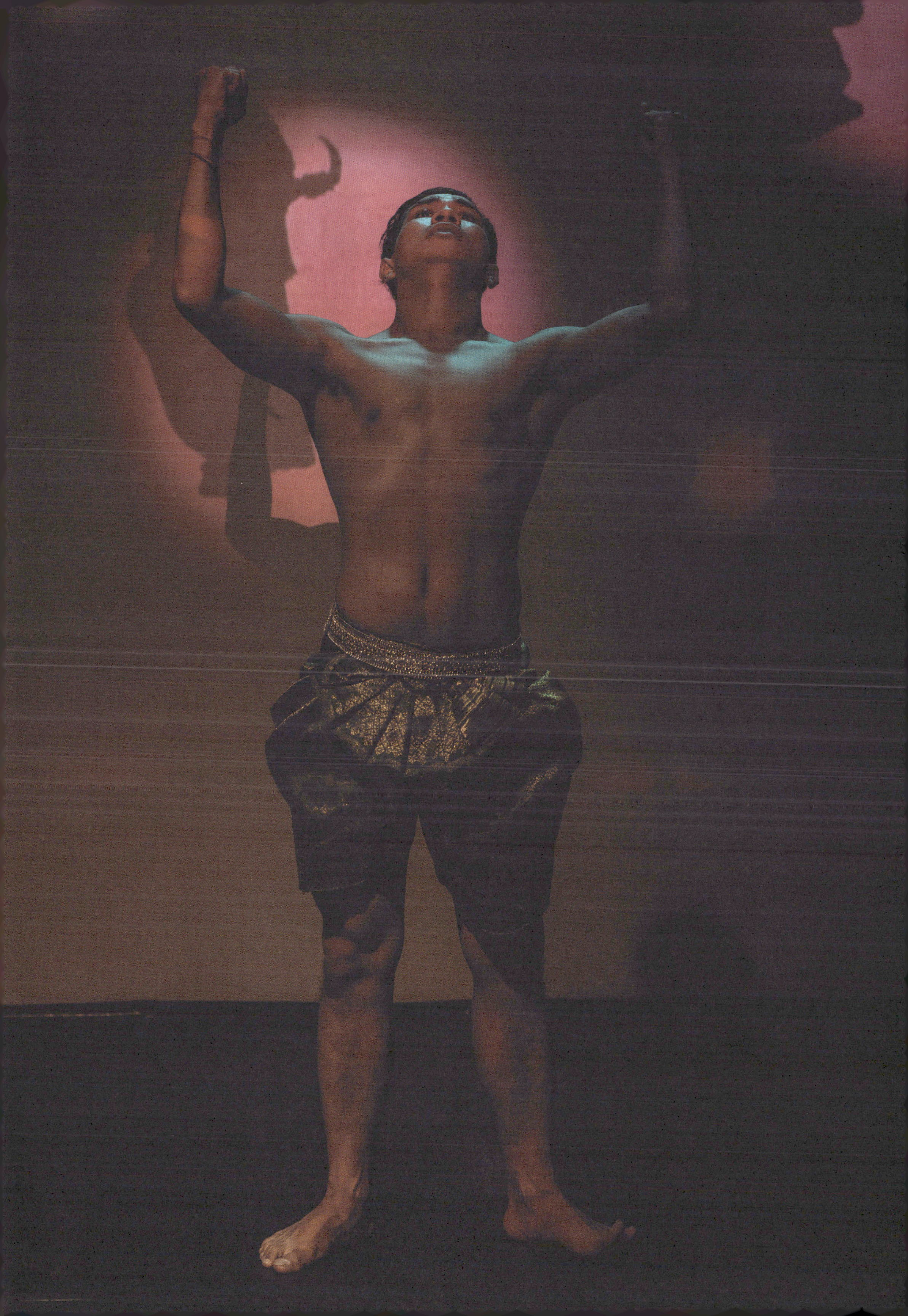

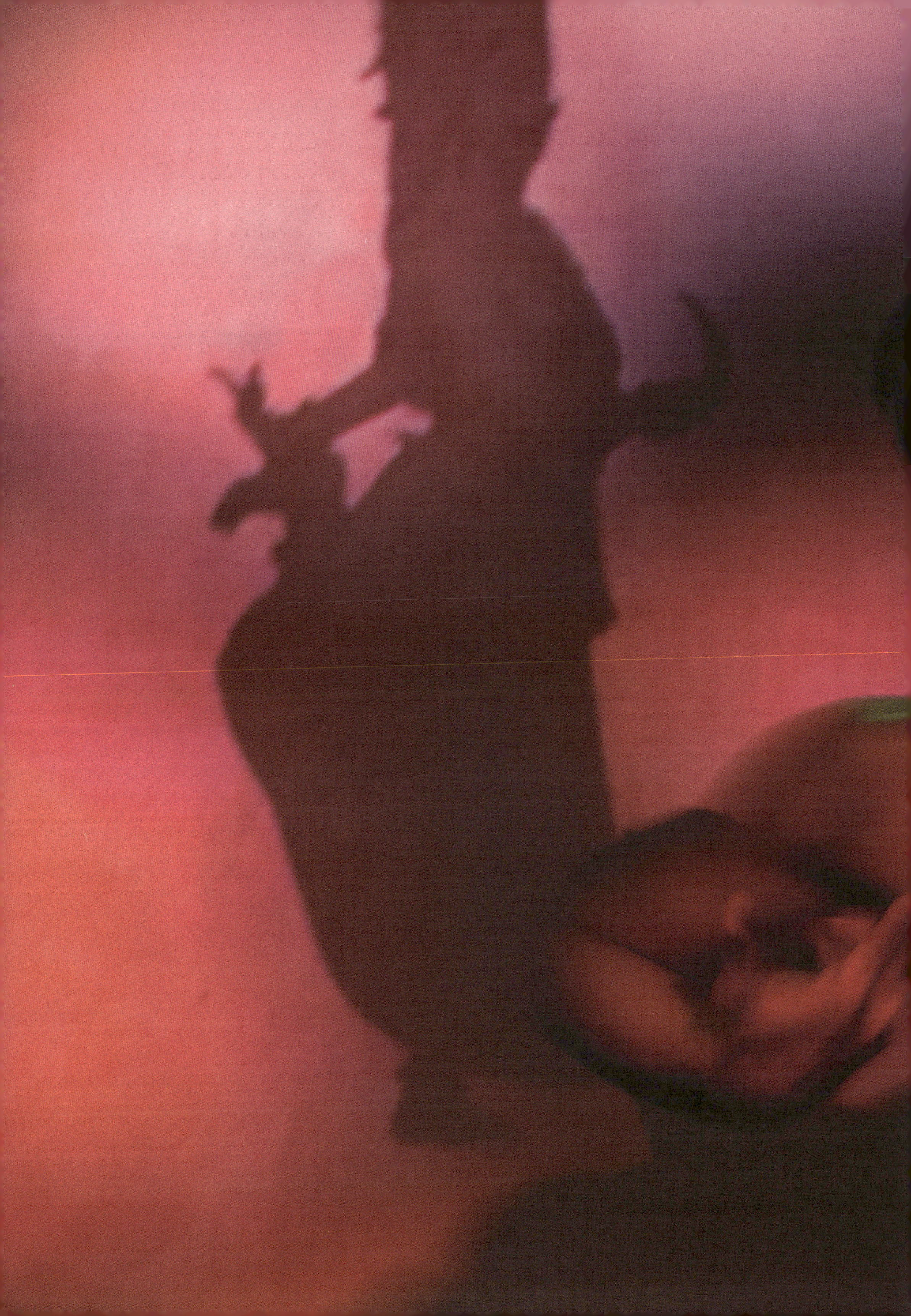

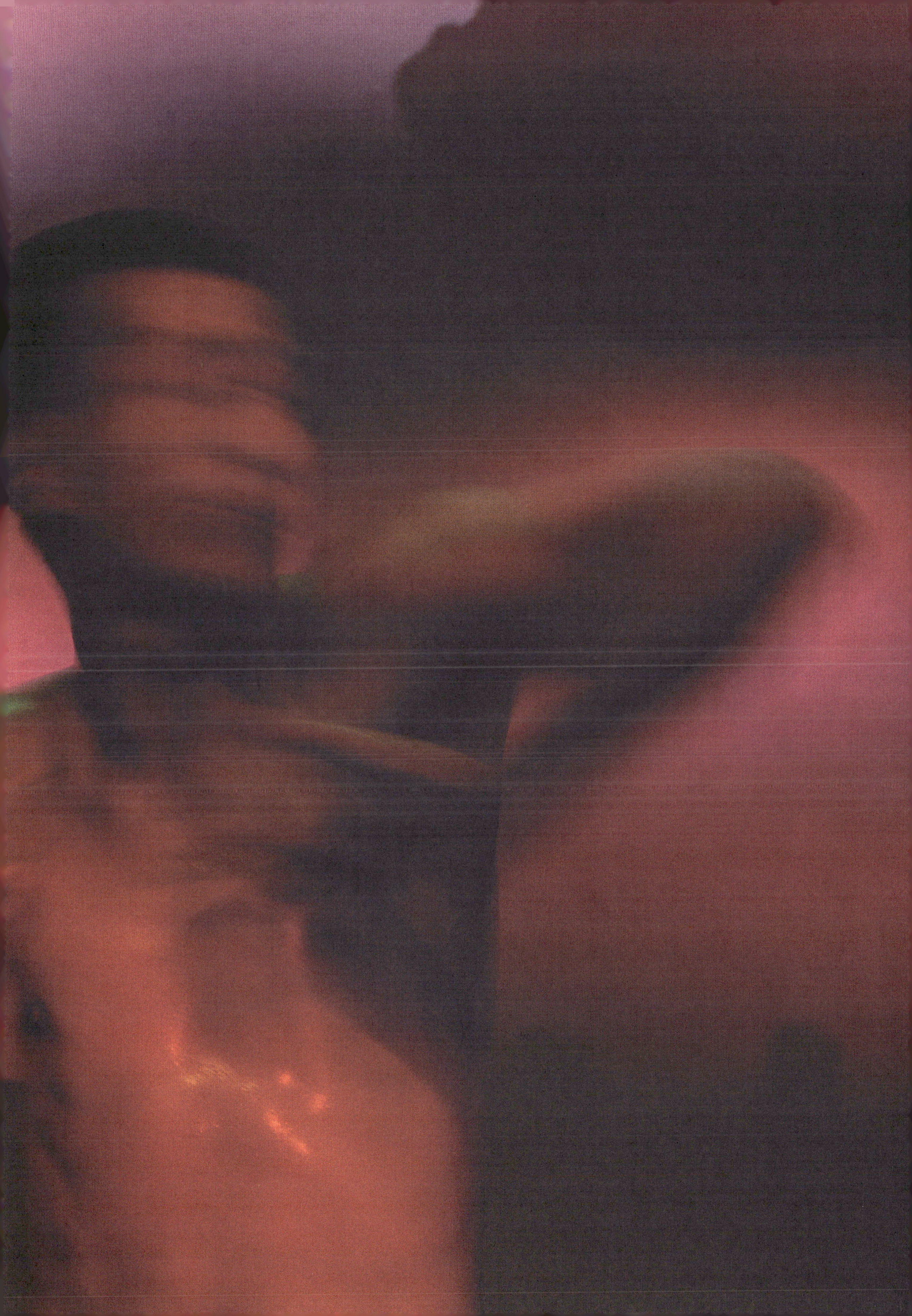

Tradition, or the Shadow of the Modern

342

YUK HUI
Interview by Cosmin Costinaş & Inti Guerrero

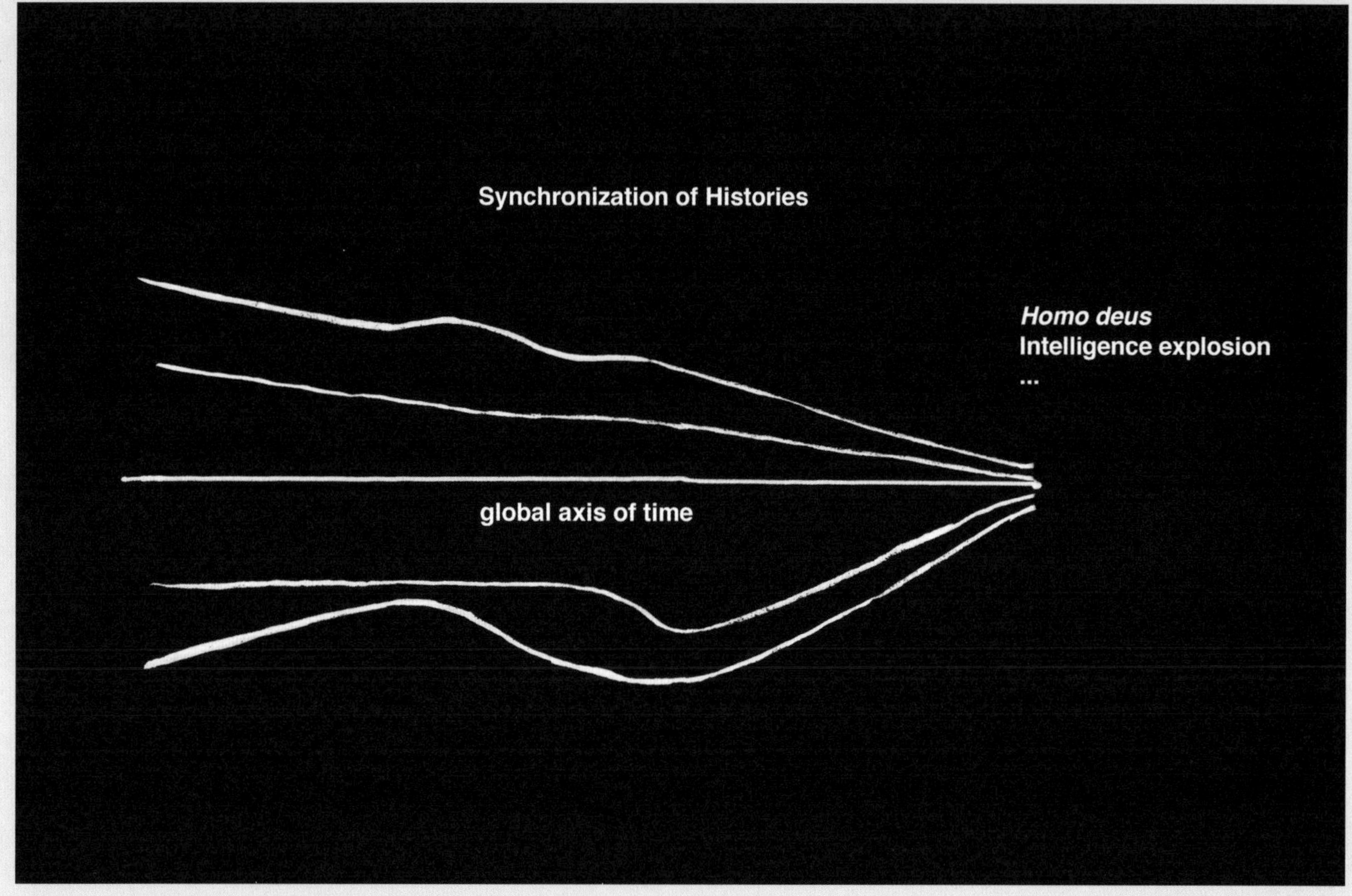

FIG 1 "Timeline of Modernization," 2019. Courtesy of Yuk Hui.

COSMIN COSTINAŞ

Let us start with this quote about you not being a traditionalist from your *e-flux* article on neoreactionary consciousness: "I appreciate tradition and still believe that the failure of all communist revolutions is due to a failure to respect tradition or draw from its forces, instead posing matter against spirit. The opposition between matter and spirit leads to a nihilism, which pushes modernization to its extreme."[1]

What is the relation between heritage and tradition? Specifically in the current Chinese context with the different instrumentalizations of the past that have happened in the last decade, as well as during the period of the Cultural Revolution and its radical attempt to reconsider, erase, and reshape Chinese tradition. Also taking into consideration the more recent attempts to project a version of the 5,000 years of Chinese history while simultaneously creating an early revolutionary tradition, and how these two coexist.

YUK HUI

This is a big question. A satisfactory answer deserves a whole book! But maybe we can start with the question of tradition: What is tradition really and how are we going to look at tradition today? A problem is that when we talk about tradition, there is a dilemma, because if we want to save the tradition or keep the tradition, then we'd have to exclude many things which may destroy or contaminate tradition. Although of course what it means to "contaminate" is another interesting question. As you know, typical traditionalists attempt to exclude something that can put tradition in danger —meaning that which would transform the way of life of people living in a certain place for a long time. This is immediatedly related to a kind of proto-fascism, because you don't want people to come in, and you don't want anything to be changed. You see the incoming force, be that arts, technology, or science, as a threat. So we see how tradition becomes an immunolo-gical barrier. On the other hand, if we give tradition away, then what do we have? We live in a time that no longer has history. So we are living in an a historical time, a time that is devoid of history because we embrace everything that is new and more and more homogeneous. But embracing everything that's new itself is not problematic. What's problematic is its homogeneity:

1 Yuk Hui, "On the Unhappy Consciousness of Neoreactionaries," *e-flux Journal*, no. 81 (April 2017), https://www.e-flux.com/journal/81/125815/on-the-unhappy-consciousness-of-neoreactionaries/.

In the process of modernization, we destroy all obstacles in order to accommodate whatever is new—for example, like what has happened in East Asia since the second half of the nineteenth century. It's another story in Latin America, because colonization took place much earlier there. And the story was also a bit different in Africa because of the European missionaries, who also came to Japan and China in the sixteenth century, and were later kicked out of the country. Now, the question is, why? Why were they kicked out in the sixteenth century and then welcomed in the nineteenth century?

This very interesting historical question was raised by the historian Arnold Toynbee in one of his lectures. He gave the Reith Lectures for the BBC in 1952, in which he raised the following question: Why did the Far East kick the Europeans out during the sixteenth century, but let them in during the nineteenth century? His answer is that in the sixteenth century the Europeans wanted to promote religion and science and technology in China and Japan. This changed the way of life of the people there, so they became un-welcome. But in the nineteenth century the Europeans realized that it wasn't a good idea to export religion alongside science and technology, so they only exported science and technology, and for the most part religion was just a byproduct of the exportation. It was therefore more easily accepted because the people from the Far East believed that using their traditional thought—Japanese and Chinese thought—they would be able to master these technologies.

They let technologies and science come in because these are merely instruments. So using Chinese thought, or Japanese thought, people would theoretically be able to master these instruments and appropriate them for their own use. This way of understanding these instances from history gives us a second way of seeing tradition—as something that was used to allow local people to transform technology. Although retrospectively we know this was in fact a failure because the process of modernization nevertheless transformed East Asia in a way that was unexpected.

For example, after the two Opium Wars in China, in the second half of the nineteenth century, China was forced to improve its military strength and to open the ports; at the same time also to build factories to strengthen industry. That continued until 1949 when the Communist Party came to power. We can see this as the continuation of modernization in a really extreme way. (You don't see this in Europe. Marx was kicked out of continental Europe, even though Marx was from Germany, he was forced to be in exile in Britain. And in Britain he had no status, he was just a freelance writer who spent every day in the British Library reading and writing.)

We're talking about the whole idea of modernization and its full force in China. There was one quote in my book that created a kind of controversy. It was a quote from Heidegger's so-called "Black Notebooks," you know, those materials that are infamous for containing antisemitic statements. They were written in the 1940s, for sure before 1949. He says, "only when communism comes to power in China, will technology become 'free.'" That one sentence, with no further explanation given, leaves the reader to speculate on what Heidegger really means. What does he mean by "free"? Free doesn't mean that there is no longer any resistance or any effort to transforming these technologies, which means that this technology will become the major force of transformation. Like, for example, what we have seen in the Cultural Revolution, when tradition was considered the remainder of feudalism. Confucianism was largely criticized because, according to certain claims, the political ambition of Confucius was to restore the feudal system, which I think is complete nonsense because we cannot call the time of Confucius feudalism following the lineage of European history.

This kind of relentless critique of tradition and all this suppression of certain locality—I prefer to use the term "locality" instead of tradition—is also the suppression of any obstacles of technological and scientific acceleration. That's what we see, for example, during the Cultural Revolution. Until recently in China it's become an imperative to restore tradition. President Xi Jinping says that by 2025 China is going to fully restore its tradition. But what does he really mean by restoring tradition? This is a question still to be answered. I wish it would be anything beyond nationalism.

I would say that I value tradition because I value the existence of different forms of knowledge, which we can find in tradition. What I value about tradition is precisely the question of knowledge — knowledge that is produced from locality, and knowledge that serves locality. You find that kind of local knowledge, for example, in many places in Latin America, in Africa, in India. And how does this traditional knowledge still have anything to do with the contemporary situations we are in today, especially when such situations are dominated by discourses on artificial intelligence, machine learning, and the metaverse, besides really fierce military and economic competitions between nation-states? What is the role of these forms of knowledge?

This is my inquiry now. Because we know that traditionalism is often associated with right-wing politics and political theory — in France, for example, and in Russia, with Aleksandr Dugin, and so on. But I think it's very naïve, if not dangerous, for people to renounce all forms of traditional knowledge just because of this association, and to go as far as even renouncing the word "tradition" itself. I think we need to reappropriate the concept of tradition. We need to transform the concept. As I mentioned, I like to use the term "locality" instead of tradition. Locality is also problematic now though, because it's been co-opted by the right, for example in France by Marine Le Pen, and in Germany by the AfD (Alternative für Deutschland), which talk about locality all the time. But I think it's not very clever to give them these words, these very important concepts, and then to step away.

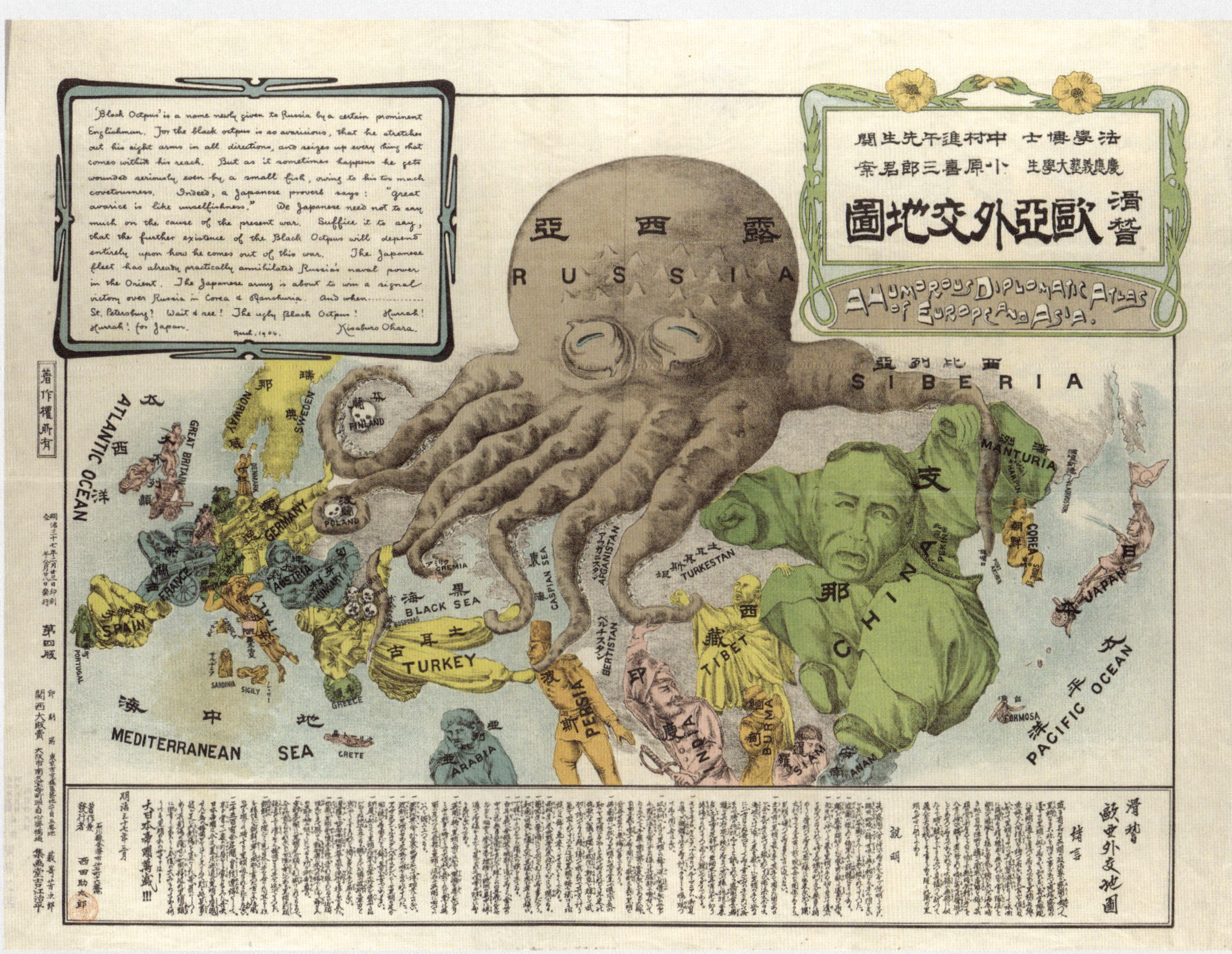

FIG 2 Kisaburō Ohara, *A Humorous Diplomatic Atlas of Europe and Asia*, 1904. 42 × 57 cm.

CC

I think that part of the Japanese right sees the current state of Japanese society as a dissolution of an ancient lineage into an anonymous and globally uniform modern paradigm, that came from defeat in World War II and from American occupation. But a significant part of the right would actually consider the modernization process, which started with the Meiji reformation in the nineteenth century, to be a successful experiment in adopting Western technology and breeding it on an uninterrupted and otherwise fundamentally unaltered traditional body. A similar proposition circulates in Iran I think, a discourse that the country achieved after the Revolution — a restoration of tradition while embracing contemporary technology.

YH

Yes. In Japan there was a slogan: "Japanese soul and Western instrument," and in China there's a similar one: "Chinese knowledge is the body and Western knowledge is only the use." So you see that there is the traditional, the Chineseness or Japaneseness, which is considered to be the soul, and then the West is considered to be the body. This is classical dualism. This is a dualism that has been proven to be a failure. We find this in Descartes and with the mechanists of the seventeenth century and early eighteenth century in Europe. After the second half of the eighteenth century it's almost banal to talk like this, but that wasn't the case for the East Asians at the very beginning of their modernization. So Japan did succeed in building a really strong country. This small country, first of all, defeated Russia in 1905. This was magic. Russia was a big and dangerous country for Europe. But it was defeated by the Japanese. Although of course both sides were supported by different European forces.

CC

It was the first time since the Mongols that European armies were defeated in war.

YH

But in a way it was also a European war, because Japan was supported by London, Russia was supported by Paris. The money came from there.

CC

But the Japanese were clearly stronger than the Russians.

YH

The Japanese had good strategies and good technologies. And they were very determined to win the war. They went on to defeat the Chinese. The success of Japan was a very important model for Asian countries. But if we go a little bit further, what happened after this time? If we look at what happened between World War I and World War II, there is another voice, which is the attempt to "overcome modernity." So what does it mean to overcome modernity? There was a conference in the 1940s among Japanese scholars that brought together a very interesting combination of people — the Kyoto School philosophers, historians, composers, writers, musicians. They wanted to overcome modernity because they saw the decadence of the West. I mean, it was not just the Japanese who called it decadence; it was people like Oswald Spengler with his *Decline of the West* (1926) and so on. They saw that Europe was surrounded by wars, so they wanted to overcome modernity as a way to also overcome the West. Because modernity is the product of the West. It comes from the West. It didn't come from Japan, it didn't come from China. The idea of this movement overcoming modernity meant they wanted to invent a new thought, a new philosophy, and a new model of development that would be different from the European one, but at the same time also allow the Japanese to develop their own thought. The humanities and sciences in Japan at that time, in the Meiji period, were very much German. If you studied medicine in Japan then, you had to learn German, because everything was written in German.The Japanese writer Osamu Dazai wrote a novel about the great Chinese writer Lu Xun (1881–1936), in which he went to Japan in 1902 to study medicine. In this biography Lu Xun was speaking broken German.

This movement of trying to overcome modernity was an attempt at reorientation, an attempt to rethink what Japanese thought is. What is Japanese culture? What is the relation between Japanese culture and modernity? What could be another way? This is very complicated and has always interested me. It has been my plan to do something about it. That is one of the reasons I came back to Hong Kong (and then we had a pandemic and nothing was possible!). The discussion has been undermined in recent years because it has tended to be condemned as mere fascism.

Our friend Ho Tzu Nyen, an artist from Singapore, has been doing a VR project in Japan. His most recent one, *Hotel Aporia* (2019), is about the Kyoto School and its involvement in the War. Overcoming Modernity is interesting and I would not want to just throw it into the rubbish. I think that group had very stimulating ideas that we can still discuss today. Interestingly, if you look at the work of the most significant thinkers in our time in Europe, people like Bruno Latour and anthropologists like Philippe Descola, they also talk about overcoming modernity, but in their cases it's about overcoming modernity within Europe itself. I think the fact that the Meiji period wasn't really a success was already recognized before World War II and that's why there was such a discussion around overcoming modernity, which was also used to justify the imperialism of Japan.

INTI GUERRERO

Could we connect this to the term you've used, "the technical singularity," and what you previously called the "synchronization" of a certain type of technology? I'm just thinking spontaneously about something like a type of technological singularity that has "won" over so called marginal(ized) technologies?

YH

For me the technological singularity is an imagination, it's a myth of technology. You imagine that one day the computer is able to reflect upon itself, which means it has consciousness. When it has consciousness, it will also have intelligence. So if you consider that one day your computer is able to do that, and everyone's computer is able to do that, and we are able to produce more computers than human beings, then we will be able to create a huge gigantic super intelligence, and this super intelligence will be more than the sum of all the intelligence in the world, because of its computational power. Then that would be the end of the human world. That would be the end of human politics, because politics, first of all, is an affair of the human, and, insofar as we are always in a political problem, it's because politics is based on human decisions, and human decisions are susceptible to mistakes and to bias and to stupidity, like what we see today in most countries around the world. So then that's actually not far from a right-wing discourse, which claims that with this super intelligence emerging, with the arrival of the singularity, we are able to build a society that is based on optimization calculated by machines. So for me this is a fantasy, but also this is an eschatology in the sense that in moving towards a singularity, all technology will be synchronized, and in doing so all cultures will be synchronized. Then there's an end point, and at that end point, a new world will be celebrated. That is eschatology. Technological singularity according to this kind of discourse is really akin to

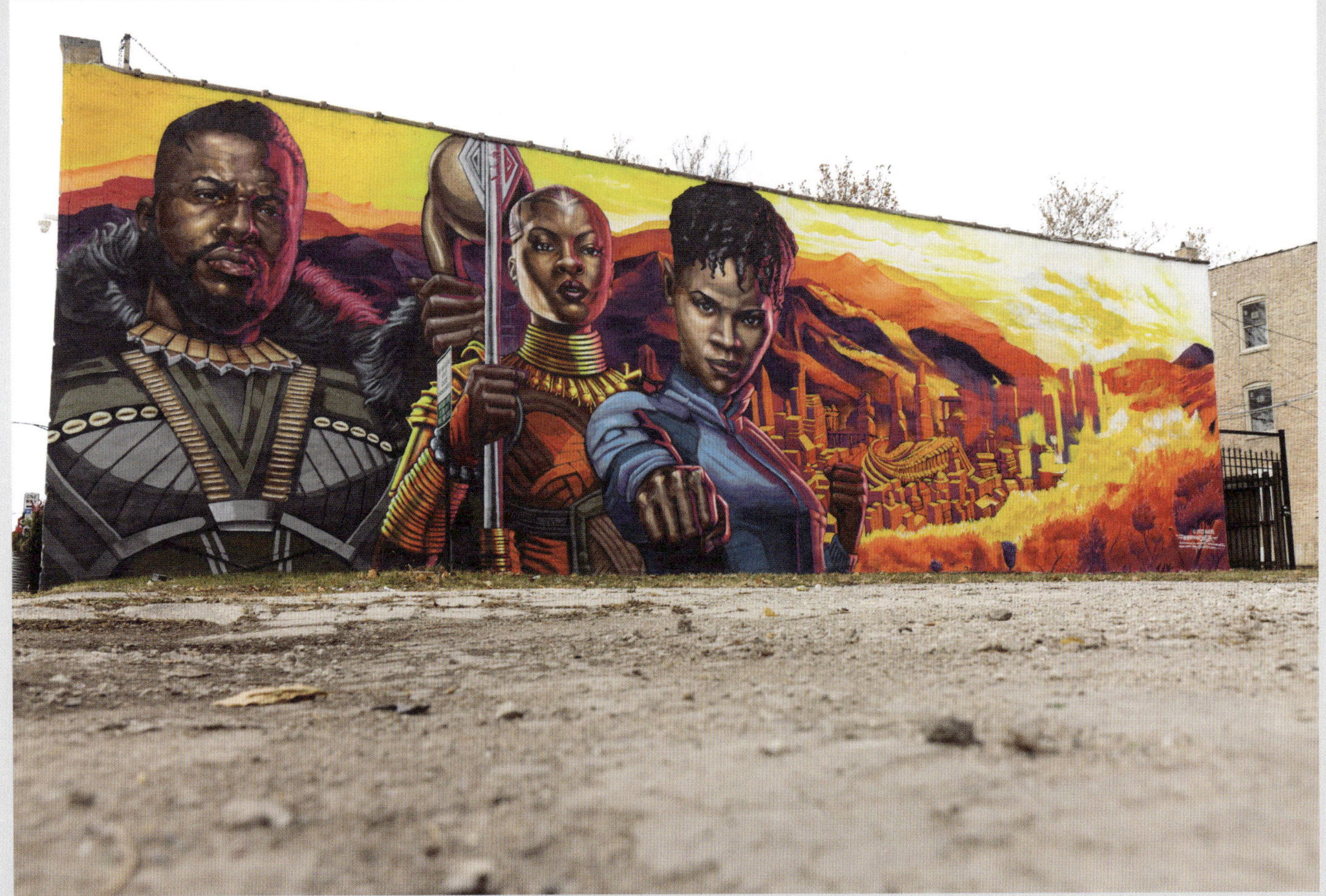

FIG 3 "Wakanda Forever" by muralist Rahmaan Statik at 606 East 61st Street in the Woodlawn neighborhood of Chicago, Illinois, December 8, 2022. STM-110246524, Anthony Vazquez / *Chicago Sun-Times*

Christian theology. This way of thinking is really something shared by many technologists today, especially in Silicon Valley. It's also a vision that is based on the belief that one day machines will be able to do all planning better than human beings. So acceleration, that's how the right wing, or even the neo-reactionaries, talk about technology and singularity. So the question within this discourse is really, What do we think of this myth of singularity? Are we going to follow this myth? Are we going to escape? If we are going to escape, how are we going to escape? For me this is a key question. In answering it we can produce another discourse of course, but we should keep in mind that it is not simply a question of inventing a new narrative; any outcome depends on the concrete development of technology, and also on the development of our relationship to technology. That's why I suggest that instead of thinking of a convergence to an end point, we think instead about the reopening of history, as an alternative to longing for the apocalypse to arrive.

IG

Regarding your invitation towards techno-diversity or -diversities, how can societies bypass racism? For example it continues to violently create hierarchies upon technological epistemes from things like ancestral irrigation to agriculture or ancestral forms of navigation in astronomy, in different cultures in the world.

CC

What is the role that racism plays? The very broad category of racism.

YH

We can see how racism is produced through technology and by technology by referring to Jean-Jacques Rousseau's *Second Discourse (A Discourse on Inequality)*. We've discussed the way the Europeans were able to enter East Asia, not as tourists but as exporters of culture. We know that Europe before the fifteenth century was really weak, and then, with modernity and the development of technology, colonization was able to take place.

CC

But was it really technology or was it more the economic system in Europe that made such expansion a critical part of its development?

YH

I think a process is an economic need—expansion, the birth of capitalism, and so on.

CC

And China had the technology to go to Europe.

YH

Although—if you have money but you don't have navigation technology or guns etc., how are you going to conquer America? When the natives are not so rare on the land and you know there's no technological difference, how would you be confident you are going to conquer them? Similarly, if the British had not been strong with their navy, we wouldn't have this story of Hong Kong today; because China was defeated in the two Opium Wars, Hong Kong was rented to Britain.

Racism is a very complicated issue which can't be explained only by technology, because there was also some biological discourse and so on. But what I was trying to say was that when we talk about racism we are actually talking about the question of inequality, and inequality not only among individuals, but also among people of different colors, people from different geographical regions in the world, because of the color of their skin, because of their system of knowledge, and what is considered "advanced," versus what is considered "traditional" or "obsolete." Traditional and obsolete—they're almost the same in the eye of modernity. Today racism of course continues to exist. And as I said, racism is not purely a question of technology, but technology plays an important role in the recognition of race and the inequalities between different cultures. For example, which cultures are considered to be behind or regressive? Even among the Jesuits in China in the early twentieth century, some came to the conclusion that the East was not about evolution. The East was about regression, stasis, immobility, while only the West was about progress, was about evolution, they thought.

So let me go back to your question—about how the development of diversity can overcome the question of racism—

CC

—or inequality, as you put it—

YH

—let's try to approach it in several ways: First of all, if technology, including military expansion and economic development, are considered to be the way we measure strength, then whoever masters AI and leads in the development of AI will dominate the world, as Putin put it in 2017. Whichever nation arrives at a technological singularity before other countries will dominate. And although on the one hand, paradoxically, this is not about race, at the same time, it also is about race, because a certain ethnic group is going to dominate, and probably not the whites. Maybe it will be the yellows, or maybe it will be like the movie *Black Panther*, and they're going to discover a specific mineral, a very powerful mineral, and then Africa will dominate the world.

On the surface it's about technological development, but this is about a national or ethnic identity that goes into developing technologies. However, the measurement of technology is very much based on a kind of "techno logos" of rationality, efficiency, and all these values that are essential to modern technology. So when I talked about developing technodiversity—to go back to the question of locality, but not only tradition—it's important to understand how locality is able to transform technologies and reappropriate technologies by renegotiating them, and that's why the relation between the human and the non-human, the human and the environment, is so key. This kind of attempt happened in Latin America, but then disappeared again, in Bolivia and Brazil. It's fundamental to pay attention to the potential to transform technology from the perspective of locality, to not simply see technology for its uses, but to perhaps even reinvent locality and reinvent thinking.

In my latest book I talk about "the individuation of thinking." It's not about keeping or maintaining tradition, nor about embracing the modern, but rather it's about how you conceive an individuation of thinking. How can you produce a thinking that can bring novelty into the locality, but at the same time allow the trans-formation of technology? This is one way to think about that, which also allows us to think about the relation between human and nature, human and non-human beings, and distance us from these mere military and economic competitions that are based on homogeneous technologies, like what is happening now with 5G microchips; it is a game of imperialism and we've had enough of this in history—do we really want to repeat?

The second way of thinking about this is to consider that within the question of race there is paradoxically an attempt to be inclusive of different races. And this is within the concept of the universal. The discourse of the universal was also somthing to do with anti-homogeneity. In a book by the historian Paul Hazard titled *La Crise de la conscience européenne* (1935), we read a rather interesting story about the French missionaries who went to Thailand, or Siam at the time, in the sixteenth century. They wanted to convert the King to Christianity, and the King replied that if there were a god, god wouldn't want this world to be homogeneous with only one religion, since it would be too easy. God would want to embrace and allow diversity under His grace. The French were shocked, because they couldn't refuse him that if god created the world then god wouldn't force everyone to be Christian. So the wisdom of the King seemed to suggest a kind of universalism that cannot be overridden by European culture.

And that continues, as we see in the Enlightenment, the crisis of the European mind is precisely the thing that must be overcome. The discourse of the universal has to justify the European expansion: colonization, wars, and later on globalization. This kind of universalism disregards race, yet we can say it is the most racist I think, because it ignores locality.

So instead of starting with the universal—instead of wanting to use the universal to mold every culture, every race—why don't we start with diversity? And from diversity through the medium of technology, look for what could be shared in common. So almost the reverse of the Enlightenment. The Enlightenment was the emanation of Europeanism. What if we start with diversity, and from diversity try to think of the different ways that contribute to commonality through what I call "technodiversity." That would give us a different geopolitical configuration from what we have today, because today we are really competing within one particular form of technology and rationality to see who gets stronger according to the rules of the game, and then whoever becomes excellent at this will dominate the world. But this is also a childish game. It's become really depressing.

CC

We wanted to introduce the subject of traditional Chinese medicine, as you often bring it up as an example of a medical episteme that operates in its own cosmology. Could you elaborate on this operation, as well as on the field of Chinese medicine itself? It has gone through its own process of modernization and integration into the capitalist system through its own set of disciplinary institutions, such as university programs and clinics dedicated to Chinese medicine. And in Hong Kong (as well as in Taiwan) you have an official hybridity between the two systems.

YH

Chinese medicine is one example I use very often. The language of Chinese medicine is a cosmological language: yin and yang, the five movements, and so on. So this is also the language of cosmology in China. That's why I said that Chinese medicine may be the best example for explaining what I call "cosmotechnics." Technologies like these, which we consider obsolete, are grounded in cosmology. And it's worth remembering that if you look at the sky in Latin America, for example, or from the South, it looks different from the sky when you look at it from Romania, let's say.

So there are different cosmologies because they're looking at the sky from different points, and therefore we have different relations to phenomena. Chinese medicine is an example of cosmotechnics not only because of its cosmological language, but also because it's an empirical science. When I say it's an empirical science, I mean that it's a product of thousands of years of practice. So it's not something fictional. It's tested on so many people, through a huge population, over thousands years. And it still works today. But if, for example, a Chinese doctor has a conversation with a Western medical doctor, and the materialist asks him or her, "Show me the ch'i (or *qi*)," how are they going to show it? Or, "Show me yin and yang,"—that's even more difficult.

With ch'i, you can actually say you can sense the pulse. But how about yin and yang? Where's yin and where's yang? You show them blood, but you cannot say where yin and yang are, and then they say, "Well then this is not scientific because in Western medicine everything is visible in terms of data. You can analyze the blood. But when it comes to Chinese medicine, it's not something that can be made visible. And it's also not something quantifiable. For example when you look at the tongue, the diagnosis of the tongue, it's based on heat and based on coldness, yin and yang. But at the same time, you cannot say it is not scientific because it's an empirical science, and empirical science is also science although it doesn't share the same epistemology and ontology as Western medicine, because as is the case with yin and yang, there are different ontological categories.

Hong Kong is going to have a new Chinese medical hospital, and last year, during the pandemic, president Xi Jinping announced that Chinese medicine will be introduced for all students from grade five in primary school. They will all have to learn Chinese medicine. This has a lot to do with national pride and national identity. But nevertheless, looking back we can say that Chinese medicine is still effective. As knowledge, not as an identity, but as knowledge it's still very valuable. If we just follow Western epistemology, we can simply throw Chinese medicine away because the two are not compatible. But we should not throw it away because it still works, and it still has so much value and potential to evolve. So this is one concrete case where we can think about how the question of locality can be used to transform technology by integrating, for example, technologies into diagnosis. A doctor I met in Beijing decided to use cameras for diagnosing the tongue. Why? She said that traditionally a doctor looks at the tongue "according to normal daylight," but the problem is that daylight changes all the time, so the diagnosis may not be right when it is early in the morning or six in the evening, or when we have to use artificial light, or in the middle of the day. So a way of dealing with this is to fix the light in the observation room, and then have cameras take pictures to make sure the tongue is always observed under the same conditions. I mean, this is only a very simple example to think about how, without giving up this full knowledge, it can easily have new interactions with modern technologies.

Twenty years ago when you were ill, you could not claim your insurance for a diagnosis from a practitioner of Chinese medicine because it wasn't considered scientific. Now perhaps it's possible to claim for it.

CC

Definitely. We have it.

YH

And now the situation has changed a bit in other ways, like in relation to what happened in the process of scientific proof for Chinese medicine. Which was done a lot, for example, in Japan, but also in China—they basically took traditional herbal products and examined their chemical components. The majority of the combinations of herbs turned out to have things like variant chemical components that were the same as those found in Western medications. If you look at what researchers at the University of Hong Kong are doing in Chinese medicine (because I have a doctor there, so I talk to him sometimes) and consider how they analyze a specific element, a specific herb, it's interesting. There are always one or two central herbs that provide the main function. And if you focus on these to find out what's inside them, then you can rationalize the prescription. Which gives some kind of scientific confidence. So this is not only about education, but also research, and also about an effort being made to strengthen the dialog with Western chemistry and medicine.

IG

Following your conversation with Brazilian anthropologist Viveiros de Castro around his concepts of Amerindian perspectivism and multinaturalism, have his ideas had an impact on your work?

YH

The contribution of Viveiros de Castro—his "multinaturalism"—is that he's trying to show, along with his colleagues including Philippe Descola, that the concept of nature that we think we know is actually problematic because it's the product of European modernity, and according to this conception of nature, it is opposed to culture. There was a funny story told by Philippe Descola in his book *Beyond Nature and Culture* (2013). It's from Henri Michaux's diary, when the author in the 1920s went to Ecuador to visit one of his friends. The next year he wanted to go back to Paris. So he had to take a boat along the Amazon river, maybe to Brazil, and then to Portugal and then back to Paris—I don't remember the route but he needed to take a boat with people from the forest to go to Brazil. So one day he arrived in a small town in Brazil, and everyone got off the boat during a stop. They had a look at the city and when they went close to the city park—there is a big park in the city—a young lady from the forest exclaimed, "Thank God, we finally have nature."

And this is surprising because for her, the forest was not nature, the Amazon River was not nature. Nature was something that was enclosed by culture, by urban space. So culture and nature are often held in opposition—I find that really profound. I use this story to explain to my students the weirdness of the modern concept of nature. The contribution of Descola, and also Viveiros de Castro, is the thought that actually there are different concepts, and different natures. There's not only one nature. And what's more, these so-called different natures contain differing relations between human and nonhuman beings.

You can also find this in China. The Chinese word *ziran* is used to translated the western term "nature," and today it is used to mean something that is not human-made, for example to refer to the river, the forest, the moutain. This translation was firstly done by Japanese scholars before it was exported back to China, but *ziran* originally means something spontaneous, or leaving a thing to itself so it can be in its own way, without suppressing or exaggerating it. It doesn't mean not touching them, it means letting them be themselves. It's very different from what we think of today as the external environment.

Similarly, it's not only the concept of nature but also the concept of technics that has to be undone and redone. And even the concept of culture. We have inherited all these categories and in our education these categories were taught as universal categories—technology, nature, culture, science. For me the issue is that we cannot resolve the problem with nature now. I was interviewed by an Argentinian leftist newspaper a few days ago and I said, "You know the machines are coming to deforest. If we change the narrative of nature, the machines are still coming."

So my negotiation with the anthropologists, including Viveiros de Castro, is to say that we will not be able to overcome modernity by singling out the concept of nature. Because a concept always exists in relation to other concepts. We cannot take it out as if it's an isolated reality. I want to reintroduce the concept of technics. That's why I coined the term "cosmotechnics." And that's why I speak about technodiversity as a response to what they call multinaturalism. I think the concept and question of technodiversity, or multiple cosmotechnics, is something that was repressed in past centuries because we have only one standard now, the Western standard, to define what is scientific and what is not scientific, what is modern and what is premodern, etc. I prefer calling it "non-modern" instead of "premodern." Things cannot be categorized as premodern or modern or postmodern. An art historian would say, "Chinese landscape painting is postmodern," but no, you can't even put it that way because by doing that you subsume it into a lineage. Premodern, modern, postmodern—and then what happens after postmodern, the singularity, which means the apocalypse. So premodern, modern, postmodern, apocalypse. That is the beautiful lineage of Christianity, of Christian time.

IG

Can you comment on how we might avoid cultural essentialisms when discussing Indigeneity today? How do you see the identitarian traps within multiculturalism in global capitalism?

YH

I think we touched on this when we discussed traditionalism. Because to essentialize it is like finding a symbol, and then you use that as an identity, as if it's a substance. But let's look at locality, let's look at tradition as a form of knowledge. We have to change this form of thinking. I constantly try to undermine the question of identity. I'd rather consider what I call individuation in thinking, meaning that two thinkings can come together—and these thinkings actually have to be incompatible. We don't have to find harmony between them; the contrary is true. We have to confront different ways of thinking. That is the only condition that can produce new thinkings. Never avoid conflict. Welcome conflict. And then we can invent. That is what I call the individuation of thinking. And incompatibility is its condition.

CC

And how do you see the identitarian traps within multiculturalism in global capitalism?

YH

Viveiros de Castro says something quite interesting: that multiculturalism assumes there are multiple cultures and one nature; that there are different cultures, but they consume the same nature. And he asks, Why don't we think of one culture with multiple natures? So we form a culture, and in this culture there are different natures. In a way it allows us to avoid the question of identity, it bypasses it, and says let's look at our everyday relation to nonhuman beings. So we change the starting point from identity, away from the narrative of what is an Indian, what is a German, what is a Hong Konger, what is a Romanian? And instead look at different ways of being with nonhuman beings. That is the starting point. I'd add that we should also look at how different forms of knowledge based on locality will be able to transform technology, but at the same time interact with other forms of thought in the world. Like an epistemological diplomacy. Currently our diplomacy is not epistemological diplomacy. It's economic diplomacy. For example, a rich country gives money to another country and says, "Now we are friends."

IG

Or vaccines.

YH

Exactly. "I give you vaccines, I give you money, and please next time when you have to vote in the UN you know who you should vote for." And you know that every day when you listen to the radio, when you look at the newspaper, that the rhetoric of diplomats is simply crazy, if not merely lies. It's scandalous. So back to the question of multiculturalism, multinationalism, and diplomacy: I propose what I call "epistemological diplomacy," and this epistemological diplomacy doesn't have to be done through the foreign minister, or the ministry of foreign affairs. This is our responsibility, the responsibility of intellectuals and curators, like what you are trying to do in this book.

CC

So we're doing this with our limited means, but what kind of institutions do you think we would have to imagine to do this? What kind of institutions could support epistemological diplomacy? What kinds of new institutional structures could be imagined in that direction?

YH

That is a very tough question. We used to rely on universities to do this, because they're the places of education. But I don't think that universities today are ready to answer these questions. Most universities are now mainly for supplying talent to industry. So we need new institutions but also new networks of institutions. Curators and art institutions have been working on this through asking questions in exhibitions and art. But for me it needs to go much further. It's not simply about the discourse of this knowledge, but it's the development of the application of this knowledge. In my case, for my interests, that means in technologies. It needs to be concrete as opposed to abstract. An abstract solidarity is, let's say, something like identity. A concrete solidarity means that we are able to produce new institutions. We are able to produce new forms of art making, be that with machines or with other operators. We are able to build new schools, new forms of technologies, new social networks for artists (not Facebook).

CC

This publication includes different perspectives on heritage and its contemporary ideological instrumentalizations, with a particular focus on conversations about the restitution of colonially looted objects in Western museums. It would be great to hear your thoughts on this.

YH

A friend of mine from Belgium has been working on this for the past three years, lobbying the Belgian government to return stolen objects to African countries, especially Congo. They have taken so much from Africa. I recall a documentary made by Alain Resnais and Chris Marker, *Statues Also Die* (1953). It's a documentary about these African objects in a museum in France, and where you find the object, the statue has this phrase written: "*origine inconnue*" (unknown origin). So these objects are decontextualized. And the question is, will these objects be recontextualized after they're returned? What does it mean to recontextualize this kind of object? For me this is a more important question than just considering this object from the perspective of private property or national property.

What would it mean to recontextualize these kinds of statues? For me this is a question of anamnesis, a question of remembering their former lives. Are we able to perform anamnesis with these objects, and what kind of anamnesis do we want to perform? Are we going to perform anamnesis of the national origin that contributes to the discourse of nationalism? What kind of anamnesis could be possible? If it is not about national identity, it is not about nationalism. It's beyond identity politics today.

CC

To directly respond to that and provoke a little bit, I think part of the conversation about these objects is that there was a triple process of erasure that happened around them. First is their actual physical removal from their context. Secondly is the decontextualization that happened alongside this act of extraction. Of course, these objects are not uniform, and they have very different functions. Some of them are religious, others have various social functions, like history telling, while others were primarily decorative objects. But whether these functions are known or partially known to the European museums, they remain invisible in that context. Thirdly, there was also this process of them being denied, in European museums, a full identity as art objects. And this is one of the most pervasive and perverse parts of the process that happened and still happens in the colonial handling of these objects. Because while the word "art" is often, albeit not always, used in relation to them, it is always with a qualifier—African art, Oceanic art, etc., which are of course

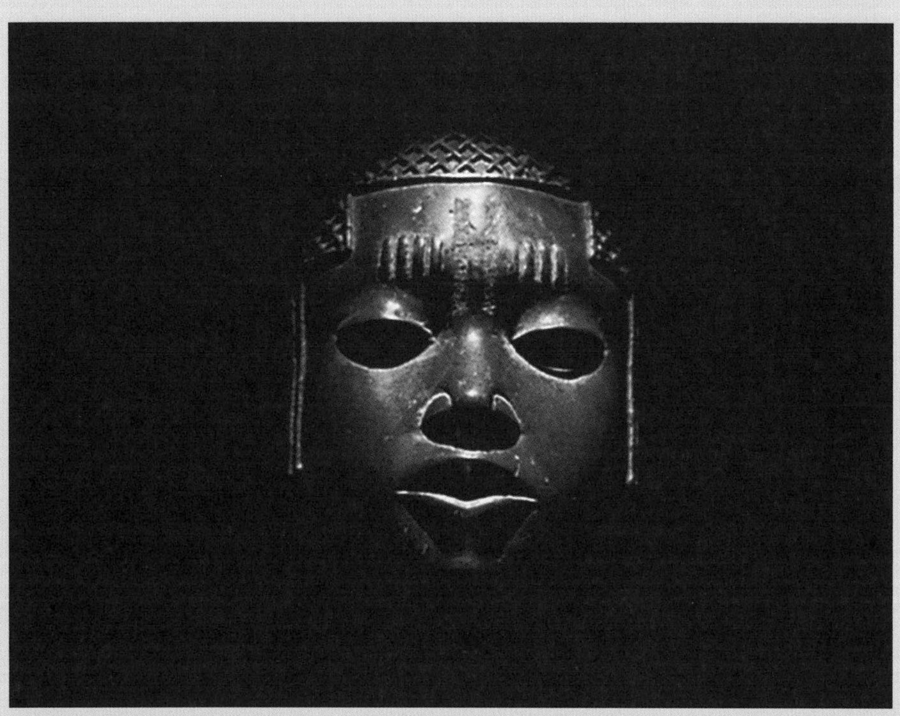

FIG 4 Chris Marker and Alain Resnais, *Les statues meurent aussi*, 1953. Film still. © Revue Présence Africaine.

fundamentally different than the unqualified art which is always the European art of the time, and which is mostly shown in different institutions and in different exhibitions. The Benin Bronzes, made in the seventeenth century, are never shown together with European baroque painting of the seventeenth century. They are shown as their own category, as not quite art. European museology even developed its own bizarre instruments for aesthetic judgment of these objects—including the fetish for their patina.

There is hope that through this process of restitution, as unlikely as it might be, a recontextualization into the objects' original functions might occur. Even if they would not always be taken to the same shrines or palaces where they were actually stolen from, which might not always exist anymore, and even if they won't perform the same functions they had in the communities that have also changed in many ways, they would at least perform other crucial functions in the process of writing multiple art histories.

YH

I think I understand the importance of having a coherent lineage of these objects. That's also a very important process because due to the finitude of human memories, anamnesis can only be performed through externalized objects such as writings and artworks. (For Plato anamnesis is fundamental for access to truth). So many stolen objects have lost their context and been excluded from History. I don't know whether you came across the opening of the Humboldt Forum in Berlin this year? There was much controversy because of criticism from art historians who were saying that this is a repetition of the colonial act, because it showed all these objects from different African countries. Even as a new institute it still repeated the same gesture! The director, art historian Horst Bredekamp, was very upset during an interview on Deutschlandfunk Kultur radio because the whole project was criticized as the continuation of the colonial project. I am not sure if it is so simple. I think the importance of having to perform anamnesis is key, as we've said. And I think European institutions should also perform their own anamnesis to readdress their past in a new form, other than exhibiting it as their glorious time. What is so tricky and interesting to think about is what kind of anamnesis one can perform through these objects in order to open different imaginations of the future, which for me is the fundamental question for creativity and curatorship.

November 2021

Contributors

Lawrence Abu Hamdan is a private ear serving industries of culture since 2007. He works across the civil, criminal, human, marital, theological, and supernatural fields from Beirut, Berlin, Dubai, and London.

Naman P. Ahuja is a curator and art historian. He is Professor of Indian Art and Architecture at Jawaharlal Nehru University, New Delhi, and Editor of Marg Publications, Mumbai.

Pio Abad's work is concerned with the personal and political entanglements of objects. Informed by the history of the Philippines, it uses appropriation to unravel official accounts and draw out threads of complicity.

Radcliffe Bailey (1968–2023) was a mixed media artist based in Atlanta, GA, who layered imagery, culturally resonant materials, and text to explore themes of ancestry, race, migration, and collective memory.

Lia Colombino is Director of Indigenous Art Museum at Museo del Barro, Director at Instituto Superior de Arte (Art Institute, National University of Asuncion), and a member of Red Conceptualismos del Sur.

Myrlande Constant is a textile artist living and working in Haiti who specializes in Vodou flags in which she employs the *tambour* technique to communicate the female gaze.

Cosmin Costinaş is a curator and writer based in Berlin. He is currently Senior Curator of Exhibition Practices at Haus der Kulturen der Welt, Berlin, and Co-Artistic Director of the 24th Biennale of Sydney.

Natasha Ginwala is a curator, researcher, and writer, artistic director of Colomboscope, Sri Lanka since 2019 and associate Curator at Large at Gropius Bau, Berlin (2018–24).

Inti Guerrero is a curator and writer based in Berlin. He is Co-Artistic Director of the 24th Biennale of Sydney, tutor of Curatorial Studies at the Royal Academy of Fine Arts-KASK, Ghent, and was formerly Artistic Director of bap, Manila.

Sven Haakanson is a leading anthropologist working in the documentation, preservation, and revival of indigenous culture, including his own native Alaskan Sugpiaq traditions.

Nikau Hindin (Ngai Tūpoto hāpū, Te Rarawa, Ngāpuhi) is a barkcloth maker dedicated to reviving and preserving this traditional Māori practice in Aotearoa, New Zealand. She is based in Turanga, Gisborne.

Hong Lysa is a Singaporean historian whose writings focus on the scripting of national histories and their contestations.

Dusadee Huntrakul is an artist based in Bangkok. His sculpture, drawings, and ceramic works are at the intersection of visual arts, archeology, and urban ecological observation.

Frances Wadsworth Jones is a jewelry designer, maker, and educator who lives and works in London. Her work uses traditional craftsmanship to render culturally diverse references.

Carol Yinghua Lu is an art historian, writer, and curator. She is Director of the Inside-Out Art Museum, Beijing.

Xiaoxuan Lu is Assistant Professor of Landscape Architecture at the University of Hong Kong. Her research focuses on the cultural landscape and geography of conflict, particularly in China and its transboundary regions.

Vali Mahlouji is a curator whose platform Archaeology of the Final Decade excavates lost cultural histories. He is an advisor to the British Museum, Art Dubai Modern, and the Bahman Mohassess Estate.

Bonaventure Soh Bejeng Ndikung is a curator, writer, and biotechnologist. He founded SAVVY Contemporary, Berlin, and is Director and Chief Curator at Haus der Kulturen der Welt, Berlin.

Nget Rady is a dancer specializing in the Cambodian classical male masked dance form, Lakhaon Kaol. He works with Amrita Performing Arts and leads the Roof Dance Team.

Maia Nuku is Curator of the Arts of Oceania at the Metropolitan Museum of Art, New York. She is of English and Māori (Ngai Tai) descent and was born in London.

Pablo José Ramírez is a curator and writer based in Guatemala and Amsterdam. He is Adjunct Curator of First Nations and Indigenous Art at Tate Modern, and Editor-in-Chief of Infrasonica.

Marian Pastor Roces is an independent curator and cultural critic. She heads TAOINC, the Philippines' only corporation curating the establishment of museums, public art projects, exhibitions, and publications.

Olinda Silvano is an Amazonian artist from the Shipibo people, a teacher of the kené art form, and a Peruvian healer. Her work communicates the language of plants in defense of the Amazon.

Frank Tang Kai Yiu is an artist based in Hong Kong. He uses a range of technologies and platforms, including ink painting, video, sound, and collaborative performance.

Cecilia Vicuña is a poet, artist, activist, and filmmaker whose work addresses ecological destruction, human rights, and cultural homogenization. She lives and works between Santiago de Chile and New York City.

Thongchai Winichakul is Professor of History at University of Wisconsin-Madison whose research focuses on the cultural and intellectual history of Siam.

Bo Wang is an artist, filmmaker, and researcher based in Amsterdam.

Yuk Hui is a philosopher from Hong Kong. He teaches at the City University of Hong Kong and his latest book is titled *Art and Cosmotechnics* (2021).

Vivian Ziherl is a contemporary art critic and curator. She is Research and Programs Manager at Kunstinstituut Melly, Rotterdam, and founder of Frontier Imaginaries foundation.

Image Credits

Unless otherwise noted, all images are courtesy of the collection from which they derive.

[FRONT ENDPAPERS]
Original artwork by Rady Nget (pp. 326–37); Myrlande Constant (pp. 110–11).

[REAR ENDPAPERS]
Original image appears as Fig. 10 on p. 314; Original image of Rosanna Raymond, "Back Hand Maiden" by Richard Wade appears as Fig. 21 on p. 64.

DUSADEE HUNTRAKUL

pp. 22–29
"There are More Monsoon Songs Elsewhere (16 Ban Chiang bracelets from LACMA collection found on www.lacma.org)," 2018. 30 × 21 cm each. Charcoal powder, soft pastel, dry pigment, white chalk, and color pencil on paper, Collection of Singapore Art Museum.

RADCLIFFE BAILEY

p. 44
Notes from Tervuren, 2012. Gouache, collage, and ink on sheet music. © Radcliffe Bailey. Courtesy of the artist and Jack Shainman Gallery, New York.

p. 45
Notes from Tervuren, 2013 Gouache, collage, and ink on sheet music. © Radcliffe Bailey. Courtesy of the artist and Jack Shainman Gallery, New York.

p. 46–47
Notes from Tervuren, 2013 Gouache, collage, and ink on sheet music. © Radcliffe Bailey. Courtesy of the artist and Jack Shainman Gallery, New York.

pp. 48–49
Notes from Tervuren, 2013 Gouache, collage, and ink on sheet music. © Radcliffe Bailey. Courtesy of the artist and Jack Shainman Gallery, New York.

p. 50
Notes from Tervuren, 2012 Gouache, collage, and ink on sheet music. © Radcliffe Bailey. Courtesy of the artist and Jack Shainman Gallery, New York.

p. 51
Notes from Tervuren, 2013 (left and right). Gouache, collage, and ink on sheet music. © Radcliffe Bailey. Courtesy of the artist and Jack Shainman Gallery, New York.

NIKAU HINDIN

p. 66
Arorangi, 2019. Kōkōwai and ngārahu on aute. Image courtesy Jhana Miller.

p. 67
Pō Ngārahu, 2019. Soot Black Night. Image courtesy Jhana Miller.

p. 68–69
Pō Ngārahu, 2019 (details). Soot Black Night. Image courtesy the artist.

p. 70
Kia Āta-Uira | Become gentle lightning, 2022. Pukepoto and kerewhenua on aute, with rattan frame. Image courtesy Seb Charles.

p.71
[LEFT] *Te Tīpare o Hine Takurua (The Winter Solstice)*, 2020. Kōkōwai (red ochre) and ngārahu (soot pigments) on bark cloth. Image courtesy Seb Charles.

[MIDDLE]
Te Ia o te Ao II (The divine flow of energy in the universe II), 2020. Kōkōwai (red ochre) and ngārahu (soot pigments) on bark cloth. Image courtesy Seb Charles.

[RIGHT]
Ira (Life Principle), 2020. Kōkōwai (red ochre) and ngārahu (soot pigments)

on bark cloth. Image courtesy Seb Charles.

pp. 72–73
Nikau Hindin laying out finished pieces for her solo exhibition *Kōkōrangi ki Kōkōwai*, 2020. Image courtesy Te Kuru o te Marama Dewes.

pp. 74–75
[1] Haylee Koroi uses a pounamu (greenstone) scraper to soften and remove water from the bast of the aute (Step 1).

[2] After making the length way cut along the stalk Hindin is peeling back the bark (Step 1.0).

[3] Here Hindin is removing the bast off the inner stalk of the paper mulberry (Step 1.1).

[4] Here Haylee is beating the cloth with a beater made from pohutukawa (Step 2).

[5] The process is called whakapaa and after making a light cut in the bark Hindin has flicked up the edges of the brown bark (Step 2.0).

[6] This is Haylee unfolding her piece of cloth after the folding and beating process. This is the final reveal (Step 2.1) .

[7] Here Hindin is peeling the outer bark off the inner bast of the mulberry paper. The process is called *whakapaa*. After making a light cut in the bark, Hindin has flicked up the brown bark (Step 2.2) .

[8] Here Hindin has managed to grip the edge of the bark and is pulling it in a downward motion against her thigh (Step 2.3).

[9] This is Haylee's piece. The creases come from the folding and beating process (Step 3).

[10] Scraping the bast and removing all the excess water. This is the step right before beating (Step 3.1).

[11] Demonstrating the beating process for Aitutaki Pa'oa revivalist Lulu (Step 4.0).

[12] Close-up of the bast that has been thoroughly cleaned and scraped being beaten on the anvil. You can see the grooves of the beater making imprints on the bast as the fibers spread out (Step 4.1).

[13] Close-up of the beaten cloth drying in the sun (Step 5.0). Images courtesy Seb Charles and Hana Burgess.

MYRLANDE CONSTANT

p. 106
Saint Nicola, 2020. Sequins and beaded flag. 79 × 89 inches.

p. 107
Erzulie Dantor, 1995–2020. Sequins, glass beads, and silk tassels on cotton. 42 × 38.5 × 2 inches.

pp. 108–9
Saint Nicola (details), 2020. Sequins and beaded flag. 79 × 89 inches.

pp. 110–11
[LEFT]
Guede, 2020. Beads, sequins, and silk on cotton. 88 × 85 × 4 inches.

[TOP RIGHT]
Scene with Brigitte and Baron, 2010–17. Sequins, beads, and silk on cotton. 62 × 87 inches.

[BOTTOM RIGHT]
Invocation of Saint Anthony, 2015–19. Beads, sequins, and silk on cotton. 47 × 60 inches.

pp. 112–13
Scene with Brigitte and Baron (details), 2010–17. Sequins, beads, and silk on cotton. 62 × 87 inches.

p. 114
Maitresse Dalia, 2021. Sequins, beads, cotton. 72 × 55 inches.

p. 115
Maitresse Dalia (details), 2021. Sequins, beads, cotton. 72 × 55 inches

p. 116
Baron Crimenel, 2021. Sequins, beads, cotton. 44 × 42 inches.

p. 117
Sirenes, 2020. Sequins and beaded flag. 82 × 103 inches.

pp. 118–19
Sirenes (details), 2020. Sequins and beaded flag. 82 × 103 inches.

CECILIA VICUÑA

p. 161
[TOP]
Magellanic penguin from ebird Macaulay Library ML 51753271. Image courtesy Noah Strycker.

[BOTTOM]
Schoolchildren in uniform, Punta Arenas, Chile. Image courtesy of Independent Picture Service / Alamy Stock Photo.

p. 162
[TOP LEFT]
Chilean student protesters march down La Alameda, the main avenue in Santiago, July 2011. Image courtesy Nicolás 15 / Wikimedia Commons.

[BOTTOM LEFT]
The sign reads: *La lucha es de la sociedad entera / Todos por la educación gratuita* (The fight is of the whole society / Everybody for free education). Image courtesy Osmar Valdebenito via Wikimedia Commons.

[BOTTOM RIGHT]
A group of Chilean students participates in the "Kiss-a-thon for education," convened on Friday, June 5, 2015, by the Federation of Secondary Students of the Metropolitan Region (Femes) in the center of Santiago de Chile (Chile).

p. 163
Naked and semi-naked rallies began soon after: "No + Lucro" "No More Profit," Santiago de Chile, 2011. Image courtesy of Kena Lorenzini Lorenzini.

P. 164
[TOP]
Cecilia Vicuña, detail of *Janis-Joe*, 1971.

[BOTTOM]
Student Rally, Santiago 2015. Standing for reproductive rights, a girl with a fetus, and my red threads. Photo by Victoria Paz Ramírez.

p. 165
[TOP]
Santiago de Chile, 2018, Gender and Equity Watchdog. Courtesy of Kena Lorenzini Lorenzini.

[MIDDLE]
May 16, 2018, Action carried out during the "March for a non-sexist education," Photograph by Matías Fuentes.

[BOTTOM]
In early October 2019, high school students in Santiago started jumping turnstiles to ska music all over the city, ostensibly in protest against a public transit fare increase of thirty pesos. Image courtesy Javier Torres Lantadilla.

p. 166
[TOP]
"*Tu rabia es tu oro.*" (Your rage is your gold). Palabrarma by Cecilia Vicuña. Photograph courtesy of Angela Torrejón/La Feli.

[MIDDLE]
"Somos el Visible Pulso de lo Imposible." We are the visible pulse of the imposible. Palabrarma by Cecilia Vicuña, Performance de Capuchas Rojas (Performance of Red Hoods) in resistance in the petrel wetland, Pichilemu. Performer: Cata Conejo@cataconejo. Photographer: Mariana Mollo @soy.arcadia.

[BOTTOM]
"Somos el Visible Pulso de lo Imposible." We are the visible pulse of the imposible. Palabrarma by Cecilia Vicuña, Performance de Capuchas Rojas (Performance of Red Hoods) in resistance in the petrel wetland, Pichilemu. Performer: Cata Conejo@cataconejo. Photographer: Mariana Mollo @soy.arcadia.

p. 167
[TOP]
Protesters at *Plaza Italia*, Santiago on October 29, 2019, during Chile's Estallido Social (Social Outburst) with a protester flying the Mapuche flag on top of the Baquedano monument. Photograph courtesy of Susana Hidalgo.

[MIDDLE]
"El Veroir Comenzó" reactivating the Palabrarmas Ver dad (Truth), GAM Gabriela Mistral Cultural Center in Santiago, 2019. Photo by Chris Chierego.

[BOTTOM]
Performing a collective ritual homage to the hundreds of people who lost their eyes to police brutality, Santiago, December 2019, GAM Gabriela Mistral Cultural Center in Santiago, 2019. Photo by Chris Chierego.

FRANK TANG

p. 198
Hong Kong Zoological And Botanical Gardens, 2020. Ink and colour on paper. 94 × 73.5 cm.

p. 199
Victoria Park, 2021
Ink and colour on paper
140 × 90 cm.

p. 200–01
Victoria Park (details), 2021. Ink and colour on paper. 140 × 90 cm.

p. 202–05
Zhongshan Park, 2022. Ink and colour on paper. 171 × 95.5 cm.

p. 206–07
Zheng Chenggong, 2019. Ink on silk. 30 × 30 cm.Photo by South Ho.

PIO ABAD AND FRANCES WADSWORTH JONES

pp. 238–47
The Collection of Jane Ryan & William Saunders, 2019. 3d-printed plastic, brass, and dry-transfer text. Installation dimensions variable. Image © Pio Abad and Frances Wadsworth Jones.

LAWRENCE ABU HAMDAN

pp. 248–61
For the Otherwise Unaccounted, 2020. 17 A3 thermographic prints.

OLINDA SILVANO

p. 300–1
[LEFT]
El mundo de matíco [The World of Matico], 2020, Dyes and embroidery on fabric. 170 × 153 cm. Lima Museum of Art. Contemporary Art Acquisitions Committee 2020.

[TOP RIGHT]
La memoria ancestral (Ancestral Memory), 2018. Xao Quené embroidery, dyed with natural pigments on mahogany and yacushapana bark with "Barra Virgen" from the Jungle's lagoon.

[BOTTOM RIGHT]
El espíritu de las madres planta (The Spirit of the Mother Plants), 2020, Natural dyes and embroidery on fabric. 137 × 152 cm.

pp. 302–3
El espíritu de las madres planta (The Spirit of the Mother Plants) (details), 2020, Natural dyes and embroidery on fabric. 137 × 152 cm.

pp. 304–5
El espíritu de las madres planta (The Spirit of the Mother Plants) (details), 2020, Natural dyes and embroidery on fabric. 152 × 140 cm.

pp. 306–7
[TOP] *Visión de ayahuasca (Ayahuasca vision)*, 2020, Natural dyes and embroidery on fabric.

[BOTTOM LEFT]
El espíritu de las madres planta (The Spirit of the Mother Plants) (details), 2020, Natural dyes and embroidery on fabric. 152 × 140 cm.

[BOTTOM RIGHT] Julia Ortiz Elias y Olinda Silvano (Reshinjabe), *Historia de la selva y la ciudad (History of the Jungle and the City)*, 2013
Oil, natural dyes and traditional shipibo embroidery on tocuyo
130 × 153 cm. Collection Miguel A. López.

RADY NGET

pp. 330–41
Soul of My Identity, 2022. Images courtesy of Prum Bandiddh.

[FRONT COVER]
Pro-democracy student leaders install a plaque declaring “This country belongs to the people” at the Sanam Luang field during a protest in Bangkok, Thailand, Sunday, September 20, 2020. Anti-government demonstrators occupying a historic field in the Thai capital on Sunday installed a plaque symbolizing the country's transition to democracy to replace the original one that was mysteriously ripped and stolen three years ago, as they vowed to press on with calls for new elections and reform of the monarchy. (AP Photo/ Sakchai Lalit).

[REAR COVER]
Frank Tang, *Victoria Park*, 2021. Ink and color on paper. Image courtesy the artist.

Acknowledgements

This publication is made possible through the generous support from the S. H. Ho Foundation Limited

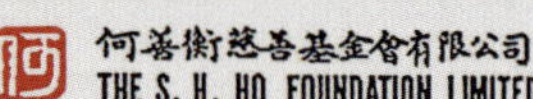

The editors would like to extend our deep gratitude to the contributors and artists to this publication, as well as to the speakers and moderators who participated in the 2018 Para Site International Conference "What to Let Go?" that took place in Hong Kong from November 22–24, 2018.

The editors are deeply thankful to:

Former and current Para Site team members

Claire Shea, Celia Ho, Jacqueline Leung, Kelly Tang, Karen Hui, and Lee Ka Wai;

Chris Wu, Ming Hsun Yu, and Nazlı Ercan at Wkshps for their tireless work on the book;

as well as our friends and family for their patience and support along the way.

The editors would also like to highlight the guidance and commitment from the following individuals

Gala Berger
Gridthiya Gaweewong
Sheela Gowda
GeeSun Hahn
Miguel Lopez
Avani Sood

Para Site Team

Billy Tang
Executive Director/Curator

Kelly Ma
Deputy Director

Celia Ho
Curator

Jessie Kwok
Assistant Curator

Doris Poon
Exhibition Manager

Jason Chen
Communications Manager

Holly Leung
Gallery Manager

Lynna Lam
*Development Intern**

*2023/24 the Arts Talents Internship Matching Programme is Supported by the Hong Kong Arts Development Council

Board

Alan Lau Ka Ming
Chair

Mimi Chun Mei-Lor
Vice Chair

Antony Dapiran
Treasurer

Sara Wong Chi Hang
Secretary

Nick Adamus
Shane Akeroyd
Bonnie Chan Woo Tak Chi
Dr. Yeewan Koon
Alan Y Lo
Adeline Ooi
Federico Tan
Honus Tandijono
Yuki Terase
Young Kar Fai Samson

Para Site Benefectors

Global Council
Shane Akeroyd
Mimi Brown & Alp Ercil
Jehan Chu
Mimi Chun & Chris Gradel
M Art Foundation
Dina Shin
Virginia Yee

Founding Friends
Stephen Cheng
COLLECTIVE Studio
David Zwirner Gallery
Alan Lau
Wendy Lee
Edouard & Lorraine Malingue
Schoeni Projects
SUNPRIDE FOUNDATION
Yuki Terase

Friends
A Pipeline
Almine Rech Gallery
Nick & Cordula Adamus-Voegtle
Nicolas & Delphine Canard-Moreau
Lawrence Chu & Natalie Chan Chu
Jane DeBevoise
Yan Du
Hawk He
Reimi Imaizumi
Jina Lee & Jae Won Chang
Jeff Li & Chuanwoei Lim
Lisson Gallery
Alan Lo
Kai-Yin Lo
Ingrid Lok & Tim Li
Magician Space
Elaine W. Ng
Justin Ng
Stefan Rihs
Fabio Rossi
Roman Ruan & Freda Yang
Angelle Siyang-Le
Tabula Rasa Gallery
Bonnie & Darrin Woo
Dayea Yeon

List of Para Site Benefactors as of January 2024

This volume is published as a reader following the 2018 Para Site International Conference "What to Let Go?"

Organized by
Cosmin Costinaș and Inti Guerrero

Editors
Cosmin Costinaș and Inti Guerrero

Managing Editor
Claire Shea

Copy Editor and Proofreader
Kasia Maciejowska

Proofreader
Kelly Ma

Book Design
Chris Wu and Ming Hsun Yu, Wkshps

Printed and bound in Hong Kong by Asia One

ISBN 978-3-95679-642-5

Distributed by The MIT Press, Art Data, Les presses du réel, and Idea Books

Published by
Sternberg Press
71–75 Shelton Street
London WC2H 9JQ
UK
sternberg-press.com

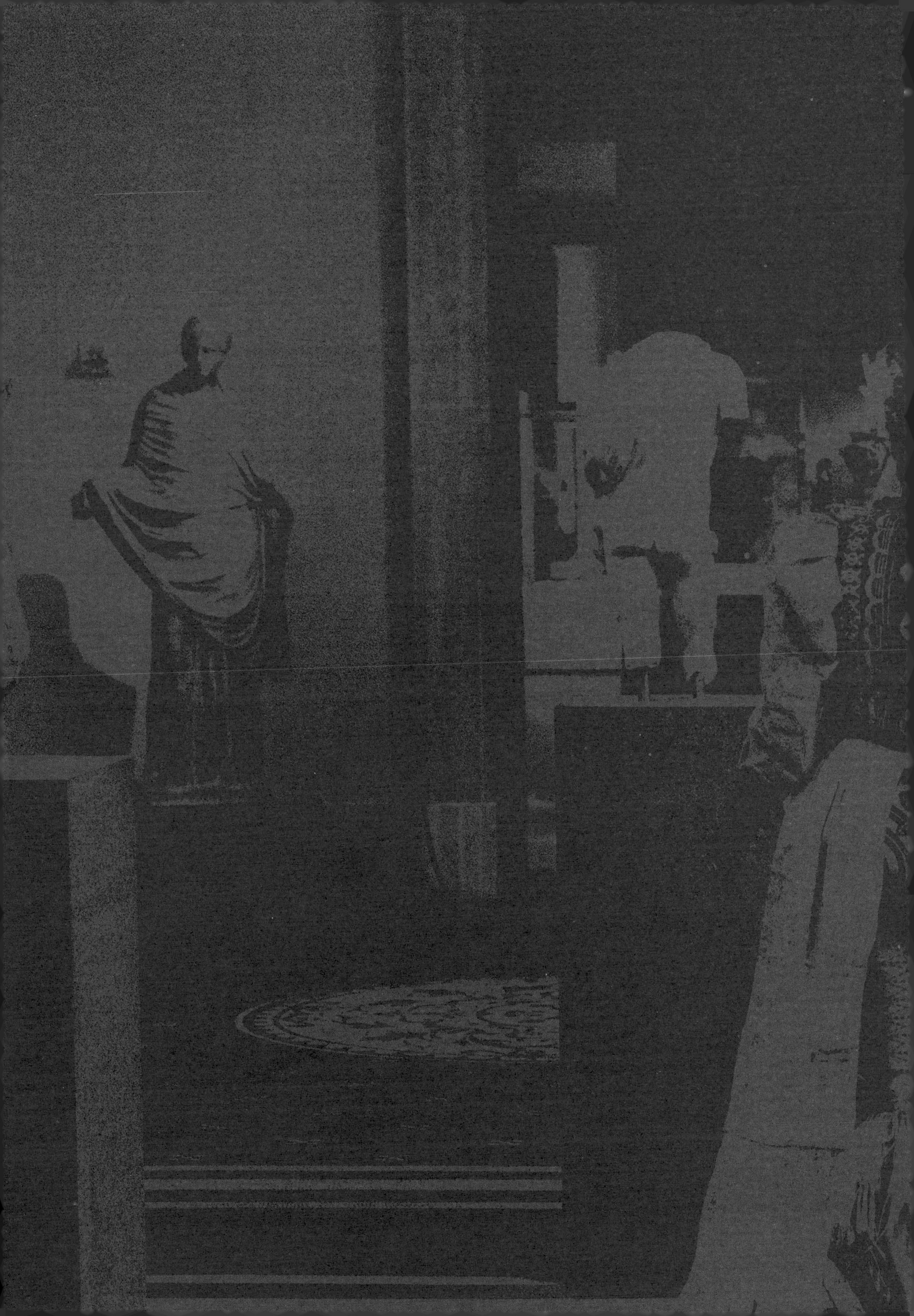